HEALING UNLIMITED

From the Editors of
Boardroom Classics

BOARDROOM CLASSICS
55 Railroad Ave., Greenwich, CT 06830

Revised Edition

10 9 8 7 6 5 4 3 2 1

Boardroom® Classics publishes the advice of expert authorities in
many fields. But the use of this material is not a substitute for
health, legal, accounting or other professional services. Consult a
competent professional for answers to your specific questions.

Library of Congress Cataloging-in-Publication Data
Healing Unlimited
  p.cm.
  Includes index.
  ISBN 0-88723-165-9

Boardroom® Classics is a registered trademark of
Boardroom® Inc.
55 Railroad Ave., Greenwich, CT 06830

Printed in the United States of America

Contents

4 • SIMPLE SOLUTIONS TO COMMON HEALTH PROBLEMS

5 • DIET AND NUTRITION

6 • FITNESS MADE SIMPLE

11 • VERY PERSONAL

12 • SECRETS OF GOOD SLEEP

19 • SIMPLE STRESS-BUSTERS

20 • GETTING THE MOST FOR YOUR MEDICAL DOLLAR

21 • HEALTH RESEARCH AT YOUR FINGERTIPS

22 • NEW HORIZONS IN GOOD HEALTH

1

Immunity Secrets

What You Need to Know About Your Immune System

Imagine a personal security system capable of neutralizing most potential dangers before you're even aware of them.

On duty all year, this security system employs a limitless pool of workers, and with minimal investment, it will be in operation for a lifetime.

Don't bother trying to hire this elite security service. It is already hard at work. This is a fair description of your body's *remarkable* immune system.

Remarkable—but not impervious. The immune system can be compromised by many things—from an ordinary cold to deadly cancers. *That's the bad news.*

The good news is that your immune defenses regularly repair themselves, and there are simple measures you can take to assist them when they have been breached.

How it works…

Basically, your immune system is a thriving swarm of billions of white blood cells, all with just two goals…

- Recognize germ invaders.
- Respond to the threat.

When bacteria enter your body—for instance, through that razor nick you got yesterday—specialized cells called neutrophils rush to the scene to virtually devour the marauders. Other cells soon come by to clean up any bacterial fragments.

Against viruses—which are more insidious than bacterial infections because they sneak into our cells and commandeer them for their own evil purposes—your immune system dispatches antibodies to tackle the attacking aliens.

More important, your immune system has memory cells that look at the viral perpetrators and remember those particular villains for the rest of your life. When antibodies recognize *and* defeat a virus, your system has established an immunity.

Vaccines and medications may be thought of, in a sense, as backups that assist a person when the immune system is overloaded.

There are a lot of microscopic threats out there. But, don't worry. We have plenty of memory cells—enough to recall every virus, bacteria or toxin that is in existence.

Why it fails…

Without an immune system, even the mildest infection would be lethal. Under normal circumstances, our immune system serves us admirably. When it does malfunction, it is usually for one good reason or another…

•Stress. Chronic, unrelieved stress is probably the most severe threat to your immune system. Along with depression, grief and anxiety, stress can trigger chemical changes, stimulating the release of neuropeptides, which adversely affect the operation of your immune system.

•Exertion extremes. Moderate exercise is necessary for basic health, of course, and that includes maintaining a healthy immune system. But, too much exertion—for instance, marathon running, mountain climbing in arctic conditions or other such strenuous activities—has been shown to temporarily depress immune system functions.

•Malnutrition. The relationship between nutrition and the immune system is still a puzzle. We do know, though, that those with poor diets are more susceptible to illness and infections, increasing the burden on their immune systems.

•Rapid and excessive weight loss, through quirky diets or periods of starvation, also drastically reduces your immune system's effectiveness.

It is natural to want to keep your immune system operating at its peak efficiency. Remember, though, that it has gotten you this far without much attention. As with a smoothly running computer, tinkering with your immune system can do more harm than good.

Routine maintenance…

•Keep stress at a reasonable level. Stress reduction is critical for your immune system to function well. If you're not addressing this common problem, make it a health-care priority.

•Vaccinations. These are key to preventing "sneak attacks" on your immune system. Follow the vaccination schedule your child's pediatrician recommends. You may be due for a tetanus booster yourself. When traveling internationally, seek medical advice on specific vaccinations you may need.

•Follow a balanced diet. Sustaining a fit immune system is another good reason for healthy eating.

But, avoid the temptation to "boost" immunity defenses through fad diets or the currently popular vitamin or mineral therapy. Such self-treatment can have serious consequences. Large doses of iron, for example, can cause dangerous digestive tract problems. And, while vitamin A is crucial to combat infections, massive supplemental doses can actually suppress vital immune functions.

•Follow your physician's advice exactly when you are ill. Take *all* medication prescribed, especially antibiotics, which we tend to discontinue using immediately after symptoms disappear.

Give your immune system time to fight your illness and recover afterward. Finally, realize that we often have unrealistic expectations for our health. A few colds a year is not a sign that something is wrong with your lifestyle. Being sick occasionally is just a part of being alive. Thanks to your immune system, so is getting well.

•Stay happy. Just as depression and anxiety can adversely affect all aspects of your health, a happy and optimistic outlook will contribute to a healthier immune system. Recent studies show that this may not be entirely psychological, but may have a neurological basis as well.

Source: David S. McKinsey, MD, codirector of epidemiology and infectious diseases at the Research Medical Center, 2316 E. Meyer, Kansas City, Missouri 64132.

To Protect Your Immune System

Your immune system is made up of white blood cells. To give optimal protection, these cells should be working 24 hours a day. They're directly affected by the quality of food you eat,* the way you behave, and the nature of your thoughts.

Dangers to the immune system:

• Excessive sugar.

• Inadequate protein.

• Inadequate zinc, iron, or manganese.

• Inadequate Vitamin C or Vitamin E.

• Diet and psychology are intimately related. Be especially cautious during times of stress, bereavement, sorrow, and trauma. They often translate into suppression of the immune function.

• Monitor magnesium intake. Most people don't get enough magnesium in their diets. And a magnesium deficiency can create anxiety symptoms. The minimum amount necessary is usually 300 to 500 milligrams a day. Under conditions of high stress, you would need more magnesium (since it's utilized very rapidly at such times). *Best sources:* Green leafy vegetables, lean meat, whole grains.

• Exercise enhances the function of your immune system by reducing stress.

*The amount of nutrients you need is best determined on an individual basis. To find out how much you need, consult a physician who specializes in disease prevention. Also useful: *Nutrition Against Disease* by Dr. Roger Williams, Bantam Books, New York.

Source: Jeffrey Bland, Linus Pauling Institute of Science and Medicine, Palo Alto, CA.

Colds/Self-Defense

Wash hands well after shaking a sick person's hand or after caring for a sick child. Colds spread mainly hand-to-hand—from infected people to healthy ones. Viruses then enter healthy bodies through hand contact with the mouth, nose, eyes and ears. Getting chilled or wet doesn't cause colds…nor does stress…although these factors may lower resistance to infection.

Source: Mark Widome, MD, is on the staff of Pennsylvania State University College of Medicine, Hershey.

Workout Warning

Brisk walks strengthen your immune system—but too-strenuous workouts can lower immunity to colds and flu. Exercising near your maximum capacity for just 45 minutes—or more—produces a six-hour "window" of vulnerability afterward. *Better:* Exercise at a moderate level—the equivalent of a brisk walk—if not training for competition.

Source: David Nieman, DrPH, professor of health, department of health and exercise science, Appalachian State University, Boone, North Carolina.

Exercise and Colds

Daily exercise speeds recovery from common colds by boosting the immune system. Women who walked 45 minutes a day recovered twice as fast (five days versus 10 days) from colds than women who did not exercise during a 15-week period.

Source: Study by David Nieman, exercise physiologist, Appalachian State University, Boone, North Carolina, reported in *The Walking Magazine*, 711 Boylston St., Boston 02116.

The Stress of a Cold or Flu

Problems: A sore throat may make swallowing painful…stuffed nasal passages may interfere with your sense of smell, leaving food tasteless…and your appetite may grow very weak.

Why you still must eat right: When your body is fighting an infection, your immune system needs even more vitamins and minerals than it normally does. When you have a fever, you utilize protein more rapidly.

Realistic solution: Eat as nutritiously as you possibly can while you are ill. Emphasize foods that are rich in protein, vitamins and minerals, yet are also soothing and easy to swallow. If you find raw fruits and vegetables totally unappealing when you're ill, forget them. Take vitamin and mineral supplements if you know you aren't eating right.

Good foods to choose…

•Soups combining meat or poultry with vegetables. Puréed soups are especially palatable when swallowing hurts.

•Yogurt or cottage cheese. Both are high in protein and they go down easy. Also try frozen yogurt or even popsicles.

•Baked potatoes. Provide minerals and vitamins, including vitamin C. Try topping one with yogurt.

•Blended juices. Drink the milder mixed juices—such as banana-pineapple-orange—for vitamin C if straight orange or grapefruit juice seems too acidic.

•Hot breakfast cereals diluted with warm milk. *Especially valuable:* Those fortified with vitamins and minerals.

•Soft scrambled eggs—or to reduce fat, use an egg substitute.

•Baked custard.

•High protein drinks such as Carnation Instant Breakfast, Sustagen, Sustacal or Ensure. For a soothing feeling, drink them warm.

The convenience factor…

Prepare in advance for cold and flu season. *Smart steps:*

•Always keep at least some of the above-listed foods on hand throughout the winter.

•Stock your freezer with homemade or high-quality commercial soups.

Advance planning is especially important for those who live alone and tend to keep little food on hand.

Reason: A cold or the flu can strike very suddenly and leave you unable to shop or cook.

Source: Judith J. Wurtman, PhD, professor of brain and cognitive science at the Massachusetts Institute of Technology. She is the author of *Managing Your Mind and Mood Through Food*, HarperCollins, 10 E. 53 St., New York 10022.

Beyond Chicken Soup: Foods for When You're Not So Well

We all know the basic principles for a healthy diet—eat lots of fiber…reduce fat consumption…cut down on sugar and salt…avoid processed foods…drink little or no alcohol. What most people don't realize, however, is that what you eat and don't eat when you're ill can make a real difference in your recovery.

What to eat for…

•Acne.

•Less processed foods and refined sugar. *Myth:* That chocolate or greasy foods are what cause acne. *Better:* Identify your own culprit foods and make it a point to avoid them.

•More zinc, found in lean beef, whole-grain cereals, dairy products, peas, beans, root vegetables and nuts…lecithin, found in egg yolks…selenium, found in whole grains and seafoods, and vitamins A, B6, C and E, found in raw fruits and green leafy vegetables. *Also helpful:* Crushed raw garlic, about three cloves a day.

•Anemia.

•Less coffee…tea…cocoa and alcohol.

•More raw vegetables…vitamin C…iron, found in meat, fish, poultry, whole-grain cereals, peas, beans, lentils, green leafy vegetables, nuts and seeds…copper, found in seafood and legumes, and zinc.

•Anxiety.

•Less sugar…tea…coffee and alcohol.

•More high-fiber foods…niacin, found in beef, poultry, milk, fish, whole-grain cereals, peas, beans, lentils, mushrooms, nuts and seeds…vitamin E…calcium and magnesium. *Also helpful:* Teas made of chamomile, lime flowers or passion flowers have a calming effect.

•Appendicitis.

•Less refined carbohydrates with sugar added.

•More high-fiber foods and water.

•Appetite loss.

•Less refined carbohydrates.

•More small but frequent amounts of food and drink...thiamine, found in bran cereals, and zinc. *Also helpful:* Teas made of fenugreek (a plant with seeds used for spices), juniper, clover or yarrow stimulate appetite.

•Arterial disease.

•Less saturated fats...cholesterol...sugar and alcohol.

•More oily fish...unsaturated fats...lecithin...raw fruits and vegetables...garlic...onions...oats...avocados...pineapple...ginger ...vitamins A, B6, C, E...thiamine and niacin.

•Arthritis.

•Less saturated fats...tomatoes...peppers ...potatoes and eggplant.

•More oily fish...raw fruit and vegetables ...zinc...copper...calcium...potassium, found in most fruits and vegetables...manganese, found in whole grains and green, leafy vegetables...selenium and vitamins A, B, C and E. *Also helpful:* Pineapple and nettle (also known as stinging nettle or Urtica)...or coriander tea.

•Bad breath.

•Less sugar...coffee and cow's milk.

•More green leafy vegetables. Also helpful: Chew parsley to fight onion or garlic breath. Chew fennel, dill, caraway seed or anise seed to disguise bad breath.

•Bedwetting.

•Less oxalate, found in spinach, strawberries and rhubarb...flavored drinks (tea, cola, coffee, cocoa) and food coloring.

•Cancer.

•Less animal fats...alcohol and salt-cured, salt-pickled, smoked, fried or charcoal-broiled foods.

•More fiber...raw fruits and vegetables... fermented foods (yogurt, etc.)...sprouted seeds ...vitamins A, B6, C and E...selenium and zinc.

•Candidiasis (yeast infection).

•Less refined carbohydrates...alcohol... milk...fruit...fruit juice...yeast...coffee and tea.

•More raw garlic...vitamin B...fresh, raw, green leafy vegetables...vegetable oils and natural unpasteurized yogurt.

•Cataracts.

•Less animal protein, fat and sugar.

•More vitamins B, C, E...manganese... selenium...zinc and raw vegetables.

•Confusion.

•Less white flour and salt.

•More raw fruit and vegetables...freshly squeezed juices...vitamins B, C, E...calcium... magnesium...zinc and lecithin.

•Diabetes.

•Less refined carbohydrates...sugar...animal protein...saturated fats...salt...alcohol... tea... coffee...cola and cocoa.

•More whole oats...beans...peas...raw vegetables...vitamins A, B, C and E...chromium, found in whole-grain cereals...magnesium...potassium...vanadium, found in fish... zinc and essential fatty acids, found in meat, fatty fish, egg yolk, whole-grain cereals, beans, peas, fruit, seeds, nuts and cold-pressed vegetable oils.

•Diverticular disease.

•Less refined carbohydrates.

•More unrefined carbohydrates...oats... raw and cooked vegetables and fruit.

•Dry eyes.

•More foods rich in vitamin A.

•Food sensitivities.

•Possible migraine culprits: Oranges... chocolate...sugar...cheese...alcohol (especially red wine)...wheat...eggs...coffee...tea... cola...milk...beef...corn...yeast...pickled fish and cured meat.

•Possible asthma culprits: Manufactured fruit drinks...nuts...milk...eggs...wheat... cheese...yeast...fish and fried food.

•Gallstones.

•Less saturated fats and refined carbohydrates (which turn into saturated fats).

•More fiber...lecithin...vitamins C and E and zinc. Also helpful: Teas made of dandelion, chamomile or parsley.

•Gout.

•Less red meat...game...organ meats...fish ...fish roe...shellfish...asparagus...cauliflower ...mushrooms...spinach...beans and peas.

•More fiber...green leafy vegetables...celery...parsley...watercress...vitamin C...magnesium...zinc...raw vegetables...juices and dandelion root or leaf. *Also helpful:* Teas made of nettle or meadowsweet (Filipendula Ulmaria).

• Impotence.

   • Less fat and refined carbohydrates.

   • More iodine, found in seafood…manganese…selenium and zinc.

• Indigestion.

   • Less refined carbohydrates…alcohol… milk…coffee…tea…cocoa…cola and fatty and spicy foods.

   • More vitamin C and zinc. *Also helpful:* Teas made of parsley, mint, chamomile, blackberry leaf or juniper berries.

• Kidney stones.

For all stones:

   • Less protein…sugar and alcohol.

   • More fiber…magnesium and water.

For calcium oxalate stones:

   • Less tea…coffee…cocoa…spinach… rhubarb…sweet potatoes…cucumbers…celery …peanuts…grapefruit…beans and carrots.

   • More magnesium and vitamin B6.

• Nausea.

   • Less large meals…fat and sugar.

   • More fresh or crystallized ginger root. *Also helpful:* Peppermint teas or chamomile.

For morning sickness:

   • More vitamin B6. *Also helpful:* Teas made of raspberry leaves or chamomile.

• Prostate problems.

   • Less meat…dairy food…coffee…tea… cocoa…cola and refined carbohydrates.

   • More essential fatty acids…fiber…vitamins C and E…magnesium…selenium…zinc and vegetables.

• Sex-drive problems.

   • More raw fruit and vegetables…vitamins A and E…magnesium…manganese and zinc.

• Smoking.

   • More vitamins B6, B12 and C…calcium …magnesium…selenium and zinc. *Note:* Sunflower seeds have a soothing effect when you're trying to quit.

• Urinary-tract infections.

   • Less animal protein…cereals…animal fat…coffee…tea…cola and cocoa.

   • More water…bicarbonate of soda…fruit and vegetables…lemon barley water…vitamin E…garlic and asparagus. *Also helpful:* Teas made of parsley, meadowsweet or borage (Borago officinalis).

Source: Penny Stanway, MD, a former senior medical officer in community health and pediatrics who lectures widely on healthy eating, childcare and breastfeeding. She is the author of *Foods for Common Ailments*, Simon & Schuster, 1330 Ave. of the Americas, New York 10020.

Infection Self-Defense

Thorough handwashing is the easiest way to avoid infection. *Key:* Apply soap or detergent to hands, and rub vigorously for at least 10 seconds before rinsing in order to wash away germs. *Best:* Water warm enough to cut through grease. Water hot enough to kill germs would harm your hands. Always wash before handling or eating food…after visiting the bathroom or changing a diaper…after handling uncooked food, money or garbage.

Source: *Mayo Clinic Health Letter,* 200 First St. SW, Rochester, Minnesota 55905.

Small Changes Can Make a Big Difference

The flood of data about health and fitness that fills the media these days can be confusing instead of helpful.

If you've been exercising or eating "right" for years—but feel frustrated and unfulfilled, you're not alone. There are very simple ways of taking charge of your life and health by tapping your inner resources in practical, effective ways. The kind of small changes we support are simple and designed to increase self-awareness, since all aspects of life are interdependent.

Example: When you're worried about something, you're likely to have an upset stomach, too. What may appear to be individual events are really interconnected aspects of a larger, more complex system.

When you master small changes, you build a fortified base from which to take further steps on your healing journey toward wellness.

Although many people associate wellness only with fitness, nutrition, or stress reduction, wellness is really much, much more. Wellness brings people into a domain of self-responsibility and self-empowerment.

Set goals for wellness…

Goals, like maps, keep you on course. And more than that, goals are like magnets—they tend to attract things that help get them accomplished. It's almost magical how this happens at times.

Often people set their sights too high and then quit completely when they don't make the grade. Approach these "impossible" goals by breaking them down into possible increments. Or, to put it another way: How do you move a mountain? One rock at a time.

Breathing reduces stress…

Stress is inevitable—you need it to stand against the force of gravity. But there are many forms of stress that may wear you down and cause a variety of health problems.

Every tense situation, or even a memory of one, causes a change in breathing. Generally, the more stressed you feel, the more shallow your breathing becomes. Breathing consciously can relieve tension, quiet fear and relieve pain.

Emotions and health…

There is a price to be paid when feelings are denied or repressed. Lethargy, boredom and a sense of deadness toward life may be the consequence. Those unaccustomed to dealing with feelings in healthy ways often seek other means to cover them up or distract themselves, such as alcohol, food, drugs, TV, unhealthy relationships or compulsive work.

Befriend your emotional self. Accept strong emotions as feedback telling you that something is in need of attention.

• Write an angry letter—then tear it up.
• Compose a poem about your grief.
• Draw, paint or dance your feelings.
• Exercise vigorously.
• Talk about your feelings.
• Let fear be there.
• Let discouragement be there.

Don't chase these emotions away. Look at them. Express them when appropriate. Then move on.

Simplify your life…

Becoming well in body, mind and spirit is not nearly as difficult as it may seem. Wellness is not a matter of accumulating something—like more data. Rather, it's realized by unburdening yourself of all that prevents the natural state of basic healthiness from being present. To become well is to become more simple.

• Simplify your life.
• Simplify your diet.
• Take time to rest your mind.
• See your loved ones as brand new every day.
• One breath, one smile, one day of seeing the sun are all precious.

The Hebrew word *dayenu*, meaning, "it is enough," captures the essence of what it means to live in gratitude for life. To live dayenu as a way of life is to be ready to embrace the mystery of each moment fully, and then let it go.

Honor your body's wisdom…

Inhabit your body. Learn to start listening to what it is saying to you and to trust what you hear. Listening to others instead of yourself, or saying "yes" when you mean "no" are just two examples of the many ways you check out of yourself. Wellness is about "coming home"—taking up residence inside your own body once again.

Reprogram yourself for health…

Current research in the field of psychoneuroimmunology verifies what folk healers have known for centuries—that thinking and emotions have direct effects upon the strength of the immune system.

The immune system is the first line of defense against disease. Strengthening your immune system consciously, through the use of imagery or nurturing self-talk, gives you a much better chance of maintaining whole-body health.

Connect to the earth for healing…

When was the last time you sat on the ground or touched the earth? Physical contact with soil, natural waters, sunlight and fresh air are healing. When stress has built up, a walk around the block is often all that's needed to restore perspective. Beyond that, in nature, you connect with forces stronger than the individual self, and this puts the big picture in the foreground.

A partnership in healing...

There will be times in your life when you need the care and attention of a helping professional—a doctor, psychologist, social worker, etc.

When looking for a helping professional, it's important to find someone willing to take the time to answer your questions, and listen to your concerns.

If you find that he/she is unwilling to do so, switch to someone who will.

Bottom line: Getting started on these small changes will help you begin to make a difference in your life. We hope that you will experience increased self-awareness and self-appreciation, that you will have a sense of greater inner strength and, above all, that you will live well!

Source: John W. Travis, MD, and Regina Sara Ryan, co-authors of *WELLNESS: Small Changes You Can Use to Make a Big Difference.* Ten Speed Press. Dr. Travis is also the director of Wellness Associates, 21489 Orr Springs Rd., Ukiah, CA 95482.

Believe It or Not...Your Personality Traits Affect Your Immune System

This concept was developed by psychologist Suzanne Ouellette, PhD, now at the City University of New York. She hit upon the idea while studying AT&T executives in the late 1970s, when that company was breaking up.

Ouellette noticed that some workers tended to get sick under the stressful conditions, while others remained healthy. Closer study revealed that the "hardy" workers shared three key characteristics...

•Strong commitment to work, relationships and other pursuits—including a sense of purpose in what they were doing.

•Sense of control. While they might not have controlled everything, they always felt there was something they could do to improve the situation.

•Acceptance of change. They saw change as a part of life—and acknowledged that it could be positive.

Executives who shared these hardiness traits were half as likely to get sick as those who lacked them.

Ouellette and a colleague have developed a four-part program for increasing hardiness...

•Find a comfortable place to sit. Focus on your reaction to a recent stressful event. Look for a word, phrase or image that describes your feelings. You might say simply that you felt bad, for example, or that you felt like a boat on choppy water.

•Jot down three ways the stressful event could have been worse, and three ways it could have been better. Explore the different scenarios in your mind.

•Develop a plan to improve the stressful situation. This plan should involve gathering other viewpoints and expressing your needs to others.

•Accept the aspects of the situation you can't change. Find a way to compensate for your lack of control via a different attitude or approach to the problem.

Source: Henry Dreher, a medical writer specializing in mind-body medicine. He is the author of *The Immune Power Personality: 7 Traits You Can Develop to Stay Healthy,* Dutton.

2

Healthier Hearts

Thousands of Heart Attacks Strike Without Warning

Most heart attacks are preceded by episodes of angina or other warning signs. Thousands of times a year, however, seemingly healthy Americans are killed by heart attacks that occur with no warning whatsoever. They are victims of silent myocardial ischemia, an insidious form of heart disease caused by painless coronary artery blockages that gradually choke off the flow of blood to the heart.

Because silent ischemia has no obvious symptoms, it's almost impossible to spot. But some people are at higher risk. *Solution:* Avoid the well-known risk factors. A single factor doubles the risk. Having two or more factors boosts risk tenfold.

Risk factors...

• Smoking. Cigarette smoke is composed of a dozen harmful gases, many of which contribute to heart disease. A smoker's pulse is 15–25 beats faster than a nonsmoker's. Six of eight smokers have reduced blood flow to the heart.

• Hypertension. Blood pressure greater than 140 over 90 damages capillaries and arteries and weakens heart muscle. Chronic hypertension forces the heart to work harder, leaving it more susceptible to ischemia—particularly after heart disease has already developed.

• High cholesterol. Levels above 240 are a primary cause of atherosclerotic plaque, the fatty deposits that clog coronary arteries. The higher the level of low-density lipoprotein (LDL) cholesterol, the greater the odds the blockages will occur.

• Obesity. One-fourth of cases of heart disease are linked to obesity, which doubles the odds of hypertension.

• Diabetes. Both juvenile and adult-onset diabetes can cause cardiovascular problems if not kept under control. Most diabetics die of heart attacks, strokes, and cardiovascular problems.

•Stress. Stress releases hormones that damage both the heart muscle and blood vessel walls. It also aggravates existing heart conditions and contributes to the development of ischemia. *Stress relievers:* Meditation, yoga, breathing exercises, and biofeedback.

•Lack of exercise. Sedentary people run a greater risk of heart disease regardless of other risk factors. Exercise is of crucial importance in staving off silent ischemia. *Note:* Persons over 35 with a personal or family history of heart disease should consult a doctor before beginning an exercise program.

Family history is also an important factor. Persons whose ancestors had coronary artery disease—especially "premature" heart disease (before the age of 55 or 60)—are themselves predisposed to the problem.

Diagnosing ischemia…

People at risk for silent ischemia should undergo diagnostic testing. *First step:* Have an electrocardiogram (ECG) during an exercise stress test. This procedure, performed in a doctor's office or clinic, costs about $200. It isn't foolproof. However, it does give doctors a pretty good picture of the heart's overall health.

Heart attack sufferers should have an exercise ECG just prior to being discharged from the hospital. Additional exercise ECGs should be arranged at six months and a year later, followed by one every two years. *Note:* There should be some kind of exertion during an ECG.

A variation of the standard stress test ECG is a 24-hour device called a Holter monitor. A small recorder worn on the belt monitors 24 hours of heart activity under normal, everyday conditions. Data is stored on a small reel of tape and played back later through a scanning device. *Cost:* $150 a day.

Doctors continue to debate whether Holter monitors detect heart disease more effectively than the conventional ECGs. However, new microprocessor-controlled Holter devices do seem to be better than standard ECGs.

If an ECG or Holter test points to heart damage, follow-up tests are advised. The most accurate test is coronary arteriography. *How it's done:* The patient is sedated and placed on a special X-ray cradle. Local anesthesia is injected into the skin covering the targeted blood ves-

sels. Long, thin catheters are inserted into arteries and veins. Dyes injected into blood vessels or heart chambers reveal obstructions and other abnormalities on X-ray movies, which are recorded on videotape and later studied.

Because arteriography is uncomfortable and somewhat risky, persons suspected of having silent ischemia should undergo radioisotopic studies before having arteriography. *Procedure:* Small amounts of radioactive isotopes (thallium 201, for example) are injected into the bloodstream. The thallium 201 shows up only in healthy areas of blood vessels. Special X-ray pictures of the heart then identify "holes" or blank spaces that indicate areas of coronary artery blockage.

An alternative radioisotopic procedure is radionuclide ventriculogram, or RVG. Another radioisotope, technetium pertechnetate, is injected into a vein, and a recording computer obtains expansion-contraction images of the heart to detect abnormalities.

Treatment…

Heart disease can usually be controlled with one of three types of drugs—nitrates, beta blockers, and calcium channel blockers. *Side effects:* Nitrates and calcium blockers can cause flushing, dizziness, and headaches. Beta blockers can cause fatigue, depression, and breathing difficulties (they're off-limits to asthma sufferers).

When drug treatment fails, doctors are increasingly using balloon angioplasty to clean out blocked coronary arteries. *Good candidates:* Older and sicker patients for whom surgery is too risky. *Procedure:* A catheter with an inflatable end is snaked through an artery in an arm or a leg all the way to the coronary arteries, where the balloon inflates and crushes areas of plaque. The success rate of balloon angioplasty approaches 90% when performed by experienced doctors, although 5% of patients experience serious complications requiring emergency coronary bypass surgery.

Bypass surgery is recommended for cases in which nonsurgical therapy fails—especially for patients who have had a heart attack and for those with obstruction of the main left coronary artery. The diseased section of artery is replaced with a section of artery or blood vessel taken from elsewhere in the body. Risks (death, heart attack) range from 1% to 5%, depending on the extent of the disease.

Source: Peter Frank Cohn, MD, chief of cardiology, State University of New York, Stony Brook, and his wife, Joan Kirschenbaum Cohn, MSW, a psychotherapist in private practice in Huntington, NY. The Cohns are coauthors of *Heart Talk: Preventing and Coping with Silent and Painful Heart Disease.*

How to Cut Your Risk Of Heart Disease 90%

Like many American families, my family was hard hit by heart disease.

My father was just 12 years old when his father died of a heart attack…and I was only 22 when the same fate befell my dad. By the time I reached my mid-30s, I too seemed headed for an early death. I was overweight, I had Type II diabetes, and my cholesterol level was elevated. According to the statistics of the Framingham heart study, my risk of a heart attack was 175% of normal. ("Normal" in our society is a 75% chance of having a heart attack in one's lifetime.)

I decided to try to cut my disease risk by adopting the 30%-fat diet recommended by the American Heart Association. *Problem:* The diet had little effect on my excess weight, diabetes and cholesterol levels.

Reversing the inevitable…

At this point, I immersed myself in scientific literature and developed an alternative approach to this problem. I cut my fat intake all the way down to 10% of calories and adopted a program of regular exercise and stress control. In a few months I lost 45 pounds, my diabetes vanished, and my cholesterol level fell so low that my risk of heart attack wasn't just normal, it was below that of someone with no family history of heart disease. My risk of heart disease fell 97%.

Bonus: I felt more relaxed and energetic than I had in years.

Here are the most common questions people ask me…

What exactly is involved with your "10% solution"? Several things. First, regular aerobic exercise. I recommend working out at least four times a week, for at least 45 minutes each time. Next, stress control. Learn to strike a balance between self, friends, family and work. Stop smoking. Get plenty of sleep. *Note:* I don't mean to gloss over these nondietary recommendations because they're all-important. But the issue of fat intake is more critical—and more often misunderstood.

What's it like to eat a 10%-fat diet? Most people think it must be terribly Spartan. In fact, while you will have to eliminate certain foods from your diet, you can continue to enjoy many of the foods you currently eat. The key is learning the subtle art of food substitution.

Illustration: A meal of broiled chicken, peas in a cream sauce, baked potato with sour cream and a dish of ice cream contains a whopping 55 grams of fat. But a similar meal of baked skinless chicken, steamed peas, baked potato with nonfat sour cream and a dish of nonfat frozen yogurt contains only nine grams. Once you get used to low-fat eating, this meal is just as satisfying—and much more healthful.

But I love fatty foods. I don't think I have the willpower to eat as you recommend. What can I do? Oddly enough, while it's quite hard to eat a *little* less fat, it's actually quite easy to eat a lot less.

Reason: If you cut back only to, say, 20% or 30% fat, your appetite for rich, fatty foods never goes away. Consequently, every meal becomes a test of your willpower. But after five to six weeks on a 10%-fat diet, your taste buds actually begin to change. Fatty foods you once enjoyed will begin to taste too greasy while foods that once seemed impossibly bland will become tastier. *Bonus:* Because you'll be eating so little fat, you'll easily lose excess weight—while never feeling hungry or deprived.

Are any foods prohibited? I divide foods into three categories—those to eat as often as you like, those to eat occasionally and those to avoid.

Emphasize…

•Breads made without oils, butter or margarine and any other whole grains or grain products.

•Pasta made without oil or eggs.

•Cereals free of fat, salt or sugar.

•Fruits, fruit juices and vegetables (except avocados and olives, which are too fatty).

•Peas, beans, lentils and other legumes.

•Nonfat dairy products.

•Tofu and other soy products.

•Egg whites.

•Lean meats, preferably fish or fowl. Up to 4 ounces daily of fish, clams, oysters or mussels, or white meat of chicken or turkey (without skin). If you want red meat, choose round steak, flank steak or other lean cuts.

Eat occasionally:

•Sugar, sucrose, molasses and other sweeteners.

•Breads and cereals made with added fat.

•Pastas made with eggs.

•Low-sodium soy sauce.

•Low-fat dairy products (one-percent fat).

•Olive or canola oil…use very sparingly.

•Caffeinated drinks…no more than two cups daily.

•Lobster, crab and shrimp. They contain too much cholesterol to be eaten regularly.

•Smoked or charbroiled foods. They contain a potent carcinogen.

Never eat:

•Fatty meats, including organs, cold cuts and most cuts of beef and pork. Poultry skin is pure fat.

•Meat fat, butter, hydrogenated vegetable oils, lard and margarine.

•Nondairy creamers and other sources of tropical oils like palm or coconut.

•Mayonnaise.

•Polyunsaturated fat, including corn oil and most vegetable oils.

•Whole-milk dairy products, including cream, whole milk and sour cream.

•Nuts (except chestnuts, which may be eaten regularly).

•Salt or salty foods.

•Egg yolks.

•Fried foods.

How can I tell how much fat I'm getting? At first you'll need to keep a food diary. Jot down the calorie and fat content of each food you eat. At the end of each day, calculate the all-important fat percentage.

Procedure: Multiply your total daily intake of fat (in grams) by nine (the number of calories in each fat gram), then divide this number by your total daily calories. If this number is above 10%, you must find ways to cut out more fat. After several weeks, you'll be able to judge your fat intake without using the diary.

How about polyunsaturated fats? Margarine, corn oil and other sources of polyunsaturated fat have long been touted as safe alternatives to saturated fats. In fact, they are *far less healthful* than once thought—and may be more harmful than saturated fats.

Recent finding: Polyunsaturated fat not only raises levels of LDL (bad) cholesterol, but also reduces levels of HDL (good) cholesterol. And now it looks as if polyunsaturated fat promotes the growth of cancer cells.

Cancer rates in the US began to rise just about the time polyunsaturated fats began to replace saturated fats in the American diet. *To be safe:* Limit your intake of all fats—saturated and polyunsaturated fats in particular.

Are there any immediate benefits to eating less fat? Absolutely. Each time you eat a fatty meal, your red blood cells become "sticky." They clump together, moving slowly through the circulatory system and clogging up capillaries. This deprives your brain of oxygen, resulting in grogginess. But when you stop eating such meals, your red cells return to normal, and your capillaries open up. *Result:* You feel calmer and more energetic, you sleep better and your complexion improves. And at the same time a subtler but even more important change is taking place within your body. The fatty plaques inside your arteries shrink and your immune system grows stronger.

Doesn't a vegetable-rich diet raise your intake of pesticide residues? No. The pesticide content of fruits and vegetables is well below that of meat—which comes from animals raised on pesticide-sprayed crops. But to minimize your intake of potential toxins, buy organic produce.

Source: Raymond Kurzweil, chairman of Kurzweil Applied Intelligence, a Waltham, Massachusetts-based computer manufacturer. He is author of *The 10% Solution for a Healthy Life: How to Eliminate Virtually All Risk of Heart Disease and Cancer,* Crown Publishers, 201 E. 50 St., New York 10022.

Height and Heart Disease

Men over five-feet, 10-inches have an 80% lower risk of heart disease than men under five-feet, five-inches.

Possible reasons: Poor childhood nutrition —or prenatal nutrition—may stunt growth and affect adult health. Also, arteries in the hearts of shorter people are narrower, possibly increasing blockage risk.

Self-defense: Short men should focus on controllable risks: smoking, blood pressure, exercise, diet, weight. Results were inconclusive for shorter women—but they should be similarly cautious.

Average height: Around five-feet, nine-inches for men…five-feet, four-inches for women.

Source: Donna Parker, ScD, an epidemiologist in the division of health education at Memorial Hospital of Rhode Island, Pawtucket, recently completed a study of more than 6,500 people.

Warning Signs of Angina Pectoris

Symptoms that can signal possible heart disease: Tightness, pressure, heaviness or constriction in the center of the chest. The discomfort may start in the shoulders—more often on the left—or spread to shoulders from the center of the chest…then move down the arms or into the neck or jaw.

Chest discomfort is diagnosed as angina pectoris when symptoms are caused by physical activity, and usually disappear within minutes after activity stops.

Warning: Angina pectoris is the most common initial symptom of heart disease in women. If you have symptoms, see your doctor immediately.

Source: Richard Helfant, MD, clinical professor of medicine, division of cardiology, University of California at Irvine, 101 The City Dr., Bldg. 53, Rm. 100, Orange, CA. He is also the author of *Women, Take Heart.* Putman.

Heart Trouble Predicator

Mental stress tests help predict who is likely to have heart trouble, over and above physical stress tests. Researchers measured the blood flow in the hearts of 126 people undergoing mental stress tests such as solving difficult math problems rapidly. They found that 27% of those who showed an abnormal response to mental stress suffered a cardiac event within the next five years—more than twice the rate of those who showed a normal response.

Source: James A. Blumenthal, PhD, professor of medical psychology at Duke University Medical School, Durham, NC.

It's Never Too Late to Start Taking Care of Your Heart

Some people mistakenly believe that if they've had bad health habits all their lives, it won't help to change now. But you can prevent—and in some cases even reverse—damage to your heart…no matter how old you are. And since heart disease is the number one killer in America, it makes sense to do what you can to prevent it.

The big four of heart health…

Lifestyle changes in four major areas can make an enormous difference in preventing heart disease.

•Stop smoking. Smoking is the greatest risk factor for coronary artery disease. It increases the chance of heart attack by 250%.

Even if you've smoked for years, stopping will improve your health. Heart rate and blood pressure will return to normal, and risk of heart attack will fall until it matches that of people who never smoked.

•Reduce blood cholesterol. The most effective way to do this is by watching your diet. It isn't just cholesterol in food that raises levels in blood, it's the saturated fat—which stimulates the body to produce its own harmful cholesterol.

The average American gets 37% of daily calories from fat. A much healthier level would be 30% or 15%.

Helpful: New food labeling regulations make it easier to estimate the fat content of the foods you eat.

Cholesterol reduction diet: Cut back on desserts and animal products—eggs, meat, cheese and other whole dairy products. Increase your intake of vegetables, dried beans and whole grains. Switch from using butter or margarine in cooking to small amounts of olive oil, which appears to reduce "bad" LDL cholesterol but not "good" HDL cholesterol.

•Exercise. Exercise benefits the cardiovascular system by strengthening the heart muscle, improving circulation, raising HDL and lowering LDL cholesterol, reducing stress on arteries and fighting the formation of blood clots.

The best kind of exercise for the heart is aerobic—the kind that uses large muscle groups for prolonged periods of time.

Examples: Biking, swimming, fast walking, running, stair climbing, rowing, racquet sports.

You're exerting yourself at the right level if you work up a sweat but don't feel out of breath. Any amount of exercise is helpful—even an hour a week. But you'll reap greater benefits if you work up to a total of at least three to four hours a week.

•Lower your blood pressure. One-fourth of American adults—and half of those over age 60—have high blood pressure, also known as hypertension. High blood pressure strains the heart muscle and damages the arterial wall, making people with hypertension more than twice as likely as others to have heart attacks.

The best way to lower blood pressure is to get the correct amount of minerals in your diet...

•Reduce sodium. Aim for less than 1,500 milligrams of sodium per day. Check food labels for sodium content. Sodium comes in many guises—the familiar table salt, as well as baking powder, baking soda, monosodium glutamate and soy sauce. Snack foods and processed foods tend to be especially high in sodium.

•Increase potassium and calcium. Many fresh fruits and vegetables are rich in potassium, including bananas, dates, oranges, cantaloupe, apples, raisins, potatoes, winter squash, lima beans, beets and broccoli. Healthful calcium-rich foods include skim milk, broccoli, spinach, fish and soybean products— particularly tofu.

In addition to these four basic lifestyle changes for heart health, research suggests several other behaviors that may help to prevent heart disease...

•Take aspirin. Aspirin reduces blood clotting and has been shown to lower risk of a second heart attack. It's possible that aspirin may help to prevent a first heart attack as well.

Recommended dose: One baby aspirin a day, or one adult aspirin tablet every other day.

Caution: Check with your doctor before taking aspirin regularly. People who have ulcers, excessive bleeding or who are on other medications may need to avoid aspirin.

•Eat fiber. Numerous studies suggest that water-soluble fiber—the kind found in oat bran and also barley, prunes, beans and other legumes—reduces LDL cholesterol in the blood.

•Eat fish. Two to three servings of fish per week can reduce heart disease risk by about 40%. *Exception:* Shellfish, which is high in cholesterol.

Fish contains omega-3 fatty acids, which lower LDL and raise HDL, and may also reduce blood clotting and inflammation in the arterial walls.

•Avoid secondhand cigarette smoke. "Passive" smoking is thought to cause up to 35,000 deaths from heart attack in the US each year. At highest risk are people who live with someone who smokes or who work in smoke-filled environments. Try to reduce exposure as much as possible—ask smokers to consider your safety...or even leave the room when someone is smoking, if you must.

•Take antioxidant vitamins. There's some evidence that vitamins C, E and beta-carotene —which seem to fight the dangerous effects of unstable molecules in the body called free radicals—lower the risk of heart disease.

If you take supplements, stick to moderate doses—1,000 milligrams of vitamin C, 400 international units of vitamin E and 10,000 international units of beta-carotene.

Caution: One study found that smokers who took beta-carotene supplements had a higher rate of death from lung cancer—so until further research is done, smokers should probably avoid these supplements.

•Learn to cope with stress. The link between emotional strain and heart disease is difficult to prove. But if you're prone to anxiety or depression, learn more about stress-fighters—yoga, meditation, deep breathing or psychotherapy. You will be helping your heart —and you'll certainly enjoy life more.

Source: Harvey B. Simon, MD, who practices internal medicine and preventive cardiology at Massachusetts General Hospital in Boston. He is on the faculties of Harvard Medical School and the Massachusetts Institute of Technology and is a founding member of the Harvard Cardiovascular Health Center...and author of *Conquering Heart Disease.* Little, Brown.

What You May Not Know About High Blood Pressure

More than 40 million Americans—about 75% of whom are adults over age 30—have high blood pressure (hypertension). Yet too few understand what they can do to possibly prevent or treat it.

Many people with mild hypertension ignore the problem or fail to spot it soon enough through medical checkups.

Danger: By the time hypertension causes medical complications, heart health has already been put at risk.

What's normal, what's not...

An initial blood pressure reading should be taken at about age three and again during adolescence. If your blood pressure is normal during this period, it should be rechecked every two or three years throughout your adult life.

If your blood pressure rises above 140/90, more frequent readings may be needed. Mild high blood pressure or Stage 1—from 140/90 to 160/100—usually requires lifestyle changes. Medication may also be necessary.

Here's what you may or may not know about high blood pressure and *what you can do to control it...*

•Being tense or nervous will not give you high blood pressure. The term hypertension refers to elevated pressure in the arteries, not to someone's personality. Many calm, cool-headed people have hypertension...many anxious, jittery people have perfectly normal blood pressures.

Nervousness may cause a short-term rise in blood pressure because of the adrenaline response. But there's no evidence that a nervous personality or even a stress-filled life causes hypertension.

•Blood pressure is variable. Your blood pressure does not remain constant. It can fluctuate by as much as 20 to 30 points a day.

Your blood pressure is at its highest during the early morning hours—just before and as you awaken—and when extra blood is needed, such as when you exercise.

It is at its lowest during sleep and restful times, dropping to the lowest point from about 1 am to 4 am.

•Blood pressure can change with the weather. Generally, your blood pressure drops during hot weather or when you're perspiring a lot. Warm weather causes blood vessels to dilate— and that lowers blood pressure.

In cold weather, blood pressure readings may rise because blood vessels constrict. Unless weather conditions are extreme, the change isn't enough to be medically significant.

•Excessive alcohol consumption can increase risk. Moderate to heavy drinking (about three to five drinks daily) can raise blood pressure over the long term.

Reason: Though large amounts of alcohol may dilate blood vessels, which can lower blood pressure, drinking also increases the heart rate, which raises blood pressure and cancels the dilation effect. Alcohol can also affect certain hormone systems that regulate blood pressure.

Cutting back on alcohol can bring levels to within normal range in some individuals. One or two drinks daily generally does not affect blood pressure, and some researchers have found that small quantities of alcohol can protect against cardiovascular disease.

Treatment…

•Exercise is good—but not all kinds. For some people, mild, repetitive exercise over time helps reduce blood pressure slightly. For others, it reduces levels significantly. It is not necessary to take up jogging or join an exercise club unless you need or prefer a structured plan. Walking or other leisure activities are satisfactory.

Warning: Isometric (pushing) exercises, like weight lifting (free weights or weight machines), should be avoided by anyone with high blood pressure or heart disease. The tightened muscles constrict blood vessels and can raise blood pressure. Avoid inversion bars and "antigravity boots," from which you hang upside down and do sit-ups. This increases blood pressure levels.

•Losing weight is the most effective nondrug method to reduce high blood pressure. Excess weight increases the volume of blood in the body, constricting blood vessels and putting extra demands on the heart, which elevates blood pressure. In some cases, losing as little as 10 pounds can return blood pressure levels to normal. If you plan to lose a significant amount of weight (more than 30 pounds), ask your doctor to monitor cardiovascular effects.

•Sex will not dramatically affect hypertension. Though sex can raise blood pressure temporarily—particularly with a new or unfamiliar partner—just minutes after the peak at orgasm, it will drop back to levels equivalent to or lower than before.

•Good nutrition can help keep levels in line. Lowering sodium intake helps some people with high blood pressure—about 20% or 30% of all cases. Others are hardly affected at all. Because most of us have too much salt in our diets, it's a good idea to cut back, regardless of your blood pressure readings.

Best way: Be aware of salt in cooking and on the table, as well as hidden sources of sodium. Many processed foods that don't taste salty—soft drinks, ice cream, breakfast cereals—are high in sodium.

Other dietary factors: Potassium—found in fresh fruits and vegetables, unprocessed meats and fish—and calcium are thought to have protective effects. Adequate calcium—800 to 1,000 mg a day for adults—rather than high doses is best. The minimum daily intake of potassium is 2,000 mg, but 4,000 mg is optimal. Daily sodium intake should be about half that of potassium.

Source: Marvin Moser, MD, clinical professor of medicine, Yale University School of Medicine. He is author of *Lower Your Blood Pressure and Live Longer* (Berkley) and *Week by Week to a Strong Heart* (Rodale Press).

Heart Healing Basics

People recovering from a heart attack, or at high risk for one, can improve the condition of their hearts by making specific dietary, exercise and lifestyle changes. *What to do:*

•*Reduce cholesterol levels.* A person's total cholesterol level should be below 200 mg/dl… and the LDL (bad) cholesterol level, below 130 mg/dl. *Recommended:*

•*Decrease cholesterol intake.* Eat no more than 300 mg daily.

•*Reduce fat intake.* No more than 30% of calories should come from fat.

•*Eat fiber foods.* 35 grams of fiber a day.

•*Maintain normal blood pressure.* That's 140/90 or better. *Suggested:*

•*Decrease sodium intake.* Avoid processed foods, canned foods to which sodium has been added and preserved and pickled foods.

•*Increase potassium intake.* This helps negate some of the bad effects of sodium. *Great sources:* Cantaloupe, tomatoes, bananas, baked potatoes, strawberries, squash and cauliflower.

•*Exercise.* At least three times a week, enough to burn off 150 to 300 calories.

• *Maintain normal body weight. Recommended:* Refer to the 1959 Metropolitan Life Height and Weight Chart.*

*Although this chart was recently updated, I prefer the 1959 version, which offers more realistic weight goals.

Source: Herman Hellerstein, MD, professor of medicine emeritus, Case Western Reserve University, Cleveland. He is coauthor, with Paul Perry, of *Healing Your Heart.* Simon and Schuster.

Never Too Late

Lifestyle changes can lower a man's risk of heart disease and premature death...even when the changes start in middle age or beyond. *Life extenders:* When men took up a moderately vigorous sports activity, they lowered their mortality risk by 23%. When they quit smoking, their death rate fell by 41%. *Less significant:* Losing excess weight, in the absence of other changes, had no effect on death rate.

Source: Study of 10,269 Harvard College alumni men aged 45 to 84, by the Stanford University School of Medicine and the Harvard School of Public Health, published in *The New England Journal of Medicine*, 10 Shattuck St., Boston 02115.

Cholesterol Confusion

Despite all that's been said and written about cholesterol in recent years, many Americans remain understandably confused on the topic. While most of us know that too much cholesterol in the bloodstream can cause heart disease, many people remain unclear on certain subtle but very important issues...

What's a healthy cholesterol level? For years, the American Heart Association and the National Institutes of Health have recommended an optimal total serum cholesterol level of less than 200 milligrams per deciliter.

But we now know that roughly *one-third* of all heart attacks occur in individuals with cholesterol readings between 150 and 200. In fact, only when cholesterol falls to 150 or lower does heart disease cease to be a meaningful risk.

Unfortunate: The average American has a cholesterol level around 220...and the average American develops heart disease.

What about "good" and "bad" cholesterol? Total serum cholesterol is made up of two different compounds—*low-density lipoprotein* (LDL) cholesterol...and *high-density lipoprotein* (HDL) cholesterol.

• LDL (bad) cholesterol forms fatty plaques inside your coronary arteries, which can lead to heart attack.

• HDL (good) cholesterol is what the body uses to remove excess LDL from the bloodstream.

Doctors sometimes use the ratio of total cholesterol to HDL as another means of gauging heart-disease risk.

Example: Someone with a total cholesterol count of 200 and an HDL level of 50 has a ratio of 200/50 or 4:1. In general, a ratio of 3.5 (200/57 is 3.5:1) or lower puts you at minimal risk for heart disease. The lower the ratio, the lower the risk—at least for people eating a traditional fatty, cholesterol-rich diet.

Exception: Vegetarians and others on a very low-fat, low-cholesterol diet less than 10% fat and virtually no cholesterol. Because they consume less fat and cholesterol and thus have less LDL in their blood, their bodies don't need to make as much HDL. Consequently, they may have high ratios yet have a reduced risk of heart disease.

What causes high cholesterol? The single biggest factor is simply eating too much saturated fat and cholesterol. In fact, in the traditional American diet, roughly 40% of calories come from fat...and foods rich in fat are often rich in cholesterol. In countries where people eat much less cholesterol and less fat and where cholesterol averages around 130, heart disease is very rare.

Eating too much fat causes not only heart disease, but also has been linked with cancers of the breast, prostate and colon, as well as stroke, diabetes, osteoporosis and, of course, obesity.

There is a genetic variability in how efficiently or inefficiently your body can metabolize, or get rid of, dietary saturated fat and cholesterol. On one end of the spectrum, some people are so efficient that they can eat almost anything and not get heart disease. On the other end of the spectrum are people who may get heart disease no matter what they eat. Ninety-five percent of people are somewhere in the middle. If your cholesterol level is less than 150, then either you're not eating very much fat and cholesterol or your body is very efficient at getting rid of it. Either way, your risk is low.

If it's above 150, begin by moderately reducing the amount of fat and cholesterol in your diet. If that's enough to bring it down below 150, that may be all you need to do, at least as far as your heart is concerned. If not, then continue to reduce the fat and cholesterol in your diet until your cholesterol stays below 150…*or* you are following a low-fat vegetarian reversal diet.

Which foods contain cholesterol? All foods derived from animals, including meats, poultry, fish and dairy products. Meat is also high in iron, which oxidizes cholesterol into a form that more quickly clogs arteries. Skim milk has almost no fat and virtually no cholesterol. "Low-fat" milk is not really very low in fat. Foods derived solely from plants contain no cholesterol.

Caution: Some plant foods, including avocados, nuts, seeds and oils, are rich in saturated fat.

Just because a food is "cholesterol-free" doesn't mean it's good for your heart. All oils are 100% fat, and all oils contain at least some saturated fat, *which your liver converts into cholesterol.*

What about the French paradox? Heart disease rates are 30% lower in France than in the US, but it is still their number one cause of death.

Despite media reports, there is no real evidence that goose liver, red wine or olive oil protect against heart disease.

Olive oil, for example, is 100% fat, and it is 14% saturated fat, which your body converts into cholesterol. The more olive oil you eat, the higher your blood cholesterol level will be. Olive oil "lowers" cholesterol only when you substitute it for oils that are higher in saturated fat. So, olive oil is not good for you, it's less bad for you.

Note: Goose liver is one of the highest sources of cholesterol.

I think the French have less heart disease *despite* their diet, not because of it. What is different is their social support. A number of well-designed studies have shown that people who feel isolated and lonely have three to five times the premature death rates from not only heart disease but also from *all* causes of death. Even in France, heart disease is much lower in the southwestern region—where they have strong social networks—than in Paris or Normandy, where the divorce rate is high.

Is it possible to have too little cholesterol? Probably not, if you lower cholesterol by changing diet and lifestyle rather than by using drugs. If you eat a very low-cholesterol diet, your liver synthesizes all the cholesterol your body needs.

Recent studies have linked cholesterol levels below 160 to an increased risk of liver cancer, lung disease, hemorrhagic stroke, alcoholism—even suicide and homicide. But just because low cholesterol is linked to these problems doesn't mean it causes them.

More plausible: Many diseases *cause* low cholesterol levels, not the other way around. Since cholesterol is made in the liver, then any disease of the liver results in reduced cholesterol production, and thus lower cholesterol levels. Many forms of cancer cause cholesterol levels to decrease, but there is no evidence that the opposite is true. One of the hallmarks of depression and of alcoholism is loss of appetite, which lowers cholesterol—not the other way around. Hemorrhagic stroke rates are slightly higher when people have very low cholesterol levels, but these account for less than 10% of strokes. Over 90% of strokes are thrombotic (caused by blood clots), and the risk of these is greatly reduced when cholesterol levels are below 160.

How often should I have my cholesterol checked? About once every two years, starting as early as age two. *To insure a reliable reading:* Find a testing lab certified by the Lipid Research Clinics. Use the same laboratory each time. Be sure to fast* for at least 12 hours prior to your test.

How can I get my cholesterol under control? Exercise—it raises HDL cholesterol.

Stress *raises* LDL cholesterol, as does eating a high-fat, cholesterol-rich diet.

So the best way to raise HDL and lower LDL is to get regular exercise, avoid smoking, practice
*Drinking water is OK.

meditation or other stress-management techniques and eat a healthful diet.

If you have heart disease: Eliminate all animal products except egg whites and nonfat dairy products…and all high-fat vegetable products, including oils, nuts, seeds, avocados, chocolate and other cocoa products, olives and coconut. In most cases this "reversal" diet not only keeps heart disease from progressing, but also reverses its course.

ConAgra, the maker of Healthy Choice, recently introduced "Life Choice Special Nutrition," a line of frozen dinners that meet the reversal-diet guidelines.

Eat more vegetables, fish and skinless chicken. Use skim milk instead of whole milk. Use as little cooking oil as possible. Avoid oil-based salad dressing. If after eight weeks your cholesterol remains high, go on the "reversal" diet.

What about cholesterol-lowering drugs? I prescribe cholesterol-lowering drugs for people with heart disease who make only moderate changes in diet and lifestyle. Why? Several studies have shown that people with heart disease who only follow the American Heart Association guidelines tend to show worsening of their disease. People who follow the reversal diet—or who take cholesterol-lowering drugs—often can stop or reverse heart disease. Diet is preferable, because you avoid the high costs and side effects (both known and unknown) of drugs.

Source: Dean Ornish, MD, assistant clinical professor of medicine and an attending physician at the School of Medicine, University of California, San Francisco, and at California Pacific Medical Center. He is the author of *Dr. Dean Ornish's Program for Reversing Heart Disease,* Ballantine Books, 201 E. 50 St., New York 10022.

Isolation…and Your Heart

San Francisco physician Dean Ornish launched a study in 1986 to see whether comprehensive changes in lifestyle could reverse heart disease. *His aim:* To find out if lifestyle changes alone could be as effective as drugs or surgery. *Important, too:* Showing that patients could maintain the sweeping changes that Ornish was proposing.

It worked: 82% of the patients with severe heart disease who enrolled in the study have shown measurable reversal of their coronary artery blockages.

Control group: After following standard treatment, they became measurably worse.

At the very least, Ornish's findings suggest that conventional recommendations for altering diet and lifestyle don't go nearly far enough.

For those who are not among the 40 million Americans afflicted with heart disease, the research may offer the first scientifically based program for preventing our nation's number-one killer. From Dr. Ornish…

Many doctors prescribe changes in diet, exercise, and lifestyle for their patients, as you do. What makes your program so different?

During the course of the study, I've been struck by the profound sense of isolation that so many people experience in our culture today—isolation from one's feelings, from other people, from the experience of something spiritual. By "spiritual," I mean the experience of feeling that while on one level we're separate, on another level we're all connected to each other and a part of something larger than ourselves. This experience may be in a religious or secular context.

In addition to emphasizing diet and exercise, my program addresses the emotional and spiritual factors in each patient's life.

To what extent is this sense of isolation directly linked to heart disease and other health problems?

A number of studies have shown that people who feel isolated have three to five times the mortality not only from heart disease, but from all causes of death when compared with those who have a greater sense of intimacy and community. Isolation generally leads to chronic stress and emotional pain.

Do we feel so isolated because we're more stressed out than ever before?

A hundred years ago, if it didn't rain, your crops wouldn't come in and you and your family might starve. That had to be at least as stressful as whether or not the fax comes in on time. *What's different:* We don't have the sense of connection and community we once had. Extended families disappeared. Even the two-parent nuclear family is now in the minority. People at work don't feel the same sense of community, given the recession and mergers and downsizing. Memberships in churches and synagogues are also declining. We pay a price for all of this.

How does your program specifically address feelings of isolation?

We teach people various techniques such as yoga, visualization and meditation, to help manage stress, and to help them identify, transform and transcend their isolation.

We also teach communication skills, which help people learn to talk to each other in ways in which others can begin to hear them. Our support group, which began as a way to exchange diet and recipe information, has evolved into a real community, a place where people feel comfortable talking about what's going on in their lives and opening their hearts to each other.

Are people really willing to deal with the underlying isolation in order to feel better?

Pain can be a wonderful motivator for change. Because any kind of change is disruptive and stressful at first, people are more content to keep things the way they are if they're just a little painful. But a heart attack can be a catalyst for real transformation. Unfortunately, most doctors haven't been adequately trained to help people take advantage of such opportunities for change.

Doesn't everything you're talking about also apply to other illnesses—and just plain stress?

Absolutely. We're focusing on heart disease as a model, because we can use high-tech, state-of-the-art diagnostic measures, including computer-analyzed angiograms and cardiac PET scans to learn how powerful—even on a physical level—these approaches are.

Most of the time, heart patients are urged to stop smoking and change their diet so they'll live longer, but efforts to motivate people to change out of fear just don't work for very long. Many—if not most—people are more concerned with getting through the day than whether or not they'll live to be 86—unless they're 85. People use alcohol, cigarettes, overeating and overwork as ways to cope with painful feelings.

Unless we address the underlying emotional pain and isolation, it's very hard to motivate people to quit smoking or change their diet or any other behaviors which, though adaptive, are unhealthy.

If fear doesn't inspire people to change, what does?

Short-term gains: Feeling better…having more energy. For those with heart disease, the chest pains tend to go away very quickly. People in the program may live longer, too, but that's not the point. It's how they live.

And, paradoxically, we're finding that it's easier to make big changes in diet and lifestyle than moderate ones.

When you make moderate changes, you have the worst of both worlds. You feel deprived because you can't eat or do everything you want, but the changes aren't enough to make you feel significantly better. But when you make comprehensive changes, you feel so much better so quickly that the choices become much clearer.

Example: When people who couldn't work or make love or cross the street because of chest pain can suddenly do all of the above without pain, they usually say, "I like eating meat, but not that much."

How does this translate for people who don't suffer from coronary disease?

Here again, it's important to emphasize the short-term gains. I began modifying my own lifestyle when I was 19—not because I was afraid of having a heart attack, but because the changes made me feel so much better. I had more energy. I could think more clearly. I had a greater sense of well-being and inner peace. I don't believe in giving up something I enjoy unless I get something back that's even better.

Do you think everyone should become a vegetarian?

That's a personal choice. What I tell people is that to the degree they move in that direction, there will be a corresponding benefit—and not only with heart disease. There's increasing evidence linking a diet high in animal products to a whole range of degenerative diseases, including stroke, colon cancer, breast cancer, prostate cancer, obesity, hypertension, gallbladder disease and osteoporosis.

It's also important to point out that several studies have shown that people with heart disease who only cut back to conform to the American Heart Association's recommended diet of no more than 30% fat generally get worse instead of better. But—if they're willing to make comprehensive changes in diet and lifestyle—they can often stop or even reverse their heart disease.

What about the person without heart disease?

You can use your cholesterol level as a rough index of how efficient or inefficient you are in metabolizing dietary fat and cholesterol. If your cholesterol level is less than 150, you're probably okay as far as your heart is concerned, because heart disease is rare at that level. If it's above 150, moderate diet changes may be all you need to bring it below 150. If that's not effective, reduce dietary fat and cholesterol still further. Most people will respond to diet alone if the diet's sufficiently low in fat and cholesterol.

Your program has several components. What ties it all together?

We put everything in the context of trying to help people heal their isolation and quiet their minds and bodies enough to experience an inner sense of well-being.

The ancient yogis and wise people didn't develop these techniques to lower their cholesterol, unclog their arteries or become better businesspeople—although the program can help us do all those things. When we quiet our minds and bodies, we may find that the peace and happiness we run around looking for outside ourselves has been right there all along.

Do participants in your study worry that if they achieve inner peace, they'll lose their edge and stop being productive and successful?

No. Most people in our program find that they become more productive without getting stressed and sick in the process. But many people confuse being relaxed with being lethargic. They confuse managing stress with avoiding it. Some people think they have to choose between an interesting, productive life and an early heart attack, or a long, boring life, mellowing out under a tree. That's not the choice at all. Athletes know the difference. When they're at their most relaxed, they perform at their highest level. When they tense up, they don't do as well.

How can people who are not in your program heal their isolation?

I encourage people to create a support group. It's unfortunate that in our culture people have to have a drug or alcohol problem to get into a community of people where they support each other and communicate openly. I encourage people to find ways to do that in their own lives, and not necessarily in the context of heart disease or any other illness.

How else can people benefit from the results of your study?

My book gives people the information and tools to follow the program themselves. And though people often buy the book hoping to reverse or prevent heart disease, what keeps them on the program is experiencing how good it feels to have an inner sense of peace and joy and well-being—not from getting or doing, but from just being. They may do the same work or have the same relationships as before, but there's a shift in attitude. They begin to realize that what they do is much less important than what they bring to it. Within any action lies the potential for isolation or for intimacy and healing.

Could one benefit from individual components of your program, such as the diet or yoga, and still see significant results?

Yes. We found that the more people changed their lifestyle, the more improvements were measured. But...people have a spectrum of choices. Our research gives people the scientifically based information they can use to make intelligent decisions about their lifestyles, giving them new hope and new choices.

Source: Dean Ornish, MD, assistant clinical professor of medicine and an attending physician at the School of Medicine, University of California, San Francisco, and at California Pacific Medical Center. He is the author of *Dr. Dean Ornish's Program for Reversing Heart Disease,* Ballantine Books, 201 E. 50 St., New York 10022.

Better Heart-Attack Treatment

Quick clot-dissolving therapy at the start of heart-attack symptoms significantly improves recovery. *Key:* Treatment within one hour of the onset of symptoms. Only 1% of patients treated that early died—compared with 10% of those treated later. *Scary:* Patients now wait an average of 80 minutes in the hospital for anti-clotting treatment.

Source: Study of more than 350 heart-attack patients, led by W. Douglas Weaver, MD, head of the Myocardial Infarction Triage and Intervention Trial, reported in *Medical Tribune*, 257 Park Ave. S., New York 10010.

and blood pressure can suddenly soar. This can lead to chest pain, heart rhythm irregularities or sudden cardiac death.

Source: Barry Franklin, PhD, director, Cardiac Rehabilitation and Exercise Laboratories, William Beaumont Hospital, Royal Oak, Michigan.

Toll-Free Heart Disease Hotline

Dial 800-AHA-USA-1 to be connected with operators specially trained to answer questions about the prevention and treatment of cardiovascular disease and stroke—the nation's number one killer.

Source: American Heart Association, 7272 Greenville Ave., Dallas 75231.

Working Wonders

A quick return to work helps first-time heart-attack victims recover emotionally. *Recent study:* Only 9% of patients who resumed working within four months of their heart attacks showed symptoms of major depression within one year after the attack. Among patients who did not return to work, 52% became seriously depressed within a year.

Source: Kathryn Rost, PhD, assistant professor of psychiatry, University of Arkansas for Medical Sciences.

Hunters, Beware

Hunters die from heart attacks *three times as often* as from firearm accidents. Hunters are often sedentary men who go out once a year in extreme cold, weighed down by heavy clothes and a heavy gun. When they sight an animal, often after hours of inactivity, their heart rate

Routine Checks Save Lives

Routine checks for HDL—high density lipoprotein, or "good" cholesterol—are good measures of heart-attack risk. HDL is crucial regardless of total cholesterol.

If HDL level is low:

In many cases, weight loss alone can diminish triglyceride (a compound made of fatty acid and glycerol) levels and increase HDL. *Also recommended:* Modify diet, exercise more and stop smoking.

Source: Elliot Rapaport, MD, professor of medicine, University of California at San Francisco.

Drinking Your Way To Better Health?

Cabernet sauvignon contains a higher level of resveratrol—a natural cholesterol fighter—than most other red wines. Consumers should be aware, however, that for resveratrol to be effective, two to three glasses of the wine must be consumed daily, not just on the weekends or at parties. *Important:* The wine should be accompanied by food, which slows the alcohol's absorption into the bloodstream.

Source: Leroy Creasy, PhD, professor of pomology, New York State College of Agriculture and Life Sciences at Cornell University, Ithaca, who originally identified resveratrol as the cholesterol-lowering substance in wine in 1991.

3

Disease Defying Tactics

How You Can Beat Springtime Allergies

For millions of Americans—up to 25% of the population—springtime brings not only a respite from cold winter weather, but also high pollen counts and weeks of nettlesome allergies.

Hay fever and other seasonal allergies result when the body *overreacts* to various types of pollen or to any of the millions of other proteins swirling about in the air.

For some unknown reason, the immune system recognizes these allergens not as what they are—harmless specks—but as dangerous threats that must be rebuffed. The immune system immediately mounts an aggressive attack against the invader. *Result:* Watery eyes, runny nose, scratchy throat, wheezing, sneezing and, on occasion, hives.

A generation ago, little help was available for sufferers of hay fever and other seasonal allergies. Today, there are effective methods not only for controlling the symptoms of an allergic reaction, but also for blocking its underlying cause.

Bottom line: While seasonal allergies cannot be cured, their symptoms can now be dramatically curtailed. There's simply no need to suffer.

To control seasonal allergies...

• Limit contact with pollen-filled air. Being indoors with the windows open is much the same as being outdoors.

Examples: On a typical windy spring day, air inside a house with open windows and screen doors contains roughly 70% as much pollen as outside air. The air inside a moving car with open windows contains roughly 90% as much pollen as outside air.

To keep pollen out: Keep doors and windows closed at all times during allergy season—both at home and in cars. Wear a filter mask while exercising outdoors, mowing your lawn, etc. On days when pollen counts are especially high, try to stay indoors if at all possible.

Pollen's secret weapon: Kids and pets. Surprisingly large amounts of pollen can hitch a ride into your home on children's clothing and on the fur of a pet dog or cat. To minimize the problem, have your kids change into house clothes as soon as they come in for the day. Put the clothes they wore in a hamper or the washer right away. Bathe pets regularly—or keep them exclusively outdoors or indoors during allergy season.

•Keep your home clean and dust free. Even if there's relatively little pollen in the air, seasonal allergies can sometimes be triggered by the combined exposure to pollen plus airborne irritants like cigarette smoke, perfume and other allergens such as household dust.* So, controlling dust helps control your allergy.

Self-defense: During allergy season, dust and vacuum your home at least twice weekly—more often in your bedroom, where you spend most of your time. To make bedroom dusting as easy as possible, remove carpeting, heavy drapes, dust ruffles, venetian blinds and other sites where dust tends to collect. Encase mattresses, pillows and box springs in zippered plastic slipcovers.

•Buy a high-quality air filter. *Best:* An electrostatic model capable of filtering particles as fine as five microns. A good unit (to filter an entire home) will cost five hundred dollars. Room-sized units are less costly, around $200. Steer clear of cheap filters— remember, you get what you pay for.

Note: If your home has a forced air-heating or air-conditioning system, install a washable filter directly to the system. Have your ducts professionally vacuumed at least once every five years.

If you have trouble locating a source of plastic slipcovers, filter masks, air filters and other allergy control products, get in touch with one of the many allergy product mail-order houses.

Helpful: Allergy Control Products, Ridgefield, Connecticut (800-422-3878) and Allergy Control Environments, Haddon Heights, New Jersey (800-882-4110).

•Find out precisely what is causing your symptoms. Allergies occurring in early spring

*Household dust is not made up of tiny specks of dirt—contrary to common belief. Rather, it's primarily a mixture of dead skin cells, fibers from clothing and furniture and the bodies and feces of insects, especially the house dust mite. This microscopic bug, harmless except to those allergic to it or its feces, feeds on sloughed-off skin cells. It thrives in bedding and upholstery.

are often caused by tree pollen, while those occurring in late spring or early summer are often grass-pollen allergies. Of course, it's possible that your allergy is not to inhaled allergens at all, but to certain foods, dust, pets, etc. If your allergy symptoms persist despite steps to keep airborne allergens out of your home, consider using over-the-counter antihistamines and decongestants, or call your doctor for additional advice. If the advice doesn't work, ask for a referral to an allergist with certification from the American Board of Allergy and Immunology to schedule an allergy "scratch test."

What's involved: Tiny amounts of many different allergens (dust, various pollens, insect feces, etc.) are placed on the skin of your arm or back. The skin is then scratched or pricked to introduce the allergens underneath the skin. Any swelling or redness suggests an allergy to the allergen applied to that site.

•Consider drug therapy. If over-the-counter antihistamines and decongestants fail to provide relief, produce unwelcome side effects, or if you find yourself using them every day for weeks on end, ask your doctor about prescription medications. These include non-sedating antihistamines and several types of nasal sprays that inhibit allergic reactions. The newer ones are highly effective against watery eyes, runny nose and other allergy symptoms.

Two additional forms of drug therapy often prove effective...

•Anti-inflammatories. Decongestants and antihistamines treat only the symptoms of allergies. In contrast, anti-inflammatories—chiefly corticosteroids and related drugs, administered via nasal spray—block the allergic reaction itself.

Caution: Steroids are powerful drugs. While they're generally administered in tiny doses, and although they break down quickly in the body, inhaled corticosteroids occasionally cause a thinning of the tissues lining the nostrils. Some patients prefer a nonsteroidal anti-inflammatory drug, cromolyn sodium, also administered in spray form. This drug, though slightly less effective than corticosteroids, has no side effects.

•Immunotherapy. This type of drug therapy is reserved for persons with severe or year-round allergies, especially those whose symptoms cannot be controlled with antihistamines, decongestants or anti-inflammatories.

What's involved: Gradually increasing quantities of known allergens are injected into the body. Injections are once or twice weekly at first. Later, the period between shots can often be stretched to four weeks. Via this process, the immune system "learns" to control its response when these same allergens are encountered in the environment.

Important: Allergy shots take weeks or even months to become effective. For this reason they must be taken on a year-round basis, even for allergic symptoms that appear only in springtime.

Source: Martha V. White, MD, senior staff fellow and pediatric allergy coordinator at the National Institute of Allergy and Infectious Diseases, National Institutes of Health, Bethesda, Maryland 20892.

Allergy News

Good news for allergy sufferers: With various preventive measures and allergy treatments now available, you can make yourself more comfortable during hay fever season this year.

Allergies: The new basics. An allergic reaction is an abnormal physical response to one of the millions of proteins in the environment. For reasons that are not entirely clear, the immune system perceives this protein—usually a totally benign substance—as dangerous to the body, and mounts an attack against it. The immune system's offensive against airborne allergens like pollen include hives, a runny (itchy, swollen) nose and teary eyes, as well as sneezing or wheezing.

In cases of food allergy, symptoms are cramps and diarrhea, often accompanied by swelling of the lips, eyes, face, tongue and throat.

Most common food allergens: Milk, eggs, fish, shellfish, peanuts, soy and other nuts. *Treatment:* Complete avoidance of the allergens. Peanuts and fish can be lethal.

The capacity to develop allergies is an inherited trait that affects about 20% to 25% of the population. Airborne or "inhalant" allergies to ragweed, dust, cats and pollen are more common than allergies to food or drugs.

If you think you may have an allergy but you're not sure what's causing it, your doctor will probably recommend the standard allergy "scratch" test.

Procedure: Small amounts of suspected allergens are placed on the skin of the forearm, upper arm or back. The area is then pricked or scratched to introduce the allergen below the skin surface. The test site is examined after 15 to 20 minutes, and if swelling and redness of the skin have developed where a particular allergen was applied, the test is considered positive for that allergen.

Treating and preventing allergic reactions…

Drug therapy for allergies will follow one of two approaches…

•it will treat symptoms of the allergic reaction…

•or prevent the reaction from occurring.

•Antihistamines and decongestants: Either over-the-counter or prescription strengths treat allergy symptoms. In cases of mild-to-moderate allergies, such medications can probably clear up the runny nose, watery eyes and itchy mouth and throat that can make spring pollen season such a trial. *Example:* Hismanal, which produces no sedative effect, is available by prescription.

•Anti-inflammatories: For more severe allergies, it may be preferable to prevent or moderate the allergic reaction itself with one of the corticosteroids administered as a nasal spray, or an anti-inflammatory drug—cromolyn sodium. Nasal cromolyn is a safe drug with few, if any, side effects. Nasal corticosteroids are topically potent agents that are quickly degraded after absorption. Therefore, the body sees only tiny amounts of steroid if the medication is used in recommended doses.

Important: If you have been relying for years on over-the-counter medication to control your allergy symptoms, it's time to consult a doctor about a more effective therapeutic regimen.

•Immunotherapy: Also known as "allergy shots," it is a third allergy treatment strategy. It is usually recommended only for people with at least moderate—but more likely severe—allergies. The goal of immunotherapy is to make allergy sufferers less responsive to their particular allergens. The starting dose is too small

25

to be effective, but it is necessary to start with tiny doses to avoid allergic reactions to the shots themselves. Therefore, don't expect to see much improvement until you reach a maintenance dose.

How it works: Small amounts of known allergens are injected into the body once or twice a week. The dose is gradually increased until an effective or maintenance dose is achieved. This controlled introduction of small quantities of "foreign" proteins provokes the immune system into producing neutralizing antibodies, but not into a full-scale counterattack that would result in an allergic reaction. Once a sufficient amount of these antibodies are circulating in the body, strong allergic reactions (and their accompanying annoying symptoms) can be prevented or significantly reduced. Once a maintenance dose has been achieved, the interval between shots can be stretched out to every four to six weeks.

Two new classes of drugs...

Nasal atrovent and antileukotriene drugs are two new classes of drugs which are being studied for their effects on allergies. Neither is commercially available yet.

Relief without drugs...

The simplest way to eliminate the unpleasant symptoms of an allergy attack is to find out what you're allergic to and avoid it.

This advice is relatively easy to follow in the case of allergies to foods or animals. But avoiding airborne allergens can be a bit more difficult to accomplish. And because people allergic to pollen or ragweed may also be sensitive to other allergens (house dust) or irritants (perfume, cigarette smoke), exposure to these secondary triggers during hay fever season may exacerbate the pollen allergy and produce some very uncomfortable symptoms.

House dust is a common allergen that often acts as a secondary trigger in people with allergies to pollen, animal dander, etc. And one of the principal constituents of house dust is the house dust mite—a microscopic insect that feeds off of discarded bits of dead skin. These mites thrive in places where you'd expect to find sloughed skin cells—in rugs, upholstered furniture, pillows, mattresses and box springs.

Battle plan...

Concentrate on the bedroom. It's where people spend most of their time...and where the house dust mite tends to spend most of its time. Put allergen-proof casings (which you can get from an allergy supply house or a department store) on the bed pillows, box spring and mattress.

Important: These coverings must have a plastic layer and a zipper and they must completely enclose the pillow, box spring or mattress. (The more expensive cases will have a cotton layer for greater comfort.) *Also:* Simplify the bedroom furnishings so it is easier to keep the room dust-free. Eliminate venetian blinds, heavy curtains, bed ruffles and canopies, stuffed furniture and bookcases that are difficult to keep dusted. Dust the room thoroughly twice a week.

Air filtration system. This can be helpful in reducing indoor exposure to dust and other allergens. *Recommended:* An electrostatic system able to filter particles down to a level of five microns. If you have a central forced air heating/air conditioning unit, a filtration device can easily be added to your existing system. If you don't have central heating, a room air purifier may handle the job adequately. *Rule:* Don't look for a bargain. The cheaper ones don't work as well as the more expensive units.

During spring allergy season, if you're allergic to pollens, grasses and other things found outdoors, reduce your exposure to these allergens when you're indoors by keeping your doors and windows closed. The same principle applies when you're traveling by car. And on dry, windy days with high pollen counts, stay indoors if you can.

When to see a doctor...

If allergy symptoms—or the side effects of over-the-counter medications—begin to interfere with your lifestyle or your ability to work ...or if they're just generally making you miserable, it's time to see a doctor about your allergies. (On the other hand, if your allergies are bothersome for only a few days each year, it's probably okay to self-treat with drugstore allergy pills.)

If you decide that you need to see a doctor, meet with your regular internist, pediatrician or family doctor first. He/she can prescribe appropriate first-line therapy to control your allergy symptoms. If, however, your symptoms don't respond to treatment, or if the side effects of the prescribed medications become difficult to tolerate, you should ask to be referred to an allergy specialist.

Source: Martha V. White, MD, Senior Staff Fellow at the National Institute of Allergy and Infectious Diseases, National Institutes of Health, Bethesda, Maryland 20892.

Autumn—Allergies' Second Season

We usually associate hay fever with the spring. But autumn allergies unleash a wicked punch—and just at one of the worst times.

Autumn allergies strike when summer's heat, vacations and other outdoor activities have taxed all our energies. They come with the increased demands of the new season—returning to school or work.

No one dies of seasonal allergic rhinitis (hay fever)—but there can be serious complications. Swelling and mucus can block drainage of sinuses and ears, resulting in sinus headaches, painful ear infections and inflammations.

Asthma sufferers may also find that autumn allergies trigger and escalate their asthma attacks to sometimes dangerous levels.

Dealing with the allergies of autumn is a concern for the 20% of us who are about to be hit. While there is no cure, there are effective steps we can take to eliminate the suffering.

How allergies strike…

Fall allergens are innocent grains of pollen released by plants as part of their reproductive cycles. We just happen to intercept the pollen before a receptive plant does.

Windblown pollen entering your nose or throat provokes a defensive response from molecules called immune globulin-E (Ig-E). These Ig-E molecules attach to special allergy cells (called "mast cells") in the respiratory tract. On further exposure of these Ig-E-bound mast cells to the pollen allergen, mast cells are stimulated to release histamine and other associated chemicals. *Result:* Nasal and throat tissues swell, mucous membranes start producing overtime, and our sneeze reflex erupts to expel the invaders—an allergy attack.

What makes autumn allergies different…

Spring's allergies are caused by a variety of plant and tree pollens. The allergens of early autumn are almost all weed pollen, most notably ragweed.

Dust is a year-round irritant to those who are susceptible. So is mold, which can be especially troublesome in the late fall.

Reason: That glorious cloak of fallen leaves is the ideal dark, moist environment for sprouting bumper crops of mold spores.

Self-defense…

•Keep the outdoors out. People tend to be most sensitive to wind-borne pollens. Keeping windows closed helps to dramatically reduce the pollen entering your house.

Weeds pollinate most heavily in the cool hours of early morning—so you may go to sleep comfortably by an open window only to wake up sneezing and congested just before dawn. Don't risk it.

Try keeping your air conditioner on—set low—for an extra month this fall. *Important:* It must have a washable filter…or, if you have central air-conditioning, you should have the unit's air ducts professionally vacuumed every three to five years.

•Clean house. A summer's worth of dust, smoke and animal hairs have visited at your house. These can provide enough irritation to detonate seasonal allergies.

A thorough housecleaning at the beginning of fall, along with regular dusting and vacuuming throughout the season, can significantly reduce the effects of autumn allergy attacks.

•Dress defensively. If pollens were sequins, after an afternoon of puttering in the yard, hiking or even shopping at a flea market, you'd look like Elvis Presley onstage. So it's a good idea to change clothes immediately when you come in, putting worn clothes in a covered hamper.

More aggressive self-defense…

•Air filters. Available for both single rooms or offices and entire houses, these filter pollutants like pollen and dust by electrical charge.

They can screen particles down to five micron levels.

•Consulting an allergist. These medical specialists may isolate the exact source of your seasonal allergy and, if it is severe enough, begin a year-round immunotherapy program to help you.

Drug treatment for autumn allergies…

There are basically two kinds:

•Antihistamines treat the symptoms of an allergy by alleviating the runny nose, watery eyes and sneezing. The most popular, which also have the advantage of being non-sedating, include Claritin, and Histamal and are available by prescription only. But over-the-counter antihistamines can be just as effective at relieving symptoms.

•Anti-inflammatories, available by prescription, prevent inflammation and the release of histamine at the cellular level. In effect, they stop the allergic reaction before it begins. Typically, anti-inflammatories are corticosteroids. Because of possible side effects—even though they're rarely consequential—a popular non-steroid nasal spray, Chromolyn, may be your physician's choice. A new anti-inflammatory, Nedocromil, also a nasal spray, is rapidly gaining widespread use.

Source: Martha V. White, MD, director, Pediatric Allergy and Research Institute for Asthma and Allergy, Washington Hospital Center, 106 Irving St. NW, Washington DC 20010.

Alzheimer's or Not?

Alzheimer's disease is a progressive disease of the brain in later life* that is accompanied by *dementia*—decline in memory, reasoning and other intellectual functions.

An older person whose mental abilities are impaired does *not* necessarily have Alzheimer's disease. There are many other causes of dementia—and many of them are treatable.

Included…

•Effects of prescription drugs—or combinations of drugs.

*Although there are some cases with victims younger than 65.

•Depression—especially if memory and concentration problems are accompanied by sleep disturbance, weight loss or diminished interest in daily activities.

•Diseases of the body's other organ systems, such as heart, kidney, lungs or blood.

•Tick-borne Lyme disease.

•Vitamin deficiencies.

•Alcohol abuse.

•Disorders of the thyroid, pituitary or adrenal glands.

To avoid misdiagnosis: Make sure the patient is evaluated by a medical professional who has special training and experience in diagnosis and treatment of diseases of the brain and aging. *Also helpful:* Seek a second opinion after any diagnosis.

Source: Robert Friedland, MD, clinical director of the Alzheimer's Center at University Hospitals of Cleveland, Case Western Reserve University, Cleveland 44106.

Alzheimer's Disease Preventive

Raise blood levels of vitamin A and beta-carotene—since insufficient amounts have been linked to Alzheimer's in recent studies. Both are antioxidants that help thwart the effects of aging. *Self-defense:* Take vitamin A and beta-carotene supplements. Nutrients from capsules are more fully utilized by the bodies of older people than from natural sources. *Caution:* See your doctor for appropriate doses of supplements—even over-the-counter ones.

Source: Arthur Winter, MD, director of the New Jersey Neurological Institute and member of neurosurgery faculty, University of Medicine and Dentistry of New Jersey.

Arthritis Can Be Controlled

Myths about arthritis abound. Many people assume that arthritis is inevitable with age… that it's invariably crippling…that it can't be treated.

Yet in my 20 years as a rheumatologist, I've rarely seen an arthritic patient who didn't feel much better after following a comprehensive course of treatment. Arthritis refers to inflammation in the joint. There are more than 100 different kinds of arthritis, which fall under two general categories:

Inflammatory—including rheumatoid arthritis, which afflicts 2.5 million people in this country. This type starts in the membrane that lines the capsule surrounding a joint. Rheumatoid arthritis tends to affect many joints, as well as muscles, nerves or other parts of the body. Inflammatory conditions are systemic in nature and influence other parts of the body. Fatigue and flu-like symptoms are common. It most often has its onset in women between the ages of 30 and 50.

Degenerative—or osteoarthritis, afflicting 36 million Americans. It is thought to result from natural wear and tear on joints and is more common in older adults...as well as younger people who have suffered sports injuries, accidents or other severe trauma to the joints.

Although we don't know the cause or cure for either type of arthritis, we have many, many resources for controlling it by relieving pain, restoring motion, slowing degeneration and helping patients lead normal and active lives.

Diagnosis, treatment...

Because there is so much prejudice about arthritis in the medical community, the disease is often incorrectly diagnosed. Just because a patient is older and has joint pain doesn't mean he/she has arthritis—and even if arthritis is present, it may not be what's causing the symptoms.

Bursitis (inflammation of the protective sac near a joint) and tendinitis (inflamed tendons) are treatable conditions that are frequently confused with arthritis.

Example: A patient complains that his right hip aches. Because the patient is 65, his doctor assumes he has arthritis. An X-ray shows some wear on the hip joint, confirming the doctor's assumption. The physician says, "What do you expect at 65?" and puts him on anti-inflammatory drugs, which don't help him. In fact, the arthritis isn't causing the pain—this patient is actually suffering from bursitis, which could be easily treated with physical therapy or steroid injections.

I urge patients who are diagnosed with arthritis not to accept the attitude that nothing can be done for them. If a primary care physician isn't sure about the diagnosis, or if treatment isn't successful in relieving symptoms, I recommend consulting a rheumatologist—a specialist in arthritic diseases.

The best approach to treating arthritis is a multi-modal one.

Medications help, but they are far more effective when used in conjunction with other factors, including physical therapy, exercise, adequate sleep, diet and stress management.

Mechanical devices such as splints and canes can also provide relief by resting the affected area.

Many of these elements are surprisingly simple—but often ignored. Commonsense remedies the medical establishment once scorned as old wives' tales are now gaining scientific support.

Though new drugs are coming onto the market all the time, I believe the real news in treatment is validation of the old treatments.

Medication...

Physicians have a whole arsenal of drugs to draw from. Mild cases of osteoarthritis may respond to over-the-counter painkillers such as acetaminophen.

More severe cases of degenerative joint diseases and cases of rheumatoid arthritis are usually helped by anti-inflammatory drugs. Most of these can have side effects, such as stomach irritation, but so many varieties are available that doctor and patient can usually find one the patient can tolerate.

Nonprescription anti-inflammatories aren't usually strong enough in recommended doses to be effective against arthritis...and increasing the dose can lead to unpleasant side effects. Talk to your doctor before taking—or increasing—any medication.

New: Capsaicin, a topical cream originally developed to treat shingles. Capsaicin is rubbed into the skin around the joint. Unlike other topical products, which provide only temporary relief, this cream appears to reduce concentrations of chemicals which lead to the pain response.

It must be used diligently—three to four times a day. Side effects can include a mild burning sensation. Capsaicin is available over the counter, but like any drug it should be used under a doctor's supervision.

For rheumatoid arthritis, gold compounds—taken orally or injected—have long been a mainstay of treatment. But these compounds have been associated with problems including rashes and kidney dysfunction—and must be closely monitored.

Other medications are also helpful for treating rheumatoid arthritis, chiefly antimalarial drugs and immunosuppressive agents—the kind used to treat cancer.

Physical therapy…

Physical therapists are vastly underutilized by physicians in general, and certainly where arthritis is concerned.

A physical therapist will often manipulate the affected area and prescribe therapeutic exercises for the patient to do at home—in order to restore use of the joints and the muscles and tendons supporting them.

Other techniques used by these health-care professionals include massage, application of heat or cold, and electrical stimulation of surrounding nerves.

Exercise…

In addition to specific exercises prescribed by a physical therapist, people with arthritis can benefit dramatically from recreational exercise, such as walking, swimming or tennis. The typical patient might respond, *I can't even move without pain—how can I exercise?* But inactivity is likely to make arthritis worse, not better.

When you don't move a painful joint, the muscles around it begin to weaken and atrophy. Scar tissue may form, and you lose mobility.

Everyone—arthritic or not—should exercise 25 to 30 minutes, three or four times a week. The key is to find the right window—enough exercise to be beneficial, but not so much as to cause great pain. It's a good idea to start very slowly—with 10 minutes of walking, for example—and note how your body responds. If your joints hurt severely while you're working out, or you feel very uncomfortable afterward

or the next morning, don't give up…just cut back to five minutes for a while. Then gradually increase the length of your workout to 30 minutes. To guard against overuse, consult with a doctor and physical therapist before you begin your program.

Diet…

Changes in diet have not generally been shown to help arthritis. *Exceptions:*

•In rare cases, eliminating certain foods from the diet, especially dairy products, provides relief for sufferers.

•Dark-meat fish—tuna, salmon, mackerel, bluefish, swordfish—are rich in oils that may have a positive anti-inflammatory effect on joints. This, though, hasn't been proven. Eating more fish can't hurt you (though I wouldn't recommend nothing but fish)…and might help.

Sleep…

The value of sleep in controlling pain is often overlooked. Arthritis patients often find themselves in a vicious cycle. Their joint pain makes sleeping difficult, and poor sleep in turn leads to more stiffness and pain.

I have found that very low doses of antidepressant medication can break this cycle by reducing chronic pain enough to ensure sound sleep.

Stress management…

Though there's no evidence that stress causes arthritis, it may make symptoms more noticeable or bothersome. Therefore, learning to deal effectively with stress is an essential part of a comprehensive treatment program.

Meditation, deep breathing or other relaxation techniques can be helpful. Yoga is gaining popularity as a relaxation method that's also good exercise.

Can arthritis be prevented?…

Theoretically, no—but there are steps we can take to reduce risk and slow progression of the disease…

•Maintain ideal weight. Obesity is a risk factor for osteoarthritis, possibly because greater weight causes more wear on the joints.

•Exercise regularly—to keep supporting muscles strong and joints moving smoothly.

•Seek medical attention early. If you notice recurring stiffness in a joint, or if it appears swollen, warm to the touch or red, see your physician. The sooner the problem is identified and treatment begun, the better the prognosis.

Source: Fred G. Kantrowitz, MD, who is on the faculty of the Harvard Medical School and the author of *Taking Control of Arthritis*, HarperPerennial, 10 E. 53 St., New York 10022.

Very Wise New Way To Treat Arthritis

Of all chronic diseases, few are as common, as physically and emotionally debilitating or as financially destructive as serious arthritis. This family of diseases now afflicts more than 37 million Americans, resulting each year in 45 million lost work days and $35 billion in medical care and lost wages...*and untold suffering.*

If you experience one or more of the warning signs—joint pain, stiffness and swollen joints—for more than two weeks, *see a doctor immediately.*

Sad: The average arthritis patient waits four years before seeking medical attention, enduring needless pain and possibly permanent joint damage.

Knowledge is power...

Arthritis patients traditionally have controlled their symptoms using some combination of exercise, rest, surgery and—most important—drug therapy.

Many different medications are now available, from aspirin and other nonprescription painkillers to a variety of prescription anti-inflammatories. Recently, however, scientists have realized that one of the most effective weapons against arthritis is *knowledge.*

Patients who learn as much as possible about arthritis gain a sense of mastery over the illness. This mastery gives them an upbeat attitude about their illness. More important, it enables them to manage their symptoms rather than simply respond to them.

Bottom line: Knowledgeable patients seem to fare much better psychologically than those who remain largely ignorant of their illness.

Here at the University of Texas, we're exploring this finding with a special training program for arthritis patients. In this program, conducted in Dallas, patients receive a sophisticated education in joint anatomy, inflammatory processes and other topics they need to know in order to discuss their symptoms with their doctors. We also teach them how to conduct a joint exam. It is crucial for keeping track of their illness.

Result: Instead of simply complaining to their doctors that their knuckles are swollen, for example, participants can report that their *metacarpophalangeal joints* have *active synovitis.*

Surprisingly, this simple ability to discuss arthritis in scientific terms is an emotionally liberating experience for most patients—especially those who've been in the dark about their illness for years. Some participants actually break down and cry upon discovering that there are specific names for what's been going on inside their bodies.

Upon returning home, most participants in our program pass along their knowledge to other arthritis patients and even to medical students and practicing physicians. Helping others in this way isn't mere charity—doing so helps confer a sense of purpose upon arthritis patients whose symptoms may have put an end to their previous careers.

However, if you can't come to Dallas, much of the material that we cover is available from health publications* and medical textbooks.

One of the best sources of arthritis information is your local Arthritis Foundation chapter. It provides free literature and conducts arthritis support groups, exercise classes and a six-week self-help course. Participants learn how to control not only arthritis symptoms, but also the fatigue and depression that often accompany the illness. If there's no Arthritis Foundation chapter in your community, contact the foundation's Atlanta headquarters at 800-283-7800.

Beyond a thorough education of arthritis, several other tools are available to keep your symptoms in check. *Most important:*

Accurate diagnosis...

Osteoarthritis and rheumatoid arthritis are by far the most common forms of arthritis.

*Recommended reading: *The Arthritis Helpbook* by Kate Lorig, RN, DrPH, and James F. Fries, MD, Addison-Wesley Publishing Co., Jacob Way, Reading, Massachusetts 01867.

Scientists have now identified more than 120 different forms of the disease, including gout and spinal arthritis.

The methods of treating these diverse illnesses vary widely. Without a proper diagnosis, you're unlikely to get the form of treatment best suited to your particular case. While a simple blood test is available to identify rheumatoid arthritis, most other forms of arthritis are identifiable only via X-rays and a skilled examination of the affected joints.

Keeping a diary...

Arthritis symptoms typically wax and wane according to the time of day and your activity levels.

Problem: Patients whose symptoms repeatedly catch them by surprise often become frustrated, depressed and reclusive.

Strategy: A diary will help you learn to "forecast" your arthritis symptoms. Use one to record how you feel at different times of the day, during and after different activities, etc. Review your comments periodically and try to detect a pattern connecting your activities and how you feel. Discuss your findings with your doctor. Changes in the pattern might suggest the need to switch to another medication or to change dosages of your current medication.

Assistive devices...

If your symptoms make everyday tasks difficult or impossible, find ways to simplify those tasks.

Example: If arthritic hands make it hard to open doors in your home, use a handle instead of a door knob—or use a loop of cloth...it is especially helpful for refrigerator doors.

For other helpful ideas, ask your doctor or physical or occupational therapist. Many mail-order catalogs* now sell assistive devices—clothing that fastens with Velcro rather than buttons, tools for grasping hard-to-reach objects, electric can and jar openers, etc.

Rest...

Besides being painful, arthritis is very tiring. Many arthritis patients think it lazy or self-indulgent to take an occasional time-out. In fact,

*The J.C. Penney Easy Living catalog is one.

it's remarkably prudent. Always pace yourself. If you start to tire, sit quietly for a few minutes or take a nap.

Use of heat and cold...

Try both to see which you find more soothing.

Exercise...

Jogging and other bone-jarring exercises aggravate arthritis symptoms. However, swimming, walking, low-impact aerobics and other gentle forms of exercise ease pain and increase joint mobility.

Especially effective: Warm-water exercise (aquatics) classes. These and other exercise programs are offered free of charge by many YMCA's and Arthritis Foundation chapters.

Weight control...

The more you weigh, the greater the stress on your joints. If you're overweight, shedding a few pounds will help alleviate your symptoms.

Source: Valerie Branch, director, patient educator program, division of rheumatic diseases, The University of Texas Southwestern Medical Center, 5323 Harry Hines Blvd., Dallas 75235-8884. An arthritis patient herself since 1982, Ms. Branch also serves on the board of directors of the North Texas chapter of the National Arthritis Foundation. For more information about the patient educator program, contact Ms. Branch at the address above.

Do You Suffer From Food Allergies?

Millions of otherwise healthy Americans needlessly endure headaches, sinus congestion, digestive problems and other symptoms, all because of a common health problem that they don't even realize they have—food allergies.

Although the complexity of modern diets makes pinpointing troublesome foods difficult, it is possible to do so—and often quite worthwhile.

Example: A friend of mine was a longtime victim of chronic muscle pain. Even I never suspected that she was suffering from a food allergy. But after carefully monitoring her diet for a few weeks, we discovered that her daily intake of chocolate and chicken was to blame for her agony.

What they do…

Food allergies can cause or worsen virtually any ailment, from a runny nose…to skin blemishes…to arthritis. Many conditions blamed on other factors are really food related…

…80% of asthma sufferers experience partial or complete relief by eliminating allergy-causing foods from their diet…

…5% of all cases of rheumatoid arthritis are believed to be caused or aggravated by food allergies…

…almost 50% of all people in the U.S. experience adverse food reactions, many of which are allergic in nature.

They're getting worse…

Although food allergies have been around forever, they pose more trouble now than ever before. *Reason:* Modern food production and transportation methods have eliminated seasonal variation in our diets.

Most of us now eat the same foods day in and day out. Strawberries, oranges and other foods that were once strictly seasonal can now be had virtually year-round.

Because processed foods contain multiple ingredients, many seemingly different items contain the same allergy-producing substances.

Example: Most breakfast cereals contain at least some wheat and the same handful of chemical additives.

This makes it increasingly difficult to avoid specific ingredients. Even people who take the trouble to vary their diets wind up with little variety.

What happens…

Constant exposure to the same foods overstimulates the immune system, releasing a flood of antibodies. The body responds as if it were being invaded by an infectious bacterium or virus. This results in a variety of allergic symptoms.

Examples: Headaches, sinus congestion, persistent coughs, rectal itching, asthma, stomach upsets, heartburn, bloating, diarrhea, constipation, urinary discomfort, eczema, rashes, prostate inflammation in men, irregular menstrual periods in women…and more.

Although food allergies usually affect the skin, respiratory tract, gastrointestinal tract or cardiovascular system, they can affect any part of the body.

People are unique in their response to foods. One person's meat is another person's poison —literally.

Example: Peanuts are full of healthful protein. But for someone allergic to peanuts, a single peanut can be fatal. In 1986, a Brown University student died after eating a bowl of chili. She was unaware that the restaurant used peanut butter as a thickening agent.

Finding the problem…

Unlike hay fever and other common allergies, food allergies are very difficult to diagnose.

Problem: The antibodies that cause food allergies cannot be measured by blood and skin tests. They are found primarily in the body's mucous membranes—and they exist in the bloodstream only in very limited quantities. The only reliable way to determine if a food allergy is causing your symptoms is to give up—at least temporarily—all suspect foods.

Many people try to identify food allergies haphazardly by skipping one food for a few days, then skipping another, and so on. Such an approach seldom works.

Reason: Food-allergy symptoms often don't occur until at least 24 hours after the troublesome food has been consumed, making it impossible to tell exactly which food has caused which symptom.

The only sure method to pinpoint food allergies is a systematic, carefully controlled diet.

The allergy-discovery diet*…

Buy a small notebook in which to record the foods you eat and any allergic reactions. Keeping a diary is essential if you are to link a food with a particular symptom. Next, give up the foods most likely to cause trouble. *Some prime suspects:*

•Cane sugar	•Coffee/tea	•Tomatoes
•Chemical additives	•Corn	•Vinegar and other fermented foods
	•Milk	
•Chicken	•Oats	
•Chives	•Onions	
•Chocolate	•Soy	

*My diet is intended for people with chronic symptoms. A once-a-year headache, for example, usually calls for no more than a simple painkiller—in many cases, the painkiller can be avoided altogether.

- Citrus fruits/ juices
- Peas and peanuts
- Wheat

Foods to eat...

In their place, substitute hypoallergenic foods.
Those less likely to cause trouble...

- Amaranth
- Apples
- Artichokes
- Bananas
- Basil
- Bean sprouts
- Beef
- Beets
- Canola oil
- Carob
- Carrots
- Celery
- Chick peas
- Cinnamon
- Cloves
- Coconut
- Cranberries
- Cucumbers
- Escarole

- Gelatin
- Ginger
- Green Beans
- Honey
- Kasha
- Lamb
- Lentils
- Lima beans
- Maple sugar
- Melon
- Millet
- Mustard
- Navy beans
- Nutmeg
- Olive oil
- Oregano
- Parsley
- Pork
- Peaches

- Pears
- Potatoes
- Pumpkin
- Rhubarb
- Rice
- Rose hips
- Rosemary
- Sage
- Sesame
- Spinach
- Squash
- Tapioca
- Thyme
- Tuna
- Turkey
- Turnips
- Veal
- Zucchini

To avoid eating the same thing every day, eat these foods on a rotating basis.

The body generally needs about six days to flush itself of troublesome antibodies. If after six days on this diet, you experience no improvement, your symptoms probably do not stem from a food allergy. However, if your symptoms do improve—or even disappear—a food allergy or allergies is probably to blame.

At that point, start reintroducing the foods you gave up. Do it one at a time to pinpoint the allergy. *Note:* To prevent a severe reaction, foods should be reintroduced only in tiny quantities.

If you reintroduce a food and it does not cause symptoms within a day, that food is definitely not the culprit. Reintroduce another food. But if you do experience symptoms after eating a particular food, you probably are allergic to that food and it should be avoided. Strike it off your diet, wait another day and then reintroduce another food. Continue until you have identified all the foods to which you are allergic.

Although people with severe symptoms to a particular food may have to give up that food forever, many people who give up troublesome foods for six months or so lose their allergies to those foods. This means foods that once caused trouble can sometimes be reintroduced into the diet, although usually only in limited amounts.

Source: Interview with John E. Postley, MD, assistant clinical professor of medicine, Columbia University, and an allergist in private practice at 903 Park Ave., New York 10021. He is the author of *The Allergy Discovery Diet*, Doubleday, 666 Fifth Ave., New York 10103.

Aspirin Miracle

A remarkable, inexpensive key to better health is probably right in your medicine cabinet. It's called *acetylsalicylic acid*—better known as aspirin.

Research suggests that one aspirin tablet, taken every other day, helps reduce risk of heart attack, certain kinds of stroke, cancer of the gastrointestinal tract and possibly Alzheimer's disease, among other serious ailments. All this for less than a penny a day.

Caution: Aspirin is not a substitute for healthy habits like eating a balanced diet, exercising regularly or not smoking, nor should it be taken regularly without your doctor's approval.

About aspirin...

Aspirin's active ingredient, *salicin*, occurs naturally in the willow tree. Willow leaves and bark have been used to relieve pain and inflammation at least since the time of Hippocrates.

Aspirin was first made commercially in Germany at the turn of the century. If it had first been synthesized today instead of a century ago, odds are it would be available only by prescription. *Reason:* Aspirin is far more complex and powerful than many people realize.

Inexpensive generic aspirin is just as effective as more costly brands. In fact, there's less difference than you might imagine. Although there are many brand names of aspirin for sale in the U.S., all the salicin found in these aspirin formulations is made by just six companies.

How aspirin works...

No one knows exactly how aspirin works. It seems to interfere with the production of *pros-*

taglandins, hormones made by the body in response to injury. Aspirin seems to reduce the pain and swelling caused by prostaglandins.

Prostaglandins are also involved in blood-clotting. By blocking prostaglandin synthesis, aspirin acts as an anticoagulant. That probably accounts for its effectiveness against heart attack and stroke.

Aspirin also seems to prevent atherosclerosis, the buildup of fatty deposits in the arteries. However, it cannot *reverse* atherosclerosis.

Aspirin and heart attack...

In the 1950s, doctors first observed that patients who took aspirin for pain while recovering from a heart attack were less likely to have a second attack.

Supporting data on aspirin's preventive value come from the Physicians' Health Study, a five-year study of more than 22,000 male doctors between the ages of 40 and 84.

Half of the subjects took a standard five-grain aspirin tablet every other day. *Result:* Subjects older than 50 who took aspirin were 44% less likely to suffer a heart attack than were similar men given a placebo (sugar pill).

If the group who took aspirin had also been eating well and getting moderate exercise, even fewer might have had heart attacks.

Researchers looked only at men. However, a subsequent study of female nurses suggests that aspirin also helps prevent heart attacks in women. Another study found that coronary care unit patients given aspirin immediately after a heart attack were about 25% more likely to survive the attack than patients who did not receive aspirin. Evidence also suggests that an aspirin a day lowers the risk of a second attack.

And stroke...

Most strokes occur as a result of atherosclerosis. When arteries are narrowed, even a tiny blood clot can block blood flow to the brain, thereby depriving the tissue of oxygen.

Aspirin apparently fights stroke by preventing atherosclerosis and thinning the blood, which helps prevent blood clots.

One warning sign of impending stroke—sometimes the only warning—is a *transient ischemic attack* (TIA). This temporary deficiency of blood in the brain is caused by a blockage of blood flow or by a piece of arterial plaque or a blood clot that lodges in a blood vessel inside the brain. *Symptoms:* Weakness, numbness, dizziness, blurred vision, difficulty in speaking.

A study by Dr. James C. Grottar (published in the January 28, 1988, issue of the *New England Journal of Medicine*) showed that taking aspirin after a TIA cuts the risk of stroke by 25% to 30%. Although aspirin is often prescribed for TIA, it is not usually appropriate for anyone with high blood pressure or an increased risk of hemorrhage.

And Alzheimer's disease...

A University of British Columbia scientist recently observed during autopsies of arthritis patients—who tend to take a great deal of aspirin—that their brains showed fewer than expected signs of Alzheimer's disease.

This observation certainly doesn't prove that aspirin prevents Alzheimer's. However, it does suggest an important avenue for future research.

And more...

Though aspirin isn't very helpful in relieving migraine pain, it may help prevent migraines. Preliminary research suggests that migraine sufferers who take aspirin regularly may be able to reduce their headaches by as much as 20%.

Aspirin seems to stimulate the production of *interferon* and *interleukin-2*—immunity-boosting proteins produced inside the body. This may explain why aspirin may prevent certain kinds of cancer...and suggests that it could be used in the fight against other immune disorders.

Finally, some evidence suggests that aspirin helps prevent cataracts, diabetes and gallstones. As with other possible uses of aspirin, these potential uses of aspirin require further study.

Aspirin precautions...

•If you're thinking about starting an aspirin regimen, check with your doctor first. This is especially important if you're taking anticoagulants...if you have diabetes, gout or arthritis... or if you are taking any other over-the-counter or prescription drug.

Caution: Aspirin should generally be avoided by anyone with asthma...ulcers or other chronic stomach problems...or an allergy to aspirin.

•If you're pregnant or nursing an infant, take aspirin only with a doctor's consent. *Danger:* Aspirin taken during the last three months of pregnancy can injure the fetus or cause birth complications.

• If regular aspirin irritates your stomach, ask your doctor about buffered or coated aspirin. Also, tell your doctor if you experience ringing in the ears or hearing loss while taking aspirin.

• Drink with caution when taking aspirin. Aspirin boosts the concentration of alcohol in the blood. If you want to drive safely after a party, for instance, you may need to drink even less or wait longer than you normally would.

• Children should not be given aspirin without a doctor's approval. *Reason:* Aspirin has been linked to Reye's syndrome, a rare but potentially fatal brain disorder.

Source: Robert S. Persky, coauthor of *Penny Wonder Drug: What the Label on Your Aspirin Bottle Doesn't Tell You,* The Consultant Press, Ltd., 163 Amsterdam Ave., #201, New York 10023.

Aspirin vs. Angina

Aspirin helps angina patients avert heart attacks. Low daily doses of aspirin—82 milligrams—cut heart-attack risk 34%.

Source: Study of more than 2,000 angina patients, aged 30 to 80, led by S. Juul-Moller, MD, Cardiology Section, department of medicine, General Hospital, Malmo, Sweden, reported in *The Lancet.*

Aspirin vs. Colon Cancer

Aspirin fights colon cancer. People who took aspirin 16 or more times a month for at least a year were 40% less likely to die from cancer of the colon. *Bonus:* Regular use of aspirin also cuts stroke risk.

Source: Study of more than 600,000 people led by Michael Thun, MD, director of analytical epidemiology, American Cancer Society, Atlanta.

How to Beat Asthma

Asthma is by far the most prevalent serious childhood disease, causing 2.5 million American children to miss 8 million days of school every year. In addition, 8.6 million adults in this country have asthma.

Although $2.4 billion is spent each year to treat the disease, the personal costs—including impaired activity and chronic fear of the symptoms—are far greater. Coping with asthma can be a never-ending puzzle and torment.

Problem: You avoid commonly recognized irritants such as dust and animal dander, yet continue to suffer repeated episodes of asthma. When the attacks begin, medications don't alleviate the difficult breathing and anxiety.

Remedy: Start a self-management program. Learn your personal triggers—allergens that cause asthma symptoms in you—and ways to avoid them. Master techniques that control the severity of your symptoms when they do begin.

Warning: Self-management techniques, though efficient, do not replace medication. Start self-management in conjunction with a physician-supervised program of asthma care.

Find your personal triggers…

Be a sleuth. Unusual substances may trigger your episodes—things that don't make the lists of irritants printed in books. *Trap:* Overlooking possibilities. A substance that is not a recognized trigger may nevertheless trouble you.

Example: New research recently revealed that aspirin is a strong irritant for 20% of asthmatic adults.

After an episode, identify substances that may have acted as triggers. Discuss them with your physician and avoid them if they are likely to irritate you. Some areas you should explore:

• Foods. Ingested food is unlikely to trigger symptoms, but food odors may. Food additives often cause problems.

Example: 10% of individuals with asthma are sensitive to sulfites, which are used as preservatives in many foods. Check labels.

• Exercise. Hard breathing cools the air passages and can trigger an attack. New research suggests that exercise causes cells in the bronchial passages to release chemicals that trigger episodes. *Mistake:* Forgoing exercise. It's a vital factor in cardiopulmonary health. *Better:* Find a program of exercise that works for you. Swimming is excellent. It combines controlled breathing, a variety of muscle movements and a calming environment. Use medication prescribed by your physician before exercising.

•Sex. The emotions and exertion of sex can trigger attacks. *Very big mistake:* Avoiding sex. Work out a satisfying sex life that won't trigger episodes. *Suggestions:*

•Don't blame sex prematurely. It may not be the culprit. Remember that bedrooms may contain irritants such as wool blankets, down pillows and dust.

•Take premedications. Preventive medicines can help if taken before sexual activity.

•Work with your partner. If exertion is a trigger, change your sexual practices.

•Avoid unfamiliar environments. Having sex in new places can bring you into contact with previously unmet triggers.

•Emotional triggers and stress. Stress can trigger asthma. *Manage it:* Identify the emotions and stresses that make you vulnerable. Practice the exercises given below.

How to handle an attack…

The American Lung Association has developed the following exercises, which are extremely effective in helping you manage anxiety and shortness of breath. Take prescribed medications at the first signs of an episode, and contact a physician if the symptoms become severe.

•Relaxation. Practice this exercise once or twice a day. When an episode begins, doing the exercise will immediately help you relax and minimize symptoms.

1. Sit upright in a chair, letting your arms hang at your sides. Breathe slowly and evenly.

2. Sit one to two minutes with your eyes closed.

3. Gently tighten the muscles in your face, making a frown. Count to 2. (Don't hold your breath.) Let your face muscles relax completely. Count to 4.

4. Clench your fists. Shrug your shoulders. Tighten the muscles in your arms. Count to 2. (Don't hold your breath.)

5. Let your shoulders drop, and let your arms hang loosely with your hands open. Count to 4. Keep breathing slowly and evenly.

6. Tighten your legs and feet. Count to 2.

7. Relax. Let all your muscles go loose, from your forehead to your toes. Count to 4.

•Breathing. When an episode begins, the natural tendency is to try to breathe faster to draw in more air. *A more effective way to normalize your breathing:*

1. Relax. Let neck and shoulders droop.

2. Breathe in slowly through your nose.

3. Purse your lips. Exhale through your mouth slowly and evenly, trying to take at least twice as long as you did to inhale.

4. Relax.

5. Repeat the pursed-lip breathing until you no longer feel breathless. If you become dizzy, rest for a few breaths.

Why this exercise works: Exhaling through pursed lips increases the pressure in your airways, keeping them open.

Source: Shane McDermott, lung disease program manager, American Lung Association, 1740 Broadway, New York 10019. Information on a full range of asthma support services, including the very successful Superstuff program for asthmatic children, is available through your local American Lung Association.

Back Protection

Ninety percent of Americans suffer an episode of severe, disabling back pain at some time in their lives. Of those, *80% recover*, with or without treatment, within a month.

Most of the remaining 20% can now be treated successfully without surgery. But the total cost of back pain in the U.S. is still a staggering $20 billion a year. So it pays to take care of your back.

Good news: Most low back pain is *preventable.* Back protection principles…

The basics are simple: Keep your back flat, not hunched…straight, not twisted…and supported. Flex and stretch frequently.

Caution: Your back may feel fine until you reach for a pencil you dropped, and—*youch!* *Reason:* Back pain occurs when cumulative wear and tear damage from postural strains or improper movement make the back vulnerable to a sudden stressful or unguarded motion.

Most troublesome areas: Bending and reaching. *Solution:* Establish healthy habits of movement to preserve your back. *For best results:*

• Use foresight. Be conscious of your back as you plan each day's activities. Avoid strain and fatigue. Get help when you must move something heavy or awkward.

• Perform a pelvic tilt. To help maintain spinal alignment before initiating *any* movement, pinch the buttocks together, tighten the stomach muscles and rotate the pelvis forward.

• Avoid twisting. A torquing motion stresses the ligaments that hold the disks in place. *Better:* When bending, squatting, lifting, lowering or reaching, position the feet forward and face the work *first*, then pivot with the feet, turning the entire body as a unit.

• Avoid reaching for overhead objects. When the arms are extended overhead, the back muscles are not able to stabilize the back. *Better:* Use a footstool, step ladder or long-handled tool for overhead tasks.

• Support objects no higher than the shoulders—and no lower than the knees. Hold objects as close to the body as possible when lifting or lowering. Plan to use intermediate steps.

Examples: Lift a box from the floor to a chair, then to the desk. Rest groceries on the edge of the cart or car trunk before continuing.

• Use the hips, arms and legs to protect the back. When bending forward over a sink, counter or other low surface, bend from the hips, keeping the back straight. Support your body weight with your arms or elbows. Squat before lifting, keeping the back straight and using the powerful leg muscles to propel upward.

• Manage your stress. Emotional stress and psychological factors can contribute to back pain. Dealing with these stresses, therefore, may help control your back pain.

Source: Robert L. Swezey, MD, medical director of the Arthritis and Back Pain Center at the Swezey Institute in Santa Monica, California, and clinical professor of medicine at UCLA. Dr. Swezey's book, *Good News For Bad Backs*, is available by calling 800-350-2998.

Say No to Back Pain

Four of five Americans report they've had back trouble—making the back pain industry a $30-billion-a-year business.

Conventional medical wisdom: Back pain is caused by structural abnormalities of the spine (such as arthritic and disc disorders), or by a vague group of muscle conditions linked to poor posture, lack of exercise or overexertion.

Conventional treatments: Surgery, traction, acupuncture, nerve blocks, biofeedback, deep massage and extended bed rest.

These approaches may bring temporary relief (through what I think is a placebo effect), but they fail to resolve the problem.

As a result, the pain recurs…and recurs. And millions of people have barred themselves from normal physical activity—from raking leaves to going to work. Back pain is the leading cause of worker absenteeism.

What's going on…

These semidisabled men and women have been imprisoned by a myth—that their backs are delicate, vulnerable structures, easy to throw out of whack and difficult to restore.

The personal and financial cost of this problem is staggering—and largely unnecessary. After 17 years of monitoring thousands of patients, I've concluded that the overwhelming majority of back pain sufferers have been misdiagnosed…that their doctors have been treating merely the symptoms of their problem, rather than its underlying cause.

Back pain, I have found, is nearly always a stress-related problem. I call it Tension Myositis Syndrome (TMS). TMS almost invariably affects the soft tissue (muscles, nerves, tendons), and not the spine, discs or vertebrae.

The good news: TMS is a harmless (though often excruciating) disorder. Most back-pain sufferers can be cured without surgery, drugs or special exercise. *Key:* The patient must fully recognize that back pain is essentially a trick played on the body by the subconscious mind.

Who gets TMS…

The notion of a mind-body connection is hardly revolutionary.

Tension is widely accepted as the primary cause of peptic ulcer, for one example. *Other mind-related disorders:* Constipation, irritable bowel syndrome, tension or migraine headaches, cardiac palpitations, eczema, hay fever.

People who fall prey to these syndromes—including TMS—are generally competitive, perfectionist types who feel compelled to excel in both family and business matters. They strive to be the best parent, the best manager, the best golfer. They are their own worst critics when they fall short.

TMS sufferers build up large stores of anxiety and anger. Because these feelings are painful, frightening and inappropriate, they are repressed.

Examples: A new father may resent the sleep he's losing...or a middle-aged woman may resent having to care for her elderly parents. Since they cannot vent their frustration at the people who are causing it, they bottle it up.

But the story doesn't end there. To divert our attention and keep hidden emotions from becoming conscious, the brain creates a defense —which diverts attention from our unkind, childish, angry, selfish feelings.

Thirty years ago, fewer people complained of back pain, but there was a much higher incidence of peptic ulcers then. When doctors and laymen came to realize ulcers were caused by tension, ulcers no longer served the brain's purpose of hiding tension. *Note:* More effective medication also has helped.

By contrast, the medical profession still ignores the emotional basis for TMS—making it the perfect camouflage for unrevealed feelings.

How TMS works...

The autonomic nervous system (a part of the brain) controls the body's involuntary functions, including heart rate, digestion and breathing. It can increase or decrease the flow of blood to any part of the body with total precision.

TMS is an abnormal autonomic activity that reduces blood flow to various tissues in the back region. Although the nervous system may be triggered by a physical event (an auto accident, a fall, a day of heavy lifting), it is responding to a psychological need.

Result: The tissues get less oxygen than normal. Depending on which tissues are affected

(muscles, nerves, tendons/ligaments or a combination), the body responds with many symptoms—sharp, aching or burning pain...tingling and numbness...pressure or weakness.

All of these symptoms should be thoroughly investigated, to rule out the possibility of tumor or some other organic illness. After that, however, patients should be highly suspicious when a doctor diagnoses a structural problem.

Example: When scans reveal that a patient's last intervertebral disc has flattened (and that its shock-absorbing fluid has dried up or leaked through the disc wall), there is a standard diagnosis—a herniated disc. The patient's back pain is promptly blamed on this condition. *Typical treatment:* Surgery.

In my experience, however, this disc pathology is a normal process of aging, almost universal after age 20. It rarely causes pain. It is no more pathological than graying hair or wrinkling skin.

I recently studied 109 patients with herniated discs. Of that group, 88% became free or nearly free of pain (with unrestricted physical activity) after following my techniques. Another 10% showed some improvement. Only two patients, who had unusually severe psychological problems, were unchanged.

I have seen similar results with people diagnosed for spinal stenosis, pinched or inflamed nerves, osteoarthritis, scoliosis, tendinitis and bursitis.

Treatment and cure...

When I see patients with acute back pain (often caused by a muscle spasm), I advise bed rest and painkillers as needed—but urge them to keep testing their ability to move around. If they assume they will be immobilized for days or weeks, they will slow their recovery.

My emphasis, however, is on the prevention of TMS attacks. *Best weapon:* The patient's own awareness of what is going on—what I call knowledge therapy.*

Once a person is truly convinced that TMS is not serious—that it is a charade to be ridiculed rather than feared—the pain stops. The brain's

*Most patients master the therapy after two two-hour seminars, and achieve permanent pain relief within two to six weeks. On occasion, small-group, follow-up sessions are required.

ruse simply doesn't work any more. *To reach that point, patients must:*

•Think psychological, rather than physical. As they become aware of pain, they must shift attention from their body to something they are worried about. The particular worry isn't important. The refocusing process short-circuits the brain's deception.

•Talk to their brain. Although this may sound silly at first, it is critical to take charge and tell your subconscious that you refuse to put up with TMS any longer.

•Resume physical activity as soon as pain has subsided. Patients must feel free to bend, lift, jog or perform any other common physical acts. Since their backs are essentially normal, there is nothing to fear—except for the fear itself, the emotion that goes hand in hand with TMS.

•Discontinue all physical treatment. Until patients renounce all structural explanations for either the pain or its cure, symptoms will persist.

Bottom line: Victory over TMS does not require any change in personality, nor a commitment to stop repressing anxiety and anger. (If this were the case, my cure rate would approach zero.)

Once patients understand and accept the true nature of their pain, they are on the path to permanent relief.

Source: John E. Sarno, MD, professor of clinical rehabilitation medicine at the New York University School of Medicine and attending physician at the Howard A. Rusk Institute of Rehabilitation Medicine at New York University Medical Center. His revolutionary book, *Mind Over Back Pain* (1984) has helped thousands of sufferers overcome back problems. Dr. Sarno's most recent book is *Healing Back Pain,* Warner Books, 666 Fifth Ave., New York 10103.

What Every Woman Needs to Know About Breast Cancer

I was 46 when I was first diagnosed with breast cancer. My tumor was 1.5 centimeters in diameter and had spread to the lymph nodes. I underwent a lumpectomy, radiation and six months of chemotherapy. Only a few weeks ago, I passed my five-year checkup with a clean bill of health.

My story has a happy ending. Looking back, though, I would have been greatly helped and comforted had I received certain information, not just from physicians but also from women who had undergone the same experience…

•Having cancer is not your fault. No one knows exactly why women develop breast cancer, but it's certainly not because they have a "cancer personality." That idea is a lot of bunk. I've seen happy, optimistic cancer patients die very quickly after their diagnosis…and I've seen negative, hostile people live long after they "should" have been dead.

Lesson: Never view cancer as your own fault. I once overheard two therapists talking about a woman whose cancer was not responding to therapy. One said, "If she could only visualize better, she could cure this." What a ridiculous notion!

There's nothing wrong with trying alternative methods of healing, such as visualization, if they make you feel happier or more in control. But no one should ever blame you for your cancer.

•You have more time than you think you do to make decisions about treatment. Like most women newly diagnosed with breast cancer, I felt I had to decide immediately about whether I'd have a mastectomy (removal of the breast), a lumpectomy (removal of just the tumor), radiation, etc. I was afraid that if I delayed treatment, my cancer would spread like wildfire.

Truth: In most cases, it's safe to take a couple of weeks to consider your options—and come to terms with your diagnosis.

Waiting also gives you the opportunity to get a second opinion—and that could help you avoid making a big mistake. Some old-school surgeons, for example, continue to recommend mastectomy even though in many cases it's just as effective—and far less emotionally wrenching—to have a lumpectomy followed by radiation.

•You'll find yourself resenting the doctor who diagnosed your cancer. Being diagnosed with breast cancer is so unnerving that women often find themselves resenting the doctor who made the diagnosis…and many find a new doctor. It's the old shoot-the-messenger feeling. You want the floor to open up and swallow him/her. But if the doctor is compassionate and competent, changing doctors at this stage is often a mistake.

•Coping with your fear is the hardest part of having breast cancer—but the fear doesn't last forever. At first, the fear that the cancer will spread and that you will die is almost overpowering. It affects everything you say, feel or do.

Eventually, the fear subsides. Although you might occasionally lapse back into fearful thinking, you get on with your life.

•Breast cancer surgery isn't painful. I was afraid my operation would cause a great deal of pain. As it turned out, neither the surgery nor the recovery period was particularly painful physically—although the drainage tube inserted in my armpit for a week or so following surgery did cause a little discomfort. I was also weepy, depressed and maybe even a little irrational after surgery…but that quickly passed.

•The timing of breast cancer surgery affects your chances of survival. Recent studies have shown that premenopausal women survive longer when tumors are removed during the second half of their menstrual cycles. Although this finding remains a matter of debate among cancer specialists, ask your doctor about scheduling surgery during the second half of your cycle, after ovulation.

•Chemotherapy affects your memory. During the months I was undergoing chemo, I experienced several memory lapses. I'd be trying to write and suddenly find myself unable to remember what it was I wanted to say next. At first I thought I had a brain tumor. I was terrified. Only later did I learn that temporary memory problems were a common side effect of chemotherapy. When they stop pouring the poison into your body, your memory returns to normal.

•Breast radiation is generally not very debilitating. Compared to chemotherapy, it's a piece of cake. It leaves you feeling a little tired, but not sick.

•Support groups are a tremendous source of emotional comfort during your recovery. Having cancer is a lonely, isolating experience. After my diagnosis, one or two longtime friends suddenly stopped calling and visiting. If your friends abandon you, realize that it's because of their fears—not because of something you did.

Even if your friends don't abandon you, they may be uncertain of how to behave in your presence. This can cause a lot of awkwardness.

You may feel, for example, that you have to crack jokes or tell funny stories just to lighten the mood. After a while, these kinds of feelings become an enormous burden.

Joining a group of other women with breast cancer can lift this burden. When you're among peers, you don't have to take care of anyone else. You're free to laugh or cry—just be yourself.

•It's important to be kind to yourself. Guilt is a constant companion when you have cancer. If you eat too much fatty cheese or don't exercise one day, you feel you're contributing to your demise. But that's just not true.

Bottom line: Chemotherapy is hard on your body and will make you feel tired and cranky. If watching the soaps and eating popcorn will make you feel better, then do it. There is no need to feel guilty.

•You don't feel like celebrating at the end of treatment. I thought that when I eventually finished my chemotherapy treatment I would be ecstatic. But when that day finally came, I found myself pleased—but also sad to say good-bye to all the doctors, nurses and technicians who had been my "teammates" for so long. Suddenly, I was alone with my enemy and no longer doing anything to fight it. Fortunately, I had a great support group to make me feel less vulnerable.

•Life after cancer can be more satisfying than it was before. Although I would never have wished cancer upon myself, I must admit that having the disease has helped me understand my real priorities in life. I no longer worry about rejection, nor am I driven to spend time trying to gain prestige and status in the business world. I want to be with my 15-year-old daughter, Anna, and make my writing as strong and beautiful as it can be.

Cancer has also made me tougher and more gutsy. After all, what can hurt me after I've had cancer? But I'm also a much nicer person now. I'm more apt to send a sympathy card or visit someone in the hospital because I know how much such gestures mean to someone who is sick and frightened.

Source: Juliet Wittman, an award-winning reporter for the *Boulder Daily Camera,* Boulder, Colorado. She is the author of *Breast Cancer Journal,* Fulcrum Publishing, 350 Indiana St., Golden, Colorado 80401.

How Women Can Lower Breast Cancer Risk

Though breast cancer isn't yet preventable, there are a number of ways a woman can reduce her risk of being among the one in nine women who get the disease…

Know your risk…

If you're already at high risk for developing breast cancer, you should be especially concerned about early detection. Begin by having mammograms earlier and more frequently than lower-risk women. Discuss this option with your doctor. *Risk groups include:*

•Women with a family history of breast cancer—a mother or sister who had the disease.

•Women who began menstruating before age 12, or who reach menopause after age 55.

•Childless women, or women who had their first child late in life. (If you are planning to start a family, having children early may reduce your cancer risk.)

•Women who are obese…have thyroid problems…took the drug DES* or whose mothers took the drug.

Promising opportunities…

•New research in genetics has identified a specific gene as playing a role in predisposing some women to certain types of breast cancer. As research progresses, we may be able to use genetic patterns to identify women at greatest risk—and watch them more closely.

•Tamoxifen, an estrogen-blocking drug that is currently prescribed to prevent recurrence of breast cancer, is now being given experimentally to high-risk women who have not had cancer. It is hoped that the drug may prevent them from developing the disease.

Watch diet…

There is a great deal of controversy about the relationship of diet to breast cancer. Some studies provide evidence for the dangers or benefits of certain foods, while others fail to support these findings. Clearly, more research needs to be done in this area. But since the food we eat affects all the cells in our body, I believe strongly that attention to diet can affect a woman's

*Diethylstilbestrol, an artificial estrogen that was used up until 1971 to prevent miscarriage in early pregnancy.

susceptibility to cancer, as well as other diseases. *The good foods:*

•Cruciferous vegetables—cabbage, broccoli, brussels sprouts and cauliflower.

•Foods rich in beta-carotene—apricots, cantaloupe, carrots, winter squash and other orange or deep-yellow vegetables and fruits.

•Sweet acidophilus milk—it may lower the levels of enzymes that generate carcinogens in the body. Tests suggest it may also limit circulation of estrogen and cholesterol, which are both thought to play a role in causing cancer.

•Garlic powder—which may strengthen the immune response of cells.

Foods to avoid…

•Alcohol. Heavy drinking has been linked to breast cancer—and beer or wine is no safer than hard liquor. Alcohol in excess can damage the liver, interfering with the functioning of the immune system.

•Smoked foods, such as bacon, sausage and hot dogs.

•Fat—although the evidence is contradictory. Breast cancer rates are much lower in Japan, where diets are low in fat. But a recent study in Boston found that a low-fat, high-fiber diet for adults did not seem to reduce breast cancer risk. It may be that fat consumption at a young age is most damaging.

Personal observations…

I have treated more than 8,000 breast cancer patients. In my own practice, I have observed that more than half the women who get breast cancer are overweight. This suggests to me that fat consumption does play a role in susceptibility to cancer. In any case, decreasing fat in the diet is good for the heart, and it certainly won't hurt you.

Food additives, pesticides, pollutants: Many of these are suspected carcinogens, and many others have not been tested for their potential to cause cancer. To play it safe, buy fresh, minimally processed meat and produce as often as possible.

The value of vitamin supplements in fighting breast cancer is not 100% clear either. I believe that adding supplements in moderation to a balanced diet won't hurt—and may help. *Most important anti-breast cancer vitamins:*

•Vitamin C, which helps to maintain tissue, keeps cells healthy and promotes healing.

•Vitamin B—important to the proper division of cells.

•Calcium and magnesium. These build healthy bones—and bone marrow is where the cells are made that produce cancer-fighting lymphocytes.

Caffeine: Good news for coffee drinkers... Coffee has not been shown to increase cancer risk. In fact, decaffeinated coffee may be worse for you. The solvents used to remove caffeine are thought to be carcinogenic. My advice is moderation: Two to three cups of coffee or 12 ounces of caffeinated soda.

Manage stress...

Stress seems to weaken the immune system so it can't fight disease as well as it should. People who have been under excessive stress are vulnerable to getting various types of cancer as well as other diseases. This is true whether stress is acute—loss of a family member...or chronic—living with an alcoholic. Stress may also affect the outcome of treatment in patients who develop cancer. Obviously, no one can avoid stress completely. *Problem:* Worrying that the stress itself might cause further damage only adds to the anxiety.

However, there are many constructive ways of handling those stresses we can't avoid...

•Social support—Ask for help from family, friends or an organized support group of people you can depend on and trust.

•Ability to vent anger. Some people feel they have to hold their feelings inside—especially after a diagnosis of cancer. But studies have found that breast cancer patients who are able to come out and express their anger about the disease survive longer than those who try to cope by showing a brave face to the world.

•Exercise. Jogging, swimming or other vigorous activities are excellent stress reducers... and contribute to overall health.

•Meditation—or other relaxation techniques. If meditating isn't for you, find other pastimes to take your mind off your anxieties, such as needlepoint, sculpting, reading.

•Good nutrition. A diet of fresh, unprocessed foods—including plenty of whole grains, vegetables, fruits and low-fat protein sources, such as beans and fish—will help keep your mood

even and your body in optimum shape.

Estrogen therapy...

Estrogen replacement therapy is often prescribed to reduce the risk of osteoporosis or heart disease in post-menopausal women. But high levels of estrogen are thought to be related to many types of breast cancer. If a woman and her doctor decide that estrogen therapy is appropriate, the dose should be kept as low as possible—and monitored carefully.

Get regular mammograms...

A mammogram can pick up tumors before they have grown large enough to feel. The earlier cancer is caught, the more effective treatment can be—and the greater the chances of preserving the breast. And newer X-ray machines expose the breast to much less radiation than in the past. Breast cancer risk increases dramatically beginning at age 38, so women 38 or older are advised to have a mammogram every other year...every year after age 50. Women in high-risk groups should have annual mammograms from age 35 on.

Breast self-examination...

No matter what your age, it's important to examine your own breasts every month—even if you're getting regular mammograms. It's important to get to know what your normal breast feels like...and you might find a lump that develops between mammograms.

Your doctor can show you how to examine your breasts. Once you're experienced, self-examination shouldn't take more than 10 minutes every month—and it could save your life.

Source: Paul Kuehn, MD, a surgical oncologist in Hartford, Connecticut, who has formerly served as president of The New England Cancer Society and chairman of the Cancer Commission for New England of the American College of Surgeons. He is the author of *Breast Care Options for the 1990s*, Newmark Publishing Company, Box 603, South Windsor, Connecticut 06074.

Better Breathing

Bronchitis relief: Blowing up a balloon, which exercises the lungs. After eight weeks of balloon blowing therapy, bronchitis patients were much less breathless, compared with members of a control group who showed no significant change.

Source: Researchers in Manchester, England.

How Not to Be One of the Three Out of Every Ten Americans Now Living Who Will Develop an Aggressive Form of Cancer

Despite constantly improving cure rates, the best odds of surviving cancer still average out at just about 50/50, and the annual statistics on cancer deaths continue to rise.

The number of deaths from lung cancer alone has risen dramatically and devastatingly since the 1930s—and the true tragedy lies in the fact that lung cancer is one of the most preventable forms of cancer.

Well-timed and scrupulously implemented prevention and early detection efforts could influence the outcome in about 80% of the 900,000 people who will develop cancer in the U.S. this year.

The simple secret to cancer prevention: A healthy lifestyle. We all have a few bad habits —*and some of them cause cancer.*

Tobacco and cancer…

Cigarette smoking has been unequivocally linked with the development of lung cancer. Smoking accounts for 85% of the lung cancers in men and 75% of those in women. Recent evidence indicates that secondary/passive smoke inhalation (from someone else smoking) can increase the occurrence of lung cancer and other diseases. Each year, 150,000 new cases of lung cancer are diagnosed. Lung cancer claims 136,000 lives annually in the U.S. alone.

Lung cancer used to be thought of as a man's disease, but it's now the most common cause of cancer death in women.

Trap: Lung cancer is very difficult to diagnose at an early or symptomless stage. And once it is detected, lung cancer will kill 90% of newly diagnosed individuals within five years. The American Cancer Society reports that lung cancer is responsible for 30% of *all* cancer deaths.

Helpful: If you quit smoking now, your risk of developing lung cancer begins to diminish almost immediately, and after 10 to 15 years, a former smoker has the same risk factor for death from lung cancer as a nonsmoker.

Many people think that pipe or cigar smoking is somehow "safer" than cigarette smoking. While pipe and cigar smokers do not face the same risk of developing lung cancer that cigarette smokers do, they are at increased risk for developing intra-oral cancers.

More trouble: Smoking accelerates the aging process, as shown by increased facial wrinkling in long-term smokers.

What's the point? *The answer seems so simple:* Don't smoke…look better…and live longer!

Alcohol-related risk…

Most heavy drinkers are also heavy smokers, a factor that can make it difficult to assign a distinct cause to some cancers. However, excessive consumption of alcohol has been associated with the development of several kinds of intra-oral cancers, including those of the tongue, the floor of the mouth, the pharynx and larynx, as well as cancers of the esophagus and liver.

Alcohol and tobacco taken together in high doses increase the risk of intra-oral cancer to 15 times that of those who neither drink nor smoke.

Useful guideline: Consumption of more than two drinks per day is generally considered injurious to health.

The role of diet and nutrition…

Researchers have estimated that diet is a factor in 30% to 40% of the cancers that develop in men…and in 60% of cancers that occur in women.

High intake of animal fats, a common dietary factor in many developed countries including the U.S., may be associated with increased risk of developing cancer, particularly cancer of the breast and colon. A high-fiber diet is generally regarded as protective against the development of colorectal cancer.

Vitamins may play a role in cancer prevention. Increased consumption of foods containing vitamin A (or carotenes) is associated with a decreased risk of cancer. Carotene-rich foods include deep yellow and green leafy vegetables, carrots and yellow fruit.

Trap: Too much of a good thing may be hazardous. Vitamin A has been found to be toxic in high doses, and exceeding recommended nutrition levels can hurt more than it helps.

Adequate dietary intake of vitamin C, found in citrus fruits as well as in some vegetables, may be associated with lowered risk of developing cancerous tumors of the digestive system.

Strategy: It's a good idea to restrict overall caloric intake and consumption of animal fat. This strategy not only lowers your risk profile for developing some cancers, it also decreases obesity, which aids early detection (a small lump is easier to detect on a thin person than on an obese person).

Whole-grain cereals and other high-fiber foods, and foods containing vitamin A/beta-carotene should become dietary staples. And brussels sprouts, cabbage and cauliflower are believed to contain enzymes that inactivate or eliminate carcinogens, so think creatively about using vegetables in meals.

Reduce your consumption of smoked or salted foods. High intake of these foods has been associated with cancer of the stomach. *Better:* Fish, fowl or lean meat for your main courses. Avoid charred or charcoal-broiled meats.

Sun exposure and skin cancer risk…

Excessive sun exposure has been definitively linked with the development of skin cancers, from easily treated basal cell carcinomas to often-deadly malignant melanomas.

The cancer-causing factor in sunlight is the ultraviolet spectrum, particularly the mid-spectrum UV light known as UV-B radiation. Fair-skinned, blue-eyed blondes and redheads are at greater risk of developing skin cancer than individuals with darker complexions, as are people who live in low-latitude and/or high altitude geographic zones.

To reduce your risk of developing skin cancer, limit your exposure to the sun, especially in the summer between the hours of 10 a.m. and 2 p.m.

Wear a hat with a brim broad enough to cover your head and neck, and apply a sunscreen liberally and often, beginning one hour prior to sun exposure. Many sunscreen creams and lotions contain PABA (para-aminobenzoic acid), an effective blocking agent. These preparations will be labeled by their Sun Protection Factor (SPF), which can range from two to 35. SPF 15 is generally recommended.

If you feel that you "must" get a tan despite the danger, be sure to tan gradually, avoiding sunburn at all costs. Begin your tanning sessions with no more than 20 minutes in the sun. Sunburn not only accelerates the aging process, but short, intense exposures to the sun are believed to be more likely to trigger the development of malignant melanoma.

Chronic, long-term sun exposure—as seen in farmers and other outdoor workers—is thought to be more likely to trigger the usually less-deadly basal cell and squamous cell carcinomas. Something as simple as wearing a polo shirt on the beach could save your life. Melanomas that develop on the torso in men are known to be particularly aggressive cancers.

No long-term studies of the effects of light from tanning lamps have been conducted—so if used, do so with extreme caution.

Early detection strategies…

People tend to think of cancerous growth as an intracellular runaway train—and in some cases, it is. But not all tumors grow rapidly.

It may take several years for a breast tumor to grow from one cell to one centimeter (about ½-inch)—and such tumors are highly curable at that stage. The key to early detection of breast cancer is periodic screening examinations even if a women is healthy or symptomless.

A good baseline physical examination should include a thorough evaluation of the skin, head and neck, and lymph nodes, as well as palpation of the abdomen and digital examination of the rectum.

Men should have a careful examination of the testes and prostate. Women should have a breast and pelvic examination with a Pap smear. Women older than age 40 should also have a mammographic examination of the breasts, and both men and women older than 40 should undergo sigmoidoscopy and stool and urine analysis to screen for colon cancer.

After having a complete doctor's physical, plan to examine yourself thoroughly once a month. Choose a date that you can remember easily—the day of your birth or the first of the month, for example—and carefully examine your skin, the inside of your mouth, and your breasts* or testes.

If you do not know how to examine yourself, ask your doctor for guidelines. It takes less time to do a thorough self-examination than to talk about it, and it can pay huge dividends if you discover a tumor early enough to easily treat it.

Bottom line…

Eliminate negative habits—smoking, excessive drinking, overeating and excessive sun exposure. Maintain positive habits—nutritious diet and regular exercise. *Result:* You will increase your health and vitality, and decrease your risk of cancer and other diseases.

*For menstruating women, breast self-examinations are best conducted three to five days after the period begins.

Source: John F. Potter, MD, professor of surgery, founder and director emeritus of the Vincent T. Lombardi Cancer Research Center at Georgetown University. He is the author of *Improve Your Odds Against Cancer*, SPI, division of Shapolsky Publishers.

Cancer Dos, Cancer Don'ts

The journey from cancer patient to cancer survivor is long, lonely and often frightening.

While there are no easy shortcuts, there are ways to lighten your burden…

•Don't blame yourself. Cancer is not caused by emotional problems or psychological trauma. There is no such thing as a "cancer personality," although certain lifestyle choices—choosing to smoke or eat a fatty diet, for instance—do make a difference.

•Don't assume your cancer will be fatal. Most cancers are curable when detected early. Some are curable even if detected at an advanced stage.

•Take an active role in your treatment. Read as much as you can. Find a doctor with whom you have good "chemistry," and participate fully in your treatment.

•Ask about side effects. We've all heard horror stories about hair loss, vomiting and other effects of chemotherapy and radiation. While these side effects still occur, they are far better controlled today than in the past. For example, nausea and vomiting are well controlled with antinausea medications.

Remember—side effects are temporary. Treatment benefits are not.

•Practice "coping" techniques. Exercise, read, listen to music, learn meditation or other relaxation techniques. Find ways to distract yourself from troubling thoughts.

•Be open about your fears. If you are frightened, tell your friends and family. They are your greatest source of emotional support…and people who feel supported tolerate their illness better, cope better with treatment and even have a better prognosis. If possible, bring someone with you when you go to see the doctor—not just for the support, but to make sure you remember what your doctor says. If no one is available, consider taking along a tape recorder to record your conversation. When we are under stress, it's hard to listen to what the doctor is saying.

•Don't be afraid to seek the help of a mental health professional. Doing so is not a sign of weakness—it's a sign of bravery and hope. Psychotherapy can boost your ability to cope with your illness…and improve your quality of life. I believe that counseling and support groups for people with serious medical illness should be considered an integral part of medical care.

•Don't worry if you occasionally feel sad or discouraged. No one can maintain a positive attitude 24 hours a day.

•Adopt a healthy lifestyle. Eat a low-fat, high-fiber diet…don't smoke…drink in moderation or not at all…and limit your sun exposure.

Source: Jimmie Holland, MD, chief of the psychiatric service, Memorial Sloan-Kettering Cancer Center, New York City.

New Cholera Strain

Highly virulent, this new strain began in southern India and has spread to Bangladesh, Japan, Malaysia, Nepal and other Asian countries. *Self-defense:* When traveling in affected areas, drink only bottled, boiled or purified water…avoid raw and undercooked seafood and uncooked foods such as salads, raw vegetables and unpeeled fruits. *Bad news:* This strain is more severe than the one that arrived in Peru a few years ago and touched off an epidemic that continues across South America. Those who have had cholera seem to have no cross-immunization to this new strain, and existing vaccines are ineffective. *Result:* Health officials fear this new strain will quickly spread around the world.

Source: Marco M. Pardi, MA, public health, National Center for Infectious Diseases, Centers for Disease Control and Prevention, Atlanta.

Chronic Fatigue Syndrome

Chronic fatigue syndrome (CFS) is a debilitating disease that has been known by many names in recent years…the Yuppie Plague, Raggedy Ann Syndrome, chronic mononucleosis, chronic Epstein-Barr disease…

Although its varied symptoms have made it difficult to identify, cases of CFS are now being diagnosed in huge numbers. I estimate that more than four million people in the U.S. suffer from CFS. I had it myself.

What causes CFS…

CFS can be triggered by anything that weakens the immune system—stress, overwork, poor diet, autoimmune disease and perhaps even a viral trigger (HHV-6, a newly discovered herpes virus, is also suspect.) *What happens:* When the body becomes run down, common organisms that many people carry come out of hiding and undergo a population explosion.

Example: Almost everyone has the Epstein-Barr virus (EBV) in his/her blood. In adolescence and early adulthood, EBV infection is often expressed as mononucleosis. In older people, EBV infection may produce CFS.

Warning signs…

CFS is so difficult to diagnose because it can strike with a number of different symptoms. Included (in order of their prevalence):

- Intermittent low-grade fever.
- Sudden onset of multiple allergies.
- Chronic sore throat.
- Chronic achiness.
- Swollen glands.
- Difficulty concentrating.
- Sudden onset or worsening of arthritic symptoms.
- Migraines.
- Hypoglycemia.
- Persistent apathy.
- Depression.
- Memory loss.

The weakness common among sufferers is not the normal fatigue at the end of a day of work. It interferes with your life, lasts four months—or longer—and often gets progressively worse.

Example: When my disease was at its peak, I was only able to stay awake for four hours at a time.

If, after a full night's sleep, you tire by afternoon, fall asleep and wake up hours later disoriented and even more exhausted, it's time to consult a doctor.

Treatment…

Although doctors are getting better at diagnosing CFS, it is important to find one who views the patient/doctor relationship as a team effort. Because the symptoms and severity of the syndrome vary from person to person, treatment must be tailored to the individual.

The best way to treat CFS is to strengthen the body's immune system. *Helpful:*

- Sleep. The liver is one of the primary targets of EBV, so prevalent in people with CFS. Because it is one of the body's major powerhouses, both the metabolism and immune system are disrupted when it is badly infected. *Result:* Fatigue.

Sleeping or resting between 9 p.m. and 3 a.m. —the time when it undergoes its regenerative cycle—gives the liver a chance to heal.

- Exercise. Exercise stimulates the metabolism, especially the digestive process. This helps the body absorb nutrients and eliminate toxins. Even though most CFS patients are exhausted, it's important to keep active.

Start slowly at first, then move into more active, even aerobic exercises—swimming, bicycling or fast walking. *Important:* Never exercise to the point of exhaustion.

•Vitamins and minerals. If you are ill, your need for particular vitamins and minerals is greatly increased.

Examples: Beta-carotene, vitamin C and zinc all aid the immune system.

Consult a physician knowledgeable in nutrition before taking any vitamins.

•Diet. Choose foods high in nutrients to supply the basic building blocks that the body needs to repair itself.

Example: Your diet should be mostly vegetables, grains, fresh fruit and—as the main course of one meal per day—fish, chicken or turkey.

It's also important that the foods you eat don't put any additional stress on your liver or immune system.

Examples: Avoid caffeine, sugar, alcohol and fatty foods.

This change of eating habits should be permanent. Although you can occasionally indulge in the things you love—ice cream, steaks, cola, etc.—the key is moderation.

•Visualization and mind/body exercises. Along with fatigue, depression and an overall feeling of ill health, CFS saps the will. And the patient's mental state is important in the healing process. Someone who is under constant stress, unhappy or feeling hopeless will have difficulty recovering.

I believe that affirmations (negative thoughts that have been changed into positive ones) and visualization exercises can help. A positive mental state tips the odds in your favor.

More information: Contact Nu-Skin International at 118 Pine St., Rockville Centre, New York 11570 for information on affirmation tapes and subliminals.

Source: Charles R. Pellegrino, PhD, an evolutionary biologist at Brookhaven National Laboratory, Brookhaven, New York. He is coauthor of *Chronic Fatigue Syndrome: The Hidden Epidemic*, HarperCollins, 10 E. 53 St., New York 10022.

New Insights Into Chronic Fatigue

New evidence suggests that many puzzling, chronic health problems resistant to treatment—from infections and allergies to the aches and exhaustion of chronic fatigue syndrome—are yeast related.

One type of yeast is regularly found on the body's mucous membranes, especially the intestinal tract and vagina. When we talk about this kind of yeast, we usually mean Candida albicans, by far the predominant type found in the body.

In a healthy man or woman, candida (pronounced can-did-a) is kept under control by so-called "friendly" bacteria living in the intestinal tract. But several factors can upset the yeast-to-bacteria balance—especially long-term use of broad-spectrum antibiotics. When this happens, yeasts grow out of control—leading to unpleasant symptoms.

Based on my critical review of continuing research, I believe there are three possible mechanisms for yeast's troublesome effects...

•Just as some people are allergic to pollens or mildew, some may be allergic to candida.

•Candida may produce certain toxins that are harmless in small amounts, but that in larger quantities weaken the immune system...leaving the body vulnerable to disease.

•Yeast overgrowth in the intestinal tract (candidiasis) may lead to changes in the intestine. In turn, these changes can cause the body to absorb and react to allergens in food.

The connection between yeast and health problems is highly controversial. Beginning with Dr. C. Orian Truss's article in the late '70s, a number of reports have linked yeast to illness, but the mainstream medical community remains skeptical.

Yet, my experience in treating hundreds of chronically ill patients, as well as similar experiences of a number of colleagues, suggests that a diet designed to curb yeast growth—along with certain antifungal medications—helps alleviate many symptoms that have proven resistant to other forms of treatment.

Do you have a yeast problem?…

There is no simple diagnostic test for a yeast-related problem. For this reason, patients must undergo a thorough physical exam to rule out other possible causes of their symptoms. *Next step:* A complete medical history.

You may have a yeast problem if you…

…have used antibiotics repeatedly over a long period of time, such as for control of acne or recurrent infections.

…have taken corticosteroids. One known side effect of nasal cortisone spray is candidiasis of the nose.

…have used birth control pills. Women on the Pill are far more prone than others to vaginal yeast infection.

…eat a high-sugar diet. A recent study at St. Jude Research Hospital in Memphis found that mice eating large quantities of the sugar glucose had 200 times as much candida in their intestinal tracts as did other mice.

…experience frequent digestive problems, such as abdominal pain, bloating, constipation or diarrhea.

…have a history of vaginal or urinary infections. Women develop yeast-related health problems far more often than men for a number of reasons. These include anatomical differences and hormonal changes associated with the menstrual cycle that promote yeast growth.

…have symptoms involving many parts of the body—for which usual examinations have not found a cause.

Treating a suspected yeast problem…

The cornerstone of treatment is a sugar-free diet. Yeasts in the digestive tract feed on sugar—and multiply. Some patients show remarkable improvement from dietary changes alone. Others need additional help—in the form of over-the-counter anti-yeast preparations sold in health-food stores…and, for more serious cases, from prescription antifungal medications.

The yeast-control diet…

•Eliminate sugar and other simple carbohydrates, such as honey and corn syrup.

•Avoid foods containing yeast or molds, such as cheese, vinegar, wine, beer and other fermented beverages, and pickled or smoked meats. Although breads are probably safe, try eliminating yeast-leavened breads for a few weeks.

Note: Yeast-containing foods should be avoided not because intestinal yeast feeds on food yeast—it doesn't. But most people with candida-related problems are sensitive to yeast in foods and can have negative physical reactions. As the candida problem improves, the sensitivity may subside…and yeast can again be included in your diet.

•Strengthen your immune system by boosting your intake of vegetables, minimally processed whole grains and other wholesome foods. Eat lean rather than fatty meats, and cut back on other sources of fat. Avoid potentially harmful additives, including artificial colors and flavors.

Some physicians recommend eliminating fruits from the diet, because fruits are quickly converted to simple sugars inside the body. I believe fruits are safe—unless your yeast-related symptoms are severe. However, I do recommend avoiding commercially prepared fruit juices, which may be contaminated with mold.

Follow this recommended diet for at least three weeks. If your symptoms subside, resume eating forbidden foods one by one. If your symptoms flare up again after you add one of the forbidden foods, stop eating that food for good.

Good news: After they show significant improvement, most people find that they can follow a less rigid diet—and can occasionally consume a bit of sugar.

Over-the-counter remedies…

Many preparations sold in health-food stores can be a useful adjunct to the yeast-control diet…

•Citrus seed extract, an antimicrobial substance made from tropical plants. Because the extract can irritate mucous membranes, it should be generously diluted with water before drinking.

•Caprylic acid, a saturated fatty acid available in tablet form. It helps keep yeast from reproducing.

Note: Some patients develop digestive problems or notice a slight worsening of yeast-related symptoms during the first week on this medication. If these don't go away within a few days, stop the medication and check with your doctor.

•Lactobacillus acidophilus, a friendly bacterium that helps restore the normal balance of intestinal flora. It is present in yogurt, especially homemade varieties. Store-bought yogurt that contains active cultures will be labeled to that effect. Be sure to buy only unsweetened varieties. Acidophilus is also available as a nutritional supplement.

•Garlic. This herb is known to stimulate the immune system…and at an international medical conference several years ago, researchers reported that garlic also seems to fight candida. Persons wary of the taste of cooked garlic—or its effect on the breath—should consider aged garlic extract (Kyolic), a deodorized supplement. It is widely available in local health-food stores.

Antifungal medications…

When a yeast-related symptom fails to respond to diet or supplements, prescription medication often helps—although the drug may take up to a year to have any effect in severe cases. *Drug options:*

•Nystatin (Mycostatin or Nilstat). In more than 30 years of use, this oral medication has demonstrated no toxic side effects. It knocks out candida in the intestines. It is not absorbed by the bloodstream, however, so it is ineffective against particularly severe cases of candidiasis.

•Fluconazole (Diflucan). This safe, highly effective anti-yeast medication has been available in the U.S. for a number of years. Unlike nystatin, fluconazole is absorbed into the bloodstream.

•Itraconazole (Sporanox). This medication is a chemical "cousin" of fluconazole, and approved for use in the U.S. Although it appears to be quite safe, a related drug, ketoconazole (Nizoral) has been linked to liver damage.

For more information on yeast-related health problems, send a self-addressed, business-sized envelope with 64 cents postage to the International Health Foundation, Inc., Box 3494-HC, Jackson, Tennessee 38303.

Source: William G. Crook, MD, a fellow of the American College of Allergy and Immunology, the American Academy of Environmental Medicine and the American Academy of Pediatrics. He is the author of *The Yeast Connection* and *Chronic Fatigue Syndrome and the Yeast Connection*, both published by Professional Books, Inc., Box 3246, Jackson, Tennessee 38303.

How Not to Suffer From Common Colds… Simple Secrets

There is no cure for the common cold—but there is a bewildering array of over-the-counter remedies that promise to relieve all its symptoms. I personally don't believe in the multi-ingredient remedies currently available. You get better results with medications that attack symptoms individually…

Decongestants…

If you have nasal congestion and a runny nose, use nose drops or a nasal spray with decongesting drugs, such as Neo-Synephrine, phenylephrine or oxymetazoline hydrochloride. These decongesting drugs, known as vasoconstrictors, really do the job.

How they work: They shrink the blood vessels and open breathing passages in the nose. Side effects: Increased blood pressure and pulse rate. *Warning:* Don't use oral decongestants. Because they work not only on your nose, but also on the blood vessels throughout your entire body, the concentrations of the drug are necessarily weak and therefore not as effective as topical decongestants.

Warning: If you use topical decongestants for more than three days, you get what is called a rebound effect—it takes more and more drops or spray to open your nose. Eventually the nose will not open without the use of a decongestant. I've seen patients who've used nose drops for weeks, and when they try to stop they can't breathe or sleep. Sometimes we have to give them steroids to get them off decongestants.

Recommended: Don't use decongestants for longer than three days. In most colds, the worst part is over by then anyway.

If your nose is still stopped up, use salt-water drops. You can make your own by dissolving a teaspoonful of salt in eight ounces of warm water.

Myth: You shouldn't stop your nose from running, because that will cause the cold to last longer. *Reality:* There is nothing beneficial about a runny nose. And since it doesn't help clear up your cold, there's no reason to endure the discomfort.

Nasal secretions are irritating to the skin of the lips and nose. To avoid skin irritations, use a petrolatum-based ointment such as Chapstick or camphor ice to keep the secretions off the skin and allow it to heal.

Cough medicines…

Two kinds of cough medicines…

•Expectorants, such as guaifenesin, supposedly loosen your sputum and make you cough more. It's difficult, if not impossible, to prove that expectorants do much of anything.

•Suppressants help if your cough is keeping you awake at night or bothering you during the day. They usually contain dextromethorphan or codeine.

Myth: Suppressing a cough can cause pneumonia. *Reality:* This is a danger only for people with chronic lung disease such as emphysema —not for normal, healthy people with a cold.

If you have a sore throat, use topical analgesics such as throat lozenges. But gargling with salt dissolved in warm water several times a day is about as effective as anything you can buy. It's much less expensive and it will give you some temporary relief.

Muscle aches and fevers…

Although these symptoms are not usually part of a true cold, people often think of colds and flu as the same thing. *Recommended:* Aspirin for adults and acetaminophen for children. We don't like to give children aspirin because it can lead to Reye's syndrome, a neurological disease. People are now also using ibuprofen for colds and flu.

Other remedies…

•Steam vapor machine. This supposedly cures colds by blowing hot steam up the nose. It may work, but it hasn't been scientifically proven effective. *Reason:* It's hard to set up a double-blind study to test it. (Can people only think they're getting hot steam up the nose?) *Related statistic:* There's a strong placebo effect with the common cold. If you give lactose, which does nothing, to a group of people with colds, a third of them will say it was helpful.

•Vitamin C and zinc. Neither of these "natural" remedies has been proven effective. Research has shown that zinc gluconate tablets, the most recent fad, are basically ineffective. In addition, zinc causes very unpleasant side effects, such as a sore mouth, an upset stomach and a bad taste.

•Antihistamines. These counteract the body's production of histamine, a substance that causes allergic diseases, such as hay fever. But studies show that the nasal secretions of people with colds don't contain elevated levels of histamine and that the effect of antihistamines on colds is minimal. They may have a slight drying effect on the nose, but you'd be better off with a decongestant.

•Antibiotics. Most people know that antibiotics do nothing for a cold and can have unpleasant side effects, like stomach upset and vaginal yeast infections. But antibiotics are helpful if there's a complication like a sinus infection or a middle ear infection. How do you know if you have an infection? It's more likely if you're a smoker, have had previous cold complications or a cold lasts longer than usual. If you suspect a complication, see your doctor. *Problem:* It's not always easy to diagnose sinus disease. X-rays are expensive, and the best in-office technique, holding a light to the sinuses, is only somewhat reliable. Doctors often prescribe antibiotics just in case—so if you want to avoid taking them unnecessarily, insist on X-rays.

•Bed rest. There is no scientific evidence that you'll get better faster if you stay in bed. However, since you'll feel better if you don't push yourself, I recommend bed rest for patients who feel really sick. *Common courtesy:* If you do stay in bed, you won't give your cold to other people.

Source: Jack M. Gwaltney, Jr., MD, professor of internal medicine at the University of Virginia School of Medicine, Charlottesville, Virginia 22903. He is one of the leading researchers on the common cold.

How to Avoid Diabetes, How to Beat Diabetes

Diabetes, one of the most widespread diseases in America, affects one person in 20 and kills many of them. It also helps heart disease, cancer, and other diseases claim their victims.

Diabetes is caused by insufficient production of, or sensitivity to, insulin, the hormone that enables the body's cells to use protein, fat, and glucose (sugar) from the bloodstream. Insufficient insulin causes glucose to accumulate in the bloodstream, where it remains unavailable for use as one of the body's basic fuels.

There is still controversy as to the exact mechanism of diabetes. Two processes seem to be involved. *First:* The body makes less insulin than normal because of abnormalities in the beta cells of the pancreas, the insulin-producing organ. *Second:* Insulin resistance rises. This means that while the body produces a normal amount of insulin, cells become less sensitive to it, and thus require more to sustain themselves.

Only 10% of diabetics have Type I (juvenile), insulin-dependent diabetes. The remaining 90% suffer from the "other" diabetes—Type II (adult-onset) diabetes.

Although Type II diabetes strikes most often after age 35 (hence its name), it can occur at any age. *Misconception:* Type II is less severe than Type I. *Reality:* It, too, is sometimes treated with daily insulin injections. Both kinds are associated with serious complications—neurological damage, kidney damage, heart disease, stroke, gangrene, and blindness.

Type II diabetes is often treated with oral medications or insulin injections. *Drawbacks:* Although oral medications usually do lower blood-sugar levels, they don't work for everyone. Sometimes they cause abnormally low blood-glucose levels. Insulin must be delivered by injection and must be carefully monitored to avoid dangerous side effects. Overdoses can lead to hypoglycemia, seizures, or coma. *Alternative:* In many cases of Type II diabetes, weight reduction, diet, and exercise may be effective.

How to avoid Type II diabetes…

Although the mechanisms of diabetes aren't well understood, two main risk factors have been isolated—obesity and family history of the disease. *More important:* Family history. People who develop Type II diabetes have a genetic predisposition to do so. While there's no way to avoid this inborn vulnerability, anyone with diabetic relatives should be aware of the risk. *Note:*

American Indians, blacks, and Hispanics are at greater risk for Type II diabetes than are members of other ethnic groups.

Controllable factors…

•Weight. 70%–80% of people with Type II diabetes are obese (at least 20% over their ideal weight). Although the relationship between diabetes and obesity hasn't been established, it seems likely that given a genetic predisposition, extra weight may well be the factor that tips the balance. Even an average middle-age spread of five or 10 pounds may increase the risk of diabetes—possibly one reason why Type II diabetes usually shows up after age 35.

•Exercise. Regular exercise may help delay or prevent the onset of diabetes in two ways— indirectly by preventing obesity, directly by improving glucose utilization. Exercise lowers insulin demand only temporarily, so it must be regular to be consistently effective. *Ideal:* Vigorous 20-minute workouts three times a week.

•Diet. While no specific diet has been proven to prevent diabetes, eating habits do affect insulin and glucose levels. *Protective:* A low-fat, high-carbohydrate diet. A low-calorie diet is helpful in maintaining weight. A low-fat and low-cholesterol diet is especially important for those at risk of diabetes, since they are also at higher risk for cardiovascular disease.

Because starches, sweets, and other carbohydrates are broken down into glucose, they were long considered taboo for people with diabetes. Now it appears that high-carbohydrate diets stimulate insulin production and lower insulin resistance, at least in some people. *Current formula:* Carbohydrates should make up 50%–60% of the diet, according to the American Diabetes Association.

Some researchers believe that high-fiber foods retard the rise in blood sugar that normally occurs after eating, thus preventing a sudden surge in insulin demand. *Best:* Water-soluble fiber, found in fruits and certain vegetables—beans, oats, peas, strawberries, apples, bananas.

Another form of diabetes, called gestational diabetes, may strike women during pregnancy. While this form of diabetes usually disappears after pregnancy, 60%–70% of the women who get it go on to develop Type II diabetes within 15 years. Pregnancy increases the insulin demand

and may reveal a genetic predisposition toward diabetes.

Warning signs…

Diabetes varies widely in type and severity. *Usual symptoms:* Frequent urination, excessive thirst, extreme hunger, sudden weight loss, irritability, weakness or fatigue, drowsiness, blurred vision, itching or recurrent skin infections, tingling or numbness in hands or feet. *Trap:* Some people with Type II diabetes have no symptoms at all or may have symptoms so mild they escape detection. In fact, an estimated 5 million Americans have Type II diabetes without knowing it.

If you experience any of these symptoms or are at risk, see your doctor for a blood-glucose test. *Normal level:* 70–110 milligrams per deciliter (mg/dl) while fasting, 120–150 mg/dl after eating. Levels differ for pregnant women. *Recommended:* All pregnant women should be screened for gestational diabetes.

Source: Francis C. Wood, Jr., MD, associate professor of medicine, University of Washington School of Medicine, Seattle.

Diabetes Danger

Poor self-testing of blood-glucose levels could cause dangerous errors in therapy. Eighty percent of the patients studied made procedural testing errors—even though 99% thought their technique was good. And 20% of the mistakes were enough to cause possible dangerous errors in treatment.

Source: Study of 75 diabetes patients one month after class instruction in self-testing, led by Karen Berkowitz, RN, coordinator of diabetes education, Grady Memorial Hospital Diabetes Clinic, Atlanta, reported in *The Medical Post,* 777 Bay St., Toronto, Ontario M5W 1A7, Canada.

Gastrointestinal Self-Defense

Next to the common cold, gastrointestinal (GI) problems cause us to miss more work and pay more visits to the doctor than any other ailment. One-third of Americans experience frequent or chronic gastrointestinal distress. *Most common problems:*

•Gastroesophageal reflux (heartburn)…a disorder of the lower esophageal sphincter (LES), the one-way valve that lets food pass from the esophagus into the stomach and prevents it from flowing backward. A loose valve allows stomach acids to back up into the esophagus. *Symptom:* A burning sensation underneath the breastbone.

•Lactose intolerance…a deficiency in lactase—an enzyme that enables the digestion of lactose, the sugar in milk.

Symptoms: Cramps, gas, bloating or diarrhea after consuming milk products. Some adults develop the condition as they age.

•Constipation…difficulty in moving the bowels. Stool is hard and dry.

•Irritable bowel syndrome (IBS)…also known as spastic colon, occurring when the bowel contracts either too forcefully or too weakly.

Symptoms: Abdominal pain, spasms, diarrhea or constipation.

•Peptic ulcer disease…a group of disorders caused by inflammation or ulceration of the mucous membrane lining the stomach and duodenum (part of the small intestine).

Symptoms: Pain or burning sensation in the upper abdomen, pain below the left rib cage, nausea, vomiting.

•Hemorrhoids…dilated veins in the rectum.

Symptoms: Pain, itching or bleeding around the anus.

Gastrointestinal myths…

Misconceptions regarding gastrointestinal disease abound. *Prime example:* Milk helps relieve ulcers.

In fact, though milk may temporarily soothe abdominal pain by acting as a buffer against stomach acid, the calcium and protein in milk actually stimulate acid secretion, further aggravating the ulcer.

Additionally, the fat in milk can relax the lower esophageal sphincter, causing heartburn. *Better solution:* Taking an antacid tablet.

Drugs for gastrointestinal conditions outsell other types of drugs. In many cases, however, drugs provide only temporary relief.

More effective: Changing diet and lifestyle habits.

Caution: Some of the standard health guidelines, particularly the high-fiber recommendation, can be dangerous for conditions such as diverticulitis (an infection in the bowel wall) or inflammatory bowel disease. Check with your doctor before starting a self-help program.

Diet mistakes...

People often aren't aware that the food they're eating may be contributing to their gastrointestinal disease...or don't know which foods are causing distress. *Six diet mistakes and how to fix them...*

•Overeating. Obesity is associated with a number of gastrointestinal disorders—including gallstones. Pressure from excess abdominal weight can force acid to back up in the esophagus, leading to heartburn. Eating too much at one sitting can produce gas and aggravate a spastic colon.

A diet that's low in calories and high in nutrition can improve a variety of gastrointestinal conditions.

•Too much fat. Fat in the diet relaxes the LES valve, contributing to heartburn. By putting stress on the gallbladder, it aggravates gallstones. Fat also adds calories and contributes to obesity. People with gastrointestinal problems should be careful to derive no more than 30% of daily calories from fat.

•Not enough fiber. A high-fiber diet makes stool bulkier and softer, relieving constipation. Fiber also fights diarrhea by absorbing water in the stool. Fiber can help relieve hemorrhoids, IBS, even ulcers, and protect against development of gallstones.

Prime sources of fiber: Whole grains, fruits, vegetables.

•Legumes. Dried beans are the exception to the high-fiber rule—they should be avoided by people with gastrointestinal problems. Legumes form gas, which is uncomfortable in itself and can produce spasms in someone with IBS or other conditions.

However, legumes are also packed with nutrients and are the basis of many healthful culinary traditions. If you don't want to give up legumes altogether, be sure to eat slowly, chew thoroughly, and stop before you feel stuffed. Or try Beano, an over-the-counter product that contains an enzyme that helps digest legumes.

•Dairy products. If you suffer from gas or bloating after drinking milk or eating ice cream, you may be lactose intolerant. Pay attention to all the dairy products in your diet—don't overlook the skim milk with your morning cereal or the cream in your coffee.

It may not be necessary to eliminate all dairy from your diet. This will depend on your level of tolerance. *Options:*

•Buy products containing enzymes that digest lactose, such as Lactaid or acidophilus milk.

•Add the lactase enzyme to milk products yourself—it's available in drop form. Or take a lactase tablet whenever you consume dairy products.

•Eat only fermented or processed milk products, such as yogurt (make sure it's made with live cultures), butter, cheese or sour cream. These contain only small amounts of lactose.

•Spices. Spicy food can stimulate acid secretion, cause spasms in the esophagus, and make heartburn, ulcers, and IBS worse. The effects are most pronounced if the food is eaten on an empty stomach.

Worst offenders: Pepper, chili powder, curry, garlic, cloves, mustard, nutmeg.

Flag foods...

In addition to applying these general diet principles, it's useful to know which foods are likely to aggravate specific gastrointestinal conditions:

•Heartburn. Avoid foods that relax the lower esophageal sphincter valve, such as greasy foods, chocolate, peppermint, nuts, caffeine. Also cut down on foods that irritate the esophagus or produce stomach acid, such as alcohol, citrus juices, pepper, chili powder, carbonated beverages, decaffeinated coffee, and milk or cream.

Also helpful: Don't eat close to bedtime, and elevate the head of your bed if possible.

•Peptic ulcer disease. Avoid the irritating foods listed for heartburn, and avoid caffeine.

•Irritable bowel syndrome and constipation. Increase consumption of unrefined carbohydrates and cut down consumption of refined flour, sugar, meat and bananas.

• Hemorrhoids. Avoid peppers and other hot, spicy foods. Increase consumption of fiber.

Other factors...

• Smoking. Smoking relaxes the LES, causing heartburn...aggravates IBS symptoms by increasing the urge to defecate...increases the incidence and severity of ulcers.

• Alcohol. Alcohol can damage the gastrointestinal tract, including the lining of the small intestine, cause gastritis and interfere with the absorption of nutrients.

• Stress. Whether or not stress is the primary cause of gastrointestinal problems, it certainly makes them worse. The entire gastrointestinal tract is innervated by nerves coming from the brain, and stress can lead to acid secretion and muscle contractions. Heartburn, peptic ulcer disease and IBS are especially affected by this brain-gut axis.

If you're stress-prone, learn how not to take on problems that others can handle. Cultivate a positive frame of mind. Practice meditation or another relaxation technique. And if stress is overwhelming, consider professional counseling.

• Lack of exercise. Moderate exercise promotes good gastrointestinal motility, prevents constipation, relieves stress and contributes to weight loss.

Caution: Excessive exercise can create gastrointestinal problems. Marathon runners often complain of diarrhea—a result of hyper-stimulation of the gut.

Important...

These recommendations shouldn't replace discussing your symptoms with your physician. Some gastrointestinal disorders may require drugs or surgery, or are signs of more serious disease.

If you suffer from chronic gastrointestinal problems, or if you experience a change in gastrointestinal function, see your doctor.

Source: Steven Peikin, MD, associate professor of medicine and pharmacology and director of gastrointestinal nutrition at Jefferson Medical College, Thomas Jefferson University. He is the author of *Gastrointestinal Health*, HarperCollins, 10 E. 53 St., New York 10022.

If You Suffer From Chronic Abdominal Pain ...Or Gas or Bloating...

If you suffer from chronic abdominal pain... or gas or bloating...if you endure frequent bouts of constipation or diarrhea...or if the need to defecate is often alarmingly urgent, you are by no means alone.

One out of every five Americans now suffers from one or more of these symptoms, known collectively as spastic colon or—more properly—irritable bowel syndrome (IBS).

IBS affects all races and age groups, although its sufferers are usually between 15 and 30 years old at the time of diagnosis. It strikes women twice as often as men. Unlike ulcerative colitis, Crohn's disease and other types of inflammatory bowel disease, IBS causes no obvious damage to the gastrointestinal tract. Yet it is often extremely debilitating.

Severe cases not only cause severe physical pain, but also disrupt personal relationships and make keeping a normal daily schedule difficult. Sex, too, yields little pleasure for many IBS sufferers.

IBS does not result from an infectious agent or from any genetic predisposition to the disease. *Causes:* Poor dietary habits, uncontrolled psychological stress and other easily remedied factors. All that's required to curb your symptoms is a commitment to avoid the mistakes that underlie them.

Causes of digestive trouble...

• Chronic anxiety. While occasional anxiety is a fact of life for most Americans, excessive or chronic anxiety disrupts the digestive process, resulting in abdominal pain and diarrhea. Fortunately, there are effective ways to curb anxiety, including regular aerobic exercise and deep breathing or other relaxation exercises.

Helpful: Avoid stressful conversations at mealtime. Also...fine-tune your time-management. If you're chronically late to work, for instance, try waking up 30 minutes earlier. *Note:* If you remain anxious even after trying these techniques, ask your doctor if you might benefit from prescription tranquilizers.

•Postponed bowel movements. People who squeeze their pattern of bowel movements into a tight, hectic schedule are sowing the seeds of IBS.

Problem: Ignoring the urge to defecate or delaying defecation until a more convenient time leads to a variety of intestinal ills, including cramps, constipation and even permanent disruption of peristalsis, the rhythmic intestinal contractions necessary for proper bowel function.

To avoid trouble: Set aside a regular time for your bowel movements. Don't rush a bowel movement, and never "hold it in."

•Trigger foods. Symptoms of IBS are often triggered by specific foods, most commonly dairy products, wheat, corn, citrus fruits and—occasionally—food additives such as monosodium glutamate (MSG). In many cases an intolerance of dairy products stems from an inability to digest milk sugar (lactose). Switching to reduced-lactose dairy foods or using special enzyme tablets remedies this problem.

To pinpoint trigger foods: Jot down all the foods you eat and any gastrointestinal symptoms. Use this "food diary" to prepare a list of safe and "trigger" foods.

•Lack of exercise. For as-yet-unknown reasons, those who exercise are less susceptible to cramping, constipation and other IBS symptoms than are sedentary people.

•Rushed meals. Chewing is the only part of the digestive process under conscious control, yet few of us pay much attention to the process.

Problem: Incompletely chewed food is very hard to digest. The harder your gastrointestinal tract must work to digest the food you eat, the likelier you are to experience cramps and other gastrointestinal symptoms.

To avoid trouble: Eat slowly. Chew thoroughly. If you need more time to eat, make extra time by waking earlier or working later.

•Drinking at mealtime. While it's a good idea to drink lots of water during the course of a day, too much liquid at mealtime dilutes the digestive juices and thus hampers digestion.

To avoid trouble: Drink no more than four ounces per meal. Don't use large quantities of liquid to "wash down" hastily eaten food. Finally, steer clear of carbonated beverages. They only add to the levels of gas in the intestinal tract.

•Social drugs. Alcohol and caffeine irritate the sensitive lining of the gastrointestinal tract. Nicotine and caffeine intensify colon cramps.

To avoid trouble: If you cannot cut these drugs entirely from your diet, at least limit their consumption. If you drink coffee as a means of stimulating a bowel movement, try herbal tea instead. Often it's the heat of the coffee and not its caffeine content that facilitates bowel movements.

•Candy and gum. They cause the salivary glands to produce more saliva, thus necessitating more frequent swallowing. While swallowing saliva poses no problem, the air inevitably swallowed along with the saliva adds to feelings of gassiness and bloating.

•Low-fiber diet. Dietary fiber helps ensure regularity by adding bulk to stools and by speeding their passage through the intestinal tract. Sadly, the average American gets only 10 to 20 grams of fiber per day (the equivalent of two to three servings of fruits, vegetables, beans or grains), half of the 20 to 40 grams of fiber needed for optimal health (five servings). *Caution:* If you decide to boost your fiber consumption, do so gradually, over a period of weeks. Upping fiber consumption abruptly worsens existing IBS symptoms. *Note:* Experiment with the various water-soluble (wheat bran) and water-insoluble (oat bran) fiber sources to determine which might work best for you.

•Overuse of laxatives and enemas. Although safe and effective for occasional use, laxatives and enemas do more harm than good when used on a regular basis. Abusers of these products often become so dependent that normal elimination becomes impossible without them. *To be safe:* Avoid these products. If you become constipated, choose oat bran, wheat bran, psyllium (Metamucil) or another bulking agent over drug laxatives. (These are most effective when taken at mealtime.) Peppermint oil offers a drug-free means of controlling cramps. A nonprescription product called Beano helps reduce flatulence and intestinal gas associated with consumption of beans. *Ineffective:* Most over-the-counter anti-gas preparations.

If your symptoms persist for several weeks even after remedying these problems, see a doctor. Chronic intestinal gas, bloating or cramping, as well as unexplained diarrhea or constipation, are symptomatic not only of irritable bowel syndrome, but also of several more serious conditions, including colitis, Crohn's disease and even colon cancer.

Source: Gerard Guillory, MD, clinical instructor in internal medicine at the University of Colorado Health Science Center and an internist in private practice in Denver. He is the author of two books on digestive disorders, including *IBS: A Doctor's Plan for Chronic Digestive Troubles*, Hartley & Marks, Box 147, Point Roberts, Washington 98281.

Everything You Ever Wanted to Know About Itching...and More

Sooner or later, we all itch. Unless the itch becomes severe, we usually ignore it...most itches eventually go away on their own.

But itching isn't *always* trivial. It can be a symptom of many serious diseases.

External causes of itching...

External causes of itching are the easiest to diagnose and treat. You can usually see the problem right on the skin. *Possible causes:*

•Allergic dermatitis. Causes very localized itching.

Example #1: Nickel—commonly used in alloys with precious metals—may cause allergic reactions on earlobes, wrists or fingers from jewelry that is worn against the skin.

Example #2: Poison ivy is an allergic dermatitis that can be identified by blisters in a linear array.

Perspiration aggravates allergic itching because wet skin is a very effective conduit for the proteins that cause allergic reactions. *Good news:* Medicines for dermatologic conditions work best when they're applied to damp skin.

•Detergents and fabric softeners. These may cause itching if they leave a residue in fabric. Bleaches may break down elastic and rubber, creating a highly irritating substance.

•Dry skin. A major itch-maker, especially in winter.

Example: Erythema craquelé is a chronic dry-skin condition that women often develop on their legs. The skin becomes shiny and looks like a dried lake bed with little cracks.

•Inflammations that itch—can be caused by fungi. *Other causes of itchy inflammations:* Viruses (such as chicken pox)...impetigo... sunburn.

•Irritant dermatitis. Often caused by tight clothing. If you itch at the waistline or in another area where clothing is tight, it's likely to be a case of irritant dermatitis.

•Skin diseases (scabies, eczema, etc.) usually cause widespread itching.

Internal causes of itching...

Internal problems cause itching all over the body, but little can be seen on the skin. No one knows why some diseases cause itching.

Possible reason: If the skin is stretched, the resulting inflammation can trigger the eruption of mast cells, which contain histamines...and histamines cause itching. *Other possible reasons:*

•Allergic reactions to drugs (including penicillin).

•Cancer (including lymphomas and carcinoma of the stomach or breast).

•Diabetes. Itching may be caused by nerve damage. Or, diabetes and some immune-deficiency syndromes predispose the skin to the colonization of micro-organisms. Although usually visible, they may be too deep in the follicles to be seen.

•Endocrine disease.

•Infectious diseases.

•Kidney disease.

•Liver disease—which includes hepatitis. Itching may be the result of bile that has accumulated in the person's skin.

•Lupus and other auto-immune diseases.

•Parasites (especially intestinal parasites— hookworm, pinworm, etc.).

•Pregnancy.

•Thyroid disease.

When to worry about an itch...

Despite the long list of serious diseases that are accompanied by itching, there's no need to panic every time you itch. Worry when other symptoms—weight loss, persistent fatigue, unexplained bleeding from the nose, mouth or rectum—accompany the itch.

If a local rash or inflammation causes itching, it's probably nothing to worry about unless it persists for longer than a few days. Unexplained itching that lasts more than a few days should probably be seen by a doctor.

Treating your itch...

Mother was right when she said, *Don't scratch!* You may obliterate a primary lesion, making diagnosis difficult. And you *can* cause an infection.

Try to treat minor itching yourself. There are many topical medicines, solutions and compounds available over-the-counter. *Effective ingredients include:* Cortisone, menthol, calamine and phenol. Some antifungal preparations not only relieve symptoms, but attack the condition itself.

If these treatments don't relieve you, consult a dermatologist, who may prescribe oral antihistamines.

Trap: Using the wrong kind of over-the-counter medication can sometimes make an itch worse instead of better. *Example:* Steroid cream will make a fungal disease spread. Steroids are wonderful for suppressing inflammation, but fungi thrive on them.

Solution: Before treating your itch, try to determine its cause.

The itching in your head: Psychological phenomena often cause itching. People concentrate on an itch because it keeps them from focusing on what's really troubling them. The itch may be keeping them from a mental or emotional breakdown.

Like back pain, ulcers and gastric distress, some people develop an itchy rash when they're under a lot of stress. Sometimes taking a few days off to relax can cause an itch to disappear.

Why we itch at night: Itching is a sensory phenomenon. If you're busy, you're concentrating on something other than the itch you might have. But at night, when you're in bed, the itch can reappear with a vengeance.

Source: Mary Ellen Brademas, MD, chief of dermatology at St. Vincent's Hospital, assistant clinical professor at New York University Medical Center and director of the sexually transmitted diseases clinic at Bellevue Hospital, all in New York. Dr. Brademas is also in private practice in Manhattan.

When You Feel Sick & Tired...There Is a Good Reason

When I was doing my clinical training at Johns Hopkins, people constantly came in complaining of being sick and tired. After submitting to routine laboratory tests that found nothing wrong with them, most of these patients were told, *Go home. It's all in your head.*

But I believed these people did have a problem. Looking for what they had in common, I found a group of real physical problems that I called Profound Sensitivity Syndrome (PS2). I found that 90% of these patients could help themselves by making lifestyle changes and learning how to handle stress.

Symptoms of PS2...

PS2 patients usually complain of several of the following symptoms...

- Alcoholism
- Insomnia
- Chronic fatigue
- Forgetfulness
- Underactive thyroid
- Trouble concentrating
- Autoimmune disorders
- Tension or migraine headaches
- Premenstrual syndrome (PMS)
- Chronic back or neck pain
- Gastrointestinal problems
- Recurring yeast infections
- Intolerance of heat or cold
- Depression
- Allergies
- Fluid retention
- Arthritis pain
- Skin problems
- Brittle nails
- Hair loss

When PS2 patients get sick, they experience symptoms much more severe than those experienced by others with the same disease. Also, PS2 patients are overly sensitive to medication and respond poorly to medical treatment.

Most PS2 patients are creative. They have vivid day and night dreams. And they react swiftly and dramatically to both emotional and physical stimuli. But they feel they can't control events that distress them or their reaction to those events. They also feel helpless in the face of their medical problems.

What causes PS2...

People who have PS2 are hypersensitive to one thing or another. Some can't stand air pollutants. Others overreact to certain foods, including sugar or salt.

Still others are hypersensitive to interpersonal relationships—they can't tolerate criticism or emotional upset.

In many ways, PS2 is like an allergic reaction to the body's own chemicals. The receptors, where the hormones hook on and do business, over-respond. So when a PS2 sufferer puts out stress hormones—specifically cortisol, adrenaline and nonadrenaline—the receptors go into overdrive. Result: A fast heartbeat, heavy sweating, confused thinking, agitation and other symptoms.

What to do if you have PS2...

Don't blame yourself...the condition is hereditary. You either have the genes or you don't. If you don't have the genes, you'll never get it. If you do have the genes, you may or may not get it—depending on how you handle stress.

Because we can't change our genes, people who suffer from PS2 must make lifestyle changes and learn stress-reduction techniques.

Rules to live by...

• Don't sweat the "small stuff." Almost everything is small stuff.

• Prioritize your time. A great deal of stress comes from not having enough time to do everything you want to do.

Solution: Pretend you have only a year to live and then decide what you want to do.

• Need no help. This is the opposite of the way it sounds. *What it means:* Express your needs, learn to say no and don't be afraid to ask for help.

Women: Let yourself say no to things you don't want to do—it's doctor's orders.

Men: Ask for help. Don't hesitate, for instance, to ask for directions when lost.

• See stress as a challenge. PS2 sufferers handle stress with doubt, uncertainty and fear, which leads to chronic hostility, anger and cynicism. And angry, hostile, cynical people are more likely to have heart attacks.

Solution: See stress as an opportunity to try your problem-solving skills.

Example: You have an irrational boss who makes your life miserable. Make believe he's ill and not really responsible for the way he acts. Treat him with compassion.

• Avoid stress in the morning. The average

person runs into 30 to 40 stressors a day. Stress increases the constriction of coronary arteries, particularly between 6 a.m. and noon, making you most vulnerable to a heart attack then.

• Do abdominal breathing. Most of us breathe using chest muscles, not abdominals. Don't suck in your gut when you take a breath... expand it.

Helpful: Pretend your stomach is a balloon—blow it up when you take a breath, and deflate it when you exhale.

• Eat a well-balanced diet. Avoid excessive salt, junk food, fatty foods, caffeine, calories, alcohol and cholesterol. Avoid cigarettes, too—of course. *Emphasize:* Foods rich in potassium and vitamins B and C, and bulk foods, including vegetables and whole grains.

• Drink at least one quart of water a day. It takes that much to wash the toxins from your system.

• Exercise. At least three times a week for at least 20 minutes each time.

• Smile. Recent research shows that smiling and other facial expressions affect your mood. If you smile, it's almost impossible to get angry. And smiling increases the blood flow to the brain.

• Have fun. Do something you enjoy every day. And laugh. Laughter is like an internal jog that relaxes muscle tension and releases beta-endorphins, the feel-good hormones.

Source: Neil Solomon, MD, PhD, who specializes in internal medicine, endocrinology, metabolism and allergy. Formerly on the faculty of Johns Hopkins University School of Medicine, he maintains a private practice in Baltimore, writes a syndicated medical column and is a consultant to major corporations. He is the author of *Sick & Tired of Being Sick & Tired*, Wynwood Press, 264 Fifth Ave., New York 10016.

Beating Knee Osteoarthritis

To beat knee osteoarthritis, keep weight down. Obesity is a known risk factor for osteoarthritis—the most widespread of all rheumatic diseases, affecting 16 million people in the U.S. *New research:* For women of average height, a weight loss of 11 pounds cuts the risk of developing osteoarthritis of the knee up to 12 years later by 50%. Even women who are of average weight—not overweight—cut their risk by losing weight.

Source: Research led by David Felson, MD, Boston University Multipurpose Arthritis and Musculoskeletal Diseases Center.

Psoriasis Psecrets, Psoriasis Psolutions

The worst thing about psoriasis for a large portion of the five million sufferers in the U.S. isn't the red, crusty patches of skin characteristic of the disease. It's the continuing embarrassment these patches cause.

To keep others from seeing the unsightly patches, these psoriatics resort to wearing high collars and long-sleeved shirts even in sweltering heat…throwing away their bathing suits… and constantly sweeping away the tell-tale flakes of skin that fall from their bodies.

Persons with severe cases of psoriasis sometimes avoid going out in public altogether. But modern, intensive therapy can help almost any patient who feels disfigured by psoriasis look normal in a bathing suit.

Today, 95% of all cases can be cleared. Though the cause of psoriasis remains unclear, doctors have developed a variety of highly effective treatments. *Key to success:* A willingness to try the many therapies until the most effective one is found.

The appearance of psoriasis-like symptoms warrants a prompt trip to a specialist. Many different conditions produce red, crusty, sometimes itchy patches of skin. Only a good dermatologist can distinguish among them…and prescribe the appropriate treatment.

For mild cases of psoriasis, sunlight alone may be all that's necessary. Ultraviolet rays retard cellular division in the skin. Usually, though, other treatments are required. *Options:*

• Tar ointments: Messy, smelly, and likely to stain clothing. Applied daily, they must be kept in place for 30 minutes to several hours, depending upon the severity of the patches. *Names:* Crude coal tar, anthralin, and Vaseline.

• Topical steroids: Clear skin completely in only 10%–20% of all patients and are impractical and ineffective if more than 15% of body surface is affected. Steroids, applied once or twice daily as a vanishing cream, produce at least some improvement in about half the sufferers. Only very potent topical steroids work…such as Topicort, Halog and Lidex. *Helpful:* Wrapping steroid-covered skin in Saran Wrap can increase effectiveness significantly—though you may not want to go to bed at night wrapped in plastic.

A new steroid, temevate, clears half of all patients. However, it can suppress the adrenal glands if used improperly. To avoid trouble, use it for two weeks, then take a week off before resuming use. Never exceed 45 grams per week.

• For small patches, topical steroids with skin patch are much more effective than topical steroids alone. *Procedure:* A bandage-like patch (called an Actiderm patch) is placed over steroid ointment- covered skin. New ointment and patch are applied every other day. This procedure clears skin within two weeks in most cases.

• Interlesional Kenalog therapy. A slow-dissolving form of the steroid drug Kenalog is injected under the affected areas. The treatment is repeated by the doctor once a month. It is very effective at clearing limited patchy psoriasis. *Cost:* $20–$40 per session…plus the cost of the office visit. Injections provide rapid results, and the treated spot usually stays clear for nine months. *Drawbacks:* Only useful for a limited number of patches. The injections are painful and, on rare occasions, can result in infections.

• Goeckermann therapy. The patient disrobes and is exposed to high-intensity ultraviolet B light (UVB) until the skin is faintly sunburned. Initially, the treatment is given daily for one month. Once the skin has cleared, the patient is placed on a maintenance schedule of three times weekly. *Caution:* Avoid tanning salons. The wavelength of ultraviolet A light they use is much less effective against psoriasis. Goeckermann therapy produces a glowing tan. Although some patients fear skin cancer, which is associated with UV exposure, the increased risk is very slight.

• PUVA—Psoralen, plus high-intensity ultraviolet A light. Psoralen, a "super tanning pill," works synergistically with UVA light to control psoriasis. This is a relatively new treatment, highly effective. *Cost:* $40 per treatment. Typically, 30-40 treatments are needed each year to keep skin clear. Produces a deep tan.

Also helpful:

•Methotrexate. This anti-mitotic drug, commonly used as a potent anticancer medication, is also effective against severe psoriasis. *Typical dosage:* Six tablets a week. *Danger:* Methotrexate is toxic to the liver. To prevent cirrhosis, certain precautions must be taken—blood tests every two weeks and a liver biopsy upon commencement of the therapy and once every two years during treatment. The doctor who administers methotrexate should have considerable experience with the drug.

•Etretinate. This treatment is highly effective against severe cases of psoriasis. *Caution:* A chemical cousin of the acne drug Accutane, etretinate (Tegison) can cause severe dryness of the skin and other minor side effects. It should not be taken by women of child-bearing potential because it causes birth defects. Any woman who has taken etretinate should wait at least two years before becoming pregnant.

•Cyclosporine A. Highly effective. Known primarily as an immune system suppressant used to prevent rejection of transplanted organs, cyclosporine is an experimental drug, available only at major teaching hospitals. *Warning:* Long-term use can lead to kidney damage and cancer.

Source: Ronald Savin, MD, clinical professor of dermatology, Yale School of Medicine, New Haven, CT. Dr. Savin, who has a private practice in dermatology in New Haven, was one of the clinical investigators of the Actiderm patch.

Permanent Ulcer Cure

When treated with antibiotics, only 8% of peptic ulcer patients suffered a recurrence within a year. A placebo-treated group had an 86% recurrence rate. *Key finding:* The primary cause of most peptic ulcers is a bacterium called Heliobacter pylori, and not gastric acid.

Source: Study of 104 Austrian ulcer patients led by gastroenterologist Enno Hentschel, MD, reported in *The New England Journal of Medicine*, 10 Shattuck St. Boston, Massachusetts 02115.

Vision: Myths & Realities

It's a *myth* that you will ruin your eyes by doing "normal" things—reading in the dark, sitting too close to the TV, etc. You may *tire* your eyes doing these things, but you won't damage them. *What will harm your eyes:*

•Ultraviolet (UV) radiation from the sun (and sunlamps) can damage the retina and may cause cataracts. This is true even on overcast days because clouds don't *block* UV radiation—they scatter it so it hits you from all directions.

Advice: Buy only nonprescription sunglasses that comply with a regulation called ANSI Z80.3. This will be stated on a manufacturer's label or in an information insert. (The regulation, from the American National Standards Institute, means the glasses adequately block harmful UV radiation.) Prescription sunglasses may provide protection that goes beyond ANSI standards for nonprescription eye wear.

•A deficiency of vitamin A may aggravate night blindness. *Recommended:* To get more vitamin A into your daily diet, increase your intake of foods such as carrots, broccoli, whole milk, liver, egg yolks, chicken and fish. *Caution:* Unlike some other vitamins, which are flushed out of your body if you consume too much, an excess of vitamin A will build up in your system and can be *toxic.*

Source: Gary E. Oliver, OD, chief of the ocular disease and special testing service, State University of New York College of Optometry, 100 E. 24 St., New York 10010.

When You Turn 50

Everyone 50 and older should be screened for colorectal cancer. According to the advisory panel the US Public Health Service, effective methods include fecal-occult blood testing and signoidoscopy (or both).

Source: Marion Nadel, PhD, an epidemiologist in the Division of Cancer Prevention and Control, the Centers for Disease Control and Prevention, Atlanta.

How to Control Constipation Without Laxatives

Over-the-counter laxatives can be very helpful for occasional irregularity. But long-term use of these remedies can cause serious health problems.

Laxative "abusers" ultimately lose the ability to have a bowel movement naturally. In some cases, diarrhea caused by laxative abuse necessitates the use of antidiarrhea medication, which then causes constipation...and so on. This can become a vicious cycle.

Fortunately, even severe cases of constipation can usually be controlled simply by drinking more water and upping the consumption of *natural laxative* foods—whole grains, peas, beans and other fiber-rich foods.

Caution: Bran, a very high-fiber food, can actually exacerbate constipation if an individual doesn't drink enough liquid with it.

The importance of water...

Adequate water intake is the simplest way to ensure regularity. But the eight-glasses-a-day rule is simplistic.

Test: You're drinking enough water if urine flows freely and is light in color. If you're not sure how much is right for *you*, your health-care provider can give you advice.

Natural laxative foods...

Crunchiness has nothing to do with fiber content...and fiber content is not altered by cooking or processing. Steaming broccoli doesn't decrease fiber content, for instance, while toasting white bread (a low-fiber food) does not increase it.

Be sure to eat a variety of laxative-quality foods. If your daily routine involves having a cup of coffee or a few prunes to "prime the pump," you may find these foods lose their effect if your daily routine is disrupted by travel, schedule changes, etc. This may be because although there is some laxative quality in the food, there is also a habit formed over a period of years.

Example: You wake up every morning, drink coffee while reading the paper and go to the bathroom. When your schedule changes, the coffee can't do the job alone.

That's why it is better to rely on a diet rich in fiber and natural laxatives.

To avoid diarrhea and/or flatulence when changing from a low-fiber to a high-fiber diet, change your diet gradually, over a period of weeks. Check with your health-care provider before making any radical change in your diet. *Often helpful:* The dietary supplement Beano.

Triple pear crisp...

This dessert—a personal favorite—makes an excellent natural laxative.

6 ounces dried pears, cored and chopped—stems discarded

1 cup pear juice, bottled

4 cups fresh pears, cored and chopped into bite-sized pieces (4 or 5 medium pears)

½ cup olive oil

⅓ cup molasses

2 cups rolled oats

1 teaspoon cinnamon

½ teaspoon nutmeg

Bring dried pears and juice to boil in small saucepan. Reduce heat. Simmer until pears are tender, about 10 minutes.

Put fresh pears into an 8-inch baking dish.

In a separate bowl, mix olive oil, molasses, oats, cinnamon and nutmeg, evenly coating the oats.

Pour tender pears and cooking liquid over fresh pears. Spread oat mixture on top. Bake in a 375 degree oven for 35 minutes, or until topping is brown and crisp.

Makes six servings. *Per serving:* 467 calories, 20 g fat, 7 g fiber, no cholesterol.

Source: Karin Cadwell, PhD, RN, coauthor of *The Natural Laxative Cookbook.* Sterling Publishing. She is also a faculty member of the nutritional consulting service Health Education Associates, Inc., 8 San Sebastian Way, Sandwich, Massachusetts 02563.

4

Simple Solutions to Common Health Problems

How to Alleviate Allergies...Naturally

Drugs are often effective at controlling itching, sneezing, runny nose and other allergic symptoms. But natural remedies sometimes do the trick *more* effectively. *Included:*

•Varied diet. The effects of food allergies are cumulative—the more you eat, the more you suffer. *Solution:* Eat a variety of foods, and rotate them in your diet to avoid taking them too often.

Example: Instead of having orange juice each morning, eat apples one day, grapefruit another, cereal another, etc.

Even if you are allergic to a particular food, you may be able to eat it and avoid allergic symptoms. *Key:* Eat the food in moderate quantities…and in rotation with other foods.

Note: Eating foods that you are allergic to, especially during the pollen season, can make hay fever worse and decrease the effectiveness of allergy medications.

Recommended: Fish, seeds and fresh vegetables contain essential fatty acids, which help fight allergies.

•Dietary supplements. *Included:*

Vitamins. Considered nature's antihistamine, vitamin C is often highly effective at reducing allergic symptoms. It works only if taken in sufficient quantities. Consult your doctor for the dosage that's right for you. *Also helpful:* Vitamins B6, A and E.

Minerals. Calcium and magnesium, selenium and zinc also help alleviate allergic symptoms. Consult your doctor for the proper dosage.

•Fresh air. Avoid airborne pollutants as much as possible—not just pollen, dust, molds and animal dander. *Included:* Industrial chemicals, solvents, household cleaners, cigarette smoke, perfume, etc.

Source: Marshall Mandell, MD, an allergist and clinical ecologist in private practice in Norwalk, Connecticut. A former assistant professor of allergy at New York Medical College, he specializes in treating allergies by identifying their causes and contributing factors. Using this approach, Dr. Mandell can treat allergies with minimal use of medications.

Back Savers

- When standing, rest one foot on a step stool.
- Bend at your hips, not at your waist.
- Avoid lying on your stomach.
- Lift heavy objects no higher than your waist.
- Sit down to put on socks, shoes, pants—don't bend over.
- Get down on one knee before picking a small child or infant up from the floor.
- When reading, don't bend your neck and shoulders—bring your book up to your eyes by placing two pillows on your lap and propping the book on top of them.

Source: *The Back Almanac,* Lanier Publishing, Box 20429, Oakland, California 94620.

Cure for Bad Breath

Brush your tongue as well as your teeth to beat bad breath. If a problem persists, floss and brush after every meal. Eat an orange or grapefruit between meals to cleanse the mouth naturally by increasing saliva production. Antibacterial mouthwashes give temporary relief by killing some oral bacteria and masking mouth odor—but are no substitute for good oral hygiene. If still a problem, see your doctor. It may be only sinusitis—post-nasal drip —or it could be more serious: Esophagitis (esophageal reflux) is caused by stomach acids flowing back up to the throat, bringing along partially digested food particles.

Source: Bruce Yaffe, MD, a physician in private practice in New York City.

How to Stop Biting Your Nails

Nail-biting (known medically as onychophagia) makes you vulnerable to severe skin infections and limits your ability to pick up and handle coins, pins and other small objects.

In severe cases—those in which nails are bitten all the way down to the whitish, semicircular "half-moon" region—permanent nail deformities are a real possibility.

Nail-biters normally try numerous remedies to curb the biting urge that include bandages, hot sauce, bitter-tasting nail coatings, relaxation tapes, hypnosis, chewing gum, etc. Sadly, these remedies seldom work.

What does work...

- Awareness. Many nail-biters chew their nails unconsciously, without realizing what they're doing. They can't stop biting their nails until they develop a keen awareness of when—and under what circumstances—they're most prone to bite. They should cultivate an awareness of where their hands are at all times.

- Manicures. Nail polish makes nails more attractive, and the better-looking our nails, the less likely we are to abuse them.

Myth: Nail polish is for women only. In fact, a growing number of men are now having their nails manicured—with clear polish that's virtually undetectable. *Cost:* $30 and up.

Especially helpful: Multi-layer (French) manicures. They cost more, but provide additional layers of protection, thus affording a stronger deterrent against biting.

- Gloves. Covered nails are not only less tempting than uncovered nails, but also are harder to reach if an urge to bite proves irresistible. *For maximum protection:* Wear gloves at all times—day and night—until the nail-biting urge dissipates. This may take several weeks—or even months. Lightweight cotton gloves are perfect for wearing at work and during sleep. If an urge to bite hits while you're not wearing gloves, lightly clench your fists until the urge passes.

- Psychotherapy. In particularly severe cases of nail-biting, short-term therapy may be helpful. In some cases, tranquilizers may be prescribed.

Source: Richard K. Scher, MD, professor of dermatology, Columbia University College of Physicians and Surgeons, and director of the nail research center, Columbia-Presbyterian Medical Center, New York City. Dr. Scher is the coauthor of *Nails: Diagnosis, Surgery and Therapy.* W.B. Saunders, The Curtis Center, 625 Walnut St., Suite 300, Philadelphia 19106.

Blister Care

Clean the area of the blister with soap and water. Pierce the blister with a sterile needle (hold the needle over a flame for 60 seconds) and drain it. You may have to repeat this as many as three times in the next 24 hours. Keep the blister covered with a bandage until it heals.

Canker Sore Self-Defense

Avoid commercial toothpastes and mouthwashes—they can irritate ulcers of the mouth. *Better:* For a month or two, brush with a paste made of baking soda and water, and rinse with warm water…for short-term pain relief, rinse with a prescription mouthwash containing viscous lidocaine, an anesthetic…apply Zilactin, an over-the-counter medication that forms a film over the ulcer, protecting it from irritants for up to six hours. To prevent outbreaks and heal severe canker sores, ask your dentist or physician for a prescription for an anti-inflammatory steroid.

Source: Brad Rodu, DDS, chairman, oral pathology, University of Alabama, Birmingham.

Better Cavity Treatment

New treatment for cavities regards them as *infections*. After existing cavities are filled, sealants are applied to prevent harmful bacteria from spreading. Then patients rinse twice daily for two weeks with a special rinse—12% chlorhexidine—prescribed by the dentist. *Also useful:* A fluoride varnish that dentists paint on patients' teeth.

Source: Maxwell Anderson, DDS, assistant professor of restorative dentistry, University of Washington, Seattle.

Cold Sore Relief

The presciption drug acyclovir (Zovirax) helps prevent recurrent cold sores (oral herpes infections)—and speeds up healing of sores that do appear. Side effects, including headaches, nausea and diarrhea, occur in about 5% of patients. *Caution:* Women who are pregnant or who plan to become pregnant should avoid using the drug except in extreme cases…under a doctor's supervision, of course.

Source: Researchers at the National Institutes of Health, Besthesda, Maryland, cited in *American Health*, 28 W. 23 St., New York 10001.

Relief for Corns And Calluses

Soften corns and calluses by adding two tablespoons of mild detergent to a half-gallon of warm water and soaking your feet for at least 10 minutes. Dry feet thoroughly. Rub a few drops of vegetable oil on affected areas for additional softening. Gently file the top layer of the corn or callus with a pumice stone or callus file. Clean with soap and water. *Caution:* Avoid medicated pads and creams. They can eat into healthy tissue and cause allergic reactions.

Source: Mark Sussman, DPM, is a podiatrist in Wheaton, Maryland, and coauthor of *The Family Foot Care Book,* Acropolis Books, 2311 Calvert St. NW, Suite 300, Washington, DC 20008.

Dental Anxiety Relief

The popular anti-insomnia drug triazolam (Halcion) is also helpful for reducing anxiety in patients with dental phobias…or in those undergoing complex dental procedures. Despite reports linking Halcion to prolonged amnesia, violence and other potentially serious side effects, the drug has proven safe and effective in three separate FDA reviews. *More:* Side effects can be minimized by using the lowest possible dose…reducing dosage for older patients…using the drug cautiously in depressed patients and those with a history of alcoholism.

Source: Charles W. Berthold, DDS, visiting scientist, Clinical Pharmacology Unit, National Institutes of Health, Bethesda. His review of triazolam was published in the *Journal of the American Dental Association*, 211 E. Chicago Ave., Chicago 60711.

Fatigue Self-Defense

Helpful: Fascination and purposefulness. A high degree of choice, concentration and enjoyment will keep energy levels high. We are seldom too tired to do what we really want to do.

Source: *Inward Bound: Exploring the Geography of Emotions* by Sam Keen, PhD, Bantam Books, 666 Fifth Ave., New York 10103.

Flu Prevention Wisdom

An estimated 25 million people in the U.S. will contract the flu this year.* *If you're one of them...*
- Rest.
- Take aspirin. *Note:* Instead of aspirin, children under 16 should take an analgesic that contains acetaminophen—Tylenol, etc.
- Use a humidifier to thin lung secretions so they can be coughed up more easily.
- Drink fluids—at least eight glasses a day.
- Take a cough medicine that contains dextromethorphan—for a dry, hacking cough.

When to call the doctor: People who are in a high-risk group** should contact their doctor right away. Others should contact their doctor only if their fever does not drop after three days. *Prevention:*
- *Don't smoke.* Smokers are much more susceptible to the flu than are non-smokers.

*Symptoms include chills, fever, muscle aches, cough, sore throat, hoarseness, runny nose, headache, fatigue.

**People who are over age 65 or under age five...anyone with chronic heart or lung disease, including asthma... people with diabetes, cancer, chronic kidney disease or anemias like sickle cell.

- *Consider getting a flu vaccine.* The vaccine is definitely recommended for people in high-risk groups and for households that include a school-aged child *and* a person in a high-risk group. *Cost:* About $8 at clinics. Doctors usually charge about $20.

Source: Paul Glezen, MD, professor of microbiology and pediatrics and head of the preventive medicine section, Baylor College of Medicine, One Baylor Plaza, Houston 77030.

Foot Pain Relief

Prevent tired, aching feet: Make arch muscles stronger. *Exercise:* Sit in a chair with several marbles on the floor in front of you and a small box nearby...pick up the marbles with your toes one by one and put them in the box. *Recommended:* Practice every day for two weeks ...then once a week to maintain arch strength.

Source: *Prime Time: A Doctor's Guide to Staying Younger Longer* by John E. Eichenlaub, MD, a general practitioner for 35 years. Prentice Hall, 113 Sylvan Ave., Englewood Cliffs, New Jersey 07632.

Gas Myth

Anti-gas food additives are ineffective at reducing flatulence and bloating associated with eating beans. *The test:* Two groups of people were fed identical fast-food meals—including six ounces of refried beans. One group's meal was treated with drops of a popular anti-gas additive containing the enzyme *alpha-galactosidase*. The other group's meal was treated with placebo drops. *Result:* Bloating and flatulence were just as common among the group with the anti-gas additive as among the group with the placebo.

Source: Thomas Rupp, MD, gastroenterologist, department of medicine, University of Louisville School of Medicine, Louisville, Kentucky.

Heartburn Self-Defense

If you must lie down after eating a big meal, lie on your *left side* instead of your right. People who lie on their left have significantly less heartburn than those who lie on their right side. *Possible explanation:* Heartburn occurs when stomach acids "reflux"—flow back up into the esophagus. Lying on your left side keeps your stomach below your esophagus… so gravity helps keep stomach acids down. *Alternative:* Place blocks under the headboard end of your bed—to elevate the esophagus.

Source: Leo Katz, MD, is a clinical instructor in medicine at Thomas Jefferson University Hospital, Philadelphia.

To Stop Hiccups

•To cure hiccups, swallow a teaspoonful of granulated sugar or eat crackers. The slight irritation in the back of the throat interrupts the hiccup cycle. *Alternatives:* Suck on a lemon wedge soaked in Angostura bitters. Or induce sneezing by sniffing pepper. Or take a sniff of something with a strong aroma, such as vinegar.

Source: *Harvard Medical School Health Letter*, Cambridge, MA.

•Rub a cotton-tipped swab gently across the roof of your mouth at the middle of your soft palate (the part that vibrates with speech). A minute of light rubbing should squelch virtually all cases.

Source: Steven Goldsmith, M.D., Baystate Medical Center, Springfield, MA, quoted in *McCall's*.

About Hives

The cause of hives—those red, itchy, raised skin blotches—is unknown for nine out of ten patients. *Best treatment in such cases:* Reassurance that the condition is not serious…and antihistamines. The side effects of stronger drugs such as cortico-steroids may prove to be more harmful than the hives.

Source: Barton Inkeles, M.D., New York Hospital-Cornell Medical Center, writing in *Drug Therapy*.

Hoarseness Preventative

To avoid hoarseness, break the throat-clearing habit by taking sips of water throughout the day…avoid smoke-filled environments… don't smoke (of course)…when using indoor heat, use a humidifier…speak in modulated tones—not loudly. If you do become hoarse, inhale steam from a hot shower…use a humidifier when sleeping…rest your voice completely—or at least at intervals throughout the day…use lozenges, gargle and sip hot tea to help relax vocal cords.

Source: American Academy of Otolaryngology—Head and Neck Surgery, One Prince St., Alexandria, Virginia 22314.

Intestinal Parasite Defense

To avoid intestinal parasites: Wash hands before eating, after cleaning up and after petting animals. When eating out, order all dishes medium to well-done. Do not eat anywhere where you suspect unsanitary conditions. Order bottled or boiled water. Consider buying a home water-filtration unit. Make sure your child's daycare center disinfects all surfaces with an antiseptic solution every day.

Source: Ann Louise Gittleman, MS, author of *Guess What Came to Dinner: Parasites and Your Health*, writing in *Natural Health*, 17 Station St. Brookline Village, Massachusetts 02147.

How to Increase Your Iron Intake

Iron deficiency is a common nutritional problem—and may be a special concern among women on low-cholesterol diets who avoid such iron-rich foods as red meat and liver.

Problem: Although there is ample iron in many vegetables and grains, it is less efficiently absorbed by the body than is the iron in animal foods.

Solution: In a recent study, a group of borderline anemic women raised their iron levels significantly when ascorbic acid (vitamin C) supplements were added to their fruit juice at each meal. The women improved their retention of iron from plant foods by more than 40% over a control group which did not receive the added vitamin C.

It is more nutritious to get vitamin C through foods than from supplements.

Plant foods rich in iron: Whole grains, nuts, beans and legumes.

Foods rich in vitamin C: Citrus fruits, tomatoes, cantaloupes, broccoli, strawberries, cabbage, potatoes.

Source: Janet Hunt, PhD, RD, a research nutritionist for the US Department of Agriculture's Human Nutrition Research Center in Grand Forks, North Dakota.

Leg-Cramp Relief

Leg cramps can usually be alleviated by firmly pinching your upper lip for 20–30 seconds.

Source: Donald Cooper, M.D., former US Olympics team doctor, in *Sportswise.*

Liver Spot Self-Defense

Liver spots can be lightened with Tretinoin cream—sold under the brand names Retin-A and Ortho. *Background:* In a study of 58 patients who applied the cream for 10 months, 83% experienced significant lightening of spots. *Follow-up:* Six months after the study, the spots had not reappeared in any of the patients.

Source: Study by Elyse S. Rafal, MD, University of Michigan, reported in *Medical Tribune,* 257 Park Ave. S., New York 10010.

Poison Ivy Self-Defense

Before outdoor work or play, use a barrier preparation on exposed skin—to block the irri-

tant action of urushiol, the oily resin on the leaves that actually causes the rash. *Recommended:* Armor lotion or Stoko-gard cream. *After exposure:* Use cleansing lotion—Tecnu—applied within eight hours—it removes urushiol and stops itching. For severe cases, see your doctor.

Source: Stephen J. McGeady, MD, director of allergy and clinical immunology, Thomas Jefferson University Hospital, Philadelphia.

Psoriasis Secret

Treat psoriasis consistently, even when no lesions are visible. *Reason:* The disease is there even when it does not produce symptoms. *Key:* Keep the skin moist and lubricated—mineral oil and petroleum jelly work well. *Also:* Avoid skin injury…practice stress-reduction at home and at work…and limit consumption of alcohol—it causes itching in persons with psoriasis. Expose skin regularly to moderate amounts of sunlight.

Source: Anil Abraham, MD, clinical research fellow, Psoriasis Research Institute, Stanford, California.

Better Scar Removal

Dermabrasion may remove scars on the face caused by surgery—but only if the procedure is done six to eight weeks after suturing. Within that time period, surgeons can even the contour differences that make scars stand out from surrounding skin. *Caution:* Dermabrasion performed before six weeks can actually make scarring worse—and after eight weeks, scar tissue begins to mature and is less likely to be dermabraded into invisibility.

Source: John Yarborough, Jr., MD, clinical professor of dermatology, Tulane University, New Orleans.

Much Healthier Skin Is Not Difficult at All

There is no secret to having healthy skin. Expensive creams and facials, special vitamin supplements and rigorous diets do not help.

Good skin is…

•Inherited. Some people are genetically susceptible to acne, for instance. Some aren't.

•Earned. A lifetime of good general health measures, staying out of the sun and avoiding fad treatments will pay off.

Diet myths debunked…

•*Myth:* Many skin problems are caused by poor diet. Bad skin that results from poor nutrition is rare in the U.S. Most people eat a relatively balanced diet. Vitamin and mineral supplements aren't necessary. And megadoses of vitamins or minerals can be harmful.

Example: Taking synthetic vitamin A tablets in doses that far exceed daily requirements can cause serious abnormalities in the nervous system.

•*Myth:* Vitamin E promotes healing and is useful in treating skin diseases. There is no evidence that rubbing vitamin-E creams or the contents of the capsules on rashes, acne or scars has any helpful effects.

•*Myth:* Drinking large quantities of water is good for the skin. Although drinking water is good for your general well-being, it does not specifically help the skin.

•*Myth:* Acne is caused by eating chocolate, sugar or greasy "junk" foods. Although the exact cause of acne is still not known, scientific studies contradict the traditional belief that diet is responsible for the problem.

Dangers of the sun…

Your skin's worst enemy is sun. The incidence of sun-related skin problems is at near-epidemic proportions.

Example: The number of cases of malignant melanoma, once rare, has increased tenfold in the past 50 years.

Although no one knows why, evidence points to a change in our sun-exposure habits. People who grew up in the past 20 years have been convinced that there's nothing wrong with getting a lot of sun. Most skin-cancer patients can recall severe sunburns in childhood and adolescence.

Best defense: Stay out of the sun or wear long sleeves and a wide-brimmed hat and use a sunscreen.

The Sun Protection Factor (SPF) listed on all sunscreens is a measurement of the exposure time required to turn the skin red while using sunscreen.

Example: A sunscreen with an SPF of 15 will allow you to stay in the sun 15 times longer than usual without turning red.

An SPF of 15 to 20 is sufficient protection for most people. Sunscreens with higher SPFs are not harmful, but they're no more effective, either.

The skin and aging…

As we get older, the number and thickness of the connective-tissue fibers that make up the skin slowly decrease. *Result:* A loss in texture, firmness and elastic rebound, all of which contribute to wrinkling.

Few of the many treatments purported to help aging are really effective.

Moisturizers work to hold water in the skin, but they do not slow the aging process. The cost of a moisturizer—and some are very costly—has nothing to do with its performance. There is no evidence to suggest that preparations with aloe or any other ingredients have special moisturizing or healing properties. Recommended: Select an inexpensive moisturizer that feels good to you.

Repairing aged skin…

•Collagen injections. The skin beneath the epidermis contains collagen, a fibrous protein that gives the skin its strength and suppleness. As we age, however, our collagen loses some of its elasticity and the amount of collagen diminishes.

Breakthrough? In the past 10 years, a purified collagen derivative has been used to correct scars and smooth wrinkles and furrows. Collagen is injected through a needle into the area to be corrected.

Drawbacks: Although the process is generally safe, the effects are short-lived—patients need another treatment every six to 12 months. Some people develop allergic reactions. Collagen injections are not recommended for people with arthritis or other connective-tissue diseases. And collagen treatments are very expensive—a single treatment may cost several hundred dollars.

•Facials. Although facials are not generally harmful, there is no evidence that they improve the skin.

•Retin-A. It is an approved, effective treatment for acne. Most recently, studies of the skin suggest that Retin-A can eliminate fine wrinkles and other signs of aging.

Result: Retin-A is being widely used for this purpose although not approved by the Food and Drug Administration for use as an anti-wrinkle cream.

Problem: Not all Retin-A users are impressed with its results as an anti-wrinkle cream. Furthermore, long-term use of Retin-A for years may have some yet-to-be-identified side effects.

Bottom line: Until we know more, I recommend that you avoid using it except as an acne treatment.

Source: Richard A. Walzer, MD, associate clinical professor of dermatology at Columbia College of Physicians and Surgeons and an attending dermatologist at Columbia Presbyterian Medical Center, New York. He is the author of *Healthy Skin: A Guide to Lifelong Skin Care.* Consumer Reports Books, 101 Truman Ave., Yonkers, New York 10703.

Natural Remedies For a Stuffy Nose

Chinese ephedra—Ephedra sinica—is an ancient medicinal herb used as a bronchodilator and a stimulant. The source of ephedrine—predecessor of pseudoephedrine, the active ingredient in Sudafed—this dried herb comes in pill form, or works well when you drink it as tea. *Caution:* No more than one cup every four hours. *Also helpful:* Bioflavonoids—available at vitamin and health-food stores. Take one or two capsules...stuffiness should clear up in about 20 minutes. *Important:* Check with your doctor before using. Ephedra is not for use by those with hyperthyroidism or prostate disease.

Source: Marvin Schweitzer, ND, a naturopath with the Center for Healing Arts, in Orange, Connecticut.

Winter Sunburn Alert

Skiing in winter sun can be harder on skin than summer sports. Because they are reflected off the snow, the sun's rays increase in intensity. *Added risk:* Skiing at a high altitude, which boosts exposure to ultraviolet rays. *Recommended safeguard:* Use a moisturizing sunscreen with a sun protection factor of 15 for winter activities on sunny days. Then apply a final "sealing" layer of petroleum jelly or a liquid foundation.

Source: Stephen Kurtin, MD, cofounder of the Institute for the Control of Facial Aging, New York.

Sunburn R$_x$

To soothe a sunburn, apply wet compresses of cool tap water for 20 minutes, three or four times a day. Coat the burned area with a lubricating lotion or cream (not a heavy ointment). Take aspirin or acetaminophen as needed. Drink lots of water. Avoid the sun until your skin has healed completely.

Source: Skin Cancer Foundation, New York.

Tiredness Preventative

Go to sleep no later than 9 p.m. at least once a week to protect your health—and your judgment—from the subtle and cumulative effects of tiredness. A few hours of additional sleep can help keep your body from falling behind. The benefits of extra sleep are not cumulative, however. Trying to bank more sleep ahead of time—in anticipation of keeping long hours for a prolonged period of time—doesn't work.

Source: Bruce Yaffe, MD, an internist in private practice in New York City.

Better Tooth Care

Better brushing: Use a gentle circular motion on both gums and on teeth. *Avoid:* Whiteners and abrasive cleaners (they remove tooth enamel), overly vigorous brushing with a back-and-forth motion—which can damage gums, teeth and tooth roots. *Recommended:* Using softer toothbrushes.

Source: Norma Wells, RDH, MPH, associate professor of dental public health sciences, University of Washington, Seattle.

Tooth-Decay Preventive

Gum chewing fights tooth decay—as long as the gum is sugarless. *Reason:* Chewing stimulates saliva flow, cutting harmful acidity in the mouth and squeezing saliva into spaces between the teeth—to rinse out harmful bacteria. *Best:* Start chewing within five minutes after eating and continue for at least 15 minutes.

Source: *University of California, Berkeley Wellness Letter*, Box 420148, Palm Coast, Florida 32142.

Trembling Hands

Trembling hands are most often due to essential tremor (ET), a treatable movement disorder. *Typical symptoms:* Patients' hands shake when reading, eating, or holding a glass. ET may also strike the head or voice. *Treatment:* The drugs Inderal and/or Mysoline lessen tremors in 60% to 70% of patients. Neurological surgery helps 80%...but its long-term effect is uncertain. *Trap:* ET is often dismissed as a sign of old age or stress...or misdiagnosed as Parkinson's disease, a more serious (and unrelated) disorder.

Source: William C. Koller, MD, president of the International Tremor Foundation, quoted in *Modern Maturity*, 3200 E. Carson St., Lakewood, California 90712.

Better Varicose Vein Treatment

Echosclerotherapy uses ultrasound to guide injection of an iodine solution into veins. Ultrasound allows precise location of proper injection points. Iodine collapses the veins, diverting blood flow and improving appearance—without surgery. *Success rate:* Echosclerotherapy successfully treated more than 80% of patients studied. *Bonus:* Patients need no hospitalization and do not interrupt daily activities.

Source: Study of 300 patients by Louis Grondin, MD, director of a vein clinic in Calgary, Alberta, Canada, reported in *The Medical Post*, 777 Bay St., Toronto, Ontario M5W 1A7.

Better Vision

Eat well, exercise and stop smoking. Conditions such as diabetes, high blood pressure and hardening of the arteries—often the result of poor health habits—damage the capillaries that supply oxygen to the retina. *Result:* Vision loss. *Helpful:* Eat a low-fat, low-cholesterol diet, exercise regularly, minimize stress, maintain a normal weight for your size and age... and schedule regular eye examinations.

Source: Arol Augsburger, OD, professor of clinical optometry, Ohio State University College of Optometry, Columbus.

Facial Wrinkle Defense

Sleep on your back. (Use a pillow under your knees, if you find that to be more comfortable.) *Also helpful:* Use a satin pillowcase. (Your face can stick to polyester, Dacron or cotton.)

Source: *Immune Power Boosters: Your Key to Feeling Younger, Living Longer* by medical-nutrition reporter Carlson Wade, Prentice Hall, Route 9W, Englewood Cliffs, New Jersey 07632.

Safe, Simple Fix for Minor Injuries

From sprains and bruises to toothache, bone fracture and postsurgical discomfort, the homeopathic remedy arnica is good for just about any type of pain caused by physical trauma. Unlike aspirin and other over-the-counter painkillers, arnica pills have no side effects.

In a 1991 English study on patients hospitalized for acute injuries, arnica relieved stiffness and improved psychological well-being in 98% of patients, compared with 57% of patients given a placebo.

Arnica works fast. One of my co-workers fell and pulled a muscle. Ordinarily, it would take a week or two for pain from such an injury to subside. Yet within three days after he started taking arnica, his pain was gone.

It may even be beneficial to take arnica before sustaining an injury. Many marathoners use it before they race. In Canada, horse trainers have begun to use arnica to coax a little more speed out of their thoroughbreds.

Arnica is derived from a mountain plant called leopard's bane. It's sold in "potencies" ranging from 6x or 6c (low potency) to 200c (high potency).

In general, higher potencies are best for chronic conditions, low potencies for acute conditions. But speak with your doctor before taking a dose.

Arnica is safe in a wide range of dosages— from one pill every eight hours to four pills an hour. If pain persists, see a doctor.

Arnica is available in health-food stores, pharmacies and mail-order homeopathic pharmacies such as Dolisos (800-365-4767). Cost: $4 to $6 for 100 pills.

Source: William Pawluk, MD, MSc, director of clinical programs, Division of Complementary Medicine, University of Maryland School of Medicine, Baltimore.

Amazing Flower Remedy

Dried flowers of *calendula officinalis* are good for burns, cuts, scrapes, acne, tonsillitis and canker sores, vaginitis, rashes, athlete's foot and sunburn.

During the Civil War, these bright orange and yellow flowers provided the major line of defense against infection. Today you can buy dried calendula flowers, ointment, tincture or spray at most health-food stores...or grow your own.

Calendula flourishes in almost any climate, whether it's planted in a pot or in the ground.

Most nurseries sell bedding plants in the springtime. Be sure to ask for *calendula officinalis*—not marigolds.

Flowers harvested between June and September are most potent. Dry them out of direct sun on a mesh screen for one to two weeks. Store in an airtight container.

Hot calendula tea helps soothe ulcers. Gargle with cool tea for inflamed tonsils or canker sores.

To make tea: Pour 10 ounces of boiling water over 2/3 cup of the flowers. Let it steep for 15 minutes. Or add five to 10 drops of calendula tincture to a cup of hot water.

Apply tincture or spray to rashes, cuts, scrapes or acne with a cotton ball. Spraying is good for sunburn, vaginitis and pinworms. Use ointment on scabs, eczema and psoriasis.

To make ointment: Melt 1/2 cup of petroleum jelly over low heat in a double boiler. Add a handful of dried calendula flowers. Heat on low for an hour. Strain out the herb and pour into a glass jar.

Source: Jamison Starbuck, ND, a naturopathic physician in private practice in Missoula, MT. She is a visiting professor at the National College of Naturopathic Medicine in Portland, OR, and the Southwest College of Naturopathic Medicine in Scottsdale, AZ.

5

Diet and Nutrition

What to Eat to Prevent Cancer

Although scientists continue to debate the role specific foods play in the development of cancer, there's now a consensus that Americans could dramatically lower their cancer risk by altering their eating habits—specifically, by eating less fat and more fiber.

The fat connection…

Most Americans consume 38% to 40% of their total calories in the form of fat—well above the 25% to 30% fat consumption considered desirable.

This makes us highly susceptible to cancer of the colon, breast, pancreas and prostate.

No one knows exactly why eating too much fat promotes the development of cancer, but the evidence—drawn from studies on both animals and humans—is compelling.

Different foods contain different types and quantities of fat…

•Saturated fats are found in beef and other meats, fried foods and poultry skin.

•Monounsaturated fats are found in peanuts, olives and a few other foods.

•Polyunsaturated fats are found in corn, safflower and other cooking oils.

•Very unsaturated long-chain fatty acids are found in cold-water fish, such as herring and salmon.

It's important to keep track of what kinds of fats you eat because nutritionists now recommend that these fats be eaten in a 1:1:1 ratio. In other words, each day we should eat equal portions of polyunsaturated, monounsaturated and saturated fats. For most of us, this means cutting down on saturated fats while increasing intake of monounsaturated and polyunsaturated fats.

To reduce your consumption of saturated fats, eat less fried foods, trim the fat off beef and other meats and trim skin off poultry. These small sacrifices have big health payoffs.

About fish: Although fish contains oils that are highly unsaturated, it's still unclear what, if any, role this oil plays in preventing cancer. There is some early evidence, however, that eating large amounts of fish reduces cancer risk and lowers serum triglycerides—lipids that may be associated with heart disease.

The fiber connection…

While we're eating too much fat, we're also eating too little fiber. On the average, Americans consume only 10 to 12 grams of fiber a day. Instead, we should be eating 25 to 30 grams of fiber every day.

Big problem: Our diet consists of highly refined, easy-to-chew foods instead of high-fiber fruits, vegetables and grains.

There are two basic kinds of fiber…

•Insoluble fiber, found primarily in wheat bran, is fiber that is not broken down by bacteria in the intestine. By helping waste pass quickly through the colon, it helps prevent colon cancer, diverticulitis and appendicitis.

•Soluble fiber, found in oat bran and in most fruits and vegetables, is fiber that is broken down by bacteria. It helps to prevent heart disease (by lowering cholesterol) and diabetes (by lowering the blood sugar).

Nutritionists now recommend that Americans should double their intake of dietary fiber …fruits and vegetables as well as grains. Pears, for instance, at 4.6 grams of fiber each, contain more fiber than any other fruit. *Other good fiber sources:* Red kidney beans (7 grams), lentils (4 grams), apples (3.3 grams), bananas (2.7 grams) and grapefruit (1.5 grams per half).

Caution: Don't consume more than 40 grams of fiber a day. Too much can be almost as bad as too little. In animals, excessive consumption has been found to cause bulky stools that can result in a form of constipation.

There also is some early evidence that alfalfa and certain other grains may actually increase the risk of developing colon cancer. *Self-defense:* Until the final verdict is in, don't rely just on grains for your fiber…eat a wide variety of fiber-rich foods.

Beyond fat and fiber…

Other than increasing fiber and reducing fats, evidence linking dietary choices to cancer is less reliable.

Still, there are things to do that probably will help prevent cancer…and which won't hurt in any case.

•Eat a wide variety of foods. This limits your exposure to any carcinogens that might be found in a particular food…and eliminates the need for vitamin and mineral supplements.

•Increase your consumption of vitamin A. A powerful antioxidant, it keeps our cells from being attacked by oxygen, and thus prevents cancer. Vitamin A seems particularly effective in helping prevent lung cancer in smokers. To a lesser extent, it also seems to help stave off colon cancer, breast cancer and lung cancer. *Best vitamin A sources:* Carrots, squash and other orange and leafy vegetables.

•Increase your intake of selenium. Selenium is a trace element found in most vegetables. To get more into your diet, eat more vegetables. *Alternative:* Selenium supplements.

•Limit your consumption of smoked and pickled foods. They have been tied to stomach cancer. An occasional dill pickle won't hurt you, and neither will an occasional barbecued meal. But a daily regimen of pickled vegetables and smoked meats is imprudent.

•Avoid obesity. Obesity is clearly linked to cancer of both the endometrium (the lining of the uterus) and the breast. Also, obese women with breast cancer are far more likely to succumb to the disease than are normal-weight women diagnosed with similar breast cancer.

Keeping track of your diet is one step toward controlling your weight. *Also extremely helpful:* Exercise.

Watching TV, working in an office and other aspects of a sedentary lifestyle all are associated with cancer.

Although it's not yet clear exactly how exercise helps prevent cancer, the incidence of colon cancer is much higher in men with sedentary occupations than men who are active. Women athletes have lower rates of reproductive-tract cancer than sedentary, out-of-shape women. And animal studies have demonstrated that moderate exercise cuts the risk of breast, pancreas, liver and colon cancer.

Caution: Too much exercise may actually be almost as bad as too little. Several studies have indicated that extreme exertion (like that necessary to complete a marathon) temporarily weakens the immune system, opening the way for infectious bacteria and viruses—and possibly the development of cancer.

Evidence: At the turn of the century, stomach cancer was common in the U.S. Now that refrigeration is almost universal—and we rely less on pickling and smoking to preserve our foods—it is a rarity. In Japan, however, where pickled and smoked foods remain common, stomach cancer rates are among the highest in the world.

• Limit your consumption of simple carbohydrates (sugars). Evolving man ate very little sugar. As a result of this, our bodies are not set up to properly digest it.

Problem: Simple carbohydrates cause the pancreas to produce a large amount of insulin very rapidly, and there is now some evidence suggesting that this can have a harmful effect on the pancreas. *Better:* Complex carbohydrates—found in pastas and breads.

• Limit your caffeine consumption. Caffeine has been tied to a variety of cancers, including those of the pancreas and bladder. More recent data suggest caffeine does not cause cancer. Nonetheless, caffeine is very clearly a potent drug, and it makes sense to consume it in moderation.

• Limit your alcohol consumption. Drinking to excess (more than a couple of drinks a day) has been linked to cancer of the mouth and throat. People who drink and smoke are at high risk. Most patients with head or neck cancer are alcoholics or near-alcoholics with poor nutritional habits who smoke regularly.

Source: Leonard A. Cohen, PhD, head of the section of nutritional endocrinology, the American Health Foundation, One Dana Rd., Valhalla, New York 10595. Dr. Cohen's specialty is in the area of nutritional carcinogenesis.

Retinol is found in animal foods—especially fish liver oils, egg yolk, butter and cream.

Carotene, which the body converts into retinol, is found in certain plants—carrots, sweet potatoes, squash, broccoli, collard greens and other fruits and vegetables colored dark yellow, orange or dark green.

Note: It makes no difference whether your vitamin A comes from plant or animal sources.

Vitamin A deficiency can lead to blindness and other health problems. Fortunately, most Americans get more than enough from dietary sources, although vitamin A deficiency is a serious threat in developing countries where the staple food is rice, since rice contains no carotene.

Some people suffering from chronic diarrhea, cystic fibrosis and certain other ailments that impair absorption of vitamin A might not get enough. For these people, vitamin supplements taken under a doctor's supervision are usually sufficient to raise levels of the vitamin to acceptable levels.

A more common threat to Americans is getting too much vitamin A—a rare but potentially serious condition known as hypervitaminosis A.

At risk: People who consume very large quantities of liver and other animal sources of vitamin A over an extended period of time…or who abuse vitamin A supplements.

Symptoms: Severe headaches, drowsiness, nausea and hair loss.

Source: Jeanne Goldberg, PhD, RD, associate professor of nutrition, Tufts University, Medford, Massachusetts. Dr. Goldberg and the renowned nutritionist Jean Mayer, who died recently, are the authors of *Dr. Jean Mayer's Diet and Nutrition Guide.*

All About Vitamin A

Vitamin A is essential for good eyesight, a working reproductive tract and healthy skin, including the epithelial tissue lining the nose, mouth, lungs, eyelids and digestive tract.

The vitamin occurs naturally in two forms:

Vitamin A vs. Strokes

Vitamin A helps stroke victims recover more quickly and completely. Patients with ischemic stroke had more complete recoveries when their blood showed higher vitamin A levels.

Possible reason: The vitamin's powerful antioxidant properties may help prevent or reverse some of the stroke damage.

Source: Study of 80 stroke patients at the Free University Hospital in Brussels, Belgium, by researchers in the department of neurology at Academisch Ziekenhuis Vrije Universiteit Brussel.

Vitamin C vs. Heart Disease

Vitamin C boosts HDL—"good" cholesterol —especially the HDL type considered most important in fighting coronary artery disease. Vitamin C is also a powerful antioxidant— helping reduce fatty deposits on arterial walls.

Source: Balz Frei, PhD, Harvard University School of Public Health.

Vitamin C and the Brain

Patients with lower vitamin C levels in their blood scored lower on tests measuring mental skills. Vitamin C is believed to help the brain use protein to make the neurotransmitters required for thinking and remembering. Food with high levels of vitamin C include broccoli, bell peppers, collards, oranges and grapefruit.

Source: Study of 260 well-educated and affluent men and women over age 60 at the University of New Mexico Medical School, reported in *Boost Your Brain Power* by Ellen Michaud, Russell Wild and the editors of *Prevention* magazine, Rodale Press, 33 E. Minor St., Emmaus, Pennsylvania 18098.

Cervical Cancer/ Diet Connection

Good news: Those women who consumed greater quantities of vitamin C, folic acid and lycopene were one-fifth as likely to develop cervical intraepithelial neoplasia, a condition that generally leads to cervical cancer. *Best*

sources of vitamin C: Citrus fruits, strawberries, cantaloupe, broccoli, tomatoes. *Best sources of folic acid:* Whole grains, fruits and vegetables. *Best sources of lycopene:* Tomatoes and other red or reddish foods, such as red peppers and ruby-red grapefruit. *Bonus:* Lycopene is actually condensed when tomatoes are processed, so foods with tomato sauce—pizza, chili, etc.— are also good sources. *Bottom line:* Follow the American Cancer Society's dietary guidelines— stick to a high-fiber, low-fat diet, that includes plenty of fruits and vegetables daily.

Source: Juliet Van Eenwyk, PhD, epidemiologist, Washington State Department of Health, who led the research study.

Cervical Cancer Diet Connection II

Diet fights cervical cancer—the ninth-most-common cause of cancer death among women in the U.S. *Key:* The B-vitamin folate, which seems to prevent a common virus that causes genital warts from entering cervical cells and causing a pre-cancerous condition in them. *Where to get folate:* Green leafy vegetables (raw, steamed or baked)…liver…citrus fruits and juices…beans. *Alternative:* A multivitamin supplement containing at least 400 micrograms of folate.

Source: Study of more than 400 women led by C.E. Butterworth, Jr., MD, department of nutrition sciences, School of Medicine, University of Alabama at Birmingham.

Vitamins to the Rescue

Vitamins fight cholesterol plaque—the primary cause of hardening of the arteries. In lab studies, vitamin C was shown to be 95% effective in preventing LDL (low-density lipoprotein—"bad" cholesterol) oxidation, which leads to plaque formation. *Also:* Beta-carotene, a form of vitamin A, was found to be 90% effective and vitamin E was found to be 45% effective.

Source: Study by Ishwarlal Jialal, winner of the American Heart Association's "Young Investigator Award," reported in *Cardiac Alert*, 7811 Montrose Rd., Potomac, Maryland 20854.

Yogurt Fights Colon Cancer

Yogurt fights colon cancer—even if you eat it only one to three times a month. *Reason:* Unknown, but possibly related to the beneficial bacteria in *active-culture* yogurt. *Bonus:* Yogurt is high in calcium—and fat-free yogurt is as effective against cancer as yogurt containing fat.

Source: Study of almost 750 colon cancer patients and an equal number of controls led by Ruth Peters, MD, University of Southern California School of Medicine, Los Angeles, reported in *Running & FitNews,* 4405 East-West Hwy., Suite 405 Bethesda, Maryland 20814.

Food and Your Brain

Your brain is a factory that produces dozens of self-made compounds that affect your intelligence, memory and mood. The starter materials for these brain chemicals come from the foods you eat.

Sugar is your brain's fuel…

Your brain's main fuel is glucose (blood sugar). Unable to store it, your brain must derive blood sugar primarily from carbohydrates —the starches and sugars in your diet. After you eat a meal, your blood sugar level rises, and then falls in a rebound reaction. If your blood sugar drops too low, your brain sends out distress signals. You may feel tired, dizzy or irritable. This can happen if you gorge on sweets or a big meal.

When you eat a complex carbohydrate, such as pasta, rather than a simple one, such as candy, it takes your body longer to process and distribute the blood sugar and thus your brain receives a bit at a time rather than a jolt.

Mind magic from meals…

When you eat a slice of pizza or a bowl of chili, you are actually downing chemicals your brain needs to send messages between its cells. Pizza, steak or any protein food contains building blocks called amino acids. Some amino acids are essential because they are vital to a healthy brain—and must be obtained from your food.

There are natural daily fluctuations in amino acids in your blood, but the combinations you ingest can cause changes that affect your thinking and mood.

If you eat meat, you may have to worry about cholesterol but won't have to worry about amino acids.

If you are a vegetarian, you have to make an effort to eat the right combinations. For example, most rice is low in the essential amino acid, lysine, while some legumes (beans) are low in another, methionine, but high in lysine.

So if you eat a meal of rice and beans, as the Mexicans do, you will have a good combination of essential amino acids. You can also get enough of these brain power substances by eating as the Japanese and Southeastern Americans do. The Japanese mix rice and bean curd. Southeasterners combine rice and black-eyed peas.

Brain boosters…

What do wheat germ, turkey, sardines and deep-green leafy vegetables have in common? They are good sources of the B vitamins that help produce the messages your brain sends out to nerve cells. Of the Bs, thiamine, niacin and B12—are particularly vital to memory and learning.

• *Thiamine (B1):* In oatmeal and green peas,* it's needed to process sugar and to maintain healthy nerves, memory, sleep and mood.

• *Niacin (B3):* In turkey and tuna,** it's necessary for red blood cells, which carry oxygen to your brain.

• *B12:* You need some meat, eggs or dairy to provide another vital chemical, B12, for your

---

*Peas contain .25 mg of thiamine per 100 grams. Oatmeal contains 4.8 mg. (Composition of Foods, US Department of Agriculture Handbook 8.)

**Tuna has 46 mg and turkey from 7.2 mg to 21.4 mg of niacin depending an the way it is served. (Composition of Foods, US Department of Agriculture Handbook 8.)

brain. This vitamin helps you keep your balance and your strength. Alcohol, estrogen pills and sleeping medications can lower B12.

Want to dance? Take a dose of former President Bush's least favorite vegetable, broccoli—or cauliflower or citrus fruits. They contain high levels of vitamin C, which aids production of a brain chemical, dopamine, necessary for coordinated movements.

Food and mood...

Do you reach for a piece of chocolate when you are feeling blue? You may instinctively be helping your brain to put you in a better mood. Chocolate raises the level of a chemical in your brain, serotonin, found to be low when you're feeling down.

If you eat when depressed, however, you may ignore the control center in your brain that tells you when you have eaten enough. In fact, most individuals with a weight problem ignore the brain's signal that says, "stop—your stomach's full."

Those who eat too fast also don't get the message. It takes about 20 minutes for your brain to receive notice from your stomach to signal you to put your fork down.

Source: Arthur Winter, MD, FICS, director, New Jersey Neurological Institute. Dr. Winter and his wife, Ruth, are coauthors of *Build Your Brain Power*, published by St. Martin's Press, 175 Fifth Ave., New York 10010.

Nutrition and Mental Illness

All food has its poisons, says an ancient Chinese proverb. *Self-defense:* Balance your poisons. In other words...eat a varied diet.

In modern society, most of us eat the same things, day in and day out. We consume so much sugary, fatty, unhealthful food it's like living in an endless birthday party.

Sad result: We develop not just physical ailments, but psychological problems—anxiety, depression, insomnia and hyperactivity...even schizophrenia and paranoia.

Good news: In many cases, it's possible to eliminate or lessen the severity of these problems simply by altering our diets.

What's going on...

Mainstream medical doctors and psychotherapists often overlook the role of food in psychological disturbances. That's unfortunate, because research over the years from MIT, the National Institutes of Health and other top institutions has shown that food does have an effect on brain processes.

In my years as a psychiatrist, I've witnessed countless instances in which a simple change of diet led to a rapid recovery of mental health. It's now clear to me that what we eat has a profound effect on what we think and how we feel.

Food, of course, is not always the culprit. Many psychological problems take years of psychotherapy before they respond, regardless of what the patient eats. But people who are experiencing emotional problems out of context to events with no discernible cause may be feeling the effects of a food hypersensitivity.

Different foods affect people differently, and any food can cause problems. But I found coffee, chocolate, milk, sugar and wheat to be the most common culprits. In many cases, my patients have been especially fond of the very food that was causing them the trouble.

Remarkable recoveries...

•Anxiety and milk. A married nurse in her 20s suffered from intense, pervasive anxiety, including terrifying choking and gagging attacks, often in public places.

So intense were these attacks that she considered herself an emotional basket case and had decided never to have children. She couldn't see how such an anxious person could be a good parent.

But in taking this woman's medical history, I began to suspect her problem wasn't psychological at all, but dietary. She had been subsisting primarily on dairy products. I suggested she give up dairy products, at least for a while, and she did.

Result: Her anxiety and choking disappeared. Within a year, she and her husband had their first child. *Note:* Resuming the consumption of dairy products would reprovoke the symptoms.

•Anxiety and coffee. Psychiatrists have long known that too much coffee can cause anxiety. In fact, caffeine is implicated in anxiety so frequently that the *Diagnostic and Statistical Man-*

ual—a guide used to diagnose mental illness—instructs psychiatrists to exclude caffeineism before diagnosing a patient with anxiety disorder.

Surprise: What many doctors don't know is that caffeine isn't the only troublesome compound in coffee. All coffees and teas—including decaf—also contain methylxanthines, naturally occurring pesticides that are a common cause of anxiety attacks. People troubled by anxiety or panic attacks should give up all coffee, tea, caffeine-containing soft drinks and chocolate.

Caution: Going cold turkey when giving up caffeine often causes severe headaches, sweating episodes and other symptoms of withdrawal. Give caffeine up gradually.

•Chest pains and milk. A 31-year-old lawyer was terrified by recurrent chest pains that he thought were heart attacks. So severe was the pain that he had been visiting emergency rooms and cardiologists' offices several times a week for more than two years.

Repeated electrocardiograms and blood tests indicated that his heart was healthy, and his doctors told him his pain was caused by hypochondria brought on by anxiety.

As it turned out, the real culprit was not anxiety but dairy products—which apparently irritated his esophagus. He gave up milk, and the pain disappeared.

•Depression and milk. A young filmmaker under my care was eager to give up film for a medical career, but he was too fearful to take the leap. Instead, he became a part-time emergency medical technician.

One day, he came into my office complaining of intestinal pain, a symptom often caused by consumption of dairy products. I told him to give up milk, because it can not only cause gripping intestinal pains, but can also show on the face as the cranky frown that he always had.

Two weeks later, his scowl was gone, and he was cheerful for the first time in years. His relationships with friends and family members had shown signs of improvement after years of decline.

Two months later, he applied to medical school. Today he is a physician.

•Chronic fatigue and chocolate. A middle-aged businesswoman was troubled by foggy thinking and by chronic fatigue so severe that it often kept her in bed for days on end. I learned she ate chocolate two to three times a week. Although this didn't sound excessive, I suggested she give it up anyway to see what happened.

Result: During her first chocolate-free month, she felt clear-headed for the first time in years. Then she ate a slice of chocolate cake at a dinner party...and spent the next three days in bed. This convinced her that chocolate had been to blame.

•Schizophrenia and wheat. A woman in her 30s had long endured symptoms of schizophrenia, including auditory and visual hallucinations that made a normal life impossible. Her symptoms were so bad at times that hospitalization was necessary—and when I first saw her, she had recently ended her fifth stay in a psychiatric hospital.

Yet even then hallucinations continued to plague her. She was able to function in society only because she was taking a powerful tranquilizer, Thorazine.

I asked about her eating habits and discovered she was eating a great deal of wheat-based products, including pasta, cakes, cookies, etc. I prescribed a wheat-free diet, and almost immediately her hallucinations vanished. A few weeks later she ate wheat, and the hallucinations recurred within minutes.

At that point, she gave up wheat and she continues to be hallucination-free years later.

Diet has not worked in every case of schizophrenia, of course. But this case illustrates the ancient saying, "One man's food is another's fierce poison." The poison (for some people) in wheat is two peptides, that act as false neurotransmitters in the brain.

•Paranoia and wheat. An obese computer executive sought my help in an effort to lose weight. I persuaded her to give up wheat, and she quickly lost 10 pounds.

Bonus: Her mood and general outlook brightened markedly. In retrospect, she realized that wheat had contributed not only to her obesity, but also to a low-grade paranoia—thinking, "The boss is saying that just to get me," which could be reprovoked on ingesting wheat again. Off wheat, she lost weight and gained equanimity.

•Drowsiness and wheat. A lawyer in his 30s was plagued by mid-afternoon sleepiness so overwhelming that he would often fall dead asleep at inopportune times—even in the middle of conversations.

Once, while visiting my home, he fell asleep in my living room. When he woke up, I asked about his eating habits and discovered he had been eating lots of bread (wheat) at fancy lunches with clients. When he gave up the bread, his afternoon sleepiness disappeared.

If you have a problem…

Ask yourself which food you would be least willing to give up—then give it up.

Wean yourself off it slowly over a few (one to three) weeks…then take note of your symptoms. Have they diminished? If so, you have probably pinpointed the culprit. If not, try giving up another food.

Good news: In many cases, it's possible to resume eating the culprit food—on occasion, and in small quantities—without having symptoms reappear.

Source: Richard M. Carlton, MD, a psychiatrist in private practice at 333 W. 57 St., New York 10019. A specialist in the relationship between food and psychological disorders, Dr. Carlton is now studying the relationship between nutrition and learning disabilities.

All About the Longevity Diet

Most Americans eat foods that are full of dyes, flavoring agents, stabilizers, preservatives and other artificial ingredients whose health effects are unknown. They're processed and refined to the point where many essential nutrients and much of the beneficial fiber are lost. And they're dripping in cholesterol, calories and fat.

Result: Heart disease, cancer, arthritis, obesity and other diet-related problems have become more and more common in American society. And our lifespans are shorter than those of people in many other developed nations.

In an effort to correct our nutritional shortcomings, the government has issued dietary guidelines. *But*—these do not go nearly far enough in restructuring our diets.

Comparison: The U.S. government recommends a diet consisting of 12% protein, 30% fat,

48% complex carbohydrates and 10% refined sugar.

This is considerably more healthful than the typical American diet, which consists of 12% protein, 42% fat, 22% complex carbohydrates and 24% refined sugar.

Far better than either diet, however, is that prescribed by macrobiotics—12% protein, 15% fat, 73% complex carbohydrates and no refined sugar.

What is macrobiotics?*…

Macrobiotics is a lifestyle principle and diet based on the living and eating patterns of humanity. Many Americans who have heard of it think of it as a mysterious and mystical way of eating and living.

Although true macrobiotics does rely on unfamiliar concepts—energy-balancing, yin and yang and more—anyone who follows its basic dietary precepts can benefit.

Foods to avoid…
- Foods containing artificial ingredients.
- Poultry, including eggs.
- Meats.
- Dairy products—including yogurt, which has wrongly been touted as a health food.
- Sweeteners—sugar, honey, molasses and artificial sweeteners.
- Refined flours or processed grains.
- Chocolate and other candies.
- Coffee, conventional teas, sodas and other caffeinated beverages.
- Fast food.

Foods to eat…
- Products that are made from whole grains —pasta, breads, rolled grains and cracked grains, including rye flakes and oatmeal.
- Whole grains—brown and wild rice, whole oats, whole rye, wheat, corn, buckwheat, millet.
- Locally grown vegetables.
- Beans, seeds and nuts.
- Fruits.
- Natural condiments. *Note:* Avoid those that contain artificial ingredients, coloring agents and preservatives.
- Soy products—tofu and tempeh.
- Pickles.

*For more information on macrobiotics, including the names of dietary counselors in your area, contact the Kushi Institute of the Berkshires, Box 7, Becket, Massachusetts 01223. 413-623-5742.

• White-meat fish.

This list represents the traditional foods that constitute the natural diet of man throughout history. As much as possible, the macrobiotic diet incorporates locally grown foods.

Why the emphasis on locally grown vegetables? Because where a person lives should dictate that person's diet.

The human body adapts to the region in which it lives. So a person who lives in the temperate zone, in which there are four distinct seasons, should avoid citrus fruits and other tropical fruits and vegetables.

Because these foods are adapted for hotter climates, they are biochemically inappropriate for temperate-zone dwellers. So-called primitive cultures practice this all the time. Eskimos, for instance, eat animal products almost exclusively. Although such a diet would be all wrong for most of us, who live in temperate climates, it is appropriate for Eskimos, who are adapted to such foods.

Similarly, many Indian, African and other hot-weather cultures make liberal use of strong herbs and spices that are inappropriate for most people living in America. For people in temperate climates, the best diet is the macrobiotic diet, with its emphasis on whole grains, vegetables and fruits, soy products and some seafood.

Macrobiotics and longevity...

A macrobiotic diet may help to prevent degenerative diseases.* It also may increase a person's longevity. Many people residing in the Hunza region of the Himalayas live to be healthy and active well beyond their 100th birthdays.**

Their secret: They follow the macrobiotic principle.

These people survive almost exclusively on vegetables and grains, with animal foods making up only 2%–3% of their diets.

Although not everyone can expect macrobiotics to see them through to such an advanced

*Macrobiotics is not a substitute for modern medical techniques. In fact, macrobiotics and medicine are complementary. Medicine is good at controlling symptoms of disease, while macrobiotics is good at taking care of the causes of such symptoms.

**Such anecdotal evidence is backed up by data collected as part of the Framingham Heart Study and other carefully controlled scientific studies.

age, the right dietary and lifestyle choices do make a difference in longevity.

How to go macrobiotic...

Because macrobiotics places such dramatic limits on diet, making the switch can be difficult for some people.

Solution: Make the transition gradually—over a period of weeks, months or, if necessary, years.

Many of the foods making up a macrobiotic diet can be found at your local health-food store. There are now 8,000 to 10,000 such stores worldwide. Virtually all carry whole grains, beans, tofu, tempeh, miso, sea vegetables and other macrobiotic foods.

Source: Michio Kushi, a leading exponent of macrobiotics and founder of two acclaimed educational organizations—the East West Foundation and the Kushi Institute. He has written several books on macrobiotics, including *The Macrobiotic Way*, Avery Publishing Group, 120 Old Broadway, Garden City Park, New York 11040.

The Japanese Secrets Of Diet...Longevity And Good Health

People are starting to realize that the traditional Japanese diet may be the healthiest in the world, both for achieving longevity and for maintaining slim and fit bodies. *Facts:*

• On average, each Japanese citizen lives 2,628 more days than we do. In fact, the Japanese live longer on average than any other people. In 1989, the average life span was 81.39 years for women and 75.61 years for men. In the U.S. (in 1987) it was 78.3 years for women and 71.5 years for men.

• Low cancer death rates. The death rates for prostate, breast and colon cancers are the lowest in the world. The prostate cancer rate in Japan is 4.6 per 100,000 people compared with 22.1 per 100,000 in the U.S. and 29.9 per 100,000 in France. The Japanese breast-cancer rate is 8.3 per 100,000 people compared with 32.5 per 100,000 in the U.S. and the staggering 52.8 per 100,000 in England. Finally, the Japanese colon-cancer rate is 9.8 per 100,000 people compared with 20.3 per 100,000 in the U.S. and 26.5 per 100,000 in West Germany.

•Low heart disease rate. The death rate for heart disease in Japan, 117.9 per 100,000 people, is the lowest in the world, almost one-third the U.S. rate of 308.8 per 100,000. In the remote island fishing village of Okinawa, which has not yet been infiltrated by Western-style diets, heart disease averages 79.5 people per 100,000.

How to eat like the Japanese…

•Consume fewer calories. The Japanese have an average daily intake of 2,600 calories, the lowest of any industrialized nation. People in West Germany, France, the Netherlands and the U.S. have the highest caloric intake, about 3,400 calories. The number of calories a person should eat every day depends on such factors as body size, physical activity, age and sex.

•Eat more fish. In certain parts of Japan, people eat about six ounces a day on average. Fish contains a much higher percent of protein than fat, and in the traditional Japanese diet, protein accounts for 15% of total calories eaten each day.

Soybeans, in products such as tofu (soybean curd) and miso (fermented soybean paste) are another important source of protein. Miso is usually served in soup. Tofu is a key ingredient in either the main dish, the side dish or the soup. Although the Japanese do eat beef, the amounts are nowhere near those consumed by Americans.

•Reduce fat intake to 15%–20% of total calories. That's significantly less than the 30% recommended by the American Heart Association.

The fat consumed in the traditional Japanese diet comes from fish and the oils in soybean products, all of which have significant amounts of omega-3 fatty acids, which are believed to protect against heart disease and cancer.

This is in contrast to the fats eaten most by Americans—saturated fats (from animal products) and partially hydrogenated polyunsaturated fats (such as salad oils).

•Consume adequate amounts of carbohydrates, fiber, minerals and vitamins. When it comes to carbohydrates, rice is the ideal staple food, superior to bread in almost every way. It has fewer calories and is more filling than bread. Because rice comes in kernels that must be carefully chewed, it takes longer to digest than bread. *Note:* Brown rice provides the vitamins that white rice loses in the milling process.

The Japanese diet is not only high in fiber, but in precisely the kinds of fiber that aid in weight loss. Seaweed, for instance, contains certain gums that slow fat absorption. Soybean fiber reduces fat levels in the blood.

•Eat more vegetables. In Japan, vegetables are in the soup, the main course and are featured exclusively in the side dishes. Boiling, called *ohitashi* in Japanese, is the most common method of preparing vegetables, resulting in fewer calories. Some vitamin C may be lost—but the Japanese eat a lot of raw fruit to compensate.

Four main types of seaweed (*kombu, nori, wakame* and *hijiki*) are a key source of vitamins and minerals. They provide all the calcium a person needs, making it unnecessary to consume dairy products that are high in fat and difficult for many people to digest. *Hijiki*, for instance, contains an incredible 1,400 milligrams of calcium per 100 grams. *Bonus:* Seaweed has no calories.

•Give up rich foods. For snacks, the Japanese opt for vegetables and fruits that are high in pectin. *Favorites:* Apples, oranges and carrots. Eating raw fruit that contains pectin helps reduce hunger.

•Drink green tea. In Japan, green tea (*ocha*) is served with every meal and drunk throughout the day. This provides the high water intake needed to fight hunger and control weight. Green tea is a nutritious alternative to pure water, because it's high in antioxidants, including vitamins C and E, which are believed to slow the aging process.

•Avoid salted, pickled and smoked foods. These have been linked to high stomach cancer rates in Japan, particularly in its northern areas, which lack fresh fruit and vegetables in the winter.

About salt: Although the average American salt intake is 12.2 grams per day, salt consumption should not exceed eight grams per day.

You'll never see a salt shaker on a Japanese table.

Source: Hirotomo Ochi, PhD, founder of the Japan Institute for the Control of Aging, Fukuroi City. He is the author of *East Meets West: Supernutrition from Japan* and *Dieting Can Ruin Your Health*, Ishi Press International, 1400 N. Shoreline Blvd., Mountain View, California 94043.

How to Lose Weight... And Keep it Off

At the age of twenty-five, after failing miserably at countless diets, Larry "Fats" Goldberg lost 175 of his 325 pounds. He lost "a whole Goldberg." Larry has kept the weight off for 32 years...even the years he was running New York City's prize-winning Goldberg's Pizzerias.

We wanted to know how he succeeded where so many others have failed, so we asked...

What's your secret?

"Controlled Cheating." I allow one day a week to eat anything I want, all day long. The Cheating Day is combined with a low-fat diet for the rest of the week, regular exercise and plenty of water. Once an ideal "goal" weight is reached, two Cheating Days are allowed.

That's all there is to it. It's simple—and it works.

How does your system work?

The major reason people can't stay on diets is they can't face the thought of a future without their favorite foods. Sooner or later they cheat, and afterward torment themselves with guilt and feelings of failure. Then they decide they lack willpower and give up their diets in despair.

But anyone can keep to a diet that only lasts six days, when they know they can eat how they choose on the seventh day. *Reasons:*

•With Controlled Cheating, you don't have to give up any foods—just delay eating them for a few days.

•Controlled Cheating takes the guilt out of cheating, because you know what you are going to do every day—when you will diet and when you will cheat.

•Controlled Cheating is a structured way of eating that imitates how normal people eat.

Overweight people benefit from learning to eat this way. Once you've started, it's easy to stay with the plan for the rest of your life—and never gain weight again.

Why does it work?

Controlled Cheating works because people simply can't eat too much in a day. *Fact:* A person has to eat 3,500 calories to gain a pound, and burn 3,500 calories to lose a pound. So if you eat about 1,500 calories a day for six days, and as much as 5,000 on the Cheating Day (a lot for anyone) you're averaging 2,000 calories a day. Subtract the 500 calories a day you burn exercising, and you are averaging 1,500 calories a day...and you're losing weight.

What are the "rules" for Controlled Cheating?

•Set your goal weight. Goal weight is something most people know about themselves. This is the weight at which you feel most comfortable, healthy and attractive. Discuss with your doctor your ideal weight and how many calories you should be eating to lose weight safely. Once you've set your Goal Weight, think of the weight you must lose in five-pound "bites."

•Choose your Cheating Day. You can pick any day of the week, but once you decide, do not change your Cheating Day.

•Follow your eating plan. Monday is usually the best day to start. But don't eat like crazy the week before you start your diet.

•Stay on the plan for two full weeks. Then you may cheat for one day.

After your Cheating Day, you must go back on your diet. You may cheat one day a week until you reach your goal weight. Weigh yourself every day.

•Reach your Goal Weight. This is a slow process. But when you reach your Goal Weight, you may cheat two days, three to four days apart, and only weigh yourself on the morning of your Cheating Days.

What is the eating plan?

I use a low-fat, low-calorie, high-fiber and complex carbohydrate, balanced diet based on the US Department of Agriculture booklet, *Nutrition and Your Health—Dietary Guidelines for Americans: Eat a Variety of Foods*, available free from the Consumer Information Center, Dept. 527Y, Pueblo, Colorado 81009. The basics:

•Eat real food. Do not use diet pills, appetite depressants or over-the-counter weight-loss aids.

•Eat a variety of foods. Be flexible.

•Eat plenty of starches, fiber, vegetables, fruits and grains.

•Eliminate fat—as much fat as possible. And …cut out the sweets, salt and alcohol. Use lean meats, low-fat milk products, unsaturated oils.

Save the grease, sugar and salty snacks for your Cheating Day.

What's the rest of the plan?

•Exercise. You must exercise, or the plan will not work. Walk more. Take the stairs. Consult with your doctor if you do not have a regular exercise program.

•Drink water. Drink at least eight to 10 glasses every day, including your Cheating Day.

Any helpful hints from your years of dieting success?

•Eat slowly. This one is hard, but it works. Put the fork or spoon down after every bite… chew…swallow. Then pick it up again.

•Eat lots of little meals. Don't skip breakfast or starve yourself.

•Eat a big breakfast, medium lunch, small dinner. Stop eating by 6:00 p.m.—or certainly by 7:00 p.m.

•Eat crunchy foods that keep your jaws busy (carrots, apples, low-cal breadsticks, etc.)

•Use low-fat and low-calorie products— such as salad dressings and soft drinks.

•Plan your Cheating Day. Look forward to your Cheating Day, and use it for the foods you truly love. Avoid cramming calories just because you can.

•Expect your weight to fluctuate. You will reach plateaus when it will seem as though you'll never lose another pound. Stick with the plan. Your body will adjust and gradually begin to lose again.

•Learn to eat only when you're hungry. *To handle cravings:* Take a walk. Drink flavored water. Fantasize about your Cheating Day. If you're really hungry, gnaw on vegetables or a bagel.

•Enjoy your food, your exercise…and your new svelte self. Controlled Cheating is a healthy way to eat that produces other healthy changes. As I followed the plan over the years, I naturally became more relaxed, energetic and positive about myself. I don't use food to counteract depression or nervousness…I no longer enjoy the feeling of being stuffed…and I crave fewer "junk" foods—though I love my grease, dough and sugar with a passion!

Best of all, I know I will never be fat again.

Source: Larry "Fats" Goldberg, author of *The New Controlled Cheating Weight Loss and Fitness Program*, Andrews and McMeel, 4900 Main St., Kansas City, Missouri 64112. Mr. Goldberg, the former proprietor of Goldberg's Pizzerias in New York City, now conducts food and other theme tours of his hometown, Kansas City. He weighs 160 pounds.

The Best Junk Foods Now…and the Worst

With the pace of life getting faster and more meals eaten on the run, snack foods are a fact of life.

Good news: Not all snack foods are terrible for your health. Some are even good for you.

Trap: Some foods that seem healthy are among the worst for you.

Biggest offender: Fat. Many junk foods are loaded with it. Fat is linked with more ills— particularly certain cancers and heart disease— than any other dietary component.

Obviously bad…

•Candy bars. Even a tiny piece is packed with saturated fat and calories.

•Chips. Potato chips get 60% of their calories from fat—even if they're labeled "no cholesterol." There are 150 calories and 9.8 grams of fat in one ounce of potato chips (10 or 12 chips), and most people don't stop with that many. Corn chips aren't much better.

Alternative: Guiltless Gourmet tortilla chips are baked, not fried. An ounce of these is 110 calories and contains only 1.4 grams of fat.

•Soda. Drinking one can of soda is like eating 10 packets of sugar and washing it down with water. And soda actually makes you thirstier—your body demands more fluids to dilute all that sugar.

Alternative: Fill a glass half with flavored seltzer and half with fruit juice. A 16-ounce glass of this refreshing drink is only about 55 calories. And the sugars in the fruit juice quickly take the edge of your appetite.

Junk foods in disguise…

Many of the foods that have a reputation for being healthy aren't. *Included:*

• Granola. It's high in fat—often saturated fat such as coconut oil. Granola bars are even worse— they require a lot of fat to retain their bar shape.

• Muffins. The old-fashioned kind Grandma made were healthful—the small, crumbly muffins that fell apart when you tore the paper off. Most of the muffins for sale now are 4½ ounces to 6 ounces, at about 100 calories per ounce, and contain as much fat as three pats of butter.

• Peanuts. People substitute a jar of peanuts for a skipped meal and think the protein in peanuts makes this a healthy choice. Peanuts do contain protein—but 74% of the calories in peanuts come from fat. A small bag of dry-roasted peanuts from the vending machine contains 170 calories and 14 grams of fat, the equivalent of almost three pats of butter.

Peanuts are also slow to be digested—your brain doesn't get the feel-full signal until you've consumed great quantities.

• Cheese. Cheese contains some protein and a significant amount of calcium. But it also has one of the highest saturated fat contents of any food. Cheese can be a good diet supplement, but it should not be a diet staple.

Best snack foods…

• Cereal…(except granola!) With skim milk and fruit, dry cereal is soothing, nutritious and simple to fix, whatever the time of day.

• Bagels. Only 160–180 calories, and almost no fat.

• Fudgesicles. If you crave chocolate, these are a great way to get the chocolate flavor without the fat. They're only about 100 calories each (35 calories for the diet version), compared with 250 to 300 calories in the average candy bar.

• Hershey's chocolate syrup. Unlike fudge sauce, which is made with cocoa butter, Hershey's syrup is made with dry cocoa powder and has very little fat. Mix it in a blender with skim milk and ice cubes for a low-calorie chocolate shake…pour it over low-fat ice milk for a sundae.

• Soft pretzels…sold in frozen food sections of supermarkets. They contain almost no fat and are similar to bagels in calorie content.

• Pizza…if you ask for very little cheese and lots of mushrooms, peppers, onions. Pizza can be a satisfying snack or light meal that's high in calcium and in vitamins A, B-complex and C.

Source: Connie Roberts, MS, a registered dietitian at Brigham and Women's Hospital in Boston, where she manages the Nutrition Consultation Service. She is nutrition editor for the *Harvard Heart Letter*, Harvard Medical School Publications Group, 164 Longwood Ave., Boston 02115.

Cut the Fat I

Better diet reduces cardiac risk. Patients who had a heart attack had significantly less chance of a second one if they stopped eating red meat, butter and eggs. *Better:* Foods high in fiber and beneficial vitamins. Of patients with modified diets, 10% died within a year of their first heart attack—but in the group that did not change its eating habits *nearly twice as many* (19%) *died.*

Source: Study of more than 400 cardiac patients led by researchers at the Medical Hospital and Research Center, Moradabad, India.

Cut the Fat II

Reduce fat in ground meat by cooking it until it's no longer pink and is in small crumbles. Drain the cooked meat, stirring it well in a colander. Return it to the kettle, cover it with very hot water and stir well. Drain again in the colander. *Result:* Using this technique in an institutional setting, the meat's fat content is reduced by 65%. Prepared this way, the meat tastes best in dishes with ample seasonings and sauces, such as chili or spaghetti.

Source: Pat Snyder, MA, RD, coordinator at the University of Minnesota School of Public Health, Minneapolis.

Cut the Fat III

How to keep weight off. Most dieters regain 30% of lost weight within a year. *Awful truth:* All the weight is back within five years. *Reason:* Failure to continue following a more healthful lifestyle after reaching target weight, and possible biological factors, such as genetic predisposition toward obesity. Food diaries—recording *every* item eaten—increase the chance of losing weight and keeping it off.

Source: Thomas Wadden, PhD, director, Center for Health and Behavior, Syracuse University.

Cut the Fat IV

Fish oil danger: Eating more fish oil can help prevent heart disease, but *too much* may cause vitamin E deficiency—which may lead to *immune-system impairment.* The problem most likely occurs in people who take large fish-oil doses in pill form. The pills also contain extra calories—they are basically gelatin capsules filled with fish fat. *Still recommended:* Eating more fish as a protein source. The extra fish oil consumed that way should be beneficial.

Source: Kevin Fritsche, PhD, a University of Missouri-Columbia expert on interactions between nutrition and immunology.

Fighting Flab With Breakfast

Eating breakfast fights flab. Overweight breakfast-skippers who began eating breakfast lost an average of 17 pounds over 12 weeks and were better able to maintain their weight loss than those who passed up breakfast. Regular breakfast-eaters consume less fat and more carbohydrates, snack less and are less hungry during the rest of the day than those who skip their morning meal.

Source: Study by David Schlundt, PhD, assistant professor of psychology, Vanderbilt University, reported in *Men's Health,* 33 E. Minor St., Emmaus, Pennsylvania 18098.

Weight Control Secrets

Last year Americans spent $32 billion on diet books, products and programs—and every cent of that vast expenditure was wasted. Dieting simply doesn't work. Dramatic, lasting weight loss—like that touted by the many weight-loss programs—is essentially mythical.

Reality: 98% of these "successful" dieters regain all the lost weight within five years…and 33%–73% wind up with metabolic changes that cause them to grow even fatter.

Typical scenario: A woman's weight is stable at 150 pounds on a diet of 2,500 calories a day. She goes on a 1,500-calorie-a-day diet until she loses 10 pounds. When she returns to 2,500 calories a day, her body continues to burn calories at the reduced—1,500-calories-a-day—rate. *Result:* She regains all the lost weight—and probably more.

This woman feels like a failure, but in truth it's the diet that has failed. Even if she holds her post-diet weight gain to the original 10 pounds, she is worse off than she was before dieting.

Reason: Although her weight has not changed, the percentage of her body composed of fat is now significantly higher, because the slight amount of muscle tissue inevitably lost while dieting is usually replaced in part by new fat cells. Each time a weight loss/weight gain cycle recurs, this increase in fat cells makes getting back to the desired weight harder.

Recent evidence has found that this "yo-yo" dieting is more harmful to a person's health than being consistently overweight.

Weight-control secret…

The key to weight control—known by 4.5 billion instinctive eaters—is to eat only when you're hungry, and not to eat when you're not hungry. That sounds simplistic, but it is the only surefire technique for controlling weight.

Dieting doesn't work because it forces people to reverse the process by which instinctive eaters avoid weight gain—that is, eat little or nothing even when they're famished and then stuff themselves when they really aren't hungry. Dieters spend so much time thinking about eating that they fail to heed the hunger/satiety signals that are the crux of weight control.

Obesity myths…

Before you can become an instinctive eater, you must shed common misconceptions about obesity. Many believe that fat people are fat because some psychological defect causes them to overeat, or because they lack willpower, or simply because they're gluttonous.

Fat people themselves get so much criticism that they too begin to believe these misconceptions.

Reality: Obesity is often hereditary. If one or both of your parents are fat, odds are that you too will be heavy—and there isn't a great deal you can do about it.

Self-defense: Naturally heavy people must realize that while they might want a model's body, they do not need such a body. They can be happy and successful with the body they have. And, contrary to what most people believe, there are no health reasons to lose weight—so long as their weight remains stable.

Exception: People who are extremely overweight—those more than 50% above their ideal body weight—should see a doctor about how they can control weight gain.

Most overweight people whose weight is constant have no more health problems than thin people. It's when they start starving themselves that they get into trouble. Yo-yo dieters are at increased risk for diabetes, heart disease and other serious ailments. Someone whose weight stays a constant 190 pounds faces fewer health risks than a person whose weight fluctuates between 120 and 160.

Most people have a sense of how much they should weigh, but this perception is often far off the mark. *Problem:* They confuse ideal and optimal weight.

•Ideal weight is that which each of us, for reasons of vanity, would like to reach. Unfortunately, many of us would have to literally starve ourselves to reach this weight…and once we reached it, we would probably be unhealthy and miserable.

•Optimal weight is that at which our bodies feel and function best. For a few fortunate people, ideal weight coincides with optimal weight. For many, optimal weight is several pounds above ideal weight.

Principles of instinctive eating…

Learning to eat instinctively does not guar-antee that you will reach your ideal weight. But it does ensure that you will reach your optimal weight, and that is more than good enough.

Illustration: One woman who attended one of my seminars had ballooned from 110 pounds to more than 200 pounds. She learned the principles of instinctive eating but for the following six months remained as heavy as ever. Then, almost imperceptibly at first, her body began to shrink. Now, several years later, she is down to a size 14. She may never again reach her ideal of size four, but she has stabilized her weight at an acceptable level. More important, her self-disgust at being overweight has ended.

To eat instinctively…

•Learn to recognize hunger. Different people feel hunger differently—some people feel a gnawing sensation in the stomach…some get a feeling of tension in their chest…others get a headache or feel weak.

Unfortunately, many signals taken to be signs of hunger are really symptomatic of illness, fatigue, sadness, nervousness or some other condition. To eat instinctively, you must learn to tell the difference.

Self-test: If you think you feel hungry but are unsure, have a bite to eat. Wait several minutes. If the sensation is somewhat alleviated, you truly were hungry. If the sensation persists, however, you were not. Do not continue eating if not hungry. Instead, go for a walk, call a friend, take a nap or do something else not involving food.

At first, it may be difficult to tell hunger from other sensations. Eventually, the process will become automatic.

•Determine what you're hungry for. The body is a machine, and, like any machine, it requires different kinds of maintenance (food) at different times. Hunger is the body's way of requesting fuel. To make sure you feed your body the right fuel, run through a mental checklist.

Protocol: Instead of grabbing the first thing that looks appetizing, break foods down into their specific attributes.

•Temperature—do you want something hot, cold or room temperature?

•Taste—do you want something sweet, sour, bitter or salty?

•Texture—do you want something smooth, crunchy, chewy or fibrous?

In many cases, you will be just as satisfied by a low-calorie, nutritious food as by a calorie-dense, nutrient-poor food. This checklist cannot reduce how much you eat or how often, but it can reduce your caloric intake and make your diet more wholesome.

Example: A hungry overeater heads to the freezer for ice cream. But after running through the food attribute checklist, she finds that she really craves not cream, but sweetness. So instead of a bowl of Rocky Road, she enjoys a ripe pear—thus providing her body with nutritious food and saving herself several hundred calories.

•Eat sitting down. Eating while standing or on the run not only encourages you to eat more often, but also makes it more difficult to tell how much you are eating. Pick one spot in your home and always eat your meals there. Don't eat in bed, while watching television, while talking on the phone or while involved in any other activity.

•Eat slowly. After the first bite of food, it may take 20 minutes or so for the body to "realize" that it is no longer hungry. Unfortunately, the average American meal is consumed in under seven minutes. By the time we feel full, we've already consumed hundreds of calories more than we needed or even wanted.

Helpful: Never rush your meal. To indulge your sense of anticipation, look at your food before eating. Chew thoroughly. If you have trouble pacing yourself, make it a point to chew with empty hands—place your knife and fork on the table while you chew and swallow. Eating slowly sounds easy, but for many people it is the single most challenging aspect of instinctive eating.

•Learn to recognize satiety. Just as instinctive eaters know how to tell when they're hungry, they're also able to recognize when they are full. Again, the process depends upon paying close attention to the signals your body gives you.

Procedure: After each mouthful of food, pause briefly to ask yourself if you are still hungry. If so, continue eating. But if you no longer feel hungry, stop eating at once. Do not let yourself eat out of habit. Do not let yourself be pressured into eating for social reasons.

•Don't be tyrannized by numbers. Many over-weight people pay such close attention to their weight, calorie counts and other numerical measures of diet that they lose sight of the natural hunger/satiety mechanism.

Helpful: Get rid of your scales, listen to your body and forget about calorie counts.

•Don't accept criticism of your body. Few of us tolerate attacks on our religion, ethnic heritage, profession, etc. Why put up with comments like, "You could stand to lose a few pounds"? Accepting such criticism not only makes obese people feel bad, it engenders a sense of hopelessness that reinforces and encourages overeating.

Better way: Love yourself at your current weight, even if that weight is well above your optimal weight. If someone puts you down for your weight, just ignore him.

Source: Steven C. Strauss, MD, a board-certified internist practicing in New York City and author of *The Body-Signal Secret*, Rodale Press, 33 E. Minor St., Emmaus, Pennsylvania 18098. Dr. Strauss's Lighten Up seminars, given in New York City and Washington, DC, teach participants to control their weight permanently without dieting.

The Anti-Craving Weight Loss Diet

Anyone can cut calories—temporarily. But diets that treat excess calories as the cause of obesity are destined to fail because they ignore the true cause of overeating—food cravings. The best way to lose weight is to understand how food cravings work, why we crave the foods we do—and how this information can help us change our eating habits permanently.

Eater's high...

People who overeat know they don't need the extra calories. They eat because they want to feel better. They're seeking a psychotropic effect—similar in many ways to the effect of drugs or alcohol on the brain.

People use food this way because life is stressful.

What we're actually looking for when we give in to food cravings is what I call the M-state—a balanced state of brain functioning that leaves us both deeply calm and highly alert at the same time.

It's the state that has been measured in people who are meditating, though structured meditation isn't the only way to reach it—other relaxation techniques are also effective.

The tastes of certain foods trigger the brain to achieve a fake M-state. It's healthy to want to relieve stress…have more energy…be relaxed…function better throughout the day. But when we seek this effect through overeating, our efforts backfire.

Problem: Cravings result from and often cause nutritional deficiencies. These deficiencies upset brain function and make the craving cycle more intense.

Example: A sweets junkie who eats a chocolate bar gets high from the release of tryptophan in the brain…that reaction saps critical nutrients, including magnesium and manganese, from the central nervous system…the brain becomes more resistant to the effect of sweets. The next time it takes more of the food to get the same effect…leading to greater deficiencies…a downward spiral. Every boost is followed by a slump…and an even stronger food craving.

To cure obesity permanently…

You can cure the process that leads to craving with a two-pronged approach:

• Physiological. Replace the missing nutrients in your body with nutritional supplements and eat foods that create a less intense but longer-lasting feeling of satisfaction.

• Psychological. Increase your level of relaxation—learn to regain the M-state without eating your craving foods.

Encouraging: People who begin to stabilize their cravings get more stable over time.

Achieve the M-state…

Although the M-state is a natural state, because life is so stressful, it's hard to reliably regain it without some kind of system.

I recommend transcendental meditation to my patients because it's widely taught and because so much solid research has been done on the process. But any relaxation technique that works for you is fine.

Some people get into the M-state simply by watching the news…some get it by walking around the neighborhood looking at gardens.

Other useful techniques: Biofeedback…religious contemplation…sensory-deprivation tanks…playing subliminal tapes. Most people find that they do best if they allow a little time for the M-state every day—once or twice, morning or evening.

Key: Dependability. The method you choose should get you into the M-state reliably.

Another natural high: Sex. Studies have proven that the euphoria, alertness and relaxation that follow good sex are second only to the sensations that are gained from meditation. People who are sexually satisfied tend not to be food cravers.

Cure your cravings…

Not everyone craves the same foods. Watch a group of coworkers unwinding at a fast-food restaurant after a stressful meeting.

One person will order fries, another will have frozen yogurt, someone will go for a soft drink, someone else will have a burger. They're all seeking a psychotropic effect—detoxing from the meeting—using different foods to get there.

Think about the first thing you reach for when you're tired or stressed. Most cravings fall into one of two categories: Sweet/starch (cake, cookies, candy, bread)—and greasy/spicy (potato chips, onion rings, steak, cheese, highly spiced foods).

To cure cravings, you need to learn to reach for balancing foods—foods that will help you reach the M-state, but in a much more stable way than the foods that you're used to…using a different brain pathway to give the overworked path a rest.

Example: A sweet/starch craver will feel more deeply satisfied by eating proteins and vegetables—properly spiced and cooked (cooked food is sweeter than raw). A greasy/spicy food craver will reach this state by eating whole carbohydrates and fruits. Without the right balance, the cravings will continue.

Crucial: Relearn to smell and taste food. Modern food processing has robbed foods of much of their taste and smell—cues that can help us know what foods are right for us.

For this reason, I urge dieters to eat organically grown, unrefined foods. Discover the enormous range of tastes in naturally prepared grains, vegetables and fruits.

If the food that you eat tastes wonderful, you'll be satisfied with less.

Source: Elliot D. Abravanel, MD, medical director of Skinny Schools, which has clinics in more than 50 cities. He is also the author of *Dr. Abravanel's Anti-Craving Weight Loss Diet*, Bantam Books, 666 Fifth Ave., New York 10103.

How Men Can Lose 10 To 75 Pounds...For Good

There are now approximately 25 million men in the United States who are considered clinically obese (more than 20% above their ideal weight).

And there are another 10 to 15 million men who are heavier than they would like to be. For men, weight-gain frequently accompanies middle age and a higher-than-average socio-economic status.

Four basic steps:

•Control stress-eating. Uncontrolled, unplanned nibbling tends to involve high-fat, snack-type foods.

•Avoid alcohol. Alcohol is high in calories and impairs judgment. In addition, it tends to work against your self-restraint when you're eating out.

Alcohol in the system slows down the body's fat-burning process.

•Decrease the amount of fat you consume. This one basic nutritional change can make a big difference in your weight.

•Increase exercise. Exercise reduces stress, helps burn more calories and produces a "post-exercise burn"—so that your metabolic rate remains at a higher-than-normal level, even hours after your workout.

Exercise also raises the levels of endorphins, resulting in a nice, drug-free "high." Sustained weight loss is virtually impossible without an ongoing exercise program. If you don't continue to exercise, any weight that is lost will almost certainly return.

First, get your doctor's OK. Then, begin a brisk-walking program five to six days a week, 20 to 25 minutes a day.

If necessary, break up your exercise into two sessions—morning and afternoon. Increase your time by five minutes per week until you're up to 45 minutes a day. You may want to eventually graduate to slow jogging or a stationary bicycle.

Smart food choices:

After 15 years of working with both male and female dieters, I've discovered that smart men are nutritionally ignorant—they just don't know what's in the food they're eating and why it can be harmful.

Example: A chef's salad and a diet soft drink is many men's idea of a healthy, low-calorie lunch...but they couldn't be more wrong. A chef's salad is a 750- to 1,000-calorie, high-fat meal, usually containing cheese and luncheon meat (each approximately 100 calories per ounce) and about 80% to 90% fat—all smothered in two or three ladles of dressing (200 to 250 calories).

Important: Don't let yourself feel deprived. While you will have to give up the notion that you can eat whatever you want whenever you want it, there is no reason you can't eat the foods you like and still slim down and improve your health. You should try to stick to the rules you have set, but you don't have to be perfect.

Source: Clinical psychologist Morton H. Shaevitz, PhD, director of the behavioral health programs at the Scripps Clinic and Research Foundation in La Jolla, California. He is the author of *Lean & Mean: The No Hassle, Life-Extending Weight Loss Program for Men*, G. P. Putnam's Sons, 200 Madison Ave., New York 10016.

Muffin Madness

The average muffin contains 800 to 900 calories—which can be 50% or more of the required daily caloric intake. *Problem:* Most muffins—even bran and sugar-free ones—aren't good for you. Breakfast should be 300 to 400 calories. Replacing a muffin with a low-fat option—even with no other dietary changes—can help you lose weight. *Weight-loss guidelines:* A man needs 12 calories per pound of body weight to sustain his daily needs (*Example:* 2,160 calories for a

180-pound man)…a woman needs 11 calories per pound. To lose weight, eat less than that number by making low-calorie substitutions for high-calorie foods and begin an exercise program. *Important:* Check with your doctor before beginning any weight-loss program.

Source: Jeffrey Fisher, MD, a cardiologist in private practice, 311 E. 72 St., New York 10021, and clinical associate professor of medicine, New York Hospital-Cornell Medical Center.

How to Eat More… Weigh Less

Most weight-loss diets don't work because they're based on deprivation. That is—counting calories, restricting portion sizes, measuring out food. Sooner or later, most people get tired of feeling hungry and deprived, and they go off their diets and regain the weight they've lost. Ninety-seven percent of those who lose weight on traditional diets—which keep fat to 30%—gain the weight back within five years.

Our data at the Preventive Medicine Research Institute are very different. We studied patients who were put on a vegetarian, 10%-fat, heart-disease-reversal diet—not a weight-loss diet. Without trying to lose weight, the average patient dropped 22 pounds the first year and kept most of the weight off for at least seven years. These people ate when they were hungry and until they were full, so they did not feel deprived.

How it's done…

•It's primarily what you eat, not how much you eat, that matters. Once you change the types of food you eat—from high-fat meats, dairy products and processed foods to low-fat carbohydrates and proteins, such as fruits and vegetables, grains and legumes—you don't have to be as concerned about the amount you eat. Even if you eat the same amount of food as before, you'll consume fewer calories. Gram for gram, carbohydrates and proteins have less than half the calories of fat.

Also, your body converts dietary fat into body fat very easily. In addition, reducing the amount of calories without changing the type of calories often causes your metabolism to slow down, whereas it stays the same or even increases on a very low-fat diet.

Bonus: Most people who eat this way discover several other benefits—more energy, the ability to think more clearly and a decreased need for sleep.

•It's easier to make big changes than it is small ones—even though this goes against conventional wisdom. We've found this time and time again. When people make small changes, such as simply reducing the fat in their diets from the typical 40% to 30% as recommended by government dietary guidelines, they feel deprived because they are not able to eat everything they want. The problem is they're not making lifestyle changes that are sufficient to achieve the desired results—weight loss, lowered blood pressure and improved cholesterol.

But when they make the comprehensive changes I outline in my program, most people generally feel so much better—and so quickly —that the choice becomes obvious, clearer and, for many people, worth making.

Also, if you continue eating meat or other fatty foods, you never really lose your taste for them. You may actually feel more deprived eating smaller portions of them than if you don't eat them at all. But if you give them up completely, your palate may adjust accordingly.

Example: If you stop putting salt on your food, initially it will seem tasteless. But after a few weeks, it will taste fine…and eventually the foods you ate before may seem too salty.

•Dining the low-fat way. Your meals can be as elaborate or as simple as you choose—either way, they can be quite delicious, hearty and beautifully presented.

My typical breakfast: Fresh orange juice…a bowl of very low-fat cereal, such as shredded wheat or Kellogg's Nutri-Grain, with some non-fat yogurt or skim milk and fruit on it…whole-wheat toast or a bagel with a little jam…and a cup of herbal tea or decaffeinated coffee.

For lunch or dinner: I might have some pasta with vegetables or oil-free marinara sauce…a green salad with oil-free dressing…and corn on the cob or a bowl of vegetarian soup—either out of the can or homemade.

There are so many familiar, simple foods you can eat—it really doesn't take any extra time to eat good, low-fat meals.

• Avoid "feeding" your unhappiness with food. Many people use overeating, alcohol or cigarettes to cope with the loneliness and emotional pain they feel—to fill the void and numb the pain.

Helpful: Meditation and yoga are powerful techniques that can help you quiet your mind enough to experience a greater sense of inner peace and well-being. Meditation is really the art of paying more attention to what you are doing. *Results:*

• You will more fully enjoy what you're doing, especially sensual activities...such as eating. When you eat with awareness, you won't need the excessive amounts of food that can lead to overweight. You'll find that small amounts will be pleasurable—one teaspoon of a rich, chocolate dessert that you really focus on will actually be more satisfying than a whole bowlful you've eaten while watching TV. Whether it's a spoonful, a bowlful or a half-gallon, at some point you are finally full. But—when you pay attention to what you're eating, that point comes much sooner.

• You will become aware of how what you're eating affects the way you feel—for better or worse.

Example: When you pay attention to how your body is reacting after eating a steak or a cheeseburger, you might find that you're feeling sleepy and sluggish, and your thinking is fuzzy.

But when you make comprehensive changes in diet and lifestyle, you may notice how quickly you feel better.

Bottom line...

There's no point in giving up something you enjoy unless you get back something that's better.

I began making these changes in my lifestyle at age 19—not out of fear of dying, but because it increased my joy of living.

Source: Dean Ornish, MD, president and director of the Preventive Medicine Research Institute in Sausalito, California. He is author of *Eat More, Weigh Less.* Harper-Collins, 10 E. 53 St., New York 10022.

How to De-Fat Your Favorite Recipes

Choosing low-fat prepared foods in the supermarket is as easy as reading labels. Preparing a heart healthy meal from scratch, however, is an entirely different matter.

If you'd like to reduce the fat content of your favorite recipes, remember the three r's—reduce, remove and replace.

• Reduce fat by spraying pots with a thin film of cooking oil instead of dumping in a tablespoon of oil...or use nonstick cookware, for which no oil is needed.

• Remove skin from poultry and all visible fat from meat.

• Replace...

...whole milk or cream with skim milk, evaporated skim milk, low-fat yogurt or homemade mock sour cream (made with eight parts cottage cheese, one part skim milk and lemon juice to taste).

...regular cream cheese with light cream cheese or homemade mock cream cheese (made with two parts each of ricotta cheese and dry-curd cottage cheese and one part low-fat yogurt).

...high-fat cheeses with skim, reduced-fat or light varieties of American, Swiss, mozzarella or Monterey Jack cheese.

...bacon with Canadian bacon or lean ham.

...one whole egg with two egg whites...or 1/4 cup egg substitute...or one egg white combined with one teaspoon of vegetable oil.

...one ounce of baking chocolate with a mixture of three tablespoons of powdered cocoa and one tablespoon of vegetable oil.

...sour cream with plain low-fat yogurt or reduced-fat sour cream.

...oil for sautéing or in sauces with beef, chicken or vegetable broth.

Source: Linda Hachfeld, MPH, RD, a registered dietitian in Mankato, Minnesota. She is the author of *Cooking aLa Heart*, Appletree Press, 151 Good Counsel Dr., Suite 125, Mankato, Minnesota 56001.

Foods...Bad and Good

Bad foods most people think are good...

• Apple juice. Very sugary. Unlike orange juice, it doesn't contain vitamin C unless it's fortified. Can cause diarrhea in some youngsters.

• Carob products. Added butter and oils make most carob-based products just as fattening as the chocolate items they're meant to replace.

• Cottage cheese. Contains about 40% fat by calories with little of the calcium found in most dairy products. *Self-defense:* Buy no-fat cottage cheese, although there's still not a lot of calcium.

• Cream cheese. As fatty as butter or margarine but with little dairy calcium. Also low in protein.

• Processed dried "fruit" snacks. Contain more sugar than actual fruit.

• Iceberg lettuce. Has little vitamins A and C and is low in fiber. *Better:* Romaine lettuce.

• Muffins. May contain more fat and calories than the donut or Danish they are meant to replace.

Good foods most think are bad...

• Eggs. High in protein with half the fat of a tablespoon of most salad dressings. *Important:* Limit yourself to three or four a week.

• Jelly. Contains half the calories of butter or margarine—and is fat-free.

• Pancakes. But only when eaten with low-fat toppings such as yogurt, brown or powdered sugar, fresh or dried fruit, jam or jelly.

• Pizza. A fairly well-balanced meal—when topped with low-fat mozzarella cheese, tomato sauce and vegetables. *Avoid:* Sausage, pepperoni and ground-beef toppings.

• Pretzels. Contain one-tenth the fat and fewer calories than potato chips. Pick unsalted varieties to reduce sodium.

• Red meat. In moderation, a good source of iron, protein, zinc and several B vitamins.

• White bread. Contains plenty of complex carbohydrates and little fat.

Source: Lawrence Lindner, executive editor of the *Tufts University Diet & Nutrition Letter,* 203 Harrison Ave., Boston 02111.

Better Weight Control

Instead of yo-yo dieting, find your *reasonable weight*—the weight you can maintain for years by eating healthfully and staying moderately active. Not only will you be healthier, you'll like and accept yourself as you are.

Source: Denise E. Wilfley, PhD, clinical director, Yale Center for Eating and Weight Disorders, quoted in *Cooking Light,* 2100 Lakeshore Dr., Birmingham, Alabama 35223.

How to Reduce the Fat in Your Food

• Sauté vegetables in a few tablespoonfuls of soup stock rather than in fat.

• Sauté and fry foods less often. Steam, broil, bake, and poach instead.

• For salads and cooking, use corn, safflower or olive oil—sparingly.

• Substitute egg whites or tofu for egg yolks.

• Use low-fat yogurt instead of sour cream or mayonnaise.

• Try low-fat cheeses such as part-skim mozzarella in recipes.

• Use ground turkey or crumbled tofu in place of ground beef.

• Thicken cream-style corn with a mashed potato or uncooked oatmeal.

• Replace nut butters with bean spread for sandwiches and snack dips.

Source: *Medical Self-Care,* Inverness, CA.

Cholesterol Basics

Results of an exhaustive, 10-year National Heart, Lung and Blood Institute study have put to rest any doubts about the links between high blood cholesterol levels and heart disease.

For most Americans, careful diet can keep cholesterol in control, particularly the dangerous low-density-lipoprotein (LDL) cholesterol. *Keys:* Cut cholesterol consumption to 300 milligrams or less per day. Keep the percentage of calories from fats to 30% or less of the daily intake. Substitute polyunsaturated fats for saturated fats in the diet.

•No foods that come from plant sources contain cholesterol.

•The most concentrated sources of edible cholesterol are egg yolks (one yolk from a large egg has 252 mg), and organ meats (three ounces of calf's liver has 372 mg).

Bacon (2 slices)	15
Beef (3 oz. lean)	77
Beef kidney (3 oz.)	315
Butter (1 tbsp.)	35
Cheese (1 oz. cheddar)	30
Chicken (3 oz. light meat, no skin)	65
Cottage cheese (½ cup 4% fat)	24
Cottage cheese (½ cup 1% fat)	12
Cream (1 tbsp. heavy)	21
Flounder (3 oz.)	69
Haddock (3 oz.)	42
Ice cream (½ cup)	27
Milk (1 cup skim)	5
Milk (1 cup whole)	34
Pork (3 oz. lean)	75
Salmon (4 oz. canned)	40
Sardines (3 oz.)	119
Turkey (3 oz. light meat, no skin)	65
Yogurt (1 cup lowfat)	17

While many fats per se have no cholesterol content, certain types of fats actually raise the cholesterol levels in the blood even if the rest of the diet contains very little cholesterol.

•Saturated fats. You can recognize these by their tendency to harden at room temperature. They contribute most to a buildup of LDL cholesterol. They include meat fats, butter, chicken fat, coconut and palm oils, vegetable shortening and even some margarines (read the label).

•Monounsaturated fats. These play a more neutral role in cholesterol chemistry, although, like all fats, they should be eaten in moderation. These are the fats found in avocados, cashews, olives and olive oil, peanuts and peanut oil.

•Polyunsaturated fats. When kept to a limited part of the total diet, these actually lower the amount of LDL cholesterol in the blood. *Good fats:* Corn oil, cottonseed oil, safflower oil, soybean oil, sunflower oil, and fats from nuts such as almonds, pecans and walnuts.

•If you are overweight, reducing will lower your cholesterol level.

•Certain fiber foods such as carrots, apples, oats and soybeans also help reduce cholesterol.

•Aerobic exercise can cut down the percentage of LDL cholesterol in the blood.

The Right Middle-Age Diet

It's not too late to change the eating habits of a lifetime when you reach middle age. As a matter of fact, it's probably a necessity because of the changes the body is going through at that time. *Most obvious change:* Slowing of the metabolic rate. Individuals who don't reduce their caloric intake after age 45 commonly gain 10 pounds a year, regardless of the amount of exercise they do. It takes 12 hours of tennis to burn off 3,500 calories, roughly equivalent to one pound.

•Steak is highly caloric, and its fat content has been linked to coronary disease and colon cancer, two potentially fatal disorders that plague older people. Chicken and fish are more healthful alternative sources of proteins.

•Because bones begin to grow progressively brittle after age 30, the body needs more calcium. But this important mineral can be absorbed effectively only by reducing the intake of protein (from meats) and phosphorous (from carbonated soft drinks). To prevent the brittle-bone problem, a calcium supplement of one gram a day is recommended by most nutritionists.

•Because many older people secrete less hydrochloric acid, they have difficulty absorbing iron and, therefore, are more vulnerable to pernicious anemia. The best source of iron is meat, especially liver. But to avoid eating too much meat, you should turn to iron-fortified foods, especially cereals. Absorption of iron is helped by intakes of vitamin C, which is abundant in citrus fruits, broccoli, kale, red peppers and brussels sprouts. For some older people, taking an iron supplement may be necessary.

•The bodies of older people often have trouble absorbing vitamin B-12, which can actually be destroyed in the body by large doses of vitamin C. B-12 deficiency can lead to anemia, particularly among vegetarians, because the vitamin is found exclusively in animal products (especially liver) and shellfish. Multivitamin supplements may be needed to insure that you are getting the right amount of each vitamin.

•Digestive problems associated with aging make fiber especially important to persons over 45. *Sources:* Whole grains, fruits, vegetables.

•Although all the evidence is not yet in, most nutritionists advise against taking vitamin megadoses. In the case of vitamins A and D, megadoses are highly dangerous. *Exception:* Vitamin E, large doses of which may help with colon cancer and the painful blood vessel spasms in the legs that older people often experience. Even with this vitamin, consult a physician before considering taking megadoses.

Source: Dr. Brian Morgan, Institute of Human Nutrition, Columbia University College of Physicians & Surgeons.

Eight Ounces of Milk

Types of milk vary in taste, fat content and nutritional value.

Here's the breakdown…

•*Buttermilk:* 90 calories, two grams of fat. Easily digested, since active bacteria break down the milk sugars.

•*Dry nonfat milk:* 80 calories, less than one gram of fat. As nutritious as whole milk, but with a flat taste.

•*Low-fat (2%) milk:* 120 to 140 calories, five grams of fat. A good choice when fat restriction is important but calories are secondary.

•*Skim (nonfat) milk:* 80 calories, less than one gram of fat. Best for dieters and those on a strict low-fat diet.

• *Whole milk:* 150 to 180 calories, eight grams of fat. Best only for children under two years old.

Source: *Berkeley Wellness Letter,* published by the University of California, Des Moines, IA.

How to Get Along Without Cream And Mayonnaise

Fat is the enemy of both the heart and the waistline. Learn to substitute yogurt and other low-fat milk products. They are tasty as well as healthy.

Yogurt…

•Thicken commercial yogurt. Line a sieve with a paper coffee filter and place it over a bowl. Pour in the yogurt and let it drain until it is the consistency you want…that of light, heavy or sour cream.

•Use the drained yogurt as a base for any dip that originally called for sour cream. (If the yogurt seems too thick, beat a little of the drained whey back into it.)

•In cooking or baking, replace each cup of cream or sour cream with ¾ cup of drained yogurt mixed with 1 tablespoonful of cornstarch. The yogurt should be at room temperature.

•In dishes such as beef Stroganoff, where the yogurt-cornstarch mixture replaces sour cream, fold it gently into the beef at the last minute …and let it just heat through.

Basic recipes…

•*Light mayonnaise:* Mix ⅓ cup thickened yogurt into ⅔ cup mayonnaise.

•*Light salad dressing:* Mix ⅔ cup slightly thickened yogurt into ⅓ cup mayonnaise.

•*Mock sour cream dressing*:* Mix 1 cup drained low-fat yogurt with 2 tablespoonfuls of wine vinegar. Add a dash of sugar (or substitute), a bit of garlic powder, and ¼ cup vegetable oil. Mix and chill.

Other good substitutions…

•Replace the cream in cream soups with buttermilk, which is satisfyingly rich, yet low in calories. To eliminate any hint of buttermilk's slightly acidic taste, add a liberal amount of mild curry powder.

•Mix 1 cup skim milk with ½ cup dry skim milk. Add to soup to thicken it. This works with all cream soups, including vichyssoise.

**The Low-Cholesterol Food Processor Cookbook* by Suzanne S. Jones, Doubleday, Garden City, NY.

Just When You Thought It Was Safe to Eat Salt...

The vast majority of foods sold in stores are laden with salt. Since we've eaten these foods for most of our lives, we're conditioned to expect the taste of heavily salted foods.

To cut down on salt intake...

• Reduce salt gradually. When people are abruptly placed on a very low-sodium diet, they develop cravings for salt that cause them to revert to their former eating habits. But a gradual reduction of salt will change your taste for salt ...so much so that food salted to its previous level will taste unpleasant. *Time:* Allow up to three months to adjust to a salt-free diet.

• Keep daily records of the amount of sodium you eat. This is now relatively easy because federal law requires most grocery store foods to be labeled for sodium content. A pocket calculator is sometimes useful as you shop, but don't think you'll have to keep count for the rest of your life. After a couple of months, separating high from low-sodium foods will be almost automatic.

• Substitute other flavor enhancers, especially herbs and spices.

• If you have children, start now to condition their taste by not feeding them salty foods. For the first time, low-sodium baby food is now on the market.

Source: Dr. Cleaves M. Bennett, clinical professor, University of California at Los Angeles, and author of *Control Your High Blood Pressure Without Drugs*, Doubleday, New York.

Tasty, Low-Salt, Low-Fat Cooking

If your doctor puts you on a no-salt, modified fat, cholesterol and sugar diet, with limited alcohol consumption, you might feel as though you're in a gastronomic straitjacket. However, the benefits are enormous—no more edema, a reduction in blood pressure, considerable weight loss and a feeling of well-being—and you can increase your food intake without increasing your weight.

Basics of the diet...

Do use:
• Low-sodium cheeses.
• Seltzer.
• Trimmed meat.
• Stews and pan drippings skimmed of all fat.
• Fish, poultry without skin, veal and lamb.

Don't use:
• Eggs, except those used in food preparation.
• Sugar. Drinks made with sweet liqueurs. Soft drinks.
• Canned or packaged foods.
• Sodas with high salt content.
• Rich and/or salty products—bacon, gravies, shellfish, organ meats, most desserts except fruit and fruit ices.

Tricks to fool the taste...

• The sweet-and-sour principle. A touch (sometimes as little as half a teaspoonful) of sugar and a dash of vinegar can add the sweet-and-sour flavor needed to fool the palate.

• Garlic. Essential in salad dressings and tomato sauces. Use it with rosemary to transform broiled chicken, broiled fish or roast lamb.

• Fine or coarse black pepper. When broiling and roasting meats and chicken, use as much as a tablespoonful for a welcome flavor. Use a moderate amount in soups, stews and casseroles (the pungent nature of pepper will not diminish in these as it will with broiling and roasting).

• Crushed hot red pepper flakes. A good flavor distraction or flavor addition. Not for every palate.

• Curry powder. Use judiciously and without a large number of other spices. Combine it only with a bay leaf, green pepper, garlic or black pepper. Add smaller amounts for rice, more for poultry or meat.

• Chili powder. Similar to curry, but you might want to add more cumin, oregano or garlic. Also try paprika, ground coriander, ground hot chilis. They're good with almost any dish made with tomatoes.

• Homemade hot-mustard paste. Dry mustard and water does wonders for salad dressing and grilled foods.

• Freshly grated horseradish. Goes well with fish or plain yogurt.

• Bottled green peppercorns. A welcome touch for bland foods.

•Plain boiled or steamed rice, cold yogurt relish, chutneys and other sweet relishes are a good foil for spicy dishes.

Cooking techniques…

•Charcoal broiling helps compensate for lack of salt.

•Steaming is preferable for fish and better than boiling for vegetables.

•No-salt soups are difficult to make palatable. *Solution:* A stockpot going on the back of the stove, to which you add bones, cooking liquid, vegetables. The more concentrated the broth, the greater the depth of flavor. Use only the freshest, ripest vegetables.

Source: Craig Claiborne, food critic.

"Good" Foods That Can Be Bad for You

•Blood-sugar-sensitive types who experience a temporary lift from sugar followed by fatigue should be cautious about fruit juice intake. Six ounces of apple juice contain the equivalent of more than five teaspoonfuls of sugar—40% more sugar than a chocolate bar. *Recommended:* Eat a whole apple or orange instead of drinking juice. The fiber dilutes the sugar impact. *Alternative:* Eat cheese, nuts or other protein with juice.

•Nondairy cream substitutes, often used by those on low-fat diets, usually contain coconut oil, which has a higher fat content than most dairy products.

•Decaffeinated coffee can lead to significant stomach acid secretion, causing heartburn and indigestion in many persons. Caffeine was assumed to be the culprit. A new study shows that decaffeinated coffee is even worse. The effect is seen in doses as small as a half cup of decaffeinated coffee. People experiencing ulcer symptoms, heartburn and dyspepsia should avoid decaffeinated as well as regular coffee.

•Most commercial products billed as alternatives to salt are based on potassium chloride. *Problem:* Although potassium chloride does en-hance flavor, it leaves a slightly bitter or metallic taste. And excessive potassium may be as bad for your health as too much salt. *Alternatives to the alternatives:* Mrs. Dash, a commercial blend of 14 herbs and spices; Lite Salt, a half-sodium, half-potassium blend. Or try adding parsley.

•One of the few proven substances that can bring on flare-ups of acne is iodine. Excessive, long-term intake of iodine (a natural ingredient of many foods) can bring on acne in anyone, but for people who are already prone to the condition, iodine is especially damaging. Excess is excreted through the oil glands of the skin, a process that irritates the pores and causes eruptions and inflammation. *Major sources of iodine in the diet:* Iodized table salt, kelp, beef liver, asparagus, turkey, and vitamin and mineral supplements.

•Chronic diarrhea, gas and other stomach complaints are often linked to lactose intolerance, the inability to digest milk. One of every four adults suffers from this problem. Their bodies don't make enough lactase, the enzyme that breaks down milk sugar in the intestinal tract. *Among the offending foods:* Milk, ice cream, chocolate, soft cheese, some yogurts, and sherbet. Lactose is also used as a filler in gum, candies and many canned goods.

•People on low-sodium diets should check out tap water as a source of salt intake. Some local water systems have eight times the amount of sodium (20 milligrams per quart) that people with heart problems or hypertension should use.

•Health-food candy is really no better for you than traditional sweets. *Comparison:* Health-food candy often contains about the same number of calories. The fat content is often as high or higher. Bars made of carob are caffeine free, but the amount of caffeine in chocolate is negligible. And the natural sugars in health bars have no nutritional advantage over refined sugars.

Sources: *Journal of the American Medical Association,* Chicago; *Dr. Fulton's Step-By-Step Program for Clearing Acne,* by J. E. Fulton, Jr., MD, and E. Black, Harper-Collins, New York; *The Sodium Content of Your Food,* Consumer Information Center, CO.

Best Whole-Grain Breakfast Cereals

Whole-grained breakfast cereals are a rich source of protein, vitamins, minerals and fiber. *Bonus:* They have relatively low percentages of cholesterol, fat and calories. *Added bonus:* Often the cheapest cereals are the best nutritionally.

What to look for:

•Cereals in which the first listed ingredient is a whole grain—whole-grain wheat, oats (rolled or flour), whole corn kernels or bran.

•Cereals with three or more grams of protein per serving.

•Avoid cereals with sugar or other sweeteners (honey, corn syrup, fructose) as a main ingredient. *Guide:* Four grams of sugar equals one teaspoonful.

•*Also avoid:* Cereals with dried fruits. They are concentrated sources of sugar. *Best:* Add your own fruits.

Caffeine Facts

•Low doses of caffeine can increase alertness and motor ability, reduce drowsiness and lessen fatigue. Small to moderate amounts of caffeine pose no health danger, according to the Clinical Nutrition Section of Boston's University Hospital. Heavy doses produce ill effects —nervousness, anxiety, irritability, headache, muscle twitch, and insomnia.

•Tolerance to caffeine varies widely from person to person. Two cups of caffeine-rich coffee make some people nervous. Others cannot survive the day without several cups. *Most sensitive to caffeine's effects:* Children and the elderly.

•The caffeine quantity in coffee depends on how it is brewed. The drip method produces a higher caffeine content than the percolator. Instant coffee contains much less caffeine than brewed coffee. Tea contains half as much caffeine as coffee, and cola drinks have even less.

How much is too much: Four cups of coffee a day (500 milligrams of caffeine) is a heavy dose for most people.

•There is no evidence that caffeine is a causal factor in either arteriosclerosis or heart attacks.

•Caffeine does not increase the blood pressure of regular users.

•Caffeine does not seem to be a cancer hazard, but other compounds (found in negligible amounts) in beverage coffee are known carcinogens in animals.

•Caffeine is a much less important factor than cigarette smoking in heart disease, hypertension, bladder cancer, peptic ulcers, and cystic breast disease.

•Caffeine stimulates the central nervous system and can help reduce boredom from repetitive tasks. It increases the body's muscle strength.

•Caffeine can relieve certain types of headaches by dilating blood vessels and reducing muscle tension.

Source: American Council of Science and Health, Summit, NJ.

Caffeine Count

•A five-ounce cup of drip-brewed coffee contains 146 milligrams of caffeine.

•Regular instant coffee has 53.

•Decaffeinated coffee has 2.

•Most soft drinks range between 33 and 44. (Diet citrus drinks, root beer, ginger ale and tonic water contain little or no caffeine.)

•A one-minute brew of tea has half the caffeine of a five-minute brew. (Steeping for five minutes can take a cup to 50 mg., depending on the leaf used.)

•*Exceptionally high in caffeine:* Non-prescriptive stimulants. The average dose is 200 mg. Even higher, diuretics and weight-control drugs.

Long-Term Weight Loss

The diet mentality just doesn't work when it comes to long-term weight loss. The straitjacket approach will probably backfire as soon as you go off the strict regimen. To be successful, you have to analyze your eating habits and change them gradually.

First, look at what's going on when you're eating. Awareness is all-important. *Start keeping a daily food diary, and review it after a week:*

•Where did you eat? Do you have food stashed in your car's glove compartment, in your nightstand and in your desk at work? Maybe you eat in too many places. *Best:* Keep food only in the kitchen.

•What position were you in while eating? Do you eat while standing up in the kitchen, lying in bed, sitting in front of the TV, or at your office desk? Learn to eat only when sitting at the table.

•With whom did you eat? Food can be a crutch for social interactions, such as business lunches or family dinners. If you pinpoint such times, you can learn to deal with them.

•What was your emotional state while eating? Were you feeling anger, stress, etc.? Did you feel the need for security, protection or comfort? Find out what food means to you.

•Were there any visual cues associated with eating? Some of us eat when the clock says noon, rather than waiting until we're hungry. If you eat at noon every day, put lunch off for half an hour and see what happens.

•What was your eating style? Paradoxically, many overeaters don't really savor their food. They gulp it down quickly, as if they wanted to get the process over with. Practice eating slowly. Taste each bite and savor each flavor. If you pace your eating, you'll consume less but enjoy it more.

•Did any practical factors influence your eating? Were you late for work, missing breakfast in the process? Did you eat an enormous lunch instead? Did you overeat when you came home from work because you were too busy for lunch? Rearrange your schedule to permit planned, unhurried meals.

Making realistic changes…

•After you became aware of how, when and why you eat, start making some behavioral changes in ways that you find most comfortable:

•Don't avoid food—manage it. There are no "good" foods or "bad" foods. You can eat small amounts of those favorite foods of yours that are forbidden by traditional diets—but be in control.

•Pay attention to portion size. We tend to use restaurant-portion sizes as a gauge. But restaurants serve much larger portions, especially of entrees, than most people really need. *Suggested portions:* Three ounces of meat, fish, or chicken, rather than the customary six to eight ounces.

•Pay attention to quality. You might just be satisfied with one small piece of Swiss chocolate as with two cheap candy bars. Half a glass of really fine wine goes a long way. A tablespoonful of real Vermont maple syrup on French toast is a pleasant substitute for drowning it in an inexpensive syrup. Develop a discriminating palate. *Bonus:* Quality foods will make you feel you're treating rather than depriving yourself.

•Keep in mind that spices don't have calories. Use garlic, pepper, vinegar, curry and other herbs and spices liberally and creatively to add sparkle to your meals.

•Be creative. Today's markets offer a multitude of products that are low in calories even though they're not in the diet-food section. *Suggestions:* Exotic fruits and vegetables. Wholegrain bread products (they're tasty, and have more fiber and fewer calories than white bread).

•Make imaginative substitutions. For example, vanilla yogurt flavored with cinnamon and nutmeg is as good as fruit yogurt and has 50 fewer calories. Half an English muffin with mozzarella cheese and tomato sauce toasted under the broiler is a delicious pizza substitute.

Source: Janet K. Grommet, a doctor of nutrition and administrator of the weight control unit (a pioneer in treating obesity) at St. Luke's–Roosevelt Hospital Center, New York.

To Avoid Food Poisoning

•Never let food cool to room temperature before putting it in the refrigerator. Slow cooling encourages the growth of bacteria.

•Do not thaw frozen foods for hours at room temperature. Allow them to thaw slowly in the refrigerator, or, wrap them in plastic and soak in cold water.

•Bacteria in raw poultry, fish or meat could contaminate your cutting board. Scrub the board after each use.

•Do not use cans that bulge or that contain off-color or unusual-smelling food. *Dangerous:* Tasting the contents to see whether they are bad.

•Lead poisoning can result from storing food in open cans. The solder that seals the tinned-steel can leaches into the contents. *Most hazardous:* Acidic foods, especially juices. They interact quickly with metal.

•Although cooking spoiled food destroys bacteria, it does not remove the poisons the bacteria produced.

Source: *Modern Maturity.*

Secrets of Better Meat Freezing

Improper freezing and thawing of meat can ruin it, or at least alter its flavor and affect its texture. *Correct procedures:*

•Rewrap the meat in heavy-duty aluminum foil or laminated freezer paper. *Reason:* Unprotected meat loses moisture when exposed to the dry cold of a freezer for a long period of time. *Result:* "Freezer burn," which causes a loss of flavor and nutritional value.

•During freezing, restrict spacing to three pounds of meat per cubic foot of freezer space. Leave room for air to circulate around each package as it freezes. *Proper temperature:* Zero degrees or lower. After the meat is frozen, push the packages tightly together to save cooling costs.

•Don't cut pieces larger than your family will use at one meal.

•Label each package with its type of meat and the date you froze it.

•Thaw the meat in the fresh food compartment of the refrigerator—not at room temperature. *Reason:* Bacteria can grow rapidly during thawing if the temperature is too warm. *Warning:* Fast cooking (for people who like rare meat) may not kill these organisms.

Source: Tom Flaherty, merchandising specialist, the National Livestock and Meat Board, Chicago.

Drugs vs. Nutrition

Don't overlook the interaction of medication and nutrition.

•Chronic aspirin users can suffer microscopic bleeding of the gastrointestinal tract, a condition that also causes loss of iron. Aspirin can also increase requirements for vitamin C and folic acid.

•Laxatives may deplete vitamin D.

•Antacids can lead to a phosphate deficiency.

•Diuretics prescribed for hypertension can promote the loss of potassium.

•In all these cases, vitamin and mineral supplements may be the solution.

Avoiding the Lure Of Megavitamins

When it comes to vitamins, the old advice is still the best: There is no reason to take more than the recommended dietary allowance (RDA) of any vitamin, except for relatively rare individuals who cannot absorb or utilize vitamins adequately. If you want nutrition "insurance," take a regular multivitamin capsule containing only the RDA of vitamins.

A megadose is 15 or more times the RDA. This is the level at which toxic effects begin to show up in adults.

Some of the medical problems adults may experience as a result of prolonged, excessive intake are:

•Vitamin A. Dry, cracked skin. Severe headaches. Severe loss of appetite. Irritability. Bone and joint pains. Menstrual difficulties. Enlarged liver and spleen. Vitamin A and beta-carotene were recently shown to promote heart disease and cancer in the CARET study. The CARET trial showed that beta-carotene plus Vitamin A supplements resulted in 28% more deaths from lung cancer and 17% more deaths from heart disease in American smokers than did a dummy pill. The Physician's Health Study of 22,017 doctors randomly assigned to take 50 mg. of beta carotene or a dummy pill every other day ended on 12/31/95 after 12 years. It showed that beta-carotene supplements provided no protection whatsoever against cancer or heart disease.

•Vitamin D. Loss of appetite. Excessive urination. Nausea and weakness. Weight loss. Hypertension. Anemia. Irreversible kidney failure that can lead to death.

•Vitamin E. Research on E's toxic effects is sketchy, but the findings suggest some problems: Headaches, nausea, fatigue and giddiness, blurred vision, chapped lips and mouth inflammation, low blood sugar, increased tendency to bleed, and reduced sexual function. Ironically, one of the claims of Vitamin E proponents is that it heightens sexual potency. The fact that vitamin E supplements are anticoagulants (like aspirin) may explain why they protect against heart attacks but promote lethal hemorrhagic strokes. Large doses of Vitamin E enhance immune activity and thus may promote progession of immune and auto-immune disease (asthma, food allergies, diabetes, rheumatoid arthritis, multiple sclerosis and lupus).

•The B vitamins. Each B has its own characteristics and problems. Too much B-6 can lead to liver damage. Too much B-1 can destroy B-12.

•Vitamin C. Kidney problems and diarrhea. Adverse effects on growing bones. Rebound scurvy (a condition that can occur when a person taking large doses suddenly stops). Symptoms are swollen, bleeding gums, loosening of teeth, roughening of skin, muscle pain.

Vitamin C is the vitamin most often used to excess. *Some of the symptoms of toxic effect from Vitamin C megadoses:*

•Menstrual bleeding in pregnant women and various problems for their newborn infants.

•Destruction of Vitamin B-12, to the point that B-12 deficiency may become a problem.

•False negative test for blood in stool, which can prevent diagnosis of colon cancer.

•False urine test for sugar, which can spell trouble for diabetics.

•An increase in the uric acid level and the precipitation of gout in individuals predisposed to the ailment.

•In approximately 10% of non-blacks and 30% of blacks born with a genetic defect which gives them high body iron, Vitamin C supplements are violently pro-oxidant. They generate billions of free radicals, promoting more rapid development of heart disease, cancer and death.

Source: Stephen Barrett, MD, and Victor Herbert, MD, JD, authors of *The Vitamin Pushers: How the "Health" Food Industry Is Selling America a Bill of Goods.* Prometheus Press. Victor Herbert, MD, JD, and Genell Subak-Sharpe, editors, *Total Nutriiton: The Only Guide You'll Ever Need: From the Faculty of the Mt. Sinai School of Medicine.* St. Martin's Press.

Safe Food Storage

•Yellow bananas can be held at the just-ripe stage in the refrigerator for up to six days. Although the peel might discolor slightly, the fruit retains both its flavor and nutrition. Ripen green bananas at room temperature first. Mashed banana pulp can be frozen.

•Nuts in the shell keep at room temperature for only a short time. Put them in a cool, dry place for prolonged storage. Shelled nuts remain fresh for several months when sealed in containers and refrigerated. For storage of up to a year, place either shelled or unshelled nuts in a tightly closed container in the freezer.

Storage times for frozen meats vary significantly. *Recommended holding time in months:*
•Beef roast or steak, 12.
•Ground beef, 6.
•Lamb, 12.
•Pork roasts and chops, 8-12.
•Bacon and ham, 1-2.
•Veal cutlets and chops, 6.
•Veal roasts, 8-10.
•Chicken and turkey, 12.
•Duck and goose, 6.
•Shellfish, not over 6.
•Cooked meat and poultry, 1.

Keep an accurate thermometer in your refrigerator or freezer. *Optimal refrigerator temperature:* 40°F for food to be kept more than three or four days. *For the freezer:* 0° is necessary for long-term storage. *Note:* Some parts of the freezer may be colder than other parts. Use the thermometer to determine which areas are safe for keeping foods long term.

Freezing leftovers:

•*Raw egg whites:* Freeze them in ice cube trays.

• *Hard cheeses:* Grate them first.

• *Soup stock:* Divide it into portions.

• *Stale bread:* Turn it into crumbs in the blender.

• *Pancakes, french toast and waffles:* Freeze and reheat in the toaster oven at 375°.

• *Whipped cream:* Drop into small mounds on a cookie sheet to freeze and then store the mounds in a plastic bag.

• *Citrus juices:* Freeze in an ice cube tray.

• *Freezing fish:* Make a protective dip by stirring one tablespoonful of unflavored gelatin into ¼ cup lemon juice and 1¾ cups cold water. Heat over a low flame, stirring constantly, until gelatin dissolves and mixture is clear. Cool to room temperature. Dip the fish into this solution and drain. Wrap individual fish pieces in heavy-duty freezer wrap. Then place them in heavy-duty freezer bags. Use within two months.

• If you do your own food canning, preserve only enough food to eat within one year. After that time, quality deteriorates.

Sources: Tom Grady and Amy Rood, coauthors, *The Household Handbook*, Meadowbrook Press, Deephaven, MN, and Joan Cone, author of *Fish and Game Cooking*, EPM Publications, McLean, VA.

Keeping Food From Becoming Tainted

When in doubt, throw it out. This is the general rule concerning food you think may have become spoiled. This includes frozen food that has thawed too long or dishes that haven't been properly handled. *Example:* Cheesecake left on a counter to cool overnight can easily go bad.

Other tips for storing and handling food…

• Keep food at temperatures below 45°F or above 160°F.

• Always keep in mind that food left away from heat or cold for two to three hours is probably unsuitable for eating. This is particularly true of foods that are moist, high in protein and low in acid.

• Refrigerate leftovers as soon as possible. Don't let them sit at room temperature for more than two hours.

• Reheat food in wide, shallow pans rather than deep, narrow ones. Place foods in a pre-heated oven, not one that's warming up.

• When refrigerating large quantities of dishes such as stews, spaghetti sauce or chili, pour them into large, shallow containers. The point is to expose the greatest mass to the preserving effects of the cold refrigerator.

• If possible, thaw frozen foods by placing them in the refrigerator. If thawing must be done quickly, immerse the food in cold water or use a microwave oven.

Cholesterol/Fat Confusion

Some fats are essential for health. In fact, some actually work to reduce your cholesterol.

The bad fats, which raise blood cholesterol, are what's called *saturated* fats. The good fats, which work to lower it, are *unsaturated* (made up of *polyunsaturated* and *monounsaturated* fats).

The difference: In general, the bad fats—saturates—are relatively solid at room temperature. They are animal products that include dairy products. *Foods with saturated fat:* Solid shortenings, fatty meats, butter, cream, whole milk. *Foods with unsaturated/polyunsaturated fat:* Liquid vegetable oils (corn, sunflower seed, safflower, soybean) and fish oils.

Exceptions: Palm and coconut oils, the major ingredients of most non-dairy creamers, are saturated fats. Vegetable shortenings are saturated fats, too. Although they contain no cholesterol themselves, they're processed in such a way (hydrogenated) that they become more saturated, which raises your cholesterol.

Rule of thumb: Always read the label. If the food contains twice as much unsaturated as saturated fat, it's acceptable.

Source: Dr. Eli M. Roth, a cardiologist, and Sandra L. Streicher, RN, a cardiologist nurse. Together they run the HeartSmart program, which teaches patients how to manage their lives after a coronary attack. They are co-authors of *Good Cholesterol, Bad Cholesterol: What You Need to Know to Reduce Your Risk of Heart Disease.*

6

Fitness Made Simple

How to Stick to an Exercise Program

• *First:* Find an exercise program you enjoy. If you enjoy it, the chances are you're going to want to stick with it.

• *Second:* Find something that fits your lifestyle. For example, something that doesn't require you to go to the mountains to hike, or require special equipment that you don't have or can't afford.

• *Third:* Make an appointment with yourself to exercise so there's always time that's scheduled in. Without that reminder, it's easy to run out of time.

• *Fourth:* Psych yourself up. You have to recognize the benefits of exercise. By doing something you like to do and getting into some consistency, if you're on a program for a while, you'll start to feel the results. You'll feel better, have some pride when you finish your workout, maybe reduce some stress. And you may notice you've gotten a little stronger or lost some weight. You can use these things and really dwell on them to help reinforce your positive mental attitude for exercise.

• *Fifth:* Morning is a good time to exercise. It helps get your day started and you get it done and out of the way.

• *Sixth:* Exercise at least three times a week. And try to incorporate activity that exercises the cardiovascular system as well as strengthens your muscles. Things like taking a brisk walk for 20 or 30 minutes, cycling, playing recreational sports or exercise classes are all valuable workouts for the cardiovascular system.

• *Seventh:* Exercise in moderation. Some people, when they get on a program, get fanatical for a few weeks, then they stop. The key is consistency, not how intense you are per session. It's much more important to have a moderate session and do it consistently over a long period of time.

Source: Jake Steinfeld, personal trainer to Hollywood stars and author of *Don't Quit*, Warner Books, 1271 Avenue of the Americas, New York 10021.

Exercise Dangers

Most people who exercise are familiar with the pains and strains that can strike their joints and muscles.

Problem: Repeated stress and shock to the body can cause stretched or torn ligaments and muscles, painful bruises and various arthritis-like conditions.

Although the best thing to do if a problem develops is to eliminate the activity that caused the problem, most people don't want to give up a sport they enjoy. They prefer to treat the problem…and continue playing.

How to treat an injury…

It's important to treat any injury as soon as it develops, to keep it from getting worse. *Suggested:*

•Pay attention to early symptoms. Serious injuries occur when the exerciser ignores the first signs that a joint or muscle area is vulnerable. *These include:*

•Redness and swelling around any body part.

•Pain in the elbow radiating from arm to wrist (tennis elbow).

•Dull or moderate pain behind the knee-cap (runner's knee).

•Pain at the bottom of the kneecap (jumper's knee).

•Pain along the shin (shin splints).

•Pain with overhead motions (shoulder bursitis) caused by activities such as swimmer's strokes.

•Pain in lower back. Pay special attention to any pain or stiffness that radiates into legs.

•Use the RICE technique to relieve symptoms of injuries. *RICE is the acronym for…*

•*Rest.* Temporarily stop performing the offending activity.

•*Ice.* Apply cold to the affected area.

•*Compression.* Use a bandage to wrap the area.

•*Elevation.* Keep the leg or arm raised.

If pain persists, but your doctor tells you that it's okay to exercise, you can minimize the symptoms of your injury by warming the inflamed area before your workout and applying ice right afterwards.

Even better: Temporarily switch to a new activity—one that doesn't place stress on the same joint. If, for instance, you've been running, switch to swimming for a while.

More help…

When simple measures fail to offer relief, see your doctor.

Although a general practitioner can treat most sports-related injuries, if you don't get significant results within a few weeks, make an appoinment with a qualified sports-medicine specialist.

Working with a physical therapist, a sports-medicine specialist might prescribe any of a number of helpful therapies. *Included:*

•Contrast baths. These alternate about five minutes of warmth with a minute of cold, but always end with cold.

•Electric pulses. Administered (painlessly) into the skin, these stimulate blood flow deep inside tissues. *More sophisticated techniques for the same purpose:* Ultrasound and high-frequency sound energy.

•Special strengthening exercises. Weights slowly strengthen the muscles near the damaged area. This helps prevent further injuries in the same spot.

•Air casts. Provide protection and support for ankle sprains, stress fractures and tendinitis. Lastraps, made of a soft, vibration-absorbing pad, support elbows, knees, shoulders, wrists, etc.

•Orthotics. Custom-made insoles for your shoes. Made of molded plastic, they help keep the foot aligned. *Warning:* They cost up to $400/pair.

No matter what happens, don't give in to long periods of inactivity. That only makes it difficult to get back on track with your exercise program.

Mistakes to avoid…

Of course, the best way to deal with exercise-oriented problems is to avoid them altogether. A small number of errors cause most exercise-related problems, and should be avoided. Although some of these are obvious, they bear repeating. *Included:*

•Weekend exercising. Taking it easy during the week, and then overdoing it on the weekends (a competitive tennis match, for instance).

•Not warming up properly. All you need is a few minutes of light jogging or swimming before going full swing into the activity.

•Using faulty equipment. Many injuries are caused by bicycles without enough air in their tires…and tennis elbow can result from using a tennis racquet with a worn-out grip.

•Not getting a thorough physical before starting an exercise program. Get a check-up prior to trying anything new. Some problems —arthritis, etc.—not treated before you start a new sport worsen.

•Neglecting to get a proper diagnosis. A bone scan, for instance, can show whether a bone was injured or whether only muscle tissue, which will heal by itself, was involved.

Source: David Hough, MD, who heads the sports medicine division of the department of family practice at Michigan State University, supervising the University's team physicians. Hough also heads MSU's Biomechanics Evaluation Laboratory.

For Fitness Highs

Nothing works as well as aerobic exercise when it comes to achieving mental and emotional well-being. Anxiety, depression—even panic attacks and phobias—can be eliminated with exercise. *How it works:* Exercise stimulates the production of…

•Beta-endorphins. The body's natural opiates, or painkillers. In large amounts, these may be responsible for the "fitness high" experienced by long-distance runners.

•Norepinephrine. Another body chemical. People who are depressed have low levels of norepinephrine.

•Body heat. Warmth during exercise leads to calm after the workout.

Benefits of exercise…

•Emotional stability. People who exercise react more calmly in stressful situations. They're less likely to feel depressed, anxious, frustrated, helpless, etc.

•Self-confidence. With greater emotional stability comes an enhanced sense of one's strengths and capabilities.

•Less bodily tension. Exercisers have a slower resting heart rate, fewer aches and pains and a general feeling of relaxation.

•A sense of control. The feeling that you command your own life is, perhaps, exercising's greatest reward.

To produce these effects, you must make a *lifelong* commitment. This means working vigorously (achieving 50% to 70% of your maximum heart rate, depending on your age and weight) for 20 to 30 minutes, three times a week.

Source: Bruce Ogilvie, PhD, one of the nation's leading sports psychologists. He maintains a private practice in Los Gatos, California. For more information, he suggests reading *The Exercise Prescription for Anxiety and Depression* by Keith Johnsgard, Plenum Publishing, 233 Spring St., New York.

How to Get Back In Shape After 40

Americans over 40 are not very physically fit. Recent Gallup polls indicate that people are more interested in exercise than ever before… and that about 40% of adults exercise aerobically three times a week. I'd say the real number is probably closer to 15%–20%—and that's too few people exercising regularly.

The physiological benefits of regular exercise—weight loss, improved HDL (good) cholesterol, lower blood pressure, decreased coronary risk, etc.—are well known. Many people, however, are not aware of the psychological benefits of exercise. Since 1977, we've done psychological testing of all patients coming to the Cooper Aerobics Center. We've found that those who are physically fit are less depressed, have a better self-image and a more positive attitude toward life. These people are just plain happier than their non-exercising counterparts.

Yet despite all the good reasons to do aerobic exercise, many people over 40 believe it's too tough, too risky or too late to start.

Nothing could be further from the truth. Surprisingly, even a modest increase in your present activity level can make a world of difference in your health and the overall quality of your life.

Whether you're beginning a fitness program for the first time or want to get back into shape, there are some important steps to follow—and pitfalls to avoid...

•Get your doctor's okay. Make sure your doctor endorses your plan. Ideally, you should first be given both a resting and a stress cardiogram. These tests should be repeated every three years or as often as your doctor recommends.

•Go slow. Don't rush into exercise. It may have taken you 20 years to get out of shape, and if you try to get back into shape in 20 days, it can be dangerous...and potentially fatal.

•Aim for just 30 minutes of sustained activity, three times a week. Even an exercise program that modest will greatly enhance your level of health and fitness.

The program...

I've created a six-week starter program, which is ideal for men and women over 40. I have found that even people with advanced heart disease or who have had bypass surgery can follow this routine with medical supervision.

•Weeks 1 to 3: Walk for 15 minutes. Don't worry about how far you get, even if it's just a couple of blocks. It's best to do this the first thing in the morning—exercise tends to be most consistent when it's done before breakfast. If that's not feasible, take a brisk walk an hour or two after dinner with your spouse, a friend or your dog. Do this three times a week, more if possible.

•Week 4: Walk for five more minutes, totaling 20 minutes each time.

•Week 5: Walk for 25 minutes each time.

•Week 6: Walk for 30 minutes each time. Alternatively, instead of walking for longer and longer periods, you may find it more challenging—and fun—to work on decreasing the time it takes you to cover two miles. Take it slow—at first it might require 45 minutes to complete the two miles. Gradually decrease your time to 30 minutes, three times a week, over a six-week period.

Caution: Walk, don't run or jog during this phase.

If, after the end of the six weeks, you don't develop any symptoms or problems—chest pains, musculoskeletal problems—you may then want to move on to a more vigorous program of slow jogging. Aim to reduce the time it

takes you to cover two miles from 30 minutes to 20 minutes. Again, do it gradually, over a six-week period.

Caution: Make sure you get your doctor's okay before increasing the intensity of your exercise program.

Walking and slow jogging are the easiest and least expensive exercises. They can be done anywhere.

But you may prefer to try something else, and there are three activities—cross-country skiing, swimming and cycling—that will produce equal, or even better, aerobic benefits.

The more varied your exercise program, the more likely you'll stick with it. It takes much more discipline to maintain the same routine month after month, year after year.

Exercise safety...

Studies show that there is, at worst, one cardiac arrhythmia for every 1,000 miles run and only one death for every 10,000 miles run—and that risk can be reduced if you follow these three basic guidelines...

1. Warm up...for three to five minutes before stretching. You should always stretch out before exercising. But many older people injure their hamstring and Achilles tendons when they stretch out because their bodies aren't as supple as they used to be. So I encourage them to walk briskly for about 1/4 mile before stretching.

2. Cool down...for five minutes after working out. Just keep walking around slowly—don't lie down or go right into your car and drive away. Never go directly into a sauna or steam room after exercising.

3. Do enough...but not too much. Moderation is the key. How do you know if your exercise routine is too strenuous for you? At the end of your five-minute cool-down, take your pulse for 15 seconds, then multiply that number by four. If you're between 40 and 50 years old, that number should be less than 120. If you're over 50, the number should be less than 100.

Bottom line...

Exercise is important, but it's no panacea. I endorse a program of total wellness, including a low-fat/low-calorie diet, stress management and the elimination of smoking.

When people tell me, "Dr. Cooper, I hate exercising," I answer, "Maybe...but wouldn't you hate dying more?" I'm 61 and have been exercising vigorously for the past 33 years. To use a gerontology term, I want to square off the curve …live life to the fullest—and then die suddenly.

If you do just 30 minutes of sustained activity three times a week, you'll substantially reduce most major causes of death—heart attack, stroke, diabetes and even cancer. What's more, you'll look better, feel better and dramatically improve the quality of your life.

Source: Leading fitness and health expert Kenneth H. Cooper, MD, director, Cooper Aerobics Center in Dallas. He is the author of many bestselling books including *Aerobics* (which coined the term), the *Preventive Medicine* series, and *The Aerobics Program for Total Well-Being*, Bantam Books, 666 Fifth Ave., New York 10103.

Walk, Walk, Walk

How would you like to shed those pounds that you've been trying to lose, *without running* a single mile, without learning anything about *step aerobics* and without ever having to hear some muscle-bound trainer advise you to "feel the burn?"

Well…the next time you get up from watching TV and head for the refrigerator, keep on walking—out the door, around the block, to the newspaper stand, to a neighbor's house—anywhere. Just walk. Doctors will tell you that walking is the *safest* way to burn fat (and keep it off). And unlike running, walking is a low-impact activity and that means much lower risk of injuries to joints, bones and muscles.

You can burn as many calories walking as you can jogging—it just takes a little longer. Walking briskly (at about four miles per hour), you burn 100 calories per mile. At that rate, a three-mile walk every day will amount to a loss of 35 pounds over the course of a year! And you get both short- and long-term cardiovascular benefits.

Important extra benefit: As those pounds drop off and you improve the overall health and functional ability of your heart, you'll find that your outlook on life improves, too—for exercise not only burns calories, but also works off stress.

Starting at square one…

Before you start your fitness walking program—or any new exercise program—it's important to check with your doctor. If you have an existing or chronic medical condition—diabetes, arthritis, high blood pressure or heart disease—you should make sure that your new exercise plan will not make it worse.

Minimum: Have a resting electrocardiogram. And if you're over 45, or a smoker or have known cardiovascular problems, a cardiac stress test is strongly advised. After you pass these tests—and there's *every* likelihood that you will—you'll know that you're up to the demands of an introductory program in fitness walking.

Initial goal: Three to five 15- to 60-minute exercise periods per week.

During these exercise periods, you should be able to increase your heart rate to more than 70% of maximum capacity.

To determine maximum capacity: Subtract your age from 220…this is your maximum heart rate. Take your pulse, at rest, for 60 seconds. Subtract your pulse rate from your maximum heart rate. Multiply the answer by 0.6. This number is your target zone. Add your pulse rate to your target zone. The answer is your *target heart rate.*

As you walk, take your pulse for 10 seconds and multiply that number by six. If your pulse is less than your target heart rate, step up your pace. If you're exceeding your target, slow down.

Before you begin your walk: Do five minutes of stretching exercises. Stretch your calf muscles by placing both hands against a wall and leaning into the wall with your left leg straight and your right knee slightly bent. Both feet should be flat on the floor. Hold this position for about 30 seconds. Repeat with your right leg straight and your left knee bent.

Stretch the muscle in the front of your thigh (the quadriceps) next. From a standing position, reach behind your back and grab your right foot with your left hand. Pull the foot toward your buttocks while keeping your right knee pointed toward the floor. (Steady yourself by holding onto a chair or railing.) Hold the position for about 30 seconds and repeat with the opposite hand and foot.

Finally, stretch the muscle in the back of your thigh (the hamstring). Again, from a standing position, place your right heel on an elevated surface (e.g., a stair). Keep your right knee slightly bent, and lean forward from the hips, extending your hands toward your right ankle. Hold the position, and repeat with your left leg.

Do these exercises *gently*. Don't bounce, and don't force your muscles if they don't do what you want them to do immediately.

The walk…

Start out at a slow to moderate pace for the first five minutes, then walk briskly for about 25 minutes. After 10 minutes at your faster pace, check your pulse. Are you at or near your target heart rate? Adjust your pace to stay within your target range.

As you walk, relax your shoulders and swing your arms to match your stride. End your walk with a five-minute "cool-down" period in which you slow your pace, and finish off the session with another five minutes of stretching exercises to prevent stiffness.

A word to the wise: If you're not a 16-year-old high-school athlete, make a mental adjustment to the popular "Just do it" slogan. *Just do it— gradually.* Go to your limit gradually and enjoy it. You don't have to leap tall buildings in a single bound your first time around the block.

And don't get tricky with your basic walking gait. Never wear ankle weights to "increase the load." You might as well hang a bowling ball off your elbow. Ankle weights will exert stresses on your joints that Mother Nature never designed into the plan—and you will suffer for it.

Fitness walking basics…

• Drink eight to 10 glasses of water a day.

• Wear light colored or reflective clothing at night or in the early morning.

• Battle boredom by listening to music or a recorded book on a portable tape player.

• If you have a blister or sprain that can be made worse by walking, don't walk.

• If you become dizzy or develop pains in your chest or your arms, stop walking immediately and go to the nearest emergency room.

If the shoe fits…

Part of the fun of starting any new sport is "suiting up." Selecting a new pair of shoes for your fitness walking program can help to rein-

force your commitment to exercise. But how do you know which shoe is right for you?

Faced with the array of athletic shoes currently on the market, let common sense be your guide. Don't buy a pair of shoes designed for running, sprinting, basketball, high-impact aerobics, etc. Buy *walking shoes*. Take your exercise socks to the store with you, and put them on before trying on the new shoes. *Important:* Always shop for shoes in the afternoon. Feet swell as the day wears on, and shoes bought in the morning can pinch in the afternoon.

What to look for: Comfort, cushioning and an appropriate degree of ruggedness. Select a lace-up shoe with good heel and arch support, a flexible sole and a good overall fit. Look inside the shoe—and feel with your hand—for any irregularities (seams, lumps, etc.) that could trouble your foot.

Once you have the shoe on, check the length by pinching the front of the shoe by your big toe. If the empty space is wider than your thumb, the shoe is too long. Check shoe width by examining the shoelace holes. When the shoe is snugly laced, the holes should be about a thumb's width apart. If the distance is greater —or less—than that, the shoe is not for you.

What about skipping the shoelace option and going for Velcro fasteners? *Bad idea.* Laces allow a shoe to conform to your foot at a number of points, but Velcro straps hold, viselike, as your foot expands.

If, after you've worn your new shoes for a while, you find that they work for you, buy another pair just like them. You'll prolong the life of your shoes if you alternate pairs. Also, shoes will have extra drying time between wearings, which decreases your risk of developing athlete's foot and other fungal conditions.

Too busy to exercise?…

Stressed-out executives with a crammed schedule and a sedentary lifestyle are among the people who could benefit most from exercise—but there are only 24 hours in a day, no matter how big the numbers are on your paycheck. No time for an exercise program? Make exercise a part of the workday.

If you're stuck at the office day and night— use the stairs. When you need to go over some numbers with someone whose office is a few floors above you, skip the elevator and get there the old-fashioned way. Or just hit the stairs for a 10-minute fitness break.

Good-quality men's business shoes are also excellent walking shoes, so, if you're a commuter, park the car a 15-minute walk from the train or bus station. You'll get your half-hour walk in every day. Women commuters will probably need to carry a change of shoes, but many do anyway.

And if you find that you've arrived early for an appointment, don't sit in the lobby looking at old magazines. Walk around the block, explore the neighborhood. You have everything —fitness, health and well-being—to gain, and nothing to lose but a few extra pounds.

Source: Daniel M. McGann, DPM, author of *The Doctor's Sore Foot Book*, William Morrow & Co., 1350 Avenue of the Americas, New York 10019.

Health, Anxiety, Ideas and Walking

Exercise doesn't have to be strenuous or punishing to be effective. Despite its economy of muscle use, walking is considered by most experts to be one of the best exercises. *Benefits:*

•Preventative and remedy for respiratory, heart and circulation disorders.

•Weight control. Walking won't take off pounds, but it keeps weight at a desirable level. (Particularly effective in keeping excess pounds from coming back, once they have been dieted off.)

•Aids digestion, elimination and sleep.

•Antidote to physical and psychological tensions.

Walking works as a second heart. Expanding and contracting foot muscles, calves, thighs and buttocks help pump blood back to the heart. This aid is crucial. The heart can propel blood very well on its own, but the body's muscles are essential to the return flow from lower regions (legs, feet, stomach). When the blood transportation system becomes sluggish because of lack of exercise, the heart compensates by doing more work. Heart rate and blood pressure rise. (Elevated pressure can be helped to return to normal by a regimen of walking.)

Best daily walking routine…

•Time. Whenever it can be fit into your daily routine. (A mile takes only 20 minutes.) People doing sedentary office work usually average a mile and a half in a normal day. Stretch that by choosing to walk down the hall to a colleague instead of picking up the interoffice phone.

•Place. Wherever it's pleasant and convenient to daily tasks. Walk at least partway to work. If a commuter, walk to the train. Walk, not to the nearest, but to the second or third bus or subway stop from the house. Get off a stop or two away from the usual one. Park the car 10 blocks farther away. Walk 10 blocks to and from lunch. Walk after dinner, before sitting down to a book, TV or work.

•Clothes. Comfortable and seasonal, light rather than heavy. Avoid thin-soled shoes when walking city pavements. It may be desirable to use metatarsal pads or cushioned soles. (The impact on concrete weakens metatarsal arches and causes callouses.)

•Length. Walk modest distances at first. In the city, the number of streets tells the beginner how far he has gone. But in the country, a walker can go farther than he realizes. *Consequences:* Fatigue on the return trip. *Instead:* Use a good pedometer.

•Pace. Walking for exercise should feel different from other kinds of walking. Some useful suggestions about pace…

•Set out at a good pace. Use the longest stride that's comfortable for you. Let arms swing and muscles stretch. Strike a rhythm and keep to it.

•Don't saunter. Sauntering can be tiring. Walking at a good pace allows the momentum of each stride to carry over into the next.

•Lengthen the customary stride by swinging the foot a little farther ahead than usual. Lengthening the stride speeds the walking pace with no additional expenditure of energy. It also loosens tense muscles, puts other neglected muscles to work and provides continuous momentum that puts less weight on the feet.

Most comfortable pace: Three miles per hour. It generally suits the average male and is the US Army pace for long hikes. With the right shoes and unconfining clothes, most women will be comfortable at that pace, too.

Source: The late Aaron Sussman, author and advertising pioneer.

Prescriptions For Walking

If you are overweight or have diabetes: Distance is more important than speed. Try to walk for 45 minutes to one hour at a self-selected pace. Heart or lung disorders: Exercise indoors in a climate-controlled, pollution-free environment, especially if the temperature is above 88° and humidity is greater than 85%. Sports injuries or arthritis in the back or lower extremities: Avoid steep hills. They stress weight-bearing joints. To reduce stress or improve aerobic fitness: Increase intensity of exercise, aiming for a 15-minute mile or better. To increase heart rate, use handheld weights, walk up stairs or hills, and pump your arms.

Source: *Walking Medicine: Lifetime Guide to Preventative & Therapeutic Exercisewalking Programs* by Gary Yanker and Kathy Burton, McGraw-Hill, 1221 Ave. of the Americas, New York 10020.

Whole Truth About Walking Shoes

A few years ago, as fitness walking began to boom, the major athletic-shoe companies announced that walkers had different needs than runners and developed a new category—the walking shoe.

The truth: Many walkers don't need walking shoes…and some walkers would even be better off with another kind of shoe.

Whether you are a casual fitness walker or a dedicated power walker (with a focus on technique, pace and heart rate), you can probably be well-served by tennis shoes, cross-trainers or running shoes—as long as they are of high quality. Running shoes can be very well-suited to walkers. Reasons:

• As you age, there is some atrophy of the fat in your foot pads—the heel pads, in particular. If you walk on hard surfaces, you will benefit from the extra cushioning in running shoes.

• People who over-pronate (roll in excessively) need the support of a straighter last (the form the shape of the shoe is built around) and stronger support features—which running shoes have.

The most important criterion in choosing a shoe is a good fit—for both length and width. Since most athletic shoes are not sized for width, the more options you have, the better.

Bottom line: When buying a shoe for walking, seek out the model that best suits your needs. Don't restrict yourself to a specific category.

Source: Tom Brunick, director of The Athlete's Foot Wear Test Center at North Central College, Napierville, Illinois.

Everyday Ways To Walk More

How to get more exercise from day-to-day activities:

•Park the car farther away from the office or train station and walk.

•Quit taking elevators. Daily climbs of 18 floors or more will increase fitness, studies show.

•Eat lunch in a restaurant at least 10 blocks from the office and stride briskly both to and from.

•Instead of driving to the shopping center, walk there. If it's too far, ride a bicycle. If there's too much to haul home, make a second trip.

•Carry your own golf clubs. And skip the golf cart, even if you're the lone walker in your foursome.

Source: *The Cardiologists' Guide to Fitness and Health Through Exercise*, Simon & Schuster, New York.

Best Home-Fitness Equipment

A home gym is both convenient and private. You don't have to travel to a health club, wait in line to use the equipment or feel like you're on display. Before investing in any piece of home equipment, however:

•Determine what kind of exercise will best meet your needs. If you have little time, consider stairclimbers, rowers and ski machines. If you think that boredom may be a problem, stay away from stationary bikes. If you enjoy walking or running, treadmills are excellent.

•Keep in mind that it's best to own more than one piece of equipment—switching back and forth between machines produces different benefits and alleviates boredom.

•Test equipment at the store. You wouldn't buy a car without giving it a test run. Put on your sweats and try at least a five-minute workout on each of several models to determine what's both comfortable and enjoyable.

•Check for safety features. If you have children, you may not want to purchase a treadmill, for instance. It's easy for small fingers to get caught under the revolving belt.

•What's available for home gyms—in order of popularity…

Stairclimbers…

Stairclimbing exercises the thighs and hips. *Note:* You're really not simulating stairclimbing. It's simply a churning of the legs up and down, with hip and knee action. *Advantage:* Short workouts…you get benefits with less time invested.

Recommended workout: Three times a week, for nine to 13 minutes. This provides the same cardiovascular benefits as walking 45 minutes five times a week.

Recommended machines:

•Good. Very basic machines, made with shock-absorbers, provide a stairclimbing motion with some electronic feedback. You can get a decent workout on them. *Drawbacks:* It's hard to get the left and right legs moving at the same speed…and it can be difficult adjusting to the machine's intensity. *Cost:* Less than $500.

•Better. Motor-run units can be set to different intensities. *Cost:* $2,000 to $3,400 (there are no mid-priced stairclimbers).

•Best. This machine uses a hydraulic system that's effective, smooth and quiet. *Cost:* $2,200.

Stationary bikes…

Stationary bikes are stable and extremely easy to use. *Main drawback:* You tire easily—your muscles give out much sooner than your cardiovascular functions.

Recommended workout: Three to four times a week, for 20 to 30 minutes.

Recommended machines:

•Good. Very basic bikes offer effective exercise without a lot of bells and whistles. They're great for self-motivated exercisers. Look for models with easily adjustable resistance, sturdy pedals and a seat height that can accommodate your body size. *Cost:* $200 to $900.

•Better. More electronics, more comfortable saddles…and they're better looking. *Cost:* $500 to $1,000.

•Best. More elaborate electronic feedback. *Cost:* $1,200 to $3,500.

Treadmills…

Many people are more successful with treadmills than with bikes or rowers. *Reason:* Treadmills require more balance and involvement, which enhances motivation.

Recommended workout: Three to four times a week, for 30 to 40 minutes of combined running and walking.

Recommended machines:

•Good. Low-priced treadmills are best for walking. *Reason:* Their motors and frames are too weak to withstand the pounding of running. *Cost:* $500 to $1,000.

•Better. These treadmills offer electronic resistance, a powerful motor and heavy-duty construction. *Cost:* $1,500 to $2,000.

Rowers…

Rowing involves more muscles than climbers or bikes and requires greater technique. Rowers are relatively inexpensive and can be easily slipped under a bed. *Drawbacks:* Rowers feel sluggish, and are not as much fun to use as climbers or treadmills. Rowing also causes back problems in some people.

Recommended workout: Three to four times a week, for 20 to 30 minutes.

Recommended machines:

•Good. These rowers have a sliding seat, are low to the ground and include electronic feedbacks. *Cost:* Less than $500.

•Best. This model is a favorite of ex-college oarsmen. *Cost:* $650.

Ski machines…

These provide an excellent workout for both arms and legs. Although the intensity of the workout is less than a workout with a climber or treadmill, the overall effect is very good. You burn a great deal of calories without a lot of discomfort.

Recommended workout: Three to four times a week, for 20 to 30 minutes.

Recommended machine:

- Best. There's really only one product in this market. *Cost:* $695.

Source: An exercise physiologist and leader in the home-fitness industry.

Home Exercise Equipment that Doesn't Take Up A Lot of Space

- Fluid-filled hand-held weights. Combining the benefits of low-impact aerobics and free weights, the *Hydrobics* workout burns up to 600 calories per hour. (For comparison, walking on a treadmill burns about 316 calories per hour.) The system consists of *Hydrohands*, a pair of approximately two-pound hand weights that can be used while walking, biking, during aerobic exercise, etc....and *Hydroburner*, an approximately three-pound, 11-inch-long cylinder that can be used during a series of 24 exercises that are described on a 60-minute videotape and instructional wall chart (both included).

Both Hydrohands and Hydroburner come permanently sealed and partially filled with a liquid solution. As it sloshes around during exercise, shocks are absorbed, putting less stress on joints—making it especially good for seniors.

Hydrohands are reported to feel lighter and more comfortable than solid weights. *Also included:* A 60-minute audiotape about the mental aspects of staying in shape and music to accompany your workout.
Hydrobics Products. 800-577-9283.*

- Free weights. *PowerBlock* is a system of high-tech free weights for a full-body workout, in a handsome stand that measures only 2½-

*Contact the manufacturer for the names of retailers in your area.

feet square and 3½-feet high. It's much more compact than traditional dumbbells. Insert the selector pin to choose how much you want to lift—from 10 pounds to 95 pounds per hand, in five-pound increments. Padded handles support the wrists for safer, more comfortable and balanced lifting action than clunky dumbbells.
Intellbell. 800-446-5215.

- Interactive exercise video game. The number-one reason why so many people abandon their exercise routines is boredom. The *Heart-Beat Personal Trainer* is an interactive video game utilizing Sega Genesis technology. It makes workouts fun. The system easily hooks up to any TV or monitor and an exercise bike or stair climber, allowing you to play a series of specially designed video games. Up to four players can program their own exercise routines into the system. The games act as personal trainers by making sure you stay within your recommended heart rate.

Example: If you're pedaling or climbing too fast, your game character starts panting and sweating...too slow, he gets sleepy and lethargic. The system constantly monitors and displays your heart rate and records past exercise sessions so you can follow the progress of your fitness program. Includes one original 16-bit video game. More games are sold separately.
HeartBeat. 800-386-7587.

- Muscle stretcher. Perfect for the pre-workout warm-up, *ProStretch PT-200* looks like a pair of automobile brake shoes connected by rods.

How it works: Place both feet in the heel cups of the semicircular devices, gently tilt back and hold the position for 30 seconds at a time to stretch the muscles of the lower legs and feet, where 75% of injuries occur. Provides a longer, more controlled stretch than simply leaning into a wall with feet flat on the ground. Helps accelerate rehabilitation. Includes an 11-minute instructional video.
ProStretch. 800-535-3629, ext. 77.

- Portable home gym. There are several compact home gyms currently on the market, but the *Lifeline Gym* is the most effective, compact and versatile available.

At the heart of the system are super-resilient stretch cords that let the user easily perform up to 20 upper- and lower-body exercises in only about 10 square feet of floor space. Simply twist the cord around the lifting bar to increase resistance from about five pounds to 350 pounds.

Also: Webbed jogging belt attaches to a door for running in place with resistance. The entire system fits into a small tote bag and weighs just two pounds.

Lifeline International. 800-553-6633.

•Slide. The newest fitness craze is called *lateral motion training* and mimics the motion of speed skaters by sliding from side to side on a sheet of hard plastic.

Benefits: Low-impact workout develops thighs and buttocks…strengthens joints…improves balance, agility and response time. *Slide Reebok* is a one-piece, six-foot portable trainer that rolls up into a tube.

Features: A nonskid rubberized bottom that will not mar floors and graduated end ramps to minimize joint impact. *Includes:* Slide socks that fit over athletic shoes and a 30-minute instructional video.

Slide Reebok. 800-843-4444.

Source: Patrick Netter, founder/owner of J.P. Netter Marketing, a health and fitness consulting firm, 10480 Kinnard Ave., Los Angeles 90024.

Better Chairing

A good desk chair can add as much as 40 minutes to your workday. *Reason:* You don't develop fatigue-induced problems…back strain, leg cramps, etc.

What to look for in a chair:

•*Seat:* Made of porous material to let body heat dissipate.

•*Front of seat:* Rounded or padded so it doesn't cut off circulation in your legs.

•*Backrest:* Extends the width of the chair, conforms to your spine, and supports the lower and middle back.

•*Height:* Your feet should rest flat on the floor. Otherwise, circulation to your feet is slowed. This also takes some of your body weight off your lower back.

•*Swivelability:* This enables you to face your

work at all times. You'll avoid eyestrain from moving your eyes back and forth.

Important: Don't sit for longer than 60 minutes at a time or you will tire your body.

Source: *Do It at Your Desk: An Office Worker's Guide to Fitness and Health,* Tilden Press, Washington, DC.

How to Sit Correctly

Even if you have the perfect office chair, you can develop physical problems from prolonged sitting unless you align your body properly. *Suggestions:*

•Keep your neck and back in a straight line with your spine. Bend forward from the hips. Do not arch your lower back.

•Use a footrest to relieve swayback. Your knees should be higher than your hips.

•Move your feet up and down frequently to ensure constant circulation.

•Move your neck and shrug your shoulders to relieve the tension that results from prolonged sitting.

Source: *Office Hazards: How Your Job Can Make You Sick* by Joel Makower, Tilden Press, Washington, DC.

Good and Bad News About Backless Chairs

Backless chairs (the kind with knee rests) can cause problems. *Among them:* Chronic knee or leg problems are aggravated by pressure from the knee rest… There's danger of sliding down the chair seat when wearing slippery fabrics… Users are unable to stretch backwards effectively. *Major advantage:* Users with chronic back pain say the chairs improve posture and relieve back strain.

Source: *The Office.*

Personalized Work-Stations Are Best

Adjustable work-stations make sense because experts don't agree on the ideal sitting posture or work-station design. Moreover, these systems make it possible for workers to adjust the stations to their own bodies, and the fact that they're comfortable minimizes their complaints.

Source: *Office Systems Ergonomics Report.*

Good Posture Tip

Stand straight to think straight. *Reason:* Good posture promotes greater lung expansion. Since more air is inhaled, more oxygen reaches the brain, increasing alertness and decreasing fatigue.

Source: Dr. Raymond Harris, chief of cardiology at St. Peter's Hospital, Albany, NY.

Exercise vs. Impotence

Exercise that's good for the heart is also a good bet to prevent arteriogenic impotence—impotence caused by clogged arteries. A healthy lifestyle, cardiovascular workouts and good nutrition all contribute to keeping penile arteries, as well as those leading to the heart, in good working condition. Of 30 million men with chronic impotence, many of the 80% with physical impotence problems, rather than emotionally induced impotence, could benefit. Exercise may be more effective than surgery in correcting the problem.

Source: E. Douglas Whitehead, MD, a urologist, director of the Association for Male Sexual Dysfunction, 24 E. 12 St., Suite 2-1, New York 10003.

How to Stay Fit While You Sit

Exercises to do at your desk to keep mentally alert, tone sagging muscles and relieve muscle strain:

•Tummy slimmer. Sit erect, hands on knees. Exhale, pulling abdominal muscles in as far as possible. Relax. Inhale. Exhale as you draw in stomach again. Repeat 10 to 20 times.

•Head circles. Drop head forward, chin on chest, shoulders relaxed. Slowly move head in large circle. Reverse direction. Do 5 to 6 times each side.

•Torso twist. Raise elbows to shoulder level. Slowly twist around as far right as possible, then reverse. Do 10 to 12 turns each way.

•Heel and toe lift. Lean forward, hands on knees. Lift both heels off floor, strongly contracting calf muscles. Lower heels, lift toes high toward shins. Do 10 to 15 complete movements.

Source: Doug MacLennon, The Fitness Institute, Willowdale, Ontario.

Exercising When You Don't Have Time

•While you talk on the phone, do leg raises, arm exercises or isometrics.

•Park your car far from the building and walk.

•Do things the hard way (walk the long way to the office, take six trips carrying things upstairs instead of saving items for one trip, shovel snow instead of using the snow blower).

•Exercise while watching TV (run in place, skip rope, use an exercise machine or do yoga, isometrics or toe-touching).

Source: Stephanie Bernardo, author of *The Ultimate Checklist.* Doubleday.

Fitness vs. Health— They Are Two Different Things

Exercise will make you physically fit—fitness being defined as the capacity to do physical activity comfortably. But, contrary to popular misconception, fitness and health are two separate things. Don't fool yourself into thinking that exercise is an all-benefit, no-risk proposition.

Three main myths about exercise and coronary health:

•*Myth:* Exercise makes your heart healthier. Exercise does make your heart mechanically more efficient—it makes it possible to do more physical activity more comfortably. But your heart isn't healthier just because it's beating more slowly. This would be true only if each of us were allotted a certain number of heartbeats per lifetime. There is no such allotment. There are people in their nineties who have had fast heartbeats all their lives.

•*Myth:* Exercise improves your coronary circulation. Exercise does not stimulate your body to grow collateral blood vessels around the heart. The only thing that does this is the clogging of your original arteries. The original idea that exercise improved coronary circulation was based on an early-1950s study done with dogs under highly artificial conditions. The tests had nothing to do with anything resembling human life.

•*Myth:* Exercise reduces your coronary-risk factors. Most hypertension specialists would agree that the likelihood of reducing blood pressure to a significant degree via an exercise program is very small. A California study of trained distance runners found that they had the same range of blood pressure as nonrunners.

Common misconception: That lower heart rate means lower blood pressure. One has nothing to do with the other. So far, a low-fat low-cholesterol diet is the only reliable way to lower cholesterol levels. It's been claimed that there are several types of cholesterol: HDL (high density lipoprotein), the "good" cholesterol…and the "bad" ones, LDL (low density lipoprotein)

and triglycerides. The latest evidence suggests that even when your HDL goes up after exercise, it may be the wrong kind of HDL. Some studies show that HDL doesn't go up with exercise and that triglycerides and LDL don't go down. There's even an important study that shows the opposite actually occurs.

•*Myth:* Exercise makes you live longer. No one really knows why some people live longer than others. Innumerable factors contribute to it, including genes, marital status, number of social contacts, resistance to stress and educational level. There's never been an unflawed study showing that exercise prolongs life. An interesting book called *Living to Be 100* analyzed 1,200 centegenarians. Avoidance of stress was a common denominator.

•*Myth:* Exercise makes you feel better. Although many claims have been made that exercise alleviates depression and anxiety, the data are contradictory. Some studies claim benefits, others don't. Some studies comparing the benefits of exercise with those of meditation and relaxation have found no difference.

Source: Henry A. Solomon, MD, author of *The Exercise Myth*, Harcourt Brace Jovanovich, San Diego.

Moving Gradually Into A Fitness Program

•Before launching any fitness program, have a complete physical examination, including an electrocardiogram. Your doctor should schedule a stress test to check on the heart's capacity.

•Don't let your new enthusiasm for getting fit make you too competitive. If you try to get back to the level of achievement you reached as a college athlete, you risk severe injury to ankles, knees, and hips.

•Don't jump into a racquet sport or a basketball league. Instead, prepare your body with a six-month program of walking, stretching and perhaps light jogging and weight training.

•Choose a sport you like as a primary activity and a complementary activity to go along with it. A swimmer might walk or jog two days a week. A runner could work with weights.

Source: Everett L. Smith, director of the Biogerontology Laboratory, Department of Preventive Medicine, University of Wisconsin, Madison.

Working Up to Rigorous Exercise

It takes middle-aged men and women six months of regular exercise (fast walking, light jogging, weight training, etc.) to work up to rigorous exercise. Even then, they should move gradually into each workout. *The steps to follow:*

• Walk or jog in place for two or three minutes.

• Do 10 minutes of stretching.

• When you move into your sport, take the first five minutes at a slow pace (a relaxed volley in tennis, for example) until you break into a light sweat.

• For the first few months, aim for 40% to 60% of your maximum heart rate. After six months, go for 70%. After nine months, shoot for 85%.*

• Take 10 minutes to cool down with slow jogging and more stretching.

• Recognize when you've done too much (if it aches to take a step the next day).

*To calculate these goals, subtract your resting heart rate from your maximum rate—220 minus your age—and multiply by the desired percentage. Then add your resting rate to get your goal. *Example:* A 45-year-old man has a maximum heart rate of 175 and a resting rate of 60. To perform at 70% of maximum, he should reach a rate of 140.

Source: Everett L. Smith, director of the Biogerontology Laboratory, department of preventive medicine, University of Wisconsin, Madison.

Swimming: The Best Exercise of All

Swimming helps the entire musculature of the body, particularly the upper torso. It tones muscles (but does not build them). *Greatest benefit:* To the cardiovascular system.

• *Best strokes for a workout:* Crawl, butterfly, and back strokes are the most strenuous.

• *Less taxing:* The side, breast, and elementary breast strokes.

• The elementary back stroke is best for survival. The face is clear of the water for easy breathing, and the limited muscle use saves energy.

• The side stroke is traditional for lifesaving. It can be performed with one arm, which leaves the other free to tow someone. It is very relaxing—and effective.

• *To build up the legs:* Hold a kickboard while swimming. This forces propulsion by the legs alone. Or swim with the flippers favored by divers. Their surface increases the resistance to the water, making the legs work harder.

Source: James Steen, swimming coach at Kenyon College, Gambier, OH.

Aerobic Ratings Of Sports

• *Best for cardiovascular fitness:* Stationary bicycling, uphill hiking, ice hockey, rope jumping, rowing, running, and cross-country skiing.

• *Moderately effective:* Basketball, outdoor bicycling, calisthenics, handball, field hockey, racquetball, downhill skiing, soccer, squash, swimming, singles tennis, and walking.

• *Nonaerobic:* Baseball, bowling, football, golf, softball, volleyball.

Source: Dr. Franklin Payne, Jr., Medical College of Georgia, Augusta, GA.

Diabetes Preventative

Once-a-week exercise lowers the risk of adult-onset (type II) diabetes by as much as 23%. *Furthermore:* Vigorous exercise from two to four times a week reduces a person's risk of developing diabetes by 38%...at five times or more per week, the risk is cut by 42%. *Danger of inactivity:* Lack of exercise contributes to as many as one of four cases of type II diabetes.

Source: Study of more than 21,000 male physicians, aged 40 to 84, reported in *The Johns Hopkins Medical Letter, Health After 50,* 5 Water Oak, Fernandian Beach, Florida 32034.

Jogging and Achilles Tendinitis

The repetitive impact of running often causes inflammation, degeneration and small tears in tendons. *Orthopedists from Boston University Medical School suggest these preventive steps:*

• Decrease weekly mileage.

• Cut down on uphill workouts.

• Prepare for running by stretching the tendons. With heels flat and knees straight, lean forward against a wall and hold for 30 seconds.

• Warm heels and tendons with a heating pad before running. After running, apply ice for 10-12 minutes.

• Elevate heels by placing small felt pads inside running shoes. They relieve tension on the Achilles tendon and contiguous structures.

• Monitor wear on outer sides of shoes. Tendons are stressed when shoe sides give no support.

• If these measures fail, consult a physician about immobilization and anti-inflammatory drugs.

Source: *American Journal of Sports Medicine.*

Easy Exercises to Strengthen Your Back

Strengthening the back and stomach muscles is the best protection against a back injury. If you have back trouble, consult your doctor before starting this, or any, exercise program.

• Flexed-knee sit-ups. Lie on your back, with knees bent and arms at your side. Sit up slowly by rolling forward, starting with the head.

• Bent-knee leg lifts. In the same position as the sit-ups, bring one knee as close as you can to your chest, while extending the other leg. Alternate the legs.

• Knee-chest leg lifts. Work from the bent-knee sit-up position, but put a small pillow under your head. Use your hands to bring both knees up to the chest, tighten the stomach muscles and hold that position for a count of 10.

• Back flattening. Lie on your back, flex the knees, and put your arms above your head. Tighten your stomach and buttock muscles and press the lower back hard against the floor. Hold this position for a count of 10, relax and repeat.

• Don't overdo the exercises. Soreness is a sign to cut back.

• Never do these exercises with the legs straight.

Source: *American Journal of Nursing,* New York.

Realities of Exercise Equipment

The sophisticated machinery that has turned old-fashioned gyms into today's health clubs is designed to offer continuous resistance during each of the movement exercises you use it for.

• Using machines is a much faster, more efficient way to build muscle strength than using weights.

• Doing all the exercises for all the muscle groups on a regular basis does not make you perfectly fit.

Strength and fitness are not equivalent. Although muscle strength is a component of fitness, you also need flexibility and heart-lung capacity. Stretching exercises make you flexible, and aerobic exercises such as running and bike riding build up your heart muscle and your lung capacity.

• Strengthening exercises do not turn fat into muscle. It doesn't work that way. People who are overweight need to follow a calorie-restricted diet and do aerobic exercises, which trigger the body to use up fat. Working out on machines only builds up muscle under the fat layer. However, combining a weight-loss program with strengthening exercises can improve body tone as the weight comes off.

• The machines are safe if you learn the proper technique for using each machine, including proper breathing, before you are allowed on the equipment alone. On the Nautilus, for example, all the straps must be secured before you start. If one is broken or missing, don't use the machine. Poor form on the machines can lead to serious injuries. So can using the wrong weight settings.

• *Good rule of thumb:* Use a weight setting that lets you do 8–12 repetitions comfortably. If you must struggle to get beyond five, the setting is too heavy. If you complete 10 without feeling any fatigue at all, it is too light. You will have to experiment with each machine to get the right setting. Then, from time to time, you can adjust the weights upward. But be cautious. Pushing yourself too hard not only invites injury, it also discourages you from sticking to the program on a regular basis.

How to Use a Stationary Bicycle

To ride without pain or injury:

• Check with your doctor, especially if you have any heart, knee, or leg problems.

• Raise the seat on your cycle high enough so that in the downward position your foot just reaches the pedal with your knee slightly bent. This is the proper mechanical position for cycling.

• Always warm up and cool down with your bicycle set on a low resistance level. After a three- to five-minute warmup, set a constant pedal speed and increase the resistance to the level of difficulty at which you want to work. Cool down with a lower resistance setting, again for three to five minutes.

• When you begin a stationary bicycle program, work at 60% of your predicted maximum heart rate. If your heart is beating faster, then you are overdoing it. As you become more fit, you can work at up to 80% of your predicted

maximum heart rate. But remember to keep the increase slow and gradual.

• Start cycling in 10-minute sessions. Then increase to 15, then 20, and then 25 or more minutes per session. Gradual increases over a period of weeks help prevent injury to muscles and joints. Once you build up your physical strength, pedal for as long as you feel comfortable.

Source: Eastside Sports Medicine Center, New York.

To Get Into Shape For Skiing

Being physically fit makes skiing more fun and helps prevent soreness and injuries. *What to focus on:*

• Muscle tone and flexibility. Stretching exercises keep your muscles long and pliable. They also warm muscles up for strenuous sports and help relax them afterward. Always stretch slowly. Hold the extended position for 20 to 30 seconds. Don't bounce.

• Do sit-ups with your knees bent to strengthen abdominal muscles (they can take stress off the back).

• Practice any active sport, from swimming to tennis, for three one-hour sessions a week.

• Jogging builds up the muscles of the lower torso and legs. Running downhill strengthens the front thigh muscles, essential to skiing. Running on uneven terrain promotes strong and flexible ankles. Biking builds strong legs and improves balance.

How to Improve Your Tennis

Here are some secrets that help tennis pros on the court:

• Psych yourself up for a big point by triggering the adrenaline response. *Here's how:* Open your eyes wide and fix them on a nearby object. Breathe deeply and forcefully. Think of yourself as a powerful, aggressive individual. Exhort yourself with phrases like "Fight!" Try to raise goose bumps on your skin—they signal a high point.

•To switch from one type of playing surface to another, practice easing the transition. If you're moving to fast cement from slow clay, for example, practice charging the net before the switch. If it's the other way around, spend extra time on your groundstrokes.

To play well against a superior player:

•Suspend all expectations. Avoid thinking about the situation. Watch the ball, not the opponent.

•Play your game. Don't try to impress your opponent with difficult shots you normally never try.

•Hit the ball deep and down the middle. The more chances for your opponent to return your shot, the more chances for him to err.

•Concentrate on your serve. No matter how outgunned you may be, you can stay in the match if you hold your serve.

Source: *Tennis* and *World Tennis.*

How to Play Good Singles Tennis After 40

Older tennis players can win and avoid injuries by using the right strategies and techniques. Pancho Gonzales, the former champion who is now a leading Seniors player, advises playing a "thinking man's" game:

•When hitting, watch the ball right up to the point where it hits the strings of the racket.

•Aim for consistency rather than winners. Older players often hit too hard.

•For power and pace, shift your body weight forward on every stroke. At impact, the weight should be completely on the front foot.

•Anticipate your opponent. *Example:* If you hit a shot to your right, it will probably be returned to your left. Be ready to move left, but don't commit yourself until the ball has been hit.

•Get the racket back quickly and all the way before each shot.

•Try to swing the same way on every shot, both for consistency and for deception. Your opponent shouldn't be able to tell from the swing if the shot is hard or soft.

•Try to hit flat shots deep to the corners, rather than underspin slices, which provide more time for your opponent to reach the ball.

•Always change a losing game. Lob frequently against opponents who are dominating plays, especially if they have a winning net game. Against winning base line players, hit drop shots to force them to come in and play the net.

•Save energy. Take plenty of time between points and before serving.

•Work on a consistent second serve. The resulting gain of confidence will lead to improvement of the first serve.

•When practicing the serve, spend time on the toss. Practice with a bucket placed where a perfect toss should fall.

•Beware of the topspin serve. Though effective, it is hard on the back muscles.

•Return serves as early as possible, and keep them low.

•Adopt sound health and conditioning practices.

•Do some weekly running and exercises. Squeeze an old tennis ball a few minutes a day to build up arm muscles, and jump rope to improve footwork.

•Rest before and after playing.

•Use a warmup jacket to speed the loosening of the muscles before play.

•During play, run with bent knees to reduce shock to knees.

•After play, apply lotion to the palm of your racket hand to keep it from scaling and blistering.

•Use the right equipment for your changed style of play. Choose a flexible wood racket, which jars the arm less than a metal racket.

•Try a lighter-weight racket more loosely strung.

Source: The late Pancho Gonzales, author of *Tennis Begins at Forty.* Dial Press.

How to Play Better Tennis Doubles After 40

Here are some more hints from Pancho Gonzales:

•Agree on strategy and signals with your partner before playing. *Most important signal:* Net players must let their partners know when they plan to cross over to intercept the return of a serve. (A clenched fist behind the back is often used.) During this move and all other moves, remember you both should be in motion...one to make the shot and the other to cover the exposed part of the court.

•Agree that the weaker player should take the forehand court. This player should be assigned to serve when the wind and sun are behind the server.

•Make sure the weaker player plays closer to the net. *Reason:* It is easier to volley in this position.

•Keep in mind that one player normally concentrates on setting up shots. This person hits the ball low to force the opponents at the net to hit up on the ball.

•The second player has the job of making the put-aways.

Source: The late Pancho Gonzales, author of *Tennis Begins at Forty.* Dial Press.

Martial Arts Schools Teach More than Martial Arts

The martial arts offer more than a simple exercise program. They build both physical and mental strengths. Students learn the skills to extricate themselves from dangerous situations and, if necessary, to defend themselves.

Styles and systems...

•Tai Chi Chuan uses slow, graceful movements.

•Karate employs powerful, focused techniques.

•Judo and Aikido make use of joint locks and throws.

Finding the right school...

•To get a list of schools, talk with friends and check out the ads in your local Yellow Pages.

•Visit the schools to observe a few classes before you sign up.

•Clarify your goals before you make a choice—do you want mainly a physical fitness and self-defense program, or are you interested in the mental/ spiritual aspects?

What to consider...

•A balanced approach to both the mental aspects (such as concentration and focus) and the physical aspects of the particular martial art.

•The temper of the fighting classes, if the school has them. Make certain that care is taken to minimize injuries. Fighting is a part of most martial arts, and you should be comfortable with the school's fighting program.

•Thoughtful answers to your questions. If the school is evasive in its explanations, it is probably not a good bet.

•Instructors create the training environment of the school. Make certain they suit you. Some people like a "marine sergeant," while others might prefer a more temperate teacher.

•Students should be brought into the regimen slowly in a progressive process. Only as a student gets used to one style should new techniques be added to his repertory.

•Make sure the school accommodates different levels of athletic ability and different ages. Inflexible standards may only frustrate you.

•Attitudes of students. Do they encourage and help each other? Or are they bullying? The attitude of the instructor is passed on to his students.

•Facilities. Is there room to practice in between classes? Does the school have exercise equipment such as weights and jump ropes? Are the locker rooms big enough for the number of students? Are there showers?

•Schedule. If you will have a hard time getting to the workouts, you probably won't go often enough.

Source: Ken Glickman, third degree black belt and Coordinator, Educational Services, Boardroom® Inc., Greenwich, CT.

Exercises that Can Harm You

The most important benefit of exercise is that, properly done, it increases longevity. But exercises that promote a single aspect of the body, such as form, stamina, coordination, speed, or strength, generally have a negative impact. *Especially dangerous are:*

•Muscle-building exercises. They can harm joints and connective tissues. Weight lifters are not known for longevity.

•Skill-producing activities. Ballet, handball, and squash require arduous training and stop-start patterns. Both are negatives for long life.

•Marathon sports. Jogging, swimming, cycling, and strenuous walking can work the body to the point of exhaustion. This is dangerous because stress and injury occur more easily during body fatigue.

•Speed-oriented activities. Those that require lots of oxygen, such as sprinting or speed swimming, can be fatal, especially for those who have not trained extensively for them.

Source: Dan Georgakas, author of *The Methuselah Factors: The Secrets of the World's Longest-Lived Peoples.* Simon & Schuster.

Alternative Exercises

•Housework (scrubbing, waxing) demands as much energy as walking three miles per hour or cycling five miles per hour.

•Climbing stairs equals playing doubles tennis or jogging five miles per hour.

•Jumping rope is equivalent to swimming 45 yards a minute or running at six miles per hour.

Source: James S. Skinner, exercise physiologist, Arizona State University, Tempe.

How Not to Become A Couch Potato

America has become a nation of couch potatoes...

•Forty percent of adults are completely sedentary.

•Only 40% of ninth graders exercise three or more times a week.

•By the twelfth grade, that figure has fallen to 32%.

Television deserves much of the blame. The average American is glued to the tube for four-and-a-half hours a day. One-third of high school students watch TV for three or more hours every school day.

Such profound inactivity can have dire consequences, the most dangerous of which is obesity. Yet—there are simple ways to get yourself off the couch. I'm 78. I had knee-replacement surgery last year. If I can manage to be active—and I can—so can you.

The dangers of inactivity...

In 1980, one out of every four Americans was obese. Today, it's one out of every three. An even larger proportion of the poor and of minority women are fat. Altogether, 38 million women and 26 million men are obese.

Obesity is also a serious problem for young Americans. One in every five children and 33% of teenagers are significantly overweight. Sadly, fat kids become fat adolescents, who become fat adults, who die prematurely.

Medical researchers have long known that being overweight is unhealthy. But only now is it becoming clear just how big a role obesity plays in many common diseases, including high blood pressure, diabetes, heart disease, breast cancer, colon cancer, gallstones, osteoarthritis and gout. Each year, 300,000 people die from obesity-related conditions.

Getting off your duff...

There's no doubt about it—exercise is the best way to control your weight. It was once thought that only vigorous exercise yielded any health benefit.

Now: Increasing evidence suggests that light to moderate activity—below the level recommended for cardiovascular fitness—also results in measurable health improvements.

Even intermittent activity—as little as five or 10 minutes at a time, several times a day—burns enough calories to help you maintain a healthy weight.

You may not have the energy to jog three miles a day. But there is no excuse for failing to get at least some daily exercise. Look for activities that are simple, convenient and inexpensive—and that involve companionship.

This is the philosophy behind "Shape Up America," my new fitness campaign. My goal is to put healthy weight and physical activity high on the national agenda. Here are some easy ideas to help you get off the couch…

At home…

My wife, Betty, and I recently moved into a three-story Washington townhouse. We could have chosen to live elsewhere. But we thought that going up and down the stairs every day would help keep us in shape.

Even with my bad knee, I walk up and down those stairs many times a day. I don't consider it an annoyance. I consider it a fitness strategy.

Climbing all those stairs certainly makes a difference. My wife and I spend one week a month in a one-story house in New Hampshire (I teach surgery at Dartmouth Medical School as well as other subjects at Dartmouth College). We notice it right away. Betty's weight goes up one to two pounds. And my knee gets stiff.

If you can't bear to give up television, at least get up during each commercial and make a circuit of your house. Do something. And don't ask someone else to fetch something for you. Get it yourself.

Don't use your TV's remote control unit. Using the remote may be more convenient, but it allows you to stay immobile for long periods of time…and "channel-surfing" only encourages you to watch more TV. *Instead:* Leave your remote control on top of the TV. If you need to change channels or—better yet—turn off the set, you'll have to get up. It's amazing how many calories you can burn via this simple trick.

So many people now have telephones in every room of the house. *Helpful:* Get rid of a couple of phones. You'll walk up to 70 extra miles a year.

On the job…

If you drive to work, park your car at least one block away and walk the rest of the way. If you take public transportation, get off a couple of blocks before your usual stop.

Don't send your assistant on errands. Do them yourself.

Whenever possible, take stairs instead of elevators or escalators. When I was a surgeon in Philadelphia 15 years ago, I worked on the third floor of an eight-story building. I used to walk from the third to the eighth floor, go down another set of stairs…and do it again.

Making exercise fun…

Outside of work, I walked almost everywhere I went. That was plenty of exercise even for a young man. If you find it boring to exercise just for the sake of exercise, try combining activities.

Everybody says the family is falling apart. Instead of sitting zombie-like in front of the TV, try getting everyone together to kick a ball around, play touch football or toss a basketball through a hoop.

A brisk walk puts into action every muscle in your body. Take the longest stride you're capable of and go as fast as you can without running. Swing your arms in an exaggerated way.

Go on a "power walk" for 20 minutes at least three days a week. If that's too much all at once, do 10 minutes in the morning and 10 minutes after work.

A word about diet…

Too many Americans—especially those trying to diet—skip breakfast. *Trap:* By lunchtime, they're so ravenous that they eat a lunch much higher in calories than it would have been had they eaten breakfast.

It's better to eat a small breakfast—a glass of orange juice and a bowl of high-fiber cereal with skim milk. This may not seem like a lot, but at lunchtime you won't eat as much.

Studies have found that when smokers see a billboard showing someone smoking, they reach for a cigarette. Similarly, the sight of a cookie jar can whet your appetite. You think to yourself, I'll just have half. But even half-cookies contain calories.

"Shape Up America" is different from other diet and exercise programs. We try to make exercise easy and incremental…simply lose a few pounds, be a bit more active and help someone else do the same.

Source: C. Everett Koop, MD, former Surgeon General of the United States. He is now a professor of medicine and surgery at Dartmouth Medical School and a senior scholar at the C. Everett Koop Institute. Dr. Koop is chairman of the fitness-promotion campaign Shape Up America, which publishes the *Shape Up America Health Letter*, Box 998, Hanover, NH 03755.

7

Getting the Best Medical Care

How to Choose The Right Doctor

There's enormous variability in the quality of medical care in this country. Very often the selection of a doctor and a hospital are the most important factors in determining the outcome of an illness.

The only way to be sure that you get the best care is to get actively involved in selecting a doctor—and then monitor your treatment. This doesn't mean you have to become a doctor or scientist—just an informed consumer.

How it works with cancer…

There's enormous variation in the quality of cancer treatment in this country. This is due to the information gap between what is known and practiced at the frontiers—at the university medical centers—and what filters down to the community physician's office where most cases of cancer are diagnosed and treated.

On any given day, you can get treatment at a university center, which gives you a good chance of recovery, and another treatment at a community hospital, which gives you virtually no chance of survival.

Example: A Connecticut study analyzed the success of several different treatments for a certain form of brain cancer in children. Patients treated at a university center had a five-year survival rate of 79%. Patients treated at community hospitals had a five-year survival rate of 24%.

The same is true for cancers that require radiation therapy. The outcome depends greatly on the institution that delivers the treatment.

In addition, there are many experimental treatments available, but only to people who search them out.

Example: Senator Ted Kennedy's son developed a rare form of bone cancer. At the time, 85% of the children with that disease died within five years. But Senator Kennedy refused to accept those odds, and his son became the third child in the world to have a then-experimental treatment. He lived. Today, using that same treatment, 85% of all children who develop that cancer live.

Experimental treatments are just that—experimental. They don't always work. But when a doctor says there's no more that can be done, he/she means there's no more he can do. At that point you have to make an effort to see if there's any research going on anywhere.

For the latest cancer treatments: Call the National Cancer Institute (800-4-CANCER) and ask for a copy of the Physicians Data Query (PDQ). This free service will alert you to experimental treatments that you may be eligible for.

Searching for excellence...

Cancer is an extreme example of how the difference between mediocre treatment and the best treatment can mean the difference between life and death. The same applies in all areas of medicine.

You also need the best...

•Family doctor. Here you're not looking for someone to treat a life-threatening illness, but for someone who's responsible for health maintenance over a long period of time.

Before you decide on a doctor, meet with him for a personal interview. *Important questions to ask:*

•What is your training?

•Are you certified by the American Medical Association (AMA)?

•Is this an individual practice, or are you a member of a group? How many physicians are in the group?

•Will I be able to see the same doctor every time I have a scheduled appointment?

•Who covers at night, on weekends and during vacations?

•How much can be done at this office—is it one-stop shopping?

•Can the rest of my family be treated here?

•Will you accept my insurance coverage as payment in full, or do I have to pay additionally?

•How long are the appointments and will they be kept on time?

After the interview, ask yourself:

•Did the doctor try to make me feel comfortable?

•Does he seem to have the quality of judgment to know when he's done all he can...and send me to a specialist?

•Specialist. Get a recommendation from your family doctor, but find out what it's based on. Many family physicians will just refer you to the doctors they've dealt with for years.

Also, call the nearest university center to get its recommendations.

At least make sure that the specialist is certified by the AMA. And find out how much of his practice is devoted to his specialty. *Trap:* In major cities where there are too many doctors and too few patients, specialists often have a general practice as well. *Better:* A doctor who spends all of his time on his specialty.

•Surgeon. The success of surgery varies enormously with each surgeon.

Example: The death rate from coronary bypass surgery ranges from 20% to 1%, depending on the surgeon who performs it.

To get a good surgeon: Check with the nearest university center for the best surgeons for your problem. Make sure the surgeon has performed the operation many times in the past year. Then ask how his track record compares with the national average.

Sometimes you have to be willing to travel to a university center outside your geographic area for the best surgeon. This is necessary for a complex problem where the procedure is performed infrequently, and only a few surgeons in the country specialize in it.

•Hospital. Mortality rates not only vary according to who performs an operation, but also according to where it's performed.

The federal government publishes mortality rates based on Medicare patients in a number of hospitals. *If you can't find out the rate from your hospital:* Call the Health Standards and Quality Bureau (410-966-8980) or the nearest regional office of the Department of Health and Human Services and get information from them.

Helpful development: Hospitals are starting to compete for patients due to empty beds. This can work to your advantage.

Example: The Eisenhower Medical Center in Palm Springs, California, took out an ad in *The Wall Street Journal* promoting the fact that they have the lowest death rate in the country for open-heart surgery.

Source: Lawrence C. Horowitz, MD, former director of the US Senate Subcommittee on Health, and medical consultant to several of the largest corporations in America.

Choosing a Doctor Made Easier... But Not Easy

If you think the smartest way to pick a family doctor is to obtain referrals from friends or coworkers, think again. No matter how good their intentions, your friends and coworkers are poorly equipped to evaluate a doctor's medical skills.

After all, a first-rate doctor might be poorly regarded by patients simply because he/she occasionally seemed brusque or uncaring. Or, a doctor with only marginal skills might come highly recommended just because he/she has a very pleasant waiting room or a genial bedside manner.

And—a doctor who is ideal for one patient might be wholly inappropriate for another. Doctors are "good" only if they meet your individual needs.

First step...

The most effective way to find a new internist or family doctor (as opposed to a specialist) is to work backward—that is, consider your own medical needs first.

•Think about what particular area of expertise would be of greatest value. This criterion should be based on your age, sex, medical risk factors and medical history.

Example I: A generally healthy person might want to pick a doctor who is board-certified in one of the four key primary-care specialties: Internal medicine, family practice, pediatrics or gynecology.

Example II: A person who has existing health problems, or who is at risk for such problems, might want to choose someone who specializes in treating those problems.

•Determine which hospital in your area is best suited to provide this care. In most large communities, this will be a university-affiliated teaching hospital, one with hundreds of beds, sophisticated diagnostic equipment and a large staff of doctors, nurses and medical specialists. (Such hospitals are sometimes called "tertiary" hospitals, because they accept referrals of difficult or unusual cases.)

Even better: A "sentinel" hospital, such as Massachusetts General Hospital in Boston, the Mayo Clinic in Rochester, Minnesota or Memorial Sloan-Kettering Cancer Center in New York City. These institutions have a range of top-notch doctors on staff and excellent facilities. They can provide you with superb medical care —or refer you to a top-quality doctor and/or hospital in your area.

Problem: Small hospitals with fewer than 100 beds, especially those in rural areas. These are often limited in the type of care they are able to provide.

•Once you've chosen a hospital, call the appropriate department there and ask to speak to the department chief or head nurse. Explain your situation, then request the names of several board-certified doctors who might be willing to take you on as a patient. Contact each doctor and set up a brief interview, by phone or in person.

Sizing up a doctor...

Because the doctors whose names you've obtained were recommended by experts and are affiliated with a first-rate hospital, they've already been screened. So even the "worst" doctor on the list is no doubt perfectly competent. Nevertheless, the interview gives you a chance to find the best one for your needs. Things to consider...

•Credentials. Though a diploma from a prestigious medical school is no guarantee of stellar medical skills, it can be reassuring. So is having completed a fellowship at a distinguished institution.

Note: If the doctor has been practicing for a decade or longer, find out whether he has been recertified. Seventeen of the 23 boards of internal medicine nationwide now periodically recertify their members. While recertification is not mandatory—nor is it a definitive indication of a doctor's ability or quality, one way or the other—it shows that he cared enough to have it done.

•Professionalism. In most states it's virtually impossible to find out if a particular doctor has ever been officially sanctioned for misconduct …but it doesn't hurt to call your state medical board to ask.

•Personality. Some patients like a tough, authoritarian doctor who tells them what to do and makes sure that they do it. Others prefer a doctor who is willing to make medical decisions jointly with patients.

Opportunity: Make sure the doctor is basically optimistic. Pessimism robs patients of hope—and hope is sometimes the only thing that pulls a person through a life-threatening illness or injury.

•Humility. No matter how vast his medical knowledge and experience, every doctor eventually confronts an ailment for which he has no solution. In such cases the doctor should be humble enough to admit his own uncertainty …and should help "quarterback" patients' exploration of alternative treatments.

Tragic: I've seen too many patients get outdated or even dangerous care simply because their doctors had grown so accustomed to one particular form of treatment that they were unwilling even to consider newer, better forms of treatment. Find out what approach the doctor would take if you developed an incurable ailment.

•Experience. All other things being equal, the best doctors generally are those who have the most experience in treating the sorts of medical problems that you're most likely to develop. Ask the doctor if he treats many patients whose circumstances are similar to your own.

•Clout. A good doctor makes sure his/her patients get the treatment they need when they need it. If you have a heart attack, for instance, you need more than a good cardiologist. You need a good cardiologist capable of immediately summoning the best cardiac surgeons and lining up a bed in a first-rate cardiac intensive care unit. Ask the doctor to describe what would happen if you had a such a medical crisis.

•HMOs: If you belong to a health-maintenance organization (HMO) or managed health-care plan, your options will be more limited. But the same principles still apply. Choose an HMO on the strength of the doctors and hospitals it permits you to use—not because it's conveniently located or inexpensive, or because it pays for comparative "frills" like eyeglasses or dental care.

Source: Robert Arnot, MD, chief medical editor of the CBS Evening News, New York City. He is the author of *The Best Medicine: How to Choose the Top Doctors, the Top Hospitals, and the Top Treatments.* Addison-Wesley, Jacob Way, Reading, Massachusetts 01867.

The Not-So-Secret Secrets Of Much Better Health

People who seek out a doctor only after a medical problem surfaces are missing an important point about good medical care—that is, a congenial, ongoing relationship with your primary doctor affords several key benefits. *Most important…*

•Quick answers to medical questions. Such a relationship gives you someone to call in case of a medical emergency or, important too, if a simple problem or question arises. It's psychologically easier to call a doctor to discuss a problem if he/she already knows you. And a doctor familiar with your medical history can give sound medical advice—and give it fast—with greater confidence than a doctor who comes to your case "cold."

•Individualized treatment. Any competent doctor knows the importance of taking a good medical history. But only a doctor familiar with your social and behavioral patterns as well as the specifics of your medical chart can individualize treatments for you. Individualized treatment means not only avoiding unpleasant or needlessly aggressive treatments, but also getting treatments that are more effective and convenient.

Example I: Because of the slight risk of barotrauma (pressure-related injury) to the ear, patients with ear congestion are usually told to avoid air travel. But a doctor familiar with a patient might be able to help a sufferer take the slight risk and take steps to enable him/her to fly, including possibly a short course of powerful anti-inflammatory steroids.

Example II: Some people with basically normal blood pressure are vulnerable to "white coat" hypertension. This condition, in which the anxiety of visiting the doctor causes a transient rise in blood pressure, is essentially harmless. A doctor who knows a particular patient is susceptible can easily make arrangements for testing to be done in a nonclinical setting. But a doctor unaware of this susceptibility might needlessly prescribe antihypertensive drugs.

•Reduced anxiety. One of the most important things that a doctor does is reassure patients when medical problems strike. A doctor who has seen you through previous medical problems will be reassuring when new problems arise. Visiting a "new" doctor typically produces a great deal of anxiety—even in the absence of a serious medical problem.

•Fewer missed diagnoses. A doctor who has treated you for years is better able to spot subtle, yet often significant, changes in your appearance and health. What's appropriate for one patient might suggest a serious problem in another—even if these results fall within "normal" ranges.

Examples: A patient whose white blood cell count has for years hovered around 4,500 cells per deciliter suddenly turns up with a count of 9,000. Because 9,000 is within "normal" range, a doctor new to this patient might give a clean bill of health. But a doctor who knew the cell count was out of line with previous counts would suspect trouble—perhaps leukemia—and could order additional tests to determine the problem. Conversely, a patient with a chronically enlarged pupil who suffers head trauma would quickly wind up getting a CAT scan or some other anxiety-provoking diagnostic test...unless the doctor knew the enlarged pupil was a pre-existing and harmless condition.

•More effective counseling. A doctor who knows you is more effective at persuading you to make good decisions regarding your diet, use of alcohol, tobacco and other drugs, and ways to cope with anxiety. Also, such a doctor is more helpful in times of personal upheaval, such as the loss of a job or the dissolution of an important relationship.

•Earlier intervention. Many family physicians are now making available to their patients quick, convenient medical tests—blood pressure tests, throat cultures, Pap smears, mammography and screenings for colon and testicular cancer. Patients in close contact with a primary physician are more apt to have problems diagnosed—and treated—at the earliest possible moment.

Source: Bruce Yaffe, MD, an eminent internist and gastroenterologist in private practice in New York City.

Beware of Faked Diseases

Nearly all of us have faked an illness at least once—as children or adults—claiming a sore throat to stay home from school or calling the boss with phony sniffles to request a sick day.

This kind of deception may be irresponsible, but it certainly isn't pathological—and the consequences are usually minor.

But some people carry this behavior to extremes. They take elaborate steps to fake illness—even going so far as to make themselves sick— just to reap the emotional rewards of the sick role, such as attention and nurturing. These people suffer from what psychiatrists call factitious disorders—those produced by human rather than natural forces.

Malingerers usually deceive for material gain —disability payments or prescriptions for narcotics. But people with factitious disorders find sickness itself gratifying.

Factitious disorders are not the same as hypochondria. Hypochondriacs really believe themselves to be ill, whereas people with factitious disorders know perfectly well that they are engineering their own illnesses.

Those who make faked illness the focus of their lives have an even more serious psychological disorder called Munchausen's syndrome. People suffering from Munchausen's may take such gruesome measures as injecting themselves with dirt or feces, drawing their own blood or undergoing unnecessary surgery.

Some even die as a result of their efforts to fake or induce illness.

When correctly diagnosed, factitious disorders can sometimes be treated successfully by mental health professionals. Unfortunately, most of these fakers aren't discovered—they're too good at what they do.

Surprise: A high proportion of factitious disorder patients are health-care professionals, with sophisticated knowledge and access to drugs and procedures that enable them to mimic symptoms quite convincingly.

If confronted with evidence of deception, people with factitious disorders typically deny it —often by abruptly checking out of the hospital or leaving town for a new city or country where no one knows them—and begin the cycle all over again.

The numbers…

Data on this subject are hard to come by, but studies suggest that roughly 1% of hospitalized patients for whom psychiatrists are consulted have factitious disorders. The actual number is probably much greater.

Based on my own experience studying and treating these conditions, I'd guess that every midsized to large hospital has at least one such patient at any given time.

In addition to the personal toll, the cost to the health-care system is enormous. Over a lifetime, one "fake" patient can run up millions of dollars in medical bills.

Why people make themselves sick…

As bizarre as their behavior may seem, many of these fakers have compelling reasons for what they do. Some feel this is the only way they'll get others to care about them. Some were abused as children…and as adults, they abuse themselves. Some simply delight in duping doctors or are excited by the plotting and secrecy involved.

Usually, however, their bizarre actions are a desperate cry for help…so they can learn healthier ways of getting attention from others.

Strange cases of self-induced illness…

• A nurse checked into the hospital with a dangerously low blood count, spontaneous bleeding, weakness and other symptoms of aplastic anemia—a dangerous condition that occurs when the bone marrow doesn't generate enough blood cells.

Close to death, she needed a transfusion of platelets—a very expensive procedure. The woman was discovered to be secretly taking methotrexate, a drug used in cancer chemotherapy. When confronted, she claimed that a friend had given it to her to build up her blood. (As a nurse, she obviously knew better.)

She demanded more tests, but the medical staff refused to perform them. When she was also found to be hoarding a narcotic painkiller, she was discharged. A few weeks later, she called from another hospital and told her former doctor, "I fooled these people—they're doing all the tests you would not do."

• A security guard showed up in a Kentucky emergency room complaining of strange nodules under her skin.

She went into the bathroom but never came out…and was found dead, surrounded by syringes and bags of yeast. Apparently, she had created the nodules by injecting yeast and other substances. This time, some of the yeast entered her bloodstream and formed a fatal blood clot.

Faking by proxy…

An even more insidious form of factitious disease is Munchausen's by proxy—in which someone induces symptoms in another person, often a child. Many of the perpetrators were themselves victims of child abuse. Others probably seek the sense of martyrdom and heroism that comes from coping with a chronically ill child…or from pretending to save someone else's life. Sadly, Munchausen's by proxy is fatal to a terribly high proportion of its victims—nearly one in 10.

What can be done?

We are beginning to understand more about factitious disorders and how to treat them. One of my more encouraging experiences was with a patient I'll call Jenny—a 35-year-old secretary who convinced her family, friends and colleagues that she had terminal breast cancer.

Though she didn't actually seek medical help, she dieted and lost 40 pounds…shaved her head to simulate hair loss…and even joined a cancer support group. The deception came to light when the group leaders reviewed her medical records and found that the doctors she'd listed either didn't exist or had never heard of her.

As it turned out, Jenny had been severely depressed after breaking up with her fiancé several years earlier. The outpouring of sympathy she'd gotten by faking cancer had helped to relieve her feelings of abandonment and isolation. Jenny and I focused on alleviating her depression through antidepressant medication and psychotherapy. We also worked to develop her skills for coping with anxiety and stress. Eventually, Jenny was able to resume a healthy life.

Despite success stories like Jenny's, psychologists and psychiatrists are only beginning to learn how to diagnose and treat factitious disorders. Offering emotional help and acceptance to these patients seems to be the most effective approach.

In the meantime, families, friends and others must learn that they're not alone in feeling frustrated and betrayed by the behavior of the pseudo-patients who have accepted their care. As more doctors come to recognize and understand these disorders, we hope to help even more people who are directly or indirectly affected.

Source: Marc D. Feldman, MD, medical director, Center for Psychiatric Medicine, University of Alabama School of Medicine, Birmingham. An expert on factitious disorders, Dr. Feldman is coauthor of *Patient or Pretender: Inside the Strange World of Factitious Disorders*, John Wiley & Sons, 605 Third Ave., New York 10158.

Diagnose Your Doctor

Asking your doctor questions is an important way to ensure good care.

Questions to ask about…

Doctor's background:

• What medical schools did you attend? Do you have any special accreditations?

• What hospitals are you affiliated with?

• What is your fee schedule?

• Can I reach you between office visits?

Recommended treatment:

• How does the treatment work?

• Are there other treatment options?

Medication:

• Exactly what dosage should I take, at which times of day?

• What are the possible side effects? If I experience any, what should I do?

• Will the medication interact negatively with alcohol or other drugs?

Source: Arthur R. Pell, PhD, author of 35 books on health and human resources management including *Diagnosing Your Doctor*, DCI/Chronimed Publishing, Box 47945, Minneapolis 55447.

How to Evaluate Your Doctor

The single most important element in good medical care is an intelligent, well-trained physician who treats his/her patients with courtesy and respect. If you're unhappy with the level of care provided by your doctor, or if you're unhappy about your doctor's attitude toward you, it's time to find someone better. *Important:* You are a consumer of medical care in just the same way you are a consumer of light bulbs, telephone service, lawn care, etc. *Never put up with a physician who…*

…doesn't answer *all* of your questions. A recent study showed that physicians listen to their patients an average of only 18 seconds before interrupting. Good doctors, however, answer patiently and without condescension all questions put to them—no matter how irrelevant or naive the questions might seem. If you've been leaving your doctor's office feeling confused, you're not receiving good medical care.

Remedy: Before making your next appointment, jot down all your questions. Estimate how long it will take your doctor to answer them, and make an appointment for that span of time—even if you'll have to pay more for the extra attention. Take the list and a watch to your appointment. Stay until all your questions have been answered. If your time runs out before you're done, *make another appointment.* If your doctor refuses to cooperate with such an arrangement, seek medical care elsewhere.

…uses too much jargon. Your doctor should be able to explain in plain English all the factors underlying a particular diagnosis or course of treatment. Your doctor should also be able to tell you with some degree of specificity how long a particular treatment should take to begin to work.

…makes you wait for appointments. The recent push to hold down medical costs has led many doctors to squeeze more patient appointments into each day. *Result:* Long waiting room stays. Of course, emergencies do arise, and an occasional delay in getting in to see the doctor is inevitable. But if your doctor is chronically behind schedule, you're being exploited.

…lacks proper credentials. While a general practitioner might be able to treat a sore throat or stitch up a laceration, thornier medical problems call for the training of a physician who is board-certified in a specific area. If your ailment isn't responding to the treatment given by your doctor, seek a specialist certified by one of the national specialty boards.

…relies too much on support staff. In a growing number of doctors' offices, a nurse takes the patient's medical history and conducts preliminary examinations. Doctors whose offices run along these lines are saving time for themselves at the expense of their patients. Capable as they are, nurses are not physicians—they sometimes miss things.

Better way: The nurse might make a brief notation about the patient's condition, but the physician should set aside the time to take patients' medical histories and to conduct all exams.

…belittles your wishes to seek a second opinion—or explore alternative forms of treatment. A good doctor not only welcomes second opinions (especially when the condition of the patient seeking the second opinion is not improving), but is a source of information about where to get one. Don't let your doctor dissuade you from seeking other opinions. Likewise with alternative therapies—a good doctor is at least willing to discuss other forms of treatment, no matter how extreme.

…places too much faith in medical tests. Arriving at an accurate diagnosis is like putting together the pieces of a jigsaw puzzle…and a medical test is only one piece of the puzzle. A good doctor realizes that even the most accurate medical test occasionally gives spurious results—*false positives* when there is no problem, *false negatives* when there is one. For this reason, doctors should always confirm test results with other pieces of evidence—physical exam, detailed medical history, the patient's specific symptoms, etc.

…fails to take complaints seriously. A doctor should always take a patient's medical complaints seriously, no matter how vague or unusual they seem.

Source: Stephen Astor, MD, an allergist in private practice in Mountain View, California and the author of *Take Charge of Your Health*, Two A's Industries, 285 South Dr., Mountain View, California 94040. A former instructor at Stanford University Medical Center and the University of California Medical Center in San Francisco, Dr. Astor is currently affiliated with El Camino Hospital in Mountain View.

How to Protect Yourself Against Disease Mongering

When it comes to treating cancer, heart disease, severe trauma and other life-threatening ailments, the American health-care system is second to none. Our doctors are highly trained, our drugs carefully screened, our hospitals chockablock with sophisticated medical equipment.

Still, it pays to remember that a desire to aid the afflicted isn't the only motive driving our health-care system. *Also at work:* A powerful and unrelenting urge to maximize profits.

In order to remain in business, doctors, hospitals, diagnostic facilities, drug and medical equipment makers, insurance companies and other recipients of our health-care dollars all need one thing—patients with health insurance. The greater their number, the sicker they are, the more drugs they take, the more tests they undergo…the bigger the industry's profits.

Problem: To get more patients, the health-care industry often resorts to an insidious form of exploitation known as *disease-mongering.*

Disease-mongering takes many forms...

•It's the surgeon who insists upon treating a minor heart ailment with costly and often risky bypass surgery—just to earn more money.

•It's the drug maker that uses manipulative ads to portray the common cold as a debilitating ailment in need of drug therapy.

•It's the diagnostic clinic that sells mammograms even to women for whom there's no evidence that they work.

•It's also the medical journalist who earns his keep by hyping minor illnesses as plagues.

No matter what form disease-mongering takes, however, the result never varies—*healthy people are led to believe they're ill or at risk of becoming ill...and persons suffering from minor ailments are led to believe they're seriously ill.*

The health-care industry knows that once we're instilled with fear, we'll take action—scheduling costly medical checkups and diagnostic tests at the merest hint of trouble...using cold remedies, painkillers and other drugs for conditions that clear up even without treatment ...gobbling prescription drugs with nasty and potentially harmful side effects...and submitting to surgery that is risky and of questionable benefit.

Watch out for trouble...

•Manipulative ads. Television, newspapers and magazines are filled with ads for sinus remedies, arthritis pills, headache relievers—and, of course, even baldness cures.

The more often we encounter these ads, the more firmly we're convinced that we need the products they promote. *Reality:* Minor aches and pains, as well as occasional cold or flu symptoms, are a normal part of life. There's no good reason to visit the drugstore every time you sneeze.

To avoid being manipulated: Each time you choose to read a health ad, ask yourself who really stands to benefit from its message—you or the makers of the product. Are there alternatives? What would happen if you took no action? *Use only those products truly beneficial to you.*

•"Man-made" diseases. While there's no doubt that broken bones and heart attacks need prompt treatment, not all medical conditions require treatment.

Example: Mild hypertension. The cutoff between "normal" and "high" blood pressure has been set arbitrarily low in this country—as a result, inflating the ranks of the "ill" and maximizing the profit potential for doctors and companies selling antihypertensive drugs. In fact, a blood pressure reading treated in this country with an aggressive drug regimen might be considered normal in England.

Blood pressure isn't the only such "man-made" disease. Elevated cholesterol level is considered a heart disease risk factor—and rightly so. But often even mildly elevated cholesterol is treated as a disease in its own right. *Result:* People who feel perfectly fine are urged to take harsh and costly drugs, even though evidence of their value is controversial.

And in an effort to sell more estrogen, drug makers are now trying to turn menopause from a natural process into a deficiency disease that needs treatment. The list goes on and on.

To avoid trouble: If a doctor says you're at risk for or already have a particular disease and urges aggressive treatment, follow the advice only if there's solid evidence that the treatment will cut your risk. Get a second opinion, and do your own research.

•Needless diagnostic tests. Doctors order far too many diagnostic tests. Each time you have a mammogram, stress test, cholesterol test, AIDS test, etc., *you're taking a risk.* Not only that you'll hear bad news, but your test results could be wrong. The test might indicate you're okay when you're really sick, for instance, or that you're sick when you're healthy.

Danger: A "false positive" causes not only needless anxiety, but also labels you as "sick" and thereby jeopardizes your insurability. It can even lead you to seek risky treatments.

Example: There have been cases in which people died during heart surgery scheduled after stress tests mistakenly indicated that they had heart disease. Similarly, mammograms are often urged for women under 40—even though young breasts are usually too dense for accurate X-ray readings.

To avoid trouble: For anyone already at reasonably high risk for a particular condition, the potential benefits of being tested generally outweigh the risk of inaccurate results. But if your risk for the ailment is very low, avoid being tested. Ask your doctor to explain your level of risk when making the decision.

Make sure the doctors with whom you discuss your case have no financial stake in performing the test.

Scandalous: Though the conflict of interest in such an arrangement is obvious, many doctors now own their own CT scanners, MRI scanners and other diagnostic equipment. The more tests they schedule, the more money they make.

•Free screening clinics. These days, free screening is being offered for everything from prostate cancer to high blood pressure. It sounds like a good idea. But in many cases these clinics are set up to bring in more patients…and are more beneficial to their sponsors than to the general public.

Problem: Unreliable readings. Some serious medical problems are missed entirely, while problems are diagnosed in persons who are actually perfectly healthy.

To avoid trouble: Be tested in a doctor's office or a diagnostic facility specializing in medical tests. Make sure the person who interprets the test results is highly experienced.

•Needless surgery. A surprisingly large percentage of operations in this country are performed needlessly—up to 25% by some respectful estimates. Certain procedures are especially likely to be performed inappropriately, including hysterectomy, back surgery, caesarean sections and bypass surgery. *Result:* Needless expense, discomfort and even the risk of fatal complications—all because a surgeon was eager to operate.

To avoid trouble: Always get a second opinion before agreeing to surgery. Many problems frequently treated with surgery can be resolved more cheaply and safely via exercise, changes in diet, physical therapy and other nonsurgical methods.

•Overbearing doctors. Americans tend to be much more deferential toward doctors than toward lawyers, accountants and other professionals we employ—and doctors rarely do anything to stop us.

Explanation: Most of us started seeing doctors when we were kids, and we still behave like kids in the presence of them.

Better way: Instead of blindly accepting your doctor's advice, make it a point to discuss all your available options.

Helpful: Calling your doctor by his/her first name—especially if the doctor calls you by yours. Doing so reminds you that you're on an equal footing with one another—that you're hiring the doctor, not the other way around.

•Overly aggressive treatment. Every good doctor knows that too much medical care is just as deleterious as too little. Unfortunately, patients often demand aggressive treatment.

Problem: While such treatment might be warranted for serious ailments, most conditions do just as well with minimal or no treatment. In fact, few medical conditions call for urgent intervention of any kind.

Certainly you should see a doctor right away for obvious injuries, severe pain or high fever. In many cases, however, it's not only safe to wait a few weeks before seeking medical care, *it's the smartest course of action.*

Reason: Many conditions improve or disappear without treatment, saving you money, aggravation and more.

Source: Lynn Payer, former editor of *The New York Times Good Health Magazine* and author of several books on medical topics, including *Disease-Mongers: How Doctors, Drug Companies, and Insurers Are Making You Feel Sick,* John Wiley & Sons, 605 Third Ave., New York 10158.

How to Cut Through Medical Mysteries That Your Doctor Can't Solve

In this age of modern medical technology, we sometimes expect our doctors to be able to accurately diagnose and successfully treat every single disease. But no doctor is always right. Many people spend years suffering from ailments that have defied the efforts of even highly trained medical specialists.

Doctors have particular trouble dealing with ailments whose symptoms fail to "add up" to a known disease. Show up at the emergency room with a broken leg or a heart attack, and odds are strong that you'll get prompt, professional treatment. Show up complaining of fatigue or vague aches and pains, though, and you'll probably have problems. *Reason:* Most doctors like to "cookbook" their way through their cases. If you don't fit the recipe, the doctor has no idea of what to make of you or your ailment.

If your physician seems unable to solve your particular ailment, don't hesitate to seek out a second opinion—or even a third…or fourth opinion.

Many commonly misdiagnosed and mistreated ailments are controllable—if you find a physician willing to make the effort.

Crucial: A willingness to consider all the possible causes of an ailment, not just the usual causes.

Commonly misdiagnosed ailments…

• Chest pain. Chest pain that cannot be linked to heart disease or some other familiar cause is often put down to a bad case of the "nerves."

But good doctors realize that once heart disease is ruled out, there remain several other possible culprits for the pain. They include spasms of the chest muscles and—more common—gastroesophageal reflux. This condition results when stomach acid splashes upward into the esophagus. It can cause pain that closely resembles that caused by heart disease.

However, unlike most chest pain caused by heart disease, pain from gastroesophageal reflux is not made worse by exertion. Gastroesophageal reflux is usually made worse by a big meal, while heart pain is only occasionally linked to eating. Eating less and avoiding aspirin and other medications that irritate the stomach are often effective against gastroesophageal reflux, as is keeping the head elevated during sleep.

• Fatigue. Many different ailments, from anxiety disorder to parasitic infections, can cause chronic fatigue. Doctors are usually quite adept at treating fatigue that can be linked to one of these ailments.

But doctors unable to pinpoint an underlying cause are too eager to blame fatigue on stress, depression or another psychological problem. In such cases, another possible culprit—chronic fatigue syndrome (CFS)—is frequently overlooked.

Once thought by many to be merely a "fad" disease, CFS is now broadly recognized as a real and often debilitating ailment. Yet only a minority of doctors are adept at diagnosing and treating it. Unlike most other forms of fatigue, CFS is often accompanied by flu-like aches and pains, sore throat, mental "slowing" and other vague symptoms. CFS fatigue is typically made worse by exercise. Other forms of fatigue are little affected by exercise.

While there is no "magic bullet" for treating CFS, many drugs are effective at treating its symptoms.

Key: Finding a physician willing to work with you to keep your symptoms in check. In most cases, CFS disappears spontaneously after two and a half to three years.

• Headache. Many so-called "stress" headaches are really caused by muscular fatigue stemming from nighttime clenching of the teeth (bruxism)…or by chronic tension in the muscles at the base of the neck (trapezius muscles). Unfortunately, few doctors ever take the time to examine these muscles, so many patients wind up taking drugs when behavioral therapy aimed at reducing stress would be far more beneficial for them.

Alternate treatments: In some cases, these headaches may also be relieved by treating the affected muscles with massage, electrical stimulation, or even injections of saline solution or by a combination of these treatments.

• Impotence. At one time, doctors thought that nine out of every 10 cases of impotence were psychogenic—caused by psychological factors, including depression and anxiety. Now we know that only about half of all cases are psychogenic. The other half are caused by specific physiological (organic) problems, including poor blood circulation in the penis.

Problem: Many men suffering from organic impotence are treated as if they have psychogenic impotence. These men waste time in psychotherapy or taking mood-altering drugs when their problem could be quickly and easily treated with minor surgery or with other, appropriate drugs.

Bottom line: Any man suffering from impotence should make sure his physician considers both possible causes before accepting treatment.

• Sleepiness. Daytime sleepiness not caused by insomnia is often blamed on depression or emotional stress, and is often treated with sleeping pills. In fact, many people troubled by daytime sleepiness are really suffering from sleep apnea. That is a condition in which sleep is disrupted scores or even hundreds of times nightly —and which cannot be controlled by sleeping pills.

Sleep apnea strikes all kinds of people but is most common among obese men who snore heavily.

Mechanism: Loose tissue inside the throat sags during sleep, eventually pressing upon and blocking the windpipe, disrupting breathing and causing the person to wake up.

In many cases, a sleep apnea sufferer's bed partner is well aware of these waking episodes —and may be instrumental in helping with the diagnosis.

Caution: Sleep apnea is more than an annoyance. It can cause fatal heart irregularities. Anyone suffering from unexplained drowsiness should suspect this condition. There are many effective methods of treating it.

• Sore throat. Doctors often treat a sore throat as if strep throat were the only possible cause. In fact, there are many other potential causes, and the antibiotics that are so effective against strep do nothing to control them. *Other possibilities:* Mononucleosis, tonsillitis, chlamydia, chronic fatigue syndrome, thyroid inflammation and more. In some cases, sore throat is caused by tenderness of the carotid arteries, a condition known as carotodynia.

Important: Don't take antibiotics unless your doctor has ruled out other possibilities. Insist that the true cause of the sore throat be found before you accept treatment.

Source: Jay A. Goldstein, MD, founding director of the Chronic Fatigue Syndrome Institute and author of *Could Your Doctor Be Wrong?*, Pharos Books, 200 Park Ave., New York 10166. Dr. Goldstein has residency training in both psychiatry and family medicine. He practices in Anaheim, California.

Questions to Ask a General Practitioner

With specialists playing ever-expanding roles in modern health care, the importance of your primary physician—the doctor you call first when illness or injury strikes—is too often diminished. To find a family doctor you trust, start by asking your friends and coworkers whom they recommend. Don't stop, though, until you've gotten satisfactory answers to these critical questions…

Is the doctor dedicated to primary care? Choose a physician whose practice is devoted primarily or exclusively to primary care.

Is the doctor willing to discuss medical problems by telephone? The more willing a doctor is to consult with patients by telephone, the less the need for unnecessary—and often expensive—office visits.

Is the doctor on time? Steer clear of physicians who routinely run well behind schedule. Ask the doctor's patients about how long they typically wait to be seen.

Is the support staff helpful and organized? The receptionist should convey information to the doctor promptly and accurately—and should be able to get the doctor on the phone in case of an emergency.

With which hospital is the doctor affiliated? The hospital should have a good reputation for patient care and comfort.

What does the doctor charge? Fees and payment options vary widely. Ask about fees for a routine office visit, a telephone consultation and a thorough exam.

How comfortable are you with the doctor? This is the most crucial issue. Doctors should not only listen carefully to the patient's concerns, but should also demonstrate genuine caring. If you have trouble communicating with the doctor, or if you simply don't like him/her, find someone else.

Source: Bruce Yaffe, MD, an internist in private practice in New York City.

How to Get the Most From Your Pharmacist

A good pharmacist not only dispenses drugs but also serves as a source of accurate, up-to-date information on drug-related topics. To get the most from your pharmacist...

Ask the right questions...

• *What is the name of the drug, and what does it do?* Find out the brand names and generic names of all the drugs you take, prescription and nonprescription.

• *When and how do I take it?* Failing to take a drug precisely as prescribed may result in incomplete treatment. Ask: *Should the drug be taken during the day or at bedtime? Should it be taken on an empty stomach or with food? Must alcohol, certain foods or activities be avoided while taking the drug?*

• *How long must I take it?* Going off a drug too early may limit its effectiveness. Continuing to take a drug for too long a period may cause undesirable side effects.

• *Does this drug contain anything to which I am allergic?* Your pharmacist should have your entire medical history, including information about allergies you have to certain drugs.

• *What are the side effects of this drug?* A good pharmacist explains in detail the drug's potential side effects—and how to minimize them.

• *Is there a generic version of this drug?* In many cases an equally effective—and less costly—generic version of your drug is available. In other cases, it's possible to save on prescription costs by buying in bulk or by switching to a different formulation of the same drug.

Caution: Certain drugs should never be bought generically. *Example:* Drugs that need to achieve a very definite blood level to work properly, or that are used to treat unstable chronic conditions, such as cardiac problems or seizure disorders. *Also:* Brand and generic sustained-release drugs may work differently.

• *How should this drug be stored?* Certain medications lose their potency quickly if stored improperly. Ask about the best way to store your particular medication.

Source: Curt Barr, PharmD. He is a member of the pharmacy faculty of Creighton University, Omaha, Nebraska. Dr. Barr also owns and operates Barr Health Mart in Blair, Nebraska.

How to Stand Up for Your Rights as a Patient

It's important for us all to take a more active role in our own medical treatment to insure getting the most appropriate care.

In medicine, information is power. Before you consent to any procedure, you have the right to know what that procedure is, its risks and benefits, its cost, what the alternatives are and the doctor's success rate with the procedure.

Important: Take advantage of your right to get a *second opinion* before agreeing to surgery. No doctor worthy of the title should object. The process will let you in on a secret known to all doctors but few lay people: There's *no universal agreement* on how to treat specific conditions. What one doctor thinks is the best treatment, another may think is the worst.

Your medical records...

Your records are confidential, but in the average teaching hospital, a patient's chart is available to be seen by at least 125 people in one day—three shifts of nurses, doctors, medical students, technicians and insurance personnel. It's the job of many of them to add to your medical records. But—when so many people have access, human error is inevitable. The standard error rate on medical records runs 3%–10%.

Imperative: Take advantage of your right to your medical records. Find out exactly what the medical profession knows about you and make sure the information they have is accurate.

The consent form...

Before undergoing surgery, you're asked to sign a consent form. The form shouldn't contain any information that you haven't already discussed with your doctor.

If there are any clauses with which you don't agree—such as allowing pictures to be taken during surgery—cross them out and bring them to your doctor's attention.

If you're being treated at a teaching hospital, you have the right *not* to be treated by medical students if you don't wish to be. If you've chosen the hospital so a celebrity physician can perform the operation, make sure it's *that* doctor who will actually do the surgery. If you see a clause in the consent form that refers to "Dr. Celebrity *or his designee*," cross it out and be sure to have a talk with your physician.

If any type of research is to be done on you, you'll be asked to sign a separate form. You're not obligated to participate in any research… and your decision cannot prejudice your care.

Refusing treatment…

You need not accept any medical treatment you do not wish to receive. You don't have the right to *demand* a specific treatment from a doctor, but you do have the right to agree—or disagree—with his recommendation.

The right to refuse treatment is a powerful one—it even extends to artificial life support—dialysis, a respirator, artificial feeding, etc.

You can't force a doctor to *help* you die, but your request to remove life-sustaining equipment must be respected.

Crucial: Leave written instructions about your treatment, and designate, in writing, someone to act in your behalf, in case you're rendered incapable of making a competent decision yourself. Legal disputes arise when a patient has lost consciousness or is otherwise unable to make his intentions known. We don't like to think about these issues when we're healthy, but if we don't think about them then, we may not be able to influence what happens to us in the future.

You can write your own *living will*, which states your wishes regarding artificial life support, but some hospitals have refused to recognize these.

Safer: Have your lawyer draw up a *durable power of attorney* (sometimes called a *health care proxy*), giving someone you trust the power to make decisions about your medical care if you can't make them yourself…and to interpret your living will if it's ambiguous. No court has yet refused to recognize this document. Keep copies where they can be readily

accessed when needed—do *not* keep them in a safety-deposit box.

Source: George J. Annas, JD, MPH, is professor of health law at Boston University School of Medicine and Public Health.

Checking Up On the Dentist

What's harder than going to a dentist? *Finding one.* And how do you know those caps fit properly or you don't have gum disease? *You don't.*

Studies show that the way a staff treats you, how an office looks and how you click with the dentist influence your perception of the dentist's competence.

Say you've selected a dentist after asking a friend for a recommendation, calling the local dental school or using the Yellow Pages. *Now what should you do?*

First impressions…

The decor has nothing to do with the care you'll get. Great dentists sometimes work in drab or archaic offices. But neatness does count. A sloppy office can often mean sloppy care.

A pleasant *Hello* and smiling faces are positive signs, too. Being seen on time may mean only that the dentist is compulsive about time—not necessarily that she/he is compulsive about redoing an imperfect crown.

By the time you're in the chair, you should have filled out a data sheet and a health questionnaire. The dentist should review your health history, noting any condition or medication that might affect your treatment. For instance, men and women with heart valve problems, even if the problems are minor, should take antibiotics before every dental session that might cause bleeding.

Prophylactic antibiotics are also essential for those with artificial hip or knee joints, heart murmurs or a history of rheumatic fever.

Caution: It's a bad sign if the dentist ignores your medical history.

The make-or-break step: Notice how the dentist reacts when you describe the reason for your visit. Is he listening carefully? Does he ask appropriate questions about your symptoms? Does he ask what other dentists have done for you? Or request your old dental records?

Caution: If you're seeing a dentist to seek a second opinion, don't blurt out the other dentist's name—or what he prescribed for you. This information may influence the new dentist's thinking.

By now, you've glanced around the place. Federal regulations require that the drill, water syringe and X-ray head be covered with disposable plastic. If they're not, be concerned. If the dentist doesn't don latex gloves before peering into your mouth—leave. Ask about the office's sterilization procedures. Most dentists will welcome the question.

The examination…

The dental examination should include not just an evaluation of your teeth but also a check for oral cancer, a soft tissue exam, probing for periodontal pockets, X-rays and—for complicated cases—diagnostic molds of your teeth.

The consultation…

Following this exam, the dentist should be able to tell you exactly what's right and/or wrong with your mouth. If you have a complex problem, the dentist should not only address your chief complaint, but should go on to examine your mouth for other possible problems. Is the dentist open to a range of treatments? For instance, does a "bad tooth" really need to be extracted, or could a specialist save it?

If you need dental implants, make sure the dentist uses an established brand that's been in existence for at least a few years. *Problem:* With more than 40 companies now selling implants, some are almost certain to go out of business. That could make spare parts very hard to find.

Important: Ask how many implants the dentist has placed—the more experienced the dentist, the greater the likelihood that your implants will be successful.

No matter what form of treatment the dentist recommends, ask to come back for a second consultation if you have questions. Be sure to bring a friend or relative as a "second pair of ears." Also, ask the dentist to write a letter summarizing his findings if the treatment plan seems confusing.

These steps can be essential to your decision-making process. A dentist reluctant to comply is not sensitive to your needs. Successful dentistry often hinges on the dynamics between dentist and patient. Make sure you and the dentist are on the same wavelength.

Ask what the dentist would do if he had the same problem—or if his father, mother, child, etc. had the same problem. *That's when you get the best treatment.*

Does the dentist try to perform every type of procedure? Or does he make referrals to specialists when necessary? Dentists who make referrals often render better care. They know their limitations and are willing to give business to other practitioners to ensure your dental health.

Checking credentials…

Look for a dentist with a full-time practice. A faculty appointment at a local dental school sounds impressive, but it may mean that the dentist sees patients only one day a week. Full-time dentists have more time to nurture, observe and treat.

If you've been going to the same dentist for a long time, you're probably satisfied…and yet you may still be wondering if the dental care you're getting is good. After all, teeth that are pain-free aren't necessarily healthy. Gum (periodontal) disease, for example, doesn't hurt.

In fact, gum disease affects 75% of the world's population, so odds are you've got at least early signs of the disease. Your dentist should probe for spaces between the gums and the roots. Deep pockets are a sign of periodontal disease. This requires a special probe. Make sure the dentist pokes around since these pockets don't show up on X rays.

What do you do if you adore your dentist and have never had a problem but would like to make certain your mouth is in good order? Every 10 years, have another dentist examine your teeth. Tell this dentist that you're simply checking up on your primary dentist.

Seeing another dentist could detect an honest slip-up. Fresh eyes sometimes pick up on things that your regular dentist has overlooked. Should you be upset if you find a problem with your primary dentist's care? Unless it's very serious, no. Be thankful. Call it to your primary dentist's attention. Most important—keep flossing.

Source: Alan A. Winter, DDS, associate clinical professor, New York University School of Dentistry, New York City. A board-certified periodontist, he also maintains a private practice at 30 E. 60 St., New York 10022.

Answers to the Most Common Questions About Dental Care

The more you understand about teeth, the better you'll take care of them and the healthier your teeth will be—now and throughout your life.

Questions patients ask...

Will this treatment hurt? It's a myth that a trip to the dentist has to be painful. With today's anesthetic techniques and fine-gauge needles, there's no reason for patients to feel pain during most dental procedures.

Before administering a Novocaine shot, most dentists now swab the patient's gums with a numbing agent so not even the needle prick is felt. Then, Novocaine is released slowly and gently so as not to create uncomfortable pressure or pain.

Some dentists are more concerned about the pain issue than others. If you're worried, ask your dentist how he/she handles the administration of anesthesia. If you're not satisfied after your first treatment, change dentists.

Of course, patients may notice some soreness later, after the anesthetic has worn off. This discomfort can be lessened with over-the-counter or prescription pain medications.

Just having my teeth cleaned hurts. Why? If you have a great deal of exposed root surface, that area of the tooth will be quite sensitive to the scraping that occurs during a thorough cleaning. A gentle hygienist can minimize the discomfort. But if you still can't tolerate the pain, ask to have a topical anesthetic painted across the gum tissue. Extremely sensitive patients might need Novocaine prior to having their teeth cleaned.

How often should I brush my teeth? You should brush and floss, using the technique your dentist shows you, at least twice a day. *Three times is even better.*

How important is fluoride? For children, whose teeth are still forming, I recommend a fluoride rinse after brushing. Fluoride slows down the buildup of plaque and makes the teeth more resistant to decay. Fluoride can also be helpful for adults who have many cavities or very sensitive teeth.

Caution: Though fluoride is safe for rinsing, it can be toxic if swallowed. Children three years old and older can be taught to swish and spit. If your child swallows more than an ounce, call a poison control hotline immediately.

Is toothpaste enough? If you brush thoroughly, even toothpaste isn't necessary, but it can help to remove plaque and freshen breath.

I also recommend using a *prebrushing rinse* such as Plax. This type of rinse is not the same as a mouthwash. Prebrushing rinses act as surfactants (similar to the action of soap), loosening the plaque and making it easier to dislodge.

What is plaque? Plaque is the sticky substance formed when bacteria in the mouth combine with the sugars left after food is broken down. Plaque adheres to teeth, and the bacteria within it can destroy the bone mineral that makes up the tooth. This destruction is what we call a cavity.

If plaque isn't removed, it hardens into calculus (a hard substance full of bacteria that are calcified—also known as tartar) and can lead to gum disease. It can only be removed in the dentist's office with special instruments.

Do I need to worry about gum disease? Periodontal, or gum, disease is a quiet destroyer. It occurs when unchecked plaque erodes the gum and bone tissue that support teeth. Eventually, the affected teeth may have to be removed.

Signs of gum disease include puffy or bleeding gums and bad breath.

But it can progress without the patient's noticing that anything is wrong. That's why it's so important not only to brush and floss on your own, but to see the dentist regularly for a checkup and cleaning. Early detection and treatment of gum disease could save your teeth.

How often should I visit the dentist? At *least* twice a year. Your dentist may recommend more frequent visits if you have a tendency toward cavities, gum disease or other dental problems.

If I brush and floss every day, do I still have to have X-rays? Yes. All the dentist can see with the naked eye are the outer surfaces of the teeth. We can't see between teeth, where a large percentage of cavities occur...or under the bone, where gum or bone breakdown might be detected...or at the root tip, where an abscess or cyst could develop. X-rays can catch these problems before they become advanced and harder to treat.

I recommend a set of bite wing X-rays at least every 18 months, and a full set of mouth X-rays every three to five years, depending on the patient's dental health.

Are X-rays safe? The amount of radiation you receive during a dental X-ray is minimal—far less than from a chest or bone X-ray. Today's machines use *very* low doses of radiation, as well as fast films that require a shorter exposure time.

What is root canal surgery? When is it necessary? If decay progresses through the top two layers into the inner part of the tooth, the nerve tissue inside the tooth can become infected... and bacteria begin to kill off the nerve. An infected nerve can be quite painful, especially if pus from the infection drains into the bone. Like any slow, long-term infection, it can also interfere with general health.

To treat this type of decay, the dentist must clear out the dead tissue by removing the nerve, which is replaced with a rubber-like material.

How painful is this type of surgery? Despite all the cocktail party horror stories, in most cases root canal surgery is not nearly as painful as the infection that brought the patient into the office. The infected area of the mouth is numbed during the procedure itself, and if there is any soreness afterward, it can be controlled with medication.

Source: Robert S. Rauch, DDS, a dentist in private practice in Milford, Connecticut. Dr. Rauch is the author of *Smile: Be True to Your Teeth and They'll Never Be False to You,* available through his office at 91 Cherry St., Milford, Connecticut 06460.

Dubious Dentistry

The incidence of tooth decay has fallen dramatically in recent years, thanks largely to the fluoridation of the nation's water supplies. That's great news for families. But many dentists, faced with fewer cavities to fill, are looking elsewhere for income...and, too often, even well-meaning practitioners have begun pushing dental care that is unnecessary, expensive or downright fraudulent. Inappropriate dental care now costs Americans more than $1 billion a year.

Good news: A little of the right knowledge is all that's required to protect your family's health and pocketbook from inappropriate dental care. *Suspect treatments:*

•Alternate root canal therapy. Standard root canal surgery involves drilling out diseased root tissue and replacing it with an inert filler material—usually *gutta-percha.* But as many as 30,000 dentists in the U.S. and Canada rely instead on a faster, cheaper, but unsafe method, in which the root is replaced not with *gutta-percha,* but with a chemically unstable formaldehyde paste.

Danger: That paste sometimes seeps into the tissue below the tooth root, resulting in pain and disfigurement and in some cases necessitating corrective surgery. In one case, a Florida woman endured 40 additional dental procedures and the removal of part of her jawbone after bungled root canal work.

Self-protection: If you need a root canal, find a dentist or endodontist with considerable experience...and make sure he uses the standard method.

•Alternate gum disease treatment. Standard treatment for advanced periodontal disease (pyorrhea) usually involves gum surgery. Since the late 1970s, however, some dentists have relied instead on a nonsurgical technique, in which gums are examined under a microscope and then cleaned with a paste of salt, baking soda and peroxide. Many patients prefer it because it's nonsurgical—and because it costs a third of what conventional surgery costs.

Problem: There is no evidence to suggest that it is effective. For severe periodontal disease, stick to surgery.

•Inappropriate TMJ therapy. Temporomandibular joint (TMJ) disease—a legitimate ailment whose symptoms include facial pain and a stiff jaw—usually responds to simple treatments including moist heat, jaw exercise, over-the-counter anti-inflammatory drugs and a temporary soft diet. But some unscrupulous dentists seem to diagnose TMJ at every turn...and to treat it they prescribe treatments that are expensive, bizarre and often harmful.

Example: The MORA (Mandibular Orthopedic Repositioning Appliance), a plastic mouthpiece that's worn continuously for many months. It can shift the position of the teeth so markedly that patients are often forced to wear braces or have their teeth crowned just to eat and speak normally again.

If you experience chronic facial pain, consult a dentist to rule out tumors, cysts and other serious problems—then try moist heat and other simple techniques. If pain persists, you may need a neurologist rather than a dentist. Some dentists work with neurologists and other pain specialists who would also be appropriate for patients whose pain does not respond to simple reversible therapies. *Note:* Some plastic appliances are appropriate for some dental conditions. If your dentist prescribes one, make sure it covers all the teeth, and that it can be removed for eating and sleeping.

•Improper implants. When properly inserted, dental implants are safe and effective. But many dentists lack the training to perform implants successfully, in some cases getting their "expertise" from a single one-hour "video course."

Common problem: Poorly fitted implants fail to attach firmly to underlying bone, resulting in loose or painful implants. To make sure implants are appropriate for your case, and to make sure the job is done well, seek out a periodontist, oral surgeon or dentist who has completed a legitimate course (they can last several months)...and who has completed at least 50 implant procedures. Also, insist upon a Brannemark or Core-Vent implant or some other implant approved by the American Dental Association.

•Inappropriate bonding and bleaching. Bonding is terrific for improving a patient's appearance. But it is not a panacea. The teeth to be bonded should be healthy, with good gum and bone support. Bonding should not be used as a treatment for loose teeth (a symptom of periodontal disease).

Bleaching done in the dentist's office is usually safe and effective. However, unsupervised bleaching done in the patient's home has not been proven safe and thus should be avoided.

In many cases in which a dentist uses bleaching, the use of porcelain laminates would be more appropriate.

•Mercury toxicity. All major health organizations recognize the safety of silver/mercury/amalgam fillings, but some dentists are recommending that these fillings be removed and replaced with either plastic, porcelain or gold—a very profitable recommendation for these dentists.

If your dentist recommends removing your silver fillings because of the mercury in them, find another dentist. *Reason:* This is an unscientific position that can lead to extensive, unnecessary dentistry.

Source: John E. Dodes, DDS, president of the New York State chapter of the National Council Against Health Fraud and a member of the New York State Health Department Fraud Advisory Council. Dr. Dodes, who practices dentistry in Woodhaven, New York, is the author of *Dubious Dental Care*, a report on dental fraud published by the American Council on Science and Health, 1995 Broadway, 16th floor, New York 10023.

What a Good Dermatologist Does

Dermatologic emergencies are rarer than other types of medical emergencies, but as anyone who's ever suffered a sudden rash or allergic reaction knows, they're not unheard of.

For this reason, a good dermatologist is accessible 24 hours a day, seven days a week—preferably via a professional answering service (answering machines are sometimes unreliable). *Rule:* After-hours calls should be returned within four hours.

Of course, accessibility isn't the only mark of a good dermatologist. *Other considerations:*

• Proper delegation of work. As a cost-cutting measure, some dermatologists are now leaving much of their routine office work to nurses or assistants. *Problem:* Assistants may lack the training to perform these procedures safely and effectively.

I believe nurses can safely take patient histories, check blood pressure, change dressings and perform the most basic procedures, such as opening pimples and administering ultraviolet treatments.

The bulk of work, however, including chemical peels and collagen injections, should be performed by the dermatologist. You're paying for a dermatologist's expertise...don't let yourself be exploited.

• Institutional affiliation. Besides being certified by the American Board of Dermatology, first-rate dermatologists are affiliated with a medical school or major hospital—or both. Such institutional affiliations confirm that the dermatologist is a skilled practitioner, up-to-date on the latest methods of diagnosis and treatment. It also indicates that he/she is in good standing within the medical community.

Bonus: If necessary, patients of a hospital-affiliated dermatologist can often get admitted to the hospital faster and with fewer headaches than patients of an unaffiliated practitioner.

• Medical philosophy. By the time certain forms of skin cancer are detected, it is often too late—they've spread and become fatal. Therefore, it's absolutely essential that dermatologists stress preventive care.

However, simply urging patients to wear sunscreen or avoid the sun is not enough. A top-notch dermatologist listens to patients' questions, then explains all aspects of prevention—how the sun damages the skin, for example, and how best to use protective clothing and sunscreen.

As an extra precaution, your dermatologist should offer a total surface examination of your skin. Such an exam, performed periodically, catches melanoma and other dangerous lesions in their earliest stages—when treatment is still effective.

Cost: $115 to $125 (often included in the price of a routine office visit). *Note:* Surface exams should be performed annually on adults with especially fair skin, every three years or so on those with darker skin. Your dermatologist should suggest what's most appropriate for you.

• Cost-consciousness. Like most doctors, dermatologists receive free drug samples from pharmaceutical salespeople. A thoughtful practitioner passes these samples along to patients, saving patients the needless expense and aggravation of filling their own prescriptions.

Source: Neal B. Schultz, MD, a dermatologist in private practice in New York City. Dr. Schultz is on staff at Mt. Sinai Hospital and Lenox Hill Hospital in New York City.

How to Use a Gerontologist

A gerontologist is a social scientist who has extensive professional training in the field of aging.

In contrast to a geriatrician—a doctor who specializes in the physical aging process and medical problems of the elderly—a gerontologist focuses on the psychological changes and social problems associated with aging. The gerontologist takes a more holistic approach to care, with an emphasis on the planning and management of *all* areas of the older person's life.

The goal of gerontology is the preservation of dignity and quality of life for the aging person.

Recently, gerontologists have begun to emphasize preventive measures for the "well elderly" and early planning for later-life management. It makes little sense to spend more effort on planning the disposition of our estates *after* death than to assure that our wishes are respected during our final years of life.

Who needs a gerontologist's services?...

As America ages, more and more people are finding themselves faced with the care of an elderly parent or relative. Often, they don't know where to turn. Many seek no help or outside support until *after* an elder suffers a severe medical incapacity. *Most common scenarios:*

• "Mother has become more forgetful and confused. She doesn't take her medication. I

141

work all day and have my own children to care for. Where do I start?"

• "I live out-of-state. I've been calling my father regularly since mother died. Lately, he seems different. The doctor says there's nothing wrong, it's just old age. I'm so worried. What can I do?"

Few guidelines exist for families confronting the transitions that occur as a family member ages.

Frequent problems…

• Little, if any planning has been done. Families may be unprepared to cope financially, emotionally or in other ways.

• Lack of information on the kind of help needed and the available options.

• Disagreement. Family members, including the older person, may not agree on a course of action.

• Red tape. The system of services available to the elderly, both government and private, grows more complicated every day.

One out of two people over the age of 80 need some type of assistance on a daily basis. But the type of help needed can range from transportation to housework to total care.

Solution: Seek expert guidance from a gerontologist who is familiar with the alternatives, qualified to give accurate advice, and skilled at navigating the maze of options.

What a gerontologist does…

Gerontologists do most or all of the following:

• Assess the needs of elderly clients and make recommendations and referrals. I help clients develop, in writing, what I call an "elder life plan," detailing the types of living arrangements they may or may not prefer.

• Guide families to support aimed at helping the older person remain independent in a home environment.

• Assist clients to prepare an advanced medical directive, or "living will," recording instructions on medical measures.

• Advocate for the preparation of power-of-attorney documents.

• Provide counseling services to the elderly and their families, including bereavement support and intervention when necessary.

• Act as advocates for the elderly.

• Perform in-home assessment.

• Provide phone consultations to family members living at a distance.

• Administer insurance claims for reimbursements, resolve Medicare, Medicaid, and other insurance problems.

• Suggest financial strategies for long-term care, by which the elderly can safeguard their assets, preserve their estates and avoid impoverishment.

• Help families resolve problems and disagreements regarding elder care.

Family conflicts…

The help of a gerontologist can be particularly valuable in soothing emotion-laden conflicts between older children and elderly parents. My premise is that families are good…that children are caring and do as much as they can. *Common issues:*

• *Control.* Who decides?

• *Money.* False expectations, miscommunications and tension over finances are frequent.

• *Where the parent "should" live.* Most often the parent shouldn't live alone, doesn't want to go to a nursing home, and may ask, "If you're so concerned, why can't I live with you?"

To find a gerontologist…

Call your local or state department on aging for a referral in your area.

Source: Gerontologist Judith S. Parnes, MSW, ACSW, founder and executive director of Elder Life Management, a private, non-profit planning service for the elderly and their families, located in Deal, New Jersey.

How to Choose An Obstetrician

When choosing an obstetrician,* it's important to find someone who offers technical competence *and* someone with whom you can be truly comfortable.

Your obstetrician should treat you as an equal in managing your pregnancy. You should feel free to ask questions and discuss all aspects of the impending birth.

*Although this article is written for women, it's also important for their partners to get involved in choosing an obstetrician. Men, too, should be working with a doctor they like and trust.

It's important to decide whether you're most comfortable with a male or a female doctor—today, 25% of all obstetricians are women.

The best way to find a good obstetrician is to develop a list of recommended doctors, and then interview each of them to find the one who best suits your needs.

Narrowing the field…

If you have a gynecologist who you trust and get along well with, it's natural to consider staying with him/her through your pregnancy.

But not all gynecologists handle births. And even excellent gynecologists aren't always good obstetricians. *To find out about yours:* Ask pregnant women in the waiting room what they like and do not like about him.

To find other doctors to interview, ask trusted friends for references. If several women mention the same obstetrician, he is probably worth looking into. But never take other opinions uncritically. Each woman's needs are different.

Other excellent sources of referrals are nurses, hospital personnel and other doctors you know.

Some women have a particular hospital in mind, having heard wonderful things about its obstetrical unit. Or they may run a high risk of complications…and want access to sophisticated technology and specialized care.

In this case, call the hospital for a list of obstetricians who practice there, and interview several.

Educate yourself…

Before you interview prospective obstetricians, read everything you can about pregnancy and birth. This will help you form opinions about the kind of birthing experience you prefer.

When you go for an exploratory interview, again, ask the other expectant mothers in the waiting room about the doctor.

Then, ask the doctor…

•Do you have a preference among the different schools of natural childbirth—Lamaze or Le Boyer?

•What kind of pain relief will be available to me if I need it? Many women today prefer epidurals—spinal injections of painkillers. Make sure that the doctor practices in a hospital where epidurals can be done.

•What preparatory steps do you take when a woman arrives at the hospital? Do you shave her…administer enemas…insert IV tubes? *Significance:* It's *not* necessary for a doctor to take these steps right away.

Example: A woman may eventually need an IV tube if her labor goes long and she doesn't eat or drink for many hours. But it shouldn't be rushed.

•Do you discourage your patients from walking around during the early stages of labor?

•Do you use any alternate means of delivery—birthing rooms, birthing chairs, etc.?

•Do you do fetal monitoring?

•If I need a Caesarean section, what kind of incision do you use? *Preferable:* A bikini cut, which leaves a less noticeable scar than an up-and-down cut.

•Who are your backups in case you can't be present at my delivery? Will I get to meet them beforehand?

•What is your fee? Most insurance companies pay only part of the obstetrician's fee. You'll pay the rest.

Note: The most expensive obstetricians are not necessarily the best. They may just charmingly cater to the wealthy.

Special situations…

If you are having a difficult pregnancy, you'll want to ask the doctor additional questions. Make sure that he has ample experience handling high-risk mothers. Ask how he would handle the various problems that might arise.

Examples: If you give birth prematurely, how would he handle premature labor? Can he make the latest technology—such as home monitors that track your contractions—available to you?

Choosing among the top contenders…

Before finally choosing, check the qualifications of the doctors you like. Many doctors who practice obstetrics are not certified by the American College of Obstetricians and Gynecologists.

Although they may have ample experience, they have less training and are not well-versed in the latest techniques. This can cause trouble.

Example: One woman began bleeding profusely in her seventh month. In the middle of the crisis, she learned that her doctor was not qualified to perform the emergency C-section she needed to save her life. A board-certified specialist had to be summoned.

Two ways to check certification:

•Ask the doctor's secretary in which specialty he holds his boards. Be suspicious if she refuses to answer.

•Look the doctor up in the *Directory of Medical Specialists*. It's available at the public library.

Source: Niels H. Lauersen, MD, clinical professor of obstetrics and gynecology, New York Medical College. He is the author of *It's Your Pregnancy: Questions You Should Ask Yourself and Are Afraid to Ask Your Obstetrician*, Fireside, 1230 Avenue of the Americas, New York 10020.

What to Ask a Surgeon

To protect against unnecessary surgery, ask the physician hard questions beforehand.

•What are the risks?
•What is the mortality rate for this operation?
•How long will it take to recover?
•What is the likelihood of complications?
•Are there ways to treat this condition medically?
•How many people have you seen with similar symptoms who have chosen not to have surgery?
•How many of these operations have you done in the past year?

Always get a second opinion.

Recovery After Surgery

At one time, doctors thought that general anesthesia rendered surgical patients unconscious—incapable of hearing events or conversations that took place in the operating room.

*No longer...*some researchers now believe that there are many levels of consciousness, and that even during *deep* anesthesia patients can hear things spoken by doctors and nurses in the operating room.

Even more surprising: What a patient hears during surgery can profoundly affect his/her recovery following the operation. Patients who hear negative comments—about the surgery or

even about seemingly innocuous topics such as the weather—tend to recover slowly and painfully.

In contrast, those patients who hear positive comments both before and during surgery tend to recover promptly and with little pain or bleeding.

Recent study: Surgical patients were divided into two groups. Members of the first group were told prior to surgery, *You will bleed less as a result of surgery.* Members of the second group were given no such reassurance. *Results:* Members of the first group experienced far less bleeding than those of the second group.

Recommendations...

Surgeons traditionally have used cloth barriers to protect the sterile field. This also keeps the patients from seeing the incision site or anything else that might prove disturbing.

I and other researchers recommend that an *aural barrier* also be set up to prevent the patient from hearing potentially unpleasant or disturbing things during surgery.

The best way to do this is through the use of a personal stereo. Listening to an appropriate tape during a surgical procedure not only blocks potentially distressing operating room conversations, it can also replace them with positive, upbeat messages.

What you can do...

Surgical patients should take a personal stereo and a tape to the hospital with them and listen to the tape during surgery. Before they enter the hospital, patients should tell their surgeon and their anesthesiologist that they would like to use a personal stereo.

What to listen to...

Some people prefer soothing music, while others may opt for meditation or relaxation tapes.

But homemade tapes that contain the reassuring voices of loved ones are generally the most effective at reducing stress and speeding a patient's recovery. To make such a tape, ask friends and family members to record simple statements of reassurance.

Example: *The fact that you are hearing my voice means that the surgery is going well and you will recover quickly...You will have a speedy recovery and will feel no pain...I love you, and I look forward to seeing you after surgery.*

The closer your emotional ties to the people on the tape, the more effective it will be. No one knows precisely why listening to these tapes is so powerful, only that they do work.

Source: Clinical psychologist John Hudesman, PhD, professor of student affairs, City University of New York. Dr. Hudesman is conducting pilot research on the role of spoken communication in recovery from surgery. He maintains a private practice in New York.

Better Breast Biopsies

New technique diagnoses cancer just as effectively as traditional surgical biopsy—but causes less scarring. It's cheaper, too. Percutaneous large-core biopsy requires only local anesthesia and uses a hollow-bore needle to remove a thin cylinder of breast tissue. The sample is then tested just like a section of surgically removed tissue. The procedure takes about one hour. *Cost:* About $850. Surgical biopsy costs about $2,400.

Source: Steve H. Parker, MD, radiologist, Radiology Imaging Associates, Englewood, Colorado.

Nondiagnosis Can Be Malpractice

A woman claimed a doctor's failure to diagnose tuberculosis in her husband led to her contracting the disease. *Judge's ruling:* The physician should have been aware of the disease—and, if he had been aware, would have been obligated to let the spouse know. Therefore, the wife has a legitimate malpractice claim even though she was not the doctor's patient.

Source: Justice Jules L. Spodek, ruling in *Ellis v. Peter,* No. 14928/92, Kings County (New York) Supreme Court, IA, Part 19.

Hospital Timing

Put off non-emergency surgery and medical tests until late fall if you can. *Reason:* In the cycles of medical education, new residents—the least experienced doctors on a hospital staff—take up their duties on July 1. Senior staff physicians often take summer vacations. *Bottom line:* The hospital is more likely to run smoothly after the new residents have worked into the routine and the senior staff is back from vacation.

Source: Jo Ann Friedman, president, Health Marketing Systems, New York.

Hospital Stay Surprise

Hospital stays vary more depending on where one lives than the ailment. In general, doctors in the East keep their patients hospitalized longer. *Longest average stay:* 13.1 days, in New Jersey. *Shortest average:* Six days, in California. *Conundrum:* Length of stay seems to have little effect on the patient's recovery.

How to Protect Yourself From Hospitals

Not long ago, American hospitals were the envy of the world—proud institutions filled with high-tech equipment and staffed by dedicated and highly skilled workers.

But growing competition for a dwindling patient population, plus a decade of government-mandated cost-cutting measures, have transformed many once-outstanding facilities into dirty, dangerous places where care is haphazard—and overpriced, too. Until recently, there was no systematic method for comparing hospitals. Patients had to rely upon recommendations from friends and family members and from their doctors. Now, however, the federal government makes available detailed information concerning mortality rates at hospitals nationwide.

These statistics—known as Medicare mortality information—cover hospitals' overall mortality rates as well as their specific mortality for surgery performed. They give a good idea of the level of care the hospital offers. The higher the mortality rate, the lower the quality of care.

To be safe: Choose the hospital with the lowest mortality score.

If your doctor recommends a particular hospital, ask about its mortality statistics. If your doctor doesn't know, check with a medical library or with the local chapter of the American Association of Retired Persons. If you have trouble interpreting the data, take a copy to your doctor and ask for help.

Of course, even superb hospitals occasionally provide substandard care. *Some of the risks faced by patients—and how to guard against them...*

Incompetent surgeons...

While no one would dispute that the majority of surgeons are competent, some are so deficient in their skills as to be downright dangerous. Yet because even a bad doctor has specialized knowledge, it's hard for a patient to evaluate the level of care he/she is providing.

Self-defense: Before engaging a surgeon, make sure he has performed the procedure in question *at least* several dozen times. Ask what percentage of these operations succeeded and what percentage failed. Finally, check up on your prospective surgeon with the state medical board. Ask for all pertinent information, including the details of any disciplinary actions filed.

Missing anesthesiologists...

Patients scheduled for surgery know the importance of a skilled surgeon, yet few recognize the key role played by the person responsible for administering the anesthetic. *Result:* Patients fail to pay attention to one of the most important details concerning surgery—the administration of anesthesia.

Self-defense: If your operation calls for general anesthesia, you may want to confirm that the anesthetic be administered by an anesthesiologist.

Important: That the anesthesiologist be present for the entire operation. In some cases the anesthesiologist leaves the room once the operation is under way, leaving the patient in the care of an anesthetist—who might not be equipped to handle an emergency.

Inexperienced or incompetent operating room staff...

Successful surgery depends not just upon a skilled surgeon and anesthesiologist, but also upon a skilled and experienced operating room staff.

Self-defense: Never submit to surgery until you know that the hospital staffers have done the procedure at least *several* dozen times previously...and make sure that mortality rates for both surgeon *and* hospital staff are low. If the surgeon or hospital lacks significant experience, or if the mortality rates are high, have your surgery performed elsewhere.

Part-time nurses...

In an effort to cut payroll costs, many hospitals have slashed the number of full-time nursing staff, relying instead upon "temps" whenever patient ranks swell. *Problem:* Even when they hold proper credentials, temp nurses often lack the specialized skills of full-time nurses. Those who are equally skilled may lack familiarity with the hospital's particular way of doing things. *Result:* Needless mistakes in patient care.

Self-defense: Before hospitalization, inform your primary physician that you prefer to be treated only by full-time personnel. If full-time nurses are unavailable, consider hiring your own. Most hospitals do allow the practice. *Note:* Temps are especially common in resort areas—places with unstable or seasonal populations.

Medication mistakes...

Getting one drug when you are prescribed another doesn't happen often, thanks to repeated checks by pharmacists, doctors and nurses.

But mistakes do *sometimes* happen—often with catastrophic results.

Example: Two patients hospitalized for heart surgery died after receiving a glucose solution instead of the heart drug that doctors had prescribed.

Self-defense: Before allowing anyone to give you an injection or pill, ask the name of the medication, the reason it was ordered and whether it is absolutely necessary for your health. If the answers you receive fail to make sense to you, ask your primary physician for a clarification.

Fatigued personnel...

Hospital personnel must be clearheaded and well-rested if they are to give patients quality care. Unfortunately, hospital rules and personnel shortages often conspire to force doctors and nurses to work long shifts, sometimes on little or no sleep. One hospital facing a severe shortage of nurses "solved" its problem by having its nurses work *24-hour shifts*. Under such conditions, mistakes are extremely likely.

Self-defense: Whenever possible, schedule surgery and major diagnostic procedures for early in the day—and early in the week—when staff members are freshest.

Inflated or inaccurate bills...

American hospitals are notorious for charging excessive prices—but that's not the half of it. At least half of all hospital bills in this country are wildly inaccurate—and the errors invariably favor the hospital.

To avoid being taken: Do not pay your bill unless you are certain all charges on it are legitimate. If you discover you have been charged for an item or a service you did not receive, or if you do not understand the bill, contact the hospital and demand a complete explanation.

Unnecessary diagnostic tests...

Beware of any doctor who recommends an expensive diagnostic test and then refers you to a specific testing facility. *Reason:* The doctor may have a financial stake in that facility—and may have found a sneaky way to pad his wallet.

Self-defense: If this situation arises, ask the doctor point-blank if he has a financial stake in the testing facility. If so, or if the doctor declines to answer your question, get another doctor. Such a relationship is unethical—and in several states, at least, is now illegal.

Passive attitude...

People who question everything else in life often are all too willing to blindly accept treatments ordered by medical personnel. Questioning your caregivers is essential, even if you cannot understand the answers. *Reason:* The very fact that you ask questions demonstrates that you expect quality care. *Bonus:* In some cases, a seemingly naive question may provoke

a doctor to reconsider a particular course of action, thereby saving money, time, discomfort or even a life.

Bottom line...

Ask any questions that occur to you. Do not worry about alienating your caregivers. Odds are they will not be annoyed. Even if they are, you're still more likely to receive quality care than someone who silently accepts the hospital's course of action.

Source: Walt Bogdanich, a Pulitzer prize-winning reporter with *The Wall Street Journal.* Bogdanich is the author of *The Great White Lie: How America's Hospitals Betray Our Trust and Endanger Our Lives,* Touchstone, 1230 Avenue of the Americas, New York 10020.

How to Get VIP Treatment in a Hospital

The first thing an admitting clerk does when you're brought into a hospital is slip a plastic tag with an identity number onto your wrist. From that point on, like it or not, you are a number to most of the hospital staff.

Being a number instead of a name can be an awful shock. It means that you have no identity—except for your symptoms, vital signs and medical treatment.

Fortunately, there are steps you can take to improve that treatment. And those steps, if successful, not only will make you feel more comfortable and human during your hospital visit, they could dramatically affect your state of health by the time you're ready to be discharged. In fact, it may be the issue that determines whether you leave alive or dead.

What you can do...

Think of a hospital as a sort of huge, complex hotel—however, one that dispenses more than food, entertainment and lodging.

As you obviously know, a hospital dispenses both life-saving and life-threatening services. A moment's inattention at a hospital can lead to tragedy.

So how do you get the hospital to treat you like a person instead of a number?

In general, you've got to use the same techniques you use in other aspects of your personal and business life. The key word is assertiveness. That's not to say you should complain and be demanding—although, as you'll see, that may be necessary under certain circumstances.

Finding the right doctor...

The first step in getting VIP treatment in a hospital should be taken long before you're admitted—and that's finding a doctor who can provide the leverage you'll need. You want someone with more than an M.D. after his name.

Every community has a clique of doctors who have "political" clout. Usually, these are physicians who serve on the local hospital boards of directors. Be aware, however, that a doctor with clout doesn't necessarily have the skills or any other attributes that make a physician a superior healer. Do you want such a person as your personal physician? Generally speaking, the answer is no, but there are exceptions. If you're satisfied that such a doctor can serve double-duty, so to speak, then you need go no further.

The drawbacks: Aside from the possibilities that such a doctor may be more expert in a boardroom than an operating room there are other potential problems.

The most serious: He may be more interested in keeping his professional calendar and the institution's beds filled than in your welfare. Of course, there are ways to get around that. If he wants to admit you to the hospital for treatment and there is any doubt in your mind about this decision, ask for a consultation.

Generally speaking, it's always wise to get a consultation for any complex medical procedure—and the likelihood is that the procedure he's recommending is relatively complex if he wants to hospitalize you. So by asking for a consultation, you're not showing lack of faith in your doctor.

Caveat: However, we've heard of many instances where doctors are annoyed when a patient announces that he would like a consultation or second opinion. If you ever face a less-than-cooperative response to such a request, it would be prudent to seek out another doctor immediately. It's well within your rights to consult with as many physicians as you wish.

The personal touch...

To guarantee better attention once you know that you're going to spend time in hospital, make a date with the hospital administrator. He may or may not be a doctor—but in any case, he is a businessman, so you can be sure he speaks the same language as you. Introduce yourself. Tell him that you're a little concerned about your hospital stay and that you'd appreciate it if he'd take a personal interest in your case.

He'll get the message, and in all likelihood, he'll take steps to be sure that you're well cared for. Now that you've made your presence known, he will probably, out of courtesy, call the head of nursing and the admitting office and tell them you are coming to the hospital and that they should be expecting you. It's just such words, without pressure, that may make all the difference in the way you're subsequently treated.

Once you're in the hospital...

Even if you've failed or haven't had the time to take the above steps, there are still things you can do to ensure good treatment, if not VIP treatment.

If you're not physically up to it, your spouse or a friend or relative may have to help you, but if you're feeling well enough, you can take the following steps yourself.

• During the admission procedure, ask what rooms are available. You may prefer a private room, or for the sake of company, you may want to share a room with someone else. If you want to share, ask about your potential partner's medical status to be sure that you can deal with his illness.

• After settling into your room, ask to see the dietitian. Explain that you understand that the hospital is not a hotel, but within reasonable bounds, and limited by doctor's orders, there are foods that you do and do not like. Itemize them. If you present your request with tact, the dietitian will probably try to meet your reasonable requests.

• Go out of your way to be polite to the nursing staff. They are your lifeline—literally. If the nurses take a dislike to you, the recuperation period will not be smooth.

• It's not tacky to provide small favors, such as a box of candy, and even flowers, on each of the three nursing shifts: the 8 A.M. to 4 P.M., the 4 P.M. to midnight, and midnight to 8 A.M. Don't offer a gratuity until you're ready to be discharged. Nurses are professionals, and most would resent the offer. But if you received extra special care from a nurse during your stay, a tasteful gift isn't inappropriate.

• Make it clear that you'd like to know what medication or treatment is being given to you *beforehand*. That will require a discussion with your doctor. Most doctors work on the premise that patients don't want to know too much, and so only provide information as it's necessary or if the patient specifically requests it.

Why you should want this information…

Unfortunately, mistakes are made now and then, but if you ask the nurse "What are these pills?" or "What exactly will you be doing to me?", and she has orders from your doctor to provide that information on request, then it gives the staff the opportunity to double-check what they are doing and it gives you the chance to say "Wait a minute!" if an obvious error is being committed.

How to complain…

If you're not happy with your care, explain your complaint firmly and politely to the nurse. If that gets you no place, ask to speak to the head nurse. And if that fails, you may have to speak to either your doctor or the hospital administrator. Usually, when you reach that level, and you're not being unreasonable, steps will be taken to satisfy your complaint and resolve your problem.

Best Hospitals for Major Surgery

Doctors who operate frequently have better safety records because they maintain their skills. *Guideline:* A minimum of 40-50 operations a year, even more for heart surgery. Aim for a hospital that does many similar operations. *Best bets:* Teaching and specialty hospitals. A good one substantially improves the chances of avoiding serious complications or death.

Patients Rights

People who are asked to sign medical consent forms are often in the worst possible psychological shape to make a decision about anything. Serious illness is a terrible shock. It brings out the part of human nature that wants to abdicate responsibility and put fate in the hands of an omnipotent being—in this case, the doctor. It's important to understand before you get sick what your rights as a patient are and what medical consent actually means.

Informed consent…

The law in this country guarantees the patient an informed consent. That means the patient must be thoroughly informed in advance about all significant aspects of the proposed treatment. Consent is necessary in all non-emergency situations in which there are invasive* procedures or treatments involving risks unknown to most lay people. This includes not only surgery but also more minor procedures such as invasive diagnostic tests or injections of any substance with negative side effects.

The essence of informed consent is what takes place between the patient and the doctor. A consent form signed by the patient does not in itself constitute informed consent. The form is simply evidence collected by doctors and hospitals as protection in case of an eventual lawsuit. In all states the patient has the right to an explanation and must understand the procedure. And in some states the informed consent must be obtained by the person performing the procedure. *Example:* The risks of anesthesia must be explained by the anesthesiologist. The explanation must be in simple language the patient can understand. If the patient speaks only Urdu, it's the hospital's responsibility to make a good-faith effort to find an Urdu translator.

Basics…

• Consent for a medical procedure on a child or unconscious adult can be given over the telephone, but hospitals and doctors will want it confirmed in writing.

*Invasive: any object entering the body through the skin or orifices.

• Consent can be revoked at any time prior to the procedure. Medical consents are not legally binding prior to the procedure, and you don't give up any rights when you sign a form and then change your mind.

• Consent must be to a specific procedure. A general consent form is not evidence of consent for those specific procedures which require that specific information be imparted to the patient to make him "informed." *Recommended:* Sign general consent forms for basic hospital care. After you're admitted, it's still the hospital's and doctor's responsibility to explain any specific procedures in order to obtain consent that's informed.

• Consent is not necessary for an emergency procedure where the patient is incompetent or unconscious and no one authorized can be located to consent. *Emergency:* Any procedure that is medically necessary to treat a condition dangerous to life or health.

What the patient must be told…

• Purpose: For what reason the procedure is being done.

• Procedure: What exactly will be done and how. What the procedure entails.

• Benefits: What the doctor hopes to achieve by performing this procedure.

• Alternatives: What else could be done besides what the doctor is recommending.

• Risks: This is the stickiest area. It gives rise to the most malpractice suits. The doctor is supposed to inform the patient about what the law calls "material risks." These are risks that are high in frequency or severity or that might have an impact on decision-making. *Example:* Anesthesia sometimes results in brain damage. This is a high-severity, low-frequency risk, but you're entitled to know anyway. Determination of the material risk varies with each procedure and the condition of each patient.

Who can consent…

• Any conscious, competent adult (over 18 in most states) can give an informed consent. A mental patient may be considered competent to consent even though he may be hallucinating, as long as he can understand objective medical data and make reasoned decisions concerning his medical treatment.

• An emancipated minor or minor who is married or a parent can give consent.

• Consent for a medical procedure on an unconscious adult can be given by: Spouses, adult siblings, parents, adult offspring, court-appointed guardians. If a hospital cannot find an authorized relative, it can go to court for guardianship.

• A parent can consent for a medical procedure on a child. A competent adult can refuse medical treatment for himself. But a parent cannot refuse treatment for a child. This issue comes up in cases of religious-sect members who don't believe in blood transfusions and parents of defective children who don't want them treated with extraordinary measures.

When you can sue…

You can sue for malpractice on the basis of lack of informed consent without other malpractice claims, irrespective of whether you were injured. The jury award may be limited, however, if you sustained no physical or psychological injury.

Occasionally an informed consent can legitimately not be taken. These are what doctors and hospitals usually use as legal defenses:

• When the risks are well-known. *Example:* An appendectomy will cause a scar.

• The patient was informed about risks, but he couldn't make up his mind and told the doctor to decide for him.

• It wasn't possible to find someone competent who was authorized to consent, and it was an emergency procedure.

• The doctor claims that knowing about the risks would adversely affect the patient's medical condition. In such a case, he is obliged to inform the family, if not the patient.

Source: Attorney Natalie J. Kaplan, a former hospital legal consultant, now in private practice in New York.

How to Handle Informed Consent

The process of giving medical consent is often so psychologically charged that many patients don't remember giving an informed consent. In six-month follow-ups, patients have been shown videotapes of their consent and still not remembered. If they do remember anything, it's having alternatives explained to them (more than any other aspect of the consent procedure).

Since making a decision about treatment of a serious illness is so traumatic, there are things you should do to be sure your decision is the right one:

•Some hospitals provide patient representatives. Ask for one to sit in on the informed-consent procedure.

•Write down all your questions in advance.

•Take notes or use a tape recorder for the answers.

•Ask the doctor for recommended reading about your illness and its treatment.

•Get second (or third) opinions.

•Take a friend or relative with you. Someone uninvolved will be cool-headed enough to get more information.

•Don't agree to anything just to get it over with. Listen closely to the alternatives and risks.

•There is usually a time gap between the time you consent and the actual operation. Use this period to do research about the procedure. Go to your hospital's medical library. If you're too ill to do your own research, ask a friend to do it.

•If you feel that the advice of your physician is more conservative than you wish, look for alternative medical sources in your area. *Example:* When statistics indicated that lumpectomies might be just as effective as radical mastectomies, some physicians were more quickly convinced than others to try the new procedure.

Source: Attorney Natalie J. Kaplan, a former hospital legal consultant, now in private practice in New York.

Understanding Hospital Talk

A hospital patient may have considerable difficulty understanding some of the jargon used by nurses and other hospital personnel. Here is what some commonly used terms mean:

NPO—Sign placed by the bed of a patient who is not to get anything to eat or drink.

Emesis basin—basin brought to patients who are sick to their stomach.

Ambulate—Take the patient for a walk.

Force fluids—Encourage intake of lots of liquid.

Void—Urinate.

IV—Intravenous.

OOB—Out of bed.

IPPB—Intermittent Positive Pressure Breathing machine to aid the breathing.

HS—Medication before sleep.

BP—Blood pressure.

HR—Heart rate.

Medication schedule…

QID—4 times a day.

TID—3 times a day.

BID—2 times a day.

OD or QD—Once a day.

OOD—Every other day.

Infection Alert

Hospital acquired infections may be caused by rings worn by hospital staff. At the hospital that was tested, two out of every five nurses had disease causing bacteria on the skin under their rings.

Source: Study at a London hospital, in *Prevention*, St. Emmaus, PA.

Mail-Order Pharmacies

Fueled by rising prescription costs, the number of mail-order pharmacies has grown dramatically since the 1980s. Few sell directly to individuals, but many people have access to them through group health insurance plans.

Advantages…

•Cost. Drugs by mail are potentially cheaper than drugs from the corner pharmacy. It's difficult to determine exactly how much cheaper because costs depend on the person's health insurance plan.

•Convenience. You save a trip to the drugstore—important for the disabled or seriously ill.

What to be wary of...

●Quality. Mail-order pharmacies—large and automated—can make mistakes. But so can drugstores. The nine mail-order pharmacies studied have elaborate quality-control systems. And the drugs themselves are produced by major manufacturers.

●Pharmacist-patient relationship. Some people want an ongoing relationship with a pharmacist. But mail-order pharmacies have toll-free numbers and include written information with the drugs.

●Time. Mail-order pharmacies ship within two days of receiving an order, so do not try to fill a prescription that you need quickly. These services should only be used for drugs that treat chronic conditions—arthritis, hypertension, etc.

●Waste. Most mail-order pharmacies fill orders for extended periods—often 90 days. If you don't need that much, you're stuck with drugs you can't use.

Source: Constance Horgan, ScD, research professor, Bigel Institute for Health Policy, Heller Graduate School, Brandeis University. She was principal investigator for a mail-order pharmacy study funded by the Health Care Financing Administration.

Health Information By Phone

As more consumers are actively educating themselves about medical issues, the demand for health information is growing dramatically.

Where to start: Contact the Office of Disease Prevention and Health Promotion, (ODPHP), at the National Health Information Center, Box 1133, Washington, DC 20013, 800-336-4797. The Center has a database of some 1,200 private and federal organizations that produce and distribute health information.

Other toll free numbers...

●National AIDS Information Clearinghouse, 800-458-5231
●National Council on Alcoholism, 800-NCA-CALL
●Alzheimer's Disease and Related Disorders Association, 800-621-0379
In Illinois, 800-572-6037

●Cancer Information Service, 800-4-CANCER
In Hawaii, 808-524-1235
In Alaska, 800-638-6070
●American Diabetes Association, 800-ADA-DISC
In Virginia, 703-549-1500
In Washington, DC, 202-331-8303
●Endometriosis Association, 800-992-ENDO
In Wisconsin, 800-992-3636
●Lung Line/National Jewish Center/ Immunology and Respiratory Medicine, 800-222-5864
In Denver, 303-355-LUNG
●National Child Abuse Hotline, 800-422-4453
●National Down Syndrome Society Hotline, 800-221-4602
●National Multiple Sclerosis Society, 800-624-8236

Source: Patricia Lynch, project director, ODPHP, National Health Information Center, Washington, DC 20013.

Health Quackery Self-Defense

If a medical treatment or "cure" has not been prescribed by your doctor but you want to check it out, call...

●The National Cancer Institute at 800-422-6237.
●The Arthritis Foundation Information Line at 800-283-7800.

Regarding other suspicious health products, send questions about specific products to the Consumer Health Research Institute, 3521 Broadway, Kansas City, Missouri 64111. Include a self-addressed, stamped, business-sized envelope and $1.

And if you think you have been harmed by a quack remedy, contact the National Council Against Health Fraud, William Jarvis, PhD, Evans Hall, Room 204, Loma Linda University, Loma Linda, California 92350.

Source: AARP, 601 E St. NW, Washington, DC 20049. The *AARP Bulletin* is distributed to members, ages 50 and over.

Yellow Pages Defense

Of medical specialists who advertise in the *Yellow Pages*, 10% lie about their training. *Self-defense:* Call the American Board of Medical Specialties to verify credentials—800-776-2378, weekdays, 9 AM to 6 PM EST.

Gender Bias

Male doctors are less likely than female doctors to order pap smears and mammograms for their female patients. Any woman whose primary doctor is a man may be improperly screened for cancer of the cervix and breast.

Self-defense: Don't wait for the doctor to recommend screening exams—ask about them.

Source: Nicole Lurie, MD, MSPH, associate professor of medicine and public health, University of Minnesota, Minneapolis. Her study of 96,962 women 18 to 75 years of age was published in *The New England Journal of Medicine,* 10 Shattuck St., Boston 02115.

What You Should Know about Medical Consent Forms

For minor ailments, doctors usually presume that their patients consent to treatment. When serious illness is involved, however, your doctor may ask you to sign a "consent form" before proceeding with treatment.

A consent form is a legal document that limits the doctor's liability should something go wrong with your care. It should be a red flag that what the doctor is proposing is risky or experimental.

Examples: Having an invasive test or surgery...or taking a new, unproven drug.

In signing a typical consent form, you limit your ability to sue for malpractice. *Exception:* If your doctor or any other medical personnel are negligent in caring for you, you can sue.

Before signing a consent form...

• Ask the doctor to explain the risks and benefits of the recommended treatment—and any alternatives to treatment. Signing the form should merely put in writing what you and the doctor have already discussed and decided.

• Read the form carefully. Have the doctor clarify anything you don't understand. Important: You have the right to amend the form as you see fit—by jotting in the margins. Indeed, you don't have to sign the form at all. But if you don't—or if the doctor disagrees with your changes—he/she may decline to provide treatment.

• Request a copy of the form to take home and show to others. That includes family members, friends or other doctors—even your lawyer, if it should become necessary. Scrutinize the form carefully before signing. If you are too ill to sign the form, a family member can usually sign it on your behalf.

Source: Norman Fost, MD, MPH, director of the medical ethics program and professor of pediatrics at the University of Wisconsin Medical School, Madison. He is the author of an article on medical consent published recently in the *Journal of the American Medical Association,* 515 N. State St., Chicago 60610.

How to Get the Best Nursing Care When You're Hospitalized

People devote lots of time to choosing a doctor. But when it comes to a hospital stay, your nurse is at least as important as your physician.

Doctors tend to make only short, infrequent visits to the bedside. Nurses are on hand 24 hours a day—not only to administer drugs and monitor your vital signs, but also to calm your anxieties and be your confidante.

To get the most from a hospital's nursing staff...

• Insist on having a registered nurse care for you. Before checking in to the hospital, call ahead to find out about the nursing staff on your ward. Ask whether you'll be cared for by a registered nurse.

153

You may be told that there is an RN on your floor—but he/she might be there in a supervisory capacity only. A floor RN is generally responsible for overseeing several patients... and will probably be stationed down the hall from your room. He lacks the time to be responsive to the needs of any single patient.

If you're told you can't be assured of an RN and that you'll have to foot the bill for a private-duty RN, write a letter of protest to the hospital administrator. If the administrator declines to comply with your wishes, find another hospital.

Be leery of any "nurse" not wearing a name tag. Recently, administrators in a hospital where I worked instructed the nurses not to wear their name tags. That way, patients could not tell whether they were being cared for by an RN, a licensed practical nurse (LPN) or a nurse's aide.

In many cities, cost-conscious hospitals have been replacing highly paid RNs with nurse's aides...and patients are unaware that aides caring for them may have been bagging groceries at Safeway a month earlier. Not surprisingly, hospital mortality rates are going up in these cities.

• Make sure your nurse is working within his/her specialty. Like doctors, nurses are often specialists. If you're in the hospital for, say, heart surgery, you don't want a nurse who specializes in pediatrics.

Problem: To meet changing staffing requirements, hospitals sometimes transfer nurses from their regular ward to another ward. "Float" nurses sometimes lack the experience necessary to provide good patient care.

Example: I'm trained as a coronary care nurse. That's been my specialty for the past 17 years. Once I was floated to an organ transplant unit, where I was asked to give a patient an anti-rejection drug. I declined. I simply didn't know enough about the drug or transplant patients to feel comfortable doing that.

• Avail yourself of all that your RN has to offer. Nurses can do more than monitor vital signs and administer necessary medications. In many states, they can administer drugs and initiate certain procedures—without a doctor's specific instructions.

Your nurse is also there to educate you. Before I give a patient a new drug, I always ask, Do you have any idea what I'm giving you? If not, I tell him the name of the drug, explain the dosage, etc.

Your nurse is also trained to act as your confidante and advocate. If you're afraid to discuss your condition with your family or your doctor, your nurse can act as the go-between.

• Don't put up with a bad nurse. If your nurse is nasty or inattentive, ask the charge nurse to find you another RN.

Source: Echo Heron, RN, critical care nurse in coronary and emergency medicine. She is the author of *Intensive Care: The Story of a Nurse* and *Condition Critical: The Story of a Nurse Continues.* Fawcett Columbine.

8

Making Pain Go Away

Toothache Relief Magic

Rub an ice cube into the V-shaped area of the hand where the bones of the thumb and forefinger meet. Numbing this area apparently blocks the passage of toothache pain impulses along nerve pathways to the brain.

Source: Researchers at McGill University in Canada, reported in *High-Speed Healing*, Rodale Press, 33 E. Minor St., Emmaus, Pennsylvania 18098.

Better Migraine Relief

Aerobic exercise significantly reduces the pain of migraines—while improving the cardiovascular fitness of migraine sufferers. *Possible:* Exercise may also help reduce the frequency, intensity and duration of migraines.

Source: Research led by Donna M. C. Lockett, department of psychology, Carleton University, Ottawa, Ontario, Canada, reported in *Headache*, Box 5136, San Clemente, California 92672.

Cutting Postoperative Pain

Painkillers before surgery cut postoperative pain in half—and lessen the need for medication during recovery. *Reason:* Surgery sensitizes spinal-cord cells, which transmit pain impulses. Taking painkillers before surgery prevents the sensitization of the cells—making post-surgical pain less intense.

Source: Eighteen-month study of surgical patients, led by Joel Katz, MD and Alan Sandler, MD, of the University of Toronto, reported in *The Medical Post*, 777 Bay St., Toronto, Ontario M5W 1A7.

Treating Bursitis, Tendinitis and Myofascial Pain

Most people think that pain, warmth and redness around a joint means they've got arthritis. But these could be symptoms of bursitis, tendinitis or myofascial pain.

Good news: Each of these conditions responds extremely well to treatment and rarely recurs. There's also a great deal you can do to prevent these conditions from recurring, or even from happening in the first place.

Diagnosis made easy...

•Arthritis causes inflammation in the joints. These other conditions cause inflammation surrounding the joints.

•Arthritis strikes many joints at once. Bursitis and tendinitis usually strike only one part of the body at a time.

•Arthritis usually has no obvious cause...the tendency to develop the disease may be inherited. These other conditions are not inherited.

•Arthritis and other rheumatic diseases can last on and off for years, even a lifetime. These other conditions, on the other hand, can be successfully treated within weeks.

Treatment...

Bursitis, tendinitis and myofascial pain all respond to similar treatment:

Apply ice to the affected area three or four times a day for 20 minutes. After 48 hours have passed, replace the ice treatment with hot packs or a heating pad.

•Rest the affected area for the first few days. A painful shoulder, for instance, can be rested by a sling.

•When the pain has eased, after two to three days, begin an exercise program with a physical therapist. This will help you avoid losing motion in the affected joint.

•Get a deep massage from a physical therapist. This is particularly helpful for tendinitis of the elbow, shoulder or ankle.

•Take aspirin, ibuprofen or other non-steroidal anti-inflammatory drugs. Doses will usually be larger than for a headache. *Important:* Follow your doctor's instructions.

•Ask your doctor about short-term treatment with corticosteroids (by local injection) to relieve severe bursitis pain. It can offer dramatic relief...which can help you avoid surgery.

Bursitis...

Tiny sacs, called bursas, act as cushions between the muscles and the tendons. Unusual stress or injury to a nearby joint irritates the bursas, which fill with fluid and become inflamed. *Joints most susceptible:* Shoulders, knees, elbows, hips, heels and big toes. *Typical problems:*

•Bursitis under the heel. Pain at the bottom of the heel when you walk. *Prevention:* Avoid long periods of walking or standing on hard surfaces. *Helpful:* Roomy, low-heeled shoes and heel pads with the centers cut out.

•Frozen shoulder. Pain in the shoulder and midway down the arm that makes any upward or backward motion difficult. *Prevention:* Don't repeat the same arm movements over and over. Don't keep your arms raised over your head for long periods of time. *Most common culprits:* Vacuuming, push-ups or any sports in which you must move your arm like a piston.

•Housemaid's knee. Tenderness and swelling over the front of the kneecap. *Prevention:* Don't kneel on hard floors for long periods of time. If you must, use a pad. Don't sit for more than 20–30 minutes without getting up and stretching. Use your thigh muscles rather than your hands when you push off from a chair. Avoid climbing stairs if you have knee problems.

Tendinitis...

Tendons, the fibrous cords that attach muscle to bones, tear and become inflamed as a result of injury. *Typical problems:*

•Rotator-cuff tear. Partial or complete tears of one or more tendons that attach your upper arm and shoulder muscles. *Consequence:* Raising an arm above the horizontal level is difficult. *Prevention:* Same as for frozen shoulder, but in some cases surgery may be necessary to repair a complete shoulder cuff tear.

•Tendinitis of the ankle. A tear of the Achilles tendon that occurs at the back of the ankle. It's quite painful and inhibits the ankle from any motion. *Prevention:* Wear comfortable shoes with proper support, and be sure to stretch before and after any form of rigorous exercise.

•Tennis elbow. Pain in the elbow when you

lift anything heavy. *Prevention:* Don't repeatedly bend or turn your elbow. *Common culprits:* Clenching your fist, clutching tools with too tight a grip, even too much handshaking. *Helpful:* Wrap foam pipe insulation, or put foam-rubber curlers, on your tool handles.

- Trigger finger. Bending the fingers is difficult. *Prevention:* Don't repeat the same hand movements for long periods. Interrupt any handwork periodically with other activities. Don't clench your fists (often a sign of stress and tension).

Myofacial pain…

A deep muscular ache occurs in the area between the neck and the shoulder blade. *Prevention:*

- Don't repeatedly reach backwards (such as when getting something from the back seat of the car).
- Don't hold the phone between the neck and shoulder.
- Don't work long periods with your head drooped forward.
- Don't sleep with your head propped on more than one pillow.

Source: Arthur Grayzel, MD, senior vice president for medical affairs, the Arthritis Foundation, 1314 Spring St. NW, Atlanta, Georgia 30309.

What You Need to Know About Headaches

What causes headaches? Are they hereditary? When the "internal messenger system" that delivers a brain chemical called serotonin is disturbed, you get a headache. Of the 60 million chronic-headache sufferers in this country, 80% to 90% have close relatives with similar headache histories.

What can I do about my headache now? For nonmigraine headaches, one aspirin tablet (325 mg)—half the recommended dose—should suffice.

Alternative I: Two ibuprofen (400 mg) or two acetaminophen (650 mg) tablets.

Alternative II: Lying down in a quiet room for one hour.

Over-the-counter analgesics (painkillers) should be taken a maximum of twice a week.

Risk with more frequent usage: A "rebound effect," in which the medication itself causes further brain disturbances. *Result:* Daily headaches. When this occurs, the patient must avoid all analgesics for at least three months.

Are migraines treated differently than regular headaches? The common migraine involves severe throbbing pain (often on one side of the head), extreme intolerance to light and sound, nausea and vomiting. Of the 24 million migraine sufferers, 10% also see an "aura" of flashing or twinkling lights about 20 minutes before their other symptoms. Migraines may last from several hours to several days.

The best time to treat a migraine is at the onset of an attack. *Problem:* Oral drugs are often useless, since the patient will throw them up. *Alternative:* Self-injectable prescription medications that alleviate symptoms for 75% of patients.

DHE (dihydroergotamine) reduces pain within 40 minutes and lasts in the body for 48 hours.

A newer drug, sumatriptan, works faster—within 5 to 15 minutes—but may need to be repeated after four hours.

It also helps to stay in a low-lit, quiet room and to place an ice pack against your temples or forehead.

Is there a cure for migraines? There is no cure, but preventive medications taken on a daily basis reduce the frequency and severity of attacks for three of five sufferers.

Examples: Beta-blockers, calcium channel-blockers, tricyclic antidepressants. *Possible side effects:* Drowsiness, weight gain, sun sensitivity, allergic reactions.

In many cases, the serotonin system "smooths out" within two years, and the drugs can gradually be withdrawn.

Can untreated headaches cause brain damage? No, but severe headaches may indicate a more serious problem—a brain tumor, a dangerous clot or tangle of blood vessels, an infection. A diagnosis can be made with an MRI or CAT scan.

Source: Robert G. Ford, MD, a neurologist and medical director of the Ford Headache Clinic, 3918 Montclair Rd., Suite 102, Birmingham, Alabama 35213. He is the author of *Conquering Headaches* (International Headache Management Inc.).

Treatment for A Stiff Neck

Stiff necks are usually caused by muscle strain. They generally go away when the strain is relieved. Heat packs are helpful. *When to see a doctor:* The stiffness is accompanied by other symptoms, such as pain in the arm...or the problem persists for more than a few days.

Source: Timothy Johnson, MD, medical columnist, writing in *The Washington Post.*

Two Things that Won't Help a Hurt Ankle

Soaking a swollen ankle in hot water does it no good. Nor does wrapping a sprained ankle in an elastic bandage.

Help for Sciatica

Sciatica, a pain that radiates down the leg, is related to damage to the discs of the spine. The sciatic nerve is formed by the convergence of a group of nerve roots coming out of the spine. Wear and tear on the discs that these nerves pass through can cause the nerves to become pinched and irritated.

Pain often subsides without treatment, but some people have recurrent and debilitating pain from sciatica. Surgery to remove the offending disc is usually not necessary. *Treatment options:*

• Rest—so as not to add to the irritation.

• Analgesics and muscle relaxants to help relieve pain during healing.

• Epidural injections of steroids.

• Physical therapy to strengthen the abdomen, improve posture and reduce stress on spine and muscles.

Source: Charles B. Stacy, MD, director of the Neurological Pain Clinic at Mount Sinai Medical Center and a neurologist in private practice in New York City. He is co-author of *The Fight Against Pain*, Consumer Reports Books.

Preventing Joint Pain Recurrences

If exercise caused your injury, you may be able to return to your former level of intensity— but only gradually, over several months... and only after carefully analyzing the mechanical problems that caused the injury in the first place.

• If the inflammation stemmed from an anatomical problem, consider replacing the offending activity with one your body can better handle. Switch from running to cycling, for example, or replace tennis with swimming.

• For job-related tendinitis or bursitis, ask your doctor to refer you to an occupational therapist. He will carefully analyze your work movements and find ways to reduce stress on your joints.

• A switch in equipment often helps. *Examples:* Wearing shoes with good cushioning and firm heel support...playing with a light, shock-absorbent tennis racket...using a cushioned pad when kneeling...and using a raised, padded bar to support your wrists when typing.

Source: David S. Pisetsky, MD, PhD, professor of medicine and immunology at Duke University Medical Center in Durham, North Carolina, and medical advisor to the Arthritis Foundation, 1314 Spring St., Atlanta 30309. He is the author of *The Duke University Medical Center Book of Arthritis*. Fawcett Columbine.

9

Coping With Medical Emergencies

It Pays to Prepare For Emergencies

Emergencies, of course, come without warning. But that doesn't mean you can't be prepared when they do arrive.

Steps to take now...

•Familiarize yourself with the emergency rooms in your area. Look into freestanding urgent-care clinics as well as hospital emergency rooms. Ask your doctor which facility is best for which type of emergency—and chart his/her recommendations on a family bulletin board.

Know where the entrance and parking area are for each emergency facility recommended by your doctor. Go for a visit. Park in a visitor's space and go in and look around. If the admissions clerk is not busy, ask how things work in an emergency.

Call your county health department. Find out the rating of each local emergency room. Level 1 facilities offer only basic emergency care...Level 2 offer more advanced care...and Level 3 are comprehensive trauma centers capable of handling the most severe, life-threatening emergencies. *Caution:* If you go to a Level 3 center for a minor cut, you may have to wait in line behind people with more serious injuries.

•*Always carry in your wallet...*
  •Health insurance card.
  •Insurance company phone number.
  •Your blood type, although it will be tested for verification anyway.
  •A list of all medications you take regularly.
  •Your doctor's name, address and phone number.
  •A brief description—written and signed by your doctor—of any health condition that might affect emergency care.
  •The name and phone number of any pharmacy where your medication history is on file—ideally one that is open 24 hours a day.

•*Keep handy in your home—and tell everyone the location of...*
  •A comprehensive first-aid manual, such as the one published by the Red Cross and sold in bookstores. Be sure that it's up-to-date.

159

•Instructions for doing the Heimlich maneuver.

•A blood pressure cuff.

•Literature on emergency treatment for any disease or condition relevant to anyone who lives or works regularly in your house—heart disease, epilepsy, asthma, etc.

•Always wear a bracelet or pendant describing any serious medical condition. *Examples:* Diabetes or severe allergies.

Learn…

•Basic first aid.

•Cardiopulmonary resuscitation (CPR) for adults and children—especially if you have a pool.

•The Heimlich maneuver.

•How to take blood pressure—even if no one in your family is hypertensive.

• *Tape to your telephones the numbers for…*

•Your family doctor and any medical specialists used by your family. List the specialty beside the name and number, just in case the caller doesn't know, for example, that Dr. Jones is a cardiologist.

•Family dentist, orthodontist, endodontist, periodontist, etc.

•Police and ambulance. Call ahead to inquire about the normal response time for each.

•Private ambulance.

•Fire department—for first aid as well as fires, in case neither your doctor nor your first-aid squad can be reached.

•Poison-control center. Ask your hospital about the location of the nearest one.

•Emergency room.

•Family veterinarian and animal hospital.

•Neighbors who could be called at any hour, especially those who have a car.

• *Read…*

•All parts of your health insurance policy pertaining to emergency care. Make sure you know how soon after an emergency you must notify the insurance company…and whether your policy offers better coverage at certain hospitals.

•Your first-aid manual.

• *For an elderly or infirm person…*

•Sign him/her up with an emergency response system.

•Provide him with a portable telephone. Make sure he keeps the telephone charged and nearby at all times—especially if he is wheelchair-bound.

•Arrange with someone—neighbor, friend or commercial elder-care service representative—to check on the person each day.

Source: Neil Shulman, MD, associate professor of medicine, Emory University School of Medicine, Atlanta. He is the publisher of *Better Health Care for Less*, 2272 Vistamount Dr., Decatur, Georgia 30333. Dr. Shulman is co-author of *Better Health Care for Less*, Hippocraene Books, 171 Madison Ave., New York 10016. He also wrote the novel *Doc Hollywood*, which was made into a movie.

Is It a Heart Attack? Or…Just a Chest Pain?

A phenomenon, known as *Syndrome X*, refers to exercise-related chest pains experienced by people who have chest pains that seem cardiac related but who have no blockages in the main arteries. In such cases, the chest pains may be attributed to one or more causes.

Included…

•Acid reflux. Acid from the stomach backs into the esophagus.

•Abnormal nerve sensitivity. Nerves leading from the heart and the esophagus to the central nervous system are inappropriately activated.

•Anxiety disorders. Panic attacks, in particular, can be associated with chest pain.

•Microvascular angina. A disturbance of the small blood vessels of the heart.

A routine angiogram *can't* detect microvascular angina. *What can:* Radionuclide angiography—measures function of the heart during exercise and at rest…or Positron Emission Tomography (PET)—a nuclear scan measuring blood flow in the heart.

Treatment: Calcium channel blockers can help chest pains caused by microvascular angina.

Source: Richard Cannon III, MD, senior cardiology investigator, National Institutes of Health, Bethesda, Maryland.

The Well-Stocked Medicine Cabinet

What you *shouldn't* have in your medicine cabinet is as important as what you put in it.

General guideline: Check with your doctor before purchasing any over-the-counter medication…or if your symptoms persist longer than a few days.

What to include…

•Pain, fever and anti-inflammatory medicines. *Recommended:* Acetaminophen (Tylenol, Datril and Panadol). It reduces pain and fever without damaging the intestinal tract. However, it is not an anti-inflammatory—it will not reduce swelling.

Aspirin and ibuprofen (Advil, Nuprin and Medipren) relieve pain and inflammation… aspirin also relieves fever. *Warning:* At high doses, both can lead to internal bleeding and wearing away of the stomach lining. *At greatest risk:* The elderly.

Aspirin is also associated with ulcers and *tinnitus* (ringing in the ears)…ibuprofen with kidney toxicity. *Self-defense:* Always take aspirin or ibuprofen with food or liquid antacids, and never exceed the recommended dosage—no more than eight regular-strength tablets a day.

•First-aid materials: Hydrogen peroxide for cleaning wounds (*not* alcohol, which is drying and more irritating), antibiotic creams, cotton swabs, gauze pads, surgical tape, adhesive bandages, blunt scissors and tweezers.

•Skin protectors: Petroleum jelly or mild moisturizers for dry skin…over-the-counter vaginal cream for mild yeast infections…hydrocortisone cream (no more than 0.5% strength) for poison ivy or other rashes.

Caution: Do not use hydrocortisone on face or genitals without consulting a doctor. And don't use it on fungal infections, such as athlete's foot or jock itch—it will make the problem worse.

•Syrup of Ipecac…to induce vomiting after ingesting a poison.

Caution: Call a poison control center before administering—vomiting makes certain kinds of toxins more destructive.

What to use less of…

•Over-the-counter cold remedies. These fight symptoms but don't cure colds. And by drying out mucous membranes, they can hamper the body's natural defenses, slowing recovery.

Antihistamines can be sedating—don't drive or operate machinery while using them.

Decongestants can constrict blood vessels and increase heart rate, making them dangerous for people with heart problems or hypertension. Talk to your doctor before taking them.

Cough medicines may contain alcohol, as well as added decongestants and antibiotics. Read the label carefully and don't exceed recommended dosages.

What to leave out…

•Diet pills. These are completely ineffective over the long-term—they work only as long as you take them. They can be addictive. And they are very, very dangerous for people with heart problems—especially *undiagnosed* heart problems—or high blood pressure.

•Decongestant nose drops. These create a rebound effect—when you stop using them, you become as congested as before…if not more. *Better:* Steroid nasal sprays, available by prescription only.

Source: Robert L. Perkel, MD, clinical associate professor of family medicine at Thomas Jefferson University, Philadelphia 19107.

Heart Attack Self-Defense

Before using CPR, call 911—if an adult is having a heart attack. Doctors used to recommend that trained rescuers give one minute of cardiopulmonary resuscitation before calling the emergency number. *New finding:* Survival and recovery rates are better if 911 is called first. *Important exception:* For children under age eight, a trained rescuer should use proper techniques *before* calling 911. All untrained rescuers should call 911 immediately.

Source: Emergency Cardiac Care Committee and subcommittee, American Heart Association, guidelines for cardiopulmonary resuscitation and emergency cardiac care, reported in *Journal of American Medical Association*, 515 N. State St., Chicago 60610.

When to Go to the Emergency Room

A hospital is advisable when *any* of these symptoms are present—and you can't see your doctor:

•Suspicious abdominal pain. Most pain in this area stems from a temporary digestive problem and will subside by itself. But if the pain is accompanied by fever, extreme tenderness or sensitivity to jarring (it hurts more when you hop), emergency treatment is called for. The same advice holds for any extreme, writhing pain.

•Visible blood in vomit or the stool. These symptoms generally point to a dangerous condition.

•Any condition that steadily becomes worse.

•Respiratory symptoms that suggest pneumonia. Although most pneumonias are caused by viruses and are self-limiting, the bacterial varieties can progress rapidly and are life-threatening. *Danger signs:* Difficulty breathing or shortness of breath, yellow-green sputum and a high fever—more than 102°F—with shaking and chills.

Your best guide in self-diagnosis is common sense. It can also be helpful to ask the opinion of a family member or friend.

Source: Mickey Eisenberg, MD, director of emergency medical services at the University of Washington Medical Center, Emergency Department, 1959 NE Pacific St., Seattle 98195.

How to Beat Hospital Emergency Room Traffic Jams

The first rule for coping with the crowded, and often chaotic conditions prevailing at many hospital emergency rooms is to seek treatment elsewhere whenever appropriate.

Severe chest or head pain, uncontrolled bleeding, loss of consciousness or breathing difficulties do call for a visit to the ER.

However, many cuts and other seemingly serious problems can often be treated safely—and with far less delay—right in a doctor's private office.

Smart strategy: Discuss with your physician before an emergency arises precisely which emergencies he/she can treat...and which call for the services of an emergency room.

Important: Know whom to contact if your physician is out of town when trouble strikes.

Key emergency room strategies...

•Know the emergency rooms in your area. Some ERs offer only "plain vanilla" service—suturing cuts, setting fractures, treating heart attacks and the like.

Others, such as trauma centers, burn centers and head treatment centers, have the specialized staff and equipment required to treat more difficult cases.

You won't always be able to pick your emergency room—there may be only one in your community, for instance, or you might be away from home when illness or injury strikes.

For times when there is a choice, however, try to pinpoint in advance the one, or ones, best suited to meet the special needs of your family members. If you have children, for instance, pick an emergency room that is capable of dealing with pediatric cases. If a family member is mentally ill, find an emergency room that has psychiatric backup. Discuss local emergency rooms with your family doctor, and with friends and family members. Do your own research, too—phone the various emergency rooms directly. In most cases, a staff doctor or nurse will discuss with you the specifics of the facility.

•Know how to call an ambulance. Although dialing 911 now works in most areas, some communities still require patients to direct-dial the ambulance dispatcher. If you're unfamiliar with the procedure in your area, consult with your family doctor—and the emergency rooms of your choice. Knowing the exact procedure often saves precious minutes that spell the difference between life and death. *Note:* Public ambulance services seldom let patients choose which hospital they'll be taken to. However, it's usually no problem to be transferred—by private ambulance, if necessary—to the emergency room of your choice after you've gotten initial treatment at the first emergency room and if you are not critically ill or unstable.

•Know your medical history. Unlike your family doctor, who is well acquainted with your medical history, emergency-room personnel have only a few minutes—if that—to find out all they need to know regarding your health. Any difficulty in taking your history delays your treatment and opens the door to potentially deadly mistakes—such as giving penicillin to someone allergic to it.

To be safe: Prepare a list detailing your allergies, chronic ailments and what medications you take, as well as the name and phone number of your family doctor and the particulars of your health insurance policy. Take this list along with you, if possible, when you head for the emergency room. If you can, also bring along recent electrocardiograms, medical tests results, etc. *Alternative:* A medical information card or—better because it is more obvious to rushed emergency room personnel—a Medic-Alert medical information bracelet. It contains all vital information on the bracelet and allows emergency room physicians to obtain much more medical information by calling into a computer bank that stores that information. For information on purchasing a bracelet, call 800-ID-ALERT.

•Alert your family doctor as soon as possible after an emergency. If you don't have time to phone before leaving for the hospital, phone as soon as possible after you arrive. Whether your physician comes to the emergency room and speaks to the staff in person or communicates with them by phone or fax, your doctor's guidance will greatly facilitate your treatment.

•Bring along a friend or family member. Having someone to talk to while you await treatment not only comforts you and helps you pass the time in the emergency room, but also gives you an "advocate" to press for better or more prompt treatment. An advocate also helps convey to emergency room personnel important information regarding your condition.

•Stand up for yourself when necessary. Emergency room patients often are troubled because they have to wait so long before being treated. Emergency rooms do not operate upon a first-come, first-served basis. Instead, all pa-

tients are evaluated using a rigid triage process—those judged sickest or most gravely injured are treated before those whose illnesses or injuries are less severe regardless of who arrived first. Attempting to "jump ahead" of others awaiting treatment is futile. Of course, triage nurses do sometimes make mistakes—serious ones. If you feel that you need immediate attention—or if your condition significantly worsens as you await treatment—speak up...fast!

Source: Stephan G. Lynn, MD, FACEP, director, department of emergency medicine, St. Luke's/Roosevelt Hospital Center, New York City.

Emergency Room Self-Defense

Most hospital emergency rooms are not equipped to treat children. *Self-defense:* Parents with kids should check out local facilities before an emergency occurs. *Essential:* Child-sized equipment—especially oxygen masks, blood-pressure cuffs, defibrillator paddles and breathing tubes... lifesaving medicines must be on-hand in pediatric formulations...doctors and nurses should have training in pediatric emergencies.

Source: Radhike Vijayn, MD, chief, pediatrics emergency room, St. Luke's/Roosevelt Hospital, New York City.

Poison First Aid Basics

This year alone, three million people in the U.S. will be the victims of accidental poisoning. More than 400,000 will become ill...and more than 500 will die.

Depending on the amount taken, many medicines—prescribed or over-the-counter—can be toxic. And accidental poisoning can occur anywhere—at home, on the job, etc.

If you suspect that someone has been poisoned...

•Check the person's physical appearance. If he/she shows signs of illness, call 911 or your local emergency number immediately.

163

If he is not breathing, administer rescue breathing and, if necesssary, cardiopulmonary resuscitation (CPR). If you do not know these procedures, find someone who does…or follow the phone directions of trained medical personnel.

- Try to determine what substance the person has ingested and in what amount. This will help medical personnel to determine the appropriate course of treatment, if necessary.
- Contact your regional poison-control center. The number can be found on the inside cover of your phone book.

Using information that you provide, the poison center will determine the danger posed to the patient and tell you what to do.

Warning: Do not administer an antidote unless directed to by a poison center or a physician. Administered in incorrect dosages, some antidotes can have serious side effects.

Source: Scott Phillips, MD, an expert in clinical toxicology at Rocky Mountain Poison Center, Denver.

- You've sliced off a finger, toe or even a flap of skin. These can often be reattached. Wash and transport the piece in anything that's clean. A handkerchief that has been ironed is always good to use.

For less serious cuts…

- Clean the cut. Use an antiseptic, such as peroxide, or tap water.
- Cover it with a clean bandage—and remove bandage when a scab forms.
- Replace soggy dressings.
- Avoid picking scabs.
- Monitor the healing process. Watch for signs of infection. *See a doctor if:*

A cut that hurt at first, stops hurting and then becomes painful again…Streaky red lines arise, leading away from the wound…You feel tender lumps either near or far away from the cut—your lymph nodes may be swelling…A pus-filled abscess forms…A fever develops.

Source: Jack Rudick, MD, professor of surgery, Mount Sinai School of Medicine, New York City.

How to Treat a Cut

When you first cut yourself, decide quickly if you need to see a doctor.

You do need medical help if…

- The cut is deep—or bleeds a lot.
- You've cut an artery. You'll know because bright red blood will spurt out.

First aid: Apply pressure on the side of the wound nearer the heart.

- You've cut a large vein—at the wrist or higher and at the ankle or higher. (A toe or finger is not critical.) *Dark* blood flows steadily from a vein.

First aid: Apply pressure on the side of the wound away from the heart.

When in doubt about what you have cut…

Apply pressure directly on the wound—*and seek medical attention promptly.*

- You've cut yourself on something dirty. If you have not had a booster within the last year, a tetanus shot is advisable.
- You've cut a hand or foot and can't move your fingers or toes.

Better Burn Advice

Nothing hurts quite the same way that a burn does. Even the smallest of burns—from a spatter of grease or the touch of a hot iron—can smart for hours or even days. Although millions of Americans suffer burns each year, most burns (more than 90%) are relatively minor…

- *First-degree burns* affect the skin's top layer, causing redness, pain but *no* blistering. They can be treated at home and heal within hours.
- *Second-degree burns* also affect some underlying skin and can cause redness, blistering, sensitivity to air and more severe pain that may not subside for several days (many sunburns are classified as second-degree burns). These burns frequently require a visit to a hospital for treatment.

Most minor burns are caused by grabbing hot objects without realizing how hot they are or spilling hot drinks or boiling water.

And most of these burns involve the hand.

Important: Hand burns must be treated more aggressively than burns on most other parts of the body. *Reason:* The hands contain many delicate muscles and tendons in a relatively small area. If not treated quickly, permanent damage can result.

Treating minor burns…

• *Run cool water over the burn.* This will ease the pain and even reverse some damage.

• *Apply salves liberally.* Several over-the-counter products, including petroleum jelly, shark-liver oil and aloe vera gel can be used to temporarily ease the stinging.

• *Monitor the burn very closely.* If it shows any signs of infection, be sure to see your doctor immediately. *Caution:* Burns are very susceptible to secondary infections. *Helpful:* Over-the-counter antibiotic products.

Things to avoid…

• Ice. Although ice can make a burn feel better, a burn packed in ice or immersed in ice water can make the injury worse. *Warning:* You can get a burn from grabbing very *cold* as well as very hot objects.

• Butter. The salt in the butter will aggravate a burn.

Second-degree burns…

Second-degree burns should be treated by a doctor…who will:

• *Cleanse and treat the burn.* It will be washed in soapy water and then rinsed with a saline solution. Fluid may be removed from unbroken blisters, and the skin left in place to provide a natural cover.

Many emergency departments use drugs containing .5% silver nitrate solution or a 1% silver sufadiazine cream. They may also be prescribed for home use. These thick creams and gels are applied over the burn, which is then wrapped in a sterile dressing.

New: Duoderm (Squibb), a sterile air-tight dressing, is used for several weeks until the body begins to generate new skin.

• *Help you cope with the pain.* Analgesics may be prescribed.

• *Know your tetanus status.* People who suffer second-degree burns require current tetanus immunization. If you haven't had a tetanus shot in five years, you will be given one.

Severe burns…

Immediate hospitalization in a facility with a burn-care unit is needed to treat severe burns.

• *Third-degree burns* adversely affect the skin's full thickness. The burned area has a white leathery appearance. Although you may not suffer from blisters or even pain (because of destroyed nerve endings), these burns are actually very dangerous.

• *Fourth-degree burns* affect the skin's full thickness *and* underlying tissues, including muscles, tendons and bones. The burned area has a blackened appearance.

Treating severe burns…

Skin-grafting procedures may be necessary. Such procedures are performed by a surgeon or plastic surgeon or burn-care specialist who take live skin from one part of the body and move it to another part to replace cells that have been destroyed and won't regenerate. In cases where large amounts of skin are needed, it may be removed from a donor's cadaver.

Note: A great deal of promising research is now being conducted in the area of skin-grafting. *Artificial skin,* for instance, may soon be put to use in the treatment of severe burns and minimize disfigurement.

Source: Steven Chernow, MD, medical director of the emergency department of University Hopital of Boston University.

First Aid for Chemical Burns

Chemical burns to the eye usually don't cause permanent damage if rinsing starts within 15 seconds. After that, chances of recovery decline rapidly. Any innocuous water fluid can be used. Continue flushing for at least 20 minutes.

Source: John Paul Wohlen, Bradley Corp. Menomonee Falls, WI, writing in *Plant Engineering.*

Summer Safety Advice

Warm weather brings a variety of fun-filled activities including family cookouts and visits to the beach…but it also brings a range of potential health hazards…

•Animal bites. Observe extreme caution when approaching unfamiliar animals and insist that your children do likewise. Use cold water to separate fighting dogs or cats—never your hands.

Bite treatment: Superficial bites from a pet call only for washing with hot, soapy water. Pet bites that draw blood, however, as well as any bite from a wild animal, require immediate medical attention—you may need antibiotics to prevent infection.

Rabies defense: Capture or kill the biting animal, if possible, and have the local health department check it for rabies. If the animal proves rabid, or if for some reason the animal cannot be tested, you must undergo a course of rabies prophylaxis—a series of five shots administered over a one-month period. Contrary to popular belief, these shots are given in the arm, not the abdomen.

Good news: Rabies is extremely rare among cats, dogs, squirrels and rodents—although skunks, bats, raccoons, foxes and cattle are sometimes infected.

•Bee stings. Avoid bright colors, perfumes, soft drinks and sugary foods while in bee territory. Instead, douse yourself with bug repellent and don white or khaki clothing, long sleeves and pants, sturdy shoes and insect netting.

Persons allergic to bee venom should carry an epinephrine injector while outdoors...and should avoid lawn-mowing, flower-picking and other activities that are likely to put them in proximity to bees.

If you're bitten: Gently remove the stinger from your skin. Use ice packs and cold compresses to minimize swelling.

•Drowning. The third-leading cause of accidental death in the United States, drowning claims more than 4,500 victims a year.

To reduce risk: Swim, snorkel and scuba dive only with a partner...wear a Coast Guard approved life preserver whenever you're on a dock or aboard a boat...never dive into water of unknown depth.

If you become fatigued while swimming, float face-down—lifting your head only to breathe—until your strength returns or help arrives. Most people can float quite easily simply by filling their lungs with air.

•Head injuries. Motorcyclists, bicyclists, skateboarders and roller skaters should at all times wear helmets approved by the Snell Memorial Foundation. Skateboard only on driveways, empty lots, parks and other traffic-free areas. Roller skate on public roads in light traffic only if you are sufficiently skilled to move smoothly and predictably.

•Heat exhaustion and heat stroke. Strenuous exercise in hot, humid weather can cause fatigue, confusion, unconsciousness and even death.

At greatest risk: Athletes, laborers, children, the elderly and persons taking antihypertensives, antipsychotics, antidepressants and certain other prescription drugs.

To avoid trouble: Consume plenty of water or electrolyte drinks (such as Gatorade), and take frequent breaks. If you begin to experience symptoms, get out of the heat immediately. Remove all clothing, then apply cool water or ice to the skin. If symptoms persist, go immediately to the emergency room. If you are with someone who has lost consciousness, call an ambulance or get that person to an emergency room.

•Lawn mower accidents. There are more than 60,000 lawn mower accidents a year.

Self-defense: Protect yourself and your family by clearing away rocks, branches and other obstacles before mowing...wearing protective glasses, sturdy shoes and earplugs...and keeping small children indoors. Never give children mower rides—the risk of falling under the blades is too great.

•Lightning. Each year, lightning causes more than 100 deaths.

To avoid being struck: During rainstorms, avoid golf courses and other large, open areas ...isolated trees, towers and other tall structures ...wading in puddles or swimming...and holding or touching anything metallic. Quickly get inside or into a car. If nearby shelter is unavailable, head for a heavily forested area.

Last resort: Crouch.

If you are struck, seek immediate medical attention. If someone nearby has been struck, immediately call for emergency medical help. Lightning causes not only severe burns, but also cataracts and potentially fatal electrical disturbances in the heart.

•Playground injuries. Last year alone, more than 250,000 children sustained playground injuries. Inspect playground facilities carefully beforehand. *Common dangers:*

•Swing sets.

•Monkey bars and other equipment situated less than six feet from fences and other obstructions.

•Equipment loosely anchored in the ground.

•Equipment not surrounded by rubber mats, wood chips, sand or other energy-absorbing materials.

•Improper spacing of rungs and steps. (Less than nine inches separation, and children's heads can be trapped.)

•Swing seats made of wood or metal rather than rubber, canvas or another soft material.

•Fine, chalky sand found in some sandboxes. It may contain asbestos-like fibers that some believe cause respiratory problems. Children should play only in sandboxes containing coarse sand.

•Sunburn. Red, blistered skin is only one result. Less conspicuous but far more ominous is the fact that even one severe sunburn boosts your lifetime risk of melanoma and other forms of skin cancer by 10%. Gradual tanning is safer, but it too can lead to cancer—and should be avoided.

Sun-taming tools: Broad-brimmed hats, UV-absorptive sunglasses and sunscreen rated at least SPF 15. Stay out of the sun between 11 a.m. and 3 p.m., the hours of greatest sunlight intensity. *Note:* The effects of sunburn cannot be undone. However, cold compresses combined with aspirin or ibuprofen will ease discomfort as your skin recovers.

•Tick bites. Insect repellent is one obvious precaution, but it also makes sense to wear light-colored clothing (dark colors hide ticks), a long sleeve shirt and long pants tucked into your socks.

Upon returning indoors, conduct a thorough head-to-toe body search. If you find a tick, gently pull it off using your fingers or tweezers. Removing a tick using a hot match or nail polish only boosts the odds that the tick's head will be left in your skin, where it can cause infection.

Warning: Anyone bitten by a tick should be extremely wary of Lyme disease and Rocky Mountain spotted fever, two serious tick-borne illnesses. See a doctor at the earliest hint of telltale symptoms—fever, headache, muscular aches or a skin rash (especially a circular rash around the bite). Both illnesses are curable if caught early. Left untreated, however, they lead to several potentially lasting ailments, including double vision, arthritis, irregular heartbeat—even death.

Source: Kelley Hails, MD, former clinical instructor of medicine, Michigan State University College of Human Medicine, East Lansing. Dr. Hails specializes in emergency medicine.

First Aid: Diabetic Coma

Thousands of people die each year because they fall into diabetic comas and do not get the right treatment promptly.

Trap: Most diabetics' family members, friends and coworkers do not know how to properly react during such a crisis.

What to watch for: Just as there are two types of diabetes, there are two types of diabetic comas:

Hyperglycemic coma...

Patients lack enough insulin to digest sugar. *Result:* They become hyperglycemic (have excess blood sugar).

Warning sign: The inability to keep down fluids.

Times of greatest risk: When diabetics are ill, their insulin requirements rise.

Timing: These comas come on gradually over anywhere from several hours to several days.

What to do: Rush the person to the emergency room. Only professionals can administer the intravenous fluids, insulin and salts needed to correct the problem.

Hypoglycemic coma...

Patients produce excess insulin and digest sugar too fast. *Result:* They become hypoglycemic (have low blood sugar).

Warning signs: Fight or flight symptoms—anxiety, tremors and agitation. People entering these comas may act inappropriately, as if drunk.

Times of greatest risk: When patients take too much insulin…or take the right amount but miss a meal…or exercise too hard.

Timing: These comas can occur very quickly, without warning. *Note:* If your child is diabetic, be sure his teachers know that comas like this may arise.

What to do: If the person is still alert and conscious, feed him carbohydrates or protein. *Best:* Six ounces of juice or skim milk. Avoid giving the person extra table sugar or excess concentrated sweets—they force blood sugar too high. This treatment can be repeated in 20 minutes if the person fails to respond adequately.

If the person cannot ingest food, get immediate medical help. If this is not possible give him a glucagon injection. All families of insulin-dependent diabetic patients should have a glucagon kit and know how to use it.

Source: James R. Gavin III, MD, PhD, William K. Warren Professor for Diabetes Studies, department of medicine, Oklahoma University Health Sciences Center, St. Francis Medical Research Institute, Oklahoma City, Oklahoma 73104.

What to Do If Someone Faints

Old-time fainting remedies are dangerous. Placing a fainter's head between his legs could cause brain damage. Most smelling salts contain ammonium hydroxide, which can cause chemical burns of the nose and lungs. *Better:* Lay the fainter on his back. Then raise his legs. Gently massage the calves to return blood to central circulation. Wait about 20 minutes and then raise the person in stages.

Source: *RN.*

Medication Warning

Sudden vision loss may occur when people with high blood pressure and a history of glau-

coma or optic nerve strokes take hypertension medications at night. *Problem:* Patients often take these drugs at bedtime to avoid dizziness …but doing so can cause a drop in blood pressure that can lead to gradual or sudden vision loss. *Safer:* Ask your doctor about taking these medications in the morning or at midday.

Source: Sohan Singh Hayreh, MD, PhD, professor of ophthalmology and director of the Ocular Vascular Unit, University of Iowa, Iowa City. Hayreh conducted a study of 200 patients with histories of glaucoma or optic nerve strokes.

Asthmatic Children: How to Avoid Emergencies

Asthma causes more hospital and emergency room admissions than any other chronic illness of childhood.

Most of these crises could be avoided if parents only knew how to monitor their child during an attack.

To tell whether a child's asthma attack is worsening as time goes by, parents have to fully understand what they should be looking for.

Signs of trouble…

•Coughing.

Look for: A cough unaccompanied by any other cold symptoms that occurs at night…or in cold air…or when the child is exercising.

Action to take: Consult with your child's physician about appropriate asthma treatment. *Note:* The usual cough remedies (suppressants, expectorants, etc.) will not be helpful.

•Retractions. The soft tissues of the chest wall sink in when a child fails to pull enough air into his/her lungs.

Look for: Indentations between the ribs and in the soft areas near the collarbone and breastbone. These changes are much more readily seen in slim children (although some slender children suck in their chest skin when they are breathing normally).

Action to take: Familiarize yourself with how your child's chest looks during normal breathing. This way, you will be able to recognize when there is a problem.

•Wheezing. This high-pitched whistling sound occurs when air passes through narrowed passages in the lungs. At an attack's onset, wheezing occurs only when the child exhales. As the symptoms worsen, the wheezing grows louder and can also be heard when he inhales.

Grave danger: The absence of wheezing in a child who is breathing out very slowly and who also shows severe retractions may mean many of the lung's airways are totally blocked.

•Fast breathing. Most children show an increased respiratory rate during an asthma attack. Fast breathing is often the first sign of an attack in a baby.

To judge whether your child's breathing is accelerated, count his breaths for a full 60 seconds…or for 30 seconds and multiply by two. *Compare your child's rate with normal breathing rates:*

- *Infants:* 25–60 breaths per minute.
- *1 to 4 years:* 20–30.
- *4 to 14:* 15–25.
- *14 to 18:* 11–23.

Sleeping children breathe more slowly. And in very young children, it's often simpler to count breaths by watching the belly rise and fall rather than the chest.

Warning: Sometimes an older child has so much trouble breathing during an asthma attack that his respiratory rate actually drops.

All parents of asthmatic children should write out a plan based on specific advice from their physician. This will serve as a guide as to when to start or add medication. If a given medicine doesn't work, the plan should spell out when the parents should try another drug or call the doctor.

Source: Thomas F. Plaut, MD, author of *Children with Asthma: A Manual for Parents*, Pedipress, 125 Red Gate Lane, Amherst, Massachusetts 01002.

Taking a Spill

Relax and give in to your fall. Try to slide as you touch the ground. Drop any packages right away. If you tumble forward, put open hands out to break the impact and protect your face. When falling backward, try to sit as you go down, to protect your spine. If you catch a foot in a hole, drop to the side that's caught.

After the fall: Breathe deeply and get up very slowly—so you won't get dizzy and fall again.

Source: *Woman's Day*, New York.

Dental Emergencies

Toothaches, broken or knocked-out teeth, fractured jaws and other dental emergencies require immediate attention.

How to minimize pain and maximize treatment until you reach the dentist…

•Bleeding. Slight bleeding is common following a tooth extraction. If the bleeding persists longer than an hour, try pressing gauze or an ice cube against the area for 20 minutes. If that fails to stanch the flow, apply a wet tea bag. *Note:* Profuse bleeding typically requires sutures.

•Broken tooth, filling or crown. Control pain with an over-the-counter analgesic—then get to the dentist as soon as possible. Be sure to take along the piece of tooth, filling or crown.

•Gum boils. These painful, pimple-like swellings form when pus from an abscess works its way to the surface. Since they are usually a sign of a serious infection or gum disease, always consult your dentist promptly if one appears. *Recommended:* Rinse your mouth with warm salt water to keep the pus draining.

•Knocked-out (avulsed) tooth. Often these can be successfully reimplanted—if you get to the dentist promptly and if the tooth is handled delicately. *What to do:* Gently rinse the tooth in water or milk, taking care not to detach any attached soft tissue. Place the tooth in water or milk, and take it with you to the dentist or the nearest emergency room.

•Mouth sores. To reduce discomfort, apply a paste of baking soda. *Also helpful:* Over-the-counter analgesics and topical anesthetics (Anbesol, Orajel, Campho-Phenique, etc.).

•Toothache. Most toothaches result from an inflamed or dying nerve, and invariably get worse until the tooth has been treated. Take an over-the-counter analgesic, and treat the inflamed area with a few drops of oil of clove. *Avoid:* Hot packs and aspirin applied directly to the gum.

Source: Jack Klatell, DDS, chairman of the department of dentistry, Mount Sinai School of Medicine, New York City. Dr. Klatell is coauthor of *The Mount Sinai Medical Center Family Guide to Dental Health.* Macmillan Publishing Co.

Big Help in Little Emergencies

•To remove a sticky bandage without pain, first soak a cotton ball in baby oil and douse the bandage with it. The oil significantly reduces the bandage's adhesion.

Source: *Parents*, New York.

•A quick, handy ice pack in an emergency is a bag of frozen vegetables (like peas or corn niblets). The bag is clean, water-tight and pliable enough to fit almost any part of the body. (It is, of course, only a stop-gap substitution.)

Source: *Harvard Medical School Health Letter*, Cambridge, MA.

•To remove a ring from a swollen finger, use a few feet of string. Slip a few inches under and through the ring toward the wrist. Then wind the long end of the string tightly down the finger toward the tip, with the loops touching one another. (In most cases this will not be painful.) Finally, take the short end of the string and pull on it toward the fingertip. As the coil unwinds, the ring is pulled along until it falls off.

Source: *Emergency Medicine*, New York.

•Muscle trick to relieve cramps and spasms: Contract the muscles in the muscle group opposite the one that is cramped. This confuses the troubled muscle, making it relax. (*Example:* If your calf cramps, tighten the muscles in the front of your lower leg to relieve the discomfort.)

Source: *American Health.*

•Treating burns with butter or greasy ointments is dangerous. Neither is sterile and either can make subsequent treatment by a doctor more difficult. *Better:* Flush a burn with cold water or immerse it in cold water for up to 30 minutes. *Alternative:* Apply cold compresses. Cover with clean bandages. Never puncture a blister. For serious burns, seek a doctor at once.

Source: Gustavo Colon, M.D., associate professor of plastic surgery, Tulane University Medical School, quoted in *Vogue*, New York.

If You're All Alone And Choking

A choking person can save himself by falling so that a table or chair hits his diaphragm, thrusting it up against the lungs. It is the forced expulsion of air from the lungs that blows out the obstruction.

Source: Henry J. Heimlich, M.D., originator of the "Heimlich maneuver" (whereby a second person saves the choker).

Family Fire Defense

•Install a smoke detector on each floor of your home. Check them monthly. Replace batteries yearly, or when they "chirp" to signal low power.

•Plan your escape. Know two escape routes from each room. Practice escaping twice a year with your family. Never use an elevator during a fire.

•Never smoke in bed or when sleepy. Make sure cigarette butts are extinguished before discarding them.

•Never leave pots and pans unattended. Turn handles inward so kids can't reach them. Don't wear loose clothing when cooking. Don't pour water on a kitchen fire. *Better:* Smother the flames with a pot lid.

•Use space heaters carefully. Keep them at least three feet from curtains and other flammable objects. Always turn them off when you go to bed or leave home.

•Teach children about the dangers of matches and lighters. Make sure they know that they are tools, not toys. Always store them out of children's reach.

Source: Operation Life Safety, American Red Cross, 523-4 Bashford Lane, Alexandria, VA 22314.

10

The Healthy Family

What Never to Ask Your Spouse

Many couples use questions to assert power ...put down their partner...express anger covertly...or to test the emotional waters....

Many questions try to force your spouse to feel or act the same way you do. *Reality:* Everyone is an individual...and you're rarely going to get your spouse to significantly change his/her behavior—he must do that himself. *What never to ask:*

- Why do you always act that way?
- Whose side are you on, anyway?
- Why must you always embarrass me?
- Why don't you think logically?

Some questions provoke answers that will either feed your insecurities or be the basis for an argument. *What never to ask:*

- Are you angry again?
- Do you think I'm getting old...fat...bald?
- Do you still feel the same way about me as you did when we met?

- Do you think I'm stubborn...bossy... sloppy?
- Are you having an affair?
- Do you think so-and-so is attractive?
- Are you sure that it's okay for my mother to visit?

Many women are frustrated and angry about their husband's unwillingness to talk about their feelings. Their questions often mask criticism. *What never to ask:*

- Why don't we talk anymore?
- Why don't you ever tell me how you feel?
- Why don't you ever ask me what I want?

Some questions are attempts to assert power and authority over the spouse. They undermine the concept of equal partnership on which a marriage should be based. *What never to ask:*

- Who taught you to do that?
- Why are you acting just like your mother?
- Isn't it your turn to take out the garbage?
- Why can't you learn to balance a checkbook...be more responsible?
- Why can't you do anything right?

Asking such questions is often a way to avoid making a statement. *Better:* Statements that start with the word "I" and express how you feel.

Source: Psychologist Edward P. Monte, PhD, administrative coordinator, senior staff therapist, supervisor and clinical director of the South Jersey office of the Marriage Council of Philadelphia, department of psychiatry, University of Pennsylvania School of Medicine, 4025 Chestnut St., Philadelphia 19104.

What Every Child Needs to Know

Real-life lessons for every child...*Life is tough ...not everybody is going to like you...there really is no free lunch.* Once these are understood, a child won't feel crippled by false expectations. Whenever something unfair happens, he'll be able to shrug his shoulders, say, "That's normal" ...and move on from there.

Source: *Pieces for Puzzled Parents* by Ray Maloney, founder of Self-Esteem Center, 726 S. Adams, Birmingham, Michigan 48009.

Stuttering Self-Defense

Childhood stuttering starts with a conflict—a child feels he/she is not getting respect and attention but is not free to protest. Since stuttering does provide attention, it is often reinforced—and persists into adulthood.

To break the cycle: Parents can lead by example by slowing down when talking—do not tell the child to speak more slowly...listen to the child carefully...pay attention when children do not stutter—not when they do. *Helpful:* A specialist.

Source: William Perkins, PhD, director of the University of Southern California's Stuttering Center, reported in *Psychology Today,* 24 E. 23 St., New York 10010.

Free Help for Your Children's Health

If your child needs expensive medical care, the bills often can be handled without going into personal bankruptcy.

There are organizations that make billions of dollars available each year to families who need help with medical expenses. And you don't have to be impoverished to qualify.

Where the money is...

• Private foundations...the most accessible sources.

• Corporations...that often will offer programs to assist employees and their families. Ask your benefits representative or human-resources director if your company has such a program.

• Government agencies...federal, state and regional awards. Grants often are not made directly to individuals, but are awarded through a nonprofit organization, such as a hospital.

• Associations that educate the public and work to combat specific diseases. Although associations don't usually give financial assistance to individuals, many offer in-kind donations—free services—such as transportation, counseling and medication.

How to apply...

Getting this money is neither quick nor easy. But it's well within the abilities of the average parent...who is willing to invest some time and effort. Steps that need to be taken...

• Research. Your library or local bookstore has guides to foundations, associations and government agencies.

• Make sure your child qualifies. *Most common restrictions:* Geographic and by disease. Make a list of organizations whose grant requirements fit your child.

• Get information and application materials. Don't call. Send a postcard to each organization on your list, requesting a grant application and guidelines. Be patient—it usually will take three to 10 weeks before you receive a reply.

• Fill out the application. This step may sound difficult, but it's no harder than filling out a college application. After you've put the first application together, you can quickly adapt it to others.

• Read the guidelines carefully. Type, don't handwrite, application materials. And keep a copy of everything you send, so you won't have to start from scratch if something is misplaced.

Typical application includes…

• A letter or essay explaining why you need the money.

• Copies of recent tax returns. Don't worry —a high income won't necessarily disqualify you, and the information will be kept private.

• Statements from your child's physicians and/ or hospital. *Helpful:* Have your doctor send this statement to you—not directly to the organization you're applying to. That way you can put it all together efficiently…and effectively.

Source: Laurie Blum, cofounder of the Los Angeles-based fundraising firm Blum & O'Hara, and the nation's leading expert on "free money" for health, education, business, etc. She is the author of 16 books on the subject, including *Free Money for Children's Medical and Dental Care* and *Free Money for Childhood Behavioral and Genetic Disorders*, Fireside Books, 1230 Avenue of the Americas, New York 10020.

Hip-Fracture Protection

Protection against hip fractures for the elderly: External hip protectors…plastic appliances built into special underwear. These appliances divert the damaging power of a fall away from the hip bones. *Result:* A 53% reduction in the likelihood of hip fractures after falls—even though only 24% of patients given the protectors wore them regularly.

Source: Study of more than 700 nursing-home residents led by J.B. Lauritzen, MD, department of orthopaedic surgery, University of Copenhagen, Denmark, reported in *The Lancet,* 42 Bedford Sq., London WC1 B35L, England.

Brain Food for Kids

It's common knowledge that children must eat the right foods to grow up healthy and strong. But it is not so well understood that children's mental functioning can suffer if they eat the wrong foods at the wrong times even if they are well-nourished. To explore how food affects learning and behavior, here's what one of the nation's leading authorities on the subject has to tell us…

How does food affect the brain?

Almost all the fuel for the brain's work comes from glucose, a sugar manufactured from carbohydrates in the diet. In addition, the brain's neurotransmitters—the vehicles for the chemical messages sent throughout the body—are composed of the same amino acids (or their by-products) that are found in food proteins.

Like drugs, foods are psychoactive. They affect how we think, feel and relate to others. Studies show that some foods can enhance problem-solving abilities, increase alertness and improve mood and behavior. Research also shows the wrong foods can impair behavior and learning. In the long run, food affects basic intelligence by shaping brain growth and development.

Is the food-brain dynamic different in children than in adults?

A child's behavioral control system is generally more fragile, and it takes less to disrupt it.

Example: Many adults skip breakfast without any noticeable ill effects. But when schoolchildren miss breakfast—as one in four frequently does—most research suggests that their attention spans and performance suffer. The effect is most pronounced among those children with attention or learning impairments, but many normal children are also breakfast-sensitive.

What should kids eat at breakfast?

Based on a recent study at Duke, we concluded that high-carbohydrate breakfasts—toast, waffles and syrup, potatoes, doughnuts—tend to have a sedative effect on the brain as the morning wears on. Again, this effect is most severe in the hyperactive and other impaired populations. Children perform better when the carbohydrates are balanced with high-protein foods—including milk, eggs and cheese.

Is milk really the ideal food that it's cracked up to be?

Milk is rich in calcium, an essential nutrient, not only for bones and teeth, but for the proper functioning of nerve cells. When schoolchildren who missed breakfast were given morning snacks of either milk or calcium supplements, they became both calmer and more alert.

We've heard a lot about the dangers of high-fat and high-cholesterol diets, even in children. Is skim milk healthier?

Children have different nutritional needs than adults. In particular, they need appropriate amounts of fat in their diets to insulate their brain nerve cells and prevent nerve crosstalk. In extreme cases, a low-fat diet can lead to brain damage. Breast milk is ideal for infants, followed by 2%-fat milk for preschoolers, then 1%-fat milk for older children through adolescence.

Can excess sugar really make children more hyperactive?

The evidence, as reflected in numerous studies over the past 10 years, is conflicting. Some research suggests that refined sugar induces inappropriate behavior, poor attention and even —in some hyperactive children—aggression. But other studies show no clear effect. In our breakfast study at Duke, we found that hyperactive children seemed to benefit when they received a sugar drink in conjunction with a high-protein meal—they quieted down. But their behavior worsened when they got the sugar drink with other carbohydrates. *Note:* When they had the sugar drink by itself, they behaved about the same as after drinking a placebo. Normal children responded similarly, though less dramatically. Again, balance was the key factor.

Are you saying that sugar itself isn't bad for kids?

I'm saying that a child's sugar craving may serve a physiological purpose—and that a parent's challenge is to manage that craving, rather than to try to eliminate it. A child typically goes through three spurts of brain growth—between three and five years of age...nine and 11...and 12 and 14. During each spurt, the brain requires more fuel, or glucose, than at other times— which might account for a child's desire for high-carbohydrate foods, including refined sugar, or sucrose. That said, fructose—the sugar found in fruits—can provide brain fuel just as well as sucrose...and will raise less havoc with the child's blood sugar along the way.

How do you handle this issue in your home?

I allow my child one refined sugar treat a day, but only one—be it a Popsicle, a candy bar or a cupcake. It's a mistake to give children uncontrolled access to the refrigerator.

Is there any food which you would ban from a child's diet altogether?

I would not give a child any drink sweetened with aspartame (NutraSweet). This substance has no nutritional value...and there is some evidence that it can provoke hyperactivity.

Do you believe in dietary supplements for children?

When children eat a balanced diet, very few need any supplementation. In fact, they are better off without it, since supplements can throw off the body's mineral balance. The one positive exception is iron supplementation for adolescent females, who lose iron in menstruation.

Source: C. Keith Conners, PhD, director of the Center for Attention Deficiency Disorders in Children at Duke University Medical School. He is the author of *Feeding the Brain/How Foods Affect Children*, Plenum Publishing, 233 Spring St., New York 10013.

Alcohol Danger For the Elderly

The older a person is, the less alcohol it takes to harm his/her body. As we age, lean body mass shrinks, water content declines, and the liver enzymes that break down alcohol become less efficient. *Result:* Alcohol concentration in the blood increases...and the level of alcohol intake that was considered social drinking when a person was younger may have the same effect as heavy drinking in someone who is older...leading to diseases of the heart, liver, and other organs.

Source: Substance abuse expert Edward Reilly, MD, professor of psychiatry, University of Texas Medical School, Houston.

Dealing with Childrens' Phobias

While most childhood fears are a normal part of growing up, parents often worry that a particular fear or pattern of fears is abnormal. In such cases, a little information often helps.

Common questions…

•Which fears are normal? All children are born with innate fears of loud noises and of falling down. As they mature and come in contact with their environment, they typically begin to fear machines, big objects, toilets, animals, strangers, leaving mom and dad.

As their imagination comes to life, children may fear the dark, sleeping alone, monsters, the supernatural, thunder and lightning.

Still later, as children enter their pre-teen years, they'll encounter social fears—fear of looking foolish, speaking in public, doing poorly in school.

•How should parents treat fears? Never belittle a child's fear or say that the fear is silly. To the child, the fear is all too real. If you shame children for their fears, the fear may disappear for a brief time…only to explode later on. *Also important:*

•Never force children to confront a fear—for example, by throwing a child who's afraid of the water into a swimming pool. Doing so may intensify the fear.

•Don't cater to a child's fear. Some parents avoid the object of a child's fear altogether, keeping a child from ever having to confront a scary situation. On the other hand, some parents say, "Oh, don't worry about that doggie," but they send another message by holding the child close to them as the dog approaches.

•How can parents keep a child's fears from snowballing? Prepare your child for new experiences gradually.

Example I: Before the first day of school, take your child to visit the school and meet the other children. Read books about school and talk about things that children do at school.

Example II: A child who fears dogs may be thinking, "This dog is going to eat me!" Let the child stand back and watch the dog as it inter- acts with others. Talk about dogs. Explain that tail-wagging and jumping can be signs of friendliness. Pet the dog while your child watches.

•What if a fear lingers…or becomes very intense? Whether your child fears spending the night out, bees and wasps, bridges, germs, etc., do not ignore the fear and assume it will just go away.

Danger: Many full-blown adult phobias—including agoraphobia (fear of open spaces or leaving the home), acrophobia (fear of heights), and fears of animals—have their roots in childhood fears that were never addressed.

Take direct action…

There are several strategies for helping your child overcome his/her fear. *Most helpful:*

•Explain that fear is a normal physiological condition. Tell your child that it's part of the fight-or-flight response that arose to protect our ancestors from saber-tooth tigers and other predators.

Assuming your child is in good health, the physical manifestations of fear are not dangerous …whether it's a rapidly pounding heart, "butterflies" in the stomach, fast breathing, lightheadedness or dizziness, trembling, clammy hands, sweating, tingling in hands or feet, etc. Make sure your child realizes this.

•Work together. Say, "We've got a problem, and we're going to solve it together. You've been waking up at night because you're afraid of the dark. Let's work on getting over this together. It's going to be fun."

•Teach positive self-talk. Explain to your child that it's possible to counter fearful thoughts by silently repeating positive ones based on real information. *Fear:* "That dog will bite me." *Positive self-talk:* "That dog is wagging his tail. He's friendly."

•Give your child correct information…what he needs to know to counteract the fear. *Problem:* Kids have gaps in their knowledge. A child who fears the dark may know something about darkness but may not understand why it gets dark or how long it takes the eyes to adjust. *Typical result:* Panic. As darkness falls, your child starts imagining monsters instead of thinking, "Wait a minute, I'm still in my room. That shape I see over there must be the lamp on my desk."

Educating your child about darkness and its effects on vision and the appearance of familiar objects may help him/her overcome fear.

Similarly, let your child know that not everything she sees or hears is true. If your daughter hears a noise and fears there is a monster under her bed, for example, explain to her, "That's not a monster, that's the water running."

• Teach your child relaxation techniques. Tension causes your child to take short, shallow breaths—and that intensifies the panic. *Fear reducers:* Deep muscle relaxation and "belly" breathing—deep, slow, rhythmic breathing from the diaphragm. Show your child how.

Four-step technique...

In *Monsters Under the Bed*, we present a four-step desensitization process for extreme or persistent fears. Say your son is afraid of the dark...

• Step one: Imagination. Use picture books, videos, television programs and "make-believe" games and stories to help your son create fear-reducing positive images. Tell a story in which he wakes up in the middle of the night, looks calmly around and goes back to sleep.

• Step two: Information. Give your son helpful facts appropriate to his age and specific fear. Educate him about darkness. Watch sunrises and sunsets together. Use an encyclopedia to study the eye.

• Step three: Observation. Use modeling to help him safely come in contact with his fears. *What to do:* Without directly comparing your son to other children, let him observe a child who goes to bed easily in the dark. Say, "Look how the child falls asleep." Or, stand with your son in a darkened room so he experiences his eyes adjusting to the dark.

• Step four: Exposure. Slowly familiarize your son to the darkness using a set of graduated activities. First, have him walk into a dark room and stay for a few seconds. Slowly increase the time spent in the dark. Play hide and seek in the dark, follow the leader in and out of darkened spaces, eat dessert in the dark. Do as few or as many of these activities as your son needs to overcome the fear.

Crucial: Set a comfortable pace—don't try to do it all in one day. Have your child use a rating scale of 1 (no fear) to 10 (terrified). If your child

signals five or greater, immediately stop what you're doing. Repeat the experience slowly until your child is more comfortable. This gives him/her a sense of control.

When to seek help...

If your child remains extremely fearful despite all your efforts, seek help from a psychotherapist specializing in fears and anxiety disorders. Before the initial visit, make sure the therapist has had previous success treating your child's specific fear.

For a list of specialists in your area, send a self-addressed, stamped, business-sized envelope to the Anxiety Disorders Association of America, 6000 Executive Blvd., Suite 200, Rockville, MD 20852.

Source: Marianne Daniels Garber, PhD, an educational consultant in private practice at the Behavioral Institute of Atlanta. She is the coauthor, with Stephen W. Garber, PhD, and Robyn Freedman Spizman, of *Monsters Under the Bed and Other Childhood Fears: Helping Your Child Overcome Anxieties, Fears and Phobias,* Villard Books, 201 E. 50 St., New York 10022.

Long-Distance Care For an Aging Parent Or Relative

In today's highly mobile society, more and more Americans are called on to provide care for aging loved ones—from a distance.

Finding good care for an aging relative can be stressful under the best of circumstances... but it can be particularly worrisome when the caregiver isn't around to provide face-to-face support and follow-up.

Fortunately, there is a way to set up and monitor an effective plan from a distance.

First, discuss care options with the older person—while he or she is still in good health, if possible.

A decline in health and independence can occur quite suddenly. While you may not feel comfortable talking about these issues, it's much easier to discuss them before things have reached a crisis point.

The conversation—or series of conversations—can take place in person or by phone. Be gentle but persistent. Your relative may not want to face the subject any more than you do …or may not be straightforward about preferences for fear of being a burden to you.

Good way to begin: "Mom, I know you're doing great, but we're all getting older. I was just talking to my kids about how I'd like things to be handled if I couldn't take care of myself. If you were to become weak or ill, what would you want to have us do?"

Explore the older person's attitudes about various care arrangements, from in-home assistance to relocation to a partial- or full-care facility.

Also, try to get a sense of your relative's financial resources…and whether savings and insurance are sufficient to pay for future care. *Helpful questions:*

•"What happened during your last doctor's visit? Perhaps we should give the pharmacist a list of your medications to make sure there are no dangerous interactions."

•"When was the last time you reviewed your will? It might be a good idea to make sure it is up to date."

•"How do you feel about (a recent life change such as loss of a spouse, retirement, moving to a new home, etc.)?"

•"You look like you've lost/gained a few pounds since my last visit. How is your appetite?"

It's helpful to think of care-planning as a partnership between the older person and the caregiver. As much of the decision-making as possible should rest with the older person…with the goal of preserving his/her independence.

Start a care log…

A care log is simply a loose-leaf notebook (or whatever filing method you prefer) that allows you to keep all the information about the older person's care in one place. You may want to set up sections for community resources, helpful friends and neighbors, travel (for your own visits), medical information and so on.

In the log, keep all your notes from phone conversations, as well as agency names and contact people, literature on available services and relevant medical, legal, insurance and financial papers.

Your care log will help the entire planning process go more smoothly. If you're asked to provide eligibility data, such as Social Security cards, proof of income or medical insurance documents, you can get your hands on it quickly. And if you need to make an emergency visit, you can pick up your log and go.

Identify problems and needs…

If you live far away from your aging relative, you must be especially observant, both during phone conversations and when you visit. The older person won't necessarily make an announcement when health begins to decline or needs change.

Watch for potential danger signs, such as weight loss…difficulty in moving around…forgetfulness…decreased ability to perform basic chores like eating, bathing or taking medications properly.

Of course, your relative may be quite open about what the problems are. But one problem could have several possible causes. You may have to do a little digging to find out the best way to address the need.

Example: Your father isn't eating properly and is losing weight. If he's too weak to prepare food, then a Meals-on-Wheels program might be all he needs. But if the problem is ill-fitting dentures…or that he's too depressed and listless to eat…or that he can't see well enough to drive to the grocery store, then the solutions would be very different. You might need to have the dentures adjusted…find someone to sit with him to make mealtime less lonely and make sure he's eating…or arrange for assistance with food shopping.

In addition to your own observations, ask friends or neighbors for their views. Someone who visits often might be able to tell you…

•There's never any food in the house, or

•There's food, but it's not eaten, or

•I've noticed that when he's eating, his dentures keep slipping out.

The informal network…

In most cases, the older person is part of a network of friends, neighbors and associates who are already involved in lending a hand.

Examples: The mail carrier who makes sure your mother picks up her mail every day…a friend from the bridge club who offers a ride when needed...a young mother from the neighborhood who brings her toddler over for friendly visits.

These people can be valuable sources of assistance and reassurance. Ask your relative whom he/she sees on a regular basis.

Also, identify people who might be willing to help but haven't yet gotten involved.

Examples: Members of the person's church, synagogue or social clubs.

Call each person in the network. Introduce yourself, explain the needs that most concern you and find out if they'd be willing to help out on a consistent schedule.

Examples: Friends or neighbors might be able to help your mother get dressed in the morning...stop by every other day to see that she's eaten a proper meal...make sure she's on top of her bills...drive her to doctor's appointments...pick up groceries once a week...call daily at a specified time and get in touch with you if there's no answer.

Formal resources...

In addition to the informal network, there are several organizations that can provide assistance.

Most communities have a host of services available to the elderly. Many are free or low-cost, although some services—especially residential—are more expensive.

Services in the home...

• Meal-delivery programs.

• Assistance with housework.

• Phone-in and personal visitor programs.

• Emergency response systems. *Example:* Electronic gadgets worn around the neck or placed in a bathroom or bedroom allow the person to signal for help.

• In-home health services, such as physical therapy or nursing.

Services in the community...

• Transportation services.

• Adult day-care centers. They provide social contact, recreation and even therapeutic activities.

• Support groups.

• A variety of housing arrangements, from congregate living (separate apartments with common facilities and possibly a staff person on call) to nursing homes providing 24-hour care.

In addition, larger metropolitan areas offer all kinds of creative services, from visiting-pet programs to traveling entertainment.

Locating these services can be difficult, since they are often administered by many different organizations. One good source of information is your company's employee-assistance program or human resources department. Many large corporations have programs to assist caregivers, ranging from information to support groups.

Another useful resource...

The National Elder Care Locator Service, 800-677-1116. Ask for the phone number of the area Agency on Aging that serves your relative's community. This agency, which is often run at the county level, may provide services—or it may function as a referral service, putting you in touch with local providers.

Be ready to describe your relative's needs specifically and in detail. Some local agencies are a pleasure to deal with—their representatives are enthusiastic, resourceful, well-trained and willing to tell you everything you need to know. Others seem more like government bureaucracies. You may be shuttled from person to person and given conflicting information. This can be especially frustrating when you're calling long-distance.

Telephone research basics...

• Call early in the morning for a quick response—before people get tied up with the day's business.

• Use a friendly, upbeat, assertive tone. Staffers encounter upset callers all day long and appreciate a friendly voice.

• Always identify yourself. Then get the name and direct phone number of everyone you talk to.

• Ask to speak to a social worker, caseworker or case manager. They are specially trained to help you zero in on the problems you and your relative are facing—and to help you identify possible solutions.

• Ask about eligibility criteria, fees and alternative options for all services offered.

• If you go in for a face-to-face appointment, find out beforehand everything you'll need to take with you—so you won't have to waste time going back for missing records and then rescheduling. I suggest making a second call before the appointment to verify this information with another representative.

•Send a thank-you note to anyone who has been especially pleasant or helpful. People appreciate this all-too-rare gesture and will be even happier to help in the future.

Set up a monitoring system...

It's not enough to put together a care program—you must also make sure that the services you've arranged are delivered consistently.

Make sure everyone in your care network—formal and informal—has your phone number. Invite them to call you collect in an emergency.

From your network resource lists, identify a few key contacts—people whom your relative trusts and with whom he/she is in regular contact. Develop a relationship with these contact people. Encourage them to call you for any reason.

Whether a service is being provided is easy to assess—simply ask the older person.

Quality monitoring is trickier. Your relative may have unrealistically high expectations...or may not expect enough. An understanding of your relative's personality will help you to interpret this feedback.

Caution: Never dismiss a complaint without first checking it out yourself or having one of your contact people do so.

Monitoring the informal network takes special tact—after all, these people are doing you a favor. One way to handle the situation is with a periodic thank-you call, coupled with a request for information about the older person.

Example: "Thanks so much for coming over every day and making sure Dad's eating. It's making such a difference. By the way, have you noticed any changes in his condition that I should be aware of?"

Not only does this give you information about your relative, it also affords the contact person the opportunity to say, "Actually, I'm only coming twice a week."

Be prepared to adjust your care plan. Based on the ability of your network to deliver, you may need to look for ways to fill in unexpected gaps.

If you're still concerned about your ability to ensure your relative's well-being from a dis-

tance, consider hiring an outside consultant—such as a family therapist, social worker or geriatric specialist. They can help you cut through red tape, explore new solutions and deal with the complicated emotions involved in caring for an aging loved one.

Source: Angela Heath, MGS (master of gerontological studies), a nationally recognized author, lecturer and consultant on caregiving issues. She is the president of Heath and Company, a Washington, DC-based consulting firm that provides aging-related services to corporations, and the author of *Long Distance Caregiving: A Survival Guide for Far Away Caregivers*, American Source Books, Box 280353, Lakewood, Colorado 80228. 800-356-9315.

Safer Glasses for Kids

Children's eyeglasses should be made with polycarbonate lenses. Kids can be very hard on eyeglasses, and regular plastic lenses are not strong enough to withstand their tough level of wear. Polycarbonate lenses, most commonly used in sports glasses, provide better protection against serious injury if glasses break during sports—or any kind of rough play. Very active children should also have eyeglass frames made for sports.

Source: Melvin Schrier, OD, an optometrist in private practice in New York City.

How to Promote Healthy Teeth in Your Child Before Birth

A baby's teeth begin to develop at approximately eight weeks in utero and continue developing throughout pregnancy. Pregnancy can also affect the mother's teeth and gums. *What a pregnant woman can do to ensure healthy teeth in herself and her child:*

•Take the vitamins your obstetrician recommends. Vitamins and minerals are the building blocks for all tissue—including teeth. *Especially important for strong teeth and gums:* Calcium... vitamin D, which aids in calcium absorption... vitamin C, which contributes to tissue formation.

• Avoid cigarettes and alcohol. Studies link both to inhibiting absorption of vitamins and minerals—sometimes seriously.

• Decrease stress. New research suggests that anxiety reduces a woman's ability to absorb important nutrients. You may not be able to eliminate all sources of stress from your life, but at least get plenty of rest—don't run yourself down.

• Take care of your own teeth. During pregnancy, a woman's body works extra hard to fight off possible infection. Gums may overreact to bacteria in the mouth, and are likely to bleed and become inflamed. To keep your teeth healthy, brush and floss regularly throughout pregnancy. Visit your dentist at least once during this period for a professional cleaning. *Important:* Tell your dentist you're pregnant, and avoid dental or any other X rays, especially during the first trimester, if possible.

Source: Robert S. Rauch, DDS, a dentist in private practice in Milford, Connecticut. Dr. Rauch is the author of *Smile: Be True to Your Teeth and They'll Never Be False To You*, available through his office at 91 Cherry St., Milford, Connecticut 06460.

Keeping Kids Safe

Ninety percent of all childhood injuries are preventable. *To avoid injury from:*

• Bicycles, skateboards, roller skates. Cyclists and skaters should wear helmets at all times. Skaters should also wear protective padding on hands and knees.

• Choking. Safety pins and coins used to be the biggest culprit—now it's food.

Special hazard: Hot dogs. They can become lodged in the throats of young children. Children younger than four should be fed hot dogs only if the hot dogs are first sliced lengthwise, then across. Choking kills more than 300 kids a year.

• Fireworks. Do not buy fireworks for home use. Instead, attend public fireworks displays. Fireworks injure more than 12,000 people a year—half of them children.

• Lawn mowers. Kids should be at least 12 years old before they're allowed to use walk-behind mowers—at least 14 years old before they're allowed to use riding mowers. Almost 10,000 children a year sustain cuts, loss of fingers and toes, broken bones, and eye injuries from lawn mowers.

Source: Recommendations from the American Academy of Pediatrics, 141 Northwest Point Blvd., Box 927, Elk Grove Village, Illinois 60009.

TV and Teenagers

The more junior-high and high-school students watch television, the worse they do on standardized tests. The correlation applies in writing, math, reading and science exams. However, researchers found no comparable relationship between fourth-graders' TV habits and test performance.

Source: Study by Illinois State Board of Education.

Prime Source Of Cavities

Dentists are right—sugar is indeed a prime source of cavities in children. Researchers replaced sugar with natural fruit purées and sugar substitutes in the diets of 73 institutionalized children ages 5–17 for five years. *Result:* 53% of the children had no cavities. None were missing any permanent teeth.

Source: *American Journal of Public Health.*

Teenagers' Special Mouth Problems

Teenagers' mouths are especially susceptible to gingivitis—inflamed and often bleeding gums. *Reasons:* Adolescents' high hormone levels increase the number of blood vessels in the mouth. *Prevention:* A dental cleaning twice a year (to prevent plaque build-up) and reduction of sugary snacks. If unchecked, gingivitis can lead to periodontitis, a more serious gum disease.

Source: Dr. Jon Suzuki, University of Maryland, in *American Health*.

Fear of Drilling

When taking a child under six to the dentist, do not announce the visit until the day of the appointment (to minimize anxiety). *Also:* If there's going to be pain, be frank about it. Let the child know that it will last only a very short time. Follow the visit with an especially pleasant activity. *Counterproductive:* Threatening a child with a trip to the dentist as punishment.

Source: Barbara Melamed, professor of psychology, University of Florida, quoted in *USA Today*.

Kind of Music Premature Babies Love

Premature babies appear to thrive on soft classical music. In one recent study, the weight of preemies increased faster than usual when doctors played Bach, Beethoven and Brahms. *Less effective:* Popular music or rock.

Source: Study at the University of California Medical Center, reported in *The Salk Letter*.

Heat and Babies' Health

It is a great mistake to think that a newborn infant cannot be kept too warm. Overzealous wrapping can cause dehydration and aggravation of fever, in some cases leading to convulsions, heatstroke and even death. A baby that has a high fever should not be wrapped or even covered if it is in a warm room. Sponge the infant with cool water to control fever and contact a pediatrician.

Source: *Archives of Disease in Childhood*.

Kids and Snow

Children shouldn't eat snow. Like water, snow can be polluted—even if it appears clean and white. Most snow, however, is only minimally dirty.

Source: Peter R. Simon, MD, a member of the American Academy of Pediatrics Committee on Environmental Health, quoted in *Parents*, 685 Third Ave., New York 10017.

Mysterious Cause Of Respiratory Problems

Wood-burning stoves can cause respiratory problems in preschool-age children, according to the results of a Michigan study.

Source: *Medical World News*.

Childhood Nosebleeds

Frequent nosebleeds in children are usually the result of rubbing the inside of the nose. *To prevent nosebleeds:* Clip the child's nails, insert a lubricant in the nose and use bedroom humidifiers in dry climates.

Don't Ignore "Growing Pains"

"Growing pains" may indicate a health problem in your child. If they occur frequently, cause a fever, change the form of the body or are accompanied by weight loss—suspect trouble. Real growing pains take place during the night, between the knee and ankle. Aspirin, massage and heat will take care of most of the discomfort.

Source: *The Salk Letter*.

Early Hearing Loss

Repeated colds and allergic reactions are experienced by one third of children in their first two years of life. *Result:* The baby doesn't hear as well as he should...which in turn hampers linguistic, mental and social development. *Recommended:* Have your baby screened for possible hearing loss, beginning at four months.

Source: Burton White, director of the Center for Parent Education, Newton, MA.

You May Be the Cause Of Your Child's Ear Problems

• A parent who smokes is more likely to raise children with chronic ear infections. When both parents smoke, their child is almost three times more likely to develop ear problems than a child in a nonsmoking household.

• Persistent middle ear effusions (fluid build-up in the middle ear) are more common in children who are exposed to cigarette smoke. Exposure to three cigarette packs' worth of smoke increases the chance of infection four times. Children who are also predisposed to allergies or nasal congestion are six times as likely to have this problem.

Source: *Journal of the American Medical Association.*

Another Reason Not to Smoke

Children of smokers are more susceptible to coughing, wheezing and pneumonia than are children of nonsmokers. *Also at greater risk:* Nonsmokers who work closely with smokers.

Causes of Bloody Stool

Blood in a child's stool usually does not indicate a life-threatening condition. But consult your physician to be safe. The source of gastrointestinal bleeding in children is often temporary stomach irritation caused by aspirin. *Other sources:* Ulcers or rectal fissures. Often what appears to be blood in feces or vomitus is something else—for example, red jello, beets, or even the antibiotic ampicillin.

Source: William Spivak, MD, chief of pediatric gastroenterology, Cornell Medical Center, New York, quoted in *The Salk Letter.*

Mono Isn't for Teens Only

Mononucleosis can strike children of any age, not just adolescents. In young children, however the disease manifests itself as a minor upper respiratory illness, not the exhausting condition associated with high school and college students.

Source: Dr. Stephen A. Spector, assistant professor of pediatrics, University of California at San Diego, quoted in *Parents.*

Scoliosis Home Checkup

Scoliosis is the abnormal (side to side) curvature of the spine that affects some growing children. The curvature displaces bone structure, causing deformity and heart and lung problems. *How to check:* Ask the child to stand straight so you can see if the spine is normal. Then, as he bends over with his arms dangling, run your hand down his spine. Feel for any side-to-side movement of the spine. If you notice anything unusual, contact your doctor at once.

Source: Scoliosis Association, 1 Penn Plaza, New York 10119.

Adopted-Child Alert

Adopted children are 10 times as likely to be hyperactive as other children. *Possible reasons:* Poor prenatal care and diet…the inability of an adoptive mother to nurse the baby.

Source: *Foods for Healthy Kids* by Dr. Lendon Smith, Berkley Books, New York.

Heart Disease and Kids

One-third of schoolchildren face a high risk of premature heart disease. *Signs:* High cholesterol levels in the blood, high blood pressure, obesity, bad exercise habits and cigarette smoking. Although heart disease usually strikes at midlife, its seeds are planted in childhood, when lifetime habits are formed. *Best:* Give children a proper diet. Watch particularly that fat- and sugar-loaded ice cream and pies and salt-laden chips and nuts are only an occasional treat. *Of utmost importance:* Establish good exercise habits. This is as vital to the child as eating, sleeping and going to school.

Source: Research by the American Heart Association quoted by Jane Brody in *The New York Times*.

A Leading Cause of Athletic Injuries

Pushing young athletes can result in "overuse" injuries such as stress fractures, tendinitis of the shoulder, bursitis of the hip and tennis elbow. These injuries in children were unheard of before the advent of organized sports programs after World War II. Even now, doctors rarely see these problems in youngsters who play sports among themselves without special coaching. (Children do not push themselves too hard.) *Most frequent cause of injury:* Inappropriate or excessive training. Children are particularly susceptible to injury when they are tired or in pain. *Remedy:* Make sure that the coaches or trainers who work with your children are sensitive to this issue and that they have a proper perspective on what a sports program is really about.

Source: Dr. Lyle Micheli, director of sports medicine, Children's Hospital Medical Center, Boston, quoted in *The Ladies' Home Journal*.

Corrective Shoe Myth

Most corrective shoes for children are of little or no value, according to medical experts polled by *The New York Times'* Jane E. Brody. Some 50%–90% of children are born with flat feet, bowlegs, pigeon toes, or other "problems." The vast majority of children outgrow these conditions naturally if given the chance.

Best Circumcision Method

An electric cauterizing needle used in conjunction with a metal clamp to perform circumcision can be extremely dangerous. Infants may suffer severe penile burns. *Best:* If circumcision is to be performed, a physician should use the traditional scalpel and clamp, or electrocautery without a metal clamp.

Source: Dr. A. Barry Belman, Children's Hospital National Medical Center, Washington, DC.

When Your Child Has To Go to the Hospital

Have a thorough talk with the doctor to find out what procedures are involved, how the child will feel, and the probable length of stay. Explain to your child—simply but honestly—what's in store. Visit the hospital (with the child, if allowed). Try to meet medical and nursing staff. Find out if you can stay with the patient overnight. Pack your child's favorite clothes (if allowed) and toys. Make sure at least one parent is there throughout the child's waking hours. That way you can both keep an eye on what's happening and allay your child's anxiety.

Source: *Parents.*

Bad-Tasting Medicine Tip

Bad-tasting medicine goes down more easily when you rub an ice cube over the youngster's tongue first. This temporarily "freezes" the taste buds to make the medication more palatable.

Source: *Practical Parenting Tips* by Vicki Lansky, Meadowbrook Press, Deephaven, MN.

Beware of Sugar In Medicine

Sugar in medicine makes it palatable to children. But it is harmful to their teeth if the medicines are taken regularly. *Best:* After taking sweet medication, children should rinse their mouths and brush their teeth.

Where the Fattest Kids in the US Live

Children who live in the Northeast are more than twice as likely to grow up obese as those who live in the West. And they're three times as likely to be super-obese. The typical fat kid is also white and lives in a large metropolitan area.

Theory: Environmental factors (such as a climate permitting year-round outdoor play) have a strong role in determining weight.

Source: Research by Dr. William Dietz and Dr. Steven Gortmaker, in *American Health.*

Why a Fat Child Shouldn't Go On a Diet

•Fat children do better when encouraged to maintain their present weight, rather than to reduce it. *Reason:* If the child's weight remains constant, he'll grow naturally into it. But a strict diet could interfere with bone and tissue growth.

Source: *RN.*

•Chubby children are more likely to become obese adults if they regain their baby fat before the age of five and a half. This "rebound" stage is the time when fat cells grow in size and number. *Advice:* Strict diets are a bad idea. But if children become plump at age three or four, encourage them to be more physically active.

Source: Research at the French National Institute of Health, in *American Health.*

How a Mother Can Help Her Child Diet

Obese children lose the most weight when their mothers diet with them. *Hitch:* If the mothers attend the same weight-watching sessions as the kids, the diet program does not work as well for the child. Mothers must be involved, but at a distance.

Source: Dr. Kelly D. Brownell, University of Pennsylvania, reporting on a study of 42 obese children ages 12 through 16.

Why Some Kids May Be Short

Fear of obesity can lead to short stature and delayed puberty among children who regularly skip meals. A recent study found that 3% of high school students were short due to poor nutrition.

Source: *New England Journal of Medicine.*

Taming Your Baby's Sweet Tooth

A baby's sweet tooth is natural, but it can be tamed by early eating experiences. *Key:* Avoiding baby foods with added sugar. *Healthful sugar substitutes:* Fruit juices plus water (for sweetened drinks). Fruits and vegetables (for candy and cookies). Unsweetened cereals (for presweetened ones).

Source: *American Health.*

Don't Feed Honey To Babies

Hold the honey for babies under one year. *Reason:* Even "pure" or "filtered" honey contains tiny amounts of bacteria. Although harmless to older children and adults, these can lead to botulism in an infant. *Symptoms:* Constipation, lethargy, feeding trouble.

Source: *Vegetarian Times.*

Hold the Salt

Infants who ate salty foods during their first 18 months tended to have a higher salt consumption at age 4. *Conclusion:* The taste for salt is acquired. If consumption can be cut early in life, that taste can be minimized—and with it, the risk of hypertension in adulthood.

Source: *Medical World News.*

Peanut-Butter Hazard

Chunky peanut butter (which has pieces of peanuts in it) is potentially hazardous to younger children. Some children don't chew as well as others, and some have smaller passageways in the throat. Peanut fragments can get stuck. *Safer:* Creamy peanut butter.

Source: *Harvard Medical School Health Letter.*

Hot Dog Danger

Hot dogs can be dangerous for children. Hot dogs are just the right size to get caught in tiny throats. *Better way:* Cut the frankfurters lengthwise for all youngsters under 10.

Source: *Time Tolls.*

More children choke to death on hot dogs than on any other food. *Also dangerous:* Cookies. *Most lethal for adults:* Steak, chicken, lobster.

Source: Research at Johns Hopkins University.

High Blood Pressure Alert

A good breakfast can help prevent children from developing high blood pressure. *Reason:* Children who skip breakfast often compensate later in the day by eating salty snacks, which then can lead to weight gain and hypertension.

Source: Robert Borgman, food science professor, Clemson University, Clemson, SC, in *American Health.*

Baby-Bottle Nipple Alert

Rubber baby-bottle nipples may contain unacceptable levels of nitrosamines, which are suspected carcinogens. *Advice:* Boil new nipples five or six times before use (using fresh water each time).

Source: US Food and Drug Administration, in the *Harvard Medical School Health Letter.*

Accidental Poisonings

Two of every three poisoning cases involve children under age five. More than 500,000 children are victims each year.

Child poisonings are most apt to occur just before mealtime. Junior will consume whatever he can get his hands on. Children frequently eat poisonous indoor and outdoor plants. *Example:* Philodendron causes swelling of the tongue and severe vomiting.

Source: New York City Poison Control Project, Bellevue Hospital Center, 27th St. and First Ave., New York 10016.

Diapering-Time Dangers

Changing diapers on a seven-month-old or older child can be dangerous, according to a survey by a Massachusetts poison control center. Starting at this age, tots have the strength and dexterity to grab objects around them and put them in their mouth. *Particularly hazardous:* All the toxic substances that surround the changing table—powder, wipes, shampoo, ointment, oil, etc. (Keep a close watch on the open safety pins, too.)

Source: *Journal of the American Medical Association.*

Common Causes Of Poisoning

Poisons aren't limited to common household products such as cleaning agents or drugs. Cigarette butts, motor oil and some brightly colored berries also can be harmful to children. Fur further details, get the long list compiled by the National Capital Poison Center.

Source: National Capital Poison Center, Georgetown University Hospital, 388 Reservoir Rd. NW, Washington, DC 20007.

•Perfumes, colognes and aftershaves cause up to 10% of accidental childhood poisonings. *Fatal ingredient:* Ethanol (alcohol), which can be harmful even in small doses.

Source: American Red Cross.

Most Dangerous Time of Day

Children are poisoned by household chemicals most frequently from 4 pm to 8 pm. That's when they tend to be bored and their parents are busy with dinner activities.

Source: Whitehall Laboratories, New York.

Home Safety Tip

Red as a danger signal is a good lesson to teach children who cannot read. Once this lesson is learned, paint red the tops of all bottles or containers at home that hold harmful substances.

Source: *Parents.*

When a Child Is Choking

When a child is choking: (1) Place the child over your lap, head down, and try four to six slaps on the back (between and below the shoulder blades). (2) If the object is not dislodged, try four Heimlich procedures. Hold the child around the waist and thrust upward with a closed fist. (3) If that doesn't work, look in the child's mouth to see if you can remove the obstruction with your fingers. (4) As a last resort, try mouth-to-mouth resuscitation. *Parent alert:* Choking is the leading cause of accidental death at home for children age six and younger.

Source: *Clinical Pediatrics.*

Dogs that Shouldn't Be Trusted

Evidence indicates that certain types of dogs pose the greatest risk to children who might be bitten by a pet. *The danger:* Dogs have a natural tendency to bite each other on the face and neck as a form of aggressive play. They might approach small children in the same spirit. Dogs most likely to exhibit the behavior include German shepherds, malamutes and huskies. *To protect kids:* Never leave a dog of any breed with a small child, even when the child seems safe in a playpen or crib. Explain to older children why they should use care when playing with a dog, even a familiar one.

Source: *Journal of the American Medical Association.*

Play that Could Hurt Your Child

Tossing an infant playfully into the air can cause brain damage, even death. *Also dangerous:* Shaking a baby out of frustration, which can lead to whiplash and brain hemorrhages. *Most vulnerable:* Infants who are two months to six months old. But to be safe, parents should avoid shaking, throwing or swinging children under two years old.

Source: Dr. David Chadwick, medical director of San Diego Children's Hospital, San Diego, CA.

Toy-Related Injuries

A sled is safer if the crosspiece that steers it is jointed, rather than rigid. *Most dangerous:* Saucers and other novelty sliders with no steering mechanism, especially when they carry more than one child.

Source: *Parents.*

•Bicycles are the leading cause of toy-related injuries to children under 15. They necessitate 594,100 emergency room visits in just one year. *Next:* Impacting with or choking on small toys, 118,000. *Others:* Skates, 61,190. Sleds, 16,600. Skateboards, 10,300.

Source: *Morbidity and Mortality Weekly Report.*

When Parents Suffer From Depression

Children of parents with serious mental depression are three times more likely to suffer similar emotional distress than the offspring of more normal parents. They are also more prone to attention-deficit disorders, separation anxiety and behavior problems, including alcohol and drug abuse. Children of parents who both suffer depression are even more at risk. A recent study showed that the rate of major depression among children with one disturbed parent was 8.3% but rose to 12.2% with two ill parents. The incidence of all kinds of psychiatric disturbances among children with one depressed parent was 16.7% and with two such parents, 23%.

Source: Dr. G. Davis Gammon, child psychiatrist, Yale University, quoted in *The Journal of the American Medical Association.*

Children and Stress

Children feel stress in the same manner as adults. *Prime root of stress:* Anxiety over school performance. *Special problem:* When a child who is naturally slower-paced is born to parents who are high achievers. They may expect too much. *Other sources of stress:* Insufficient playtime…minimal contact with the extended family (grandparents, aunts, uncles, cousins)…peer pressure to keep up with fashions and trends…too much responsibility too soon…excessive TV watching.

The Secret Key To Personality

Being the first of many brothers and sisters, an only child, a middle child or the lastborn plays a major role in determining your personality. Understanding this role of birth order can help you know yourself and improve the way you deal with others at home or at the office. Although there are many exceptions, this is the general pattern:

•Only children may have a low sense of self-esteem in social situations.

•Firstborn children are expected by their parents and siblings to be serious and responsible.

•Middle children often become competitive.

•Lastborns are often carefree and funloving.

Birth order, of course, determines personality only in combination with other forces:

•Who runs the family?

•What do the parents expect from their children?

•How do children relate to their brothers and sisters?

On a practical level, if I were hiring the oldest of seven siblings, I wouldn't automatically assume that this person knows how to lead. I would ask about his role with his brothers and sisters.

Interpretations…

If he said he couldn't wait to get out and left home at 15, I wouldn't think that person would be a good manager. On the other hand, if he said he had been second-in-command after his mother, I would think he had already learned something about management. Birth order only suggests general patterns that help us understand personality.

•Only children…

Children without siblings may have parents who overprotect them. Everything is done for these children who are left very much on their own. Their problem is that they have no one to learn from.

Unless they have cousins or friends to play with, only children have no sense of the impact they make on kids their own age. Without feedback from playmates, only children may develop a low sense of self-esteem in social situations. Only children also tend to have a hard time at negotiating and often don't know how to handle conflict.

•Firstborns…

Firstborns have a hard time because parents have a lot riding on these kids. The parents' self-esteem comes from the way the firstborn responds. As a result, firstborns aren't usually given much room to be on their own. (I often think it would be easier on firstborns if there were a "disposable training baby" that parents could us to practice their parenting on.)

Later, and often ironically, younger brothers and sisters look up to the firstborn to show them the way. *One result:* The attention from parents and siblings helps the firstborn develop a sense of responsibility, and that may be why firstborns have a high rate of achievement in later life.

•Second and middle children…

By the time the second child arrives, the parents have had more experience and are usually more relaxed. Secondborns have an older brother or sister to learn from so they can say, "Oh, that's how folks react to that. I'm going to try something else." From watching how their older siblings operate, secondborns can benefit socially. They're more easygoing and relaxed with others.

One problem secondborns may face is pressure if their parents have decided on only two children. The second is it—there aren't going to be any more. If the secondborns feel this pressure, they may become more wary and defensive.

In two-children families, if the children have a disagreement, they don't have another sibling to turn to. The luxury of large families is the variety of relationships that can develop among siblings. However, if the three children are of the same sex and close in age, the middle child tends to feel lost or forgotten.

Middle children can become worry children with problems. The problems, of course, are rooted in their need for attention. Middle children get a lot of practice in seeking attention that can make them very competitive in later life.

In some cases, the middle child has a network of close friends outside the family and may well even "adopt" a friend's family.

•Lastborns…

Lastborns are often treated as babies for their entire lives. It's a struggle for them to be seen by their brothers and sisters as an equal. Lastborns may also feel guilty if they surpass an older sibling in school or some other competition: "I'm outranking my brother and I shouldn't."

But being the youngest can be enjoyable. Watching older siblings teaches lastborns a lot. Their parents aren't concerned enough to follow their every step, and a child can benefit from that benign neglect.

Lastborns often become high achievers because they've watched all the choices made by their older siblings and then selected the path that best suits them.

Source: Dr. Bunny S. Duhl, co-director of the Boston Family Institute, Brookline, MA.

An Only Child Isn't So Bad Off

The only child may not be as bad off as many people believe. A recent study at the University of Texas concluded that only children are happier in adulthood than are people with brothers and sisters. *Reason:* They develop greater self-esteem in childhood, which remains with them in later life. Although onlies are sometimes thought to be spoiled and selfish, the positive effects of this status outweigh the negative ones.

Source: *American Demographics,* Ithaca, NY.

Recent studies show that the size of a family matters far less than its social and economic status—and the presence of both parents in the

home. *Other findings:* Compared with children with siblings, only children are just as popular with peers…express the same degree of general happiness in their adult years…are just as healthy, both physically and mentally…score higher in intelligence tests…have higher academic aspirations…reach higher levels of education…and attain more prestige on the job.

Source: Research by Toni Falbo, PhD, associate professor, University of Texas at Austin.

Different Child— Different Treatment

Treating your children equally isn't always possible—or desirable. Don't be afraid to take into account the differences in your children—age, intelligence and maturity, for example—when granting privileges or setting rules.

Coping with Sibling Rivalries

Anyone who is not an only child can testify to the profound effect of the sibling relationship. Our research shows that it is a mistake to emphasize only the jealousy and rivalry. The same children who are at each others' throats one minute are also capable of great affection, concern and attachment to brothers and sisters. Even before the age of three, a child is capable of understanding the feelings of a baby sibling and showing empathy for the infant.

Observations and insights…

There are patterns in families that may help parents better understand how sibling rivalry is triggered. Once mothers and fathers see what is happening, techniques for minimizing conflict between siblings make more sense. *What we found in our research:*

•In families where there is an intense close relationship between the mother and firstborn daughter, the girl is usually hostile to a new baby. A year later, both children are likely to be hostile to each other.

•Firstborn boys are more likely than girls to become withdrawn after a new baby's birth. Children who withdraw (both boys and girls) are less likely to show positive interest in and affection for the baby.

•In families where there is a high level of confrontation between the mother and first child before the birth of a sibling, the first child is more likely to behave in an irritating or interfering way toward the new baby.

•In families where the first child has a close relationship with the father, there seems to be less hostility toward the new baby.

•There is no indication that a child whose parents prepare him for the birth of a new baby with explanations and reassurances reacts any better than a child who wasn't prepared. *More important:* How the parents act after the new baby is born.

•Inside the family, girls are just as physically aggressive as boys.

•Physical punishment of children by parents leads to an increase in violence between children.

•Breastfeeding the new baby can have a beneficial effect on firstborns. *Reason:* Mothers who breastfeed tend to find distractions for the older child during feeding. This turns a potentially provocative time into a loving situation where the first child is also cuddled up with the mother, getting special attention while the baby is being fed.

Dealing with sibling rivalry…

•Don't blame yourself. Much sibling rivalry is unavoidable. There's no way you can blame a mother for an intense relationship with her firstborn child.

•Try to minimize a drop in attention to the first child. This change in attention is dramatic —not just because the mother is occupied with the new baby, but because she is often too tired to give the older child the kind of sensitive, playful focus he or she received in the past. *Recommended:* Get as much help as possible from the father, grandparents, and other relatives and friends. The mothers we studied were exhausted. A month after the new baby came,

half were still getting less than five hours' sleep a night. *Also:* Quarreling between siblings increases when the parents are under stress. Anything that alleviates the mother's fatigue, depression, and irritability is likely to lead to a decrease in bickering and teasing among the children.

•Keep things stable. A child's life is turned upside down when a new baby arrives. Toddlers of around two and three appreciate a stable, predictable world in which the daily schedule of events—meals, naps, outings—can be counted on. In families where the mother tries to keep the older child's life as unchanged as possible, there is less disturbance.

•Talk to the older child about the baby as a person. Involve him or her in caring for the baby. In families where the mother draws the older child in as a helper for the new baby, there is less hostility a year later.

•Be prepared with distractions for the older child. An older child gets demanding the moment the mother starts caring exclusively for the baby, but mothers who are prepared with projects and helping tasks head off confrontations.

•Recognize and avoid favoritism. Our current study shows that mothers intervene three times as much on behalf of a second child, although the second is equally likely to have been the cause of the quarrel. (The first child's feeling that parents favor the second is realistic.) Parents tend to intervene on behalf of younger children because they see them as more vulnerable to abuse. But our studies show that older siblings tend to hold back because they know their aggression is disapproved of, while younger ones often physically attack brothers and sisters because they feel they can get away with it. Parents neglect to impose the same standards of behavior on the babies in the family.

•Be firm in consistently prohibiting physical violence. In the context of a warm, affectionate relationship, this is the most effective way to minimize sibling rivalry and to keep jealousies in check.

•Try to keep your sense of humor and your perspective when a new baby is born. Things will get better sooner than you think. By the time the infants in our study were eight weeks old, many of the firstborns were adjusting quite well.

Source: Judy Dunn, coauthor with Carol Knedrick of *Siblings: Love, Envy & Understanding,* Harvard University Press, Cambridge, MA.

Growing-Up Myths And Realities

The study of human emotions is in its infancy, but a growing body of research has begun to dispel some harmful myths. These new insights can be helpful and reassuring to parents. *Important new findings:*

•Negative events in infancy do not irreversibly damage the mental health of the adult. Some repair is possible if the environment becomes more benevolent.

•The behavior of an infant doesn't provide a good preview of the young adult. A one-year-old's tantrums don't foreshadow teenage delinquency, for example. Many infantile qualities disappear as their usefulness is outgrown. Adult behavior becomes more predictable after the age of five than it was before.

•Human beings are not saddled with a fixed "intelligence" or "temperament" in every situation. These qualities are related to context and can vary in different circumstances.

•A biological mother's physical affection is not basic to a child's healthy emotional growth. More important is consistent nurturing from primary caregivers, related or not, female or male. The key is a child's belief in his own value in the eyes of the caregivers.

Charting emotional development…

Developmental psychologists, long led by the Swiss theorist Jean Piaget (1896–1980), have been able to chart the stages of human intellectual growth with great success. They have found that our cognitive capacities (languages abilities, spatial skills, reasoning capacities, etc.) mature in a uniform, orderly sequence from infancy to adulthood.

A growing amount of evidence suggests that our emotional capacities also emerge in an orderly progression. But the interaction between biological factors—the growth of the brain and central nervous system—and developing emotional and cognitive skills is highly complex.

Studying human emotions poses many new problems. It is much harder to provoke, identify and measure a feeling than to test, for instance, whether a child understands the concepts "larger" and "smaller."

One problem is limited terminology. For example, because we apply the same "angry" to a two-year-old that we apply to an adult, it is easy to assume that the experience is the same for both. But we err in judging children's emotional reactions by adult standards. And words for feelings do not identify the sources or objects of our emotions.

The stages of emotional growth…

The first three to four months: The emotional reactions a very young infant displays are associated with the events he or she encounters. The introduction of a stuffed toy might provoke a reaction of interest. The sudden slamming of a door might cause an infant to startle. Distress is a response to physical discomfort, relaxation, to gratification. All are familiar emotions to new parents. However, mothers can easily misinterpret their babies' facial expressions and actions. An infant's pushing the mother away, for example, may be seen as anger rather than as distress or fright.

Four to twelve months: As the infant's mental ability develops, new emotions appear. Fear of unfamiliar adults and sadness or anxiety at separation from a primary caregiver are examples of emotions that require the ability to compare the events of the present with the events of the recent past. The removal of a favored toy may provoke anger, as the baby is able to relate the loss to another person as its cause.

One to four years: With the recognition of standards, including self-generated goals, comes an increased repertory of emotional reactions. A two-year-old may show frustration when he is capable of imagining a tower of six building blocks but can balance only four of them before they tumble to the floor. Likewise, he will show satisfaction at a successfully completed task.

Late in the third year comes the understanding that one could have acted otherwise—guilt. And by the fourth year, children can identify with people who lead them to feel pride in a parent's intelligence or shame at a sibling's dishonesty.

Five years and up: During the fifth and sixth years, a child begins to compare himself or herself with others on desired qualities. We then see the emergence of such emotions as insecurity and confidence. *Problem:* A child in a large peer group can compare himself with a pool of children and will find many children who have qualities superior to his own. He is therefore more likely to feel inferior if he is in a large peer group rather than in a small one. *Better:* Smaller classrooms with students of equal ability. *Important:* To be motivated, children need a reasonable expectation of success. *Key:* Reasonable goals.

Adolescence: The hormonal changes that occur in puberty permit a degree of sexual emotion not known is childhood. The adolescent also begins to examine his own beliefs for logical consistency and discovers many incompatible ideas. *Example:* Parents are all-knowing and always right, but my parents exhibit imperfections.

The ability to review ideas also allows an adolescent to recognize seemingly insoluble problems such as rejection by a lover or fatal illness. *Result:* A feeling of helplessness or depression. This may explain the popular misconception that teenagers are moody.

Source: Jerome Kagan, PhD, professor of developmental psychology at Harvard University and author of *The Nature of the Child,* Basic Books, New York.

Babies and Strangers

When infants reach the age of six to eight months, most are upset by a stranger rushing toward them, especially if a parent is not right there. *Reason:* The baby has just come to realize that other people are separate individuals and doesn't know how to handle the stranger. *Best:* When approaching a baby for the first time, smile at the infant from a distance, talk in a low tone to other people in the room, and walk very slowly and casually. Don't rush up to the baby.

Source: Robert B. McCall, PhD, senior scientist, Boys Town Center for the Study of Youth Development, writing in *Parents,* New York.

A Father's Role

Stay-at-home fathers contribute to precocity in babies. In one study, infants averaged six to 12 months ahead of schedule in problem-solving tasks when their fathers stayed home and mothers went off to work. Their social skills were comparable to those of the average baby 19 months older. *Probable reason:* The babies were getting love and attention from both parents.

Source: Research by Kyle Pruett at Yale University, quoted in *The Salk Letter,* Boulder, CO.

Girls Will Be Girls

Baby girls who favor one hand over the other show faster intellectual growth than those who don't. But no such relationship was found in baby boys. *Possible reason:* Sexual differences in neural anatomy.

Source: Study at California State University in Fullerton.

What Happens at Age Six

Boys and girls show similar traits up to age six, according to a recent study of 275 children. The researchers found no significant sex differences in timidity, aggressiveness, activity or intelligence. And both genders were treated similarly by parents. *What did matter:* Birth order. Firstborns are generally pressured to achieve more, whereas later children get more unconditional praise and warmth.

Source: Study by Eleanor Maccoby, Stanford University.

When a Child Won't Share

Toddler possessiveness can be a healthy sign. *Reason:* When a two-year-old guards toys before sharing them, the child is showing increased self-awareness—a natural stage of development. *Bottom line:* Don't insist that your toddler share toys right away. Support the child's possessiveness, then help negotiate.

Source: *Parents,* New York.

What the Experts Say About Security Blankets

Most children give up a favorite blanket or stuffed animal by the age of seven. But some cling for years. *Key:* The less importance you attach to the blanket, the sooner the child will grow away from it. *Steps:* Start early (from the age of two) to build the child's self-esteem. Allow the child to make choices regarding meals, clothes, friends, books and games. If blanket-clinging persists, distract the child with a live pet or a new toy, book or game. Don't feel angry or guilty about the reliance on the blanket. Child psychiatrists agree that a security blanket is a natural and normal attachment for most youngsters. But if a child still needs it into adolescence, seek professional consultation.

Help for Southpaws

Left-handed children should be supplied early on with left-handed scissors and spiral notebooks with bindings on the right side. *Also:* Ask the teacher to seat the child at a left-handed desk. (Most schools are able to cooperate.) Aside from practical help, these measures will reinforce the child's self-esteem.

Source: *Working Parents,* New York.

Unattractive Children

Unattractive children usually develop other assets that enhance their personalities. *Examples:* Loyalty. A capacity for intimacy. The ability to share interests and feelings. *Result:* They often have an edge in the quest for success and happiness over the much more attractive children who have lived with undue emphasis on physical qualities. *The most important trait:* Self-assurance. The person who has this quality quickly overcomes any possible deficiencies in physical appearance.

Like Grandmother, Like Granddaughter

High-energy, strong-minded women often rebel against their own mothers, but they still need a female role model. *Readily available:* One of the grandmothers. Usually it will be the powerful grandmother whom the granddaughter will choose—the one who is similarly strong-willed.

The skipped-generation effect is also involved. If the mother's mother was very strong, chances are the mother is weak because her will was broken early. The strong-minded daughter, in effect, overthrows her own mother to copy the behavioral outlook of the maternal grandmother.

Insight: The daughter does not have to rebel against the grandmother, unless the older woman raises her. The grandmother has the advantage over the mother of not eliciting the day-to-day rebellion that is part of exercising daily authority over children.

This latching onto the grandmother occurs when the daughter is old enough to be verbal and has the capacity to differentiate between grownups. The older woman's days of struggle are behind her. Relative to the mother, the grandmother is calm and secure.

The grandmother needs to be available, but proximity is not as important as interaction. Sometimes all the grandmother and granddaughter need is a few weeks together once a year. Often the grandmother's house is a refuge where the granddaughter escapes the authority of her mother or of both parents.

The mother's reaction can range from accommodating and supportive to competitive and suppressive. *Point:* If the mother is jealous of a close relationship between the daughter and grandmother, that is her problem, not the child's. If the grandmother is a positive influence, she should be welcome. A child needs many affirmative adult role models.

This interaction is primarily a phenomenon of women. Although there is some role-modeling between grandson and grandfather, the line of descent in males is not as defined as in females. The women in a family are more available to one another and therefore exert more overt influence. *Contrast:* The males are generally less self-revealing to each other.

If you are really trying to learn what makes a certain woman tick and you cannot pick up the necessary information by knowing her parents, then look at her grandmother, especially on the mother's side. She will probably supply the insights as she presents the model that the granddaughter emulated.

Source: Martin G. Groder, MD, a psychiatrist and business consultant who practices in Chapel Hill, NC.

Dr. Seuss Was Right

Preschoolers who learn to recognize rhymes become better readers later on, according to a recent study. And when low-scoring children were trained in sound recognition, their reading levels improved far more than those schooled in concepts and categories.

Source: Study at Oxford University, in *Psychology Today*, New York.

A Plus for Early Writers

Children who write at an early age almost always become good readers. Moreover, early writing helps teach children to structure and plan, to develop a concept of self and to become aware of others by considering their audience's point of view.

Source: *Growing Up Writing* by Linda Lamme, Acropolis Books, Washington, DC.

Starting-School Tip

The first day of school usually proves unsettling for young children. Don't make things worse by painting too rosy a picture of what it will be like. *Instead:* Be honest. Tell your child it may be confusing, with teachers forgetting names and some children crying. Don't forget to point out, though, that things will soon improve.

Source: *The Salk Letter*, New York.

What's In a Name?

Unusual first names have no bearing on a child's academic performance or social behavior. This was the conclusion of a recent study of more than 23,000 students. Previous research in the field had failed to consider a child's ethnic background.

Source: *The Chronicle of Higher Education*, Washington, DC.

Budding Entrepreneurs

Persistence is the most essential quality in children who display an enterprising bent. *Example:* Typical young entrepreneurs will try selling calendars and, if they don't make any money, they'll say the idea didn't work. They detach failure from themselves personally... and just go on to another idea.

Source: Marilyn Kourilsky, economist, University of California at Los Angeles, quoted in *Inc.*, Boston, MA.

Early-Training Surprise

In a follow-up look at a group of adults whose mothers had been interviewed on parenting practices when the children were five, two patterns emerged. The children who had been subjected to the strictest feeding schedules and toilet training have the highest need to achieve as adults. The youngsters whose mothers were most permissive about sex and aggression (allowing masturbation and fighting with siblings, for example) show the highest need for power as adults. Practices the researchers expected to relate to adult characteristics did not show clear correlation in the study. How warm the mother was with the infant, or how long the child was breast-fed, long assumed to be important to a child's well-being did not match up directly with specific adult traits.

Source: Study by psychologist David McClelland, Harvard University, reported in *Journal of Personality and Social Psychology,* Washington, DC.

Youthful Creativity

Stressing success may make a child less creative. *Reason:* A child under too much parental pressure will try only the things he does well, rather than exploring new ideas. *Also critical:* An ability to accept criticism and even to tolerate being laughed at.

Source: Dr. Joyce Brothers.

How to Talk and Listen to Your Kids

The beginning of wisdom is silence. Then comes listening. It's not easy to hear what another person is really saying. Yet hearing is what children need most from their parents. To be an effective and caring parent, one needs to develop the ability to hear not just the words but the feelings those words try to convey. One needs to learn to listen with empathy.

What is your child really saying?
Example: A child comes home from school shouting, "I'm never going back to school. Do you know what my teacher did? She punished me because she caught me passing notes. She even called me names."

Many parents react to such an outburst with anger. They feel that their child has misbehaved and that they must discipline him so that he will not do it again. But this reaction is not helpful. It only makes the child who was angry at the teacher also get angry at his parent. When we hear only what the child did, not how it made him feel, we are unable to understand or be of help.

From their parents, children have a right to expect understanding, because what they need is help not with their behavior but with their feelings. A child who feels right usually behaves right.

Rule for parents: When a child is upset, no matter what the reason, even if he brought it on himself, the first thing he needs from his parents is a response that will take care of his disturbed feelings. *How:* By reflecting the feelings back to him: "You mean the teacher called you names in front of the whole class? That must have been very humiliating. No wonder you're so upset." *Result:* The child's anger will diminish and he'll be able to return to school.

Many parents may feel that this response doesn't teach the child anything, that he will misbehave again. But the teacher has already taken care of this behavior. The child does not need additional lessons in behavior. What he needs is his parents' understanding of his feelings.

Empathic listening…

Empathic listening is the ability to put oneself in another person's place and understand where that person is coming from without imposing one's own point of view. Only with an open mind can one listen empathically and hear even unpleasant truths. *Problem:* Listening with an open mind doesn't come naturally, especially when it concerns our children. *Reason:* We have a vested interest in them. They reflect on us. We're so busy trying to make them into the kind of adults we need them to become—beautiful, brilliant, athletic, popular, etc.—that we can't afford to listen empathically. Our first reaction is more likely to be, "How will this behavior affect Jane's future?" than, "My daughter Jane (whom I claim to love) is very upset."

We're also afraid to hear the truth from our children. *What we fear:* Feeling like a bad parent. Disruption of the status quo. Being forced to confront ourselves or them. Getting angry. Having to say no. Having to enforce limits. Being disliked. Feeling helpless.

What to do about it...

It isn't dangerous to hear what our children are saying as long as we remember that we don't have to do anything about it. Most parents feel that when a child talks about a problem, they have to do something. In reality, the only thing a parent needs to do is to help the child feel better so that he can think rationally and use good judgment.

It's very important that we let our children solve their own problems in order for them to develop self-confidence, autonomy and a feeling of competence. When children don't feel competent, they become anxious. This is why it is not a good idea to solve children's problems for them. The only problem children can't help themselves with is their negative feelings. That's where they really need our help. Once these feelings are gone and the child feels good about himself, he'll be able to figure out what to do. When our child shares a problem with us, it's preferable to say, "I wonder what you can do about it," rather than, "I think you should do thus-and-such."

The secretive teenager...

When teenagers are not communicative, parents need to ask themselves, "What do I do when I talk to my child that makes it so difficult for him to talk to me?" We tend to blame our children, claiming there is something wrong with them. *What's really happening:* Every time a child has shared something really important, we have probably reacted negatively.

Today's parents say, "You can tell me everything." But do we really mean it? We usually get angry when children tell us things we don't want to hear. To mean it, we must really be prepared to listen empathically to information that may upset us. *Example:* Should your teenage daughter announce to you that she is pregnant, it would be more caring and effective to

be able to respond with, "How terrible for you. I'm so glad you could share this with us. Can we be of help?" than to scream, "How could you have done this to us, after all we've done for you?"

Source: Alice Ginott, PhD, psychoanalyst and lecturer on communication in caring relationships.

How Parents Can Help Their Adolescent

The transition to adolescence is a difficult time both for children and for parents. But parents can create an environment that will make it easier for everyone involved to weather this stressful preadolescent passage.

Entry into adolescence begins between the ages of 10 and 13. The process is earlier than it used to be and is much more condensed.

We look for the physical changes, such as body growth, hormonal functioning and appearance. But right before that, changes usually show up in feelings and moods, an increase in sexual drive and aggressiveness. Children eat a lot more and are more self-centered. They regress. *Example:* Boys tell toilet jokes.

Another symptom: Seventh-grade slump. Schools are often sensitive to dips in students' performances in the seventh and eighth grades. Parents need to be supportive but also must set limits so that the child doesn't go under completely. Be aware that there will be some slippage. That doesn't mean the youngster has suddenly become stupid or will never work again.

Development stages...

Latency, the stage prior to adolescence, is a period of mastering self, work, play and social relationships. In the uneasy transition to adolescence, youngsters are no longer involved in mastery. In fact, sometimes it looks as though it's all been lost. It hasn't been. The tasks of early adolescence are difficult.

The major task for the child is disengagement from parents. He experiences a conflict between the upsurge of drive and pullback to the early parental relationship. He acts older and then younger. He progresses and regresses.

The parent must disengage from the dependent child of the earlier period. The adolescent doesn't need as much nurturing and attention to his physical comfort. The parent must step aside in those areas and let the child do his own growing up.

The parent is heading toward middle age at the same time the child is heading toward adulthood. That's often painful.

Mistakes parents make…

•Parents too often pull the child back into the nurturing, dependent status. The child may go along because it's hard to give that up.

•Parents tend to enter adolescence with their children…by dressing like the child, getting involved with his friends, becoming a participant.

Neither of these attitudes helps the child, although he may enjoy it at the moment. Both are keeping the child with the parent at a time when he needs support in disengaging.

The healthy child will openly rebel at these and other ways by which parents hold on. This is preferable to the child's staying fixed in an earlier mode—looking like an adolescent but never engaging the most important adolescent task.

Expect some stress and conflict. No one disengages easily, whether he's 2½ or 12½.

The parents of adolescents still have to be parents. Limits are still necessary, perhaps even more so. Let children know what you expect, but be reasonably tolerant. They are still not up to assessing the reality of the dangers of drugs, alcohol or herpes. Rules and regulations for social life are important.

Strategies…

There is a big jump in cognition at adolescence. A child is capable of much more abstract thinking and introspection. Despite all the turbulence, you have much more to work with. A parent can engage in a dialogue and work out compromises. A lot depends on the earlier relationship with the child.

Try to work on a rational level first. *But remember:* You are the parent. You have a certain awareness of the child's needs. *Ask yourself:* Why do I need to keep the child as a baby (which is not going to help him)? What do I need to be a parent who knows what's safe and what's reasonable? It's the ability to recognize one's own motivation that distinguishes parents who can handle their child's adolescence from those who can't.

Different growth rates…

Physical appearance becomes an important factor at this time. The child whose growth spurt comes early has a definite advantage. Those kids do better both academically and socially. Peer groups are important, and physically advanced children get more positive response.

The girl who doesn't get her period until after her friends or the boy who doesn't grow as quickly often needs more support from the parent. Such children see what is happening to their friends, and they get anxious, they worry, they act out.

Gender differences: By age 13, girls are two years in advance of boys. This makes it harder on boys because girls are more interested in them than they are in the girls. Parents sometimes become anxious, too.

Change for parents…

During this transition, parents must shift. They have to find new sources of gratification away from their children and accept limitations. They can't control as closely as they did earlier.

The child will no longer tell you everything, which is actually positive. He won't be as responsive or as responsible.

Bottom line: The child has to change. But it's equally important for the parent to change as well.

Source: Pearl-Ellen Gordon, PhD, a child psychologist in private practice in New York.

Teen Years Aren't All Bad

Most teenagers get along fine with their parents, despite their gripes. In a recent poll, 71% rated their relationship with Mom and Dad as good or excellent…and 84% said they confide in their parents. Most agree with their folks on politics, religion, moral issues and careers. *Biggest complaint:* Insufficient freedom and understanding.

Source: Survey by *Seventeen*, New York.

How to Deal with Troubled Teenagers

Anyone with adolescent or young adult children who reads a newspaper account of a young person apprehended for a violent crime must look at their own child and wonder "Would I have recognized the depths of my child's problems?" or "Would I have known how to handle such a situation any better?" Dr. Anne de Gersdorff, an analyst and chief psychologist at the Austen Riggs Center, a private psychiatric hospital in Stockbridge, MA, that specializes in treating young adults, addresses these important issues...

How can parents tell if their teenage children are troubled enough to need professional help?

Adolescence, which can last from puberty into the early 20s, is a difficult and moody time for everybody. Many healthy youngsters go through transitional problem periods and bouts of depression which are a normal part of growing up. Some disturbed young people act up enough to be referred for help by their schools or local police. More worrisome are the quiet, withdrawn students who keep up at school but don't really function at full throttle. *Danger signs:* A teenager with no friends and little or no peer involvement. Long periods of withdrawal and obvious unhappiness. Extended depression and passivity (just sitting around and watching television for weeks at a time, for example). Lack of interest in school or work with no motivation to participate in activities.

Should adolescent suicide threats be taken seriously?

Yes. Adolescents are melodramatic, and many of their emotional outbursts must be taken with a grain of salt. However, a suicide threat, whether made dramatically or not, should be treated with respect and considered a genuine call for help.

What is the best way to approach a young person about getting professional help?

Show your concern for his unhappiness and suggest that talking to someone outside the family about it might be useful. Assure your child that you want him to feel comfortable and free to talk with the therapist, and involve the youngster in the search for one. Don't impose your choice of a therapist on the child.

What if you think your youngster needs counseling, but the child refuses to go?

This situation is not unusual. By the time the family feels that a child is beyond its reach, communication has probably already broken down. The youngster will assume that you think he is crazy and that's why you want him to see a therapist. He has to prove he is not crazy by refusing to go. *Better approach:* Suggest that the whole family has a problem and might benefit from counseling. In truth, family counseling can help parents and siblings to manage living with a disturbed youngster whether that youngster responds to therapy or not.

How do you find the right therapist for your child?

You want a professional—either a man or a woman—with training in psychotherapy and experience in working with young people. A psychiatrist or certified social worker (ACSW, CSW or MSW) could qualify. A psychiatrist is a medical doctor and can prescribe drugs, but many psychologists and CSWs work with hospitals and clinics and can make referrals for medication if they think it is necessary. Get recommendations from trusted physicians, friends, mental health clinics or social agencies. *Three essentials:* The therapist's training and credentials should check out; the young person must find the therapist easy to talk to; the therapist should be willing to talk with you without violating the confidentiality of the therapist-patient relationship. You and your child should interview several candidates before making a choice, and the child should have two consultations with the chosen therapist before making a long-term commitment.

If the relationship between the child and the therapist is privileged, what rights do parents have?

The relationship is privileged and should be respected. Your child must feel free to tell the therapist anything that is on his mind, without fear of anyone else's knowing about it. But you have every right to a general discussion of the problem to help in opening up communications with your child. Parents too often feel so guilty that their child is in trouble that they withdraw from his life just when he most needs their support and understanding. The therapist can help you with that understanding.

What if you feel the therapy is not helping or is progressing in a way that disturbs you?

Don't be afraid of your own common sense. If, for example, you feel your child is more disturbed than the therapist indicates, ask for psychological testing. It may point up problems to the therapist or, even better, reassure you.

If you question a course of action recommended by the therapist, you do have recourse. Request a consultation with another therapist (go back through the list of people you interviewed earlier). The consultant will interview the therapist, the patient and you, and give an evaluation of the situation.

Obviously, if your child's therapist resists either the testing or the consultation, you have grounds for changing therapists.

Four Signs that May Mean Trouble

A child's moodiness is usually a temporary condition that can be dissipated quickly with a little extra attention and affection. Signs that the situation might warrant professional help: 1) A dramatic change in behavior that persists more than several weeks. 2) Prolonged changes in eating or sleeping patterns. 3) Poor peer relationships. 4) A sudden change in communications (your child is hostile or won't talk to you).

Source: *A Child's Journey: Forces that Shape the Lives of Our Young* by Julius Segal, PhD, McGraw-Hill, New York.

Why Kids Shouldn't Go to Rock Concerts On School Nights

Rock fans who attend concerts on school nights will struggle in class the next day. *Reason:* After bathing their ears and brains with abnormally loud sounds, students will be able to hear only lower frequencies in a normal auditory setting. They'll be hearing their teachers as though pillows covered their ears. Their powers of concentration will be adversely affected, and they will not be attuned to the world in general.

Source: Paul Madaule, director, the Listening Center, Toronto, Canada.

Drugs and Peer Pressure

Peer pressure to try drugs and drink alcohol is experienced by school-children as early as fourth grade. About one-quarter say they are pressured by peers to try beer, wine, liquor or marijuana. *Motivation:* In the lower grades, to feel older. In the middle grades, to fit in. And in high school, to have a good time.

Source: A survey of 500,000 students by the *Weekly Reader,* Middleton, CT.

Why a Child Becomes an Addict

Addicts are made, not born. According to a study by the National Academy of Sciences, children are more likely to become drug or alcohol abusers if they are physically abused, lied to or humiliated, or if their parents are addicts. *Other potential causes:* Deprivation or over-indulgence, shifts from too much to too little discipline or praise.

How to Talk With Your Child About Sex

Parents who want to give their children mastery of the facts about sexuality have to start early in the child's life. That's when to begin, too, to build the attitudes they will need to enjoy themselves as sexual beings and to respect the sexuality of others.

A child is born sexual, just as he or she is born with the capacities of walking and of talking. Parents delightedly help children to develop their ability to walk and talk but rarely treat sexual pleasure the same way. Once you understand and accept your children's sexuality as normal and beautiful—the same as their other human endowments—you'll be free to help them in their sexual socialization.

Sexual socialization…

The process of socialization starts in infancy. We socialize our children in other natural functions such as eating. We praise them for using a spoon instead of plunging their hands into the cereal bowl and for other appropriate eating behavior.

A child also needs the guidance and support of parents in developing appropriate sexual behavior that fits in with the parents' own cultural norm and value system. *The beginnings:*

- Establish a sense of intimacy and trust with a newborn by touching and holding it. The cuddling, kissing and hugging should continue —do not stop when the child reaches three, when some parents feel awkward with physical demonstrations of affection, especially with boys.

- When you start the game of naming parts of the body, include the sex organs. Avoidance of the area between the waist and the knees causes confusion and lays the groundwork for problems in adult life.

- Don't interfere with a child's natural discovery and enjoyment of self-pleasuring. Genital play is normal. At six or eight months, a child learns to put its hand where it feels good. Don't slap on a diaper, pull the hand away or look upset or disapproving. Leave the child alone. As the child gets older, teach what you consider appropriate behavior. You don't want your child masturbating in the supermarket or living room even at 15–18 months, so you pick up the child and, smiling, carry it to its bedroom. Explain that the place to pleasure yourself is in your own room with the door closed —that sex is good but should be private.

- Parents need privacy, too. Tell children: "When our door is closed, you don't come in without knocking and being invited. When we see your door closed we'll do the same for you. Everyone likes privacy during sex games." This is when you can introduce the idea that sex games are something people who love and respect each other can play together.

- Sex play between children is usual. If parents banish the play, it will only drive the child underground. It's better to keep the lines of communication open and to reinforce socially appropriate sexual play. *Inappropriate:* Sex play with someone older. Child molestation is more commonly practiced by someone in the family or known to a child than by a stranger. *The message:* "You don't have to let anyone touch your body if you don't want them to. You are in charge, and you can say *No.* Tell me if anyone gives you a hard time."

Communication…

Few parents are aware of how much sex education is transmitted before nursery school by attitudes and body language—how parents react to scenes on TV, the tone of voice or facial expression in sexual conversations or situations, significant silences.

Children delight in affection openly expressed between their parents. Withholding such demonstrations can indicate sexual hang-ups.

Don't avoid opportunities to discuss sex or to answer questions. Always speak only the truth. You may wish to withhold some of the details until later. Explain appropriate behavior outside the home. "In our family, we are open with each other about sex. But most other families don't talk about it the way we do. So, we keep what we do private. It's a good thing to respect what other people believe."

A child who doesn't ask questions by the age of four or five has gotten the idea that the parent is uncomfortable about sex, that sex is not an open topic or he was not given straight answers. But parents should be the ones to give children sexual information. Initiate a discussion. *One idea:* Tell your child about your own questions when you were the same age. If there is no response, try again another day to prove you're available.

Choose a time when you (or both parents) are alone with the child and have plenty of time. Be encouraging about behavior that is appropriate or shows maturation. Give recognition to a good line of thought. Respond positively, even if you are criticized.

Common mistakes…

The most damaging mistake is to associate sexual parts of the body with dirt, ugliness or sin. Guilt and shame transmitted about such a wonderful part of our human birthright will never be erased.

Parents should never lie. They may have to tailor the truth to the level of the child, however. *Example:* To a three-year-old who asks, "Do you have to be married to have a baby?" the correct answer is, "No, you don't, but…" Then you go into your own value system about why marriage is important—on a level that a three-year-old can understand.

Talking with children about sex should be a shared responsibility. A harmonious front is important. Both parents should be clear on attitudes towards standards and rules and on what they agree and disagree on. If there are differences of opinion, call them that. Undermining the other parent shakes the confidence of the child in the one who's doing the undermining. Children trust parents who are for each other.

After six…

If you have laid groundwork between birth and six or seven, then you can take advantage of the major learning years until 12. Before puberty is when to pour in reliable information about sexually transmittable diseases, reproduction, etc. Keep the lines of communication open. Give opinions when they're asked for. Avoid judgments—they tend to close off discussions. Express your own values frankly and give sound reasons. Young people will respect them, even if they don't share them.

Source: Mary Steichen Calderone, MD, former medical director of the Planned Parenthood Federation of America and co-founder and president of SIECUS (Sex Information and Education Council of the US), New York.

When *Not* Knowing Can Be Harmful

Ignorance about sex doesn't make people less promiscuous. Rather, it makes them feel guiltier—and more likely to have impulsive, unprotected sex. Lack of knowledge leads to irresponsible sexual behavior. *Research finding:* Sex education classes do little to change students' overall values.

Source: Robert Pollack, professor or psychology, University of Georgia, in *Self,* New York.

Teenage Confidential

Virgins can become pregnant as the result of heavy petting with a boyfriend. If the male ejaculates outside the vagina, sperm could reach the vulvar mucosa, causing inadvertent insemination. It is important for youngsters to know this, since they often engage in this kind of sexual activity without realizing the risks.

Source: Dorothy DeMoya, RN, and Armando DeMoya, MD, writing in *RN,* Chicago, IL.

Misplaced Guilt

Victims of child abuse are more likely to feel guilty than their abusers. In one study, half the victims of sexual abuse said they felt guilty "for disrupting the family or revealing the act." (Only 5% voluntarily reported the abuse.) But less than half of actual abusers either expressed any guilt or felt responsibility for the act.

Source: *Sex Care Digest,* Piscataway, NJ.

How a Child Can Protect Himself

Child molesters are often deterred if the child simply yells or screams. Yelling helps the child translate fear into anger and overcomes the initial panic response. *Good phrases:* "Stop it!" or "Get away!"

Source: *Your Child Should Know* by Tamar Hosansky, Berkley Books, New York.

Why Some Adults Prefer Bad Kids

Many people who consider themselves sentimental child lovers actually have fond feelings only for docile, respectful children. They cannot embrace independent, free-thinking, quirky or opinionated children who are critical of adults.

Problems: The defiant child magnifies adult impotence. The vulnerable child reminds us of our own frailty. The self-sufficient child proves we're not indispensable.

Result: Some adults find it easier to believe that children are intrinsically bad. This frees them from responsibility, allowing them to be cruel and punitive.

Source: Letty Cottin Pogrebin, author of *Family Politics*, McGraw-Hill, New York.

Another Kind of Child Abuse

Emotional abuse can stunt children's social growth, undermine their self-esteem, and lead to later mental disorders. *Worst:* When negative interactions between parents and children become repetitive.

Common forms of abuse: Criticism that tells children that they're "bad" or worthless, rather than singling out a specific behavior. Constant teasing with the child as the butt of the joke. A failure to praise good behavior.

Source: *Parents*, New York.

Violence that Leads To More Violence

Children who see physical violence between their parents are six times more likely to abuse their own spouses after they marry. If those children were also hit by their parents as teenagers, they are 12 times more likely to abuse their spouses.

Source: National survey of family violence, cited in *Medical Aspects of Human Sexuality*, New York.

Pitfalls of Too Much TV

Heavy TV viewing lowers school achievement in all children. Bright kids are hurt the most. One explanation…Good students generally come from homes with books, magazines and stimulating games and have parents who encourage their use. The more time spent on TV, the less is left for these mind-sharpening activities.

Source: *Gifted Children Newsletter*, Bergenfield, NJ.

To Break the TV Habit

If your kids watch too much TV, you could restrict their viewing to one hour per day (makes children more discriminating viewers). Watch along with them; then discuss (or disagree with) the program's "message" (makes them more critical viewers). Or, substitute family games, reading or athletic activities.

Major Parental Failing

Poor discipline is perceived as the major failing of today's parents. In a recent poll, 37% said that parents were "too lenient" and that children "have it too easy." *Second worst failing:* Child neglect.

Source: Poll by The Gallup Organization, Inc.

When Not to Shout At Your Kid

Shouting at children under age five—even in dangerous situations—only confuses them and eggs them on. Very young children, according to recent research, react to the context in which words are given. A shouted command like "Don't chase that ball into the street!" has a lot of energy in it. To a toddler, that energy is interpreted as encouragement. (A shouted instruction to an older child—if the technique is not overused—will get his attention and, quite likely, his obedience.) *Most effective with under fives:* Give commands in a soft or moderate tone of voice.

Source: The late Lee Salk, former clinical professor of psychology in psychiatry and pediatrics, The New York Hospital Cornell Medical Center, writing in *The Salk Letter,* New York.

The Right and the Wrong Way to Punish

Hitting a small child as punishment only sets up a destructive pattern of escalation. Each occasion requires harder blows, and the relationship between parent and child deteriorates. *Better:* Withdraw a privilege or cancel a planned excursion.

Source: Lilian G. Katz, professor of early childhood education, University of Illinois at Urbana-Champaign, writing in *Parents,* New York.

•Don't withhold the allowance to punish a child. *Reason:* Doing so imbues money with moral and emotional values, which could distort financial decision-making later on. *Better punishment:* Temporarily withhold a non-monetary privilege such as television.

Source: *Better Homes and Gardens,* New York.

Danger of Material Rewards

Material rewards actually discourage children from learning or achieving for its own sake. When you pay your child for an accomplishment, you literally steal the personal satisfaction that came from doing it. *Better:* Offer children strong approval to enhance their self-esteem.

Source: *The Salk Letter,* New York.

When Both Parents Work

When both parents work, children need help in coping with extra stress and pressure. *Suggestions:* (1) Don't yell at the kids. Be sure to tell them what they do right. (2) Be on time. Children may feel neglected or become scared when parents aren't home at the set hour. (3) Think smaller. Instead of ordering children to clean up their room, tell them to put away the toys. (4) Communicate with the kids. Leave a cheerful note or taped message for them to find.

Source: *Execu-Time Letter,* Lake Forest, IL.

Help for "Latch-Key" Kids

Children left alone after school because both parents work often feel lonely or frightened. But two new services are helping the nation's estimated four million "latch-key" kids cope with the stress. One is a self-help program of the Campfire, Inc., youth organization. It consists of eight one-hour sessions that teach children how to act in normal and emergency situations when they're home alone. The other is Phone Friend, a Pennsylvania volunteer service that counsels children over the phone.

Source: *A Letter from Dr. Lee Salk.*

How to Choose a Safe Day-Care Center

A decent day-care facility offers clean quarters, good food, reasonable safety precautions and regular naps. Beyond that, parents should look for:

•A stable staff, with relatively little turnover …specialized training in child development or psychology…staff members assigned to specific children.

•A staff-to-child ratio of no less than one to three for infants, one to four for two-year-olds, and one to eight for children age three to six.

•Ambitious activities (trips to a zoo, a tour of the firehouse), but no heavy academic instruction.

•A welcoming attitude toward parental involvement, including unannounced visits.

Sources: *Newsweek,* NY.

Traits to Look for In a Babysitter

The ideal babysitter is warm, patient, outgoing, well-adjusted and interested in your child. *Caution:* Very domineering people will undermine your relationship with your child. People who are depressed or have other emotional problems will be more concerned with themselves and will not see to the emotional needs of your child.

Divorce and the Kids

Younger children (under the age of six) suffer less emotional damage in the long run, a new study suggests—even though they show the most distress at the time their parents break up. *Theory:* Younger children forget about life before the divorce more quickly than older ones.

Source: Study at Ohio State University in *Psychology Today,* New York.

•Divorce hurts preteen sons more than daughters, especially as they approach puberty. *Reason:* Boys of this age have an increased need for their same-sex parent. But 90% live with their mothers after a divorce.

Source: Study by John Guidubaldi, chairman of the Early Childhood Department, Kent State University.

•Single-parent children are more than twice as likely to get a divorce in adulthood as children from traditional homes. They also generally leave school earlier and earn less money.

Source: Study by sociologist Daniel P. Mueller of the Amherst H. Wilder Foundation, in *USA Today.*

When to Put Off A Divorce

Father hunger commonly strikes young boys when families are split by divorce and the mother retains custody. Symptoms include insomnia, nightmares about the missing parent, and uncontrollable rages or crying jags. *Most at risk:* Boys between 18 months and 32 months. They need a man around for gender identification. *Treatment:* Frequent visits with the father, including a tour of his new living quarters. Even better, couples should consider postponing divorce to a less crucial stage of a boy's development.

Source: Alfred A. Messer, MD, an Atlanta-based family psychiatrist, in *The Wall Street Journal.*

Living Better with Adult Children

We have entered the era of the nesters: Adult offspring (past age 18) who are living in the parental home. Twenty million young adults are proving Thomas Wolfe wrong. They *can* go home again, and they're at least 25% more likely to do so than they would have been 15 years ago.

Nesting is a temporary phenomenon. Your children want to be self-sufficient. At least 90% come home for financial reasons. Education and housing cost more these days, and an entry-level job's paycheck buys less.

The great majority of nesters are "reroosters." They've tried independent life, if only at a college dorm. Maybe they've lost a job or gone through a failed romance or a divorce. They're coming home to lick their wounds before venturing out again.

Six of our eight kids are grown, and all six have moved in and out at least a couple of times. (Our record-holder has completed six round trips.) At first it was a shock. I'd figured I owed them only 20 years apiece.

Over the years, however, it's become a very positive experience for us. Nesting offers parents a chance to develop close, adult relationships with their children. At last they can enjoy their kids as individuals, apart from the burdens of childrearing or the stresses of adolescence. It's time to reap the results of all that labor.

But, if mishandled, nesting can be hazardous to the family—even destructive. It can strain the parents' marriage and hurt the nester's growth. *Key:* You can't dictate to nesters nor smother them with indulgence. You must seek the middle ground. Your nesters need to make their own decisions to ease their transition to independence. *Guidelines:*

• Release your parental authority. When children reach adulthood, they should be treated accordingly. It's time to reshape your old roles. This adjustment can be toughest for fathers, who (like my husband) often deal with their children as authoritarians.

• Don't be too generous with advice or financial aid. For many parents, excessive giving may be an unconscious attempt to control the nester. *Our motto:* Don't offer, but don't refuse. Try to find a solution that preserves the nester's responsibility. *Example:* Your nester approaches you for an emergency loan. Rather than simply forking over the money, you agree to co-sign a bank note.

• Communicate. Sulking may be tolerated in a 10-year-old, but there's no excuse for it in adults. The issue may be trivial—breakfast dishes that don't get cleared, ice cube trays that are never refilled. But if resentment is allowed to build, the entire family will suffer. Speak up about what's bothering you.

• Don't perform a nester's personal business. As adults, they are responsible for walking their dog, getting up in time for work and paying their taxes. They might as well learn now… there will come a day when you won't be around to bail them out.

• Share household chores equitably. Make a written list. A 23-year-old bachelor's standard of cleanliness may not mesh with your own.

• Ask that they contribute something toward room and board. My survey found that nesters with full-time jobs pay an average of $75 a month. (One-third pay nothing at all.) *Fair formula:* Propose that our nester pay 15% of take-home pay. Don't feel guilty about this. You're teaching a key survival skill: How to handle money and live within one's means. (If you really don't need the money, you can put it aside as a nest egg for when your nester leaves. But keep this a secret, or you'll defeat your purpose.)

• Remember that it's your roof and mortgage. If your adult children want to live in your home, they must abide by your rules and value system. In part, this is just basic consideration, such as limiting telephone or bathroom time. But it also applies to drugs or premarital sex. If you feel uncomfortable with certain behaviors, it's your right to forbid them. (Flexibility helps. Much as you might despise cigarettes, for example, you might let a nester smoke in his or her bedroom.)

•Keep in mind that house rules stop at the front door. What nesters do outside is their own choice, unless they bring their problems home (no drunk driving or drug dealing condoned). Our study found that curfews are unrealistic. Like it or not, much of a young adult's social life happens after midnight.

•Reject the notion (quite popular in this culture) that nesters are failures. Ignore any friend who suggests the same. You know better.

•Set a target departure date before the nester moves back in. This could be three months after college graduation or six months after a divorce. The date can be modified later on. But by affirming that your nester's stay is temporary, you'll relieve much anxiety on both sides.

Source: Monica Lauen O'Kane, author of *Living with Adult Children,* Diction Books, St. Paul, MN.

Drinking and The Elderly

Drinking by the elderly causes as many hospital stays as heart attacks. *Cost to taxpayers:* $230 million a year through Medicare. *Highest alcoholism rated:* Alaska, with 77 hospitalizations per 100,000 people. *Lowest:* Arkansas with 19 per 100,000.

Source: Study of more than 87,000 Medicare hospitalizations during 1989, led by Wendy Adams, MD, Department of Medicine, Medical College of Wisconsin, Milwaukee, reported in *Journal of the American Medical Association,* 515 N. State St., Chicago 60610.

Your Job and Your Spouse

Occupational hazards of your job can harm, or even kill, your spouse. *Possible cause:* Occupational stress and environmental hazards—such as workplace toxins—are carried home by one spouse and shared with the other. *Also:* The way one spouse interacts with the world rubs off on the other, so that the careless atti-

tude of one may make the other more accident-prone.

Source: Psychology professor Ben Fletcher, PhD, University of Hertfordshire, United Kingdom. His study of occupational hazards was reported in *Longevity,* 1965 Broadway, New York 10023.

Free Health Care For Your Family

If the high cost of health care threatens to break your budget, look into the many free or nearly free sources of drugs, examinations, diagnostic procedures, etc., that are available.

Medications…

•Doctors have drawers full of drug samples. Ask for a free sample of any drug your doctor prescribes. This lets you see if the drug is effective *before* you pay for an expensive prescription.

•Drugs, checkups and treatment are usually provided free of charge to people who participate in studies sponsored by drug manufacturers.

If you suffer from a serious health problem, find out if any relevant research is being conducted in your community—and see if you're eligible to participate. Ask your doctor or call a local medical school or teaching hospital.

Drawback: Study participants must sign a release form waiving their rights in case of an adverse reaction.

•Most drug manufacturers also offer medications free of charge to poor people.

Medication advice…

•Pharmacists are much more knowledgeable than many people realize. Take advantage of this knowledge. Each time you fill a prescription, request advice and printed materials relevant to your ailment. Few pharmacists charge for such services.

Dental care…

•State-of-the-art dentistry—including X rays and cleanings—is available free or at reduced cost at most dental schools or schools of dental hygiene.

If there's no dental school in your area, cut a deal with a young dentist just opening a practice.

More free information…

•Free lectures on health topics are held at local hospitals, community centers, community schools, public libraries, nursing homes, YMCAs, YWCAs and activity centers for the elderly.

•The Food and Drug Administration (FDA) will answer questions about food safety, drugs, cosmetics and medical devices. Check your phone book for the nearest district office of the FDA.

•Questions on workplace noise, psychological stress, chemical and physical hazards, carpal tunnel syndrome, etc., should be directed to the National Institute of Occupational Safety and Health, 800-356-4674.

•Literature on 1,000 rare and not-so-rare diseases is available from the National Organization for Rare Disorders (NORD), 800-999-6673 (GO NORD on CompuServe).

•For recorded information on hundreds of diseases, health tips for travel, disease prevention, statistics and more, contact the Centers for Disease Control and Prevention, 404-332-4555.

•For cancer information, call the National Cancer Institute's Cancer Information Center, 800-422-6237.

Source: Neil Shulman, MD, associate professor of medicine, Emory University School of Medicine, Atlanta. He is publisher of *Better Health Care for Less* newsletter, 2272 Vistamount Dr., Decatur, Georgia 30333. Dr. Shulman is coauthor of the book *Better Health Care for Less*, Hippocraene Books, 171 Madison Ave., New York 10016.

Most Commonly Asked Questions About Kids' Health Care

Despite the seemingly endless array of childhood ailments, concerned parents often find themselves seeking answers to the same basic questions about their children's health…

•How can I find a good doctor for my child? While a pediatrician is the most obvious choice, family practitioners and internists often make equally good doctors for children.

Interview different types of doctors, then pick one with a pleasant, caring attitude…a willingness to talk directly with your child as well as with you…a clean, orderly office…and a good system for fielding after-hours phone calls. Make sure your child gets along with the doctor and that the doctor accepts your health insurance plan.

Caution: If the doctor belongs to a group practice, ask that you be allowed to make appointments specifically with him/her.

Ask if the doctor can provide you and your child with videotapes, pamphlets, and other educational materials regarding specific health issues. They're a big help when illness strikes —or during puberty.

•Does my child need an X ray? In addition to being costly, X rays, CAT scans, magnetic resonance imaging and other diagnostic tests are typically frightening to children, risky and often unnecessary.

They should be administered only if their findings will have a direct bearing on your child's treatment. If your child has a cough, for example, a chest X ray is generally unnecessary—unless the doctor has reason to suspect a serious lung ailment. Before agreeing to any test, question the doctor thoroughly to make sure it is necessary. Key questions:

•What's the name of the test?

•Why is it necessary?

•What will it reveal that you don't already know?

•What will happen if the test is not performed?

•What are the possible side effects?

•Is a less-invasive test available?

•Are childhood immunizations safe? Most states require that all children be immunized against eight diseases—diphtheria, pertussis (whooping cough), tetanus, measles, mumps, rubella (German measles), poliomyelitis, and Haemophilus influenza type B (bacterial meningitis). These vaccinations, typically administered between the ages of two months and 16 years, are generally quite safe.

Exception: Pertussis. Half of all children who receive this five-dose vaccine develop fever, and one in 310,000 develops mental retardation or another permanent disability. Yet because pertussis is such a serious disease, it is still prudent to have your child immunized.

To minimize risk: Insist that your child receive the recently approved acellular pertussis vaccine. It's less likely to cause dangerous reactions than the old vaccine, which remains in use.

The pertussis vaccine should never be given to any child who is over age six, who has a fever or has already had pertussis. Any child who experiences fever, shock, persistent crying, convulsions, or neurological problems after the first pertussis shot should not receive any of the additional pertussis boosters.

• Is circumcision a good idea? While most doctors now agree that circumcision is not medically necessary, the procedure does seem to have certain benefits.

Compared with uncircumcised males, circumcised males experience fewer urinary-tract infections during infancy and reduced incidence of venereal diseases in adulthood. They also appear less likely to transmit the virus that causes cervical cancer to their female sex partners.

Like any surgical procedure, circumcision has drawbacks, including the possibility of infection, bleeding and—because anesthesia is rarely used—severe pain. Few insurance policies cover the procedure.

How to proceed: Discuss all options with your pediatrician, including the use of anesthesia if you do opt for circumcision...and the possibility of delaying the procedure until your son is older—but not more than one year old. Ultimately, the decision is a personal one.

• My child has recurrent throat infections. Should his/her tonsils be removed? Tonsillectomy is neither necessary nor particularly effective at curing recurrent ear or throat infections, even though doctors often urge surgery.

When it's appropriate: Only if the tonsils become so swollen that they interfere with the child's breathing, or if lab tests indicate the presence of abscesses behind the tonsils.

In all other cases, it's best to treat such infections with antibiotics.

• What about chronic ear infections? Ear infections (otitis media) are especially common among children of smokers. If you smoke—stop. New mothers should try to avoid bottle-feeding their children. Recent research suggests that breast-feeding helps prevent earaches. Beyond this, there's no real consensus on treatment.

The American Academy of Pediatrics recommends use of oral antibiotics (usually amoxicillin), although some of the most recent research casts doubt on their effectiveness. The surgical insertion of drainage tubes through the child's eardrums (tympanostomy) can cause serious complications, including severe infections and hearing loss.

Conservative approach—to discuss with your doctor: At the first sign of pain, give your child acetaminophen (Tylenol) or another non-aspirin painkiller. Every two hours, place two drops of warm (not hot) olive oil into each ear canal. *Also helpful:* A heating pad held against the ear.

• Do children's hospitals offer better pediatric care than general hospitals? Many parents seem to think so. In most cases, however, the standard of care in children's hospitals is no better than that in general hospitals with good pediatric sections. If your child requires inpatient surgery, pick a hospital that performs that surgery on a routine basis.

• My child's doctor refuses to give me details of my child's medical care. What can I do? Parents sometimes fail to realize that all doctor-patient relationships are private. When your child is very young, of course, you are by necessity intimately involved in all aspects of his/her medical care. As children approach puberty, however, they may wish to keep some aspects of their medical care private. Parents should respect that right.

Source: Charles B. Inlander, president of People's Medical Society, the nation's largest consumer health advocacy organization. He is the coauthor of several books on medical topics, including *Take This Book to the Pediatrician with You*, People's Medical Society, 462 Walnut St., Allentown, Pennsylvania 18102.

All About Healthy Pregnancies...and Healthier Babies

Many women know that if they're pregnant, they should watch what they eat and drink, stop smoking, see their doctors—and read up on pregnancy, labor and child-rearing. All this is good.

But to wait until the pregnancy test is positive before making these changes is not good.

That's like preparing a meal by dumping all the ingredients in a bowl, and reading the recipe afterward. The time to read the recipe is before you mix the ingredients together. And the time to prepare for pregnancy is before you conceive.

The fetus is most vulnerable very early in pregnancy—including the weeks before you know you're pregnant. Most organ systems are formed within eight to 12 weeks of conception—and most birth defects occur during that period.

I suggest to my patients that they view pregnancy as a 12-month process that begins when they first think about becoming pregnant.

Nutrition...

An undernourished mother—and that could include a seemingly healthy woman who's dieting to keep her weight down—is more likely to have a baby whose growth is retarded. Growth retardation is associated with disorders such as cerebral palsy, mental retardation and metabolic problems.

Being overweight causes more problems for the mother than for the baby. A woman who eats heavily and gains too much weight during pregnancy may have a bigger baby that's harder to deliver. And heavy mothers have a higher incidence of diabetes, toxemia (pregnancy-induced hypertension) and phlebitis.

Before you stop using birth control, have your doctor assess your eating habits, and compare your weight and height against commonly available data for ideal weight. If you're significantly underweight, you should improve your nutritional status and approach your ideal body weight before trying to conceive.

If you need to lose weight, do it before, not during, pregnancy.

There's nothing mysterious about eating properly during pregnancy. You don't have to weigh or measure your food. Eat a balanced diet, with a variety of foods from the major food groups. Pay particular attention to protein,

calcium, fruits, vegetables and fiber. Your doctor can give you more specific guidelines.

Taking a vitamin and mineral supplement can't substitute for a balanced diet, but it can help to ensure that you're getting the minimum requirements for yourself and your baby.

Especially important: Iron, folic acid, calcium.

Excess alcohol during pregnancy is known to be harmful to the fetus...but we don't know at what quantity it presents a problem.

An occasional alcoholic drink may not be dangerous, but to be on the safe side, I recommend that my patients avoid alcohol completely during pregnancy—and do the same while they're trying to conceive.

Exercise...

Exercise is an important part of a healthy life, and a woman who works out regularly can continue to exercise throughout her pregnancy. While there's no evidence that exercising will make the fetus any healthier—exercise does benefit the mother.

As the mother gains weight over the nine-month period, being in good shape will make her daily activities easier. A physically fit mother may also be better able to tolerate the strenuous physical demands of labor. But there's no evidence that fitness can shorten the duration of labor or lower the risk of complications.

If you're a couch potato, don't suddenly take up exercise when you learn you're pregnant—you'll put your body under stress. It's better to start an exercise program before you try to conceive.

Beware: Exercising strenuously, especially in hot weather, can raise your core body temperature, increasing the risk of birth defects. If you work out, make these modifications in your exercise program as soon as you stop using birth control:

•Don't wear warm clothes while exercising.

•Don't exercise in a warm environment.

•Reduce the length of your workouts to between 15 and 30 minutes.

•Reduce the intensity of your workout. Don't push yourself until you're huffing and puffing—you should have enough breath left to talk. Keep your heart rate under 140 beats per minute.

•Avoid saunas and hot tubs.

Environmental risks…

As soon as you consider becoming pregnant, evaluate your exposure to chemicals, radiation and other hazards at home and at work.

Examples: Pesticides, weed killers, household cleansers, formaldehyde in carpets and pressed-wood products, X rays.

We have very little information about the effects on pregnancy of chemical and other environmental hazards.

Rule of thumb: If you're not sure about the safety of a substance, and you can realistically avoid it, do so.

You don't need to be paranoid or live in a sterile environment, but if there are modifications you want to make, you should make them now—before you become pregnant.

What about the VDT controversy? Studies suggesting that women who work at video display terminals have a higher incidence of miscarriage have not held up to proper scrutiny—too many variables were involved in these studies. If you are concerned about VDT radiation, you should pay attention to the work stations near you more than your own—more radiation is emitted from the back and sides of a computer than from the front.

Smoking is a reproductive poison. Women who smoke have a higher incidence of infertility, miscarriage and babies with birth defects …as well as serious complications during pregnancy. If you haven't stopped smoking, stop when you discontinue your form of birth control. (If you're already pregnant and still smoke, stop—the hazard continues throughout pregnancy.)

Recreational drugs are also dangerous to the fetus. The time to stop taking these drugs is before conception.

Medical problems…

If you have a condition such as diabetes, high blood pressure or lupus, it's important to have a reproductive checkup before you try to conceive.

You and your doctor will want to be sure the disease is under control, and that any medications you're taking are appropriate to continue during pregnancy.

You should also make a point to discuss with your doctor ahead of time how pregnancy will affect the disease—and vice versa. Don't wait until you're pregnant to find out.

Even if you're not aware of any chronic medical condition, it's a good idea to have a pre-conception checkup. Make sure your tests—such as a Pap smear—are up to date. A medical problem identified after you're pregnant generally is more difficult to diagnose and treat.

Example: If you discover a breast lump while you're pregnant, you may be reluctant to have the X ray that would aid in diagnosis…or the surgery and/or chemotherapy that might be part of the recommended treatment if you weren't pregnant.

You should also find out whether you're immune to rubella, also called German measles, which is known to be associated with birth defects. About 15% of the population is not immune. If you're among them, get immunized at least three months before you try to conceive.

Source: Barry Herman, MD, assistant clinical professor of obstetrics and gynecology at UCLA and co-author of *The Twelve-Month Pregnancy*, Lowell House, 2029 Century Park East, Suite 3290, Los Angeles 90067.

All About the Oppositional Child

The oppositional child is a source of frustration and bewilderment to parents.

The oppositional child is consistently aggressive, argumentative, uncooperative and in conflict with others—especially parents, teachers and other authority figures…

- Yelling doesn't help.
- Reasoning doesn't help.
- Threats of punishment are ignored.
- Actual punishment doesn't seem to bother the child.

Parents may wind up feeling as though nothing they do will make a difference.

The oppositional child's point of view…

The key to dealing with the oppositional child is to see the world the way the child sees it.

People of any age want to have control over their lives. Control helps us feel that our lives are ordered, predictable and secure.

While children feel that they have very little control in a world run by adults—some of them seize control aggressively...others by being overly dependent.

Oppositional children go after control assertively and forcefully, by manipulating the emotions of others.

They may not be able to take away their parents' car keys or send them to their rooms—but they can enrage and frustrate them. That's why angry confrontation makes the problem worse—the child has won by causing parents to focus their emotional energy on him.

Parents, too, want to be in control...

Parents tend to try to control children by force—overpowering them, out-arguing them—or trying to reason them into seeing things the parent's way.

But using force with an oppositional child actually reinforces his/her behavior. You wind up with a noisy turf battle—and the child continues to control the emotional atmosphere of the home.

Trying to reason with the child is equally ineffective. Kids are smart—they can see when the parent is emotionally invested in bringing them around to the parent's point of view. This only reinforces the child's sense of control.

Handling the oppositional child...

Paradoxically, we can actually have much more control by recognizing the child's need for control. When the child feels understood, he's more likely to come over to our side.

This does not mean stepping aside and letting kids "do their own thing." Children are inexperienced in the ways of the world and need our guidance.

By virtue of age, wisdom and experience, parents are the natural leaders in the home. But leadership is demonstrated more effectively through communication than force. A wise leader solicits and takes into account the needs and desires of each family member...then makes the final decision.

Understanding is not the same as agreement. You don't have to approve of what your child is doing...but if you understand what motivates his behavior, you'll be less likely to act in ways that encourage it.

Tactics that don't work:
- Making threats that won't be carried out.
- Shouting to make a point.
- Making sweeping generalizations such as You always...You never...etc.
- Trying to reason with the child.
- Interrupting.
- Withholding affection.
- Trying to convince the child to agree with you.

What parents can do...

- Control their own emotions. The parent needs to develop a sense of detachment from the child's difficult behavior. That doesn't mean hiding your emotions—that would be impossible. It does mean allowing your child the room to make his own mistakes.

Trap: When a child does something we don't approve of, we tend not to stop at the behavior—we try to change the child's emotions and opinions as well.

The child's problem then becomes our problem...and he's once again in control.

Detachment isn't easy. Instead of thinking, *Well, 12-year-olds do that kind of thing,* parents tend to think, *No 12-year-old girl is going to control me.* But adults, too, are capable of maturing throughout life. We must be honest with ourselves and continually strive to develop insight into our thoughts and actions.

- Set clear, consistent boundaries. Rather than guiding by giving orders, offer choices that indicate the limits of behavior. Let the child know ahead of time which behaviors will result in punishment—and what those consequences will be. Avoid excessively harsh or aggressive punishment, particularly spanking. And don't ever punish when you're not in control of your emotions. Call a time-out first.

Example: Missing curfew results in loss of use of the car for a week. If the child exceeds the boundaries, impose the consequences—without lecturing or getting emotional about it. Parents don't have trouble getting the first part right. A teenager comes in at 3 a.m. and the parent says, You know that you're supposed to be home by midnight. It's 3 a.m.—no more car this week.

The problem arises when the parent then starts to lecture or harangue the child: *I told you to be in by midnight! I tried to be fair! Now you've broken the rules again—I can't believe it! How do you expect me to trust you?*

Children may test the boundaries for a while to find out whether parents are serious. This is when it's especially important not to get emotional—just keep enforcing the rules.

•Read between the lines. Kids aren't skilled in verbal communication. It's often difficult for them to put what they feel into words. Often, it's through their behavior that they express what's going on inside.

With practice, parents can learn to cut through the offensive behavior and respond to the emotion beneath.

Example: A child who shouts *I hate you!* may mean, *I hate being told I can't do something!* or *I have no power in this family, and it's not fair!*

A parent's usual tendency is to tell the child why he shouldn't feel that way. A more effective response might be, *It feels pretty bad when I tell you what to do. I know you hate that.* This allows the child a right to his feelings.

A non-opinionated, nonjudgmental response will encourage the child to reveal more layers of emotion until he feels understood…and once he feels understood, he's more apt to cooperate.

This response is difficult for parents. The parents who haven't mastered detachment fear that they are telling the child—go right ahead and hate us—we're rotten people. But when the child knows his feelings are accepted, the feelings will pass much more quickly.

•Don't give advice unless the child asks for it. You may have useful insights, but the child won't benefit from them unless he's interested. He can usually work out his own solutions if you listen in a nonjudgmental way.

•Work on building a positive relationship with your children. The oppositional child is crying out for attention, so make sure he's getting enough of the positive kind. *Recommended…*

Spend time playing games and talking with your children.

Be generous with physical affection for your child.

Note: This is easier with pre-adolescents than with teenagers. Older children—who look to their peers, not their family, for support—may resist your attempts to enter their world. But it's important to show your willingness to build rapport.

Invite your child on outings—or to a one-on-one dinner. Don't give him a hard time if he turns you down. Even if he says no, continue to invite him to other activities in a no-big-deal way.

Or try a chat before bedtime. A child who's winding down at the end of the day may be more receptive to building rapport.

Source: William Lee Carter, EdD, a psychologist at Child Psychiatry Associates in Waco, Texas, and author of *Kidthink*, Word Publishing, Inc., East Tower–Williams Square, 5221 North O'Connor, Suite 100, Irving, Texas 75039.

Protect Your Child From Sports Injuries

More than twenty million children are active in some form of organized sports in this country. In the coming year, one in three—close to 7 million—will suffer an injury requiring the attention of a parent…or doctor…or both.

High school athletes alone will suffer one million sports-related injuries, including 20,000 that will require surgery.

Many of these injuries can be prevented. Actively involved parents can help minimize problems. *Key safety guidelines…*

•Beware of the injury-prone child. Not all children are suited for all sports. If a child has had multiple injuries—concussions, fractures, severe sprains, etc.—over the course of two seasons, it's time to consider switching him/her to a different activity.

Typical adjustment: From a physical team sport to an individual sport, where the chances for injury are less.

Example: A young person may lack the strong foot control to perform safely in soccer …but may have great hand-eye coordination for tennis.

•Watch out for overuse or stress injuries. Stress injuries have become epidemic over the last 10 years…even among the under-12 set.

Reason: Children are competing harder—and during more months out of the year—than ever before.

Solution: Take six months off from all sports. Then choose just one to resume the following year.

•See to it that your child is adequately conditioned. Good conditioning can enable a child to safely absorb a fall or collision. Pre-activity warm-ups are vital, but teenagers also need physical preparation months before their season starts.

Examples: Swimming, biking or running for endurance...weight-training for strength...stretching for flexibility.

Caution: Overstretching can lead to back and sciatic nerve injuries.

•Make sure that your child isn't overmatched by much larger athletes. A 12-year-old pitcher who stands 5-foot-6-inches tall and weighs 130 pounds can terrify a smallish 10-year-old batter.

Injury prevention: Ask the coach to outfit all batters with a plastic face mask...switch your child to a league that uses the new, softer baseballs.

•Check out the coach's priorities. A win-at-all-costs syndrome leads to many unnecessary injuries.

Danger signs: A track coach who pushes tired runners on when they are obviously unfit to continue...a football coach who keeps a player in a big game despite a significant injury that could get worse.

•Watch the weather. Whenever the temperature is over 85 degrees and the humidity exceeds 70%, coaches and parents should be on the lookout for heat illness.

Symptoms: Abnormal movements and bizarre actions. In some severe conditions, practice should be suspended.

Hot-weather precautions: Urge coaches to schedule practice sessions for early morning or evening...require loose white clothing...provide rest in the shade between sessions...make water available at all times and see that it is consumed.

•Insist that your child use appropriate safety equipment. This applies to practices as well as games. Children tend to neglect safety because they think they are indestructible. It's up to parents and coaches to see that safety headgear, mouthguards and running shoes fit properly and are not worn out.

Source: John F. Duff, MD, a practicing orthopedic surgeon and director of the North Shore Sports Medical Center in Danvers, Massachusetts. He is author of *Youth Sports Injuries: A Medical Handbook For Parents and Coaches*, Collier Books, 866 Third Ave., New York 10022.

Your Children...School And Other Transitions

Some children are naturally adventurous—they jump into any new activity or environment with relish. Others, however, are much more cautious and pessimistic about change.

While edgy behavior about the unknown is perfectly normal, there are ways for parents to help make dramatic transitions less stressful for their kids.

Empathic listening...

Most important: Take your child's feelings seriously. Don't minimize his/her concerns by saying, There's nothing to worry about. That just tells him that he has no right to his feelings. It may also convince him that there is something wrong with him for feeling that way.

More helpful: Acknowledge those feelings and say, *I can see that this might be scary for you.* Then, follow up with an encouraging comment, showing him that you have confidence in his ability.

You also shouldn't assume your child is worry-free just because he hasn't told you that he's anxious. Often, it's hard or embarrassing for kids to articulate what they're afraid of.

Instead of waiting for your child to bring up the subject, do so yourself. If you can help your youngster find the words to talk about his fears, you'll be better able to address his questions and concerns as well as let him know you're available to listen.

Providing structure...

These are two techniques that will help you provide the structure and familiarity that kids need to feel more at ease with transitions.

•Preparation. Help your child retain his sense of control by including him in the planning stages. Rehearse potentially difficult situations so that he can practice acting appropriately.

• Ritual. Having special rituals is reassuring to a child—it gives him something familiar to fall back on. Rituals don't have to be elaborate, but they do need to have a certain regularity. They can be as simple as reading a story aloud at bedtime or talking over problems while sitting in a favorite chair.

Common transitions and ways to handle them…

First day at a new school:

Preparation: Visit the school with your child before classes begin. Show him where the bathroom and lunchroom are. Have him meet the teacher, if possible. If he will be walking to school, walk there with him a few times beforehand…if he'll be taking the school bus, go with him to the bus stop for a dry run.

If an older relative, neighbor or friend attends the same school, arrange to have him show your child around the first day.

If your child is worried about his ability to talk to kids he doesn't know, try some role-playing.

Example: You could say: *Let's pretend we've just gone to the lunchroom and somebody sits down next to you. You could ignore him, or you could say, "Hi, I'm Paul—what's your name?" Pretend I'm this new person and let's practice.*

Rituals: You might help your child pick out the next day's clothes and lay them out the night before…send him off with a special wave …serve a favorite snack each day when your child comes home from school.

When a friend moves away:

Preparation: Remind your child that he can stay in touch with his friend, even if they live miles apart. Find the friend's new town on a map. Explore the feasibility of exchanging visits. Go shopping for farewell cards. Help your child plan a going-away party for his friend.

If you have a going-away party, take Polaroid pictures of the friend with each of the guests…and make sure everyone goes home with a photograph.

Rituals: Consider allowing your child to call his friend long-distance on special occasions, such as birthdays and holidays. In addition to letters, it might be possible to exchange a monthly fax. Ask your child to think of other ways to stay in touch.

Moving to a new city…

Preparation: Reassure your child that even though he'll be far from his friends, they won't forget him.

Take him with you to the post office to buy change-of-address cards and help him fill them out to send to his friends.

Let him know what to expect on moving day …will a moving van arrive? Will you drive to the new house, or take a plane or train? Suggest that he draw pictures of the old and new houses.

Rituals: Have a farewell open house for the friends your child will be leaving.

Caution: In your attempt to pack light, don't just throw out toys your child has outgrown. Let him choose which ones he wants to take along. Once he gets used to the new house, he may decide he's ready to give some of them away.

When parents go out of town…

Preparation: Talk to your child about the person who will be looking after him while you're away, and about your expectations.

Example: Aunt Ella will be staying with you. I'll tell her about your favorite book. She knows you're supposed to be in bed by 8:00—no later.

If a new babysitter will be staying in your home, make sure your child meets that person a day or two before your departure.

To avoid misunderstandings, go over house rules with the caregiver—in the child's presence. If your child will be staying at a relative's home, explain that this person's rules may not be the same as yours. Be as specific as you can: *Grandma only wants you to eat at the table— not in front of the TV. And once dinner's over, the kitchen is closed.*

Arrange to phone your child at a certain time each day.

Rituals: Make sure the caregiver understands the daily rituals that are important to your child, and encourage him to maintain them as consistently as possible.

Example: Preparing for bedtime might involve reading a storybook aloud, then a hug and a bedtime chant (*Good night, sleep tight…*).

When a parent returns to work…

Preparation: Before you start a new job, show your child around your office. This will help him have a vivid mental picture of you when you're at work—one of the ways kids cope with separation.

Give him a transitional object—something he can associate with you, such as a stuffed bear from your own childhood or a handkerchief doused with your perfume. Ask him to make a painting or drawing that you can hang in your office. This is particularly helpful for pre-schoolers.

Rituals: If time permits, some families enjoy sitting down to breakfast together. Have a snack ready in the refrigerator so your child can help himself when he gets home from school. Set up a daily phone call from the office.

When you get home from work, spend a little low-key time with your child before you plunge into dinner or housekeeping chores. You might want to play a game on the living-room floor or hold him on your lap while you sit in a rocking chair.

Remember, it takes time to adjust to any new situation, but adjustments will become less stressful as situations become more familiar.

Source: Nancy Samalin, founder of Parent Guidance Workshops in New York and consulting editor and columnist for *Parents* magazine. She is author of *Loving Your Child Is Not Enough: Positive Discipline That Works* and *Love and Anger: The Parental Dilemma*, Penguin Books, 375 Hudson St., New York 10014.

Words That Get Parents Into Trouble with Their Kids

Even though our intentions are good, it's easy for parents to use words or phrases with children that are insensitive at best—hurtful at worst—and that actually work against the results we want.

This is especially true when we're annoyed, frustrated, tired or stressed. We react automatically and don't even think about what we're saying.

One of the quickest and best ways to change this pattern is to watch out for red flag words. These are usually short, simple words that almost always escalate any conflict with a child —or a spouse or anyone with whom we have a close relationship.

By becoming aware of these words, we can substitute expressions that are more likely to result in cooperation and understanding.

Words to avoid…

Most red flag words occur at or near the beginning of a sentence.

If—usually followed by *you*—when used as a threat.

• *If you do that again, you'll be sorry.*

• *If you don't get in that bathtub, there will be no story tonight.*

• *If you keep leaving your clothes all over the floor, I won't buy you any more this year.*

Many children perceive a threat as a challenge and may repeat the offense just to see what the parent will do.

These threats are often impossible to carry out. We make them when we're least rational— and often when we've lost control of the situation. And, if we don't follow through on the threat, the child stops taking us seriously—we lose the ability to be authoritative.

In addition, a threat that is irrational or out of proportion relative to the offense doesn't teach the child anything about the realistic consequences of his/her behavior.

Better: As soon as or when. These phrases are more positive and less punitive. They encourage you to stay rational—and make a statement that can be followed through.

• *As soon as you've taken your bath, we'll have a story.*

• *When you've hung up your jacket, we can play a game.*

Who started it? Obviously, this question applies to an argument or fight between two or more children. But think about it: Have you ever heard any child answer I did?

This question implies that we are looking for somebody to blame rather than trying to resolve the problem effectively. The result is likely to be even more fighting or finger-pointing.

Better: Take a neutral, problem-solving approach.

• *You two have a problem. There's only one book here, and you both want it at the same time. What can you do about that?*

Instead of looking for a bad guy, you're helping the children work out a solution to the problem.

Why—especially when followed by don't you, can't you or won't you.

• *Why don't you pick up your things?*

• *Why can't you keep your hands to yourself?*

• *Why won't you listen?*

These questions are unanswerable. In fact, we're not even asking why because we want a rational answer. Instead, we are really just blaming or making a critical statement. Children are not likely to cooperate when they feel they are being accused.

Another common use of the word why is *Why did you...*as in, *Why did you hit your sister?*

Children don't usually know why they do things. They're basically impulsive—and don't think before they act. You're likely to get a useless response such as, *I don't know, I felt like it*, or, *Because she's a dork.*

Better: Leave out the why and change the question to a clear, firm, non-accusatory statement.

• *There will be no hitting.*

• *Those toys need to be picked up.*

• *I would appreciate your hanging up your jacket without my reminding you.*

Never, ever and always.

• *You never think about anybody else.*

• *When will you ever learn?*

• *You're always such a slob.*

These words can become self-fulfilling prophecies. They hurt a child's self-esteem and discourage him from trying to change. What they really say to the child is, *You're a disappointment...you're hopeless.*

Better: Be concrete—describe your expectations clearly and specifically.

• Instead of *You never do anything I ask*, try *It's your job to take out the garbage, and that needs to be done this afternoon.*

• Instead of *You never pick up after yourself*, try *I expect the blocks to be put in the toy box.*

You...plus a negative adjective, noun or phrase.

• *You're impossible.*

• *You're selfish.*

• *You're spoiled.*

• *You're a clod.*

• *You're acting like a baby.*

At worst, these are global statements about a child's character, which he can't change, as opposed to statements about his behavior, which he does have some control over. Even when they address his behavior, the statements are perceived as accusatory and negative. Accusations put people—children and adults alike—on the defensive, and a defensive person isn't likely to be reasonable.

You-statements can be destructive to a child's self-esteem. Like always and never, they can be self-fulfilling prophecies and are not likely to encourage your child to cooperate.

Better: Instead of telling your child what's wrong with him, talk about yourself, and keep it short. Try *I'm mad*, which is much more effective than *You're bad*. An I-statement encourages the child to take your feelings seriously—and respect them.

Beware: I think you're bad does not qualify as an I-statement—it's still a you-statement that happens to start with I.

Another alternative is a brief, impersonal reminder about house rules, such as *The rule is no TV until you've finished your homework.*

Source: Nancy Samalin, founder and director of Parent Guidance Workshops in New York. She is consulting editor and columnist for *Parents* and author of *Loving Your Child Is Not Enough: Positive Discipline That Works* and *Love and Anger: The Parental Dilemma*, Penguin Books, 375 Hudson St., New York 10014. 800-253-6476.

The Most Common Mistakes that Parents Make with Teens...and How Not to Make Them

One of the most effective ways to help your children become happy, successful adults is to create a warm, supportive environment in your home during their teenage years. You'll also get along much better under the same roof. *The most common mistakes parents make with their teenage children...*

• *Mistake:* Indiscriminate threats. Parents often make threats when they're angry. Then once the heat of the moment passes, they don't bother following through on them. *Result:* Your word will mean little, and your teen will believe that he/she need not pay attention to you —or any other authority figure. Promise disciplinary action only if you really mean it.

• *Mistake:* Setting unrealistic goals. Teens whose parents expect too much of them eventually become discouraged, and chronic discouragement sets many teenagers on a path toward personal crises. *Better:* Encourage them and don't expect perfection.

Be careful with praise, which celebrates the results of your child's efforts. Encouragement celebrates your child's effort—regardless of outcome. Effort is what you should reinforce.

• *Mistake:* Nagging about trivial issues. If you disapprove of your teen's views or behavior, it's acceptable to say so. But don't let essentially trivial issues—hair length, matters of style, for instance—drive a wedge between you and your teen. Adolescents dress, talk and behave in ways distasteful to their parents just to see if their parents will continue to love and respect them. Your teens will grow up to be fine, well-adjusted adults despite dozens of wrong choices.

• *Mistake:* Interrupting while your teen is talking. Make a conscious effort to listen. Don't be judgmental. Listening is one of the best ways of showing your love.

When talking with them, remember that simple questions deserve simple answers. Teenagers quickly "tune out" parents who talk to excess—especially those who utter too many sentences beginning with *When I was your age...*

• *Mistake:* Hiding your feelings. If your teen asks your opinion, be open and direct—but not controlling.

Example: If your teenage daughter asks how she looks, and you think her skirt is too tight, tell her so. She might wear the dress anyway, but she'll at least respect your candor.

Call things as you see them, but don't think you can say anything you please just because you're the head of the household. That's unfair —and also counterproductive. *Better:* If you've been inconsiderate of your teen, apologize, and when appropriate, ask for forgiveness.

• *Mistake:* Invading your teen's privacy. If your teen seems to use your home only as a place to eat and sleep and catch up on phone messages—congratulations—you have a normal child.

Rather than pry into your teen's affairs, help him cultivate a sense of independence. Unless you suspect a major problem, don't read his notes or go through his drawers or closets. And never listen in on phone conversations.

• *Mistake:* Overlooking irresponsible behavior. Don't let your teen get away with shirking responsibility. If he says something hurtful and then asks for a lift to soccer practice, for instance, say that you can't do it. Odds are, he will quickly sense that something is wrong and apologize for his behavior. Or, you arrive home and find that your teens have failed to get dinner started, as you had asked. Don't yell. Instead, say, *Goodbye, kids. I'm going out for dinner with your father/mother.*

But don't overreact. A youngster who spills a glass of milk needs a rag to wipe it up, not a lecture on clumsiness. The same holds true for teens. Don't blow up over insignificant things. Don't berate your teen for every minor transgression.

• *Mistake:* Ducking tough issues. Discuss problems well before they crop up. This will give your teen time to prepare to confront them rationally.

Example: If you have a 13-year-old daughter, now is the right time for the two of you to discuss problems that might arise when she turns 16.

Traditionally, mothers have discussed sexuality with their daughters, fathers with their sons. This is not always the best approach. *Reason:* An adolescent girl knows how she feels about love and sex. Her father can give her a sense of how adolescent boys feel. Likewise, a teenage boy needs to hear his mother's perspective about girls and dating. In fact, both of you may want to have this discussion with her/him.

• *Mistake:* Acting like your teen. Parents often try to behave like teenagers in a misguided attempt to fit in with their kids' lives and experiences. In fact, teens want and expect parents to behave like parents. They're uncomfortable around parents who act like they do.

•*Mistake:* Making teens do things your way. Be willing to let them fail when they make the wrong choice.

Example: Consider giving your teen the choice of mowing the lawn or using his allowance to hire someone else. A teen who opts for the latter quickly realizes that he has less money for compact disks, movies, etc. Occasional failure helps the person understand the importance of personal responsibility.

•*Mistake:* Making their lives hassle-free. Occasionally helping your teen with homework is okay—as long as your help is requested. But offering help when none is needed encourages your child to be overly dependent upon you. Intervene on your child's behalf at school and elsewhere only when absolutely necessary. This will help your teen develop problem-solving strategies and learn to anticipate them before they occur.

•*Mistake:* Spoiling their fun. If your teen asks to go dancing or camping, don't carry on about how worried you'll be.

Bottom line: If you've decided it's okay for your teen to do something or go somewhere, outline potential problems to prepare him for issues he might not have anticipated.

•*Mistake:* Putting your teen on the spot. Never ask your teen to perform for friends or relatives without first asking permission. Certainly, avoid disciplining your teenager in front of friends. Wait until the two of you are alone.

Adolescence is a time of low self-esteem. The pressures of high school, dating, schoolwork and competitiveness may be greater than your teen lets on. Odds are your teen is well aware of his flaws without your pointing them out.

Source: Kevin Leman, PhD, a Tucson, Arizona-based psychologist, author of *Smart Kids, Stupid Choices: A Survival Guide for Parents of Teens*, Dell Publishing, 1540 Broadway, New York 10036.

Imaginary Friends are Useful for Children

They help kids entertain themselves and develop their imaginations. Imaginary playmates usually befriend children between the ages of two-and-a-half and six. Boys and girls are equally likely to have them. Only children—and ones at least five years older or younger than the closest sibling—are more likely to have imaginary friends. *Helpful:* Give your child space and privacy with the friend. Never belittle him/her for talking to someone invisible. Play along—within reason. Keep your distance—children want to control these friends themselves.

Source: Charles Schaefer, PhD, psychologist and professor, Fairleigh Dickinson University, Hackensack, NJ.

Appreciative Kids Are Made—Not Born

Complaining is natural, but thankfulness requires the power of observation.

Helpful: Explain to children how even the poor today live better than the rich did 100 years ago...that until relatively recently, cars, telephones and computers didn't exist...that not many years ago, millions of people died of pneumonia, infections and other maladies that today are easily treated.

Aim: Contentment depends not so much on having more, as on appreciating what we already have. Always demanding more is a common trait among children. Parents should help by teaching them the inner joys of contentment.

Source: Reuven Bar-Levav, MD, a psychiatrist in private practice in Southfield, Michigan, and author of *Every Family Needs a CEO: What Mothers and Fathers Can Do About Our Deteriorating Families and Values.* Fathering Press.

11

Very Personal

Health Care Dilemma

Half of all medical costs are incurred in a person's last five days of life. The decision about where to die—in a hospital or at home—must now be given serious thought.

Source: *150 Ways to Be a Savvy Medical Consumer* by Charles B. Inlander, president, People's Medical Society. 462 Walnut St., Allentown, Pennsylvania 18102.

Antidepressant Fights Impotence

The drug trazodone...usually used against depression...has been found to prolong erections by keeping blood from draining out of the penis prematurely. Trazodone may help men who can achieve erections but cannot maintain them—because of arterial damage caused by cigarette smoking, high cholesterol or groin injuries.

Source: Research led by Irwin Goldstein, MD, professor of urology, Boston University Medical Center, reported in *The Journal of Urology*, 428 E. Preston St., Baltimore 21202.

Sex and Kidney Transplants

Kidney transplants improve sex for impotent men who undergo the transplants. In one study, the impotence rate dropped from 49% to 25%.

Source: Leslie R. Schover, PhD, staff psychologist, Center for Sexual Functions, Cleveland Clinic Foundation.

For Women Only

Endometriosis is a disorder in which the *endometrium*, tissue that normally lines the ute-

219

rus, implants and grows elsewhere in the body. *Common sites:* Ovaries, fallopian tubes, surface of the uterus and ligaments attaching the uterus to the back.

Symptoms: Painful periods, heavy menstrual bleeding, spotting between periods, pain with intercourse (especially during deep penetration), lower back pain and painful bowel movements. More severe cases can lead to scarring and infertility.

It's estimated that 15% of American women will develop endometriosis sometime during their reproductive lives. The majority of cases are mild—though the severity of the condition is not always related to the amount of pain. A woman with very few tissue growths may experience more pain than a woman with a much more advanced case.

Who is susceptible…

Major factors associated with endometriosis include:

•Age. Endometriosis is a disease of the reproductive years—the teens to mid-forties. It is most common in women 25 to 40 years old. When the condition appears in postmenopausal women, it's usually in connection with another factor, such as a tumor that is generating estrogen.

•Delayed childbearing. Women in their twenties with several children are less likely to develop endometriosis than women who have children later or don't have them at all. Pregnancy suppresses both the menstrual flow, which is thought to stimulate endometriosis, and the hormones, such as estrogen, which cause endometrial tissue to build up inside the uterus…and wherever else it's implanted.

•Heredity. In one study, 7% of women diagnosed with endometriosis had a *first-degree relative* (mother or sister) who also had the disease, as opposed to only 1% of women without endometriosis. Seven percent is not a very high figure, but the findings suggest a slight genetic tendency toward the disease.

Still, we don't know what causes endometriosis.

Primary theory: Retrograde menstruation—menstrual flow backs up through the fallopian tubes and into the abdominal cavity. Endometrial tissue that was supposed to be ejected by the body is implanted instead. Retrograde menstruation may be more likely to occur if a woman's cervical opening is narrow—which could be another reason why endometriosis is more common in women who have never had children.

It's also possible that an immunological deficit might make tissues more susceptible to implantation.

The *infertility* associated with endometriosis may result from adhesions on the ovaries, or blockage of the fallopian tubes by implanted tissue. In addition, the endometrial tissue itself produces hormones that may interfere with ovulation. Infertility could also be an indirect result of other symptoms.

Example: Women who experience severe pain during intercourse are more likely to avoid sex.

Preventing endometriosis…

There's no way to guarantee against developing endometriosis, but certain measures can be helpful…

•*Start your family early*—if it's practical to do so. If a woman has a strong family history of endometriosis, and she and her husband are wondering whether to postpone parenthood until she moves up in her job, she might be wise to have children now and devote time to her career later.

But for a 25-year-old single woman to consider artificial insemination—or marriage to the wrong man—to ward off the possibility of endometriosis would be foolish. Eighty-five percent of women don't get the disease—and of those who do, most have only mild cases. Effective treatment is available. The statistics aren't strong enough to support basing such an important life decision solely on fear of endometriosis.

•*If you're using birth control, take the Pill.* Like pregnancy, oral contraceptives suppress the menstrual cycle, minimizing the buildup of endometrial tissue.

•*Exercise and keep your weight down.* Physically fit women have more regular cycles and lighter menstrual flow than overweight, sedentary women. Though the connection with endometriosis hasn't been proven, staying in shape can't hurt.

Ineffective: Avoiding tampons, diaphragms or the cervical cap…avoiding sex during menstruation. These measures were recommended as ways to prevent endometriosis—*but* they have not been scientifically shown to decrease risk.

Diagnosis and treatment...

In the past, endometriosis was difficult to diagnose because it mimics other disorders, such as urinary tract infection or irritable bowel syndrome. During the last decade, *laparoscopy* —a simple surgical procedure in which a thin, telescope-like instrument is inserted through a tiny abdominal incision—has made diagnosis much more accurate.

Treatment options:

•Pain control. Women with very mild cases, or who aren't concerned about getting pregnant, may choose simply to relieve the pain—with over-the-counter anti-inflammatories, such as Motrin, or an antiprostaglandin.

•Surgery. After being located through laparoscopy, the growths are destroyed by cutting, cauterizing with electrical current or vaporizing with laser energy. In very severe cases—such as when tubes and ovaries are bound together —partial removal of the organs, or a complete hysterectomy may be advised. Hysterectomy was far more common in the past. Today, it is reserved for women with disabling pain who don't wish to have children.

•Drug therapy. Hormonal therapy is effective against growths that are small but too widespread to make surgery practical. As with surgery, patients who have mild endometriosis show a high fertility rate after drug treatment.

Drawbacks: Side effects can be unpleasant. And the drugs are expensive—$300–$400 per month, for six to nine months.

Types of drugs...

•*Danocrine (Danazol)*, a male hormone derivative taken orally. *Side effects:* Weight gain, acne, growth of facial hair—all reversible when therapy is stopped.

•*Synthetic hormones.* They are known as GnRH agonists (*brand names:* Lupron, Synarel). These act on the brain rather than the ovaries, creating an artificial menopause or low-estrogen state. The drugs are injected once a month, or taken twice a day in the form of a nasal spray. *Side effects:* Hot flashes, vaginal dryness, decrease in breast size. These side effects are also reversible after the drugs are discontinued. *Note:*

Treatment is usually limited to six months—if continued longer, bone loss can occur.

Extremely rare...

In fewer than 1% of patients, endometrial cancer may develop in the implanted tissues. Treatment is available, and the prognosis for these patients is excellent.

Source: Owen Montgomery, MD, instructor in obstetrics and gynecology at Thomas Jefferson University, 111 South 11th St., Suite 68210, Philadelphia 19107.

Menopause Without Medicine

Menopause myth: Decreased production of the female hormones estrogen and progesterone inevitably causes women to experience extreme physical discomfort, emotional turmoil and sexual dysfunction...and their only recourse is to take hormones.

The truth: Many women do experience physical and emotional changes during menopause. But these changes aren't necessarily disruptive. And some 20%–25% of all women breeze through menopause without any problems at all.

Most helpful: Becoming informed. Although talk shows routinely discuss the most personal subjects, from family conflicts to sexual aberrations, menopause is still practically taboo. Women approach this time of life not knowing what faces them. That uncertainty can be frightening and lead a woman to feel she's not in control of her life.

In fact, many symptoms can be prevented, or at least partly relieved, by healthy habits such as exercise and proper nutrition...beginning well before menopause. Both help the body to normalize hormone levels.

Also effective: Vitamin E, which has been used since the 1940s to minimize symptoms including hot flashes, vaginal dryness and mood swings. Start at a low dose—100 iu per day—and gradually increase dose (to a maximum of 1,200 iu) until you notice an improvement. *Important:* Consult your doctor before making any dietary changes.

The estrogen debate…

Hormone replacement therapy—usually estrogen plus progesterone—can be highly effective against osteoporosis and heart disease. It can also relieve some of the physical and emotional discomfort associated with menopause. But it also carries risks…and it is not the only option.

Estrogen taken alone is associated with higher risk for cancers of the uterus and breast. Estrogen and progesterone—taken together—may increase the risk for breast cancer.

Hormone replacement is definitely appropriate for some women, especially those at high risk for heart disease and osteoporosis…or who are truly debilitated by other symptoms. But too many doctors tell their female patients, "You're 50, it's time to start hormone replacement therapy," without evaluating the woman's own situation and cancer risk.

Menopause is highly individual—not all women experience all symptoms, or to the same degree. Treatment should be individualized as well. And natural remedies, particularly proper nutrition and exercise, should certainly play a part.

Osteoporosis…

Osteoporosis—progressive loss of bone—is one of the most common, and potentially debilitating, problems of menopause and post-menopause. About one in three women have this condition by age 75, characterized by bones that are highly porous—hence, prone to fracture.

Most at risk: Thin, fine-boned, fair-skinned women, especially if they don't exercise regularly.

Prevention—through calcium intake and exercise—is key. It's important to get enough of both during the bone-building years (to about age 35)—and afterward.

Calcium target: 1,200 mg per day before menopause, 1,500 mg after. Though you should eat plenty of calcium-rich foods such as milk and broccoli, you would have to drink four cups of milk a day to get 1,200 mg of calcium! Broccoli: 16 cups/day!

For this reason, I believe every woman over age 35 should be taking calcium supplements. *Best source:* Calcium carbonate or calcium citrate tablets. Dolomite and bone meal are not desirable because they are poorly absorbed and frequently contain trace amounts of lead and other toxins.

For best absorption, calcium should be taken with magnesium and vitamins C, K and D.

Don't overdose on vitamin D—too much can be toxic. Best sources are vitamin D-fortified milk, multiple-vitamin supplements and sunshine—20 minutes a day. Studies show that women who don't get out in the sun have a higher incidence of osteoporosis. And, phosphorus can leach calcium out of the bones, so go easy on red meat, colas, sugar, coffee and alcohol.

Weight bearing exercise also helps to build and retain bone. *Best:* Walking, jogging, dancing, weight-training. Swimming is not a weight bearing exercise. *Minimum schedule:* 20-plus minutes a day, four times a week. More is better. *Important:* Always consult with your doctor before starting any exercise program.

Women who benefit most start exercising in their teens, twenties and thirties and continue to do so. But it's never too late. Women who begin a moderate exercise program in their eighties can slow—even partly reverse—bone loss.

Hot flashes…

Up to 80% of menopausal women experience hot flashes—which usually feel like a surge of heat that may start with the head and then encompass the entire body. Some women sweat so profusely throughout the day and night that they have to change their clothes or bed sheets.

Episodes are often triggered by small changes in room temperature or eating spicy foods.

Hot flashes seem to be related to an overabundance of the brain hormones FSH and LH. Before menopause, they are kept in check by estrogen and progesterone. As the body adjusts to hormonal changes over a period of several years, the hot flashes tend to become less frequent and less intense. *Natural remedies:*

•Exercise is a hormone normalizer and can lower the levels of FSH and LH in the body. However, if you aren't used to working out, exercise will act as a stimulant and make the problem worse. If you're out of shape, begin exercising very gently and gradually.

•Good nutrition also seems to have a normalizing effect. *Important:* Avoid stress on the adrenal glands by eliminating or cutting down on sugar, fat and caffeine.

• Vitamin E…usually at levels of about 400 to 800 iu per day.

Sexual changes…

Women are certainly not fated to stop enjoying sex at menopause. The myth that post-menopausal women are asexual is partly based on our society's equating sexuality with youth… and on a lack of accurate information.

In fact, increased levels of testosterone—no longer tempered by high production of estrogen and progesterone—can lead to increased sex drive in menopausal women.

Freedom from the need to use birth control can enhance sexual enjoyment. And since the speed of sexual response slows with age in men as well as women, some women find that they are now more "in sync" with their partners' sexual timing.

It's true that the vagina becomes shorter, thinner, drier and less elastic. That can make intercourse uncomfortable. But these changes are usually controllable—with vitamin E, lubricants or with estrogen either taken orally or applied as a cream.

In addition, the vagina becomes more alkaline, making infections more common. Drinking cranberry juice and eating yogurt may help restore the pH. Drinking lots of water helps flush out bacteria.

Kegel exercises—contracting and releasing the pubococcygeus muscles (the ones you use to stop the flow of urine when going to the bathroom)—can improve muscle elasticity and tone in the vaginal area.

Abdominal exercises help to strengthen the muscles surrounding the sexual organs.

Mood swings…

In the past, physicians may have dismissed mood swings at menopause as female hysteria.

We now believe that emotional changes may be a result of lower estrogen levels. It could be that when estrogen decreases, there's a corresponding decrease in endorphins—the brain chemicals which create a feeling of well-being. *Most helpful:*

• Understanding that the condition is normal …temporary…and that you're not going crazy.

• Exercise, which is thought to raise endorphin levels.

• Relaxation techniques such as meditation, yoga, prayer—or simply taking time for quiet reflection. Regular, focused relaxation is a highly effective mood balancer—and can help you cope with physical changes as well.

Source: Linda Ojeda, PhD, CNC, a consultant and lecturer on nutrition and fitness and the author of *Menopause Without Medicine.* Hunter House, Inc. Dr. Ojeda has done extensive interviews with physicians in the UK and US.

Exciting Prostate News

A new medication, Proscar, can shrink an enlarged prostate gland and improve urinary flow —averting surgery for this common problem of aging men. *Importance:* Benign prostate enlargement accounts for 1.7 million doctor's office visits a year—and 400,000 operations. *Manufacturer:* Merck & Co. *Price:* Approximately $2/day. *Side effects:* Minimal. *Drawback:* Proscar reduces one's PSA (prostate-specific antigen) level, which is sometimes elevated with cancer. This could result in a missed diagnosis of prostate cancer.

Source: E. Douglas Whitehead, MD, FACS, a New York City urologist, Director of the Association for Male Sexual Dysfunction, 24 E. 12 St., Suite 2-1, New York 10003.

Chlamydia Cure

Better cure for sexually transmitted disease: A new drug, azithromycin, cures chlamydia infections with just one dose, compared with currently used medications that require two doses daily over seven to 10 days. *Big benefit:* A single-dose treatment ensures patients get the full amount of drug required.

Source: Study of 138 cases at the University of Iceland, reported by Vincent Andriole, MD, professor of medicine, Yale University School of Medicine, in *The Medical Post,* 777 Bay St., Toronto, Ontario M5W 1A7.

Hemorrhoid Horrors

Everyone has hemorrhoids—that's simply the name given to the cushion-like network of blood vessels lining the anus. Unfortunately, millions of people also suffer the pain, inflammation, itching, and even bleeding of hemorrhoidal inflammation. *Shocking statistic:* Nine out of 10 Americans experience these hemorrhoidal symptoms by age 50. The problem strikes men and women with equal frequency.

There are several causes of hemorrhoidal inflammation. *Most significant:* Chronic constipation. The additional pressure on the rectum that constipation produces can cause blood vessels to swell and become inflamed. Prolonged periods on the toilet also put considerable pressure on the anus. People who read, listen to the radio, or talk on the telephone while defecating face an increased risk of developing symptoms. A normal bowel movement takes no more than a few minutes.

Other factors: Pregnancy (it increases pressure in the lower abdomen), family history, overuse of enemas. Children who were forced to relieve themselves at certain times of the day regardless of the urge to do so often develop problems—and can have them again later in life. Parents should always let nature take its course.

Lack of exercise and jobs requiring long periods of standing or sitting have been cited as aggravating factors, but there's little evidence of this.

Inside, outside…

There are two types of hemorrhoids—external and internal—and consequently two kinds of inflammation. External inflammation occurs when blood vessels around or just inside the anus swell. If a blood clot develops in one of these vessels, it stretches the sensitive skin and causes severe pain.

This clot can develop in people of all ages and is usually brought on by strenuous physical exercise. The clot is usually small and firm, yet tender. In most cases, it softens on its own within a few days. If it's very painful, a doctor can speed the healing process by making a small incision so that the clot may be removed. This procedure is done on an outpatient basis. *Cost:* $75–$200.

More common and more troublesome than external hemorrhoidal inflammation is internal hemorrhoidal inflammation. Internal hemorrhoids are blood vessels and connective tissue that line the anus and lower rectum (anorectal passage). When these vessels swell, they narrow the passage.

This problem is barely noticeable in young people. As people age, however, hemorrhoids loosen, become elongated, and slowly descend the anorectal passage toward the anus.

Result: Stool entering the anorectal passage can be passed only with substantial straining, injuring the lining. This increases pressure in the rectum and causes the blood vessels there to become engorged with blood. The vessels become progressively weaker and bleed easily during bowel movements.

Interesting: Since the mucous membrane surrounding the hemorrhoid have no nerve endings, there's no pain.

Bleeding is often the first sign of irritated internal hemorrhoids. However, colorectal cancer, polyps, and other serious conditions can also cause bleeding. See a doctor for an accurate diagnosis.

Four degrees of trouble…

Hemorrhoidal symptoms develop in four progressive stages. All are helped by changes in hygiene and diet, but drug therapy or surgery is sometimes necessary.

•First degree: Blood vessel cushions are slightly swollen but usually go unnoticed. Hard stool occasionally causes bleeding. *Help:* Stool-softening drugs, available by prescription.

•Second degree: Hemorrhoids begin to protrude during bowel movements. But the connective tissue is still strong enough to draw the hemorrhoids back within the anus. *Symptoms:* Irritation, itching, and slight burning. *Help:* Warm sitz baths. Sit in plain warm water for 10 to 15 minutes. Over-the-counter remedies, such as hemorrhoidal ointment and suppositories, soothe irritated skin but do nothing to shrink hemorrhoidal tissues—contrary to manufacturers' claims.

• Third degree: Hemorrhoids don't retract on their own and must be carefully pushed back into the anus. *Help:* Suppositories containing steroids or cortisone, which help shrink swollen tissues and relieve pain.

• Fourth degree: Reinserting the hemorrhoid becomes difficult or impossible. Bowel movements are painful. *Usual treatment:* surgery.

Self-help…

Hemorrhoidal symptoms can often be prevented or improved by simply preventing constipation. *Crucial:* Regular exercise and a balanced diet with high fiber content. Laxatives are not the answer. After prolonged use, they damage the lining of the colon and make constipation worse.

Fiber passes through the intestinal tract virtually undigested. Its soft, bulky consistency speeds the passage of feces and lessens the strain of bowel movements. *Bonus:* Since it retains water, fiber also softens the stool.

Fruits, vegetables, breads, and cereals are excellent sources of fiber.

Good toilet habits and anal hygiene are also important. Try not to postpone bowel movements, and cultivate a schedule for defecation. But don't strain just to stick to your schedule, and don't prolong your toilet time by listening to the radio or reading.

Keep the area around the anus clean and dry. Wipe gently, but thoroughly, using soft, moistened toilet paper. Then gently pat dry.

Some symptoms that seem to indicate hemorrhoidal inflammation are really indications of other problems. Perianal warts, soap allergies, and psoriasis can all cause itching. Fissures (tiny cracks in the skin surrounding the anus) and anal abscesses (infections near the rectum) cause severe pain.

Professional help…

The simplest, least painful, and most widely used treatment for severely swollen hemorrhoids is rubber band ligation. *Procedure:* Protruding hemorrhoidal tissue is tied off (ligated) with a tiny but strong rubber band. This stops blood flow and kills the hemorrhoidal tissue, causing it to fall off within a week. No anesthesia is required. Aspirin is usually sufficient to control pain. *Cost:* $45–$130. Rubber band ligation can be performed in the doctor's office.

Less severely inflamed hemorrhoids can be shrunk via drug injections. They can also be welded to the rectal wall through a technique called photocoagulation, in which infrared light is used.

Traditional hemorrhoid surgery, hemorrhoidectomy, is less popular now because these other measures are so effective. It requires local anesthesia and a few days of recuperation. *Cost* (including surgeon's fees, hospitalization, and diagnostic tests): $2,500.

Laser hemorrhoidectomy is still being evaluated for its effectiveness, and cryotherapy, which destroys tissues through rapid freezing, has not lived up to the great expectations doctors once had for it.

Source: Peter A. Haas, MD, a colon and rectal surgeon at Henry Ford Hospital in Detroit and clinical instructor of colorectal surgery, University of Michigan, Ann Arbor. Dr. Haas has written numerous medical journal articles on hemorrhoids.

Reducing Urinary Incontinence I

Bladder training—educating women about urinary function and scheduling urination for specific times—significantly reduces urinary incontinence.

Study: Patients were asked to urinate on a schedule of every 30 to 60 minutes initially—and to empty the bladder as much as possible during these times. If subjects needed to void before these times, they were told to use relaxation and distraction techniques to suppress the urge as long as possible. Urination times were increased to up to three-hour intervals for those who kept on their schedules.

Results: 75% of the women were able to improve their bladder control by at least 50%. Twelve percent achieved complete bladder control. *Problem:* Urinary incontinence affects almost 40% of women aged 60 and over.

Source: J. Andrew Fantl, MD, professor of obstetrics and gynecology, Medical College of Virginia, Richmond.

Reducing Urinary Incontinence II

A non-surgical device has proven to be very successful in the treatment of bladder-control problems among women. *Eighty percent improvement:* In a recent study, more than four out of five women reported improved bladder control after six weeks using a device that electrically stimulates the pelvic floor for 15 minutes twice a day. Other studies of behavior modification or exercise in the treatment of incontinence have done equally well—with cure rates of up to 40%.

Problems: Some women may not want to spend the time using the device, and many physicians still see surgery as the most reliable cure for bladder-control problems.

Source: Peter K. Sand, MD, director of urogynecology, Evanston Hospital, Evanston, Illinois.

How to Fight Impotence With Diet...Not Drugs Or Surgery

By age 65, about one quarter of all men find it difficult or impossible to achieve an erection during lovemaking. And only rarely is that impotence truly psychological.

To blame: In more than 80% of these cases, impotence can be traced to a poor diet. *Tragic:* Most doctors overlook diet as a possible cause of impotence, simply because few medical schools teach anything about nutrition.

Self-defense: Before you submit to drug therapies or surgery for an impotence problem, make sure your diet and lifestyle have been fully evaluated.

What happens...

The same high-fat and cholesterol-heavy diet that can cause hardening of the arteries and stroke are prime causes of impotence. *Reasons:*

•Blood vessels in the penis are damaged by atherosclerosis.

•Too much dietary fat can cause obesity, which can cause diabetes. Diabetes injuries penile nerves.

Impotence quiz...

To rule out other causes of impotence, ask yourself:

•Do I drink? Alcohol temporarily blocks erections.

•Do I smoke? Both tobacco and marijuana have been linked to impotence.

•Do I take any prescribed medications? Many heart and hypertension medications—diuretics, beta blockers, calcium channel blockers and anticholinergics—cause impotence. *Alarming:* One antihypertensive drug, Aldomet, causes impotence in a large number of patients who take it.

Other culprits: Antiulcer drugs, antidepressants and drugs (including estrogen) that suppress male hormones.

The diet solution...

•Limit fat intake to between 5% and 10% of daily calories. Concentrate on grains, beans, potatoes, fruits, vegetables.

•Try the herbal extract yohimbine. Made from the bark of an African tree, yohimbine decreases blood flow out of the penis. It's available by prescription in capsules (Aphrodyne, Yocon and Yohimex) or as a natural bark in health-food stores.

Source: Internist John A. McDougall, MD, medical director of the Lifestyle and Nutrition program at St. Helena Hospital, Deer Park, California.

Testosterone Trap

Eating a fatty meal causes men's testosterone levels to drop significantly one to four hours afterwards. In a study of healthy men aged 23 to 35, their testosterone levels fell about 30% after they ate a meal deriving 57% of its calories from fat. Eating a meal with no fat or very little fat (2% of calories from fat) had no impact on testosterone levels. The researchers believe that if a man eats a fatty meal only occasionally, it probably won't affect his sexual performance but that a man's habitual consumption of fatty foods may have a negative effect.

Source: Wayne Meikle, MD, professor of medicine, University of Utah Medical Center, 50 N. Medical Dr., Salt Lake City, Utah 84132.

Impotence: The Miracle Treatment

Almost any impotent man can again have erections if, with a urologist's help, he learns to self-inject special drugs into his penis. The treatment's success rate: 80%.

Better drug mix…

Since the 1980s, two medications have been used together. Papaverine causes erections. Phentolamine helps sustain them. Papaverine, though, can cause internal scars of penile tissue, adding to erectile problems. It can also lead to erections which last too long (more than four hours) and can damage the penis.

New addition: Prostaglandin E-1 (PGE-1) augments papaverine's effect. Less or no papaverine need be used so fewer side effects occur.

Finding the correct dose of the two- or three-drug mixture requires several office visits. The urologist also teaches the man, or his partner, how to inject the drugs into the base of the penis. (The needle is tiny and the injection virtually painless.)

The patient reports how the drugs work when he is alone with his partner (such erections frequently are firmer and longer lasting than erections he has at the doctor's office). Then the final dose is determined and the man takes home a one- to three-month supply of the drugs. (With time, a higher dose may be needed.) The injections are to be used no more than every two days.

Vital: A man must immediately call his doctor or an emergency room if he has a rigid erection for more than four hours. (This situation can be life-threatening.)

Twice yearly, the patient must also have a blood test to check his liver function, which may be affected. Periodic visits to his urologist

are also advised to make sure no internal scars have developed.

Note: Because this drug program is new, some doctors allow its use for only two years. Most allow longer use because the drugs are used in tiny amounts.

Also, the treatment does not work on men with severe atherosclerotic penile vascular problems, and many men drop out after treatment is started due to lack of spontaneity, reduced quality of erections with time and fear of unknown long-term complications.

Rate of complications, mainly prolonged erections: Less than 5%.

Cost: About $1,000–$3,000/year. Insurers may not pay. Those interested should consult with their insurance company.

Source: E. Douglas Whitehead, MD, FACS, a New York City urologist, Director of the Association for Male Sexual Dysfunction, 24 E. 12 St., Suite 2-1, New York 10003.

How to Choose the Right Contraceptive

There are hundreds of different contraceptives on the market today, each claiming to be more effective—and to have fewer side effects —than the next. In fact, different contraceptives are right at different times in life and for people with different lifestyles, medical histories and sexual habits.

Cervical cap…

A small plastic or rubber cap that is placed over the cervix.

•Effectiveness: 71% to 98%. The effectiveness of the cervical cap depends on how carefully it is positioned over the cervix.

•Side effects: Risk of toxic shock syndrome if left in place too long. Sometimes it irritates tissues surrounding the cervix. It is not yet known whether these changes increase the risk of cervical cancer.

•Popularity: Widely used in Europe, but only recently available in the US.

•Other advantages: May be left in place for 48 to 72 hours.

•Other disadvantages: Smaller than the diaphragm and therefore more difficult to insert and more easily dislodged during intercourse.

•Best for: Women in stable relationships where insertion before sex is not a problem. Women using either the cervical cap or the diaphragm should be well-informed about the correct insertion and removal of these devices.

Condom...

Placed over the erect penis, it physically prevents sperm from reaching the cervix. Typically used together with spermicidal foams or jellies.

•Effectiveness: 85% to 97%.

•Side effects: None.

•Popularity: Use of the condom has risen sharply during the current AIDS epidemic, although condoms are not 100% effective in preventing the spread of the disease. Used by 12.2% of couples, the condom is exceeded in popularity only by sterilization and the Pill.

•Other advantages: No prescription is needed...readily available almost anywhere...reduces transmission of venereal diseases and AIDS.

•Other disadvantages: May break or leak. Must be put on just prior to intercourse. Reduces sensation for the male.

•Best for: Anyone concerned about venereal disease or AIDS should use (or insist their partner use) a condom. Easy availability without a prescription makes the condom, used together with spermicides, the best choice for those having infrequent coitus and in situations where individuals have not decided on a long-term contraceptive solution.

Diaphragm...

A hemispherical cup that is filled with spermicide and inserted over the cervix.

•Effectiveness: 71% to 98%. As with the cervical cap, effectiveness depends heavily on how carefully it is positioned over the cervix.

•Side effects: Increased incidence of urinary tract infections.

•Popularity: Used by 8.3% of couples, it is the fourth-most-popular contraceptive method in the US.

•Other advantages: Unlike other barrier methods (condoms and foams), it can be inserted up to several hours before intercourse.

•Other disadvantages: A consultation with a physician is needed for prescription and fitting. The diaphragm must be inserted before beginning intercourse. Its position must be checked and additional spermicide must be added prior to each coital episode.

•Best for: Many women who are concerned about potential side effects of the Pill and intrauterine device (IUD) have turned to the diaphragm. As with the cervical cap, it is best for women in stable, supportive relationships where insertion before sex is not a problem.

IUD...

There are currently two types of intrauterine devices that can be inserted into the uterus by a physician. One has progesterone incorporated into the plastic material. It can be used for a limited time before it must be removed.

The other type utilizes copper that adheres to the plastic and can be left in place for several years. IUDs produce an inflammatory reaction in the uterine wall, and, in some unknown way, prevent implantation and pregnancy.

•Effectiveness: 95% to 98%.

•Side effects: Menstrual periods often last longer in IUD users, and some users experience cramping and increased menstrual flow. Infections, including those leading to pelvic inflammatory disease, may cause sterility.

•Popularity: Fifth-most-popular form of birth control. It is used by 7.3% of all couples.

•Other advantages: A single visit to the doctor is all that's needed. Insertion of an IUD provides contraception for up to five years (at which time the IUD should be replaced).

•Other disadvantages: Because of the heightened risk of pelvic inflammatory disease, doctors are not as eager to prescribe IUDs as they once were. Recent legal action has also caused IUD prices to soar.

•Best for: Women older than 30 who have decided against having children but wish to avoid sterilization. *Note:* Women in monogamous relationships are less likely to get pelvic inflammatory disease.

The Mini Pill...

Contains the hormone progestin, which causes the formation of a thick mucus barrier in the cervix that prevents sperm from reaching the uterus. The Mini Pill also inhibits the release of eggs by the ovaries and makes implantation of fertilized eggs more difficult.

• Effectiveness: 96% to 98%. The Mini Pill is not quite as effective as the standard estrogen-containing Pill.

• Side effects: Irregular menstrual bleeding, increased rate of ectopic pregnancy, depression.

• Popularity: Only 1% as popular as the standard Pill.

• Best for: Women who are breast-feeding, and women who for medical reasons cannot take the standard Pill but want to use an oral contraceptive.

Norplant…

Matchstick-sized rods are surgically implanted beneath the skin of the woman's upper arm. These rods, which slowly release the hormone progestin, remain effective for up to five years.

• Effectiveness: 99%.

• Side effects: 30% to 40% of women using Norplant experience irregular menstrual cycles, especially during the first three months of use. Although Norplant uses the same hormone found in many oral contraceptives, it generally causes fewer side effects because its dosage is lower.

• Popularity: Growing in popularity.

• Other advantages: Just as effective as oral contraceptives.

• Other disadvantages: Requires minor surgery to implant—and later, to remove—the six contraceptive rods. The procedure, which requires only a tiny incision, can be performed in a doctor's office in less than 10 minutes. Relatively expensive—$350 for the device, plus $250 to $750 for the implant surgery.

• Best for: Women who want a highly reliable form of birth control without the bother of having to take a daily Pill.

Oral contraceptives for men…

Despite intensive research in this field, no male contraceptive pills are yet available in the US. Researchers hope to develop a pill that prevents production of viable sperm.

• Drawback: There would be no way for a woman to determine whether or not her partner was consistently taking these pills.

The Pill…

Several different types are available, in a variety of dosages. All work by preventing the release of eggs from the ovaries.

• Effectiveness: 97% to 99.9%.

• Side effects: Some women experience nausea, breast tenderness, weight gain, yeast infections, hair loss and depression. The more serious side effects of the Pill are especially common in women who smoke and women who are over 35 years old. These side effects include heart attacks, strokes, blood clots in the lungs and high blood pressure.

Note: Most side effects are related to the dosage of the hormones estrogen and progestin contained in the Pill. Women should find out from their doctors if they can get by with a lower-dose Pill—many equally effective formulations are available.

• Popularity: The most popular reversible contraceptive method. It is used by 28.6% of couples practicing birth control today.

• Other advantages: Does not interrupt lovemaking…the most effective method for preventing pregnancy aside from sterilization… reduces pain during periods for some women.

• Other disadvantages: Requires a doctor's prescription. Must be taken every day even when no sexual activity occurs.

• Best for: Women under 35 with regular periods and who suffer no undesirable side effects during use. Not recommended for women who are forgetful or who have erratic daily schedules. Also not recommended for smokers.

Progestin shots…

An injection every two to three months prevents eggs from being released.

• Effectiveness: Up to 99.7%.

• Side effects: Irregularity or loss of periods. The shots sometimes make it harder for women to have children even after the injections have been stopped.

• Popularity: Used commonly throughout developing countries.

• Other advantages: Very convenient—four to six shots per year provide continuous contraception.

• Best for: So far these shots have been used mainly by women living where other contraceptive methods are too expensive or unavailable. Because of their convenience and high rate of effectiveness, they may gain wider acceptance in the next few years.

Spermicides…

Includes foams, creams, jellies and vaginal suppositories. Inserted into the vagina several minutes prior to coitus. These agents kill sperm.

- Effectiveness: 70%–92%.
- Side effects: Few. Rarely, allergic reactions may occur.
- Popularity: Used by 2.4% of couples as the sole method of birth control.
- Other advantages: No prescription is needed. Provides some protection against venereal diseases.
- Other disadvantages: Messy. Relatively high failure rate when used alone.
- Best use: Along with a condom, diaphragm or another form of contraception.

Sponge…

A polyurethane sponge that contains the spermicide Nonoxynol 9 is inserted into the vagina before intercourse.

- Effectiveness: 80% to 91%.
- Side effects: Irritation due to the spermicide has been reported. Infections and toxic shock syndrome can occur if it is left in too long.
- Popularity: Approved by the FDA in 1983, it is still growing in popularity.
- Other advantages: No prescription is needed. It remains effective for 24 hours and need not be replaced before each act of coitus.
- Other disadvantages: Relatively high failure rate. Some women have difficulty removing the sponge.
- Best use: Because of its relatively low effectiveness, the sponge is best used in combination with a condom.

Sterilization…

How it works: Women…the fallopian tubes, which carry eggs from the ovaries to the uterus, are tied or clamped shut in a relatively simple and low-risk operation. Men…a vasectomy can be performed in a doctor's office in less than 15 minutes. It consists of making a small incision in the scrotum and cutting the vas deferens, the two tubes that carry sperm to the penis. Although a small to moderate percentage of sterilization cases are reversible, this procedure

should be undertaken only as a final decision in family planning.

- Effectiveness: 99.6% to 99.95%.
- Side effects: All of the usual risks and side effects of minor surgery. Women may have irregular menstrual bleeding.
- Popularity: Sterilization is the most popular method of birth control in the US. Used by 21.9% of women and 10.8% of men for a total of 32.7% of all couples.
- Other disadvantages: The procedure is often irreversible. Some people have difficulty adjusting psychologically to being sterile.
- Best for: Women and men who are certain that they do not plan to have any children in the future and who do not mind undergoing surgery.

Timed abstinence…

Also known as the rhythm method. Intercourse is avoided around the time of ovulation. The approximate time of ovulation is determined by counting days from menstruation, by monitoring changes in body temperature or by noting changes in the consistency of vaginal secretions.

- Effectiveness: 76% to 97%, depending upon the method used to detect ovulation. Monitoring body temperature is the most reliable.
- Side effects: None.
- Popularity: Used by 4% of couples in the United States.
- Other advantages: Accepted by the Roman Catholic Church.
- Other disadvantages: Requires abstaining from sex for a significant part of the month—often when a woman's desire is strongest. In addition, the failure rate is relatively high. When fertilization does occur while using this method, the fertilized egg is more likely to be in suboptimal condition. This may cause a slightly higher rate of birth defects and miscarriages.
- Best for: Couples who do not want to use other methods of birth control, especially for religious reasons.

Withdrawal…

The penis is withdrawn from the vagina prior to ejaculation.

- Effectiveness: 77% to 84%.
- Popularity: Used by only 2% of couples in the US. Widely practiced in Europe and Japan and where other methods are unavailable.

• Other disadvantages: Sexual dissatisfaction for both partners.

• Best: When no other contraceptive method is available and when a relatively high risk of pregnancy is acceptable.

Source: Robert Morris, MD, director of obstetrics and gynecology, New York University Hospital, and Livia Wan, MD, professor of obstetrics and gynecology, New York University School of Medicine, 550 First Ave., New York 10016.

Condom Risk

Old condoms rupture far more frequently than new ones. *Study:* 262 couples were asked to test about 5,000 condoms over a four-month period. *Result:* Less than 5% of brand-new condoms ruptured during intercourse. But condoms a year or two old broke about 10% of the time...and seven-year-old condoms broke about 19% of the time.

Source: Research by Markus Steiner, BA, contraceptive use and epidemiology division, Family Health International, Research Triangle Park, North Carolina.

Sex and the Middle-Aged Couple

In almost two decades as a practicing sex therapist, I have encountered nearly every sexual problem imaginable. Yet for all their differences, most couples—especially middle-aged couples—share a remarkably similar set of concerns, including passion, fidelity and compatibility. Here are the questions I get most often, along with my answers.

My husband fears he is losing his virility. What should we do?

This is an especially common question. In my view, the problem stems not so much from the realities of aging, as from the cultural fallacy that a man must be physically powerful to be a good lover. Compared with younger men, men in their 60s and older do take longer to get an erection and to achieve orgasm, and

their orgasms are often less intense. But these changes need not hamper a man's ability to enjoy sex and to be an exciting lover. In the vast majority of cases, a middle-aged man's growing self-knowledge and life experience can more than compensate for the slight decline in his physical capacity.

Crucial: A willingness to take sex more slowly and deliberately, with less emphasis on performance and more emphasis on the pleasures of stroking and caressing. For men of any age suffering from impotence or other forms of sexual dysfunction, effective treatment is available. Some cases of impotence have specific, reversible physiological causes. These should be investigated by a urologist.

Will menopause ruin our sex life?

Many middle-aged women worry that menopause will destroy their libido and ruin sex for themselves—and their partners. Menopause can bring about certain physiological changes —vaginal dryness or a loss of sensation, for example. Fortunately, these problems are usually treatable, via the use of lubricants, estrogen replacement therapy or homeopathic herbal remedies. Moreover, many women find that menopause actually improves their sex life. Following menopause, for instance, sex is often more spontaneous, as there is no longer any need for contraception.

Bottom line: As long as both partners are emotionally prepared for menopause, there is no physical reason that it should interfere with sexuality.

We have fallen out of sync sexually. Why?

Middle age affects men and women quite differently. Many women find middle age a time of sexual liberation. After years of relative inhibition—brought on in part by the time constraints and emotional demands of childrearing—middle-aged women begin to seek greater satisfaction from lovemaking. They have become more comfortable with their bodies, so they are more willing to experiment sexually, and they start to want more from their lovers. Unfortunately, this increasing sexuality among middle-aged women often clashes with the changing sexuality of their husbands. *Reason:* Unlike their wives, middle-aged men often find themselves becoming less, rather than more, interested in sex.

Happily, this rift can usually be repaired. *Crucial:* Honesty, communication, playfulness, tenderness, an openness to sexual experimentation and self-exploration, including masturbation. However, where there are specific sexual problems or dysfunction, sex therapy is essential. In such cases, the couple may be asked to refrain from sexual intercourse while learning once again to derive pleasure simply by touching and through foreplay. Forgoing intercourse in this manner seems strange to most couples who have been having intercourse for decades. But the payoffs in enhanced pleasure and greater intimacy are well worth the effort. For couples willing to work together with love and sensitivity, middle age can be the time during which they first learn how to make love, rather than merely copulate.

What's happened to my sex drive?

In some cases, a loss of libido can be traced to a crisis outside the marital bedroom: Serious illness, a death in the family, the loss of a job, failure in business, increased work load, unresolved feelings of anger or resentment, etc. All can cause one or both partners to lose interest in sex. Happily, desire usually returns upon the resolution of the crisis. All that's required is a little patience.

Other cases of waning desire are more complex. For example, some people find their libido diminishes the more intimate they become with their partner. A middle-aged man may lose interest in his wife because they know each other so intimately…and in the same way a middle-aged woman can lose interest in her husband. In such cases, the trouble usually stems from some early emotional trauma resulting in a fear of intimacy. For couples who feel this phenomenon is playing a role in their relationship, the best solution is psychotherapy.

Why doesn't my spouse turn me on anymore?

Your premise is wrong. Your spouse doesn't turn you on, nor does he/she turn you off. Each of us is responsible for turning ourselves on and off. If you are no longer aroused by your spouse's loving touch, the question to ask is, *Why am I turning myself off?* In many cases, the answer can be traced to unexpressed or unresolved feelings of anger or resentment. If you

have difficulty becoming aroused, scan your mind for such feelings, then discuss them with your spouse. In other cases, a spouse unwittingly sabotages the arousal process by reviewing a mental list of his/her partner's flaws.

Better: Run a list of his/her good points. Instead of letting your thoughts wander, try focusing directly on yourself, on just how pleasurable it is to be held and caressed. Remember, the brain is your most sensitive erogenous zone.

Why do my spouse and I argue so much these days?

For most couples, middle age is the time when the kids leave home and strike out on their own. This emptying of the nest seems innocuous enough. In many cases, however, it profoundly alters the emotional dynamic that exists between a husband and wife.

Reason: After years of concealing their sexuality and focusing on childrearing, the couple suddenly find themselves alone, with nothing and no one to keep them apart. *Typical:* Points of conflict that once were glossed over "to spare the children" flare up into big fights.

Good news: While often scary, fighting is not without its practical side. It helps couples negotiate important emotional boundaries, providing emotional "space" when necessary. A more congenial way to accomplish the same thing, however, is to learn to state your needs directly to one another, and not wait until resentment turns into a fight. If you feel grouchy, for instance, ask your mate for a couple of hours alone. That way you can create some distance without causing a fight. But, remember, a little fighting is healthy.

We just don't have time for sex anymore.

Many couples who complain of not having enough time for sex are really filling their time with other activities—often so that they can avoid intimacy.

And no wonder. Though they can't admit it, even to themselves, most people are terrified by true intimacy. All too many of us grow up in dysfunctional households, seeing our parents argue, suffering harsh discipline and perhaps even abuse or incest—all from the first people with whom we are close, our parents. As we grow older, we fear intimacy out of a sense of self-protection. If you really want to have sex and be intimate with your partner, you can find ways to make the time.

Source: Dagmar O'Connor, PhD, lecturer in psychiatry at Columbia University, New York City. A practicing sex therapist for two decades, Dr. O'Connor was the first Masters & Johnson-trained female sex therapist in New York City. She is the author of *How to Make Love to the Same Person for the Rest of Your Life—and Still Love It* and *How to Put the Love Back into Making Love*, Bantam Doubleday Dell, 666 Fifth Ave., New York 10103.

Secrets of Much Better Sex

If you're experiencing difficulties in an intimate relationship, professional sex therapy might be the solution. Helpful questions and answers:

Why do people begin sex therapy?

The reasons vary. Men typically begin therapy because they're experiencing problems with erection or rapid (premature) ejaculation. Women may be having trouble experiencing orgasm. Many men and some women are also concerned about lack of sexual desire. In addition, some women experience vaginismus, a spasm of the vaginal opening that precludes penetration.

What causes these problems?

A culture that teaches women not to feel good about sexuality and puts pressure on men to perform is the major cause of sexual problems. Lack of desire often stems from the disruption of a couple's sex life following the birth of a child—abnormal only if this disruption persists more than a few months. Lack of desire also may be symptomatic of a power struggle within the relationship.

Don't measure your sexuality by someone else's standard. There is tremendous variation in human sexual response. Sex therapy can help determine what's right for you.

Does eliminating a sexual problem also eliminate its underlying cause?

It's the other way around. If you are having other problems in your life, clearing up sexual issues won't change them. *Key questions:* How do you expect your life to change once you resolve this problem? Could things be worse?

The issues exposed by therapy can be exceedingly complex. *Examples:* The wife of a man experiencing impotence may be reluctant for him to solve his problem—if he can't get an erection, he cannot be unfaithful. Her insecurity may cause her to sabotage his therapy. A husband may be afraid that if his wife becomes turned on sexually, he might not be able to satisfy her.

Is sex therapy all talk?

No. Almost every sex therapist gives homework assignments. Whatever the problem, I don't want my clients just talking about it. I want them experimenting and changing their behavior.

What kind of homework assignments?

Most homework assignments start out with masturbation and feelings about the body. For women especially, feeling good about their bodies is essential to having satisfying sexual relationships. If you're concerned about your appearance, it's hard to be turned on.

Masturbation is helpful because it teaches you about your body and its responses. *Common mistake:* Masturbating in one way only. Many women assume one unvarying position when masturbating—maybe with their legs crossed, or on their stomachs. They train themselves to achieve orgasm in a way that is nothing like what happens during lovemaking. Men often masturbate in such a way that they train themselves to be rapid ejaculators. They may have spent their teenage years masturbating as quickly as possible because they didn't want to get caught. However, masturbation can also be used to retrain yourself, to learn new techniques.

What other assignments do you give?

This really depends on what the problem is. *Example:* People unable to tell their partners what they like can become less inhibited by fantasizing about such conversations ahead of time. People who have no difficulty achieving orgasm during masturbation, but do have trouble with a partner, might try masturbating with the hand not ordinarily used. This provides the experience of imprecise stimulation.

Couples can learn a great deal about each other simply by exploring each other's genitals. *Suggestion:* Take time to really look at each other with the lights on. Show your partner areas of particular sensitivity. In this way you can quickly and playfully teach your partner a tremendous amount about your particular sexual needs.

One exercise involves setting aside 45 to 60 minutes for lovemaking—longer than most couples spend—and devoting at least 30 minutes to kissing, stroking, massage, manual and/or oral stimulation of each other's genitals. *Important:* Most women need at least 20 minutes of foreplay to achieve orgasm.

How long does sex therapy last?

Some sexual problems are very easy to treat. Generally, women who are preorgasmic (have never had orgasms) and those with vaginismus can be treated in 10 to 20 weeks. Men who are rapid ejaculators take around 15 to 20 weeks. Women who are orgasmic with masturbation but not with a partner, and men who have erection problems are a little tougher.

Hardest to treat: Lack of desire. This may take a year or more—and the success ratio is rather low because it's often not a sexual problem but a symptom of a problem in the relationship.

Is lack of desire a common problem?

We are seeing more cases involving lack of desire, and our fast-paced lifestyles are usually to blame. If both partners are continually exhausted and under a great deal of stress, they may not have the energy to have sex. It is a very physical activity. Set aside time in your busy schedules for intimacy, when you are both feeling relaxed. *Interesting:* Until recently, lack of desire was ignored. Women didn't feel they should desire sex anyway. So they weren't distressed to find this part of their relationship missing. It just wasn't talked about.

What are other major causes of problems?

Unexpressed anger and resentment, boredom—not putting enough energy and creativity into the sexual relationship—and stress and fatigue can all have a negative effect.

Can sex with a sex therapist help?

Never. That totally confuses the issue.

What about surrogate therapy?

This is used occasionally, but it must be done in conjunction with psychotherapy. Usually, surrogate therapy is used in treating men. Sometimes a man has so many problems and is so anxious that he can't find a partner. He sabotages himself at every turn. But a few positive experiences with a trained sexual surrogate can relax him and build his confidence to the point where he can find a partner. Surrogate therapy is generally inappropriate if the client already has a partner. Few women are interested in surrogate therapy, because women are generally less able than men to disconnect sex from emotion.

Is it important to treat both partners as a couple?

That is ideal. I try to meet with both partners whenever possible. Even when I work with one person, it's best if I meet the partner. I want to know who they are, and how they are going to respond. People whose partners go into therapy alone often feel threatened. This is perfectly normal. After all, their mates are telling someone else about their intimate relationship…and they may worry that they're being blamed for the problems. The partner in therapy must be aware of these things.

How do you tell your partner that you think you need sex therapy—without hurting feelings?

Don't place blame. Tell your partner that you would like to go into therapy because you really want a better sexual relationship for both of you. Emphasize that you would like to do the therapy jointly. If your partner refuses, seek therapy alone.

When is a doctor required?

I send my clients to a physician for medical screening whenever I have reason to suspect that there is an underlying physiological problem. Someone experiencing a lack of desire or who has never had any desire should go to a physician for a complete workup. A woman who has vaginismus because she has experienced pain with intercourse, or a man who has had soft erections for his entire life, or is experiencing them after a particular operation or after taking medication, should have a physical.

What causes failure?

Failure is common when people neglect to do their homework. If you are sitting there talking about your problems but not going home and doing anything, it is usually a sign that you are resisting change for some reason.

If things are not going well, it is often a good signal that you haven't found the right issue, and you need to delve deeper—or look in another direction entirely. Midway through treatment I might find out that one partner really wants a divorce, and just hasn't been straight about it.

This partner may be doing everything to sabotage the therapy, because he or she doesn't want to have a better sexual relationship...because he or she doesn't want to stay married...or because he or she happens to be having an affair that provides more happiness than the marriage.

How do I find a sex therapist?

Ideally, you'll know someone who can recommend a therapist from personal experience. Or call the psychology department of the nearest university and ask for a referral. You can also contact the American Association of Sex Educators, Counselors and Therapists (11 Dupont Circle NW, Suite 220, Washington, DC 20036, 202-462-1171). This organization publishes a directory of sex therapists throughout the US.

What happens next?

First, set up a face-to-face interview. Ask the therapist how he or she would approach this problem. Has the therapist treated this problem before? Was the treatment successful? How does he or she feel about treating this problem?

What to ask yourself: "How do I feel about this therapist? Am I comfortable talking to him or her? Do we share the same basic values?" Therapy doesn't work when the therapist tries to impose his or her values on you. If what the therapist has to say antagonizes you, or if you find yourself arguing continuously, find someone else.

How much does sex therapy cost?

Typically, $65 to $100 per session. Ask about fees before setting up the first appointment. Some therapists may give an initial consultation at no charge.

Source: Lonnie Barbach, PhD, a practicing sex therapist and member of the clinical faculty of the psychiatry department, University of California, San Francisco. Dr. Barbach has written several books on sexual topics. Most recently she edited *Erotic Interludes* (Doubleday), a compilation of erotic stories written by women.

Bed Size and Better Sex

King-size beds—often associated with sexual passion—are not necessarily ideal for intimacy. *Reason:* The larger the bed, the easier it is for partners to keep their distance from each other, especially if, for some reason, they're already avoiding each other. A smaller bed may actually provide greater opportunity for more physical contact and intimacy.

Source: Shirley Zussman, EdD, editor of *Sex Over Forty*, Box 1600, Chapel Hill, North Carolina 27515.

Erections During Sleep

All healthy males get erections while sleeping. Most get an average of four or five per night, each lasting about a half-hour. Although erections usually occur during dreams, they are not associated with the content of dreams. They are totally nonsexual—even infants get them.

Source: *Superpotency: How To Get It, Use It, and Maintain It for a Lifetime* by Dudley Seth Danoff, MD, FACS, urologic surgeon on the clinical facility, UCLA School of Medicine. Warner Books.

Hypertension Drug Fights Prostate Problems

Terazosin (brand name *Hytrin*) has been used for years to treat high blood pressure—it works by relaxing the body's smooth muscles. For men with prostatic obstruction, it works on the smooth muscle in the prostate and bladder neck, allowing urine to flow better.

Success rate: Hytrin alleviates troublesome symptoms in about two-thirds of patients. Side effects are rare, but include a drop in blood pressure, dizziness, sleepiness, mild flu-like symptoms and impotence.

Important: A thorough checkup by a urologist prior to treatment to identify the cause of the urinary problem.

Source: E. Douglas Whitehead, MD, FACS, a New York City urologist, Director of the Association for Male Sexual Dysfunction, 24 E. 12 St., Suite 2-1, New York 10003.

Impotence: How to Solve It

If you're one of the 10 million American men who suffer from chronic impotence, acknowledge your problem and seek help. Odds are very good you can be helped. A wide variety of treatment options, ranging from drug therapy to surgery, are very effective.

Impotence myths…

Myth: Impotence is an inevitable consequence of aging, to be accepted with resignation. *Fact:* Men often are able to perform sexually well into their 80's.

Myth: Impotence renders a man infertile and unable to achieve orgasm. *Fact:* Impotence rarely interferes with the ability to ejaculate. It does not damage sperm or impede the sex drive.

Myth: Ninety percent of all cases of impotence are caused by psychological problems. *Fact:* Although medical science would have agreed just a few years ago, today the figure has been revised to 50%. The other half can be traced to specific causes—diabetes, arteriosclerosis, nerve damage, neurological disorders, uremia in kidney patients, endocrine disorders, alcoholism, and certain medicines. Make sure you and your doctor determine the source of your problem before choosing a course of treatment.

Psychological vs. physical causes…

If you sometimes wake up with an erection, your problem may be either psychological or physical. Psychological problems are best treated by a psychologist or sex therapist. If you never have an erection, your problem is probably physical. You'll need an extensive medical examination.

Choose a doctor with a specific interest in male sexual dysfunction. Such doctors distinguish between psychological and organic causes and among the five specific types of physical impotence:

•Hormonal impotence. Some cases of impotence are caused by a hormonal imbalance that can be detected with a simple blood test. Hormonal impotence is generally correctable.

•Drug-induced impotence. Drugs taken for high blood pressure or depression occasionally cause impotence as a side effect. *Helpful:* Adjusting the dosage or switching to another drug. Impotence can also be a result of alcoholism or drug abuse.

•Vasculogenic impotence. Diminished circulation in the penis can be a cause, too. The problem is caused by lesions in the arteries in or leading to the penis, the veins by which blood leaves the penis, or both. Such lesions can usually be spotted on an angiogram or arteriogram. Other tests can be performed in a doctor's office to identify cases of venous abnormality. Surgery corrects many of these cases of vasculogenic impotence.

•Neurologic impotence. Damage to the nerves necessary for erection can be caused by multiple sclerosis, diabetes, stroke, spinal cord injuries or tumors, injuries to the groin or pelvic nerves.

•Post-traumatic/pelvic surgery. More than 650,000 American men have been rendered impotent by vascular or nerve damage sustained during radical pelvic surgery for prostate, bladder, or colorectal cancer.

Surgical remedies…

Surgical techniques developed over the past five years are 60%–75% effective in curing vasculogenic impotence. For those with an arterial problem (deep dorsal vein arteriolization), a bypass that restores blood flow to the penis restores potency in 60%–65% of patients.

For those with impotence caused by a loss of the trapping mechanism by which blood is obtained and held in the penis (caverno-venous leak), a procedure called venous ligation has proved 70%–78% effective. The procedure, in which veins are tied off, is simple and relatively risk-free. *Recovery time:* One and a half days. Venous ligation is most useful for men under age 50.

Some men with neurologic impotence respond well to a program of self-injections using vasoactive drugs. For many men in their late fifties and sixties, this can be an effective form of treatment in selected patients. *Risk:* Scarring in 4%–8% of patients. Careful follow-up is needed.

Vacuum erection devices…

These *non-invasic* devices have established themselves as an effective therapeutic alternative in carefully selected patients. *Limitations:* Should only be used for 20 minutes.

Implants…

Once the only other option to psychotherapy or drug therapy, implants are still the major treatment for most impotent patients. Consider implants not as a last resort, but as one of several options. They're particularly attractive to men averse to injections and to those for whom revascularization surgery has failed.

Types of implants:

•Paired silicone rod prosthesis. Consisting of semirigid, flexible rods implanted in the penis's two chambers that normally fill with blood during an erection, this prosthesis produces a permanent but concealable erection.

•Inflatable prostheses. *Two types:* A self-contained device into which fluid is pumped for a controllable erection…and a paired inflatable device that includes a separate pump located beneath the scrotum.

In many cases, you should be the one to choose which type of implant to get. See samples of each type. Your urologist should have these available and will be qualified to implant them. Be sure to include your partner in the discussion. Consider your lifestyle.

Helpful: Avoid unrealistic expectations. Implants cannot heal a troubled marriage or make your penis longer.

Source: William L. Furlow, MD, F.A.C.S., codirector, Center for Urological Treatment and Research, 2201 Murphy Ave., Suite 115, Nashville. Dr. Furlow is also attending physician at West Side, Baptist, and Park View hospitals in Nashville.

Sex Education Helps Older Adults

Participating in workshops to learn about the physiological and psychological changes that occur in the sexual response during aging helped older couples (ages 50 to 70) who were experiencing erectile dysfunction. The workshop participants reported significant increases in knowledge and in sexual satisfaction, com-

pared with couples who did not participate in the workshops.

Source: Arlene Goldman, PhD, instructor in psychiatry and human behavior, Jefferson Medical College, and psychologist for the Jefferson Sexual Function Center, Thomas Jefferson University Hospital, Philadelphia.

Prostate Trouble

The prostate is a chestnut-sized gland below the bladder that produces fertility-promoting substances. It is susceptible to enlargement and cancer—especially in middle age. *Scary statistic:* Prostate cancer kills more men than any other form of cancer except cancer of the lung. This year it will strike approximately 85,000 Americans, causing 26,000 deaths. Incidence of prostate cancer is on the rise.

Many men have prostate cancer without being aware of it. Autopsies performed on 50-year-old men show that between 30% and 50% have microscopic evidence of prostate cancer (even though it may not have been related to the cause of death).

By age 80, that figure is between 50% and 80%. Clearly, the risk of prostate cancer increases with age.

Scientists aren't sure exactly what causes prostate cancer. Recent studies in Japan suggest, however, that sexual activity plays a role. *At highest risk:* Men who become sexually active when very young, have many sexual partners, marry late, or stop their sexual activity early. Levels of the male hormone testosterone, which stimulates the prostate and affects sexual drive, could be a factor. Testosterone seems to stimulate tumor growth.

Discovery…

Prostate cancer doesn't always cause obvious symptoms. In about 25% of men with advanced cases, however, there is pain in the pelvis and spine, the ribs, and the long bones. Most cases of prostate cancer are detected during routine rectal exams.

The American Cancer Society currently recommends that men have annual rectal exams after age 40. During the exam (known as a digital exam), the physician places his gloved finger into the rectum and examines the prostate for lumps. *Cost:* $60 when performed by a urologist, $20 when done by a family doctor.

A new technology, transrectal ultrasonography, uses high-frequency sound waves to detect tumors that are too small to be detected with a digital exam. *Comparison:* A digital exam can locate tumors half a centimeter in diameter or larger. Ultrasonography can spot tumors less than half that size. Biopsies are then performed to confirm the presence of cancer. *Cost:* $100–$150.

At one time, treating prostate cancer by radical surgery was likely to cause impotence. But today, many treatments are effective without serious side effects. *Options:* Surgery, external radiation, internal radiation, and hormone therapy. Treatment is tailored to each individual, based on age, health, and tumor size.

If the cancer has not spread, surgical removal of the prostate (prostatectomy) or radiation therapy offers the best chance of cure. If it has spread, removal of the testicles (orchiectomy) or treatment with estrogen is most appropriate.

A new technique known as the Walsh nerve-saving method reduces the incidence of post-surgery impotence from 90% to 20%–50%. And the 5%–10% of surgical patients who become incontinent can be treated in several ways, including the use of an artificial urinary sphincter.

Other treatments have side effects as well. Some 30% of the patients undergoing radiation therapy also become impotent. Orchiectomy can inhibit the libido. Estrogen therapy can cause heart attacks and blood clots in 6%–8% of cases.

Prostatectomy costs about $15,000 and requires seven to nine days of hospitalization. Implanting radioactive pellets in the prostate (to treat small tumors) costs about $10,000, with five to seven days in the hospital. External radiation therapy for advanced cancer costs about $7,000 for 35 treatments spread over six to seven weeks. Orchiectomy can be done on an outpatient basis for about $1,500.

Chemical castration for patients with advanced disease can be achieved with the drug leuprolide, which blocks the release of testosterone. This $250-a-month drug, which can cause hot flashes, has to be injected daily.

The second leading prostate problem is enlargement, also known as benign prostatic hyperplasia (BPH). This occurs when the gland swells and begins to press upon the urethra. Half the men past the age of 40 have at least microscopic evidence of BPH.

BPH symptoms: Difficulty in initiating urination, the need to urinate frequently at night, slow urination, dribbling.

Surgery for enlarged prostate, known as transurethral resection of the prostate (TURP), involves the insertion of a telescopic instrument down the urethra into the prostate. TURP requires three to four days of hospitalization. *Cost:* About $10,000.

Bleeding and incontinence may develop following TURP. There may also be fertility problems, since the surgery occasionally causes ejaculation into the bladder. Very rarely, some men complain that they enjoy sex less following surgery.

Alternatives to surgery: A drug called dibenzyline reduces difficulties with urination in about 30% of patients. There also are antiandrogen medications that interfere with the action of testosterone, which in turn helps shrink the prostate.

Source: Dr. Gerald Chodak, professor of urology, University of Chicago Medical Center.

More Facts About Impotence

Half of all men experience at least one period of impotence in their lives lasting several weeks or more. Their partners can help ease the problem by taking the matter seriously, but not personally…by learning about impotence…and by dealing with it promptly.

Without quick treatment, a man who has trouble getting an erection only 10% of the time may become fully impotent. *Culprit:* Stress arising from his failure to get an erection pumps adrenaline through his body. This drains the blood from the penis and stops any incipient erection. Anti-panic drugs can help in many cases.

Facing reality…

The partner of a man experiencing impotence should acknowledge the problem by saying, "We have a problem. What should we do about it?" She should suggest a doctor's appointment to investigate potential physical causes, the reason underlying some bouts of impotence.

Obstacle: Too many internists know too little about treating sexual dysfunction. To find one who does, ask the local medical society to recommend a medical sex therapist. Or consult the human sexuality program at a nearby university medical center.

Men under 50 years of age often experience impotence because of external factors—drinking, smoking, certain medications (tranquilizers, heart drugs, antihypertensives, anti-anxiety drugs).

In men over 50, about half of all cases of impotence have a physical component—most commonly poor circulation in the penis. In such cases dietary precautions might prevent a heart attack as well as improve sex. To help prevent circulatory problems, men should reduce consumption of fried foods, fats, and other high-cholesterol dishes.

A man whose problem is purely psychological will be able to have erections in the morning—or while dreaming—or under non-sexual circumstances, when the pressure to perform isn't on. A man who suddenly finds himself unable to have any erections should see a doctor immediately. *Common cause:* Serious depression.

A woman's response…

A woman whose partner experiences impotence shouldn't lash out at him. He's vulnerable and needs support. *What to say:* "Am I doing something wrong? What can I do to improve things?" Typically, the problem disappears after a few weeks. If it persists, and a skilled doctor has ruled out physical problems, therapy for one or both is a good next step.

Sometimes a man's impotence feeds the vulnerabilities of his partner, who may assume he no longer loves her. In fact, it may be only that their lovemaking skills are poor and that sex has gone stale.

Women must remember that men slow down sexually as they age, and most older people need fantasy for full sexual enjoyment. The time between erections (refractory period) lengthens.

Myth/reality…

Impotence rarely occurs in men who don't have feelings for their partners. It's often the most caring men, fearing they'll displease their partners, who tend to suffer from impotence.

Myth: The newly liberated woman's aggressiveness saps men's potency. *Reality:* Partners of impotent men are more likely to be too passive.

Many men function best with call girls, who tend to be very active. The woman should take an active part in lovemaking and be interesting and creative, not subservient.

Sometimes the woman's fears are well founded and her partner does wish to end the relationship. If so, she must face facts and take it from there.

Source: The late Helen Singer Kaplan, MD.

Avoiding Pain

Pain—and sex: Pleasurable vaginal and clitoral stimulation reduce pain to a measurable extent in women by raising their pain thresholds. The effect is analgesic (specific loss of pain sensation) rather than anesthetic (general loss of sensation). Tactile responses other than pain are not affected.

Source: Research led by Beverly Whipple, PhD, RN, associate professor of nursing, Rutgers, State University of New Jersey.

Single Doesn't Mean Lonely

Most older single people aren't as lonely as is commonly thought. In a recent survey, only 2% of unmarried men and women over 50 said they were "almost always" lonely. Another 14% were "often" lonely, and 35% felt that way "sometimes." But 50% were "hardly ever" lonely.

Source: *Love, Sex and Aging* by the editors of Consumer Reports Books. Consumers Union.

How Often Do People Cry?

Many men (55%) cry at least once a month, and 73% of them feel better afterward, a recent study found. Women cry five times as often, and 85% of them feel better. *Most common crying time:* Between 7 P.M. and 10 P.M., while watching a movie or visiting with friends or relatives.

Source: *What's the Difference? How Men and Women Compare* by Jane Barr Stump, William Morrow & Co., Inc., New York.

The Tall and Short of It

Tall women are usually more independent than short women and more likely to strike out on their own. Short women, on the other hand, are more apt to marry and have children.

Source: *The Height of Your Life* by Ralph Keyes, Warner Books, New York.

Making the Most Of a Midlife Crisis

The notion of a midlife crisis has developed only over the last 20 years. People used to stick with bad marriages, boring jobs and what Thoreau called "lives of quiet desperation." There was no real expectation of personal satisfaction. Several factors—a longer life span, increased mobility and the influences of the sexual revolution—have changed all that. Now people expect to live long, healthy lives that are both professionally and personally fulfilling.

Today, somewhere between age 33 and age 52, the majority of individuals in our society go through a midlife crisis. It involves questioning all the values they'd previously taken for granted. In a frantic desire to reject the past, a person undergoing midlife crisis often acts impulsively and destructively, squandering his hard-earned financial security or breaking up his family. But a midlife crisis can be a time for creative changes rather than destructive ones. Make the most of your own midlife crisis by understanding what it's all about and seeing it as an inevitable and positive part of your growth as a human being.

Midlife crisis defined…

A midlife crisis involves a period of self-examination sparked either by internal awareness of mortality or by an outside event, usually involving a loss of some kind. *Typical:* A divorce, loss of a job, death of a friend or family member, children leaving home. Or, there may simply be an awareness of change in oneself—the realization that life is half over. We see the first signs of aging and realize we're mortal. The awareness of mortality leads to an internal questioning process whereby we start to evaluate what we've done with our lives so far. The search for meaning begins.

Questions we typically ask ourselves: What do I want to do with the rest of my life? Do I really want to stay at my current job for the next 20 years? Am I really happy in my marriage? How would I like my life to be different?

There are many regrets to mull over. The childless regret never having had children. Parents regret not having spent more time with theirs—or not having more. Some people regret never having tried for the career they always dreamed of. Others feel that they missed opportunities to travel or find adventure.

How to handle your midlife crisis…

It's crucial to recognize that a healthy life involves balance. People tend to go to extremes. Some want money and success. Others will sacrifice anything to be loved. Midlife is the time to find the sense of balance within yourself. *Suggestions:*

•Stop measuring success by money. This is the current American mistake. Ask yourself what you missed in the making of the buck. Many people feel they lost contact with their children as they were growing up. It's important to realize when you've made enough and can begin to spend it. Use your goodies for yourself. It's not wise to leave them all to children, who generally tend to dissipate an inheritance they didn't work for.

•Don't dive into anything. It took you lots of years to get to where you are…and you don't have to make any instant decisions. Don't be the stereotypical midlife male who throws it all over to run off with a young girl, only to later regret his impulsive decision. Lifetime family and friendship networks are very important and should be preserved if at all possible.

•Learn to grow up. Changing your life doesn't have to be an either/or decision. Life is neither good nor bad. Today, it's one thing, tomorrow, another. Life involves balance plus movement. *Keys to maturity:* Keep moving. Stay active, and always be self aware. Tune in to your thoughts and feelings—your entire being.

•Head off a crisis. Make changes before the axe falls. *Example:* The 45-year-old executive who sees that his new boss is a 34-year-old whiz kid and his coworkers are 25-year-old MBAs making a third of what he does. The tuned-in midlife exec sees the handwriting on the wall and gets out on his own terms.

•Change is not so much doing as undoing. If you've spent your life giving to others and sacrificing yourself, start seeing what you can give to yourself. If you've spent your life focused on yourself, start paying attention to others. Learn to undo whatever narrow force has been controlling your life so far. Then you'll be able to broaden your ability to experience and enjoy all of life.

•Don't be afraid to fantasize. The language of fantasy comes out of one's whole being and life experience. It's a beautiful language because it can lead to realizing that one's fantasies can possibly be achieved. When you really want something, your energies go in that direction. If you don't fantasize, you won't make a move. *Example:* My oceanfront house in Montauk came out of a fantasy I had during a fishing trip back in 1954.

•Don't break up your marriage over an infidelity. You may have to come to peace with your spouse's having had an affair. If he or she is a good husband or wife and loves the children, and something solid and good still exists between you, you don't have to break up. Expand your awareness instead...and give up the rigid notion that there can be only one true love forever.

•Learn to be open with your spouse. In a crisis that threatens a relationship you must learn to be open. With the average couple, neither one really wants to hurt the other, but boredom sets in and leads slowly to a crisis. The partners realize there's no more excitement, fun or laughs. *How to create excitement:* Trust each other with your inner thoughts and feelings. Share sexual fantasies. Join a therapy group for couples.

•Stop living by the "shoulds." Learn to be who you are rather than who you "should" be. People who live lives of quiet desperation are doing what they think (or someone else thinks) they "should" do rather than what they really want to do.

Source: Milton M. Berger, MD, a psychiatrist and co-director of the American Short-Term Therapy Center, New York.

Unreliable Erections? New Injection Technique Is Extremely Effective

About 20 million American men have what urologists call "unreliable" erections. In other words, they're frequently unable to achieve—or maintain—a rigid erection.

Occasional impotence is nothing to worry about. But if erection problems routinely make sexual intercourse difficult or impossible, it's time to ask your doctor about self-injection therapy.

This new technique is safe, easy to use—and effective in four out of five cases.

Self-injection therapy is good for men of all ages. For young men, whose unreliable erections may stem from anxiety, the injections allow them to relax and enjoy sex.

Injections are also effective for older men, whose impotence may be linked to heart disease, prostate cancer or diabetes.

Exception: Self-injection may be ineffective for men with severe vascular problems. For these men, it may be necessary to surgically implant a penile prosthesis.

Practically painless...

When I first tell my patients about self-injection therapy, they are usually horrified. Actually, the injection is practically painless. The needle is extremely thin and only a half inch long. It is inserted into only one side of the penis near the base, which is surprisingly insensitive to pain.

About 30% to 40% of men feel a slight ache following the injection. Fortunately, this pain can be reduced or eliminated simply by reducing the dose. Only about 1% of men who try self-injecting find that they cannot have sex because of the pain.

The syringe is filled ahead of time. You initiate foreplay, then excuse yourself to administer the injection just before intercourse. Some men inject before foreplay, so that sex becomes even more natural.

The entire process takes less than a minute. It's as easy as putting on a condom. The erection occurs as it would naturally, gradually getting firm in five to 15 minutes.

The doctor will make the injection the first time—to demonstrate the technique and to make sure the patient responds.

Until recently, the drug of choice for self-injection therapy was the muscle relaxant papaverine. It relaxes muscles surrounding the arteries in the penis, allowing them to fill with blood and create a good, firm erection. However, recent studies have shown that, over a period of years, papaverine injections cause formation of scar tissue inside the penis. *Result:* Unsightly lumps and bumps.

For this reason, many urologists are now using *prostaglandin E1*. This muscle relaxant affords good erections with little risk of scarring.

What about vacuum pumps?

Some men refuse even to try self-injection. Many of these men ask instead about using a vacuum pump to achieve an erection.

This device consists of a plastic cylinder, into which the penis is inserted. Air is removed from the cylinder with a pump, creating a partial vacuum around the penis and allowing blood to flow into the penile tissue to yield an erection.

The truth is, vacuum pumps are more painful than injections. *Reason:* To maintain a vacuum-created erection, you must place a tight rubber band around the base of the penis. And a man's partner will always know he's using the pump. *Reason:* It takes 15 to 20 minutes to get the erection with a pump…the base of the penis must be shaved…the rubber band is visible…and the penis must be covered with special gel to create a seal with the base of the pump.

Do not expect self-injections to transform you into a sexual athlete overnight. Injections won't boost your sex drive or fix a relationship. Injections work best with couples who were already having good sex despite their inability to have intercourse.

If you seek treatment for impotence, ask your family doctor to recommend a urologist who specializes in erectile dysfunction…or contact the urology clinic at the largest medical center in your area and ask for a referral.

For more information, contact the Impotence Information Center, Box 9, Minneapolis 55440. 800-843-4315.

Note: A wife or girlfriend may tell her mate that his impotence doesn't bother her. Even if that's really the case, impotence often ruins a man's self-image. I always tell my patients, *Don't do it for her. Do it for yourself.*

Source: J. Francois Eid, MD, director of the Erectile Dysfunction Unit at New York Hospital–Cornell Medical Center in New York City. He is the coauthor of *Making Love Again: Regaining Sexual Potency Through the New Injection Treatment.* Brunner/Mazel.

12

Secrets of Good Sleep

All About Sleep

New and exciting findings in sleep research have helped many stay healthier—both physically and emotionally—and work better.

Insomnia…

•Most adults need seven-and-a-half to eight hours of restful sleep to function well.

•Teenagers do better with 10 hours.

•One-fifth of the US population complains of the inability to fall asleep or to stay asleep.

Costs of sleep deprivation: Irritability, falling asleep at work, wavering attention and not fully processing the outside world.

Example: Driving a block past where you planned to turn.

Tension—physical or psychological—keeps us from relaxing sufficiently to fall asleep. People are literally "taking their worries to bed." *Solution:* Learn techniques for coping with stress and "winding down" before bed. Relaxation techniques are also helpful.

Example: Write a worry diary each night and "close the book" before getting into bed.

Helpful: Don't associate the bed with wakefulness. If you can't sleep, get up and read, sew, or watch TV until you feel sleepy. *Also helpful:* Avoid sleeping pills and alcohol.

Snoring…

An estimated 10 million snorers are disturbing the sleep of another 10 million "snorees." The problem occurs as throat tissues loosen with age. It escalates with weight gain and alcohol intake.

Solution: Tone up, sober up and avoid sleeping on your back. *Helpful:* If necessary, snorers can train themselves to sleep on their sides by wearing a T-shirt with tennis balls sewn into a pocket down the spine.

Sleep apnea…

If snoring is not controlled, it can lead to apnea, episodes in which the airways collapse, the sleeper stops breathing and often awakens with a snort, gasping for breath. *Caution:* Apnea can be life-threatening. See your doctor, or go to a sleep center in your area for treatment.

Solution: Often the interventions used to control snoring—weight loss, no alcohol, sleeping side to side—prevent apnea. *Useful:* An oral appliance similar to a boxer's toothguard prevents the tongue from falling backward, cutting off airways, when the sleeper rolls on his back. For serious cases, a nose mask and compressor creates continuous nasal airway pressure to keep passages open.

Sleep and chronic pain...

People with painful conditions, such as arthritis, often find their pain prevents them from having a deep, restful sleep.

Solution: Sleep deepens when the body temperature falls. As the temperature rises—generally after five o'clock in the morning—you begin to wake up.

Helpful: Deepen your sleep by taking a twenty-minute very hot bath—about 103°F—two hours before bedtime, then reading or relaxing as the body's internal thermostat pulls the temperature down.

Sleep and learning...

Researchers have found that REM (rapid eye movement) sleep is a very active brain state during which learning consolidation takes place and new information is put into long-term memory. *What this means:* Before a test or presentation, you will remember new learning better if you allow for some active dream time.

Recommended: Go to bed for several hours of deep sleep. Get up about 2 a.m. and study. Then go back to bed from about 4 a.m. to 9 a.m. for your REM sleep, which builds up during the last third of the night. When you wake up, you'll know the material you just studied.

Body clock research...

Recent research has focused on the use of bright light to help night-shift workers—from medical and industrial personnel to astronauts—adjust their sleep-wake cycles with timed exposures to sun-strength light. Researchers are working to determine the best times and minimum durations subjects must be exposed to light.

Example: Pre-travel "light treatments" to prevent jet lag.

Dream research...

Dreams appear to be important for processing emotional information, revising our moods and maintaining a stable sense of self from one day to the next.

New findings: A study conducted at Rush Presbyterian-St. Luke's Medical Center of men and women going through a stressful divorce found that 80% of those who were clinically depressed began to dream earlier in their REM sleep and had longer, more active dreams than those who were not depressed. Their dreams were often painful, and they felt miserable when they woke up.

Key finding: One year later, these people had recovered from their depression without the help of drugs or psychiatric treatment. Those who didn't dream earlier were still depressed. *Conclusion:* Our dreams act as our own inner therapist, helping us to work through troubling emotional material.

Exciting: There is growing evidence that "lucid dreaming" techniques—learning to recognize an unpleasant dream and change the outcome—can help people to improve their moods and hasten their emotional repair work.

Sleep terrors...

People with sleep terrors—almost always young men—do not dream, but rather awaken in terror from deep sleep, often behaving bizarrely.

Examples: Striking their partner, insisting housemates hide or flee.

These men tend to over-control their behavior and feelings. Their emotions are never expressed. *Helpful:* Teaching them how to dream, so their emotions have a healthy outlet.

Source: Rosalind Cartwright, PhD, director of the Sleep Disorders Service and Research Center, both at Chicago's Rush Presbyterian-St. Luke's Medical Center. She is the author of *Crisis Dreaming*, HarperCollins, New York, 10 E. 53 St., New York 10022.

How to Get Rid Of Nightmares

A nightmare, technically, is a frightening dream that wakes you. Its contents are no different than the contents of a normal dream. *What is different:* How you react. How we respond to our dreams is affected by how we feel both physically and emotionally. Eliminate nightmares by getting rid of things that can cause you to react badly to your dreams.

These include...

•Medications. Certain drugs can increase the incidence of nightmares, including beta blockers, tricyclic antidepressants, sleeping pills, nasal sprays.

Solution: Ask your doctor about changing prescribed medications.

•Stress. Feeling on edge increases your susceptibility to nightmares.

Solution: Use stress-reduction and relaxation techniques...and exercise.

•Illnesses. Any illness that makes you feel bad can cause nightmares.

Solution: With minor illnesses, the nightmares will go away as you get better. If they don't and other nightmare-causing factors are ruled out, see your doctor for an evaluation.

•Miscellaneous problems. For many, nightmares have no obvious cause.

Solution: Figure out what's causing the nightmares by making a connection between them and real life—think metaphorically. *Example:* A nightmare about being assaulted may be a metaphor for feeling threatened or intimidated by your boss, a friend or relative.

Alternate solution: Confront a recurrent nightmare by imagining how you want it resolved before you go to sleep. *Example:* A person who dreams he's being followed by a stranger can imagine that the person is simply a friend who wants to say hello.

Source: Milton Kramer, MD, director, Sleep Disorder Center, Bethesda Oak Hospital, Cincinnati.

Sheep for Sleep

Counting sheep really does help people who have trouble falling asleep. It focuses the mind on a meaningless, repetitive pattern and prevents disruptive thoughts from creeping in. *Related strategies:* Count backwards from 786 by 17s...imagine writing the numbers one to 100 on a blackboard, erasing each number in sequence, then doing it again from 100 to one.

Source: *Overcoming Insomnia: A Medical Program for Problem Sleepers* by Donald R. Sweeney, MD, PhD, Putnam Publishing, 200 Madison Ave., New York 10016.

Better Sleep Strategies

About 80 different types of sleep disorders currently plague millions of Americans. To decrease your chances of developing one, follow these sleep-saving strategies:

•Limit caffeine intake to no more than 500 milligrams (mg) a day. A typical cup of coffee contains 200 mg to 250 mg of caffeine. Tea, soft drinks, candy, medicines, etc., also contain caffeine. Avoid caffeine after 6 p.m.

•Avoid using alcohol as a sleep-inducer. In addition to being habit-forming, even small amounts of alcohol (as little as a glass of wine) can cause insomnia in the middle of the night, when its effects wear off.

•Avoid smoking before bedtime or during the night. Nicotine is also a stimulant that disrupts sleep.

•Avoid heavy meals before sleep. A light bedtime snack, however, can help. *Best:* Milk, which contains the sleep-inducing amino acid tryptophan. *Note:* Avoid the drug, L-tryptophan, which the FDA has warned may be unsafe.

•Avoid snacking in the middle of the night. This reinforces insomnia.

Source: Charles Reynolds, MD, professor of psychiatry and director, Sleep Evaluation Center, University of Pittsburgh Medical Center. His recent editorial, "The Implications of Sleep Disturbance Epidemiology," appeared in the *Journal of the American Medical Association*.

How to Fall *Back* to Sleep

Agony: Awakening in the middle of the night and not being able to fall back to sleep. *Prime cause:* Advancing age. People over 50 have middle insomnia. Those under 50 often have difficulty falling to sleep.

How to cope: Do not become angry when you find yourself awake at 3 a.m. Anger only excites you, preventing sleep. Instead, fix your mind on a single relaxing image. *Example:* Visualize a flickering candle. If you are still awake after 30 minutes, go to another room. Watch an old movie on TV, or read a book or magazine. When you feel sleepy, return to bed. If sleep still eludes you, go back to the other room and read some more. *Frustrating and useless:* Tossing and turning in bed, waiting for sleep to arrive.

Preventive steps...

• Eliminate daytime naps if they have been a habit.

• Do not go to bed too early. This only increases the chances of middle insomnia.

• Set your wake-up alarm an hour earlier than usual. This makes you more tired for the following night. Advance the alarm by 15-minute increments until you are sleeping through the night. Then slowly extend your sleep period until you are back on a normal schedule.

Source: *A Good Night's Sleep* by Jerrold S. Maxmen, M.D., Contemporary Books.

Profile of an Insomniac

Chronic insomniacs are less active physically and mentally during the day and are also less involved in their work and with other people than good sleepers. Insomniacs are also more preoccupied with self, quieter...and, oddly, less worried. They spend more time watching TV during the day, shopping and relaxing. Good sleepers pass their time studying, working and doing active things around the house. *Unknown:* Whether the habits of insomniacs are the result of poor sleep or its cause.

Insomnia-prone people are generally unable to discharge anger and stress outwardly. Insomniacs are characteristically inhibited, anxious and depressed. Their internalized emotions lead to physiologic activation, preventing sleep at night.

Source: Study conducted by psychologists at the University of California, San Francisco, and the Pacific Graduate School of Psychology, Palo Alto, CA.

Relaxation May Be the Key

Insomnia is often stress-related and is frequently treated by relaxation therapy. Sleeping pills can cause morning drowsiness and poor-quality sleep. *Some techniques:* Hypnosis, progresive relaxation (tensing and relaxing muscle groups), biofeedback (including relaxation and breathing exercises), meditation (focusing the mind on a single point), and yoga. It's important to reduce outside stimuli—no reading, eating, or TV-watching in bed. *Avoid:* Worrying, especially about getting to sleep.

Sleeping Pill Alert

Avoid sleep medications until the source of insomnia is traced. *Reason:* The drugs can be harmful, even deadly, to people with sleep apnea (a disorder in which breathing ceases momentarily).

How Much Is Enough?

Much of the anxiety about getting enough sleep stems from the myth that everybody needs eight hours of sleep every night. While eight hours is what most people need, many really need far less. Cases of individuals requiring less than one hour of sleep a night have been documented.

Realistic sleep requirements for adults range from five to six hours to nine to 10 hours. Children, of course, need more sleep than adults. But probably the greatest discrepancy between sleep need and sleep amount occurs in teenagers. They still need almost as much sleep as children do, but they begin to adopt adult sleep schedules.

Source: Mark Chambers, PhD, a clinical psychologist at the Stanford University Medical School, Sleep Disorders Clinic, 211 Quarry Rd., Stanford, California 94305.

13

Self-Defense

The Electricity/Health Connection

Electric razors may heighten leukemia risk, according to a scary new study—but they aren't the only electrical appliances that could cause cancer.

Details of a study by the authoritative Batelle Institute: Men who used electric shavers more than 2½ minutes/day were twice as likely to get leukemia as those who didn't.

Probable cause: Electrical fields from plug-in razors disrupt cell division controlled by the pineal gland. This study shows an effect from intermittent electromagnetic fields. Previous studies found higher cancer risk only in people exposed continuously to such fields—at work or at home (power lines, computer terminals, electric blankets, etc.).

Self-defense…

Limit exposure time—or maintain a safe distance from the following sources of electromagnetic fields…

• Electric shavers. Use only if in a rush or away from home.

• Hair dryers. Minimize home use—professional users should avoid holding at chest height.

• Massagers/vibrators. Minimize use.

• Microwave ovens. Pregnant women should avoid using while standing in front of these… all users should stand at least three feet away. Have a technician check oven door seal periodically for radiation leakage.

• TV. To find a safe distance for any set, use a portable AM radio: Tune to a spot between stations to get static…turn up volume…turn on TV and—holding the radio two to three feet away—back up until static starts to fade.

• Laser printers, fax machines and photocopiers. Should be at least four to six feet from the nearest worker's desk—pregnant women should avoid use entirely.

• Electric blankets. Discard those made before early 1990…look for new models that emit no electromagnetic radiation…or—turn on blanket an hour before bedtime to warm bed, then turn off and unplug the blanket before getting in.

Source: Researcher and educator Robert O. Becker, MD, Lowville, New York. He is the author of *Cross Currents*, Jeremy Tarcher, Inc., 9110 Sunset Blvd., Los Angeles 90069. The book is about electromagnetic radiation and your health.

Bacteria Dangers

Boiling drinking water before use will not make the water safe. *Problem:* Boiling only kills off bacteria—it won't remove many heavy metals and other toxic chemicals such as lead, asbestos, copper and trihalomethanes (carcinogenic by-products of chlorination).

Result: Even water labeled "distilled" could still be contaminated. *Worse:* Boiling actually concentrates harmful substances in the water left after evaporation.

Self-defense: Run tap water for several minutes before use to remove lead…buy a quality home water filter to remove other substances—even from commercial bottled waters, which could possibly have the same contaminants.

Source: Robban Sica-Cohen, MD, is a physician with the Center for Healing Arts in Orange, Connecticut.

Mouthwash Danger

High-alcohol mouthwashes may raise a person's risk of developing oral cancer by as much as 60%. *Danger threshold:* Mouthwashes with an alcohol content of 25% or higher (as indicated on their labels) have been implicated in mouth, tongue and throat cancers.

Theory: Alcohol acts as a solvent in the mouth, making tissues more vulnerable to carcinogens.

Source: Research by the National Cancer Institute, reported in *Working Mother*, 230 Park Ave., New York 10169.

Blood Transfusion Self-Defense

Even if recent reports suggesting that a previously unknown virus might be causing an AIDS-like illness prove false, transfused blood is not now—and never will be—risk-free.

Risks: Despite rigorous screening methods now in place at blood banks across the US, one of every 250,000 units of blood contains HIV, the virus that causes AIDS…and one of every 2,500 units contains the viruses that cause hepatitis B and C, which can be just as deadly as AIDS.

Because of these risks, doctors and patients alike are increasingly wary of transfusions. When blood loss from surgery or trauma is especially severe, however, it's important to remember that receiving a transfusion is sometimes far less risky than not having one.

If you need a transfusion following a severe injury or emergency surgery, whether or not you receive tainted blood is essentially a matter of chance. But if you're scheduled for elective surgery, certain precautions can help lower your risk…

• Find a conscientious surgeon. While all good surgeons try to avoid giving transfusions, some try harder than others. The more conscientious your surgeon, the smaller your risk.

• Bank your own blood. Before you're scheduled for elective surgery, ask your surgeon about autologous blood donation. With this technique, you will receive blood not from an anonymous donor, but your own previously donated blood. Costs will vary, depending on what procedures are necessary.

Exception: Patients suffering from severe anemia and certain other conditions are not candidates for autologous transfusion.

• Insist on blood-saving surgical techniques. One way to reduce the need for transfusions during thoracic (chest), orthopedic (skeletal) and other forms of surgery where bleeding is often severe is to collect and then re-transfuse blood from the patient's surgical incision. The process—known as cell-salvage—uses sophisticated equipment not found in every operating room. Ask your surgeon beforehand if the hospital has the necessary equipment and if he/she is experienced in its use.

Source: Mark Feinberg, MD, PhD, assistant professor of medicine, microbiology and immunology, University of California at San Francisco.

Snug Necktie Warning

Snug neckties are bad for health—they restrict oxygen flow to the brain and constrict the vital carotid arteries, important blood carriers in the neck. That makes it harder to think. *Common problems:* Headache, sweating, tension. A weight gain of just five pounds can do it. A too-tight shirt collar can have the same effect.

Source: Bruce Yaffe, MD, is a physician in private practice in New York City.

How to Protect Yourself When Buying Seafood, When Eating Seafood

Seafood and fish are an excellent protein source that is low in saturated fat, light on calories and high in vitamins, minerals and the omega-3 fatty acids that help reduce the risk of heart disease.

But there are risks. More than 80% of the seafood eaten in the US has not been inspected for chemical or microbial contaminants. Fortunately, there are things that you can do to enjoy maximum health and minimum risk…

•Avoid chemical contaminants. When you buy fish, choose younger, smaller ones, since they've accumulated fewer contaminants. Low-fat, offshore species like cod, haddock and pollack are especially good choices. Always trim the skin, belly flap and dark meat along the top

or center, especially when it comes to fatty fish such as bluefish. Don't use the fatty parts to make sauce. Don't eat the green "tomalley" in lobsters or the "mustard" in crabs.

•Avoid natural toxins. When traveling in tropical climates, avoid reef fish such as amberjack, grouper, goatfish or barracuda, which are more likely to be contaminated. Buy only seafood that has been kept continuously chilled, especially mahi-mahi, tuna and bluefish, which produce an odorless toxin when they spoil.

•Avoid disease-causing microbes. Bite for bite, raw or undercooked shellfish is the riskiest food you can eat.

Self-defense: Don't eat shellfish whose shells remain closed after cooking. Do not eat raw fish or shellfish if you are over 60, HIV-positive, pregnant, have cancer or liver disease or are vulnerable to infection. Cook all fish and shellfish thoroughly. Raw clams, oysters and mussels should be steamed for six minutes.

•Don't buy fresh fish that has dull, sunken eyes, or fish that smells "fishy." Do not buy ready-to-eat seafood that is displayed too close to raw seafood.

Source: Lisa Y. Lefferts, an environmental health consultant in Hyattsville, Maryland, who specializes in food safety, environmental policy and risk assessment.

Toilet Seat Danger

You can catch diarrhea, intestinal bugs and hepatitis from toilet seats. *Trap:* When toilets are flushed, a fine mist of water that could contain contagious fecal bacteria rises and lands on toilet seats and flush handles. *Best defense:* Clean your toilet three times a week with disinfectant…avoid using public rest rooms—especially the most popular middle stall…stand before flushing.

Source: Dr. Charles Gerba, University of Arizona.

How to Protect Yourself from Pesticides, Fertilizers, Preservatives, etc.

Although there is no way to avoid dangerous toxins entirely, certain precautions can dramatically reduce your exposure to them. *What to do:*

•Eat less fat. Because most pollutants are fat-soluble, eating less fat (especially animal fat) automatically reduces dangers of potentially dangerous toxins. *Avoid:* Fatty meats, gravy, lard, meat drippings, ice cream, butter, sour cream and deep-fried foods.

The average American gets 45% of his/her calories from fat—far too much. *Better:* Get no more than 30% of your calories from fat.

•Eat a wide variety of foods. Limiting your diet to a small number of foods eaten again and again is risky, since any single food can be a source of unknown toxins. *To minimize risk:* Balance your exposure to food toxins by eating a wide variety of foods.

•Eat more fiber. Before 1960, many scientists considered fiber useless from a dietary standpoint. It's now clear, however, that fiber not only speeds the passage of dangerous toxins through the intestinal tract, it also binds to and neutralizes them before they do damage. *Bonus:* The cabbage family contains indoles—potent anticancer chemicals.

•Eat organic. Conventionally grown produce—especially apples, broccoli, carrots, celery, peaches, pears and spinach—often are laced with dangerous pesticides. Organic produce, although not entirely safe, is usually far safer.

Even better: Grow your own produce. A home garden can yield tasty, wholesome greens with only a few minutes of work a day.

•Peel fruits and vegetables. Bananas, corn, grapefruit, melons, oranges and other produce with peelable "wrappers" are usually safe. *Reason:* Most—but not all—pesticide residues are thrown out with the peel.

Also peel carrots, potatoes, beets, onions and other root vegetables, as well as shiny waxed vegetables—green peppers, cucumbers and apples. And remove the outer leaves of cabbage, lettuce, kale, endive, spinach and similar vegetables.

•Eat lower on the food chain. Since toxins become more concentrated with each successive predator, you should limit your intake of swordfish, tuna, beef, pork and big game animals. *Better:* A vegetarian or semi-vegetarian diet. A little chicken or fish won't hurt, but avoid red meat.

•Eat natural foods. Instead of trying to determine which additives are safe and which are harmful, choose foods that are as close to their original, natural state as possible.

Examples: A fresh orange is safer than frozen orange juice, which is safer than powdered orange drink...a potato is better than instant mashed potatoes, which are better than potato chips.

Eating natural foods cuts your food additive intake by 90%. When you do buy processed foods, choose those with a minimal list of ingredients.

•Avoid moldy nuts, grains and seeds. Aflatoxin, a mold that grows on peanuts, grains and seeds, is a strong carcinogen. You can reduce your aflatoxin intake by avoiding locally processed peanuts and peanut butter (which don't have to comply with federal aflatoxin standards).

Scary: Several members of former President Jimmy Carter's family have died from pancreatic cancer. For years, the Carter family ran a peanut company in Georgia. Did something—perhaps aflatoxin from moldy peanuts—cause the same form of cancer in the Carter family members?

•Avoid raw animal foods. Americans could avoid 275,000 cases of diarrhea a year simply by washing and cooking food properly. *Crucial:* Cook all animal food. Avoid undercooked pork, unpasteurized milk and raw fish (sushi). *Good news:* Most fruits and many vegetables can be safely eaten raw...after they have been thoroughly washed and/or peeled.

•Keep foods refrigerated. All foods contain bacteria, and storing food at room temperature causes these bacteria to multiply rapidly. To stunt bacterial growth: Keep foods in the refrigerator or freezer.

•Wash foods. All food that is neither peelable nor organic must be washed with warm, soapy water. Ivory soap shavings make a good, low-cost soap.

•Avoid chemically "dirty" foods. Seventy-eight percent of the pesticide risk in the American diet comes from just 15 foods—tomatoes, beef, potatoes, oranges, lettuce, apples, peaches, pork, wheat, soybeans, beans, carrots, chicken, corn and grapes.

Although it's hard to eliminate these items from your diet, try to avoid them in their most highly processed forms—ketchup, beef jerky, etc.—in which toxins are most highly concentrated.

Also avoid foods that contain excessive levels of chemical residues—unpeeled baked potatoes, spinach, raisins, raw sweet green pepper, collards, strawberries, squash, frankfurters, dry roasted peanuts, pumpkin and milk chocolate.

•Avoid very hot foods and beverages. People who consume large quantities of extremely hot foods face an elevated risk of cancer. *Possible explanation:* Repeated burning and healing of sensitive tissues in the mouth and throat causes alterations in DNA...and this leads to cancer.

•Buy local—and in-season. Produce shipped from distant sites is usually picked green, sealed in wax or gassed with preservatives—all of which boosts toxin levels. Similarly, fresh produce sold out of season has probably either been shipped from abroad, which makes it suspect, or gassed with preservatives and stored for months.

•Avoid burned foods. "Blackened" forms of steak, fish and other protein-rich foods contain highly carcinogenic compounds. Eat your meats medium rather than well-done.

•Avoid foods that contain natural toxins. Eat no more than one cup of mushrooms weekly. Avoid regular consumption of potato skins and parsnips.

•Avoid "perfect" produce. Sixty percent of the pesticides used in the US are for cosmetic purposes only. Shiny, blemish-free apples and fluorescent oranges look appealing, but odds are they've been heavily sprayed with potentially dangerous chemicals. Organic produce looks less appealing...but is actually more healthful.

•Take precautions with fish. Small fish are safer than big fish, because they are lower on the food chain. *Avoid:* Bluefish, striped bass, swordfish, shark, shellfish, raw fish, fish organs, fish fat and fat drippings. Also avoid fish caught in the Great Lakes, upstate New York and big city bays. Eat no more than half a pound of tuna weekly. *Good news:* Salmon is surprisingly toxin-free.

•Buy American. Imported produce often contains banned pesticides and unacceptably high levels of federally approved pesticides.

•Eat more oats. Oats are so hardy that they thrive without heavy applications of pesticides. Eat more oat-based bread and cereal products.

•Use no peelings. Although peels from oranges and other fruits are often vitamin-rich, they tend to be full of pesticide residues.

•Buy Western produce. Produce grown in the humid American Southeast generally needs more pesticide and fungicide applications than food grown in the comparatively dry West.

•Drink less alcohol. Alcohol poses several health risks, including an increased risk of cancer...and most forms of alcohol contain impurities that pose additional risks. *Least risky:* Gin, vodka, beer and white wine. *Most risky:* Bourbon, whiskey, European fruit brandy, cream sherry, port wine and Oriental wines.

Bottom line: If you drink, do so in moderation. Pregnant women, motorists, heavy-equipment operators, American Indians and Asians should avoid alcohol altogether.

•Eat less liver. Liver is full not only of vitamins, minerals and protein, but also concentrated pollutants.

•Watch out for risky food containers. Avoid foreign-made plates and glassware, which may contain leaded glazes...and milk in wax cartons—choose plastic containers instead. Minimize use of canned foods, since lead can leach from the can into the food...and soft plastics, including soft-drink bottles and sandwich bags. Never store food in opened cans.

Source: Patrick Quillin, PhD, RD, vice president for nutrition services, Cancer Treatment Centers of America, Tulsa. A frequent lecturer on nutrition, Dr. Quillin is the author of several books, including *Healing Nutrients*. His most recent book is *Safe Eating*, M. Evans and Co. Inc., 216 E. 49 St., New York 10017.

Another View on Pesticides

Despite bad press over the years, chemical pesticides do not pose a danger to the average consumer. And they do serve a very important purpose—killing insects and preventing plant disease, which can devastate crops. Personally, I favor conventionally grown produce—foods grown with pesticides—to produce grown organically. It's less expensive, better looking and not at all dangerous.

What's going on: Pesticides are very toxic in their original form, but break down quickly after application. By the time produce gets to the market, its pesticide concentration is either very low, or the pesticide has degraded into nontoxic compounds.

Downside to organically grown produce: It is often less visually pleasing, with insect bites, more bruises, etc...significantly more expensive...and disease can be transmitted if the crop was grown with manure that was not treated for dangerous microorganisms. And... studies suggest there is very little—if any—difference in nutrient content and flavor between organically grown and conventionally grown produce.

Common sense: Whether you buy organically or conventionally grown produce, wash it before you eat it.

Source: Robert Shewfelt, PhD, associate professor of food science, University of Georgia Experiment Station, Griffin, Georgia 30223.

Computer Health Hazards

As computers have become commonplace, so have problems for people who use them—eyestrain, headaches, back problems and injuries to hands and fingers. And though conclusive evidence isn't in yet, there is a possibility of injury from radiation emitted by computer monitors.

Unless people and companies take steps to avoid these risks, they jeopardize the gains computers are designed to achieve...not to mention risking an increase in medical claims and lawsuits.

How injuries occur...

Companies and home users alike have been slow in anticipating computer health problems because computers look similar to their benign forerunners—typewriters.

But computers are very different, and the difference is largely responsible for the injuries.

Examples: It's more difficult to read a computer screen than a typewritten page. Computers also let users work at a steady, concentrated rate without the breaks that typewriting normally requires—changing paper and ribbons, using correction fluid, etc. *Results:* Eyestrain, headaches and muscle pain.

In addition, users' hands remain in the same position for almost everything they do—scrolling to a new page, deleting a paragraph or even calling up a new file. If a user has a modem and a speaker phone, he/she may even use the same hand position to make a call and take notes on the conversation. This can be injurious, as can repetitive motions.

Most common computer hazards...

•Eyestrain and headaches. These are typically caused by poor-quality monitors, glare from the screen and/or the failure of monitors to tilt to the optimum position for the user to see both it and the keyboard. *Solutions:*

•High-quality monitors. The quality of letter image, known as definition, is far more important than whether the type appears in green or amber. The Human Factors Society, in conjunction with the American National Standards Institute, has developed standards for monitors. (A listing of those standards is available from the Human Factors Society at Box 1369, Santa Monica, California 90406.)

•Adjustable monitor stands. These stands allow each user to set the monitor at the best tilt and distance for his/her own specific use.

Worth considering: Adjustable workstation surfaces. These devices let you raise, lower or tilt the entire workstation surface to fit your individual physical needs.

•Hand/wrist injuries. Brought on by repetitive motion or holding hands in awkward positions for extended periods, these injuries cause pain, numbness and loss of mobility.

Carpal tunnel syndrome, most likely caused by a combination of repetitive motion, excess force and awkward wrist posture, is currently the most publicized of these. It afflicts secretaries and others who spend long hours at a computer or typewriter keyboard. In this condition, compression of finger nerves leads to loss of feeling and possible paralysis.

The condition is frequently treated through surgery, but may recur if you go back to the same work conditions and habits. *Solutions:*

•Frequent breaks—ideally, five- to 10-minute breaks every two hours. *Note:* Workplace studies show that breaks work best when they're staggered, not when a whistle blows and the whole staff stops at the same time.

•Adequate education for users, to be sure they know both how to use the computer and how to prevent or minimize physical injury.

•The best keyboards, those which provide cushioning, auditory or tactile feedback and user-friendly key arrangements. Educated computer users themselves are usually the best judges of keyboards. For a second opinion, check with the Human Factors Society. In a year or two, it may be possible to buy a completely new type of keyboard that's designed to accommodate a person's normal hand position. (It's slightly raised in the center.)

•Adjustable workstations—consider the same ones recommended earlier for eyestrain problems.

•Make physical fitness a priority. Physically fit people are less likely to suffer from computer-related ailments than those in poor health. For businesses, a company wellness program is an effective way of maintaining employee health. Such a program can also catch injuries at an early stage, when the company can more easily correct the problem. Companies not large enough to fund a wellness program can now contract with private health services.

•Radiation injuries. This is still a very controversial area because evidence is far from complete. At this stage, dangers from lengthy exposure to extreme-long-frequency radiation emitted by computer monitors have not been conclusively ruled out. But the dangers haven't been convincingly demonstrated. Keep abreast of research. Companies should get advice from legal counsel.

The stress factor at the office...

Even computer operators who work in the best-designed environments are prone to injury if they're also under stress. The most common causes are demanding supervisors and, ironically, computer programs that monitor operators.

Signs of worker stress: High turnover, frequent absences, low job satisfaction.

If you suspect supervisors are at fault, look into giving them additional management training. If the monitoring system is causing stress, it usually pays to hire a consultant who can redesign it.

New monitoring systems now being developed promise to be almost user-friendly. The National Institute of Occupational Safety & Health, for instance, has experimented with monitoring systems that spot the types of errors that operators make when they're tired or under abnormal stress. When it spots these conditions, the computer advises the operator to take a rest.

Source: Marvin Dainoff, director of the Center for Ergonomic Research and professor of psychology at Miami University, Oxford, Ohio 45056. A former researcher at the National Institute of Occupational Safety & Health, Dainoff is the author of *People and Productivity*, MDA Books, 8606 Empire Court, Cincinnati, OH 45231.

Computers and Health

Working at a computer—even for an extended period—usually does not cause eyestrain, headache or blurred vision. However, it can aggravate existing eye problems. *Self-defense:*

•Keep the computer screen 20 to 24 inches from eyes and no more than 20 degrees below eye level.

•Place document holders close to the screen and at eye level.

•Dim or turn off overhead lights.

•Every 15 minutes or so, glance away from the screen. Focus on a more distant object to relax eye muscles.

•Install low-wattage (60-watt or less) bulbs in desk lamps. Adjust lamps so that light does not shine directly into eyes or onto the screen.

•Cover the computer screen with a glass or plastic antiglare filter. *Best:* Filters approved by the American Optometric Association.

Source: James Sheedy, OD, PhD, associate clinical professor, School of Optometry, University of California, Berkeley.

Dangerous Medicines: Prescription Drugs that Don't Always Do What They're Supposed to Do

For better or worse, Western medicine relies heavily on pharmacological treatment for ailments great and small. But all drugs have the potential to cause adverse reactions…any drug can be misused…and, because the human body is a complicated network of interrelated systems (circulatory, respiratory, nervous, digestive, etc.), all drugs can provoke responses in the body beyond what they are designed to do. These responses are known as side effects.

While most of the medications on the market today are quite safe and effective, there are many drugs—several among the most commonly prescribed drugs in the United States—that can be classified as questionable.

What makes a drug questionable?

A drug is questionable if…

•It is ineffective in treating the condition it is supposed to treat.

•It can have harmful side effects…and safer alternatives exist.

•It is often overprescribed or inadequately monitored by doctors, misused or abused by patients.

The most questionable drugs in the US.…

•Ulcer drugs (Zantac, Tagamet). These best-selling drugs work great—if you have an ulcer.

Problem: They are usually prescribed in large doses. But most ulcer patients fare very well after a few months on half the dosage, and some can stop taking the drug after two months—once the ulcer quiets down. If the ulcer recurs (and many won't), the drug can be resumed.

Worse problem: These drugs are widely prescribed to people with mild heartburn, indigestion or other vague, poorly defined abdominal pain not due to an ulcer. These conditions are often "self-limiting." They get better by themselves in a few days. This leads many patients to credit their recovery to whatever medication they are using. But 40% of these patients also get better when given a placebo. *Better:* Avoid pepperoni pizza and beer.

•Arthritis drugs (Indocin, Feldene, Motrin). The nonsteroidal anti-inflammatory drugs that are usually prescribed for arthritis do work to diminish pain and inflammation.

Problems: They are often prescribed indiscriminately when other alternatives exist. They can be costly and they can have dangerous side effects, such as gastrointestinal bleeding and kidney damage.

Example: Feldene has caused numerous deaths from internal bleeding, especially in older adults.

Better: Coated aspirin works well. And a recent study, published in the *New England Journal of Medicine,* found that acetaminophen (Tylenol) is just as effective for many arthritis patients.

Key: It must be used regularly to provide consistent relief, control symptoms and prevent flare-ups.

Caution: Some physicians may have a bias against older or over-the-counter drugs. Look for a doctor who will work with you to find the best dosage levels for you.

•Cholesterol-lowering drugs (Mevacor, Colestid, Lopid, Questran). These relatively new drugs are helpful for patients with extremely high cholesterol levels, especially in combination with a low-fat diet, regular exercise and weight control. But studies have shown many patients do well with diet and exercise alone.

Problems: The drugs are very expensive and can cause side effects, such as gastrointestinal problems. And the effects of their long-term use are still unknown.

Worse: Due to recent "cholesterol hysteria," these cholesterol-lowering drugs are being widely prescribed to people whose cholesterol levels are not high enough to warrant drug treatment, and for whom they are ineffective. They can even be counterproductive, if people who believe they are controlling their cholesterol by taking a pill avoid diet and exercise.

Many patients also respond well to supplemental niacin (vitamin B3), although supplemental niacin, too, can have side effects ranging from skin flushes to liver damage.

• Pain control (Darvon, Darvocet). The popularity of Darvon is mystifying, since it is known among physicians to be a "bad drug"—having overdose potential and also being potentially habit-forming.

Problems: It is no more effective than aspirin or Tylenol, and it can be habit-forming. Additionally, the risk of overdose is greater and it costs more.

• Alzheimer's drugs (Hydergine, Pavabid, Vasodilan). These drugs have been prescribed as cerebral vasodilators, which allegedly open the arteries to improve blood flow to the brain and improve memory.

Problem: They don't do anything at all. One study found that Alzheimer's patients treated with Hydergine—the 11th-most-precribed drug in the world—deteriorated faster than those given placebos.

Note: Vasodilan and Pavabid are also completely ineffective in treating vascular problems in the legs. Pavabid has been of limited benefit to some people when used to treat impotence.

• Insomnia and anxiety drugs (Valium, Xanax, Librium, Halcion, others). While tranquilizing drugs work well to relieve severe anxiety, they are often prescribed for too long a period of time and they are used excessively to treat insomnia.

Problems: These insomnia and antianxiety drugs are addictive, they become ineffective with long-term use (repetitive use merely prevents withdrawal symptoms) and their side effects can include drowsiness, mental confusion and rebound sleeplessness.

Better for insomnia: Go to bed at the same time every night, take a walk after dinner, don't drink coffee at night and, if you're over 60, avoid napping during the day. If all else fails, visit a sleep disorder clinic.

Caution: Some doctors are reluctant to recommend nondrug solutions to insomnia—and some patients demand medication.

• Depression (Prozac). Prozac clearly works for many patients suffering from severe clinical depression.

Problem: Due to a combination of fashion fad and excessive marketing, it is being used far more widely than is prudent with a new drug.

Trap: It is being prescribed, unmonitored, for patients with mild symptoms.

While there is some concern about scattered reports of patients who became violent while taking Prozac, no conclusions have been reached, particularly since physicians tend to try new drugs on patients whose illness has been hardest to control.

Recommended: Rather than being used as a drug of first choice, Prozac should be reserved for patients with severe symptoms who don't respond to or cannot tolerate other antidepressants. Patients taking Prozac should be monitored closely.

• Blood pressure drugs. This is an area in which medication is underused.

Problem: Physicians are often reluctant to treat hypertension in the elderly. However, a recent study has shown pharmacological treatment of high blood pressure in the elderly to be safe, effective and very desirable.

Dosages...

As people age, their sensitivity to certain drugs increases, their livers become less able to metabolize drugs, they generally have more body fat in which drugs can accumulate and their kidneys are less efficient at clearing drugs from the system.

In addition, they are more likely than younger people to use one or more prescription medications. Therefore, older adults are more likely to have an adverse reaction to a drug or combination of drugs.

Caution: Recommended dosages, even on drugs commonly used by the elderly, are often calculated too high. Whatever your age, ask your doctor to monitor your medications closely. *Aim:* Fewer drugs at lower dosages.

Source: Jerry Avorn, MD, an internist and geriatrician. Dr. Avorn is associate professor of medicine and director of the Program for the Analysis of Clinical Srategies, Harvard Medical School, Boston, Massachusetts.

How to Avoid the Yeast Trap in Your Own Body

Yeasts are microorganisms that occur naturally in the body. They live primarily on the skin and mucous membranes, including the intestinal tract.

The most common species of yeast in humans is *Candida albicans.* No one is sure what yeast's function is, except to quickly decompose the body once we die.

Yeast are usually harmless under normal circumstances. But when they multiply too rapidly, they create problems. Many unexplained or puzzling symptoms may actually be the result of uncontrolled yeast. *Included:* Anxiety, depression, indigestion, diarrhea, fatigue, difficulty concentrating and cravings for sugar or alcohol.

A number of factors contribute to yeast overgrowth. *Most common:*

• Antibiotics…by killing friendly bacteria in the digestive system that normally keep yeast under control.

• Stress on the immune system…including poor diet, heavy metal in the diet (including lead and mercury), pesticide poisoning, viral infections.

• Excessive sugar in the diet. Just as bread yeast will grow quickly in the presence of warm sugar water, the yeast in our bodies flourishes on carbohydrates—multiplying and dividing as fast as every 20 minutes.

Yeast overgrowth contributes to four major types of problems…

• Local infections…such as thrush and diaper rash in babies, vaginitis and skin rashes—particularly the uncomfortable rash under the breasts that many women experience during hot weather.

By inflaming the lining of the digestive system, yeast can also lead to heartburn, gas, bloating and alternating constipation and diarrhea.

• Production of toxins. One of these is ethanol, a metabolic by-product. It is absorbed into the bloodstream just like the ethanol in liquor.

Acetaldehyde is produced as ethanol is broken down…and is six times as toxic to the brain as ethanol.

One theory holds that these substances interfere with the enzymes responsible for sugar transport across cell membranes. *Result:* Abnormally high or low blood sugar, with symptoms such as lethargy, weakness, headaches—especially a few hours after eating. Sugar transport problems also seem to be associated with sugar cravings and easy weight gain.

Interference with sugar transport may also lead to brain symptoms such as difficulty thinking clearly, insomnia, depression, panic attacks and even trouble with balance. Yeast may well be a factor in causing learning disabilities and hyperactivity in children.

• Altered immune system…leading not only to infection but to chemical and food sensitivities. The mechanism for this is not completely understood. One explanation is that yeast damages the intestinal lining, which ordinarily filters out chemicals and large food particles, keeping them from entering the body. When the lining is damaged, incompletely digested substances may be absorbed into the bloodstream and treated like foreign invaders. The body responds with allergic reactions.

Over time, the immune system may react to a greater and greater variety of foods and chemicals. Common allergens may include foods and chemicals such as perfumes, car exhaust, dry-cleaning products.

•Nutrient depletion. Yeast seems to compete with the host—your body—for certain nutrients from food, especially B vitamins and magnesium. Under normal circumstances, acidophilus and other friendly bacteria in the digestive system act as net producers of these nutrients. Yeast overgrowth can lead to nutrient deficiencies.

Diagnosis...

There is no completely effective way to diagnose yeast overgrowth.

Cultures will only show that yeast is present in the body—not how much is present. Blood tests can detect antibodies against *Candida*, but because all of us have some yeast in our bodies, we all have some antibodies against yeast.

The best diagnosis is to try a treatment program and see whether symptoms clear up. If the symptoms do clear up after treatment, you may have a yeast problem. *Caution:* This program should not replace a doctor's advice and care.

Treatment plan...

The treatment program involves several parts, all of them important.

•Medication...to kill excess yeast. *Recommended:* The generic drug Nystatin. People sensitive to Nystatin can try Nizoral or Diflucan—these may cause liver problems in some patients, but the problems are reversible when the drug is discontinued. Nonprescription products containing caprylic acid are helpful to some patients, though not as effective as prescription drugs.

Most cases respond to medication within three months. Drugs should be discontinued one month after symptoms have stabilized.

•Lactobacillus supplements...to build up friendly bacteria in the intestinal tract. *Recommended:* One to 10 billion organisms per day (available in some kinds of milk and in capsule form). Continue for one month longer than drug treatment.

•Diet. The yeast-control diet is based on three principles...

•Eliminate foods that feed yeast—all refined sugars and refined carbohydrates and, until symptoms are under control, fresh fruits. (Complex carbohydrates, such as whole grains and vegetables, should be included in the diet.)

•Eliminate foods containing yeast, fungus or fungus residues.

Examples: Wine, beer, vinegar, mushrooms, yeast breads, all cheeses except cottage, ricotta and cream cheese.

•Eat enough food. A diet that's too low in calories can weaken the body, creating additional symptoms and interfering with the healing process.

After four weeks of this regimen, gradually add back the restricted foods, one at a time. However, continue to avoid refined sugar, other refined carbohydrates, fruit juice and alcoholic drinks indefinitely.

•Vitamin supplements...both to repair damage to the immune system and to replace lost nutrients. *Recommended:*

•A standard multivitamin supplement.

•Additional B-complex vitamins (four to six times the RDA).

•Vitamin C (2,000 to 8,000 mg daily, broken down into two to four doses).

•Calcium and magnesium, in a 1:1 ratio (600 to 1,000 mg calcium and 600 to 1,000 mg magnesium per day).

•Zinc (15–60 mg per day for a few months, then down to 15 mg).

•Exercise...to improve sugar metabolism, reduce stress and strengthen the immune system.

Best: Aerobic exercise, such as walking, jogging, swimming, bicycling or aerobic dancing. *Goal:* Work gradually up to three 30-minute sessions a week.

Source: Dennis W. Remington, MD, coauthor of *Back to Health: A Comprehensive Medical and Nutritional Yeast Control Program,* Vitality House International, Inc., 1675 N. Freedom Blvd., Provo, Utah 84604.

High-Tech Medical Dangers

The medical profession is more sophisticated and high-tech than ever before. It can effect treatments and cures that would have been considered miracles only 10 years ago.

But the health-care system is also more dangerous than ever.

With more diagnostic tools and surgical options available, many more opportunities exist for physicians to make mistakes or to act on incomplete knowledge. The wrong doctor—or the wrong lab test or the wrong surgery—is dangerous and even deadly. More than 200,000 Americans die each year, according to authoritative estimates, because of their doctors' negligence.

To survive the modern health-care system, patients must be assertive, informed and ready to protect themselves from myriad hazards, including...

•Misdiagnosis. It happens more than you think. A study of 1,800 autopsies from 32 hospitals found a diagnosis error rate of 20%. Half the errors—180 cases in all—led to the patients' deaths. *Most commonly overlooked:* Pulmonary embolisms, peritonitis and pulmonary abscesses ...all life-threatening conditions.

Self-defense: In any diagnosis that would lead to surgery or an invasive test, always get a second opinion. Do this as soon as possible. And be sure to go to a disinterested doctor, not a referral (or worse, a partner) of the first physician. The rate of confirming second opinions is significantly higher when coming from referrals.

If the second opinion conflicts with the first, don't simply accept the one you want to hear. Get a third opinion—even a fourth—until you are able to find a clear consensus on your condition.

•Faulty medical equipment. A butcher's scale must be inspected annually...but a doctor's blood pressure cuff may never be checked. The tremendous advances in today's technology have aggravated the problem. Modern doctors often rely too much on their equipment and not enough on their clinical training and instincts. And they may lack the training to use the equipment properly or they may be so specialized that they miss the larger picture. *One result:* 22%–40% of X-rays are misread.

Self-defense: Take it upon yourself to look at every one of your X-rays and read every test report. If you can't understand a report, ask your doctor to translate it into English. If a reading seems suspicious—say a blood pressure reading of 160 when you've never before had a problem—get a second test with different equipment. Talk directly to the practitioner who conducted the test.

•Laboratory errors. More and more doctors do lab work at their offices these days. It's a big money-maker for them...and it's also hazardous to your health. Doctor-operated labs have doubled the error rates of independent or hospital laboratories, which are monitored far more tightly by the state. And even these are not fail-safe. As many as 35% of pap smears produce false positives or false negatives. The former can lead to an unneeded hysterectomy, the latter to an untreated cancer.

Self-defense: Ask your doctor to send all lab work outside. (If he/she resists, find a new doctor.) Ask for a second test whenever lab results seem questionable, or have a different type of test. (A biopsy, for example, may turn up different results than a culture.) It may be smart for women to get two pap smears each time.

•Hospital infections and errors. A hospital is the most dangerous place in the world for sick people. One out of every 10 patients gets a new infection inside the hospital. Many of these are fatal...and 80% are preventable. In addition, a good hospital will have a 2%–3% error rate in medicating their patients. On average one patient in this country every minute gets either the wrong medicine, too much or too little or is dosed at the wrong time. This problem has worsened with the recent nursing shortage, since more nurses come out of "pools" and there is less continuity of care.

Self-defense: Never let anyone in the hospital touch you unless they first wash their hands... or use equipment on you that hasn't been obviously sterilized. If your medication changes, ask why before you take it. See written orders for the change. If you still have a question, wait until you can talk to the doctor directly. And if you are too ill to do all of the above, have someone you trust by your side, 24 hours a day.

•Alcoholic, drug-addicted or incompetent doctors. The local medical society knows who they are...but they keep the information confidential. You'll know, too, if your doctor shows up bleary-eyed, mumbling or wobbly. The problem is that many impaired doctors—and particularly surgeons—are not as obvious.

Self-defense: If you have any question about your doctor's competence, give yourself the benefit of that doubt and leave. There are, after all, 549,000 other physicians out there. If you're scheduled for surgery at a certain hospital, get to know some nurses there. (You probably have a friend of a friend who knows someone.) Ask them off-the-record what they think of Dr. So-and-So. If they express any doubts or criticisms, find a new surgeon.

Source: Charles Inlander, president of the People's Medical Society in Allentown, PA, and coauthor of *Medicine on Trial.*

Questions to Ask Before Having An Operation

Item: Four of every five Caesarean section deliveries are unnecessary.

Item: Half of all post-operative infections are preventable—many simply by hospital personnel washing their hands.

Item: Some patient "surgicenters" may legally employ surgeons who have never been board certified.

If any of this surprises you, you're among the majority of Americans.

We readily grill a car salesman, yet when it comes to surgery, we routinely accept medical opinions without question.

That's a mistake—one with potentially serious consequences. Questioning surgical procedures—all of them—and being an involved, participating patient is your most important consideration when you are facing surgery.

Actually, your first and best step is to approach your surgeon as a service provider. You're a consumer...and it's your right to ask questions. Which questions should you ask?

Ask the doctor...

• *What are the alternatives to this procedure?* Temporary pacemakers are commonly implanted during cardiac surgery. But noninvasive pacemakers, with electrodes attached outside

the chest, have proven to be effective in 94% of patients. This is typical of the alternatives to many surgical procedures that should be discussed with your physician.

• *How much experience do you have with this procedure?* Studies show that surgeons who more often perform specific procedures tend to do them better. Experience, though, isn't the only factor when selecting your surgeon. Many veteran surgeons, for instance, continue to perform Halsted mastectomies, an outdated operation that is avoided by younger physicians who are attuned to more modern technologies.

This illustrates, incidentally, the importance of second opinions. Nearly 80% of some procedures may not be recommended by a second opinion. If there is disagreement between your first and second opinions, don't hesitate to seek a third or even a fourth opinion. The key here is consensus.

• *What are your fees?* You should ask, and get in writing, your doctor's fees—from him, not his secretary. *Important:* Fees are often negotiable.

Ask the hospital...

• *What are your nosocomial infection rates?* Nosocomial infections are those that are developed in the hospital. About 10% of all patients get them, usually because of flaws in hospital sanitation procedures. Hospital personnel are usually reluctant to discuss their nosocomial infection rates. If so, your doctor should be able to provide them. If the rates are around 5%, the hospital is probably doing a good job controlling infections.

• *What kind of training and experience does the surgical support staff have?* Insist on meeting your anesthesiologist. Also ask to see the certified nurse anesthetist, if one is going to be present during the operation. Discuss what he/she will be doing throughout the operation. In a nonhospital setting—a hospital outpatient department, physician's office or free-standing surgery center—the anesthesiologist's qualifications are crucial. He should be board certified in anesthesiology. Like others on the surgical staff, he should be trained in CPR.

State laws vary governing surgery outside of hospitals. Some facilities may use surgeons who are board eligible but not board certified…so check.

• *How do you handle emergencies?* This is especially important in nonhospital surgery. For example, is an ambulance on standby to transport you to a hospital if an emergency arises? Does the facility have a written agreement with a nearby hospital to accept patients in trouble immediately, or will you have to be processed through an emergency room? Every surgical facility should be happy to discuss the ways in which surgical complications are handled.

• *How often is this procedure done here?* Recovery rates for coronary bypass surgery are noticeably higher in hospitals where 100 or more of them are done annually. The hospital should be able to inform you of its experience with specific operations.

Ask the anesthesiologist…

• *What kind of anesthesia will be used?* Local (anesthetizing a small portion of the body for a short time), regional (affecting a larger body area, like the epidural that numbs the entire abdominal region) and general anesthetics (which affect the whole body for an extended time) are all possibilities. Be sure you know which one will be used and why.

• *What's going to happen to me?* Your anesthesiologist can be helpful by explaining exactly what you'll experience while he prepares you for the operation, what happens when you're "under" and what to expect as you come out of the anesthesia.

These kinds of questions may seem excessive. However, they serve two vital functions.

•They provide you with valuable information.

•Your questions alert doctors and hospital personnel to the fact you're informed and interested.

Several studies have shown that involved patients who question surgical procedures receive above-average treatment during their hospital stays. When you interact with your surgeon, anesthesiologist and others on the surgical staff, you're no longer "the laparoscopy in room 213." You're an individual personality.

By involving yourself in the operation, the doctor and hospital staff become involved with you, and they're much more likely to do their best with someone they know.

Source: Charles B. Inlander, president of The People's Medical Society, Allentown, Pennsylvania 18102. He is the author of *Good Operations, Bad Operations,* Viking, 375 Hudson St., New York 10014.

Home Cholesterol Test Trap

Don't rely on the results of home cholesterol tests to assess your risk of heart disease. These tests don't give an accurate assessment of a person's cholesterol level—they give only a total count, with no breakdown for "good" and "bad" cholesterol readings. One's cholesterol level varies day to day—sometimes by as much as 30 points—so people may overestimate or underestimate their levels. *More drawbacks:* If you squeeze your finger to withdraw a few drops of blood onto the test plate, it can either dilute or concentrate the cholesterol level. And home tests, of course, don't take into account other heart-disease risk factors—family medical history, body weight, blood pressure, physical activity level, smoking habits, etc. There is no substitute for going to your regular doctor for this test.

Source: Bruce Yaffe, MD, an internist in private practice, 11 E. 84 St., New York 10028.

Shoe Savvy

High-heeled shoes shift most of the wearer's weight to the front of the foot. *Result:* Calluses …hammertoes…blisters…Achilles tendinitis… Morton's neuroma (an inflammation of the nerve between the third and fourth toes). Shoes with narrow, pointed toes can cause ingrown toenails …corns…bunions. *Help for feet:* If you must wear high heels—elevate tired feet…soak them in a warm-water bath…massage them gently.

Source: *University of Texas Lifetime Health Letter,* 7000 Fannin St., Houston 77030.

Cleaner Trap

Rug- and upholstery-cleaner danger. These common cleaners sometimes contain toxic chemicals—naphthalene, perchloroethylene, oxalic acid, diethylene glycol. *Safer:* Sweep and vacuum rugs and furniture regularly. *Helpful:* Sprinkle dry cornstarch, baking soda, borax or cornmeal before beginning to vacuum.

Source: *The Solution to Pollution: 101 Things You Can Do to Clean Up Your Environment* by Laurence Sombke, MasterMedia Limited, 17 E. 89 St., New York 10128.

Medication Warning

Sudden vision loss may occur when people with high blood pressure and a history of glaucoma or optic nerve strokes take hypertension medications at night. *Problem:* Patients often take these drugs at bedtime to avoid dizziness …but doing so can cause a drop in blood pressure that can lead to gradual or sudden vision loss. *Safer:* Ask your doctor about taking these medications in the morning or at midday.

Source: Sohan Singh Hayreh, MD, PhD, professor of ophthalmology and director of the Ocular Vascular Unit, University of Iowa, Iowa City. Hayreh conducted a study of 200 patients with histories of glaucoma or optic nerve strokes.

How to Protect Yourself Against Your Drinking Water

Americans are concerned about their drinking water—and rightly so. Roughly 20% of households have dangerous levels of lead in their tap water…and the once-sporadic cases of bacterial and industrial-chemical contamination seem to be occurring with increasing frequency.

Yet despite the real and ever-growing threat, there are effective ways to protect yourself and your family.

What's the biggest threat? By far the biggest threat is lead. Ingestion of lead causes a wide variety of serious health problems. Children who drink lead-tainted water often sustain irreversible brain damage—resulting in reduced IQ scores, short attention spans and other mental problems. (These problems are also common among infants born to mothers who drink lead-tainted water while pregnant.)

In adults, lead poisoning can cause kidney damage, high blood pressure and brittle bones. It can also cause brain damage, although adult neurological tissue is less sensitive to lead than children's neurological tissue.

Exposure of skin to lead-containing water—during a bath or shower, for example—is not considered dangerous.

How does lead get into tap water? It leaches into tap water as the water passes through lead-containing pipes or plumbing fixtures. Homes of all ages can show lead contamination from leaded solder joints or lead alloy pipes.

Even if your water pipes are made of plastic, however, faucets may still be leaching lead into your drinking water. *Reason:* Even faucets touted as "lead-free" are allowed by federal law to contain up to 8% lead.

The lead can also come from outside your home. In some parts of the country—including parts of New York City, Boston, Chicago and the Pacific Northwest—the municipal water systems are built with lead-jointed pipes. Even water from private wells can be contaminated with lead.

Bottom line: Any home can have lead in its water.

What can I do to protect myself? Have your tap water tested. Your local water utility may provide you with a free test kit—or may be able to recommend a water-testing agency in your area.

Test kits are also available from…

•Suburban Water Testing Labs, 4600 Kutztown Rd., Temple, Pennsylvania 19560.

•National Testing Laboratories, 6555 Wilson Mills Rd., Cleveland 44143.

•Clean Water Lead Testing, 29½ Page Ave., Asheville, North Carolina 28801.

A typical test requires two water samples. The first sample is taken early in the morning, when the water has been sitting overnight in your home's pipes. The second is taken after the water has been running for one minute.

Even if the first sample contains dangerous concentrations of lead, the second sample will not in nine out of 10 cases.

So I can eliminate the threat of lead simply by purging my water for one minute? Yes, in most cases. But purging your faucet once in the morning—the old advice—is not really valid. *Reason:* Lead leaches into water much more rapidly than previously thought. If it's been more than a few minutes since the last time you drew water, purge the tap again. To save time and water, keep a gallon pitcher of water from a purged tap in your refrigerator.

Can't I just boil my water? No. Although boiling water generally gets rid of bacteria, it does not eliminate lead or other heavy metals.

What if purging my tap water doesn't get rid of lead? Get a water-purification system…

•Cation-exchange filters remove 80% to 90% of lead.

•Reverse-osmosis filters remove 90% to 95% of lead.

•Distillation units remove nearly 100% of lead. Unlike cation-exchange or reverse-osmosis systems, they do not need periodic filter-element changes. But unlike these other systems, distillation units do require electricity.

Caution: Filter makers generally specify a schedule for changing the filter elements on cation-exchange and reverse-osmosis units. But an element that lasts six months in one home might last half as long in a home with higher concentrations of lead.

Self-defense: Until you get a sense of how long the filter element lasts in your home, have your filtered water tested for lead every four months or so. Periodic testing is no longer necessary once you know how long the filter continues to work.

What about bottled water? Bottled water is another safe—and generally less costly—option. We've tested a variety of brands. All have proven safe with respect to lead. Just to be sure you're getting pure water, however, choose bottled spring water over bottled water from a municipal water supply. *Even better:* Distilled water. It's cheaper than spring water and should be absolutely free of lead or any other impurities.

What about germs? Very rarely do water supplies become contaminated with E. coli or other potentially harmful bacteria or parasites. When this happens, local water authorities are generally quick to alert people to the problem—which is easily solved by boiling your tap water or switching to bottled water until the microbes are eliminated.

Bacterial contamination is uncommon in the US because almost all municipal water is now chlorinated. Unfortunately, when chlorinated water comes into contact with dissolved organic matter commonly found in municipal water systems, trihalomethanes (THMs) and related compounds are created.

THMs are suspected of causing cancer of the colon, rectum and bladder. Federal regulations now set the maximum allowable THMs at 100 parts per billion (ppb), and this will likely be reduced to 50 ppb within the next couple of years.

How can I tell if my water contains dangerous levels of THMs? Contact your local water authority. If levels of THMs have approached or exceeded the 50 or 100 ppb level in recent months (or if you're simply worried about the accuracy of the water authority's records), simply let water stand in an open container for at least six hours before using. Most of the THMs will dissipate if the water is exposed to air in this fashion.

Another way to get rid of THMs is via a granulated activated carbon (GAC) filter. GAC filters remove more than 80% to 90% of THMs…and they are equally effective at filtering out most organic industrial pollutants that may have found their way into your tap water.

Caution: GAC filters do not remove lead.

Source: Richard P. Maas, PhD, associate professor of environmental studies, University of North Carolina, Asheville, and director of the university's Environmental Quality Institute, the nation's largest research center on tap water purity.

The Hidden Enemy

Lead levels reported by your local water supplier may not accurately reflect the lead in the water in your home. To have your water—or soil or china—tested for lead, contact your state's certification office for a list of state-certified laboratories. To obtain a list of state certification offices, call the EPA Hotline (800-426-4791). Tests cost about $15.

Source: Environmental Protection Agency, 401 M St. SW, Washington, DC 20460.

Prescription Trap

Standard drug doses are often higher than necessary, especially for older patients with chronic illnesses. *Risks:* Side effects...and excessive costs. *Self-defense:* When starting to take a new drug, ask your doctor if it would be prudent to begin with less than the usual dosage. This dosage can then be gradually increased, as necessary, without crossing into the toxic range.

Source: Marvin M. Lipman, MD, a clinical professor of medicine at New York Medical College, writing in *Consumer Reports on Health*, 101 Truman Ave., Yonkers, New York 10703.

The Dangers of Tobacco

By now, most Americans are well aware that smoking causes lung cancer. But tobacco is a far bigger villain than most of us could ever imagine. Cigarettes, pipes, cigars, snuff and chewing tobacco kill more than 434,000 Americans each year—accounting for almost one out of five premature deaths in this country.

Lung cancer is just the *first* in a long and harrowing litany of tobacco-related problems.

Other tobacco dangers...

•Addictiveness. While some people have likened the addictive potential of nicotine to that of heroin, the good news is that tens of millions of people have been trying to quit smoking.

•Back pain. Smoking is probably a major risk factor in recovery from back pain (the leading cause of worker disability in the US) because poor oxygen levels of those who smoke prevent lumbar disks from being adequately oxygenated.

•Bladder cancer. Smoking causes 40% of all cases of bladder cancer, accounting for more than 4,000 new cases annually.

•Breast cancer. Women who smoked heavily, more than one pack per day, and who started smoking at an early age are 75% more likely to develop breast cancer than nonsmoking women.

•Cervical cancer. Up to one-third of all cases of cervical cancer—12,000 new cases a year—are directly attributable to smoking. Women who smoke are four times more likely to develop the disease than are nonsmoking women.

•Childhood respiratory ailments. Youngsters exposed to parents' tobacco smoke have six times as many respiratory infections as kids of nonsmoking parents. Smokers' children also face an increased risk of cough, chronic bronchitis and pneumonia.

•Diabetes. Smoking decreases the body's absorption of insulin. *Also:* Smoking exacerbates the damage of small blood vessels in the eyes, ears and feet of diabetics.

•Drug interactions. Smokers need higher than normal dosages of certain drugs, including theophylline (asthma medication), heparin (used to prevent blood clotting), propanolol (used for angina and high blood pressure) and medications for depression and anxiety.

•Ear infections. Children of smokers face an increased risk of otitis media (middle ear infection).

•Emphysema. Smoking accounts for up to 85% of all deaths attributable to emphysema.

•Esophageal cancer. Smoking accounts for 80% of all cases of esophageal cancer, which kills 15,000 Americans yearly.

•Financial woes. A pack of cigarettes (which costs the manufacturer less than 20¢ to make) sells for about $2.50 a pack—nearly $1,000 a year for a pack-a-day user.

•Fires. Smoking is the leading cause of fires in homes, hotels and hospitals.

•Gastrointestinal cancer. Preliminary research indicates that smoking at least doubles the risk of cancer of the stomach and duodenum—the portion of the small intestine just downstream from the stomach.

•Heart disease. Smokers are up to four times more likely to develop cardiovascular disease than nonsmokers. *Mechanism:* Carbon monoxide and other poisonous gases in tobacco smoke replace oxygen in the blood cells, promote coronary spasm and cause accumulation of clot-producing platelets.

•Infertility. Couples in which at least one member smokes are more than three times as likely to have trouble conceiving than nonsmoking couples.

Explanation: Tobacco smoke interferes with the implantation of a fertilized egg within the uterus. It reduces the number and quality of sperm cells in a man's ejaculate and raises the number of abnormal sperm cells...and increases a man's risk of penile cancer. Women who smoke are more likely to miscarry or deliver prematurely than nonsmoking women. Some scientists now theorize that toxins in the bloodstream of pregnant smokers pass through the placenta to the fetus, sowing the seeds for future cancers.

•Kidney cancer. Smoking causes 40% of all cases of kidney cancer.

•Laryngeal cancer. Smokers who smoke more than 25 cigarettes a day are 25 to 30 times more likely to develop cancer of the larynx than nonsmokers.

•Leukemia. In addition to tobacco smoke condensate, better known as tar, tobacco smoke contains several powerful carcinogens, including the organic chemical benzene and a radioactive form of the element polonium, both of which can cause leukemia.

•Low birth weight. Women who smoke as few as five cigarettes daily during pregnancy face a significantly greater risk of giving birth to an unnaturally small, lightweight infant.

•Mouth cancer. Tobacco causes the vast majority of all cancers of the mouth, lips, cheek, tongue, salivary glands and even tonsils. Men who smoke, dip snuff or chew tobacco face a 27-fold risk of these cancers. Women smokers—because women have tended to use less tobacco—face a six-fold risk.

•Nutrition. People who smoke tend to have poorer nutrition than do nonsmokers. Smokers also have lower levels of HDL (good cholesterol).

•Occupational lung cancer. Although a nonsmoker's risk of lung cancer increases six times due to prolonged occupational exposure to asbestos, that risk jumps to 92 times in an asbestos worker who smokes.

•Osteoporosis. Women who smoke experience menopause on an average of five to 10 years earlier than nonsmokers, causing a decline in estrogen production—and thinning bones—at an earlier age.

•Pharyngeal (throat) cancer. Last year, cancer of the pharynx killed 3,650 Americans—the majority of these deaths resulted directly from smoking.

•Premature aging. Constant exposure to tobacco smoke prematurely wrinkles facial skin and yellows the teeth and fingernails.

•Recovery from injury or surgery. Wound and bone injuries of smokers take a longer period of time to heal. Smokers also have a greater risk of complications from surgery, including pneumonia (due to weaker lungs), and remain in the hospital for longer periods.

•Stroke. Smoking increases the risk of stroke two-fold both among men and women.

Special danger: For women who smoke and use oral contraceptives, the risk of stroke is ten-fold.

•Tooth loss. Use of snuff or chewing tobacco causes gum recession and tooth abrasion, two frequent contributors to tooth loss.

Source: Alan Blum, MD, family physician, Department of Family Medicine, Baylor College of Medicine, Houston. Dr. Blum is the founder and president of Doctors Ought to Care (DOC), c/o Department of Family Medicine, Baylor College of Medicine, 5510 Greenbriar, Houston 77005, an antismoking group long-recognized for its service to public health.

How to Avoid Becoming a Victim Of a Violent Crime

From purse-snatching and car-jacking to assaults, rapes and kidnappings, violent crime has become a frightening fact of everyday life. While there's little you can do to control the rise of these crimes, there are ways to limit your chances of becoming a victim.

In your car…

• *Car-jacking self-defense:* Unlike professional car thieves, who have no wish to encounter car-owners, car-jackers are out for a thrill—and violence for them is thrilling. Tell yourself now that if someone tries to pull you from your car or demands your keys, you will behave passively and give them the car. When the event occurs, you should instinctively give up the vehicle rather than panic and fight back.

• Keep doors locked while driving. Close windows in slow traffic and at red lights. When coming to a stop, leave enough room between you and the car in front. This will allow you to maneuver around the vehicle if necessary.

• Pay attention to your surroundings. Car-jackers almost always approach on foot. Avoid self-absorbed distractions, such as combing your hair, fumbling with cassette tapes, etc.

• Park under a street light or as close as possible to the mall or well-lit buildings and stores. Avoid parking next to potential hiding places, such as dumpsters, woods, etc.

• Scan parking lots before approaching your car. Try to walk with other people, or ask a doorman or security guard for an escort.

• Have your key ready in your hand as you approach your vehicle. Look inside the car and around the outside before getting in. *Caution:* On some new cars, all doors will unlock when the driver's door is unlocked—a dangerous feature if someone is hiding outside the passenger door. If you do sense danger, retreat to a place of safety and call the police immediately. Do not confront an intruder.

On the street…

• Carry purses and briefcases close to the body—but be able to release them if necessary. *Avoid:* Shoulder straps across the body, straps wrapped around the wrist. People have been dragged by the straps and injured in purse-snatchings. If someone tries to take your wallet or purse, let it go. *Useful:* "Fanny pack" belts and pouches seem to be an unattractive target for street thieves.

• On the bus or subway, do not sit next to an exit door or place briefcases or purchases on an empty seat. Robbers tend to grab valuables as they are leaving and while doors are closing.

• If you are held up, do not resist. Most armed robbers only want your money. *Problem:* Many will turn to violence if they are alarmed or disobeyed. Surrender your valuables quickly.

At home…

• Keep doors and windows locked, especially after you turn in for the night. Keep curtains drawn after dark. Most home intruders are opportunists.

• Install deadbolt locks with reinforced strike plates on front and back doors. A few dollars will purchase a reinforced strike plate that secures the door frame to the first wall stud. Locks like these are also deterrents.

• Secure sliding glass doors by placing a broomstick or piece of wood along the interior track and by blocking the dead space in the upper channel that allows the door to be lifted off the track.

• Consider installing an alarm system. Ground-floor windows can be equipped with an alarmed jamming stick for $30 to $40.

• Never confront a burglar. If you come home to a door that's ajar or has been tampered with, leave the scene immediately and call the police. If you wake up to find an intruder in your bedroom, pretend to be asleep until he leaves.

• Don't depend on your dog to alert you. Most people command their dogs to stop barking when a stranger arrives. Many a dog has slept through a burglary or been seduced by a doggie treat.

• Do not open the door to strangers. If you have to hire an unfamiliar repairman, ask someone to be with you at home or plan to be on the phone when he arrives…or pretend there is someone else at home. If a repairman or stranger arrives at your door unannounced, do not let him/her in. Lock the door and call his office for verification.

• If you think you hear a prowler, call the police. Don't assume it's just the wind, that the police are too busy or that they might get mad if no one is there. It is always better to feel foolish than to be a victim.

• Unless you are well-trained, do not keep a gun in the house. People who are untrained with firearms are more likely to have them stolen or taken away from them by intruders, who may have arrived unarmed. If you do keep a gun in the house, the gun and ammunition should be stored separately.

Caution: According to law, in order to shoot an intruder on your property, you must be "in fear for your life." This does not mean in fear of losing your TV and jewelry.

•Know your neighbors. Neighborhood watch programs and "telephone trees" to alert neighbors of strangers in the area are very effective.

At work…

•Know your neighbors. Set up a building-wide security policy to identify visitors. "Business watch" programs for merchants in shopping areas are highly effective, too.

•Team up in pairs to use public restrooms or locked rest rooms located in public hallways. Avoid using remote stairwells alone.

•Keep the office's doors locked when working late, on weekends or early in the morning.

•Do not get on an elevator with someone who makes you feel uncomfortable or unsafe.

•When traveling on business, ask a bellhop to accompany you to your hotel room and to check it before you enter. Avoid ground-floor rooms. Make sure that the phone is working and that security numbers are provided. Never open the door to someone you're not expecting. If someone knocks unannounced, call the lobby for verification.

At play…

•Exercise with a partner, or take along a dog or stick while jogging. Avoid isolated parks and paths. Wear glasses if you normally need them, and do not use a stereo headset. Avoid loose clothes that are easy to grab.

•At parks, beaches or other recreation areas, know where the ranger or lifeguard stations are located. Leave expensive cameras, jewelry and credit cards at home or locked in the trunk of the car. Do not use recreation areas after hours.

In all situations…

•Make direct eye contact with people around you. This sends a message of confidence, an effective deterrent to violent crime. Criminals seek passive, distracted victims, who make easy targets.

•Trust your instincts. Humans are extremely instinctive. *Important:* Tune into the messages.

Some of the most common statements police officers hear following a crime are, "I had a feeling I shouldn't have walked to my car"…"The guy gave me the creeps, but…"

Bottom line: If a situation makes you nervous, avoid it. Learn to respect your instincts and act on them.

Source: Patricia Harman, a crime-prevention officer with the Prince William County, Virginia, police force. Harman, who conducts lectures nationally on personal safety, is the author of *The Danger Zone: How You Can Protect Yourself from Rape, Robbery and Assault,* Parkside Publishing, 205 W. Touhy Ave., Park Ridge, Illinois 60068. 800-221-6364.

More Crime Avoidance Tactics

While no one deserves to be a victim of violent crime, in many cases it's our own careless behavior that renders us vulnerable.

Crime-inviting habits…

•Failing to be vigilant. People often fall victim to violent crime simply because they think "it can't happen to me"—or because they fail to notice obvious threats. *To avoid trouble:*

•Be alert. Walk with your head upright.

•Steer clear of secluded parks, stairwells, laundry rooms, etc.

•If you suspect you're being followed, head for the nearest store, gas station or other busy public place.

•Check the back seat before getting into your car.

•Give a wide berth to dark foliage, alleys, doorways, parked cars and other likely hiding places.

•Don't use cash machines.

•Flashing cash or jewelry. If you must carry lots of cash, separate the bills into two pockets. In one carry a cash reserve, in the other, the money needed for the next purchases.

Better: A money belt or a zippered wallet suspended from a neck cord and worn under your shirt. Women carrying a purse should grip it inconspicuously under their arm. Keep jewelry hidden under clothing whenever you venture into potentially dangerous areas.

•Being too trusting. Don't make the mistake of falling prey to crime simply because you're afraid to risk hurting the feelings of an innocent person. *To avoid trouble:*

•Trust your instincts. If someone looks even slightly suspicious, take evasive action. Turn and walk in the other direction. Cross the street. Step into a store. Get on—or off—an elevator.

•Don't stop if someone suspicious tries to flag you down while you're driving—it could be a setup for a car-jacking.

•Teach your children about child molestation. Instruct them to never trust any stranger about whose legitimate authority they have any doubt.

•Being needlessly confrontational. These days, giving vent to our anger and frustration—gesturing offensively or "staring someone down"—can quickly escalate into violence. *To avoid trouble:*

•Be courteous to all strangers—even to motorists who cut you off or provoke you in some other manner. Use your horn only as a warning device, not as a means of letting off steam.

•Being an easy mark. Street criminals generally prey upon those least able to fight back—the elderly, women with small children, intoxicated people, people burdened with packages or fumbling with car or house keys, etc.

Precautions:

•Don't drink to the point of intoxication.

•Don't be overburdened with packages.

•Have your keys ready before you reach the door.

Bottom line: The greater your alertness and apparent physical capacity, the greater your safety.

•Failing to lock up. Never leave your house or apartment or go to bed without first locking your doors and windows.

Keep car doors locked at all times as well. If your car conks out at night, try to stop beneath a street lamp and wait for the police. If someone else offers help, stay in your locked car. Shout to the person to call the police.

Self-defense: Keep five envelopes in your glove compartment each containing change for a phone call and the name and number of a different friend or family member. If someone stops to help, crack the window and give them

an envelope. Tell the person there is 25¢ and a phone number to call. Ask them to call until they reach someone.

Most important…

If you are ever confronted by a criminal, do not resist. Many street criminals are desperate drug addicts who feel little compunction about taking a life.

If threatened with a knife or gun, comply with all demands quickly but cautiously. Turn slightly to the side so your body presents a smaller target in case a gun accidentally fires. Make no sudden motions, and explain all movements in advance to make sure your actions are not misinterpreted as threats.

Source: Richard L. Bloom, founder of the Crime Deterrent Institute, Houston. A frequent lecturer on crime prevention and victims' rights, Bloom is the author of *Victims: A Survival Guide for the Age of Crime*, Guardian Press, 10924 Grant Rd., Houston 77070. 800-771-8191.

What to Do If There's A Burglar in the House

Outdoor lighting, alarm systems, timers that automatically turn household lights on and off, and other precautions all help protect your home from burglary.

Just as important as taking steps to keep burglars outside is planning what to do if someone makes it inside. *Most important:*

•Create a "safe haven." Inside every home should be a specially equipped room where occupants can retreat in case of an attack or intrusion. This room—ideally a bathroom or bedroom—should have a window or some other means of escape…a solid-core door with a one-inch deadbolt that latches from the inside …a telephone…and a list of emergency phone numbers. If your home is equipped with an alarm system, install a panic button inside your safe room.

•Develop an escape plan. Know the fastest way out of your house from every room. Periodically rehearse your escape. Make sure windows, doors and other escape routes can quickly be opened from the inside.

•Don't go to investigate. Confronting a burglar face-to-face can turn a simple burglary into an assault or even murder.

More prudent: Leave the investigation to the police. If you arrive home and find evidence of a break-in, don't go inside. The intruder might still be there. Leave the premises immediately and call the police.

If the burglary takes place while you're inside, lock a door between yourself and the intruder—ideally that of your safe haven—and telephone the police. If you cannot reach a phone, open a window and yell for help.

If it's possible to escape without risking an encounter with the burglar, then do so. Call the police from a neighbor's house.

•Remain calm. If you come face-to-face with an intruder inside your home, try not to panic. The more level-headed you are, the more likely you'll be able to think of a way to defuse the situation...and the less threatening you'll appear to the burglar.

If you don't provoke him, odds are he/she won't harm you. Most burglars just want to get out of the house once they've been detected. Don't attack or attempt to hold him until the police arrive. Just give him a wide berth so he can escape.

Most important: Fight only if attacked. Then use any weapon at hand—a knife, scissors, a heavy object, a canister of irritating chemical spray, etc. A gun is useful only if you know how—and are willing—to fire it at the intruder. If you wield a gun tentatively, he might take it away and use it against you.

Source: Richard L. Bloom, founder of the Crime Deterrent Institute, Houston. A frequent lecturer on crime prevention and victims' rights, Bloom is the author of *Victims: A Survival Guide for the Age of Crime*, Guardian Press, 10924 Grant Rd., Houston 77070. 800-771-8191.

Most Common Indoor Pollutants

Indoor pollution may be as much as 10 times worse than outdoor pollution. *Most common pollutants:* Asbestos...carbon monoxide...sulfur dioxide...formaldehyde (especially in new homes built of plywood and other cheap materials)...aerosol sprays...cleaning products...dry-cleaning chemicals...and cosmetics. *Highest risk:* Well-insulated homes that trap pollutants inside.

Source: Report by the Consumer Product Safety Commission, in *Moneysworth*.

Safe Asbestos Substitutes

Insulation alternatives to asbestos. When asbestos is removed from buildings, replace it with:

•Fibrous insulations (fiberglass, mineral wool). Easiest to install but lack durability for industrial use.

•Calcium silicate. More durable, but must be cut with a saw, increasing installation costs.

•Cellular glass. Lightweight and moisture-proof, best used underground where temperature is consistently low or in areas where chemicals are used. Difficult to cut and may shatter.

•Foam plastics (urethane and polystyrene). Lightweight and very efficient but tend to shrink under high heat and ignite more easily than other materials.

Source: *Energy User News.*

Hot Tub Hazard

Communal hot-tub bathing sometimes causes severe infections. Several cases of major ear infections were traced to a tub where the redwood itself was harboring the infectious organisms. Other users developed skin infections requiring intravenous antibiotics. *Recommendations:* Adequate chlorination, disposable liners for redwood tubs, frequent cleaning of the filtration system and maintenance of the pH at 7.5

Source: *Internal Medicine News*, New York.

Germiest Spots In the House

Disease-causing bacteria are very much at home the same places you are. They're most populous in kitchens and bathrooms. *Germiest spots:* Sinks and bathtubs, U tubes, dishcloths, cleaning cloths, facecloths and bathmats. Surprisingly, researchers found toilets to be relatively germ-free. It may be that flushing is an effective disinfectant.

Source: *New Scientist.*

How Hair Driers Can Become Lethal

Bathtub electrocutions are often caused by appliances that aren't turned on at the time. If an appliance is plugged in and falls into the tub, the water will complete the circuit. *Most frequent cause of electrocution deaths:* Hair driers.

Christmas Tree Safety

Keep a natural tree's base in water until ready to set it up. (Cut the butt end diagonally one or two inches above its original cut, fill the holder with water to cover the cut line and refill as necessary.) Keep both natural and plastic trees away from heat sources. Get rid of the tree when the needles begin to fall off in great quantities.

Source: *Mothers Today.*

Pretty Plants That Can Be Dangerous

Many common plants are poisonous and can be fatal. Included are daffodils, buttercups, lily of the valley, sweet pea, oleander, azalea, rhododendron and yew. Warn children not to eat anything you're not absolutely sure is safe. *If poisoning occurs:* Call the nearest poison control center and your physician. If possible, collect a sample of the plant for identification, and estimate the amount consumed.

How to Fight Noise Pollution In Your Neighborhood

To squelch noise pollution within your house: Line a wall with bookshelves filled with books …keep closets filled with clothing…plug all openings around pipe fittings and electrical outlets with fiberglass. *To insulate from outside noise:* Use weatherstripping and caulking to close all openings in outside walls…keep storm windows closed whenever possible.

Tip for Gaggers

If you gag when the doctor applies a tongue depressor, it helps to sing "Ah" in falsetto. You may feel silly, but you'll avoid the scary gagging reflex.

Bugproof Clothing

Best bugproof clothing for mosquito, blackfly and no-see-um country is lightweight, waterproof rain gear of Gore-Tex, Klimate or coated nylon. These breathable fabrics are so tightly woven that bugs bounce off as easily as raindrops. The garments have tight closings at wrists, neck and ankles and can be adapted to different temperatures by changing the number of layers worn beneath. *Extra protection:* Take a head net and light cotton work gloves for badly infested areas.

Source: *Sports Afield.*

Lightning and Your Health

The odds of being struck by lightning are low. But they could be made a lot lower by taking a few simple precautions during a thunderstorm: (1) Move indoors quickly or get into your car. (2) Get off and away from golf carts, bicycles and motorcycles. Put down your golf clubs. Keep away from tractors or metal farm equipment. (3) Stay away from wire fences, clotheslines, metal pipes and rails. (4) If caught in an open area and your hair stands on end, drop to your knees and bend forward with hands on knees. Do not lie flat on the ground. (5) Never seek shelter under a tree.

Source: National Oceanic and Atmospheric Administration, reported in *Modern Maturity.*

Dangerous Dog Play

Games of tug-of-war or fetch in which the owner tries to pull something from the pet's mouth may be dangerous. By learning to clamp hard onto passing objects, even good-natured dogs become potential biters.

Source: *The Weekend Dog* by Myrna M. Milani, Rawson Associates, New York.

Diseases You Can Catch From Your Dog

The family dog may pass on contagious diseases, particularly streptococcal sore throats. About 100 diseases can be transmitted from animals to humans. *Point:* If the family is bothered with persistent infections, especially sore throats, take the dog to the vet for testing. When the dog is cured, the family problem with diseases may also disappear.

Source: *Ladies' Home Journal.*

Small Pet—Big Danger

Pet turtles can be hazardous to their owner's health. They're often reservoirs of salmonella bacteria. Even though selling turtles under four inches long is illegal, they're still available in many pet stores.

Source: *The Harvard Medical School Health Letter.*

Pesticide Danger

Many unlabeled, so-called "inert" ingredients in pesticides, such as mercury, cadmium, lead, benzene, trichlorethylene, arsenic and asbestos are actually extremely dangerous substances. A recent investigation by the Environmental Protection Agency revealed that 50 of the inert ingredients used in pesticides are known or suspected carcinogens or are highly toxic; 30 are active ingredients in other pesticides. Presently, the law requires that only active ingredients be labeled on pesticides, even if inert— and toxic— ingredients make up most of the product.

Motor Oil Warnings

Do-it-yourself mechanics should avoid prolonged skin contact with used motor oil. It may be carcinogenic. *Suggested precautions:* Wear gloves—or at least wash the oil off as soon as possible. Discard oil-soaked clothing. Don't tuck oily rags in pockets or under your belt. Discard the used oil at a designated disposal location.

Source: Environmental Protection Agency.

Office Pollution Prescription

To avoid office pollution: Keep carbonless copy paper stored away in closed cupboards (the chemical can be irritating). Never tear paper (it generates troublesome chemical dust). Keep copying machines outside the room you work in. Make sure your office is well ventilated and no warmer than 68°F.

Source: *Ultrahealth* by Leslie Kenton, Delilah Communications, Ltd., New York.

How to Keep Your Medical Records Private

Confidential medical information, often revealed without a patient's consent or knowledge, can seriously damage a career, boost insurance premiums and cause embarrassment. Sometimes you can protect yourself.

Risk factors...

•Socially stigmatized medical conditions. Venereal disease, alcoholism, sexual dysfunction, nervous conditions and the like can endanger your reputation and your job.

•Company plans. Any conditions for which you file a claim may come to the attention of your employer. Common problems such as diabetes, heart disease, cancer or even insomnia may effect your future with the company.

•Seeing a specialist. You may have a verbal agreement with your family doctor not to release any but the most specific or innocuous information to other sources, such as employers or insurance companies. Although doctors are usually good about protecting information, they routinely disclose medical histories to other physicians without the patient's consent. Since you do not have a personal relationship with the specialist, knowledge of your record may proliferate from here.

•Computerized records. Purchasers of health insurance should be aware of the Medical Information Bureau, a computerized service that keeps extensive medical records on over 11,000,000 Americans for their insurance company subscribers. The computer stores medical information and may also contain personal items, such as participation in dangerous sports, drunk-driving citations, criminal associations and large life insurance purchases.

How to protect yourself...

Use the doctor/patient relationship. The basis of confidentiality is largely contractual and is not covered by laws. Review this issue with your doctor or any specialist you go to. You might devise a written form for each physician requiring your permission for the release of any information about yourself.

Never sign a blanket medical release form. The only medical release forms you should sign should specifically identify the following: Information to be released, who is releasing the information and who is to receive it. Releases are not self-limiting as to time. A form you signed 10 years ago can still be used to obtain information.

Do not use your company insurance plan in sensitive areas. If you need treatment for an emotional problem, venereal disease, etc., pay for it yourself if at all possible.

Legitimate inquiries...

Insurance companies, potential employers and current employers all have the right to know a fair amount about your health. However, if you protect yourself as outlined, you can minimize the information revealed in a legitimate inquiry. Physical examinations required by a current employer have been upheld in the courts and so must be complied with. The American Occupational Medical Association, to which company doctors belong, has a code of ethics provision precluding occupational physicians from turning over a patient's full record.

Getting access to your records...

•You have a right to see your medical records in about half the states. In states that don't have specific statutes, your legal right to see your records would probably be recognized by the courts.

•You do have a right to rebut what your medical record says. In states with right-of-access, you can challenge by filing a lawsuit.

Bottom line: Take preventative action before confidential medical information about you has reached the wrong parties.

Source: Robert R. Belair, former counsel to the National Commission on Confidentially of Health Records. He is coauthor, with Dr. Alan Westin, of *Medical Confidentiality: A Guide for Practitioners, Administrators and Other Users of Personal Health Data,* Aspen Systems Corp., Rockville, MD.

Sunglasses on Cloudy Days?

Sunglasses help on cloudy days, too. Clouds stop the sun's light but not its eye-damaging ultraviolet (UV) radiation. *Self-defense:* Sunglasses with maximum UV protection. *Note:* Sunglasses with yellow lenses are best for cloudy days, when darker lenses can be bothersome.

Source: Melvin Schrier, OD, optometrist in private practice, 539 Park Ave., New York 10021.

Medicine Bottle Trap

Cotton packed in bottles to keep pills from breaking during shipment can pass germs from one user to the next. This is one way that viruses and other illness are passed throughout a household. *Important:* Remove cotton when the medicine bottle is opened.

Source: Bruce Yaffe, MD, an internist in private practice, 121 E. 84 St., New York 10028.

Too Many Dangerous Chemicals Are in Too Many of Our Homes

According to the Environmental Protection Agency's estimates, the average household contains between three and 10 gallons of hazardous chemicals—and many of them are organic compounds that vaporize at room temperature.

In the effort to save money by sealing our homes to reduce heating and air-conditioning bills, and by becoming do-it-yourselfers for many tasks once left to professionals, we expose ourselves and our families to high levels of these toxic substances.

Read the label...

"We are all guilty of not thoroughly reading labels," according to Charles Jacobson, compliance officer, US Consumer Products Safety Commission.

If vapors may be harmful, it doesn't do much good to read the label after you have used the product and inhaled the vapors.

Important: Read the labels before buying a product to select the safest in a category. If you find any of the 11 ingredients listed below on a container, avoid buying it. If you must buy it, use extreme caution when working with these dangerous chemicals...

1. Methylene chloride. A widely used solvent, it is in pesticide aerosols, refrigeration and air-conditioning equipment, cleansing creams and in paint and varnish removers. Some paint strippers are 80% methylene chloride. Its toxic effects include damage to liver, kidneys and central nervous system. It increases the carbon monoxide level in the blood, and people with angina (chest pains) are extremely sensitive to the chemical. Methylene chloride has been linked to heart attacks and cancer.

2. Dichlorvos (DDVP). An investigation by the National Toxicology Program of the Department of Health and Human Services revealed a significant leukemia hazard from this common household pesticide. It's been widely used in pet, house and yard aerosol products since the 1950s. The EPA has had DDVP in special review since February, 1988, and it has been considering banning it from food packaging.

3. 2,4-D. A weed killer related to Agent Orange—which allegedly caused health problems in exposed Vietnam veterans, 2,4-D is widely used by home gardeners and farmers. It does not cause acute toxicity, but its long-term effects are scary—much higher incidence of cancer and non-Hodgkin's lymphoma has been associated with its use among farmers. The National Cancer Institute also reports that dogs whose owners use 2,4-D on their lawns have an increased rate of a type of cancer closely related to human non-Hodgkin's lymphoma.

4. Perchlorethylene. The main solvent employed in the dry-cleaning process, metal degreasing and in some adhesives, aerosols, paints and coatings, it can be absorbed through your lungs or your skin. The most common effects of overexposure are irritation of the eyes, nose, throat or skin. Effects on the nervous system include dizziness, headache, nausea, fatigue,

confusion and loss of balance. At very high exposure it can cause death.

5. Formaldehyde. An inexpensive and effective preservative used in more than 3,000 household products. They include disinfectants, cosmetics, fungicides, preservatives and adhesives. It is also used in pressed-wood products —wall paneling, fiberboard and furniture and in some papers. There are serious questions about its safety. It is estimated that 4% to 8% of the population is sensitive to it. Vapors are intensely irritating to mucous membranes and can cause nasal, lung and eye problems.

6. Benzene. Among the top five organic chemicals produced in the United States, this petroleum derivative's use in consumer products has, in recent years, been greatly reduced. However, it is still employed as a solvent for waxes, resins and oils and is in varnish and lacquer. It is also an "antiknock" additive in gasoline—thus, make sure your house is well ventilated and insulated from vapors that arise from an attached garage.

Benzene is highly flammable, poisonous when ingested and irritating to mucous membranes. Amounts that are harmful may be absorbed through the skin. *Possible results:* Blood, brain and nerve damage.

7. Cyanide. One of the most rapid poisons known, it is used to kill fungus, insects and rats. It is in metal polishes (especially silver), in art materials and photographic solutions.

8. Naphthalene. Derived from coal, it is used in solvents, fungicides, in toilet bowl deodorizers and as a moth repellent. It can be absorbed through the skin and eyes as well as through the lungs. It may damage the eyes, liver, kidneys, skin, red blood cells and the central nervous system. It has reportedly caused anemia in infants exposed to clothing and blankets stored in naphthalene mothballs. This chemical can cause allergic skin rashes in adults and children.

9. Paradichlorobenzene (PDB). Made from chlorine and benzene, it is in metal polishes, moth repellents, general insecticides, germicides, spray deodorants and fumigants. PDB is also commonly found in room deodorizers. Vapors may cause irritation to the skin, throat and eyes. Prolonged exposure to high concentrations may cause weakness, dizziness, loss of weight and liver damage. A well-known animal cancer-causing agent, the chemical can linger in the home for months or even years.

10. Trichloroethylene (TCE). A solvent used in waxes, paint thinners, fumigants, metal polishes, shoe polish and rug cleaners. Tests conducted by the National Cancer Institute showed TCE caused cancer of the liver. A combination of alcohol ingestion with exposure to trichloroethylene can cause flushing of the skin, nausea and vomiting.

11. Hydroxides/lye products. These include automatic dishwasher detergents, toilet bowl cleaners, fire proofing, paint remover and drain cleaners. Ingestion causes vomiting, prostration and collapse. Inhalation causes lung damage. Prolonged contact with dilute solutions can have a destructive effect upon tissue, leading to skin irritations and eruptions.

Source: Ruth Winter, author of *A Consumer's Dictionary of Household, Yard and Office Chemicals,* Crown Publishers, 201 E. 50 St., New York 10022.

Car Emergency Equipment

- Flashlight with fresh batteries.
- Flares or warning reflectors.
- Extra washer fluid.
- First-aid kit.
- Drinking water and high-energy food.
- Booster cables.
- Extra fan belt and alternator belt.
- Fully inflated spare tire.
- Tool kit (including jack, lug wrench, screwdrivers, pliers, adjustable wrench and electrical tape).

Extras for winter driving:
- Tire chains and traction mats.
- Ice scraper.
- Warm clothing or blankets.
- Square-bladed shovel.
- Extra antifreeze.

Coping with Car Trouble On the Highway

Unexpected breakdowns on the open road are frustrating and can be very dangerous.

How to avoid them:

Practice preventive maintenance. Have your car checked before you set out on a long trip.

Likeliest sources of trouble: Battery, tires, belts and engine hoses.

Be sure you have emergency supplies, such as flashlights, flares and basic tools, and that your spare tire is inflated.

At the first hint of trouble, move off the road, activate your emergency flashers and only then assess the problem.

Fix the things you can yourself.

If your car is overheating, you may be able to let it cool down and then proceed slowly to a gas station if you know one is nearby.

If you are really stuck, wait for help. Major highways are regularly patrolled by troopers. Less traveled roads may require a Good Samaritan.

Don't leave your car. An abandoned car is vulnerable to theft and vandalism. And in winter, you are vulnerable to the elements.

To signal for help, raise your hood or your trunk lid as a distress signal. Hang a white handkerchief or colored scarf from it. If you have flares or reflectors, set them out (in those states where they are legal).

Run the motor (and heater or air conditioner) only 15 minutes out of every hour, keeping a window slightly open to guard against carbon monoxide poisoning.

If you are a woman alone, keep the car doors locked and the windows rolled up while waiting. This gives you a protected vantage point for sizing up strangers who approach the car.

When help arrives, describe your car problem clearly so a service station can send the proper equipment. Beware of helpful strangers who are not mechanically inclined. Using battery jump cables incorrectly can cause an explosion or ruin your alternator. Improperly hitched tows can ruin your automatic transmission.

You must stay calm and be patient. If this is too upsetting a proposition for you, consider investing in a car phone or CB radio so that you can get help sooner.

Source: Francis C. Kenel, PhD, director of traffic safety, American Automobile Association, Falls Church, VA.

Your Car Radio

Don't turn on your car stereo during the first five minutes of your drive. Use that time to listen for noises that could signal car trouble.

Organize your stereo tapes before you leave, so you can pick them out without taking your eyes off the road.

Keep all tapes within easy reach.

Don't wear headphones while you drive. A safe driver must be able to hear the traffic as well as watch it.

Wait for a straight patch of road before glancing at the stereo to adjust it.

Read your tape cassette titles at eye level so you can see the road at the same time.

Source: *High Fidelity,* New York.

Driving in Hot Weather

Inspect the auto radiator for leaks, and check the fluid level.

Check all hoses for possible cracks or sponginess. Make sure all connections are tight and leak-free.

Test the thermostat for proper operation. If it does not operate at the proper temperature, overheating could occur.

Inspect the fan belt for cracks and proper tension. Belt slippage is a common cause of boilovers. It also drains electrical power.

If loss of coolant has been a problem, check for water seepage on the water pump around the engine block.

Don't turn off the engine when the temperature warning light goes on. If stuck in traffic, shift to neutral, and race the engine moderately for 30 seconds at two-minute intervals.

Shut off the air conditioner to avoid further overtaxing of the cooling system.

Turn on the heater for a few minutes. It may help.

If the radiator continues to overheat, drive the car off the road, turn off the engine and raise the hood.

Wait at least half an hour before removing the radiator cap. Then do it very slowly and carefully, with the help of a towel or thick rag. Keep your face turned away from the radiator.

If your car has a see-through overflow catch tank, replace any loss of coolant. Don't touch the radiator.

If the fluid level is low, restart the engine while adding cool or warm water as the engine idles.

Source: Automobile Association of America.

Preparing for Cold Weather Driving

•Radiator coolant. Read the label on your antifreeze to be sure you make the right blend of water and antifreeze. The antifreeze keeps your radiator from freezing and cracking; the water, even in winter, keeps your car from overheating.

•Battery condition. Your car needs three to four times more starting power in winter than in summer. Have a mechanic do a complete battery draw and load test. If your battery fails, a recharge may save it for another year. Otherwise, invest in a new one.

•Windshield washer fluid. Frozen fluid in the washer tank is dangerous. Use a premixed commercial fluid. Check that the hoses are clear, and clean the washer nozzles out with a thin piece of wire.

•Electrical system. Make sure the distributor cap, points, condenser, ignition coil, spark plugs and spark-plug cables are in good shape. Borderline components that still function in summer will give out in cold weather.

•Hoses and belts. If they are cracking or fraying, replace them.

•Tires. If you have all-season tires, be sure the tread is still good enough to give you traction on slippery roads. Otherwise, put on snow tires. *Important:* If you have a front-wheel-drive car, the snow tires go on the front. Store summer tires on their sides, not on the tread. (Storing on the tread causes a flat spot and an unbalanced tire.) Inflate stored tires to only 50% of their operating pressure.

•Windshield. Apply antifogging compound to the inside.

•Cleaning. Clear dead bugs off the radiator by hosing it from the inside of the engine compartment. Pick out dead leaves and debris from the fresh-air intake box of the ventilation system.

•Stock up. Buy flares, an aerosol wire-drying agent, a scraper and brush, chains and a military-style collapsible trench tool for emergencies. Keep a lock de-icer at home and/or at the office.

Driving Small Cars Safely

In a severe crash between a large car and a small one, those in the small car are eight times more likely to be killed. *Defensive strategies:*

Wear seat belts. A belted occupant of a small car has the same chance of surviving as the unbelted occupant of a big car in a crash between the two.

Keep your lights on at low beam full time to increase visibility.

Be aware that light poles and signs along the road may not break away as designed when hit by a lightweight compact car.

Respect the inability of larger vehicles to maneuver or stop as quickly to escape a collision.

Dealing with Trucks On a Highway

To pass a truck:

Blow your horn or blink the headlights to indicate your intentions.

If it's raining, pass as quickly as possible to reduce road spray.

After passing, speed up to avoid tailgating.

When following:

Maintain a distance of 20–25 feet so the truck driver has a complete view of your vehicle.

Be prepared for a possible truck shift to the left (even when it's signaling a right turn) as the driver makes sure he clears the right curb.

Stay at least one or two car lengths back so as to remain in the truck driver's line of vision. This is especially important on an upgrade, where the truck may roll back a few feet.

Source: *Canadian Vehicle Leasing's Safe Driving Bulletin,* as reported in the *National Association of Fleet Administrators Bulletin,* 295 Madison Ave., New York.

How to Brake on Ice

Start early.

Squeeze the brakes with a steady pressure until just before you feel them begin to lock.

Ease up, and slowly repeat the pressure.

Disc brakes do not respond well to pumping (the old recommendation for drum brakes). They will lock, causing you to lose control of the car.

Source: National Safety Council, Chicago, IL.

Accidents with Aggressive Drivers

Violent and aggressive drivers are dangerous when they get into an accident. If you're in an accident with one, stay calm.

Don't escalate any argument.

Copy down the other driver's license number immediately.

If you are threatened, leave at once.

Call the police so that you won't be charged with leaving the scene of an accident…but do it from a safe distance.

If your car is disabled, lock the doors and wait for the police to arrive.

Which Cars Bring The Most Injury Claims

Imported small cars are more dangerous than large models. This is confirmed by the record for insurance claims filed by persons injured in crashes.

Is the economy worth the risk? Forty-five percent of the general public think so. *Contrast:* Of corporate executives asked the above question, 83% said the small cars are worth the risk.

Other groups polled who also opted overwhelmingly for the riskier small cars: Investors, lenders, federal regulators, Congressional members and aides.

Source: *The Highway Loss Reduction Status Report.*

Safety Seats for Children

Ninety percent of the young children (under 5 years of age) killed in car accidents each year would have survived if they had been in safety seats. *Reason:* They can slip out of full-sized seat belts or be knocked out of an adult's arms by any impact.

For infants, experts recommend a molded plastic bucket that holds the baby securely with its back towards the front of the car to protect the child from flying glass. When they are too big for that model, graduate to a child seat. These face forward, have racer-type harnesses and are padded.

Two types: Tethered (a strap gets anchored to the car) and non-tethered. Both are safe when properly installed. Shop for one that's been crash-tested by the manufacturer. *Safest place to install:* The center of the back seat.

Winter Driving Safety

Reinforced tire chains on the rear wheels reduce braking distance on ice by 50% (compared to regular tires).

Conventional snow tires without studs actually are slightly inferior to regular tires for stopping on ice.

Radial tires offer no advantage over regular tires when driving on ice. On snow, they help only if they have special snow treads.

Small, light cars have less start-up traction on ice than standard-size cars. But they perform somewhat better when it comes to braking on ice.

Dental Surgery Self-Defense

Eat more of the right things prior to surgery to ensure faster healing. *Reason:* Nutrients, particularly vitamin C, calcium and fiber, aid in combating infections and help tissues heal. *Also:* Mouth pain following dental work tends to diminish the desire to eat, so excess nutrients need to be "stored up" prior to surgery.

Source: Winston Morris, DMD, orthodontist-endodontist and lecturer for the Academy of General Dentistry, quoted in *USA Today.*

Barbecue Self-Defense

Protect against possible cancer-causing chemicals created when foods are grilled by wrapping foods in foil...using a drip pan that does not rest directly on coals...partially pre-cooking foods that require longer cooking times...using low-fat or nonfat basting sauces...not charring or overcooking foods.

Source: Christine Murray, editor, *American Institute for Cancer Research Newsletter,* 1759 R St. NW, Washington, DC 20009.

Stroke Self-Defense

Warning signals of stroke: Sudden weakness or numbness of the face, or arm or leg on one side of the body...or sudden dimness or loss of vision, particularly in one eye...or loss of speech or trouble talking or understanding speech or sudden, severe headaches...or unexplained dizziness, unsteadiness or sudden falls. Call a doctor as soon as symptoms appear.

Source: Edward Cooper, MD, president, American Heart Association, 7272 Greenville Ave., Dallas 75231.

The Alcohol/Cancer Link

Recent media reports about alcohol's potential benefits to the cardiovascular system have obscured one inescapable fact—that drinking raises the risk of breast cancer and several other forms of cancer. This increased risk far outweighs the reduction in the risk of cardiovascular disease.

New finding: Alcohol's negative effects begin with as few as two drinks a week. Women who have three drinks a week, for example, are more than three times more likely to develop breast cancer than women who don't drink alcohol.

My advice: Forsake alcohol entirely. If you must drink, limit yourself to one drink a week. In addition, avoid lotions, shampoos, mouthwashes and other personal-care products that contain alcohol. Recent evidence suggests that even skin contact with alcohol raises your overall cancer risk.

Source: Charles B. Simone, MD, is the author of *Cancer & Nutrition,* Avery Publishing Group, 120 Old Broadway, Garden City Park, New York 11040.

Osteoporosis Self-Defense

Calcium and vitamin-D supplements significantly reduce the risk of hip fractures among elderly women. The supplements also lower the risk of other types of fractures—and are safe to take at any age.

Source: Study of more than 3,200 ambulatory women, aged 69 to 106, led by Marie Chapuy, PhD, Institut National de la Sante et de la Recherche Medicale, Lyons, France.

Sun Screen Basics...
How to Protect Yourself

The US is facing a growing epidemic of malignant melanoma, the deadliest form of skin cancer.

Why this dramatic increase? Believe it or not, a study published recently in the *Journal of the National Cancer Institute* suggested that sunscreen might be to blame.

This study found that while sunscreens did prevent sunburn, they offered no protection against skin cancer. By permitting humans to stay out in the sun longer without getting burned, the researchers reasoned, sunscreens might have the perverse effect of raising one's risk of skin cancer. It is an unsettling notion, to say the least.

To clear up the confusion...

•Do you continue to recommend sunscreen? Absolutely. Over the past 20 years, countless studies have shown sunscreen to be effective at preventing both sunburn and skin cancer. A single study—even a provocative study like this one—is not enough to overturn decades of careful research.

Of course, this study—which was performed on mice, not humans—should serve to remind all of us that sunscreen is not 100% effective. Wearing it does not give you complete freedom to bask in the sun all day.

Better: Avoid sun exposure as much as possible...and wear a hat, a long-sleeved shirt and long pants whenever possible. These strategies are especially important for people who burn easily.

•What type of sunscreen is best? Look for a sunscreen that offers protection against both forms of ultraviolet light—UVA and UVB. UVB poses a greater threat of sunburn and skin cancer than UVA. But UVA can still be harmful if you're in the sun for prolonged periods of time.

Your sunscreen should have a sun protection factor (SPF) of at least 15...and if you're headed for the beach or pool, it should also be water-resistant. With an SPF-15 sunscreen, you can remain burn-free for 15 times longer than you would with unprotected skin.

In regions where the sun's rays are particularly strong—near the equator, for instance—use sunblock in addition to sunscreen.

Rationale: Sunscreen creates a chemical barrier between sunlight and your skin. Some rays still get through. In contrast, sunblock uses zinc oxide, talc or another opaque material to create a physical barrier that keeps out all rays.

Problem: Sunblock is messy and unattractive. Consequently, it is not appropriate for covering large areas of skin. I recommend using it only on two high-risk spots—the nose and the rims of the ears.

Avoid suntan lotions containing mineral oil, cooking oil or cocoa butter. These products merely lubricate the skin. They do not block out harmful rays.

•How should I apply a sunscreen? Apply it liberally to all areas of skin that will be exposed to the sun. Do so at least 15 minutes before heading outdoors, so it has a chance to be absorbed.

Pay special attention to easily overlooked areas—your feet, earlobes, a bald spot, the backs of your hands, the tops of your ears, the nape of your neck and the tip of your nose.

Reapply at least once every three hours for as long as you're in the sun. Even with water-resistant sunscreen, it's prudent to reapply after going into the water or perspiring heavily.

•I stopped sunbathing years ago. Do I still need sunscreen? Yes. Your skin is at risk anytime you venture into sunlight—whether on the beach, in your backyard or on a brief walk. Sunscreens are not just for the beach!

In spring, fall and summer, applying sunscreen should become part of your daily routine. Rub it on just after your morning shower.

For office workers, a single morning application will suffice. If you work outdoors, reapply sunscreen frequently during the day. Even in winter, it's a good idea to wear sunscreen if you plan on being outdoors for more than a few minutes.

Source: Perry Robins, MD, associate professor of dermatology at New York University and president of the Skin Cancer Foundation, 245 Fifth Ave., Suite 2402, New York 10016. He is the author of *Sun Sense*, which can be ordered through the foundation. $14.95.

14

The Healthy Traveler

How to Get More Out of Your Travel

•Take along a small tape recorder when you travel. This is easier than jotting notes or trying to find the time to keep a diary.

•Interview people you meet along the way. Ask them all about their lives, occupations and backgrounds. This will preserve the facts and actual voices of interesting people you meet.

•Tape guided tours. Guides give out lots of information that is forgotten during the excitement of a tour but can be enjoyed later.

recommendations. Go to an out-of-town newsstand for Sunday papers and "city" magazines.

•Talk with people who live in, work in or often visit your destination. Ask for recommendations of things to see and do on your off-hours.

•Schedule your first week back. Set up lunches and meetings in advance, to avoid losing time when you return.

•Tell your secretary exactly when you plan to call in. That way, she will surely be at her desk, with the necessary messages and materials at hand. She can also deal more effectively with callers or employees who need to know when they'll have answers from you.

How to Enjoy Business Trips More

Before you go:
•Learn about local hotels, restaurants and theaters, so you won't be at the mercy of bad

What to Tell Children Before a Business Trip

Children resent business trips and private vacations taken by parents. They feel you would rather travel than be with them.

To minimize hurt feelings:

• Explain the nature of your trip. Speculate on the problems they would encounter if they accompanied you.

• Leave behind a list of activities for them to do while you are gone. Perhaps lend them the family camera for taking pictures of what they do.

• Stash little gifts they can open on different days during your absence.

• Give each child a bonus of spending money.

• For young children, tape yourself reading a few favorite stories. The children can play them when they feel lonely.

Source: Kay Kuzma, author of *Prime-Time Parenting*, Rawson Wade Publishers, New York.

Making a Business Trip Less Stressful

• Take only work you can realistically do. Report writing that requires copious files and conferences with colleagues is out.

• If you like to bring back presents or postcards for your children, purchase these at the airport as soon as you arrive.

• Make things easy on yourself. Most people will accommodate out-of-towners by driving to their hotels or holding meetings at airports. Trying to find your associate's suburban home by flashlight or dealing with downtown rush-hour traffic is frustrating.

• If you don't want to rent a car and can't justify hiring a car and driver, compromise. Cabbies will often agree to drop you off and pick you up throughout the day for just the fare plus a fat tip.

How to Make the Most Of Your Time in Unfamiliar Towns

• Be a part-time tourist. An hour or two between appointments gives you enough time to check out the local aquarium, museum, library, antique district, park or waterfront. Major tourist attractions are often located near enough to a city's business district for you to mix meetings with pleasure conveniently.

• Have a great meal. Do some advance research, and equip yourself with a list of the best restaurants in each city on your itinerary. Then, when your free time coincides with a mealtime, invest instead in a delightful hour of gourmet adventure.

• Look up old friends. Perhaps you can share that gourmet meal with a college friend you haven't seen in years, or surprise an uncle or cousin with a call or visit.

• Take pictures. If you're into photography, you know that a new environment frequently yields new visions and special scenes and subjects. Keep your eyes open and your camera ready.

• Go gift shopping. On autumn trips, carry a list of holiday gift ideas for friends and family. Use even a spare 15 minutes to pop in on the local boutiques and specialty shops. Charge and send your purchases, and when you get home they'll be there, all ready for your December giving.

• Bring busywork. When you're too tired to kill time on the move—or it's raining or the neighborhood is threatening or everything is closed—you should have something to do in your hotel room other than watch TV and order room service. Try catching up on a pile of periodicals or going through seed catalogues.

Source: Letty Cottin Pogrebin, author of *Family Politics*, McGraw-Hill, New York.

Making the Most of Travel Time

Some people claim that they can work on airplanes, trains or boats, but you may not be one of them. *If you, too, are unable to concentrate while traveling:*

• Go to sleep. Traveling is a natural soporific. Catching up on your sleep will give you an edge when you arrive.

• Find someone to talk with. Walk around and see if anyone who looks interesting has a copy of the *Official Airlines Guide* (which frequent travelers carry) or other travel guides. Start talking about travel, and you'll learn a few things.

• Clean out your wallet or briefcase. This is something you always mean to do but never get around to.

• Write letters. They don't take much concentration.

Killing Time Creatively At Airports

• Make phone calls. Check into your office, pick up a dozen phone messages and return eight calls before being driven from the public phone by the furious stares of others waiting to use it.

• Write letters or pay bills. Bring notepaper, envelopes, bills and your checkbook. Use your briefcase as a desk.

• Shop for the unexpected. Airport gift shops are notoriously glitzy. And at first glance, the merchandise in every gift shop looks alike except for the city etched into the beer mugs. But you may well find a Pierre Cardin belt at a bargain price in Cleveland, live lobsters in Boston and sourdough bread in San Francisco.

• Read indulgently. Buy a spy novel if you usually lean toward business books. Pick up a foreign magazine and test your French. Indulge in a crossword puzzle magazine or cartoon book. Read the local papers.

• Get a haircut or shoeshine. Men have the edge here. Although airport barber shops sometimes advertise "unisex," I've never seen a woman in any of them. Bootblacks will gladly shine a woman's shoes.

• Jog. With throngs of people running to catch their planes, no one will know you are just jogging along the concourses to kill time. Leave your coat and carry-on bag under someone's watchful eye while you run.

• People-watch. This is a surprisingly diverting pastime, especially for hyperactive types who don't often stop to observe the world around them.

• Eavesdrop. Airports are great places to tune in on some fascinating conversations—one as melodramatic as a soap opera dialogue, another as funny as a Mel Brooks sketch.

• Think. If you're uninspired by the above alternatives, you can simply stare out at the landing field, letting your mind go blank. Or you can give yourself a specific problem to mull over. Sometimes the brain does a better job of thinking at rest than it does under pressure.

Source: Letty Cottin Pogrebin, author of *Family Politics*, McGraw-Hill, New York.

Getting a Good Airplane Seat

Getting the seat you prefer on an airplane has become an increasing problem.

• If you're assigned to a seat you don't like, go back to the desk when all the prereserved seats are released (usually about 15 minutes before flight time). Prime seats for passengers who didn't show up are available then.

• If you discover on the plane that you don't like your seat, don't wait until the plane takes off to find a better one. Look around the plane, and the second before they close the door, head for the empty seat of your choice. Don't wait until the seat-belt sign goes on.

• Prereserve a single seat on a nonjumbo where the seats are three across and you'll increase the odds of getting an empty seat next to you.

• Ask for a window or aisle seat in a row where the window or aisle is already reserved by a single. The middle seat between two singles is least likely to fill up.

Know When Not to Fly

Avoid flying if you have had:
- A heart attack within four weeks of takeoff.
- Surgery within two weeks.
- A deep-diving session within 24 hours.

Don't fly at all if you have:
- Severe lung problems.
- Uncontrolled hypertension.
- Epilepsy not well controlled.
- Severe anemia.
- A pregnancy beyond 240 days or threatened by miscarriage.

Source: *Pocket Flight Guide/Frequent Flyer Package.*

Your Ears and Air Travel

- Avoid flying with a cold or other respiratory infection. A cold greatly increases the chances of your suffering discomfort, additional fluid buildup, severe pain or even rupture.
- Take decongestants. If you must fly with a cold, or if you regularly suffer discomfort or pain on descent, decongestants can give real relief. For maximum effect, time them to coincide with the descent (which begins half an hour to an hour before landing). Use both oral decongestants and a spray for best results. *Suggested timing:* Take quick-acting oral decongestants two to three hours before landing or slow-release tablets six to eight hours in advance. Use nasal spray one hour before landing. *Caution:* If you have hypertension or a heart condition, check with your cardiologist about taking decongestants.
- Don't smoke or drink. Smoking irritates the nasal area, and alcohol dilates the blood vessels, causing the tissues to swell.
- Try the Valsalva maneuver. While holding your nose closed, try to blow through it as though you were blowing your nose. This will blow air through the ears. Do this gently and repeatedly as the plane descends. *Warning:*

Don't use this method if you have a cold, as you'll be blowing infection back into the middle ear. Use the tried-and-true routines of yawning and swallowing instead. They can be quite effective if the problem is not too severe. Chew gum and suck candy. *Aim:* To activate the swallowing mechanism in order to open the eustachian tubes.

- If your ears are stuffed after landing, follow the same routine. Keep on with decongestants and gentle Valsalvas. Temporary hearing loss and stuffiness may persist for three to four weeks. If the symptoms are really annoying, a doctor can lance the drum to drain the fluid. If pain persists for more than a day, see a doctor.
- See a doctor before flying if you have a bad cold, especially if you have a history of ear pain when flying. If you absolutely must fly, the doctor can open the eardrum and insert a small ventilation tube that will allow the pressure to equalize. The tube should eject by itself in a few weeks…or you can go back to your doctor.

Source: Neville W. Carmical, MD, attending otolaryngologist, St.Luke's-Roosevelt Hospital Center, New York.

Coping with High Altitudes

One out of three travelers at altitudes of 7,000 feet above sea level (Vail, Colorado, for example) experiences some symptoms of altitude sickness. By 10,000 feet (Breckenridge, Colorado), everyone is affected. *Common complaints:* Headaches, nausea, weakness, lack of coordination and insomnia.

To minimize the effects:
- Take it easy the first two or three days. Get plenty of rest and don't schedule vigorous activities.
- Eat a little less than usual. Avoid hard-to-digest foods such as red meat and fats. Carbohydrates are good.
- Drink more liquids than usual. (Breathing harder in dry air causes you to lose water vapor.)

• Avoid alcohol, smoking and tranquilizers. Their effects are compounded at high altitudes.

Flyer's Health Secrets

• Taking your mind off the motion can help your body restore equilibrium without drugs. *How to do it:* Close your eyes, or concentrate on a spot in front of you, and hold your head as steady as possible. Then focus your attention on your breathing or on alternately tensing and relaxing your muscles. Continue to concentrate until the nausea has vanished.

• The low air pressure in an airplane's interior can aggravate some medical problems unless precautions are taken. Gas trapped in the colon can expand, causing severe discomfort or cramps. People with heart or lung diseases should check with their doctor in advance to discuss requesting supplemental oxygen.

• Don't fly with a serious sinus problem. If a sinus is blocked, the trapped air inside expands and can lead to serious infection. Improve drainage prior to ascent and descent with decongestants or nose drops.

• The arid atmosphere of pressurized cabins encourages evaporation from the skin's surface, drying the skin. *Remedies:* Avoid beverages that contain alcohol or caffeine (they both have a diuretic action). Drink plenty of water during the trip and afterward.

Getting to and from the airport:

• Arrive early to avoid stress.

• Schedule an appointment at the airport. If you're in a strange city, try to get your last appointment of the day to meet you there a few hours before your plane leaves. Why should you be the one to do all the running?

• Join an airport club. Most airlines have them. Choose the one that belongs to the principal carrier flying from your city. Then you can relax in comfort while you wait for your flight. *Benefits:* Special services to members, such as a separate check-in desk.

Source: *Healthwise* and Commission on Emergency Medical Services, American Medical Association, Chicago.

What You Should Put in Your Traveling Gear Box

A practical travel kit should include:

• Swiss army knife (complete with scissors, small screwdriver, nail file and clippers).

• Safety pins.

• Large Band-Aids.

• Styptic pencil.

• Small tin of aspirin.

• Two packets of antacid tablets.

• Dental floss.

• Two pairs of shoelaces.

• Small sewing kit.

• Sample bar of soap.

• Two packets of cold-water laundry detergent.

• Envelope of talc.

• Four feet of cord to tie your suitcase together if it has been damaged in transit.

Source: *Medical Economics.*

Health Hazards Of Flying

Although crashing is the most obvious and dramatic threat faced by airline passengers, the risk of going down is so small as to be almost negligible. *More realistic threats:*

• Dry/oxygen-deficient air. Air inside an airliner cabin contains only 2% to 20% of normal relative humidity—and about 25% less oxygen —than air on the ground. Cabin air is about as thin as the air atop a peak 6,000 to 8,000 feet high.

For most passengers, dry, oxygen-poor air presents no particular problems beyond dry skin and thirst. But for those afflicted with certain chronic cardiovascular and respiratory ailments—especially heart disease, asthma and bronchitis—cabin air can be life-threatening. *To avoid trouble:*

•Drink at least one glass of bottled water for each hour you're aloft.

•Avoid alcohol, coffee, tea, colas and other beverages with a diuretic effect.

•Sit with your legs elevated to prevent blood clots in your lower legs—a real possibility if flight-induced dehydration is severe enough to cause your blood to pool and thicken.

•If you begin to feel breathless or faint while flying, ask a flight attendant for oxygen. Federal law requires airliners to keep oxygen tanks on board for just such an emergency. If your breathing difficulty persists, ask if there's a doctor on board.

•Reduced air pressure. As an airliner climbs to its cruising altitude, air pressure inside the cabin falls. Most passengers recognize this phenomenon by the familiar "popping" effect that occurs when air that's inside the ears is squeezed out. Unfortunately, not all the effects of reduced air pressure are as benign.

Dangers:

•Severe intestinal gas, toothache and—far worse—sudden hemorrhaging of stomach ulcers, ovarian cysts or surgical incisions.

•Reduced air pressure can also cause the bends in scuba divers who fly too soon after diving. And, a boy wearing a plaster cast developed gangrene when air trapped beneath the cast expanded and cut off circulation in his arm.

To avoid trouble: Wear loose-fitting pants while flying, and avoid beans and other gas-producing foods for several hours before takeoff. If you suspect you have any loose fillings, have them repaired before your departure. If you've been diagnosed with ulcers or ovarian cysts, or if you've recently had surgery, consult a doctor before flying. Do not fly with a plaster cast. Never fly within 12 hours of scuba diving (24 hours if you've dived below 30 feet or have been diving for several days).

•Contaminated air. Long notorious for poor ventilation and stale air, airline cabins have gotten even stuffier in recent years.

In the interest of cost-cutting, cabin air on most flights is now being recirculated for 12 minutes at a time.

In the past, cabin air was recirculated for only three minutes at a time before fresh air was pumped in.

Result: Cabin air is depleted of oxygen and laden with disease-causing germs, carbon dioxide, carbon monoxide and other contaminants—especially on flights where smoking is permitted.

Stale, contaminated air can cause coughing, shortness of breath and headaches, as well as eye infections, colds, the flu and even lung cancer.

To avoid trouble: Use a saline nasal spray to keep your nostrils clean and moist (the greater the moisture in your nostrils, the more effective they are at filtering contaminants from the air). On smoking flights, sit as far as possible from smokers.

•Radiation. Modern airliners fly in the upper reaches of the atmosphere, where cosmic and solar radiation is particularly intense. The longer and more frequent your flights, the greater your exposure. In most cases, this extra exposure causes no apparent problems. Under certain conditions, however, it can cause birth defects, infertility and cancer.

To play it safe: Pregnant women should avoid flying during the first trimester, when rapidly dividing cells in the fetus are especially vulnerable to radiation.

Persons who spend more than 11 hours a week on an airplane should monitor their radiation exposure with a radiation film badge (dosimeter) worn at all times while aloft.

Frequent flyers should have regular checkups by a doctor who specializes in aviation medicine. For a list of flight doctors in your area, contact the Aerospace Medical Association at 703-739-2240 in Arlington, Virginia.

Source: Farrol S. Kahn, founder of the Aviation Health Institute in Oxford, England, and author of *Why Flying Endangers Your Health: Hidden Health Hazards of Air Travel*, Aurora Press, Box 573, Santa Fe, New Mexico 87504.

Secrets of a Much More Comfortable Flight

Airline travel may be fast, but it is not always comfortable. Too often, travelers, especially those seated in coach, are crammed into confining seats, fed factory-produced meals and confronted with delays or lost luggage. Flights can be made more bearable, however, if you know how to work the system.

Getting a good seat...

Most travelers don't want to sit in the middle seat of a row. But if you're late checking in for a crowded flight, you're almost certain of getting one. *Problem:* Airlines automatically assign aisle and window seats first, even if the two passengers in a row are traveling together.

You can improve your chances of getting an end seat by asking the agent at the check-in counter to search the passenger list for two travelers with the same last name in the same row. Request the middle seat in that row. Chances are the other two passengers are related and will want to sit together, leaving you either the window or aisle seat.

Storing luggage...

Finding room for your carry-on luggage is always challenging. It is best, however, not to wait until you arrive at your seat to store your bags. Instead, put them in the first overhead compartment after you pass through the first-class cabin.

These compartments will likely be empty, since they are for the last passengers that board. In addition, you won't have to carry your bags to your seat as you enter or to the front as you exit the plane.

Better baggage handling...

Bags that have first-class or priority tags attached are usually first to come off the plane into the baggage claim area. Even if you're traveling in coach, you can benefit from this quick service by getting one of these tags.

Sometimes the airlines will give you a first-class tag if you ask for it. If not, try to find an old one from any airline. You can even make one up in advance by having a brightly colored card stamped with the word "priority" and laminated at a local printer. This will attract the attention of the baggage handlers.

Getting an upgrade...

Just because you have enough frequent-flier miles to qualify for a better seat doesn't always mean you'll get one, especially if the flight is crowded.

In fact, you may actually stand a better chance of getting one if the flight is overbooked. In this situation, airlines commonly offer free tickets to passengers turning in their tickets. If you hear this announced, immediately notify the check-in personnel that you're still interested in upgrading.

Reason: A surprising number of first-class travelers give up their seats for free tickets, opening up space in the forward cabin.

A more comfortable flight...

Strong sunlight is a common problem that travelers face when flying during the day. It often forces you to travel with the shade down. To avoid the sunny side when traveling eastbound, request an A, B or C seat. When traveling westbound, request a seat on the other side of the cabin.

Source: Randy Petersen, who travels up to 400,000 miles a year and is editor of *InsideFlier*, a magazine for frequent fliers, 4715-C Town Center Dr., Colorado Springs 80916. 800-333-5937.

Travel and Your Health

Simple precautions before you leave home can keep health problems from spoiling your vacation.

Timetable: Start your planning at least six weeks ahead. Check with your doctor...or call the Centers for Disease Control at 404-639-1610 for information on health risks at your destination.

New: There are now travel medicine clinics where people can get advice on immunization, coping with jet lag and other travel/health concerns. To find one, check with local *teaching* hospitals. Beware of clinics that sign you up for an exhaustive battery of shots. Few shots are required for most travel.

Recommended: Make sure tetanus, diphtheria and polio boosters are up to date. *Also advisable:* The hepatitis-A gamma globulin shot.

Malaria…

Malaria in many regions is now resistant to chloroquine, the traditional malaria preventive.

Still effective: Mefloquine (*Brand name:* Lariam). Like chloroquine, this drug is taken orally once a week during the trip and for four weeks upon return. *Caution:* Mefloquine is dangerous to people taking high blood pressure medication such as beta-blockers.

Best preventive: Don't get bitten. *Also helpful:* Wear DEET-containing insect repellent…screen off your sleeping area and spray your bedroom before retiring…burn a mosquito coil. Repellents containing higher percentages of DEET don't give better protection—they just last longer than lower-strength DEET compounds.

Traveler's diarrhea…

Diarrhea is fairly simple to prevent and treat. *Prevention guidelines:*

•Watch what you drink. Carbonated beverages kill diarrhea-causing germs, so stick to carbonated beverages such as soda, beer or mineral water *with gas.* Don't drink tap water, or water served from jugs or re-capped bottles. If you must have ice in your drinks, don't drink the melted ice. Hot drinks made from boiled water are safe.

•Watch what you eat. *Safest:* Food that's freshly prepared and served steaming hot—hot enough to burn your tongue…fruit you peel yourself…most citrus fruit. *Avoid:* Salads and most other raw food…sauces left on the table …rewarmed food…hard-to-wash fruits…watermelon, which may have been injected with water during cultivation.

If you do suffer from diarrhea, you can usually clear up symptoms within a day by taking a quinolone-type antibiotic (such as Cipro), in combination with loperamide (*Brand name:* Imodium A-D).

Preventive measure: Chewing two Pepto-Bismol tablets four times a day gives up to 65% protection. Never follow this regimen for longer than three weeks. Don't use it at all if you have chronic gastrointestinal problems.

Important: Keep prescription drugs in their original containers when abroad. Failing to do so can lead to customs hassles. If you fall seriously ill while abroad, contact the nearest US Consulate or Embassy for a referral to a qualified English-speaking doctor.

Source: Charles Ericsson, MD, professor of medicine at the University of Texas Medical School in Houston and a member of the Scientific Advisory Committee for the International Society for Travel Medicine.

Dry Eyes Preventive

Helpful: Don't sit directly in the flow of air conditioning…cover eyes occasionally with a wet cloth or paper towel…remove contacts before a flight. Don't use over-the-counter eye drops to relieve airplane-induced dry eyes. Most contain vasoconstrictors, which shrink blood vessels—eliminating red eyes—but they don't add needed moisture.

Better: Wetting solutions used by contact lens wearers are effective—whether or not one wears contacts. "Artificial tears" are also good.

Source: Melvin Schrier, OD, an optometrist in private practice in New York City.

Advice for Allergic Travelers

Plan to go away on vacation during the height of allergy season…in your home town. *To minimize risk of pollen exposure:* Travel to a beach resort or go on an ocean cruise.

Also recommended: Limit your early-morning outdoor activities—pollen levels drop later in the day…keep hotel air conditioning on during the night to clean, cool and dry the air.

Source: Sidney Friedlaender, MD, clinical professor of medicine, University of Florida, Gainesville.

Doctors and Medical Facilities

Any cruise ship carrying more than 50 passengers is required to have a licensed physician on board. But the quality and level of facilities vary greatly. Check with your travel agent about the qualifications of the ship's doctor, especially if you have special medical needs.

Source: Douglas Ward, a founding member and president of International Cruise Passengers Association and author of *Berlitz Complete Guide to Cruising and Cruise Ships*. Berlitz Publishing Co. Inc.

Smart Overseas Travel Strategies

•Carry a medical ID card. It should be encased in plastic and should list your allergies, current medications, chronic illnesses, surgical history, next of kin, insurance information and your doctor's name and phone number. Make sure the card is filled out *legibly*—preferably in the local language.

Also: Wear a Medic Alert necklace or bracelet (available from the Medic Alert Foundation, 800-432-5378).

•Carry drugs in their original containers. Prescription labels can help local doctors identify medications in an emergency. And drugs in their original containers are unlikely to arouse suspicion at border crossings.

Source: John Connolly, EdD, author of *How to Find the Best Doctors, Hospitals and HMOs for You and Your Family*. Castle Connolly Medical Ltd.

To Minimize Jet Lag...

Upon boarding the plane, set your watch to the time of your destination and immediately assume its sleep/wake schedule. *Upon arrival:* Don't nap during the day—or, if absolutely necessary, take only a one-hour nap. Spend time outside the first few days after your arrival —sunlight helps reset your internal clock. Avoid consumption of caffeine, alcohol or sleep medications.

Source: James D. Frost, Jr., MD, professor of neurology, Baylor College of Medicine, Houston.

Easier Travel With Children

Many hotels have begun catering to families with infants and children. Many will allow up to two children to stay free in their parents' room.

Also: Rooms are childproofed and kits with toilet-lid locks, night lights and door alarms are often available to parents...changing tables have been installed in all (men's and women's) public rest rooms...diaper pails, strollers and cribs are usually available free of charge.

Many hotels also run on-site "camps" with adult-supervised, age-appropriate activities for children.

Note: Cost and availability vary by hotel.

Source: *Good Housekeeping*, 959 Eighth Ave., New York 10019.

Better, Healthier Eating On the Road

Use travel time as dieting time...drink lots of water and avoid alcohol...never use travel as an excuse to overeat...pay closer attention to what goes into your mouth...exercise regularly...don't try to eat exactly as you do at home —this will only lead to frustration and more overeating.

Source: *Healthy, Wealthy & Wise: A Step-by-Step Plan for Success Through Healthful Living* by fitness consultant Kris Edstrom, MS. Prentice-Hall.

Safer Hotel Stays

Select a hotel with interior corridors that provide limited access...close the door securely whenever you're in your room and use all locking devices provided...make sure sliding glass doors, windows and any connecting room doors are all locked...do not display your guest-room keys in public or leave them on restaurant tables, at the swimming pool or anywhere else they can easily be stolen.

Source: *Consumer Reports Travel Letter*, 101 Truman Ave., Yonkers, NY 10703.

Safety in Remote Areas

First-aid kit for remote areas should contain topical antibiotics and steroids...gauze dressings...athletic tape...saline eye irrigator...bandages...moleskin...sunblock...pain reliever... cold and diarrhea medicines...antacid...if necessary, water-purification equipment.

Source: *University of Texas Lifetime Health Letter*, 7000 Fannin, Houston 77030.

Dengue Fever Is Making a Comeback

Visitors to tropical areas of the world should use insect repellent, especially in the early morning and late afternoon. Hotel windows should be kept closed unless they are screened. Dengue fever was once nearly eliminated in the tropics of Latin and South America—but to date in 1995, more than 190,000 cases have been reported and epidemics are now occurring in many countries of the region. No vaccine or therapy is available.

Source: Duane J. Gubler, ScD, dengue specialist, Centers for Disease Control and Prevention, Atlanta.

Aging Parent and Travel Self-Defense

When aging parents travel, make sure their medical conditions are known. Give information to the tour guide, ship's doctor or other responsible person. Make sure their regular doctors know of the travel plans. Help them pack comfortable clothes—especially footwear for any walking they may be doing. During a trip, aging parents should maintain eating, drinking and sleep habits. It can be tempting to change those habits, but that can lead to health problems. *For cruises:* Choose a large ship if there are special medical problems. Larger ships usually have more complete medical facilities.

Source: *Aging Parents and You* by Eugenia Anderson-Ellis, expert on longevity as it affects business and family, Verona, VA. MasterMedia Limited.

Healthier Travel

•Pack a copy of the prescriptions for any drugs you take in case you lose your medicine.

•Carry prescription medications in a purse or carry-on bag, not in checked luggage, which could be lost or delayed.

•Take along a list of emergency telephone numbers, including those of the US embassy or consulate in every city you are visiting.

•Carry insect repellent if you will be outdoors, and adrenaline or antihistamine if you are allergic to stings.

Important: Buy travel insurance that covers medical needs and cancellation due to illness before you go abroad.

Source: Recommendations by the North Shore University Hospital's International Travel Medicine Service, Melville, NY.

15

Secrets of Longevity

Living Life to The Fullest... In the Later Years

Aging is so often thought of in our society as an entirely negative experience. So—we spoke with 40 people over the age of sixty about their experiences in aging.

We asked each person: What can you say in praise of age? Their answers were inspiring...

Maturity turns out to give us a chance to do many new things and to develop ourselves in new ways. Suggestions from the people we interviewed...

Develop a new avocation...

It's important to develop a vital, challenging interest that you can take up when you retire. This is especially important for people who, after years of work, have grown tired of their jobs. They look forward to retirement and then find themselves bored, with too much time on their hands, and become depressed or even ill.

If you develop an avocational interest that's an alternative to your work well in advance of retirement, you will be able to make the transition with much less stress and sense of loss.

Example: Radio and television broadcaster Art Linkletter has used his "retirement years" to start a new career as a writer, using his personal experiences of aging as the basis for his work. His most recent book, *Old Age is Not for Sissies,* which focuses on the joys and pains of late life, has become a national bestseller.

Retirement is a full-time job...

A regular job consumes 35 or 40 hours a week—more if you factor in commuting. But if you're retired, you're retired 24 hours a day, seven days a week. And you alone have the responsibility for how your day turns out. Structuring your own time is a skill that has to be learned. That's particularly so if you've spent your life in a corporation, where a lot of structure was provided. Some retired people can't find enough activities they enjoy to fill their time, while others, like former Time-

Warner executive Dick Munroe, find retirement to be busier than full-time work. "I love what I'm doing. I love not doing what I used to do", explains Munroe, "I'm just doing too many things and I should fix that!"

So find things you love to do and learn to say "no" to anything else.

Value your own experience…

Americans undervalue experience. We're so hooked on youth that we haven't yet recognized that inexperience isn't always a virtue, and knowing what you're doing isn't a handicap.

For people who stay open to change and growth throughout their lives, the mature years can prove to be unexpectedly rewarding.

Writer May Sarton told us she was glad to be old. She had solved a lot of problems that are very anguishing for young people, and she had come to terms with her own life in ways that made life much easier.

The late Norman Cousins spoke very specifically about being in the harvest years. He told us that he was using everything he had ever learned, everything he had ever done or known, and using it better than he ever had before. He could accomplish things with greater economy of effort than when he was younger.

The more you learn, the more you will ultimately be able to do. In a long life, you will have time to develop skills you don't have now but would like to. And when you have assembled them you will be able to use and truly enjoy them.

Become wise…

You don't necessarily grow wise as you grow old. Wisdom isn't a part of the biological process of aging. But you can work to develop it. Wisdom comes from wrestling with our experiences, making sense out of them…enjoying life's pleasures, letting go of its sorrows and mistakes and moving forward.

Many of the people that we interviewed found great security in the knowledge gained through aging of what their moral values were and what's valuable in life. Dancer and choreographer Bella Lewitsky told us: "As I've aged I've grown more confident in my own values and at the same time more tolerant of differences."

Take time to enjoy the simple things in life…

We have the idea as we come into the later years that if we do nothing, or very simple things, we're not using our time very well.

But even the very famous people that we interviewed found pleasure in simple things, like Peanuts creator Charles Schulz. "I'm great for doing nothing," he said. He still draws his comic strip several hours a day, but he also likes to just sit, to watch television and play with his dog. He likes the feeling of comfort that he receives from simple and quiet activities.

Writer Eve Merriam—who died only recently—talked about how she relished the change of seasons, particularly the coming of spring, finding what she called daily joy in the colors and fragrances of the trees and flowers.

Explore your inner life…

Young adulthood and middle age don't leave us much time to explore the heart and spirit deeply. As the outer life shrinks, there's room for a great deal of inner growth for most people. Although we continue to need the nourishment of other human beings of all ages in our lives, we also need quiet and solitude to explore the inner self.

Through this self-exploration, many of the people we interviewed developed a strong spiritual sense as they grew older—and found that to be one of the richest aspects of aging. This spirituality was often connected with a reverence for nature.

Clarinetist Rosario Mazzeo finds his spiritual connection in nature and takes long walks in the woods every day.

The challenge of physical changes…

There's general agreement that the worst thing about aging is the physical erosion that often accompanies the later years—the slowing up of the body.

The attitude that you take toward your physical aging is extremely important. Actor Hume Cronyn spoke about the lines on his face: "Let them get deeper—particularly the laugh lines!" *Important:* Deal with physical limitations and needs, to care for yourself. Then move past them and focus on the many satisfactions that are possible out there.

While the body is subject to deterioration, the person inside has a continued capacity for growth, whatever the body's age.

Understand the value of life…

The best way to get the most out of life is to come to terms with mortality. Actor Jason Robards told us that to him, life is like a hotel—everybody checks in and everybody checks out. Once he fully grasped this, he was able to truly savor each day.

It is in fact the sense of the preciousness of time that we acquire as we get older which should fill our later years with a new richness and intensity.

Songwriter and singer Burl Ives finds that contemplating death gives him a renewed sense of joy in life.

Forget the myths…

If we want a richer later life, we have to take responsibility for achieving it. We can't accept the myths that "old is over," and that only youth matters. We must learn to appreciate and give thanks for the many gifts that aging brings us.

Source: Phillip Berman and Connie Goldman, authors of *The Ageless Spirit: Reflections on Living Life to the Fullest in our Later Years,* Ballantine Books, 201 E. 50 St., New York l0022.

The Healthiest Places To Retire in the USA

Your lifestyle at any stage—including retirement—contributes more to your health than the place where you live. For that reason, the healthiest cities for retirees are those that support a low-risk lifestyle. *America's healthiest cities for retirement:*

•Eugene, Oregon. A university town that's rich in parks and offers myriad fitness activities. A temperate climate allows outdoor exercise year-round.

•Prescott, Arizona. With pure air filtered by deep pines, it offers endless fitness activities, a rich cultural life and adult education at two colleges.

•Sun Cities, Arizona. The best controlled-age community (no children allowed), these twin cities are immaculate and safe. Volunteer, cultural and educational opportunities abound. So do splendid recreational facilities.

•Kerrville, Texas. My home, it has pure air and water, lovely hills all around and fine facilities for exercising body and mind. Living costs are low.

•Mount Dora, Florida. A pretty, safe, livable town, it offers excellent biking, hiking, swimming and more. Nearby Orlando provides rich cultural programs.

•Durango, Colorado: Laid-back and surrounded by spectacular mountains, it has a strong fitness orientation. Its people are energetic, upbeat and well-educated.

•Boulder City, Nevada. This safe, casual town offers fitness activities such as hiking, swimming, tennis and canoeing. *For rich culture:* Las Vegas is nearby.

•Bradenton, Florida. Near glamorous Sarasota, with its rich cultural and educational life, lies more affordable Bradenton, offering outdoor walking, swimming, tennis and fitness classes, among other pursuits.

Source: Norman D. Ford, author of *The 50 Healthiest Places to Live and Retire in the United States,* Ballantine Books, 201 E. 50 St., New York 10022. Ford has been living the low-risk lifestyle for more than 30 years without a day of illness.

How to Change Your Biological Age

Gray hair, wrinkled skin, growing flabbiness, loss of vitality and reduced resistance to injury and disease…

To most Americans, these are harbingers of old age, unwelcome but inevitable milestones along a path that leads inexorably to the grave. In fact, recent research suggests something quite different—that the body's gradual decline stems not from the passing of years but from the combined effects of inactivity and poor nutrition. So no matter what your present health status or your chronological age—regular exercise and improved eating habits will lower your biological age.

Benefits: Reduced body fat...increased muscle mass...strength increases of 200% to 300%...increases in aerobic capacity by 20% or more...and reduced risk of heart disease, diabetes, osteoporosis and other age-related ailments.

Your goal should not be to become immortal, but to remain healthy and vigorous for as long as possible...and to compress the inevitable period of decline preceding death from several years into a few weeks or months.

To gauge your biological age: Forget how many birthdays you've marked...instead consider how you stack up in terms of the 10 key "biomarkers" identified by our lab...

•Muscle mass. As Americans move from adolescence into old age, we lose almost seven pounds of lean body mass each decade—a rate that accelerates after age 45.

Reduced muscle mass leads not only to reduced strength, but also to an increased risk of heart disease and diabetes, reduced aerobic capacity and a slower metabolism (which promotes gain of fat). All because of bad habits like driving instead of walking or riding a bike, taking elevators rather than stairs...and because we're all too willing to let younger friends and relatives do chores we should do ourselves.

Good news: Those who remain physically active lose little muscle tissue as they age. All it takes is 20 to 30 minutes of aerobic exercise two or three times weekly.

•Strength. Between the ages of 20 and 70, the average American loses about 30% of his muscle cells—including a large proportion of "fast-twitch" cells needed for sprinting and other high-exertion exercise.

Unchecked, this loss of muscle leads eventually to sarcopenia, the severe, debilitating weakness that makes independent living impossible.

Good news: While we cannot prevent loss of muscle cells, a weight-lifting regimen will compensate by boosting the size and strength of the cells that remain.

Myth: Weights are appropriate only for young people and bodybuilders. In fact, I've watched frail 90-year-olds use weights to boost their arm and leg strength by 200 to 300%—with just a few weeks of twice-weekly weight-lifting sessions.

Essential: Ten repetitions of 10 lifts with a weight that should leave your muscles completely fatigued. If not, add more weight.

•Metabolic rate. Because more energy is needed to maintain muscle than fat, the less muscle tissue in your body, the slower your metabolism—and the fewer calories you must consume to maintain ideal body weight. Beginning at age 20, the average person's metabolic rate drops about 2% per decade. Thus the average 70-year-old needs 500 fewer calories a day than the average 25-year-old.

Problem: Many middle-aged Americans continue eating as if they were 20. *Eventual result:* Obesity. To fight fat, eat fewer calories and get enough exercise to maintain your muscle mass.

•Body fat percentage. In most cases, advancing age brings not only muscle loss but fat gain. Even if our weight (as measured by a scale) changes little, the ratio of fat to lean in our bodies can rise markedly over the years.

The body of the average 25-year-old woman is 25% fat, for example, while the average 65-year-old woman is about 43% fat.

For men, the numbers rise from 18% fat at age 25 to 38% at 65.

Danger: Excessive fat leads to chronic disease and premature death.

Especially dangerous: Fat around the waist. It's far more unhealthy than fat on the buttocks or thighs.

To lose fat and gain muscle: Combine a low-fat diet with regular exercise.

•Aerobic capacity. To gauge fitness, doctors often measure the body's ability to process oxygen during exercise. The greater this aerobic capacity, the faster oxygen is pumped throughout the body—and the fitter the individual. Like other biomarkers, aerobic capacity often declines with age. Typically, by age 65 it is 30% to 40% below its level in young adulthood.

Good news: Regular, aerobic exercise—the kind that causes huffing and puffing—will raise your aerobic capacity no matter what your present age. The longer and harder your workouts, the greater the benefit.

•Blood-sugar tolerance. For most Americans, aging brings about a gradual decline in the body's ability to metabolize blood sugar (glucose). So common is this problem that by age

70, 20% of men and 30% of women are at increased risk of diabetes, a potential killer.

At special risk for problems: The overweight, the sedentary and those who eat a fatty diet.

Good news: A low-fat, high-fiber diet, combined with regular exercise, will cut your diabetes risk. Be sure to include both strength-building and aerobic exercise in your routine.

• Cholesterol ratio. As most of us already know, a high cholesterol level boosts your risk of heart disease. But total cholesterol isn't the only thing that counts.

Very important: The ratio of total cholesterol to HDL (good) cholesterol. For older people, the ideal ratio is 4.5 or lower. A person whose total cholesterol is 200 and whose HDL is 50, for example, has a ratio of 200/50, or 4.0.

To lower your ratio: Stop smoking, lose weight, reduce your intake of fatty, cholesterol-rich foods (especially animal products) and exercise regularly. Exercise is the only way to boost HDL levels.

• Blood pressure. In many parts of the world, advancing age brings little if any change in blood pressure. In the US, however, where older people tend to be both overweight and sedentary, blood pressure does rise with age, often spiralling far above the maximum "safe" level of 145/80.

To keep pressure in check: Stay slim, don't smoke, get regular exercise and limit your consumption of fat, salt and alcohol. If these steps fail, pressure-lowering drugs may be necessary.

• Bone density. As we age, our skeletons slowly become weaker and more brittle. While some mineral loss is inevitable, the severe and potentially deadly condition known as osteoporosis is not.

Prevention: Although consuming at least 800 milligrams of calcium a day will retard the loss of bone, that alone rarely does the trick. *Also needed:* Weight-bearing exercise, such as walking, running or cycling.

Not helpful: Swimming and other forms of exercise that do not subject the long bones to the stress of gravity.

• Body temperature regulation. Compared with young people, old people sweat less, get less thirsty and excrete more water in their urine. These seemingly minor changes—plus the loss of muscle tissue needed for efficient shivering—hinder the body's ability to regulate its internal temperature, raising our risk of dehydration in summer and hypothermia in winter.

Good news: Staying fit keeps the "thermoregulation" mechanism in tip-top shape. *Note:* In healthy, well-hydrated individuals, urine is almost clear. Bright yellow urine suggests dehydration.

Source: William J. Evans, PhD, chief of the human physiology lab at the Human Nutrition Research Center on Aging, a Boston-based facility operated jointly by the US Department of Agriculture and Tufts University. Dr. Evans is the coauthor of *Biomarkers: The 10 Keys for Prolonging Vitality,* Fireside Books, 1230 Avenue of the Americas, New York 10020.

Slow Down Aging and Enjoy Life Much More

There's no way yet to stop aging, but new research suggests that we can slow the process —perhaps even extend the maximum human-life span to 150 or 160 years. Not everyone would live to such a ripe old age, of course, but even the average life span might be lengthened by about 40 years—to 120. *Better:* We may be able to extend a vigorous, productive middle age into our seventies, eighties, even nineties.

While there's no conclusive proof in humans, animal research at UCLA laboratories has shown that a special high-nutrient/low-calorie diet prolongs life by as much as 50%. This diet should work for humans, too. *Reason:* The basic mechanisms of aging are essentially the same in most mammals. The special diet also retards the deterioration in coordination, learning and other mental functions that occurs with age.

Caution: The high/low diet is not recommended for people under 20, who need extra calories and nutrients for growth, or for pregnant women.

The high/low diet...

Goal: To consume all the essential nutrients in as few calories as possible. There's no limit on the number of calories you consume. This varies from person to person. But the high/low diet should lower your set point (the weight you normally gravitate to) by 10%–25%. This makes for maximum metabolic efficiency. After 4–6 years on the diet, your total body fat should be halved. *Exception:* Those already very thin won't lose as much weight on the diet—but their metabolic efficiency and health will still improve.

Plan: Consume about 1,500 high-nutrient calories a day. If you lose weight rapidly, increase the calories. If weight loss is slow, decrease the calories. The fewer calories you consume, the harder it is to get enough of each nutrient. *Crucial:* Choose foods judiciously.

• Avoid empty calories—sugar and alcohol, for instance, which have plenty of calories but almost no nutrients.

• Choose foods that, calorie for calorie, pack a big nutrient punch.

• Avoid fat. It has almost twice as many calories per gram as protein or carbohydrates but fewer nutrients. Only 8%–20% of calories should come from fat.

• Eat the best protein—fish, skinless poultry or a combination of legumes (beans, peas, soybeans) and grains. Protein needs vary, but 60–90 grams a day are usually sufficient.

• Choose healthful carbohydrates. Eat a lot of fresh vegetables and fruits, and complex carbohydrates (brown rice, potatoes, whole grains, etc.). They're packed with vitamins and minerals.

• Include fiber. It adds bulk to the diet with virtually no calories. *Recommended intake:* 40–60 grams a day, about half from cereals (bran, whole-grain breads) and half from fruits and vegetables. *Best sources:* Apples, pears, peaches, oranges, rolled oats, beans.

Combining foods in certain ways also yields more nutritive value. *Example:* There are eight essential amino acids. Most meats contain all eight, but other proteins, such as cereals, grains and vegetables, contain only some amino acids. However, combining two incomplete proteins —beans and rice, for example—can provide a complete protein. Although the principles are simple, finding an acceptable diet—balancing the calories and amounts of fat, protein and carbohydrate, along with the nutrition values of hundreds of foods—is an enormous job of calculation. If you have a personal computer, there is a program available to do these calculations for you.* If not, start out with a basic low-fat diet plan such as Weight Watchers, Pritikin or the one outlined in my book *The 120-Year Diet*.

Vitamin supplements…

Why not just eat a minimum of calories and get all your vitamins and minerals in a daily pill? Because we haven't yet identified all the substances necessary for human health. Vitamin pills contain only those substances we know about, not the ones we don't. *Also:* Many nutrients seem to be absorbed better from food than from supplements. However, to avoid possible borderline deficiencies, take a daily supplement that includes the recommended daily allowance (RDA) of most vitamins and minerals. *Important:* Check the label for date of manufacture. Vitamin E should be used within six months, others within 18 months.

The value of exercise…

There's no proof that exercise enables humans to live longer. In fact, some evidence suggests that exercise accelerates aging slightly. However, exercise more than makes up for that deficit by improving cardiovascular fitness and stabilizing blood sugar. *Bottom line:* Moderate exercise does much more good than harm. *Ideal:* Jogging 15–20 miles a week or the equivalent. More than this produces no additional cardiovascular benefits.

Avoiding disease…

In addition to extending life span, the high/low diet also helps stave off the major killer diseases—cancer, heart disease, diabetes, stroke, osteoporosis. This increases even further the chance of living to a healthy old age. *Prevention tips:*

• Heart disease. Cut intake of fat and cholesterol. Stick with unsaturated vegetable oils. Monounsaturated oil, such as olive oil, helps reduce blood cholesterol. *Also beneficial:* Omega fatty acids, found in fish, especially salmon, mackerel and herring.

• Hypertension and stroke. Consume less than 2 grams of sodium daily. Boost intake of magnesium and calcium, as deficiencies in these minerals can cause hypertension. *Recommendation:* 1 gram of magnesium and 1–1.5 grams of calcium daily, either in the diet or in a supplement.

*Dr. Walford's Interactive Diet Planner works on IBM computers with graphics capability. Available from the Longbrook Co., 1015 Gayley Ave., Suite 1215, Los Angeles 90024.

•Diabetes. Keep thin and physically fit. Get enough fiber, and make sure you consume the recommended daily allowance of chromium. *Good news:* The high/low diet has prevented diabetes in mice.

•Cancer. A low-fat, high-fiber diet helps prevent cancer. Eat a lot of fresh cruciferous vegetables (broccoli, cabbage, cauliflower, brussels sprouts, turnips). *Also helpful:* Vitamin C, 500–1,000 milligrams (mg) daily…bioflavonoids, 100–200 mg daily…vitamin E, 200 mg of alpha-tocopherol daily…beta-carotene, 25,000 International Units daily…and selenium, 100 micrograms daily.

Source: Roy L. Walford, MD, professor of pathology, University of California at Los Angeles School of Medicine, and a member of the National Academy of Sciences Committee on Aging. Dr. Walford has written numerous scientific books and articles, including *The 120-Year Diet*, Simon & Schuster.

Never Too Late To Quit Smoking

Those who quit smoking—even after age 60—have better lung function than those who continue to smoke.

Source: Millicent W. Higgins, MD, National Heart, Lung and Blood Institute, Bethesda, Maryland, and leader of a study of 5,200 men and women 65 years of age and older.

How We Can Slow Our Aging Processes

Today, people are living longer, but enjoying it less. Many of us fear old age as a period of declining powers and failing health. But if we learn to replace that fear by a positive attitude, an enhanced physical and spiritual awareness of our bodies and a sensible pattern of activity, we can expect to enjoy the blessings of a vigorous and healthy old age.

A century ago, less than one person in 10 reached the age of 65. Most of those who did live that long had been worn out by a lifetime of inadequate nutrition…widespread disease …backbreaking physical labor. Their remaining years were difficult not because they were old, but because their bodies were in a state of breakdown.

Today, relieved of those harsh external pressures, most of us will live well into our 60s and 70s…and the physical disease and mental breakdown we fear in old age is largely a result of internal stress we can learn to avoid.

People age differently…

Your well-being depends far less on your chronological age—how old you are according to the calendar—than on two other indicators…

•Biological age tells how old your body is in terms of critical life signs and cellular processes.

Every individual is affected differently by time …in fact, every cell and organ in your body ages on its own timetable.

Example: A middle-aged marathon runner may have leg muscles, heart and lungs of someone half his age, highly stressed knees and kidneys that are aging rapidly and eyesight and hearing declining on their own individual paths.

Most 20-year-olds look alike to a physiologist …but at 70, no two people have bodies that are remotely alike.

•Psychological age indicates how old you feel. Depending on what is happening in your life and your attitude to it, your psychological age can change dramatically within a very short period.

Examples: An old woman recalling her first love can suddenly look and sound as if she has just turned 18…a middle-aged man who loses his beloved wife can become a lonely old man within a few weeks.

Aging is reversible…

It is not news that psychological age can decrease. We all know the old proverb: "You are as old as you feel." And—now scientists have learned that biological aging can be reversed.

Example: Muscle mass is a key factor in the body's overall vitality…and it was believed until recently that it inevitably declined with increasing age. But Tufts University researchers discovered that isn't so. They put 12 men, aged 60–72, on a weight-training program. After three months, the men could lift heavier boxes than the 25-year-old workers in the lab…and milder weight-training programs proved equally successful for people over 95!

That's not all the good news for aging bodies. The Tufts team found that regular physical exercise also reverses nine other typical effects of biological age…

- Reduced strength.
- Lower metabolic rate.
- Excess body fat.
- Reduced aerobic capacity.
- Higher blood pressure.
- Lower blood-sugar tolerance.
- Higher cholesterol/HDL ratio.
- Reduced bone density.
- Poorer body temperature regulation.

To get optimum benefits from exercise, the type and amount have to be expertly tailored to your individual constitution. You don't have to be a fitness freak to gain from exercise…just 20 minutes of walking three times a week improves the cholesterol/HDL ratio. No expert advice is needed to benefit from another important route to longevity…a balanced lifestyle.

A study of 7,000 Southern Californians found that the longest-lived followed seven simple rules:

- Sleep seven to eight hours a night.
- Eat breakfast.
- Don't eat between meals.
- Don't be significantly over- or underweight.
- Engage in regular physical activity…sports …gardening…long walks.
- Drink moderately…not more than two alcoholic drinks a day.
- Don't smoke.

The study found that a 45-year-old man who followed these rules could expect to live another 33 years…but if he followed only three of them or less, he would probably die within 22 years.

Role of stress…

The human body reacts to stress by pumping adrenaline and other powerful hormones into the bloodstream. This "fight or flight" response provides energy for taking rapid action and is vital when you are actually faced with pressing external danger.

But it makes your metabolism work in the direction of breaking your body down instead of building it up.

If it occurs too often or continues too long it produces lasting harmful effects including muscle wasting…diabetes…fatigue…osteoporosis …hypertension…effects typical of aging.

That is why a major contribution to the aging process in modern life comes from situations that do not present real physical dangers but produce dangerous levels of stress.

Example: Our cities are full of unavoidable noise, a serious source of stress. Studies have shown increased levels of mental disorder in people who live under the flight paths near airports…elevated blood pressure in children who live near the Los Angeles airport…more violent behavior in noisy work environments.

Fortunately, we have discovered a number of measures that can reduce the aging effects of stress and other hazards of modern life.

To reduce stress and slow the aging process…

- Experience silence. Research has shown that people who meditate have higher levels of DHEA, a hormone that protects against stress and decreases with age. Spending 20 minutes twice a day in calm silence pays great benefits in detaching you from the mad bustle of the world and finding your true self.
- Avoid toxics…not only foods and drinks that stress your system, but relationships that produce anger and tension.
- Shed the need for approval by others…it's a sign of fear, another stress factor that promotes aging.
- Use relationships with others to learn your own self. People we love provide something we need…those we hate have something we need to get rid of.
- Change your inner dialogue. Change from "What's in it for me?" to "How can I help others?" Selfishness is bad for you. Psychologist Larry Scherwitz found that people who used the words "I," "me," "mine" most often in their conversations had the highest risk of heart disease.
- Be aware of your body's needs. The body only recognizes two signals…comfort and discomfort. You will be healthier if you learn to respond to its signals.

Example: Don't eat by the clock…eat when you're hungry…stop when you're full.

• Live in the moment. Much stress comes from living in the past or the future instead of the present.

Example: If you're angry at something that already happened…or fearful of something that may happen…your stress can't produce any useful result now. When those feelings occur, bring yourself back to the present.

• Become less judgmental. Don't get stressed by other people's decisions…your viewpoint may not be right for them.

• Stay in contact with nature. It will make you feel you want to stay around to enjoy it longer…and your body will respond.

Source: Deepak Chopra, MD, executive director for the Institute for Mind/Body Medicine, San Diego, California. He is the author of *Ageless Body, Timeless Mind: The Quantum Alternative to Growing Old*, Harmony Books, 201 E. 50 St., New York 10022.

Life Span and Diet, Life Span and Exercise

Although most Americans have come to accept 70 or 80 years as a normal life span, scientific literature suggests that humans are capable of living far longer. My continuing research has convinced me that a life span of 100 or even 120 years is not only possible, but normal—given the right lifestyle. *Sad:* Because we eat too much of the wrong foods and exercise too little, most of us succumb to heart disease, cancer or some other avoidable condition long before we should.

Good news: By combining a special diet with regular exercise and a positive mental outlook, it's possible to stretch your life span to the limit.

Reduce your consumption of protein…

Most of us were raised to believe that the more protein we ate, the better our health—and no wonder. Over the past several decades, the meat and poultry industries have spent countless millions of dollars on ads promoting eggs for breakfast, a hamburger for lunch and steak for dinner. Similarly, the dairy industries have encouraged consumption of milk, cheese and yogurt.

Yet just because we've been conditioned to believe that a diet rich in animal protein is healthful doesn't mean that it is. In fact, it isn't. Nutritionists have known for decades that while the body needs some protein for synthesizing enzymes and building tissues, too much protein wreaks havoc in the body. It weakens the heart, speeds deposition of fatty plaques in the arteries, saps the immune system and promotes the formation of free radicals, a class of compounds implicated in the aging process.

The evidence against protein…

In 1904, scientists at Yale University discovered that athletes who were fed for six months on half their usual allotment of protein not only thrived, but actually developed greater speed, strength and stamina.

Similar results were obtained in a 1937 study conducted at Cornell University.

And in a landmark study completed just two years ago, scientists from Cornell and the Beijing School of Preventive Medicine showed that eating a diet low in protein dramatically reduces the risk of diabetes, heart disease, breast cancer, colon cancer and several other life-threatening ailments.

The 6,500 Chinese participating in the study remained remarkably thin even though they consumed roughly 20% more calories than their American counterparts.

For some reason, however, word of these remarkable findings has failed to become known within our general population.

Americans continue to eat far too much protein. In fact, the average American adult eats 120 to 130 grams of protein a day. But with the exception of pregnant women, victims of severe burns and those severely debilitated by disease, we need only about 50 to 60 grams. That's approximately one gram for each three pounds of body weight.

Eating less protein will enable you to lose weight and lower your blood pressure and cholesterol levels while slowing the aging process and raising your immunity.

It will make you more energetic and will lower your risk of heart disease, diabetes, cancer and several other life-threatening diseases. It will help you to live a full and vigorous life for as long as possible.

To reduce your intake of protein, boost your consumption of fruits and vegetables while limiting your intake of meat and dairy products to a single serving per day. (One serving equals an egg, a three-ounce portion of meat or fish or a cup of yogurt.)

Don't worry—you can get all the protein you need from rice, beans, pasta, bread and cereals and other vegetable foods.

And contrary to popular belief, there is no need to eat vegetable sources of protein in any particular combination. You'll be fine as long as you get at least one serving each of grains, vegetables and legumes a day.

To make certain that there are no gaps in your nutrition, you should take a daily multivitamin and mineral supplement. *Recommended:* Beta carotene (6.6 milligrams), vitamin C (1,000 mg), vitamin E (400 mg) and selenium (200 micrograms).

Exercise every single day…

Exercise yields so many health benefits that it's hard to keep track of them all.

…It burns calories, allowing you to eat more without gaining weight.

…Lowers your risk of heart disease and cancer.

…Boosts your strength while reducing your cholesterol level.

…Keeps your bones strong and your joints flexible.

…And much, much more.

A recent study of 17,000 Harvard alumni found the death rate for men who burned more than 2,000 calories a week during exercise was 28% lower than for less active men.

While 30 to 60 minutes of exercise a day is best, you can get by on as little as 10 minutes. Any type of exercise will do—walking, jogging, bicycle riding, aerobics, etc.

Just make sure that you exercise every day and that your pulse climbs above 120 beats a minute, the threshold level at which the heart and lungs begin to reap significant benefits.

Important: Check with your physician before beginning any regular fitness program.

If you have trouble sticking to your exercise regimen, try committing yourself to it one week at a time.

At the end of the first week, commit yourself to a second week…and then to another and another.

By the time you've been exercising for a month, you'll be so accustomed to a daily workout that skipping even one day will cause fatigue, insomnia and irritability. Exercise will become part of your normal routine.

Keep a positive mental attitude…

Many people grow complacent as they grow older, choosing to sink into a comfortable chair and reminisce about the way things used to be rather than living in the present. *Problem:* Living in the past destroys your *raison d'être*—that's French for "reason for being." Once that's gone, it's easy for infirmity and illness to get a foot in the door.

Better way: No matter what your age or your present health status, try to live for today. Be hopeful. You might not be as energetic as you were at one time in your life, and there may be days when you feel less than chipper, but strive to remain open to new challenges, and set new goals. These goals can be short-term, such as losing five pounds (within a safe period of time), or long-term, like starting a new business or even running a marathon. Just set them, and then try your best to accomplish them.

When setbacks occur—and they inevitably will—try to view them not as impassable roadblocks or as personal failures, but as opportunities for new achievement and growth.

Your optimism will help ward off depression and reduce psychological stress.

And the less stress you experience, the lower your blood pressure, the slower your pulse and the stronger your immune system…which ultimately means the longer your life.

Source: Art Mollen, DO (doctor of osteopathy), founder of the Southwest Health Institute in Phoenix, Arizona. Dr. Mollen writes "The Art of Feeling Good," a nationally syndicated newspaper column, and is the author of *Dr. Mollen's Anti-Aging Diet*, Dutton, 375 Hudson St., New York 10014.

The Secrets of Staying Vital and Fully Involved Forever And Ever and Ever

In her book, *The Fountain of Age,* Betty Friedan confronts and challenges society's negative assumptions about growing older. Her view of aging as a time of adventure, self-expression and possibility promises to change the way men and women approach their later years.

Friedan explains what she discovered in her meetings with vital older Americans and her research into the science of aging...

What is society's current image of aging? In a certain sense, we're in such enormous denial of aging that we don't have an image of it.

It's difficult to find any images of older people in the media—certainly few that portray aging as a new, valuable period of human life. All the people we see depicted as doing anything important, worthwhile or enjoyable are young. When we do think about the subject of aging, it's as a dreaded pathology of deterioration and decline—sickness, senility, incontinence, nursing homes. But these ideas distort the new reality of growing older.

What is that new reality? The fact is that only 5% of Americans over age 65 are in nursing homes at any one time. Only 5% of Americans over age 65 have Alzheimer's disease or any other kind of senility. Life expectancy today is nearly age 80 for women and over age 72 for men...up from about age 45 for both sexes at the turn of the century. We're looking at a whole new additional half of life. It's open not just to a few exceptional people but to virtually all of us.

Yet there are no road maps or role models for us to follow during this period. We're only beginning to study the opportunities that emerge in our later years—that weren't even visible in our youth.

What are some of the unique opportunities and strengths that come with age? I interviewed many women and men who were having no problems moving into their 60s, 70s and 80s. They remained vital and continued to grow—and they weren't as hard to find as I had thought they would be.

Their experiences confirmed what much recent research has suggested—that if you can break free of the obsession with youth that is so pervasive in our culture, you become more and more authentically yourself...more distinctive in your style and less concerned with what other people think.

People are surprised by the changes in themselves. They're not driven any more by the inhibitions and conflicts that tore them apart in their youth. There's enormous liberation in that.

There's also a kind of crossover that occurs in sex roles. Men and women become much more comfortable with characteristics that they used to associate with the opposite sex.

I know men in their 60s and 70s who have discovered the delight of fixing up the interior of a house, picking out every item, bringing a true artistic sense to a task they might previously have left to their wives.

Women become much more comfortable with the aggressive side of themselves... though I think that shift is less dramatic than it used to be, since younger women are now moving to express that side as well.

Many people think of getting older as a time when sexuality declines. Does the nature of intimacy change as we age? Thank goodness, love can be different at different stages in life. Years ago, the Kinsey studies revealed that for men, sexual potency peaks at around age 17. Adult men who hold themselves to that teenage sexual standard will find that all of intimate life becomes fraught with anxiety.

I believe that intimacy can evolve and develop with age. Many people continue to enjoy sex well into their later years—but they also recognize that love can express itself in many ways. It is not true that you have to love the way you loved at age 17—or not love at all.

When men and women talked to me about their sexual relationships, they indicated that they had begun to discover a second language of love that's not measured in terms of the sexual performance of youth.

One man in his 70s, who was living with a woman, told me that he was technically impotent because of the medication he was taking after a heart attack. But he added, "I have never had such a complete and wonderful sexual experience. My whole body has taken the place of my penis. I've stopped worrying about my own performance, and I'm able to be with my lover completely in a way I never could before."

This kind of wholeness of mind, body and soul might sound like an impossible ideal of love—but in a simple sense, it is achievable when people are no longer driven by the standards of youthful sexuality.

Given that at least some physical decline is probably inevitable, how can people stay vital and involved as they get older—and reap the full potential of these years? Not everyone I interviewed was out jogging a 12-minute mile. I spoke to people who were recovering from strokes, dealing with serious arthritis or who had had bypass surgery, knee operations, cataract surgery—and yet who seemed to be the essence of vital age, embodying the strengths we've been talking about.

Yes, this or that piece of the body might show some debility. But as long as you continue to grow and develop, whatever it is that makes you human—your spirit, your whole—comes to dominate. There's a mystical quality to this transformation that is very powerful—and that is something you can draw upon.

On a more practical level, I don't have any how-to's…but massive research has shown that, in addition to not smoking, three major elements contribute to a long and vital life:

• Purposes and projects. Unfortunately, older people are often forced out of jobs that they're not ready to leave…or they choose to retire and find themselves frustrated and listless without the structure and challenge their jobs provided. Purposes and projects are important at any age but especially during postretirement years, and I have met people who were very creative in finding them.

I ran into a doctor who had always loved classical music. When he retired from medicine, he took a songwriting workshop—and now he's writing popular songs and loving it.

A woman in Atlanta told me about her father who retired from the post office in his 60s,

then went into a year-long depression. He began volunteering with so-called senior citizens. Developing new interests motivated him to go back to school. He got a college degree in his late 60s and became a counselor, working with older people and helping them to get beyond depressions like the one he'd experienced himself.

• Bonds. Part of vitality is feeling that you're part of the community…having intimate ties beyond your own family…regularly going out of the house to meet others.

For both these elements to be part of your life, several other characteristics are necessary.

The first is the ability to respond to change—in both yourself and the community around you. You have to be flexible enough to create new purposes and projects if you leave a job or are forced out of one.

You need to be able to nurture new bonds if your grown children move away or your spouse dies.

These tasks require the willingness to risk—even if you have avoided risk before, whether because everything was already laid out for you or because you were afraid of being rejected. They also require you to control your own life by making your own choices.

These challenges may feel uncomfortable, but they force you to use yourself to your fullest human capacity…encouraging growth and vitality.

• Meaning, I believe, is the other essential characteristic of an involved life—a sense of working toward something beyond yourself…of being part of the continuum of life.

Starting and working with the women's movement and participating in its continuing evolution has helped to provide that meaning for me.

But you don't have to have found a social movement to have meaning in your life. Being involved with the lives of my children and grandchildren has been profoundly meaningful to me as well.

I know an older couple who planted a tree in their community that won't bloom until after they've died.

Contributions that people make to their families and their communities—contributions that will live long after they're gone—are among the most powerful sources of meaning.

What kinds of living arrangements would help older Americans retain their vitality through the years? Though many people build good lives for themselves in retirement communities, even the most luxurious of these are really adult playpens, walled off from the rest of the world.

I don't think this country needs more retirement communities or nursing homes. What we need are more measures that enable people to live in the larger community—whether they stay in their own homes or in some kind of shared facilities.

I think it would be healthy for us all to have more intergenerational housing available. Such arrangements could provide the support systems that allow older people to participate in community life as long as possible, even in the face of physical deficiencies. They would also provide younger people the opportunity to benefit from the many, many strengths of older generations.

Do you think such changes are likely to happen in the near future? I think it will all happen sooner than anyone could predict. I sense it from the response to my book—not only 60- and 70-year-old readers, but 30-year-old readers are seizing the book with relief and telling me they can now look forward to the future.

Once marketers and the mass media establishment discover that the 39-to-70-plus market is just as productive and profitable as the 18-to-39 segment—if not more so—we'll be seeing new images, products and innovations faster than we can imagine.

Source: Betty Friedan, founder of the National Organization for Women, the National Women's Political Caucus and the National Abortion Rights Action League. She teaches at the University of Southern California and New York University and is author of several books including *The Feminine Mystique* (1963) and, most recently, *The Fountain of Age,* Simon & Schuster, 1230 Avenue of the Americas, New York 10020.

Aging Isn't All Bad

Intelligence doesn't necessarily decline with age and neither does an individual's learning

ability. Crystallized intelligence—the ability to make judgments and solve problems by using one's accumulated information—actually increases over the years. Memory loss due to age is usually confined to unimportant matters, such as phone numbers. The key factor is mental alertness. People who stay socially and mentally active suffer no decline in mental powers.

Source: John Horn, psychologist, University of Denver, University Park, Denver.

Happiness Doesn't End at 55

In our youth-oriented culture, the idea that older people are less satisfied with life is generally accepted. This is not true. Older people tend to expect less, and, therefore, they usually adjust more easily to changes. They are more inclined to look on the bright side of situations.

Source: Results of a survey of 9,000 workers of all ages made by Anna Herzog and colleagues for the University of Michigan.

Ages of Greatest Happiness

The greatest happiness usually comes not in youth, but in old age. Men generally are happiest during their middle sixties, women, during their seventies. *Unhappiest time:* Early fifties for men, late forties for women.

Source: *Pathfinders* by Gail Sheehy, William Morrow & Co., New York.

Best Resisters of Age

Our personalities needn't grow old. Although the machine we call our body changes, even breaks down, the thing inside that says "I" can remain quite constant. *Who resists age the best:* Creative people.

Source: Observations of British poet Stephen Spender.

Early Retirement Controversy

•Retirement is not responsible for a decline in health, contrary to the prevailing belief. The Veterans Administration recently examined 200 retired men aged 55–70, along with 409 men of comparable age who had continued to work. *Result:* The retired men were no more likely to suffer from health problems than were the working men.

Source: Report in the *American Journal of Public Health,* New York.

•Early retirement could shorten your life. A survey showed that men who retired at 62 died younger than those who worked until 65. At age 74, the survival rate for the later retirees was 13% higher. *Trap:* Boredom often leads to overeating, oversleeping and inactivity, which, in turn, increase vulnerability to heart attack.

Source: A government study of 64,000 people born between 1900 and 1910, reported in *American Health,* New York.

Sex and Aging

Contrary to general belief, sex remains a vital part of most people's lives into their seventies and even beyond. A survey of 4,246 men and women aged 50–93 found that:

•More than 75% of married couples in their sixties have intercourse. *Average frequency:* Once a week.

•More than three-quarters of single men (widowed, divorced or never married) remain sexually active in their seventies. So do half the single women that age.

•Six out of 10 married couples in their seventies still have regular intercourse. *Average frequency:* Three times a month.

•Common ailments (arthritis, diabetes, heart disease) cause little decline in sexual activity.

Source: *Love, Sex and Aging: A Consumers' Union Report* by Edward M. Brecher and the editors of Consumer Reports Books, Little, Brown and Co., Boston.

Aging and the Mind

Forgetful older people may be the victims of a self-fulfilling prophecy. In fact, recent research suggests that people's ability to make complex judgments and solve problems increases well into their eighties, assuming they stay healthy.

What older people lose: Abstract reasoning abilities (used in situations such as playing chess). But even here the decline is generally slight and slow.

Who loses the least: People who are socially involved, mentally active and flexible in dealing with new experiences. *Key:* You'll stay sharper if you reject the stereotype of a helpless old age.

Source: Research by John Horn, psychologist, University of Denver, reported in *The New York Times.*

Help for Fading Memory

Short-term memory tends to fade as you age. But you can stay sharper longer by avoiding vitamin deficiencies (particularly of B_{12})…limiting yourself to no more than two alcoholic drinks a day…keeping your blood pressure down…staying mentally active through reading, writing, crossword puzzles, etc.

Source: *The Washingtonian,* Washington, D.C.

•Walking helps to keep your mind young, according to a recent study of 200 elderly people. After a four-month program, the subjects all showed improvement in reaction time, short-term memory and reasoning power.

Source: Study by the Veterans Administration.

Senility's Earliest Signs

Poor memory and decreased concentration. These may be related to poor nutrition. It was observed that individuals without good diets and adequate vitamin intake were the first to suffer these mental insufficiencies.

Source: *Journal of the American Medical Association,* Chicago, IL.

Understanding Aging

Contrary to popular myth, the psychological problems caused by the stress of the aging process can be treated successfully. With properly supervised medication and psychological intervention, many disorders in thinking and behavior to which older people are subject can be minimized and, fequently, reversed.

Stress factors that contribute to problems of aging: In addition to the normal declines in intellectual function and memory that are to be expected, elderly people also must cope with the increased likelihood of physical illness, loss of family and friends and often a general loss of esteem in the community. These factors produce tremendous stress of the kind that frequently leads to mental confusion and depression. Organic Mental Syndrome (OMS) is a state in which the elderly person becomes disoriented and suffers intellectual impairment of a fairly constant kind. The important thing is to recognize that some kinds of OMS are reversible. It should be determined at the outset which sort the elderly person has.

A confused state of long duration is not necessarily irreversible. There are many long-standing conditions that can cause such confusion. The reversal or amelioration of these conditions will, most of the time, lead to reversal of the elderly person's symptoms. *Most common causes of reversible OMS:*

•Medication. This can cause problems because of the drug itself or because the person has taken an overdose, as elderly people frequently do. Just about any kind of medication can cause confusion of this sort. Elderly people are extremely susceptible to drugs. *Reasons:* The liver and the kidneys, which excrete drugs, don't work as efficiently in older people as in younger ones. Drugs remain in their bodies longer. Fat, which stores drugs, is present in a higher ratio in the bodies of older people. Cardiac function is not as good in an older person, so not enough blood gets to the brain. *Result:* Drugs build up unpredictably in the body and cause confusion. It is vital to carefully supervise any medication older people take.

•An undetected illness. This includes heart conditions, abdominal problems, cancer and diabetes. Undetected diabetes is a particularly common cause of confusion in persons of any age, including children. Even a minor infection, such as an upper respiratory infection that would make a younger person merely sick, can cause OMS in an old person. *Other causes:* Thyroid abnormality, alcoholism, nutritional deficiencies and anemia.

•Disorientation. The simple fact of being put in a hospital for any ailment can lead to a state of confusion in an older person.

Common effects of OMS: Older people very often become paranoid as a result of their confusion. It's very hard for older people to admit to themselves that they've misplaced an item, or that they don't know what's going on, or that they've forgotten something. As a result, they make up stories. "The building superintendent stole my watch." "My daughter stole my dress." Paranoid states of this kind are eminently treatable. In fact, this is the easiest OMS condition to reverse. It responds very quickly and very well to low doses of a major tranquilizer. The side effects are very few, but careful supervision of older people taking this drug is still important. Buildup in the system can lead to oversedation.

Depression is a very common cause of confusion in the elderly. It can be treated with a high degree of success by an antidepression medication such as Elavil. *Possible complications of antidepressant drugs:* They can be dangerous to old people with cardiac problems. A good many old people are easily oversedated by them. They also sometimes cause orthostatic hypertension, a condition in which the blood pressure doesn't rise quickly enough when a person moves from a sitting to a standing position. This can result in fainting or falling. *Other possible side effects:* Constipation, urinary retention, dryness of the mouth and glaucoma.

What to do when an older person shows symptoms of OMS:

•Avoid arguments and head-on confrontations with them. Older people who insist that someone is stealing from them will continue to protect their stories. It's useless to tell them it's not true or to imply that their confusion is caused by mental deterioration. It is far better to

303

be understanding and to begin establishing more structure in the older person's life. Check up on the elderly on a regular basis, or arrange homemaker visits.

• Don't assume that they can continue to take care of themselves. Older people who show signs of confusion should not, for example, be permitted to ride a bus alone. And don't fall into the error of refusing to acknowledge that the older person has become confused or is showing signs of disordered behavior at home. Very often, not only the older people deny they have a problem—their children or other relatives deny it as well.

• Arrange for a thorough physical examination. If the symptoms are especially severe, that should include a neurological workup with a brain scan. But don't stop with a physical or allow a general practitioner or anyone else to decide there's "no more to do" for the older person. The next step should be a geriatric center, which specializes in medical and psychological problems of the elderly. *Aim:* To determine whether the OMS is reversible. A neurological exam and psychological testing can usually determine that very quickly.

Where to go for help:

• Hospitals. Most of them have geriatric centers. Any hospital should be able to refer you to a geriatric internist and psychiatrist.

• Social agencies for the elderly. Virtually all have resources that can help in arranging treatment by geriatric specialists. They can also help arrange for home care or visiting nurses and provide information about what benefits are available from Medicaid and Medicare. They can give information about the many benefits available in areas such as housing. Many benefits are available for elderly people, despite the recent government cuts.

• Day hospitals. These are places where elderly people can spend the day in activities that help increase reality-orientation or in other supervised recreation. Day hospitals can enormously ease the burden of caring for a confused elderly person.

• Senior citizens centers. These are important resources, like the day hospitals, which can provide the day-to-day structure that elderly people need in their lives. It's important that the elderly person who shows signs of confusion not be allowed to sit home staring at the four walls all day. (This is also true for elderly people who are not confused.) Senior citizens centers are equipped to handle confusion if it is not too severe.

Source: Michael Levy, MD, a psychiatrist in private practice, New York.

Exercise Helps The Elderly

Exercise keeps the joints from becoming stiff and immobile and may even strengthen the bones themselves. *Reason:* The pull of muscles on bones often stimulates the bones to acquire calcium. *Best exercises:* Flexing and stretching. Gently bend, extend or rotate the neck, shoulders, elbows, back, hips, knees and ankles. *Best aerobic exercise:* Walking. *Also beneficial:* Swimming, dancing, riding and using an exercise bicycle.

Source: Consumer Info Center, Pueblo, Colorado.

Sugar Alert

Sugar is also tougher on your body as you grow older. Healthy people, ages 22–30, have twice the insulin-binding abilities of people ages 40–59. *Result:* Older people become more glucose-intolerant.

Source: *Diabetes*, New York.

Aging Parents

Before moving aging parents in with you, consider…who will bear the brunt of the extra work? Is that person willing? Are there any old family feuds that could flare up? On the other hand, grandparents are often revitalized by their grandchildren. And the children enjoy contact with an older person as confidant and guide rather than authority figure. If you can't take your parents in, remember that regular, supportive contact is more important than money, whether they live independently or in a nursing home.

Source: Stanley Cath, MD, Family Advisory and Treatment Center, Belmont, MA, cited in *Levinson Letter*, Cambridge, MA.

Help in Caring for An Elderly Parent In Another City

As our population becomes older and more mobile, a growing number of middle-aged people are trying to care for elderly parents or relatives who live a considerable distance away. Even if the relative is nearby, the busy "child" simply may not have the time or skills to devote to caretaking. Government services are little or no help, since they're focused mainly on the indigent, not on the older person who has been prudent enough to plan ahead. People who have any kind of means generally prefer to pay for what they need.

A number of private services have gone into business in response to this need. Usually run by social workers, they find and coordinate services for the elderly who want to remain at home but are no longer able to care totally for themselves.

How they work...

Agencies provide what they call "case management." *This includes the following:*

•Assessing the individual situation, either in the home or at their office. The assessment determines what is needed. This can include anything from helping balance a checkbook once a month to supervision of 24-hour-a-day nursing care.

•Finding the right staff to do what is needed. As professionals in the field, these agencies know where to locate reliable housekeepers, homemakers, cooks, nurses, physical therapists, companions and medical assistants. They interview and check references on whoever is hired. Even out-of-the-ordinary needs can be filled.

•Supervising whatever arrangement is made. This is one of the most valuable services provided. You can hire help on your own to care for a parent, but there is no guarantee that the person you hire will fulfill his or her responsibilities.

Good supervision should consist of:
•Managing money.
•Submitting bills to lawyers and families.
•Checking on whether the client is getting regular exercise and recreation.
•Checking medication.
•Determining the need for psychological or other consultation.
•Making sure medical appointments are kept.
•Assessing menus, taking into account good nutrition and individual taste and eating habits.
•Handling anything else that comes up.

The case manager should do basically what you would do if you could. She also should take a personal interest in your parent, treating him or her like a human being and taking individual needs, feelings and preferences into account.

Example: One of our clients loved classical music but was too ill to go to concerts any longer. We made sure that recordings of his favorite music were played for him regularly.

Costs...

Private case management isn't cheap, especially considering that the cost is in addition to homemaking, nursing or whatever else is needed. Agencies generally charge about $50 an hour. An initial assessment runs $100–$350. If a medical doctor accompanies the social worker to the home, for instance, the bill will be in the higher range. Monthly case management can run from $500 to $1,000 for supervision of a round-the-clock situation. Some agencies bill on a flat-fee basis rather than hourly. If less service is needed the bill will be lower.

When calculating costs, take into account fees of approximately $6–$18 an hour for homemaking or nursing, depending on the level of care needed, plus case management.

Evaluating agencies...

What to ask:
•Will the agency do an assessment in the home? (Some do only a phone or office interview with you.) A home assessment is important, to see how the elderly person relates to the environment and to determine if any struc-

tural changes can be made to improve safety or comfort.

•What is your gut feeling about the case manager? Experience and a caring attitude can be more important than fancy credentials.

•Will the agency be on call 24 hours a day? Will it give you a home phone for after-hours emergencies?

•Does the agency have access to and familiarity with the latest medical home-care equipment, such as heart monitoring?

•Will the case manager visit your parent's home at least once a week?

•Can the agency have a private ambulance summoned if necessary, or is it dependent on public services?

•Will the agency give you and your family regular reports and tell you about anything else that might relieve your anxiety? Will it give you advice on how to deal with your sick relative?

•Is there an M.D. on its staff who can consult with the family physician? Does it have access to psychiatric consultants and other medical consultants?

•Will the agency tell you when it thinks the time has come for nursing-home care? At a certain point, your parent's home can become more of a jail than a home.

How to find a good agency...

This is the hard part. A recent Brown University study counted 22 such private agencies in seven states. These don't even begin to fill the need. Indications are, however, that new services will be springing up in response to the burgeoning demand.

Our agency will help you find a social worker or agency in any area of the country to assess an elderly parent's condition and arrange for necessary services. There is also a national consultation service in Maryland that makes such referrals.*

Other sources:

•The local Congressional office in your parent's district is a good place to start and should give you a few leads.

•Elder law lawyers offer a new specialty for protecting the assets of the elderly. Ask your own lawyer for a referral, or try a few trust and

*Aging Network Services, Suite 821, 7315 Wisconsin Ave. West, Bethesda, MD 20814.

estate lawyers. Elder law lawyers are trust and estate specialists.

•The local university may have a gerontology program, which gives a new master's degree in the care of the elderly. You might find an individual or agency through such a program.

Source: Gerontologist Gloria A. Scherma and psychiatrist Kenneth L. Caccavale, MD, directors of Multi-Comprehensive Consulting Service, Inc., a private agency providing case management for the elderly, located in New York.

How to Find a Good Nursing Home

Most families postpone as long as possible the decision to use a nursing home. Once the decision is reached, the process of selecting a good facility is so painful that often they move too fast. *Good advice:* Give your parent time to get used to the idea. Meanwhile, investigate every possible choice thoroughly.

How to begin: Get lists of not-for-profit, community-based homes from your church, fraternal order or state agency on aging.

Costs: If your parent's resources are small, Medicaid may provide financial support for nursing home care. Homes offering complete care in metropolitan areas usually charge $50–$80 per day (depending on the amount of care required). Some require a large advance gift or admission fee. (Health insurance sometimes covers nursing homes.) Patients paying their own way may be eligible for Medicaid assistance after their savings run out. Check the rules in your state.

Evaluating a nursing home...

1. Accreditation, license and certification for Medicare and Medicaid should be current and in force.

2. Best to arrive without an appointment. Look at everything. The building and room should be clean, attractive, safe and meet all fire codes. Residents should not be crowded (ask about private rooms; sometimes they're available at a reasonable extra cost). Visit dining rooms at mealtime. Check kitchen, too. Visit ac-

tivity rooms when in session. Talk to residents to find out how they feel about the home.

3. Staff should be professionally trained and large enough to provide adequate care for all residents.

4. If the home requires a contract, read it carefully. Show it to your lawyer before signing. Some homes reserve the right to discharge a patient whose condition has deteriorated even if a lump-sum payment was made upon admittance. *Best:* An agreement that allows payment by the month, or permits refunds or advance payment if plans change.

5. Find out exactly what services the home provides and which ones cost extra. Private duty nurses are not included. Extras, like shampoo and hairset, can be exorbitant. (A box of tissues can cost a dollar.) Make a list of the "extras" your parents will need for a comfortable life. Try to supply some of them yourself.

Before you decide on a home, you and your parent should have a talk with the administrator and department heads. Find out who is in charge of what, and whom to speak to if problems arise.

Source: Sheldon Goldberg, American Association of Homes for the Aging.

More on How to Pick A Nursing Home

Placing a troubled, dependent relative in a nursing home is a heart-wrenching ordeal. To ease the way, know when a nursing home is the only answer. *Deciding factors:* When there is a loss of control of bodily functions, a loss of memory or an inability to perform the basic activities of daily life, such as shopping, cleaning and dressing. People do not age physically and emotionally at the same rate.

Never coerce a person into a nursing home. Rather, open the decision for discussion. When possible, have the person accompany you when you shop for the proper home.

The nursing homes with the best reputations, highest staff-to-patient ratios and longest wait-ing lists are non-profit. That is, they are run by churches, fraternal orders and charities. *Hitch:* Only about 25% of all homes are non-profit.

The majority of nursing homes are for profit, or proprietary. Other differences among homes:

•Health-related facilities emphasize personal, not medical care. These are generally non-profit homes.

•Skilled nursing facilities are for patients with serious mental and physical disabilities. Most of these places are proprietary.

Non-profit homes usually charge a flat, high monthly fee with no extras for added services. Proprietary homes ask a lower monthly fee with extra payments for services. Always be certain that you understand the rates and service charge.

Many proprietary homes don't take Medicaid patients. The amounts paid by the state and federal health plans aren't always enough to cover the costs. Patients without any money should be placed in a non-profit home.

To select a home, start by asking the patient's physician, relatives and friends who have gone through a similar experience for information. Also, get information from your state's departments of health and social services.

Begin the search long before it becomes necessary to find a home. *Caution:* Many emotional problems among the elderly occur during the waiting period because of the stress of being in limbo.

Since this is an emotional experience, take a close friend with you when you inspect nursing homes. The person will look for things that you forget.

What to seek in a home:

•Good location. The right home is close enough for convenient visits. Avoid places in run-down or dangerous neighborhoods. *Best:* A residential area with gardens and benches.

•Well-lit, cheery environment. Doors to the room shouldn't have windows. This is a home, not a hospital.

•The home's affiliation with hospitals and associations. And, find out how many patients are on Medicaid. If the number exceeds 50%, the home is not likely to provide adequate care.

•A professional staff. There should be a full-time or regularly visiting doctor with specialized knowledge in geriatrics. The total number of registered nurses, licensed practical nurses and nurses' aides should be at least 40% of the number of beds.

•The residents. Nothing speaks better for a nursing home than active, vital patients. Observe the staff to see if they treat residents with respect. Talk to the residents and ask for their complaints. *Bad signs:* If more than 3% of the residents are in the hospital at one time. If patients are still in bed or in bedclothes at 11 am. If many residents are catheterized to avoid linen-changing. Ask what happens when a patient is hospitalized. Is the nursing home bed still available afterwards?

•Handrails in hallways and bathrooms.

•Smoke alarms in public areas and each room. Ask to see the latest fire inspection report and note the date.

•The dining room should be clean, bright and inviting, with no dirty trays around. Are special diets adhered to?

•The residents' rooms should be comfortable and attractively furnished. Be sure the room can be personalized with pictures, plants, knick-knacks. Drawers should be lockable.

•Happy patients are those plugged into the outside world. Newspapers and large-print books should be readily available. The home should show movies, bring in entertainers and provide outside trips. *Other necessary activities:* Gardening, workshops, education courses, lecture series and discussion groups. Find out about religious services and provisions for voting.

•Special services should include visits by a licensed physical therapist and workable therapy equipment that the patients can use. *Visits by other specialists:* Speech therapists for stroke victims, audiologists, dentists, psychiatrists, optometrists and podiatrists.

What to watch out for:

•Patients who are sedated to keep them quiet.

•The home asks for a large sum of money up front.

•Doctors who hold gang visits (they see 40–50 patients during each call).

•You are denied visiting rights to the kitchen, laundry and library.

•The Patient's Bill of Rights isn't displayed.

Before you leave: Stand in the home and feel the ambience. Ask yourself if you would like to live there. Return to the place several times. Arrive at least once unannounced. The best time to visit is 11 am or 7 pm.

To monitor nursing homes for abuses: Put small pen marks on the patient's body and bandages to check frequency of bathing and bandage changes. Visit at mealtime. Get weekly weight checks of the patient to be sure nutrition is adequate. Learn the names of the nurses and aides on all shifts to determine who's responsible for the patient's care.

Source: Texans for Improvement of Nursing Homes, Houston.

Life Savers for Aging Parents

Give smart gifts...

•Send a love letter, listing all the things you love about the person.

•Make a birthday board of all the family birthdays or a video tape of a family event.

•Tape an interview of your parent to help your family get to know him/her better—and to keep for future generations.

Make the phone friendly...

•Make a list of frequently called numbers in large type that can be posted near the phone.

•Buy a telephone that will make things easier...large buttons for easier dialing...no cord, so there's no tripping and no running for the phone...speed dialing, which cuts down on the phone numbers an elder needs to remember or find.

•Send a book on tape. If eyesight has degenerated, books on tape provide a terrific alternative to TV and radio.

Ease travel stress...

•Make an index card in bold, block letters containing all flight information, a contact number with a calling card number and the name of the person picking your parent up at the airport.

•Make sure that your parent puts any medication in his carry-on bag, in case the checked luggage gets lost.

•Bring another person along to the airport to escort your parent while you check the baggage and park your car.

•Request a wheelchair or courtesy cart in advance for airports with long concourses.

•Help your parent board early.

•Request a kosher or vegetarian meal—they're often fresher and lower in sodium than the usual fare.

Source: Tracy Green and Todd Temple, coauthors of *52 Ways to Show Your Aging Parents You Care*. Thomas Nelson Publishers.

Strategies for Lifelong Health

Eating low-calorie, nutrient-dense foods—those containing as many nutrients as possible per calorie—may increase your life span.

Over time, you'll become substantially younger in…

•Form (body shape).

•Feature (appearance).

•Function (how well your body works, including your brain).

You'll improve your eyesight and hearing, sharpen your intelligence, reduce your need for sleep, have more pep and enhance your sense of well-being.

A nutrient-dense diet diminishes hunger—since it works continuously to provide energy and a sense of fullness.

Perhaps most important, you'll increase your resistance to colds and flu as well as more serious diseases, including…

•Clogged arteries and heart disease.

•Breast, lung and liver cancer. At least 70% of overall cancer risk is related to diet.

•Leukemia.

•Inflammation of the large bowel (diverticulitis). More than half of Americans older than 50 have diverticula, balloon-like outpouchings of tissue that can become swollen and painful.

People who start the antiaging diet at age 20 could theoretically live to age 140. But you'll extend your age whenever you start if you follow the program consistently. Even if you never become thin, simply dropping below your usual weight—and staying there—will extend your life.

Seven simple steps…

1. On the same day each week, weigh yourself before breakfast. Decide if you want to aim for weight loss and health promotion only, or add the life-extending element of the antiaging plan. To extend your life, you'll have to reduce your weight at least 10% and preferably 20% below your set point (usual weight). After four weeks of rapid weight loss, you will work towards slow, steady weight reduction.

2. Have a complete physical. Discuss your plan with a trusted and receptive doctor.

Ask whether there's any medical reason you shouldn't strictly limit your calorie intake indefinitely. If you go on the plan, have basic tests done (blood pressure, pulse, total cholesterol, High-Density Lipoprotein [HDL] cholesterol, fasting blood sugar, tests for autoantibodies and white blood cell count) after four to six months…and then annually. Test results should show improvement quickly.

3. Choose between rapid orientation and gradual orientation. For the gradual route, eat one low-calorie, high-nutrient meal during the first week, two such meals during the second week and so on until you're participating fully.

For other meals, eat wholesomely and sensibly. Meanwhile, cook and freeze meals you'll need later. Seek out local restaurants that serve dishes consistent with your goals. Prepare your friends and family for the big change you're making in your life.

4. Avoid caffeine, sugar and dairy products other than nonfat ones. Base all your meals on foods derived from plants—grains, beans, rice, pasta, breads, vegetables and fruits. Eat red meat and poultry in small amounts only, if at all. Start with 1,800 calories a day. If you're losing weight too fast, slowly increase your intake to a maximum of 2,200 calories a day.

5. Begin and maintain a program of moderate exercise with your doctor's approval. A

good way to start is to take a brisk 30-minute walk three times a week.

6. Take one multivitamin/ mineral pill a day. It should provide about 50% of the Recommended Daily Allowance (of the major vitamins and minerals). Also take…

• 500 milligrams of vitamin C.

• 300 to 400 International Units (IU) of vitamin E.

• 100 micrograms of selenium.

• 25,000 IU of beta carotene (toxicity levels for beta carotene are not yet known).

Optional: 0.5 to 1 gram of magnesium…0.1 milligram of chromium in organic form…and 20 milligrams of coenzyme Q10 (CoQ10), an essential part of the membranes of the energy factories of the cell that may help prevent cancer.

Note: It is important to check with your doctor before taking these or any supplements.

7. Plan how you want to spend your longer, healthier, more vigorous life.

Antiaging eating…

• Sprinkle two tablespoons of wheat germ (flakes) on salads, soups, hot and cold cereals or casseroles daily.

What to buy: Refrigerated, unprocessed wheat germ found in health food stores tends to be fresher than the processed kind sold in supermarkets.

• Add a heaping tablespoon of oat bran or wheat bran flakes, which provide 10% of daily fiber requirements, to salads, soups, cereals or casseroles.

• Sprinkle brewer's yeast (a powder), one of the healthiest of all foods, over grains or salads…stir it into stews…toss it with unbuttered air-popped popcorn with a little low-sodium soy sauce to make it stick.

• Substitute fresh lemon juice for salt, salad dressing and sauces on steamed vegetables.

• Discover the world of healthful whole grains…amaranth, barley, bulgur, millet and wheat berries.

• Choose dishes that are steamed, broiled or roasted (without butter) in restaurants…avoid those that are sauteed, fried, braised, creamed or escalloped.

Lessons from the East…

These foods, commonly used in Japanese cooking, are nutritional wonders with almost no calories…

• Shiitake mushrooms. These large, meaty fungi are filling and loaded with healthful minerals as well as fiber and vitamin D. Fresh ones are great in vegetarian stews and stir-fries. Dried ones must be soaked in hot water for 15 minutes before cooking.

• Seaweeds contain vitamin B6…calcium…iron…possibly vitamin B12 (usually sparse in vegetarian diets) and vitamin D. These two seaweeds are popular:

• Kombu. Cut into strips with kitchen shears. Add in first stages of cooking soup. Before adding to a stir-fries or casseroles, cover strips with water and soak for 10 to 15 minutes or until soft. Add, minced, to recipes for leafy green vegetables.

• Nori. The thin, dark-green sheet wrapped around sushi rolls. Cut or tear pieces and add to stir-fries and casseroles. Toast a sheet and crumble it over salad, rice, vegetables or baked potatoes.

Anyone who requires a low-salt diet should avoid nori, which has a high-sodium content.

Resources…

If you can't find specialty items in your local stores or markets, you may be able to get them by mail from Walnut Acres, Penn Creek, Pennsylvania 17863. 800-433-3998. Williams Sonoma, Box 7456, San Francisco 94120. 800-541-2233.

The anti-aging kitchen…

Organizing your pantry simplifies planning and cooking. *For example:*

• Alphabetize spices for easy access.

• Store grains, legumes and dried pastas in one-quart glass jars labeled with large letters.

• Spend half a day each week preparing and freezing enough nutrient-rich dishes for the following week.

Source: Roy L. Walford, MD, who spent two years sealed in Biosphere 2 in the Arizona desert as team physician. A leading gerontologist, Dr. Walford is a professor of pathology at University of California, Los Angeles, School of Medicine. Building on his previous book, *The 120-Year Diet,* is his latest book, *The Anti-Aging Plan: Strategies and Recipes for Extending Your Healthy Years.* Four Walls Eight Windows.

16

The Mind/Body Connection

New and Healthier Way of Looking at Life

Heart disease, cancer, AIDS and other life-threatening illnesses bring pain and suffering, to be sure. But they can also bring a new and healthier way of looking at life...of distinguishing that which truly matters in life from mere distractions.

Of course, it's best to learn these invaluable lessons *before* you're diagnosed with a life-threatening illness...

•Don't be afraid to show your vulnerabilities. Almost all of us were raised to be strong in the face of adversity, to put on a "brave front" no matter what. *Problem:* Acting one way when we're feeling another way saps our vitality, leaving us vulnerable to depression and illness and resentful of the world. We wind up with few friends and little support to help us through life's inevitable crises.

Better way: Admit your frailties. If you feel you need help, ask for it—and be willing to help others.

Exercise: Next time someone asks how you're doing, admit your true feelings. If you feel fine, say so. But if you feel lousy, admit it. Being honest might be hard at first, but it paves the way to honest, caring communication. That's essential for good health and happiness.

•Relinquish your need to be in control. As a young doctor, I thought the key to life was to get things done. My daily routine involved jotting down and then ticking off entries on "to do" lists. When I failed to get everything done, I got nervous and frustrated.

As I grew older and got in closer touch with my feelings, I came to realize that life is inherently disorderly. Now I know that living well means forgetting about rigid schedules. It means learning to find happiness, fulfillment and tranquility in the face of disorder.

Lesson: Stop trying to control all situations. Don't be a slave to your intellect. Make plans, but don't be upset by redirection. Something good may come of this redirection.

•Learn how to say "no." Our parents and teachers taught us that it's rude to say "no" to others. So when people ask for favors or tell us how to behave, we give in to their wishes.

Danger: Saying "yes" when you'd rather say "no" may be good manners, but it's destructive to our health. Doing so keeps us in unfulfilling jobs and makes us bitter. It leads us to do things we detest, and it distracts us from the things we cherish. We wind up resentful and possibly ill.

Better way: Stand up for yourself. If you don't want to mow the lawn, pursue a particular career, etc.—don't do it. I'm not asking you to be selfish or needlessly rude. I'm merely asking you to have enough self-esteem to stand up for yourself, to pursue life on your own terms, to realize that you can say "no" when someone asks you to change your plans.

•Confront your fears. People in crisis often seek peace of mind by burying or denying their fears. But real peace of mind comes only when we confront our fears head-on.

What to do: First, define exactly what it is you're afraid of. Don't say, "I'm afraid of dying." Be specific.

•Are you afraid of pain?

•Or what a medical treatment might do to you?

•Or that no one will take care of you?

Once you've pinned down your exact fear, find a metaphor for it. I tell patients to imagine their fear as a tiny baby crying in a crib. I tell them to pick up the baby, caress him/her, and see what happens. This exercise shows people that they're distinct from their fears and suggests that they, and not their fears, are in control. Learning to control fear is very reassuring.

•Live in the moment. If you spend all your time ruing the past or fearing the future, you'll have a hard time deriving any pleasure from the present. To fight this tendency, remind yourself that death could come at any moment. Don't let that thought frighten you. Just try to assimilate it into your psyche. Once you do, you'll be freer to enjoy a blue sky or a poem or the presence

of a loved one. *Ultimate goal:* To approach life with a childlike sense of awe and wonder.

•Identify your true feelings. Ask a child what he wants to do, and you'll get 40 answers.

Ask an adult, and the response will likely be, "I don't know. What do you want to do?" Adults have a hard time knowing what to do—for an afternoon or a lifetime—because they're so out of touch with their feelings that they've lost track of what really matters to them.

People without emotions live almost like automatons. Helen Keller used to ask, If you had three days to see, what would you choose to see in those days? Your answer to this question will teach you about what you truly love in your life.

•Define pain and suffering in positive terms. When I ask my lecture audiences if they think life is fair, they usually answer with a resounding, "No!" But I believe that life is fair. All of us experience difficulties, problems, pain and losses. But while some people give in to self-pity, others retain their vitality and optimism—even in the face of terminal illness.

Lesson: We should not only avoid suffering, we should respond to it in a constructive manner.

Strategy: Redefine whatever pain you're feeling as labor pains. Just as the anticipation and joy of bringing a new baby into the world can help to ease a mother's suffering during childbirth, other types of pain will seem less awful if you view them as integral to the process of birth you're undergoing.

Examples: The pain of chemotherapy leads to the birth of a person who is cancer-free…the pain of divorce leads to the birth of a happy single person.

•Refuse to be a victim. To some extent, we're all prisoners. Some of us are prisoners in the literal sense. Others, suffering from some debilitating ailment, are prisoners of our own bodies. Still others are imprisoned by emotional scars from a difficult childhood or a violent crime. No matter what form your prison takes, you don't have to feel or behave like a victim.

Example: Franklin Roosevelt could have pitied himself after polio left him wheelchair-bound. Instead, he became president of the United States.

Bottom line: No matter what befalls you, retain the ability to choose what sort of life to lead.

Source: Bernard S. Siegel, MD, a noted lecturer on healing and the founder of Exceptional Cancer Patients (ECaP), a nonprofit support group for people with cancer, AIDS, or other life-threatening illnesses. A retired surgeon formerly on the staff of Yale University School of Medicine, Dr. Siegel is the author of three books, including the just-published *How to Live Between Office Visits: A Guide to Life, Love, and Health,* HarperCollins, 10 E. 53 St., New York 10022.

How to Make the Most Of the Good…and the Bad…in Everyday Life

While no intelligent person seeks to become a victim of serious illness, violent crime, or emotional or financial problems, crises of this sort occur almost inevitably, but are not without their positive aspects.

Crisis can serve as spiritual "wake-up calls," reminding us of our own mortality and demonstrating the need to improve our lives.

Example: Many people find that a diagnosis of cancer—though terrifying—shows them for the first time in their lives what's truly important. As a result, these people make changes that are both liberating and long-overdue—becoming more open and loving…adopting a more healthful lifestyle…finding more meaningful work… forgiving old enemies…abandoning loveless relationships.

Tragically, in advanced cultures such as our own, people tend not to embrace crises but to shun them. We expect to progress smoothly through each stage of life, floating effortlessly forward and avoiding pain. This is a crazy notion. Crises are inevitable, and without them we'd never learn how to progress to the next stage.

Primitive cultures know better. In certain parts of Africa, tribal ceremonies are designed to create crises in the lives of "initiates" making the transition from one stage of life to another.

Example: When a boy becomes a man, for example, he is stripped of belongings and kept briefly in isolation, away from friends and family members. This disorienting experience forces the boy to confront and then overcome his own fears. So, the ceremony that marks a boy's coming of age actually helps him hone the emotional and spiritual resources he'll need as a man.

What lesson can we draw? Simply to face painful crises not with dread or resentment, but with a sense of optimism and gratitude. Look for meaning in them. Do so, and you'll learn things that cannot be taught in any other way.

Philosopher Kahlil Gibran: "Pain is the bitter pill of the inner physician that cracks the shell of our understanding."

A similar view is discernible in Chinese ideograms. The symbol for "crisis" is a combination of the symbols for "danger" and "opportunity."

Of course, this is not to deny that crises are very stressful, very painful…and very challenging experiences. They certainly are. But there are certain steps that can make crises easier to bear —and more likely to bear fruit. *Most important:*

•Pay close attention to your physical needs. *Key points:*

Breathing. Rapid, shallow breathing breeds anxiety. *More soothing:* Diaphragmatic breathing, practiced several times a day. *Procedure:* Inhale deeply through your mouth, exhale fully, then take a breath through your nose. Feel your belly inflate like a balloon. Then exhale, and feel your belly deflate.

Tension. To keep tension from turning into pain…several times a day, shut your eyes and scan your muscles for tightness. Stretch until the tension eases.

Nutrition. The better you eat, the better your ability to handle stress. *Helpful:* Avoid sugary, fatty foods and tobacco. Minimize intake of alcohol. Eat lots of whole grains, vegetables and fruits.

Rest. To beat insomnia, try meditating while in bed. If you're not lulled to sleep, at least you'll get some rest. *Also helpful:* Soothing music (use earphones to avoid disturbing your partner).

•Spend time alone. Solitude helps heal our deepest spiritual wounds. No matter how busy your schedule, set aside a few minutes each day to be alone. Garden, go for a walk, meditate, listen to music, etc. Don't watch TV. Cultivate your sense of spirituality, either within an organized religion or on your own.

•Get psychological help. Crises are not your fault, nor are they some kind of divine punishment for your sins. If you find yourself blaming yourself for your problems, or if you feel overwhelmed by powerful emotions, fight the temptation to "tough it out." Get help. *Caution:* Whether you pick a grief group, illness support group, 12-step program or some other form of therapy, make sure it helps you grow and change. Avoid any form of help that keeps you feeling sick, dependent or victimized.

•Be realistic. There's just no point in worrying about things that lie beyond your control. *Helpful prayer:* "God grant me the serenity to accept the things I cannot change, the courage to change the things I can and the wisdom to know the difference."

•Try not to worry. A noted anthropologist has these simple rules for living...

- •Show up.
- •Pay attention.
- •Tell the truth.
- •Don't be attached to the results.

Most of us are good at obeying the first three rules, and not so good at obeying the fourth. Resolve to obey all four rules. If you do your best, what more can you ask of yourself?

•Use positive affirmations. Practiced on a daily basis, they help boost your sense of mastery over life. *What to do:* Facing a mirror, close your eyes and recall a moment of great serenity in your life. Focus on the sense of peace, vitality and safety this memory evokes. Then open your eyes and say aloud, "Good morning, how are you? I am alive and I am grateful, and today, for the benefit of myself, my family and all beings, I will (insert your desired goal here)." Repeat two or three times. (Adapted from an exercise of Dhyani Ywahoo.)

•Be kind and loving. In a crisis, the last thing someone needs is criticism. That holds true whether the crisis is yours or someone else's. Instead, be kind-hearted, loving and altruistic. Do favors. Volunteer to work in a soup kitchen or hospital. *Helpful poem:* "May I be at peace.

May my heart remain open. May I know the beauty of my own true nature. May I be healed."

•Focus on happiness. At the core, all people are not only wise and compassionate, but also happy. Joy is your birthright, not just an ephemeral goal. Remember that, and you'll be less likely to give in to despair during tough times. *Helpful:* If you're unhappy now, smiling—just smiling—can help you feel less sad.

Shakespeare: "Practice a virtue if you have it not."

•Don't be passive. If you wish to escape a difficult situation, don't leave everything to prayer or vague wishes. Action is also required.

Example: An old man prayed that he would win the lottery, then chastised God when his prayers went unanswered. God shook Her head and said, "For heaven's sake, at least you could have bought a ticket!"

•Be patient. If you're not getting what you want, perhaps you're getting what you need.

Example: While you might prefer a speedy resolution to a crisis, a protracted crisis might lead to a deeper healing.

Don't demand or expect a prompt end to your troubles. Pray not for a crisis to end, but for the strength and courage to endure it.

Source: Joan Borysenko, PhD, formerly a member of the faculty at Harvard Medical School. Dr. Borysenko is now the president of Mind/Body Health Sciences, Inc., an educational firm that conducts seminars on health and spirituality, 393 Dixon Rd., Salina Star Route, Boulder, Colorado 80302. Dr. Borysenko is the author of three books. Her most recent one, *Fire in the Soul*, provides coping strategies for everyday life. Warner Books, 1271 Avenue of the Americas, New York 10020.

The Best Kind Of Medicine

Hot chicken soup is beloved by sick people. Yet the tender loving care that usually accompanies it may be at least as helpful to the patient. Levels of agents in the immune system that fight colds and viruses rose when subjects in a test saw a movie about Mother Theresa as she worked with the poor in India. Levels of these agents stayed high as the viewers later recalled times when they had been cared for by others.

Source: Research done by psychologists David McClelland and Carol Kirshnit at Harvard University as reported in *Psychology Today*, New York.

The Healing Power Of Hope

Hope helps heal the sick and may even keep you from getting ill in the first place. Heart disease and sudden death are more likely to strike a person who is troubled by bereavement, divorce, business failure or retirement. Cancer victims with high "hope scores" did significantly better in fighting their disease.

Source: Studies by the American Psychiatric Association, cited in *Medical World News,* Houston, TX.

Pets and Good Health

Pet owners are healthier, in general, than people who do not own pets. They have lower cholesterol and triglyceride levels than non-owners...and are less likely to suffer from nervousness, insomnia, stomachaches, headaches and other minor health problems. *Bonus:* New pet owners—especially dog owners—experience increases in psychological well-being and self-esteem.

Source: Study by researchers at the Baker Medical Institute in Australia, and the Companion Animal Research Group at Cambridge University, England, reported in *The Medical Post*, 777 Bay St., Toronto, Ontario M5W 1A7.

Trust Your Instincts

Trust your instincts about your health—don't just rely on your doctor's report. Several large surveys have shown that an individual's perception of his/her health—rated as excellent, good, fair or poor—is frequently the best predictor of his mortality and is often more accurate than a standard examination by a physician. In one study, people who rated their health as "poor" were seven times more likely to die within four years than those who rated their health as "excellent." These results illustrate how important it is for individuals to communicate with their physicians about their general well-being, as well as their perceptions concerning any existing health problems.

Source: Ellen Idler, PhD, associate professor of sociology, Institute for Health Care Policy and Aging Research, Rutgers University, New Brunswick, New Jersey.

Health Benefits Of Doing Good

Those who help others also help themselves in some very practical, tangible ways. A national study gives evidence that helping others, through volunteer work and community services, contributes to better health and stress reduction.

•Of the volunteers studied, 95% reported that regular personal helping gives them an immediate physical feel-good sensation.

•Over time, the benefits of helping include feelings of increased self-worth, calmness and relaxation, and better general health, including far less pain in chronic conditions.

•Those who volunteer weekly reported improved physical and emotional health.

Creating the helping society...

Older volunteers: A 1976 federal study of the Retired Senior Volunteer Program found that, at 98% of the sites surveyed, volunteers reported significant improvement in their emotional and physical health.

Students: Young people through the college level should also participate in personal contact community service. Younger children can write letters or draw pictures for nursing home residents—older students can visit emergency room patients or mentor a younger, less privileged child.

Source: Allan Luks, executive director of Big Brothers/Big Sisters of New York, Inc., and coauthor of *The Healing Power of Doing Good: The Health and Spiritual Benefits of Helping Others*, Fawcett Columbine Books, 201 E. 50 St., New York 10022.

315

Loneliness...and Health

Feeling lonely is not the same as *being alone.* While many lonely people have fewer friends than those who say they aren't lonely, some socially isolated people enjoy being that way and don't feel lonely at all.

Key: Loneliness reflects our *expectations*—and how well our relationships are meeting them.

Expectations are formed partly by the kinds of relationships you've had in the past and partly by social norms.

Example: A 26-year-old graduate student with plenty of friends, but no steady girlfriend, feels lonely because many of his friends are getting married and he wishes he had a romantic relationship.

• Who is lonely?

Loneliness strikes men and women about equally. However, men are much less likely than women to *admit* they are lonely.

To some degree, loneliness is inversely correlated with *social support.* People are not as likely to feel lonely if they have other people available that they can turn to for help with the problems of living.

Examples: Lending money...offering a ride when their car breaks down...listening to complaints about the job.

This connection is less true as people age. Older people have *fewer* social supports, yet are less lonely than younger people. Middle-aged adults are slightly less lonely than college students...and the *least* lonely group is the elderly. *Possible explanations:*

• *Attitude differences between generations.* Today's elderly may have been less lonely throughout their lives than later generations—perhaps because they were brought up to be more stoical or to expect less. This explanation implies that when today's young people are elderly, they *will* be lonely.

• *Increased confidence and social skills.* As we gain life experience, we may become more skillful in attracting others into our lives.

• *Adjusted expectations over time.* As we grow older and face the reality of loss, we may learn to cope better with being alone.

• *Survival of the least lonely.* We can't overlook the possibility that lonely people may be dying earlier than those who are not lonely.

• Loneliness and health.

A number of studies have established that deficits in social support are related to illness and mortality.

James House, a sociologist at the University of Michigan, reviewed many studies of social isolation and subsequently found that mortality rates are higher among individuals who reported having only a few friends...or who were unmarried or divorced.

The clearest data on loneliness and its links to health comes from Janice Kiecolt-Glaser and Ron Glaser at Ohio State University. Their research has found loneliness to be associated with deficits in immune function. These associations have been found across a range of ages and lifestyles.

One of the most consistent findings is that lonely people have a greater number of antibodies to the Epstein-Barr virus (EBV), a precursor to mononucleosis. Virtually all of us have been exposed to EBV and carry some antibodies to it, but an elevated level of these antibodies is considered an indicator of impaired immune function.

We only know that loneliness is *associated* with these immune system deficits. We don't know that loneliness *causes* them.

In addition, no one has yet proved that deficits in immune function actually increase the likelihood of someone's becoming ill.

• Why people are lonely...

Some research has suggested that problems in early childhood attachments might lead to loneliness later in life.

Example: Having your parents get divorced when you were very young.

It's also possible that the behavior of lonely people may discourage social contact. Warren Jones, a psychologist at the University of Tennessee, has studied the interactions of lonely people with others.

He found that lonely students are more focused on themselves, and view themselves and others more negatively than students who don't describe themselves as lonely. These characteristics may be preventing them from forming satisfying friendships.

•How to be less lonely…

While little careful research has been done on the effectiveness of interventions for loneliness—there are some promising strategies…

•Cognitive therapy. Exploring and challenging the negative assumptions of lonely people might encourage them to take social risks… and make them more attractive to others.

•Social-skills practice. Some university counseling centers and community mental-health clinics offer group workshops on overcoming shyness. Role-playing and other methods can help lonely people build confidence and learn to interact more successfully with others.

•Changing the environment. Many people have trouble forming relationships not because of any deficit in social skills, but because they're not spending time in the right places.

Example: Loneliness is a common reaction to moving to a new city. Work is the basis for many people's social lives. If you have little in common with your colleagues other than the fact that you work together, you'll be at a disadvantage in finding people to socialize with.

In fact, it can be dangerous to overemphasize a lack of personal and social skills as a cause of loneliness. Studies have shown that people who focus on their situations—and try to do something to change them—are more successful at overcoming loneliness than people who blame their own presumed personality defects.

Successful relationships are largely a function of *proximity and similarity*…being in settings where you are likely to meet people who share your interests, education level, socioeconomic background, age or hobbies.

Example: Trying to meet people of the opposite sex in bars, or even many singles groups, is highly *unlikely* to result in satisfying long-term relationships. The people you meet there may be pleasant, but the odds are you'll have nothing in common with them…and the future of such relationships is not promising.

Think about what you are interested in and where people with the same interests as yourself are likely to be found—then go there. People too often overlook this seemingly obvious but effective strategy.

Source: Daniel Russell, PhD, a social psychologist and associate professor in the College of Medicine at the University of Iowa. With psychologists L. Ann Peplau and Carolyn Cutrona, he developed the UCLA Loneliness Scale, which has become a standard instrument used by psychologists to measure loneliness.

All About Holoenergetic Healing

The word "healing" comes from the same root as "wholeness"—a sense of connectedness, of being one with ourselves, other people and the world around us.

In my 25 years as a physician and surgeon, I have come to view illness as separation, and healing as the restoration of our natural state of wholeness.

Our individualistic, highly rational society encourages the illusion of separation—the belief that our minds are somehow separate from our bodies and that people are isolated from one another. It takes energy to maintain separation—energy which is often experienced as pain or illness.

I have coined the term "holoenergetic healing" to describe a method that allows us to dispel the illusion of separateness and to heal using the awareness and energy of the whole.

Unconditional love—for self as well as others—is a crucial element of this method. Love isn't just the stuff of poets and mystics. It's also a profound tool for facilitating the body's natural healing processes.

I have done laboratory experiments which suggest that focused, loving energy can create results not dreamed possible…it may affect bacterial growth in test tubes, unwind and entwine DNA molecules, and inhibit the growth rate of tumor cells in tissue culture.

Return to source…

Holoenergetic healing is certainly not intended to replace Western medicine. The medical practices developed by Western society are of tremendous value in treating acute illness, serious infection, trauma and other disorders.

But these practices represent only part of the healing tools available to us today. We can benefit greatly by making use of both approaches.

The holoenergetic model allows us to go beyond relief of symptoms and connect with the fundamental source of separation. This is frequently a long-past, deeply troubling experience, which we interpreted in a way that initially helped us to cope...but ultimately cut us off from a part of ourselves.

Example: Someone who was punished and humiliated as a child for something he/she didn't do may have carried into adulthood the unconscious belief, "No matter how hard I try, I'm bad and deserve to suffer." One way he expresses this loss of faith in his right to happiness is through the physical pain of illness.

Other common themes that may be expressed through illness include difficulties in accepting love, receiving pleasure, expressing anger, forgiving and trusting.

Holoenergetic healing gives us a way to identify and understand these limiting patterns and beliefs, release them, and replace them with life-affirming feelings of safety, nurturance and love.

The process consists of four basic steps, which I call the *Four Rs of Holoenergetic Healing:* Recognition, Resonance, Release and Reformation.

•Step 1: Recognition...

With this step, we gather information about the symptom or quality we want to change. We draw on the insight of the rational mind (later, we'll access the intuitive mind as well) by entering into a state of relaxation and asking ourselves these questions:

•What do I want to change?

•Why do I want to change now?

•How do I see myself contributing to the present circumstances?

•What does having this illness or issue in my life allow me to do, be or have...and what does it keep me from doing, being or having?

•What outcome—both inner experience and outer result—do I want to create?

•Step 2: Resonance...

Drawing on the nonrational, intuitive aspects of the mind can help us rediscover the source of limiting patterns...the times in life when we unconsciously made significant decisions that influenced or blocked our later health and well-being. *The process:*

•Close your eyes, breathe deeply, and focus your attention on the symptom you want to change.

•While keeping this idea in mind, allow yourself to notice where in your body your awareness is drawn. Focus your attention on that area and become aware of any sensations there—such as pressure, tension, tingling or throbbing.

Example: With a migraine headache, the attention might be drawn to a throbbing spot behind the temple.

•Give that sensation a shape, such as a bright red ball—or any other form that works for you.

•Imagine yourself entering inside the shape. As you penetrate this image with your mind, deep emotions are likely to come up. Allow yourself to feel these emotions...and to travel back mentally to an earlier time when you had similar feelings. Begin to explore the beliefs and emotional patterns you formed around this issue.

•Delve even more deeply inside to discover the positive value of this pattern. This might include messages or warnings the pattern has for you...the security it provided... other legitimate needs that you would now like to meet in healthier ways. Give this positive intention a symbolic form, such as the sun, a flower, a waterfall or spiritual figure.

•Step 3: Release...

This step uses breath, intention and imagery to break up the undesirable pattern.

•Until now in this process, you have been imagining yourself inside the shape of your troublesome physical symptom. Now it is time to withdraw your mind from inside the form— but keep in your mind's eye the new image of your positive intention.

•Release the old, dysfunctional form by taking a deep breath and expelling it forcefully —and with it, your picture of the symptom (that bright red ball). Imagine the old form collapsing like a ruptured balloon. Move your hands forcefully away from your body as though to extract the energy. Inhale and expel one more clearing breath. Experience the feeling of freedom from your old pattern.

• Step 4: Reformation…

By releasing the old form, you have created a void—which you can fill with positive energy during this step.

• Focus your attention on the healing symbol you created for your positive intention in Step 2. Visualize that image and its healing qualities filling the area of your body that has been giving you trouble. Transfer your healing image into that area of your body with your next indwelling breath. You may also wish to fill the area with the image of healthy-looking organs or tissue…or with new, healthy beliefs about yourself.

• Complete the healing process by experiencing the gift of unconditional love. Become aware of a sense of complete, nonjudgmental love for every fiber of your being. Feel this love as a light moving throughout your body, until it flows out from the top of your head like a rainbow fountain of loving energy. Know that this love is your essence, always, even when you're not aware of it.

Source: Leonard Laskow, MD, a fellow of the American College of Obstetrics and Gynecology and former chief of OB/GYN at the Community Hospital of the Monterey Peninsula in Carmel, California. He conducts seminars on healing at medical centers, universities and other institutions worldwide and is the author of *Healing with Love*, HarperCollins, 10 E. 53 St., New York 10022.

Words to Use To Protect Your Health

With medical costs rising astronomically and no relief in sight, it's increasingly important for Americans to reduce their dependence on outside experts—and take at least some control of their own health care. One of the best tools for doing so is also one of the most basic—language.

There are many ways that language can be used to affect our health—for both the good and the bad. *Included:*

• Messages that we give ourselves. Whether we're aware of it or not, most of us talk to ourselves continuously.

Pessimistic, helpless messages ("I feel terrible, and there's not a thing I can do about it") tell the body to give up.

Positive messages ("I can stand this discomfort, and I will feel good again") help the body to fight illness.

• How we respond to others. Chronic exposure to hostility has been found to be a risk factor in many diseases—and the primary risk factor in heart disease.

We can't always avoid hostility and conflict, but we can learn to use language to deflect a verbal attack and spare ourselves mental and physical strain (see below).

• Metaphors we use. Visualization can be an effective healing tool in dealing with illness.

Example: A visualization patient is advised to imagine the disease as an army of enemy invaders, and the immune system as a good army destroying the invading forces.

But images of war and destruction are only helpful to individuals comfortable with military themes. For others, violent imagery may work against the healing process by equating illness with violence and slaughter.

As an alternative, focus on fixing rather than killing.

Example: Think of your immune system as a gardening crew pulling up weeds…or a road crew fixing potholes in the street…or a piano tuner restoring harmony to an out-of-tune instrument.

• Doctor/patient relationships. When doctors and patients don't communicate well with each other, patients wind up with poor health care.

A pain phobic society…

What we tell ourselves about pain has a profound impact on our well-being. Television commercials bombard us with the notion that pain is terrible—that no one should ever hurt even a little. But pain is a normal part of life.

That doesn't mean that discomfort should be ignored. If running makes your shins hurt, rest …don't push yourself for another mile.

Pain alerts us to our limitations, and chronic discomfort may be an indicator of a physical condition that requires medical attention.

People who panic every time they're in pain end up spending a lot of money needlessly on doctors and drugs, without appreciable benefits. In fact, their fears—and the drugs' side effects—may make them feel even worse.

Coping with pain...

If you're plagued with chronic or acute pain, instead of telling yourself, "I can't bear this," substitute the thought, "I can stand this pain for 15 minutes."

Then spend that 15 minutes doing something you enjoy—gardening, playing music, absorbing yourself in a challenging project at work. At the end of 15 minutes, you're likely to find that the pain is gone.

If not, say, "I can stand this pain for another 15 minutes." You'll notice that the pain ebbs and flows. This attitude enables you to go on with your life, instead of focusing your life around the pain.

Another way to cope with pain is to keep a journal. Describe what the pain feels like and what sets it off. Compare it with something that has a similar distinguishing feature and name it.

Example: "My pain is like an earthquake—sudden and unpredictable."

As you start to define your pain and give it boundaries, you will see it less as an overwhelming force that's controlling you, and more as an object...which you can control.

Deflecting attack...

We can relieve ourselves of a great deal of stress by learning not to get hooked into other people's hostility.

Verbal attacks aren't always easy to recognize. Someone can be smiling, or using words like "sweetheart" and "darling," and still be sending a hostile message. *Key:* Verbal hostility has a characteristic melody in which many words are emphatically stressed.

Examples: "Why do you always think only of yourself?" Or "I'm only thinking about what's best for you."

There are several ways to deflect verbal hostility...

•Remember that nobody can fight alone. If you refuse to fight, even the most hostile verbal attacker will give up.

•When in doubt about how to handle an attack, try the boring baroque defense. Treat the attack as if it were a serious, rational question or statement, and talk the other person into a coma.

The idea is to answer in such excruciating detail that the attacker has no fun at all. *Example:*

Attacker: "Why can't you ever stick to your diet?"

Boring baroque defense: "You know, that's an interesting question. I think it has to do with when I was a kid in Wisconsin, and our family ...no, maybe it was when we were living in Illinois. Yes, it must be Illinois, because that's when my uncle was working for the Post Office, and..."

This technique won't work if you let sarcasm creep into your voice. You must keep your tone serious.

How to talk to doctors...

It's easy to become resentful when dealing with doctors, especially if the doctor is brusque, uses jargon or acts condescending. Unfortunately, in our society, inequality is built into the doctor-patient relationship.

Acting resentful, however, will not help you achieve your health goals. The doctor is as trapped in the system as you are, and communicates in doctor-speak because he/she has been taught to.

Your doctor is a channel through which you get access to medicine, surgery and other treatments that affect your health. Annoying your doctor makes about as much sense as annoying your computer or arguing with a traffic light.

To get what you need, learn to interact with your doctor effectively...

•Before your appointment, make a list of things you want the doctor to know and any questions you need answered. Don't leave the meeting until those subjects have been covered to your satisfaction—even if you have to repeat your questions several times.

•Remember that a meeting with a doctor is not a social conversation. Don't worry about being entertaining or bouncing the conversational ball back and forth.

•Keep each question or statement to 18 seconds at most. Research shows that's the longest period of time doctors allow patients to talk before interrupting them.

•Don't try to talk like a doctor. If you've been feeling short of breath, say so—don't say you have dyspnea. Using medical jargon may be taken as a challenge—the doctor may try to top you by using even more technical language, and you won't get your questions answered.

Your goal isn't to impress the doctor, it's to get the information and care that you need.

Source: Linguist Suzette Haden Elgin, PhD, who teaches communication skills to health-care professionals nationwide. She is the author of *Genderspeak: Men, Women, and the Gentle Art of Verbal Self-Defense*, John Wiley & Sons Inc., 605 Third Ave., New York 10158.

Breathing for Relaxation

One benefit of Zen meditation is the breathing exercise. It helps you clear your mind and relieve stress. Try this exercise when you are tense or need to think more objectively:

First get into a comfortable position, either standing or reclining. Then take a deep breath, slowly, through your nose. Hold the breath for a second and try to push the air down to your stomach. (Your exhalation should be slower than your inhalation.) *Important:* Concentrate on the flow of your breath going in and out.

Source: Shihan Tadashi Nakamura, founder and chairman of the World Seido Karate Organization in New York.

Dr. Herbert Benson Tells What Wellness Is All About

Anyone with exposure to the media these days knows it's a good idea to exercise regularly, eat a low-fat diet and learn to cope with stress. The media have also devoted plenty of attention to the interaction between mind and body…and to the ways that lifestyle choices can affect this interaction.

Yet few people understand how to apply these principles in their daily lives. They may follow some of the rules and yet still feel tired, edgy, anxious or unable to think clearly. They may not actually be sick, but they don't have the vigor they'd like. They don't feel well.

More than treating disease…

Wellness involves fostering life habits that prevent illness, promote faster healing when we do get sick and enhance vitality whether we're ill or not.

Sadly, the many health-promoting behaviors available to us are often viewed as independent activities that have little bearing on each other.

At the Mind/Body Medical Institute, founded in 1988 at the Deaconess Hospital/Harvard Medical School, a whole-life approach to wellness is taken.

Each year there are 7,000 patient visits to these mind/body clinics for consultation or to attend workshops. Patients are taught how to manage their health using an integrated approach that emphasizes relaxation, nutrition, exercise and cognitive work.

Many healing approaches stress one or two of these factors. In our program, all four are viewed as a package. Although not a substitute for traditional medical care, this four-part package yields results far more dramatic than those obtained using any single method. *Examples:*

•Insomniacs become normal sleepers.

•People with high blood pressure learn to lower their pressure and maintain that new level—often without any medication.

•Depressed or anxious people report having more energy and better moods.

•People with chronic pain pay fewer visits to the doctor, feel less upset and angry about their condition and begin to lead more active lives.

Optimum health maintenance draws on the wisdom of the individual and the knowledge and skill of the medical establishment. But because self-care has historically received so little attention in our culture, the role of the individual is stressed.

Contract for health…

For many people, the struggle is not so much *knowing* what to do to improve their health. It's actually *doing* what they know they should do. One way to make this transition is to make a formal contract with yourself—*in writing*. This contract need not be complicated.

Write down a *realistic* long-term goal in each of the four areas—such as stopping smoking, exercising more, losing weight, etc. List short-term goals you can make toward this goal. Set a deadline for reaching both short-term and long-term goals.

Example: Cut back to two cigarettes a day by next week.

Sign the form in the presence of a witness—someone who's willing to support and encourage your efforts.

Record your progress. If you fail to meet any of your short-term goals, reevaluate your plan and choose steps that are more attainable.

Your good intentions will become reality as you integrate the following four areas of wellness into your life…

•Part 1: The relaxation response.

Life is full of large and small stressors—traffic jams, arguments, the death of a loved one, etc.

The body reacts to these stressors by releasing adrenaline and other hormones. This process leads to an involuntary physiological reaction called the *stress response*—a state of arousal marked by increases in metabolism, heart rate, blood pressure, breathing rate and muscle tension.

Over time, the stress response takes its toll, resulting in headaches, backaches, indigestion, chronic anxiety, insomnia and general unhappiness.

By using an inborn bodily response called the *relaxation response*, you can *voluntarily* undo the effects of the stress response—*decreasing* heart rate, blood pressure, breathing rate and metabolism and producing a sense of deep calm.

The relaxation response does more than counteract stress. It boosts your sense of confidence, leading you to try out new, healthful behaviors—thereby facilitating lifestyle changes that promote health and well-being.

There are many ways to elicit the relaxation response—deep breathing, meditation, prayer, progressive relaxation, yoga…and even aerobic exercise for people who can't stand to sit quietly.

All these methods share two basic elements—*focused repetition* of a sound, mental image or physical activity…and *passive* disregard for distracting thoughts.

For most people, the simplest way to elicit the relaxation response is to…

•Sit comfortably with your eyes closed. Relax your muscles.

•Breathe gently and naturally.

•Silently repeat "one" or another word, phrase or sound each time you exhale. (Instead of a sound, you might want to focus on the sensation of the breath itself as it flows through your nostrils.)

If thoughts intrude, don't worry. Just say to yourself, "Oh, well," and return to the repetition. Continue for 10 to 20 minutes, once or twice a day.

To deal with everyday stresses as they occur, use the *mini-relaxation response*. Just take a few moments to focus on your breathing or a repeated sound. You'll immediately feel calmer—and better able to deal with aggravation.

To generate the relaxation response using exercise, simply move in time with your breathing, while repeating your focus sound with each exhalation. Gently disregard distracting thoughts as they occur, always returning to your focus.

•Part 2: Nutrition.

Each passing week seems to bring a new fad diet purporting to cure one disorder or another. However, most experts agree on the basic principles of good nutrition.

These principles are spelled out in *Dietary Guidelines for Americans*, published by the US Departments of Agriculture and Health and Human Services: Eat a variety of foods…maintain healthy weight…choose a diet low in fat and cholesterol…eat plenty of vegetables, fruits and grains…consume sugar, salt and alcohol in moderation—if at all.

Knowing these principles and adhering to them are two different things. It might help to spend some time in a relaxed state thinking about what eating means to you.

Do you eat as a means of coping with stress or fatigue? If so, it would be more productive to eliminate the stressor, learn to cope with it more assertively, or simply get more rest.

Do you associate good nutrition with deprivation and boredom? Not true—a healthy diet can be delicious and satisfying. Many current cookbooks are packed with recipes that use healthful ingredients in flavorful and exciting ways.

Think about other barriers to eating better... and make a contract with yourself to address them.

•Part 3: Exercise.

Regular exercise improves emotional, as well as physical, well-being. It also boosts your sensitivity to your own body, so you'll be more likely to recognize potential health problems before they become serious.

There's no one right way to exercise.

Try to get at least 10 to 20 minutes of vigorous, heart-pumping (aerobic) exercise three to five times a week...plus muscle toning (weight training or calisthenics) twice weekly. If that's impossible, remember that any form of movement is better than none.

Problem: Half the people who start ambitious exercise programs abandon them within six months. Pick the type of exercise that's most enjoyable for you.

Examples: Walk or run with your dog...take stairs instead of elevators...run errands by bike instead of car...take a brisk walk at lunchtime.

Caution: If you're older than 40 or have a medical condition, check with a doctor before beginning any exercise program.

•Part 4: Cognitive work.

Our thoughts have a profound effect on our emotions, physical state and motivation to take care of ourselves.

Often without our even realizing it, our minds keep up a nearly constant stream of mental chatter. Much of this mental chatter is negative.

Examples:
•"That person doesn't like me."
•"What's that supposed to mean?"
•"I'm such an idiot."
•"This isn't fair!"
•"That person is a jerk."
•"I'm always doing the wrong thing."

When we give ourselves negative messages, our bodies as well as our minds react negatively.

We can improve our well-being by learning to recognize and change these habitual thoughts. Whenever you notice yourself feeling tense, anxious or frustrated—whether from a traffic jam, a work snafu or a fight with your spouse—do the following:

•Stop and breathe—to interrupt the thought pattern.

•Reflect—to identify the negative thought ...challenge it...rob it of its power.

Notice how you talk to yourself about the stressful situations that have just happened. Are you making unrealistic assumptions about life?

Examples:
•"Life should be fair."
•"I have to be perfect to be accepted."
•"Circumstances should arrange themselves for my convenience."
•"When things go wrong, it's because there's something wrong with me."

Try not to view yourself as a victim of circumstance or unfair treatment. Instead, reframe the situation as a problem. Consider what you can do to solve the problem, then take action.

If you're quick to criticize yourself, practice coming up with alternative explanations of troubling events.

Example: If a proposal at work is rejected, your automatic assumption might be, "I did a lousy job and my boss hates me."

Deliberately force yourself to review at least three other possible explanations, even if you don't immediately believe them...

•"The proposal was fine, but we don't have the budget for it."

•"The boss was impressed by my initiative— it's just this particular idea that he didn't like."

•"He liked the idea but wasn't sure he could sell it to his superiors."

Humor is helpful. Finding a way to laugh at yourself and the situation is one of the fastest ways to improve your mood—and your health.

Be patient with yourself as you apply these wellness principles. Change doesn't happen quickly—or in a smooth, linear fashion. But as you adopt more health-promoting habits, you'll find that you handle the setbacks—as well as the victories—with greater ease, energy and confidence.

Source: Herbert Benson, MD, associate professor of medicine, Harvard Medical School, and chief of the division of behavioral medicine, New England Deaconess Hospital, Boston. He is the author of more than 100 scientific publications and four books, including *The Wellness Book* and *The Relaxation Response* (Fireside, 1230 Avenue of the Americas, New York 10020).

How to Relax...

Chronic stress, if left unchecked, eventually can lead to high blood pressure, heart attack, stroke and physical and emotional burnout.

Important: The ability to relax. By this I don't mean sitting back in an easy chair and propping up your feet (although that's a start). True relaxation means retraining your nervous system not to overreact to events —to produce only the level of arousal needed for any situation.

Reducing a person's nervous-system arousal level...

•Slows the pulse.

•Loosens and relaxes muscles.

•Warms hands and feet.

•Slows breathing.

•Slows production of adrenaline and other potentially destructive chemicals.

•Extends the attention span and enables effective response when a crisis does occur.

Although there are numerous techniques used to promote relaxation, I have found that biofeedback is especially effective.

Common misconception: Biofeedback requires complex and expensive high-tech equipment.

Reality: Although certain relaxation skills are best learned with such machinery, several highly effective techniques can be mastered just by paying close attention to your body.

Relaxation and breathing...

Crucial to the relaxation response is slow, paced breathing. Too often we breathe rapid, shallow breaths. This overstimulates the nervous system. *Result:* Headaches, dizziness, faintness, lightheadedness, vertigo, numbness, palpitations, pain and more.

Similar problems can be brought on by doing precisely the opposite—holding your breath and taking big gulps of air. Excitement and fear often cause us to breathe rapidly or hold our breath. Unfortunately, the faster we breathe or the more we hold our breath, the more nervous we feel.

Many people breathe with the upper chest instead of the abdomen. Abdominal breathing promotes relaxation, while chest breathing promotes arousal. Make sure that your stomach goes out as you inhale, then goes in during exhalation. If not, you are breathing with your chest.

Self-test: Place your left hand on your chest, with your thumb in the notch between your collarbones. Place your right hand on your belly. Notice which hand moves as you breathe. If your left hand moves more than the right, you are breathing with the upper chest. Continue to practice your breathing until the belly hand moves and the chest hand remains still.

Breathe at a calm, easy pace. *Best:* Eight to 12 breaths a minute. Count to three or four while breathing in through your nose, pause for one count, count to three or four while exhaling, then pause for a count and begin again. This pattern may seem uncomfortable at first, but after about a week it will seem entirely natural.

Practice slow, paced breathing at home, at work, in elevators, at traffic lights, before making phone calls, while making love, etc.—or anytime and anywhere you find yourself feeling stress. Doing so is remarkably calming.

I have developed several exercises to promote relaxation. Do these with a friendly, caring attitude toward yourself. Don't demand too much of yourself. Practice the exercises regularly, or the symptoms of stress may return.

Paced breathing exercise...

Find a quiet room where you won't be disturbed. Sit in a comfortable, supportive chair or lie on the floor. (If you choose the floor, put a pillow under your knees to relax your lower back.)

Don't use a bed right away, because beds are associated with sleep. Although you can use paced breathing to promote sleep once you are adept at self-regulation, you have to acquire the skill first. *Procedure:*

•Take a deep breath and hold it as you tighten your right fist. Maintain tension for six to eight seconds.

•Breathe out and relax your fist.

•Repeat two more times, letting the relaxation spread into your fingers and wrist.

•Take another breath and tense your left fist. Hold for six to eight seconds.

•Relax and breathe out.

•Take another deep breath and tense both fists. Hold for 10 seconds.

•Relax and breathe out, letting your muscles become loose and limp.

•Pace breathing for three or four counts.

•Tighten your forehead and bite down. Hold for six to eight seconds.

•Relax and breathe out.

•Take another breath, then tighten your legs from the buttocks to the toes. Hold for six to eight seconds.

•Relax and breathe out.

•Letting your breathing slow, breathe for two to three cycles.

•Take another deep breath and tense your entire body. Hold for eight to 10 seconds. Important: Don't try to tense your muscles with 100% effort—50% to 70% is fine. And it's okay if your muscles tremble.

•Relax and breathe out. Let your muscles become loose, limp and relaxed.

•Repeat the total-body tension part until you become as relaxed as you can. Enjoy the sense of relaxation.

•To end the exercise, count to three slowly and open your eyes. Stretch and yawn before getting up.

If you start and end each day with this exercise, you will feel much less nervous, your heart rate will slow and your blood pressure will drop—not just during the exercise, but for a couple of hours afterward.

Don't do the exercise on a full stomach. *Best:* When you wake up, before breakfast or lunch, at the end of the workday, the middle of the evening, or at bedtime. Consult a physician if you experience pain.

Muscle relaxation...

Except during exertion, our muscles should be long and loose, not tight. People waste a lot of energy through muscle tension, especially in the jaw, back, forehead and shoulders. Some people wake with jaw pain because of nighttime jaw-clenching. This exercise will help you avoid tight muscles. *Procedure:*

•Take five or six slow, paced breaths.

•Wrinkle your forehead and frown while relaxing your body.

•Take a couple of slow breaths.

•Relax your forehead and scalp and tighten your eyes by squinting.

•Take two or three slow breaths, holding the tension.

•Relax your eyes.

•Take one or two slow breaths and tighten your jaw muscles as if you were biting down.

•Hold for two breaths, then relax.

•Tighten your forehead, eyes and jaw. Hold the tension for one or two slow breaths.

•Relax. Enjoy the relaxation in your face and head. Breathe slowly.

•Lean your head forward until your chin rests on your chest. Hold the position for a couple of breaths.

•Bring your head back up until it rests against the chair or floor. Push it back gently for one or two breaths.

•Relax your neck. Then take a deep breath and raise your shoulders up toward your ears.

•Take one or two slow breaths and relax your shoulders. Tighten your right hand into a fist.

•Take two or three slow breaths.

•Relax your fist. Let the relaxation flow into the rest of your body. Breathe slowly.

•Repeat with your left hand and arm. Relax.

•Tighten both fists at the same time and take two or three slow breaths.

•Relax both fists. Then tighten both arms.

•Take two or three slow breaths. Relax.

•Feel the tension easing away. Notice how relaxed you're feeling.

•Take a deep breath and hold it for several seconds. Breathe out and relax.

•Tighten your abdomen, pull in your stomach and hold your breath.

•Exhale and relax your abdomen. Your sense of relaxation should be increasing.

•Arch your lower back while keeping the rest of your body relaxed.

•Take one or two slow breaths and relax.

•Tighten your buttocks. Hold for one or two slow breaths. Relax.

•Tighten your calves for one or two breaths. Relax.

•Push your toes forward and down.

•Hold for one or two breaths.

•Relax. Your entire body should be relaxed.

•Continue the slow, paced breathing for a minute or two. Your heart should now be pumping slowly, and your body should feel limp and warm and relaxed. *Say to yourself:* I feel calm, relaxed and alert.

•To end the exercise, count to three, then open your eyes and stretch.

Source: Keith Sedlacek, MD, medical director, Stress Regulation Institute, 239 E. 79 St., New York 10021. He is the author of *The Sedlacek Technique. Also available:* Two audiotapes under the same title that give detailed instructions on stress-reduction exercises, $17.45/set. Both are available from the Stress Regulation Institute.

Better Health Through Relaxation Response

Most of us have experienced the power our minds can exert over our bodies. You dream that you are being chased—and awaken perspiring, your heart pounding in your chest. A mosquito buzzes in your ear—and soon you are scratching all over. You feel insects crawling on your skin, even when nothing is there!

Audiences at *Lawrence of Arabia* flocked to buy drinks. These moviegoers were not really suffering from a lack of liquids, but their identifications with scenes of hot deserts provoked in them overwhelming thirst.

Conditions our minds perceive to be real become real for our bodies through the messages transmitted by our brains.

The faith factor…

Physicians have long been aware of the im-portance of their patients' beliefs in effecting cures—from the life-preserving will to live to the less dramatic but much more common placebo effect, in which a patient believes a treatment will help him, and therefore it does.

It has been estimated, in fact, that 75% of all patients who visit their doctors have conditions that will eventually get better by themselves. Only 25% are illnesses or injuries that require specific medication or surgery.

For many, the simple act of seeing a trusted physician is enough to bring relief. The doctor's reassuring manner interacts with the patient's faith in modern medicine and in his doctor's ability, producing measurable physiological changes in the patient. Even without direct medical intervention, the patient's condition improves. Any treatment is likely to have greater success if the patient has a profound faith in his physician's efficacy or a belief that a higher spiritual force is at work in his body.

The relaxation response…

Deep relaxation or meditation also produces physiological changes in the body…lowered heart rate and blood pressure, slowed breathing and brain waves, and a generally reduced rate of metabolism. Physicians call this set of physiological changes the *relaxation response.*

The process reverses the self-perpetuating cycle of anxiety, in which worries trigger the central nervous system to react (heart rate and blood pressure increase, identifying anxiety, which again triggers the central nervous system …aggravating the symptoms of stress-related ills).

Regular practice of the relaxation-response technique has proven benefits: Relief from headaches, backaches, hypertension, hyperventilation, panic attacks and insomnia; reduction of high blood pressure, angina pectoris pain and cholesterol levels; enhancement of cancer therapy and other specific treatments; increased inner peace and emotional balance.

The procedure is simple:

(1) Assume a comfortable position in a quiet environment.

(2) Close your eyes and consciously relax your muscles.

(3) Breathe slowly and naturally.

(4) On the exhale, repeat a focus word or phrase of your own choosing.

(5) Maintain a passive attitude, gently dismissing intrusive thoughts and returning to your focus words.

(6) Continue for 10–20 minutes, once or twice a day.

Combining the relaxation response with the faith factor…

The human mind exerts its power over the body better when it is provided with a positive focus for belief—faith in a healer or a pill, for example. Likewise, patients show improved response to the relaxation-response technique when they choose a positive focus word or phrase that has deep personal meaning. (Avoid words such as health or calm, which might draw your attention to your medical problems.)

Example: A Greek Orthodox patient was told to practice his relaxation-response technique. His doctor suggested that he focus on the number *one.* A few days later his condition had worsened. The doctor learned that that patient had negative associations with the word one, and together they arrived at *Kyrie eleison.** The patient then improved rapidly.

Choosing a focus word or phrase with personal meaning can activate and reinforce your belief system, providing a more calming effect on your mind than a neutral—or negative—focus word. But more importantly, it will increase the likelihood of your regular practice of the technique.

Suggestions…

The technique works best on an empty stomach, so plan your sessions accordingly.

Try to suspend your expectations, and do not worry about how well you are doing. Noticeable result may take four to six weeks—or longer—so allow your practice to become as routine as brushing your teeth.

It is normal for your mind to wander. When thoughts intrude, quietly return to your silent repetition.

Place a clock or a watch where you can peek
*Lord, have mercy.

at it. (Don't set a jarring alarm.)

Allow yourself a few minutes when your session is over to just sit quietly with your eyes closed. Jumping immediately to your feet may produce a slight dizziness.

The ultimate benefit of the relaxation-response technique is to reinforce your belief in your body's capacity to heal itself—and thereby its ability to do so.

Source: Herbert Benson, MD, associate professor of medicine at the Harvard Medical School and chief of the division of behavioral medicine at New England Deaconess Hospital, Boston.

Meditation— The Wonder Drug

Using meditation, people can explore their pain to determine what is physical and what is of the mind.

Result: They often find that their pain is being worsened by their thoughts and feelings about it.

Example: A person's back pain makes him irritable, anxious and depressed. This causes muscle tension…which in turn causes more pain.

Relieving pain…

Meditation teaches people to pay attention to their pain and explore the physical sensations.

Because a person's thoughts and feelings can greatly compound or reduce his pain levels, changing how pain is perceived changes how it is actually experienced.

For pain-reduction purposes, meditation should be performed 45 minutes a day, six days a week.

Source: Jon Kabat-Zinn, PhD, director of the Stress Reduction Clinic, University of Massachusetts Medical Center, and author of *Full Catastrophe Living*, Delacorte-Dell Books, 666 Fifth Ave., New York 10103.

Ancient Secrets Of Good Health

Ayurveda, an ancient system of mind/body medicine from India—at least 5,000 years old—says that each of us is unique—physically, emotionally and intellectually. In order to keep ourselves healthy, we must each be aware of our different innate tendencies.

According to Ayurveda, there are three operating principles—*doshas*—that control body functions. Every cell in our body needs all three to survive.

•Vata. Allows the body to breathe, circulate blood, digest food and send nerve impulses to and from the brain.

•Pitta. Processes food, air and water through the system.

•Kapha. Holds the cells together and forms muscle, fat and bone.

The three body types...

Corresponding to the doshas are three basic body types. Your body type depends on which dosha dominates your body. Characteristics of...

•Vata bodies:

•Overactive with a light, thin build. A fast metabolism lets them eat anything and not gain weight.

•Characterized by rapid movement, both mental and physical.

•Learn quickly...and forget quickly.

•Get hungry at any time of day and digest irregularly.

•Sleep lightly, especially when stressed. Tend towards insomnia.

•Energy, both mental and physical, comes in bursts.

•Love excitement and change and won't keep to a routine.

•Pitta bodies:

•Medium build. Usually fair-skinned and freckled with sensitivity to the sun and hot weather.

•Sharp hunger, sharp thirst. Can't skip meals easily.

•Tend towards anger and irritability under stress.

•Very enterprising, with a sharp intellect and precise, articulate speech.

•Live by their watch and resent having their time wasted.

•Others find them too demanding, sarcastic and critical.

•Kapha bodies:

•Solidly built with good physical strength and endurance. Thick, cool, smooth, often oily skin.

•Slow metabolism with a tendency to gain weight. Don't get hunger pangs. Slow to digest. Seek emotional comfort from eating.

•Tranquil and relaxed, slow to anger.

•Need more sleep and wake up more slowly than the other types.

•Mull things over for a long time before making a decision.

•Happy with the status quo and respectful of the feelings of others.

Most people are combinations of two types, with one type predominating.

The importance of knowing whether you are a Vata, Pitta or Kapha type is that you can focus your diet, exercise, daily routine and other measures to prevent disease.

Getting into balance...

The dosha that is the most likely to go out of balance is the one that dominates your body type. Vatas need to be careful about aggravating their Vata, Pittas their Pitta and so on.

If you are a two-dosha type, both doshas are candidates for causing problems.

•Vatas. By nature, a Vata person is cheerful, enthusiastic and resilient. If you are a Vata type and have retained these qualities, you are very likely to be in balance.

But Vatas generally don't enjoy the best health. They often suffer from unexplained aches and pains, difficulty sleeping and excess anxiety.

Signs of Vata imbalance:

Insomnia...anxiety...impatience...short attention span...restlessness...low appetite...constipation...dry skin...excess gas...high blood pressure...lower back pain...intolerance to cold ...nerve pain...muscle spasms.

The key to balancing Vata: Regular habits. Stop grabbing bites to eat here and there, exercising in fits and starts, going to bed at odd hours. Get plenty of rest...stay warm and avoid drafts...eat a lot of warm, comforting foods that soothe and satisfy…eat three meals a day… drink a lot of warm fluids…take a long bath or shower in the morning—moist heat is good for Vata aches and pains…avoid mental strain… make surroundings light and bright…don't use stimulants, including alcohol, coffee, tea and nicotine.

• Pittas. Of all the body types, Pittas are gifted with the most innate drive, aggression and energy. They attack life head-on and relish challenges.

But this inner drive is often the source of their undoing. Pitta gives you a fiery energy. If you abuse it, it will burn you up. The workaholics of this world are generally out-of-balance Pittas, especially if their emotional undertone is angry and compulsive.

Signs of Pitta imbalance: Anger…resentment …intolerance of delays…rashes…excessive hunger or thirst…bad breath…hot flashes… heartburn…ulcers…sour body odors…hemorrhoids…patchy complexion…bloodshot eyes …yellowish feces or too-yellow urine.

The key to balancing Pitta: Moderation. Don't push yourself too hard. Take time to wind down from activity…meditate regularly…keep home cool…eat lightly, avoiding overly hot food and fatty foods…avoid stimulants…take a tablespoon of castor oil before bedtime every four to six weeks…avoid strenuous exercise…spend a lot of time outdoors…add laughter to your life.

• Kaphas. Kapha people are naturally steady and slow, which makes them dependable and strong. But out-of-balance Kaphas cling to the status quo. They need the stimulation of new sights and sounds, people and events.

Signs of Kapha imbalance: Mental inertia… depression…procrastination…oversleeping… greed…intolerance of cold… sinus or chest congestion…fluid retention…skin pallor…aching joints…high cholesterol…frequent cold… weight gain…allergies…asthma…cough…sore throat…cysts…diabetes.

The key to balancing Kapha: Stimulation. Seek variety in life…don't overeat…reduce sweet foods…stay warm…avoid dampness…drink warm fluids during the day…exercise regularly

…take it easy when you are sick and need to recuperate.

Source: Endocrinologist Deepak Chopra, MD, former chief of staff of New England Memorial Hospital in Stoneham, Massachusetts, and founder of the American Association of Ayurvedic Medicine. His most recent book is *Perfect Health: The Complete Mind/Body Guide,* Harmony Books, 201 E. 50 St., New York 10022.

Placebo Effect Is Shown To Be Twice as Powerful As Expected

"Hurry, hurry—use the new drugs while they still work!" a 19th-century French physician urged his colleagues. He may not have known why faddish drugs work on credulous patients, but the fact that they do has been borne out by scientists studying the power of the placebo to cure.

Trusted physician power…

New findings show that the placebo effect—in which patients given an inactive treatment believe it can cure them—is most powerful when a trusted physician enthusiastically offers a patient a new therapy.

In a study of more than 6,000 patients being given experimental treatments for asthma, duodenal ulcer and herpes, two-thirds improved, at least temporarily, even though rigorous tests later found the treatments medically useless. They were then abandoned.

The old rule of thumb among medical researchers was that only about one-third of patients will show some improvement when given a placebo. The results of the new studies reveal the effect to be twice as powerful as was thought.

These and other findings that the placebo effect can be far stronger than had been widely assumed are leading some researchers to call for stricter standards for testing new medications. Others are proposing that physicians try to capitalize on the placebo effect in treating their patients in order to marshal the body's own healing powers.

"I argue that instead of just trying to control for placebo, we should try to maximize it," said Dr. Frederick Evans, a psychologist at the Robert Wood Johnson School of Medicine in New Brunswick, New Jersey. "If a doctor believes in what he's doing and lets the patient know that, that's good medicine."

While many people think a "placebo" is simply a sugar pill or other medicine with no active ingredients, the term has a broader meaning. The "placebo effect" includes any improvements in a patient not specifically due to a particular ingredient in a treatment, like a drug or surgical procedure. These "nonspecific," or placebo, effects may be due to causes ranging from a patient reporting relief from symptoms in a subconscious effort to please a well-liked physician, to actual biological improvement.

Testing the placebo effect…

To assess the potency of the placebo effect during the burst of enthusiasm for a new medical treatment, researchers reexamined data from initial clinical trials of five procedures that had at first seemed highly promising, and then later were shown to be useless. The procedures included surgical removal of the glomus—a structure near the carotid arteries in the neck—to treat asthma, and gastric freezing for duodenal ulcers. They also included three treatments for herpes simplex virus—the drug levamisole, organic solvents like ether, and exposure of dyed herpes lesions to fluorescent light.

"In these studies, the doctors treating were also those evaluating the symptoms, which is what happens in a typical physician's office," said Dr. Alan H. Roberts, a psychologist at the Scripps Clinic and Research Foundation in La Jolla, California, who led the research. The results were published in *Clinical Psychology Review.*

The physicians, who offered the treatments as part of an early clinical trial and believed in their efficacy, told their patients the various approaches were new and promising. With both physicians and patients having high hopes for a cure, the resulting placebo effect was potent. Because these were very early trials of new drugs, no control groups were used.

Of a total of 6,931 patients receiving one or another of the five treatments, 40% were report-ed to have excellent results, another 30% had good outcomes, and only 30% were reported to have "poor" results, Dr. Roberts and his colleagues found.

Yet in later trials, when patients who received the treatments were methodically compared with control groups of patients who received placebos or nothing at all, "the effectiveness disappeared," said Dr. Roberts.

Psychological factors…

Dr. Roberts believes that for relatively mild medical problems, under the best conditions, the placebo effect will produce positive results in roughly two-thirds of patients. The effects would not be nearly as strong for serious diseases such as AIDS or cancer, he said: "In the more severe disorders, the placebo effects would be mainly in terms of patient's subjective complaints, not their physical symptoms."

In Dr. Robert's view, the improvements associated with placebos are caused by factors like patients subconsciously exaggerating improvements of their symptoms in order to please their doctors, and doctors who hope for positive results skewing their evaluations of symptoms favorably.

The notion that the placebo effect is due to biological changes from patients' hopes being raised is met with skepticism by Dr. Roberts. But other researchers disagree.

"Could an enthusiastic physician and a believing patient create a clinical improvement in a patient?" said Dr. Ronald Glaser, a virologist at Ohio State University Medical School. "That question has haunted drug studies. But there may well be a psychological effect with a significant biological outcome, if you extrapolate from data showing that psychological factors like stress can affect viruses like herpes. It's definitely one possible explanation."

The herpes virus is one of Dr. Glaser's specialties. With his wife, Janice Kiecolt-Glaser, a psychologist, he has studied the effects of people's emotional swings on the replication of herpes virus.

"We've found herpes viruses are responsive to stress, improving or worsening depending on a patient's emotional state," said Dr. Kiecolt-Glaser. "Since herpes virus is quite responsive to psychological influences, the first wave of physicians' enthusiasm could well have a beneficial medical effect."

Dr. Roberts is not the first researcher to find that the placebo effect can account for improvements in more than one-third of patients, a ratio proposed in the 1950s by Dr. Henry Beecher, one of the first to do research on the placebo.

Patients most likely to benefit…

"The range for placebo recovery I've seen varies from zero to 100%," said Dr. Arthur K. Shapiro, a psychiatrist at Mt. Sinai Medical Center in Manhattan. "Different factors combine to produce the magnitude of a placebo. For example, in my own research with 1,000 patients, those who like their physician most and who were most anxious showed the greatest improvement from placebo."

Such findings on the power of the placebo are bringing calls for revising the way in which new treatments are tested. In order to be sure the benefits attributed to experimental treatments are not simply due to placebo, tests of new medications now use a "double-blind" design, in which neither the physician nor the patient knows what medicine is being given, and some patients are given a nonactive treatment.

"There is a false sense of security about the scientific tests of drugs, particularly psychiatric drugs," said Dr. Roger Greenberg, a psychologist at the State University of New York Health Science Center at Syracuse.

One of the main problems with the standard double-blind test, said Dr. Greenberg, is that patients and physicians alike can very often tell who is getting the active medication and who is getting the placebo because only the true medication has side effects. This can lead to placebo enhancement of the seeming effectiveness of the medication being tested.

Unblind "double-blind" test…

"In instances when researchers have asked patients and physicians to guess whether they were using the active medication or the placebo, the results are sobering—in one such study, 78% of patients and 87% of their physicians could tell," said Dr. Greenberg. "That means the so-called 'double-blind' is not really blind."

For that reason, Dr. Greenberg proposes that in addition to the medication being tested and the

usual inert placebo, tests of new drugs should include an "active" placebo, which produces side effects but has no medical consequence. And, in the most rigorous test, a physician other than the one giving the medicines would make the evaluations of improvement.

In an analysis of 22 studies of antidepressants, Dr. Greenberg and colleagues found that if, in addition to the new drug being tested, some patients were given an older antidepressant as a control, the new drug was only one-quarter to one-half as powerful as was reported in studies without the comparison drug, in which the new drug was pitted only against an inert placebo.

The research finding, published last year in the *Journal of Consulting and Clinical Psychology* by Dr. Greenberg and his colleagues, concludes that current standard practices for drug testing often exaggerate the potency of new medicine.

"In general," said Dr. Greenberg, "the better a study is controlled, the blinder it becomes and the smaller the difference becomes between the real drug and the placebo."

Source: Daniel Goleman, PhD, is the former editor of *Psychology Today* and a fellow of The American Association for the Advancement of Science. He writes about health and human behavior for *The New York Times*.

Cancer Support Groups

Despite all the hoopla over advances in drugs and surgery, one of the most powerful weapons we have against cancer is simply talking about it.

Study after study has shown that cancer patients who participate in support groups live longer than those who face the illness on their own. If you find that hard to believe, consider our recent study of women with breast cancer.

If detected early, breast cancer is easily treatable. Once the tumor has spread to other parts of the body, however, breast cancer must be thought of as a chronic rather than a curable illness, and the risk of dying from it is much higher. We decided to study how we might help women to face this threat honestly, but in such a way that it enriched their lives and those of their family members.

Our study, which began in 1985, involved 86 patients with advanced breast cancer who had undergone standard medical and surgical treatments for their disease. Fifty of the women were assigned to participate in a support group. Thirty-six "controls" did not participate in a group.

How support groups work…

Our first goal for the women participating in the support group was to help them establish a new social network. These women—many of them new to the process of psychotherapy—were facing death. They were grieving and in pain and feeling isolated.

At first, we worried that talking about their illness might make these women feel worse instead of better. And they were reluctant to discuss their feelings in a room full of people they did not know.

To help break the ice, we tried to foster an atmosphere in which it was possible to talk about the "hard stuff." We encouraged the women to focus on common experiences—things they shared rather than things that set them apart.

Example: Many women discovered they shared a fear of telling their husbands just how frightened they felt.

Living longer—and better…

Watching each other grapple with death helped these women in two ways. First, it showed them how to cope better with the specifics of disease and treatment. Second, it helped them learn to face their own mortality.

The women participating in the group gradually learned to air their true feelings and to accept the support of loving friends and families. They also learned self-hypnosis to "turn down" the pain and anxiety associated with cancer.

Eventually, they reached the point where they could say, "I don't like the idea of dying, and it will sadden me that I can't do what I've wanted to do in the world, and that I will not be with the people in my life I love and care about. However, I am going to make the most of the time I have left."

As a result of their participation, the women were less anxious and depressed. In addition, they lived significantly longer than women who did not participate in the groups.

In fact, the average survival from diagnosis until death was 18.9 months for women who did not participate in the support group—and 36.6 months for the women who did. Two of the 86 original patients are still alive. Both were in the support group.

Our support group made living with cancer easier. The women in the group found they were not alone. As a result, they felt less fearful and less depressed. They were more likely to adhere to their treatment regimens. They ate better, slept better and exercised more than women not participating in the group—who, despite having a similar disease, tended to feel demoralized and alone.

Bottom line: Health care is more than just drugs, surgery and other methods of physical intervention. It's support from caring doctors and nurses—and often some kind of group counseling with other patients.

Psychological support pays…

In this country, we have long underemphasized compassion, support and stress management and overemphasized costly high-tech procedures. The latter are important, but they are only one portion of medical care.

In managed-care organizations, psychological support for medical illness is often considered an unnecessary expense. The fact is that such psychological support reduces unnecessary office visits and diagnostic tests because it helps patients deal better with a very serious illness.

Self-help suggestions…

If you have cancer, take steps to get the emotional support you need. Ask your oncologist about cancer support groups in your community. Participate! *Also helpful:*

•Take care of yourself. No matter what path your cancer takes, keep yourself comfortable and rested.

•Be direct and open with your family—but don't discuss things with them when you feel especially tired or stressed. Open lines of communication are especially crucial between husbands and wives. If your spouse's illness frightens or frustrates you, let him/her know. If you have children, tell them that you do not want to leave them. Make sure they know that they are not to blame. Finally, encourage them to be helpful to you—even if it means something as simple as giving you a glass of water.

•Don't worry about others' reactions to your cancer. Your illness is likely to arouse strong feelings in friends and family members. Don't try to control these feelings.

•Know your limits. Don't trivialize your illness. Be direct with yourself and with others about what you can and cannot do.

•Set priorities. Focus your energy on that which is most important to you. If you need help in accomplishing a certain task, don't be afraid to ask for it.

•Tell your physician what you are really scared about. Let him/her know what kind of care you prefer.

•Be optimistic. Face the worst—but hope for the best. Be honest with yourself and those around you.

Beyond breast cancer…

Our findings have just been confirmed at other institutions and with other types of cancer. At the University of California, Los Angeles, similar support groups extended the survival of people suffering from malignant melanoma. At the University of Southern California, the same happened with persons suffering from lymphoma and leukemia.

Another support group starting…

We are now recruiting patients for another support group study. In this study, we want to teach the participants to live rich, fulfilling lives no matter how little time they have left. After all, the real issue for all of us is quality of life, not quantity. And life is about using the resources at your disposal to do what you want to do. It's about cherishing close relationships.

Some people spend an entire lifetime and never accomplish these things. Others can accomplish these things in two months.

Source: David Spiegel, MD, professor of behavioral sciences and director of the Psychological Treatment Laboratory, Stanford University School of Medicine, Palo Alto, California. He is the author of *Living Beyond Limits*, Times Books, 206 E. 50 St., New York 10022.

How to Help Your Brain

The brain works best in a cool room (65° Fahrenheit). *Also helpful:* (1) Diffused light (either natural or artificial light reflected from the ceiling and walls). (2) Upright posture, with the back bent slightly forward.

Source: *The Brain Book* by Peter Russell, E.P. Dutton, Inc., New York.

Some Plain Truths About Your Brain

A popular misconception concerning human potential is that only 10% of the brain is ever utilized. This leads to the logical assumption that 90% of the brain is idle, waiting to be activated. *Common belief:* If people could only learn to stimulate and direct that latent brainpower, they could accomplish the work of a genius.

Plain truth: The brain does not lie 90% fallow awaiting the proper inspiration. That statement about 10% of the brain being in use is perpetuated by purveyors of the human-potential movement. The brain cannot be increased tenfold through application and drive. It's an illusion that vast multiples of brainpower are available. Although additional skills requiring greater application of the brain can be learned, they require special methods of application.

Some truths and fallacies…

•The quest to master such skills as deductive reasoning, musical achievement, martial arts, meditation or creative expression requires an enormous investment of time and effort. *Fallacy:* The messianic, utopian concept that relies on tapping the power of unused brainpower. *Fact:* This leaves out the most important ingredient—the work effort.

•Innate abilities are important. There are several forms of intelligence, which include the verbal, logical, spatial, musical and interpersonal abilities, as well as the body abilities of athletes and dancers. The brain has many capacities, but most people have innate abilities in only a few of these areas, not in all. *Fal-*

lacy: You can become an accomplished master in anything you attempt if only you can persuade your brain to cooperate.

• The brain works in ways that are far from understood. The exact function of the "unused" brainpower isn't clear. Indeed, the precise—or even approximate—amount of unused brainpower isn't provable in any way. Little of the brain is a wasteland—each portion has its purpose. *Example:* Memory is apparently spread around the brain mass, and any bit of a memory can reconstruct the entire experience. Thus the brain has the tremendous ability to reduplicate itself. If parts of the brain are damaged or destroyed, the remaining portions can often take up much of the load without serious impairment of human activity. In this way, most of the brain is in use all of the time. It is not lying idle.

• The brain has a built-in rate of forgetfulness. While a person strains to fill the brain's neurons with new information, the brain is busy actively unloading previously stored information. *Needed:* A sophisticated, realistic awareness of those factors in order to achieve personal growth.

Personal growth…

• Personal growth is a positive commitment that is aided by in-depth reading and conversations with those who have done it. Search out people who are skilled in a field in which you wish to advance. Learn about the dedication required and the attitudes that will help to make your effort fruitful.

• Never forget the level of application demanded. *Depressing cycle:* Beginners start out wildly enthusiastic, eager to master a chosen endeavor, such as playing the violin or unraveling the secrets of Zen. But they have been oversold on self-development without effort, and they quickly become discouraged at the first patch of difficulty. Do experimental trials before making a total commitment. Try a class, session, interview or book. Be certain you are ready to give yourself to the project.

• Be aware that such achievement requires personal commitment. You must have the fortitude to overcome discouragement, persevere when the spirit is weak, and stay with it despite long odds. Many creative people develop blocks from the fear of defeat or failure. The term "wri-

ter's block," for example, describes a creative person who has temporarily lost the courage to take the risks that writing entails. Similarly, a "negative attitude" is a defense employed by people hoping to avoid the pain of failure by rejecting their chances of success.

A positive mind-set is best: You are then more likely to be courageous. And it will be easier to find a purpose and the strength to accomplish the objective.

Bottom line…

All people who are accomplished in a given field share one vital quality—the willingness to work hard. That quality is learned and trainable. *Requirement:* The willingness to disbelieve those who claim that everything is simple once that mythical 90% of the brain is activated.

Postscript: Some people do not want to make the effort to grow. They are content with what they are, character faults and all. That's all right! Knowing your limits and accepting yourself are also part of realizing your potential.

Source: Martin G. Groder, MD, a practicing psychiatrist and business consultant in Chapel Hill, NC.

Working from Both Sides of Your Brain

Have you ever felt "of two minds" about something? There's a valid reason for it. *Try this mini-quiz:*

1. Without looking at your watch, do you know about what time it is? (a) Yes. (b) No.

2. Do you believe in intuition, hunches, and horoscopes? (a) Yes. (b) No.

3. Are you goal-oriented in almost everything you do? (a) Yes. (b) No.

4. As a student, did you prefer (a) algebra or (b) geometry?

5. Would you rather (a) do the talking or (b) listen?

6. Do you prefer your activities to be (a) planned in advance or (b) spontaneous?

7. Are you well-organized, a maker of lists and schedules, etc.? (a) Yes. (b) No.

If your answers are predominantly a's, you are very likely left-brained. Conversely, if most of your answers are b's, you are right-brained. What does this mean?

• The split-brain theory.

In 1981, the most exciting news in the scientific community was neurosurgeon Roger Sperry's proof of the split-brain theory, for which he was awarded a Nobel Prize.

Sperry's proof confirms that the two hemispheres of the human brain house separate, though sometimes overlapping, skills. (The two halves communicate through a central connector, the corpus callosum.)

The left brain is logical, verbal and linear, while the right brain is visual, emotional and intuitive. You use your rational left brain to add a line of figures or to make a speech. You use your more spontaneous right brain to imagine yourself on a tropical island as you drive in rush-hour traffic. You shift back and forth between the two hemispheres, depending on the tasks you are performing.

Sperry also proved that individuals tend to prefer one side of the brain to the other. The degree of preference or dominance (known as "brain bias") profoundly affects each person's thinking style, physical and mental abilities, personality and job performance. As people develop and learn to depend on the skills of one half, they tend to neglect the other. *Bottom line:* Although you cannot change your brain bias, you can develop the abilities of the less-preferred half through exercise and practice. You can increase your brain power by learning to use both sides of your brain.

• Thinking styles mirror brain bias.

One thinking style is not better or smarter than another, any more than right-handed people are more dextrous than left-handed. But your ability to function in the work world is indisputably related to your thinking style and your sensitivity to the styles of others.

Example: A left-brained secretary, typically tidy and efficient, might be driven crazy by a messy, absent-minded ad executive who stares out the window all day. This boss might see the secretary's efforts to impose neatness and order as an irritating waste of time. The secretary, though, would undoubtedly see the exec's daydreaming as unforgivable when he should be clearing his desk. In truth, the left-brained

secretary is unable to work efficiently in a cluttered, chaotic environment, while the right-brained ad exec comes up with his best ideas while staring out the window. These coworkers need each other and would get along better if they understood each other's brain bias. The secretary's need for structure and the boss's for flexibility are as real—as physical—as the need for well-fitting shoes or a bright reading lamp.

By learning to recognize the characteristics of brain bias, managers can place their staff in positions that will better suit their talents and temperaments.

• Group bias.

Like individuals, companies, organizations and groups exhibit brain bias as well.

American business (and Western society as a whole) has traditionally valued the skills of the left hemisphere: Logic, speech, attention to detail, efficiency, order. But the most effective managers successfully combine left-brain abilities with creativity, warmth, and the talent to perceive an overall situation—skills from the right hemisphere.

Although the computer has taken over many of the more tedious left-brain tasks, the spontaneous associations, sensitivity to others and inventiveness of the right brains cannot be replicated. American management (like the much-lauded Japanese) is learning to rely more sincerely on right-brain skills. A study of executives who acknowledged the validity of insights and hunches—right-brain talents—showed that those with the greatest reliance on intuition had the highest profit records.

Some of America's most successful companies are enrolling workshops devoted to whole-brain thinking. Sophisticated tests, including biofeedback, are used to measure brain bias. Exciting new techniques help the individual to develop his or her less-preferred side and to recognize when and how to switch to the "task-appropriate" hemisphere.

For the left-brained, increased access to the right brain leads to improvements in memory, creativity, communication and social skills. The right-brained sharpen their verbal and organizational skills when they learn to "switch left."

Examples of switching techniques:

Your mind wanders in meetings (right-brained). Switch left by taking notes or planning a question to ask. Use your right brain to imagine yourself in the speaker's position. Why does he think that point is important? Where did she get her data? You'll find your interest renewed.

You are facing a problem. Use your left brain to define the problem as clearly as you can. Write it down in simple language. Then free your right brain with "internal brainstorming." Let your ideas about the problem flow, and jot down or tape your associations, no matter how wild. Include your feelings. Do not stop to judge your thoughts. Later, using your left brain again, evaluate your ideas one at a time, focusing on the useful ones. Finally, employ your whole brain to recognize a solution and to fill in the details.

Additional exercises for problem solving: Imagine the extreme opposite of the situation. Assume the role of someone else. Reverse your objective. Suppose that all your information is wrong.

Learning abilities thrive on challenge, risk and variety. Without these elements, people stagnate.

Source: Jacquelyn Wonder, communications and creative management consultant, Denver Corporate Seminars.

Truth About IQ Scores

IQ scores and achievement are closely linked in men—but not in women. In one study, two-thirds of the women with genius-level IQs (170 or above) were housewives or office workers.

Source: *What's the Difference? How Men and Women Compare* by Jane Barr Stump, William Morrow and Co., Inc., New York.

How to Expand Your Thinking Power

Over the past few years, there have been important developments in our understanding of effective thinking and how to teach it.

Because of the well-publicized decline in Scholastic Aptitude Test scores and other indicators of educational achievement, most of this effort has been directed at students. But there's every reason to believe that many adults suffer from the same kinds of difficulties as schoolchildren. Research shows that the means are now available for adults, as well as children, to improve their reasoning skills.

Reasoning power...

When we think of reasoning, we think of *formal* reasoning—that is, mathematical, logical or symbolic thought. But one of the most important areas in which people need skill is *informal* reasoning. In fact, 99% of our reasoning is informal, the kind you would use to figure out what house to purchase, what stock to invest in, what job to take, to whom you offer a job and so on.

Yet our research shows that four years of high school, four years of college and even four years of graduate school do little to sharpen one's informal reasoning skills.

A characteristic pitfall of informal reasoning is incompleteness. People fail to take advantage of the information they have to investigate an issue thoroughly. Most people neglect to argue both sides of a case or to develop more than one or two lines of an argument. In informal reasoning, since every line of argument is only probable, not absolute, you need to develop several lines to be convincing.

Example: We did research into how people think about everyday issues such as the litter-reducing effect of a 5¢ deposit on bottles. People commonly give the most obvious response: "Litter will be reduced because people will return the bottle to get the 5¢." And that's about it. Or they get a little more sophisticated with: "If you return the bottles all at once, it's not such a burden." But these responses aren't sufficient to sort out the issue thoroughly. One overlooked issue, for instance, is that the majority of litterers aren't at home. They are at outdoor picnics or in parks. It's much more of a burden for them to save the bottles than to toss them.

Another pitfall is overlooking counterexamples. People are prone to sweeping generalizations. We've done research on statements such as, "Art is creative," a natural, conventional belief. The catch is that there are lots of counterexamples, such as dime-a-dozen ocean scenes or clown paintings. Thinking more acutely will lead to the conclusion that art isn't necessarily more creative than anything else, unless it's original or very unusual.

Creative thinking…

In this area, there's a gap between understanding and practice. People are full of sensible advice about what to do in difficult situations. They know you should be thorough, use what you know, look at both sides of the question, challenge your own assumptions, try to imagine a different approach to break the mind-set you're in, put the problem aside for a while and come back to it, and so on. There's one catch… most people seldom follow their own advice.

Tricks of the trade…

It's not true that simply knowing a little about how to think well guarantees that one will think well. Forces in human psychology tend to undermine our best thinking. One of the simplest is the effort required. Carefully critical or creative thinking requires more work, exacting a price in terms of effort expended and frustration encountered, even though the result may be better.

Also, your personal bias in favor of a particular conclusion may prevent you from exploring the other side. Just to think in another direction is almost painful because it seems to put at risk everything you've invested so far.

If you pay attention to what you already know about thinking, you'll improve your reasoning skills:

•Using analogies and metaphors. Deliberately ask yourself, "What am I assuming?" If art is creative, for example, does that mean business is noncreative? This will lead you to think about the real meaning of creativity.

•Not getting bogged down in a particular line of reasoning. Deliberately step outside it. *Suggestion:* Take 10 minutes to think of the problem in a completely different way. If that doesn't work, you've lost only a little time.

•Paying more attention to the aesthetic aspects of the problem than to the pragmatic ones. The aesthetic and pragmatic are really the same thing seen through different windows. By looking through the aesthetic window, you get a fresh hold on the problem. *Example:* If you're designing an inventory system, it shouldn't only be functional but should also solve certain difficulties in keeping track of things in an easy, elegant way.

•Looking at how you're being conventional. Break that conventional set. Watch out for clichés. Avoid timeworn and obvious answers.

•Being self-conscious. It's a myth that self-consciousness is a barrier to effective thinking. Be aware of the way you do things. Do you brush aside problems, or do you take them seriously? Do you look for opportunities to think about something a little longer, or do you pass them by? Don't be put off by the initial awkward feeling that self-consciousness will give you. As with any skill, the more you practice, the easier and more natural it becomes.

•Opening up to ideas. Don't dismiss suggestions with "That's just common sense" or "I already do that." Common sense isn't always common practice, and if you think you already do it, you probably don't. Research on actual behavior tells us that people don't accurately perceive whether or not they follow their own advice. Typically, they don't.

If you want to take a course in thinking, look for one that requires a lot of small-group work over a substantial period of time. The one-shot workshop typically washes out in a couple of weeks. The extended program that meets for six to 20 weeks and keeps at the objectives in a persistent, fresh and involving way can really remake a person's pattern of thinking.

Courses are common, but quality differs widely. Investigate the course carefully, including the teacher's credentials, before taking it.

Source: David N. Perkins, PhD, senior research associate in education, Graduate School of Education, Harvard University, Cambridge, MA.

The Power of Positive Imaging

Over and over again, I've seen that when people begin to think positively about what they want to accomplish and how to do it, the chances are very good that they'll reach their goals.

One of the most important elements of positive thinking is positive imaging. That is, creating a picture in your mind in which you actually visualize yourself doing whatever it is you want to do. These pictures—and the suggestions they generate—can have a powerful effect.

When they apply: Visualization can work for virtually any personal or professional goal. Sports figures have long used visualization techniques to improve performance. Even health problems can be alleviated through effective imaging. All it takes is a defined goal, a logical process of achieving it and an attitude that says, "I truly want to meet that goal."

Breaking barriers...

Consider the four-minute mile. It appeared to be insurmountable, the Mt. Everest of track. Nobody seemed able to break that four-minute mark. Roger Bannister did it, however, in 1954 ...and within 15 years, 274 men had run a four-minute mile or better. Bannister's accomplishment changed the mental image of the race for those who followed.

There are many similar stories. I know a top golf pro who had never stroked a putt until he heard—in his mind's ear—the thud of the ball dropping into the cup. And baseball players visualize themselves at the plate, watching for the pitch and taking the perfect swing. Through the process of concentrating on a realizable goal and "seeing" it reached, they fulfill their true potential.

Finding direction...

Obviously, putting positive imagery to work is like using any other tool. First, set reasonable goals. Second, believe you're capable of reaching them. Third, work at changing your thought habits.

I once met a young man raking leaves on a golf course. He told me he wanted to get somewhere in life. But he didn't know where he wanted to be, when he wanted to get there... or even how to get there. My advice to him... Go think about it, and then write down and show me what you want, when you want it and so forth.

This young man later told me he aspired to be a foreman at a nearby factory. He showed me his timetable. He had developed his plan, but he still had one obstacle to overcome—he didn't think he had any ability beyond that foreman's job. But positive imaging proved him wrong, and now he runs that factory!

Mind over matter...

This type of imaging works. I have no doubt about it. I once knew a 97-year-old man, the oldest practicing physician in New York. He was one of the healthiest people I've ever known. How did he stay so healthy? He encouraged his organs to do their jobs and do them well. Every morning this man jumped out of bed and paid homage to his body, starting with his brain and working down. He'd thank God for his wonderful stomach, kidneys, liver and so on. And then, he'd tell these organs how much he appreciated the fine job they were doing. He venerated his physical organs and visualized them doing well.

He was living proof that you can improve yourself by seeing yourself as vigorous and vital. But it wasn't just the veneration of his organs that kept him so healthy. His appreciation of his body helped him conduct his life in a manner that was supportive of his health.

Images and expectations...

Developing images of your own performance is only one side of the coin. You also have the opportunity to help yourself and others by applying mental imagery to the people with whom you work. Perhaps there's someone in your business with whom you're always at odds. You've developed an enemy relationship with this person. You don't like each other.

Solution: Think of this person as someone you like, someone who can work with you. Create in your mind an image of the relationship restored. Put aside your negative feelings and begin to treat this person as a valued friend and associate. You won't see immediate results, but over time, you'll find that this person is responding to you in a more positive way. *The lesson:* Be aware of your expectations of others. People are likely to deliver what you expect them to.

The mind is a powerful tool, and you'll be pleasantly surprised by the results of positive imagery. You won't always accomplish everything you visualize, but you'll do much better than you would believing you'll never reach your goals.

Source: The late Dr. Norman Vincent Peale, author and lecturer, New York.

Some Reasons to Consider Acupuncture

Many health problems can be helped by acupuncture. The sex and age of patients are not important factors, but their attitude is. They must not fight the treatment mentally. They should be believers.

The sensation of the needles varies among patients. Some feel only the slightest prick and others find it painful. The more pain a patient feels, the more resistance and stress there are in the related part of the body. As in deep massage, where the patient must "work through" the pain to get real relief, we help him get through the painful part of acupuncture until he gets some positive effect. Actually, acupuncture goes even deeper than massage because it stimulates the nervous system.

Problems that respond to acupuncture…

• Back pain. First, we ease the discomfort by working on the circulation in the spinal area. Then we try to analyze the cause of the problem. It could be posture, weight, or a poor mattress. Or the patient may need a better diet and more exercise. The object is to keep the pain from recurring. *Success rate:* 95%.

• Insomnia. We try to relax the natural functions of the body through the nerve system to get the patient into a natural rhythm of feeling energetic when he wakes up and sleepy at night. *Success rate:* 90%.

• Addictions. Whether the substance is cocaine or nicotine, the user must want to shake the habit. Acupuncture helps people get into a healthier, more energetic cycle. When cocaine users feel good naturally, they won't need the high from the drug. With smokers, we try to counteract nicotine withdrawal symptoms by reprogramming nerves to the lungs and the adrenal gland. *Success rate with patients who really want to quit:* 80%.

• Excess weight. Businesspeople do a lot of nervous eating. Acupuncture relaxes them and strengthens their sense of well-being. They can then better burn off fat and control eating. *Success rate:* 80%.

• Depression. Many people don't know how to cope in our kinetic society. They tire and get nervous too easily. We give them more energy with acupuncture and a combination of herbs and vitamins. *Success rate:* 80%.

• Hearing loss. We can help if the problem is the result of some (but not all) kinds of nerve damage. *Success rate for hearing improvement:* 80%.

• Impotence. Sometimes people lose sensitivity and desire because they are tired. Acupuncture can contribute to general well-being and appetite and can specifically stimulate the nerves of the sex areas. *Success rate:* 70%.

• Hair loss. Acupuncture can increase circulation to the scalp and may be helpful to men under 50. I take this treatment myself as a preventive measure.

General therapy…

Acupuncture should be your first therapy rather than a last resort. We recommend monthly treatments for general good health. These "tune-up" sessions rejuvenate the thyroid, lymph and digestive glands to head off other problems before they surface. For a specific problem, such as back pain, patients usually need 10 visits for sustained relief. Expect to pay around $50 for a visit of 45–60 minutes.

Look for a good acupuncturist who is certified by your state's licensing board. If you find a practitioner by word of mouth, be sure he has the proper credentials.

Source: Zion Yu, a 20th-generation acupuncturist in Beverly Hills, CA.

How Hypnosis Works

The sharp voice of your boss/teacher/spouse startles you. "You haven't heard a word I've said!" "I'm sorry," you explain. "My mind was on something else."

Sound familiar? If you have been so absorbed in a train of thought that you were barely aware of the activity around you, chances are you were in a state similar, if not identical, to a hypnotic trance.

Trance is a state that occurs naturally in the vast majority of people, a state of aroused intense concentration—the opposite of sleep—that can occur spontaneously whether one intends it or not. And hypnosis is, quite simply, the formal use of this natural capacity for attentive, receptive concentration.

Our everyday consciousness is balanced between whatever our attention is focused on and our awareness of peripheral activity. The hypnotized person is able to focus his attention entirely on a single issue while increasing his peripheral awareness.

Health-care professionals regularly use hypnosis to treat problems ranging from chronic pain to fear of flying. The use of hypnosis is an active part of a wider trend to enlist the strengths and resources of the individual patient in his or her own healing.

Hypnosis is not something that is done *to* you. You are not in someone's power. You do not "go under" or "pass out." Rather, hypnosis seems to be a matter of shifting attention to the right hemisphere of the brain (the side that is more emotional, visual, creative and analogical) while the left brain (verbal, analytical and rational) "idles." Hypnosis is something that people can be taught, quickly and easily, to do for themselves—a technique that can give them greater control over their lives than they have ever had before.

Who can be hypnotized?

About 30% of people are not hypnotizable. This group includes persons who are mentally ill, who have suffered brain damage, who are of very low intelligence, or whose ability to concentrate has been otherwise impaired. The remaining 70% of the population have a measurable amount of "trance talent." Ten percent of people have the ability to achieve a light trance. They are known as "ones" on a scale of zero to five. About 50% have medium ability. They are the twos and threes. Finally, there are the remaining 10%, the highly hypnotizable fours and the ultra-talented fives.

An individual's capacity for achieving the trance state seems to be a given and does not change appreciably over time.

One indicator of trance capacity is the eye roll. The subject, seated comfortably, is asked to roll his eyes toward the top of his head and at the same time to close his eyelids slowly. The amount of white showing just before the eyes close indicates the degree of trance capacity. "High rollers" (the easily hypnotizable) have no iris showing. "Low rollers" (poor candidates for hypnosis) are barely able to roll their eyes.

Personality traits also indicate trance talent. People with a strong preference for the left-brain mode (practical, analytical) fall on the low side of the scale—the zeros and ones. People who are distinctly right-brained (creative, intuitive) are the fours and fives.

How does treatment work?

Just because a person has little trance talent does not mean that hypnosis can't help him. Motivation is equally important. For example, a person who is highly motivated to quit smoking through hypnosis has a high probability of success, even if he has only modest trance talent. And motivation can be increased.

Hypnosis increases our responsiveness to suggestion, whether the messages are directed by a hypnotist or later reinforced through self-hypnosis. A general rule for success seems to be to accentuate the positive. *Example:* Suggesting to the smoker that cigarettes are poisonous to the body...that we need our bodies to live... and that we are as responsible for our bodies as for a beloved child or pet.

Ways hypnosis is helpful...

Although hypnosis cannot do anything that psychotherapy can't, it does greatly accelerate the process. Hypnosis has been particularly successful in the following areas:

•Overcoming phobias. The success rate for one-time treatment of fear of flying is higher than for any other clinical syndromes, and many other phobias are overcome with hypnosis.

•Eliminating undesirable habits. Symptoms such as hair-pulling, teeth-grinding and nail-biting are overcome.

•Conquering addictions, such as those to nicotine, food or caffeine. Hypnosis has proved least successful with alcohol and drug problems, possibly because these substances interfere with a person's ability to concentrate.

•Controlling pain. Subjects are taught techniques to "filter the hurt out of the pain" with impressive results. Migraine headaches, childbearing, dental work and, in some cases, even major surgery can be rendered painless, while the subject remains relaxed and awake.

•Mastering insomnia and anxiety. The sensation of "floating," often mentioned to describe the feeling of trance, is particularly useful in problems relating to anxiety. In the "screen technique" a subject is instructed to make his mind a blank screen and to place his anxieties on one half of it while conjuring up a restful scene on the other half. He can then focus entirely on the second screen until he is calm.

•Enhancing concentration, memory and creativity. When the constraints of left-brain thinking are temporarily relaxed, "creative leaps" are facilitated.

As a person gains control over one problem through hypnosis, his self-respect is increased, and he may gain control in other areas.

There do not seem to be any negative effects associated with hypnosis. The Svengali-like hypnotist creating a zombie-killer is pure myth.

Hypnosis by itself is not the same thing as treatment. You don't visit a hypnotist to have a tooth extracted, and you shouldn't expect medical treatment from anyone who is untrained in medicine. Referrals to accredited practitioners of hypnosis can be obtained from your physician or from a professional association.*

Hypnosis is not useful for everyone. But for the 70% of us who are gifted with trance capacity, it is a quick, simple, inexpensive and pleasurable way for us to truly use our minds.

*American Society of Clinical Hypnosis, 2400 E. Devon Ave., Des Plaines, IL 60016; Society for Clinical and Experimental Hypnosis, 111 N. 49 St., Philadelphia 19139.

Source: Herbert Spiegal, MD, clinical professor at Columbia University's College of Physicians and Surgeons and a doctor in private practice in New York.

Self-Hypnosis Secrets

The word *hypnosis* is actually a misnomer. The Greek word for "sleep," it is actually the opposite of sleep. While hypnotized, you're tuned in to what the hypnotist is saying. It's basically an altered state of consciousness in which there is heightened attention. It is useful for giving yourself certain suggestions that will "take you someplace you want to be."

Hypnosis can be used to help you stop smoking, overeating, using drugs or drinking excessively, or to control any other compulsive behavior. It can help you overcome anxiety, give you relief from pain, or help you get to sleep. In these stressful times, hypnosis is an invaluable relaxation technique. It uses neither magic nor hocus-pocus, but our untapped human potential to cure some of what ails us.

Hypnosis at its best…

As a therapeutic tool, hypnosis is most effective as an adjunct to treatment rather than as a treatment itself. *Exception:* Pain control or other nonpsychological problems can be helped by hypnosis alone. Many problems that seem simple are actually multifaceted, and no one-shot treatment can provide a lasting cure.

For any self-hypnosis technique to be meaningful, it must be tailored to you as an individual, to reflect your particular problem. *Example:*

A man goes to a hypnotist to lose weight because he has a family history of diabetes and is terrified of getting the disease. His self-hypnosis technique will include visualization of an insulin needle, being hooked up to a kidney machine, etc. If you want to lose weight but don't have this particular fear, your technique will be quite different. Each person has to find the one that works best for him or her.

Hypnosis also works as a diagnostic tool to uncover the secret fear that is keeping a person from reaching a goal. I ask my patients while hypnotized to visualize themselves without the problem they've come to me to cure. During the visualization, I ask them, "What's wrong with the picture?" *Example:*

A happily married overweight woman, when asked what was wrong with the picture while she was visualizing herself at her ideal weight, said,

"I'm cheating on my husband because I'm getting more attention from men and feeling sexier." In order for self-hypnosis to work for this woman, she had to confront her fear and deal with what she perceived as a threat to her marriage.

Hypnosis will work only for the highly motivated person who isn't looking for an instant magic cure but is willing to make some sacrifices to reach the goal.

Using images...

The visualization of images during self-hypnosis, both negative and positive, is at the heart of the technique. The hypnotist aims to find out what your hot button is. Then you work on coming up with an image that will have a strong impact. You close your eyes and imagine yourself as a character in a movie. *Examples:*

• You want to stop smoking. Visualize yourself 10 years from now in a chest specialist's waiting room. The receptionist calls you into the doctor's office, telling you your X-rays have just been developed. The doctor points to a dark mass on the X-ray and tells you it's inoperable. Nothing can be done. You have only six weeks to live, and you'd better start making arrangements for your family.

• You want to lose weight. Visualize yourself at your favorite restaurant with your usual dinner companion. Dinner is over, and the waiter asks if you want dessert. Your partner orders chocolate cake, but you ask just for coffee. See yourself watching that person eating the cake without feeling deprived or competitive.

Important: The scene you visualize should be as detailed as possible. The type of image used will depend on the problem. Negative images can be very useful with something that you can avoid completely, like cigarettes, alcohol or drugs. For such substances, negative imagery also serves as an aversion technique. If you hypnotize yourself and imagine that the first drink will taste like urine, a strong aversion to alcohol can be created.

Negative imagery doesn't work in weight control, however. You can't give up food completely, and no matter how often you imagine a chocolate-chip cookie tasting like sawdust, eventually you'll try one and it will taste good. The point of self-hypnosis for weight control is

to take a rational approach to food, so that it becomes just food—not comfort or friendship.

Hypnotizing yourself...

I teach people self-hypnosis in two or three sessions. During the first session I take a detailed history of the problem in order to tailor the hypnotic routine individually. Then I hypnotize the person, later explaining how it can be done at home, repeating the process until the person feels comfortable doing it alone. *How it works:*

• Sit down near as little distraction as possible, preferably at night, in a comfortable chair you usually don't sit in. Roll your eyes up, keep them there, take a deep breath and hold it. Close your eyes slowly, exhale very deeply and normally, and concentrate on a floating sensation. Feel the sensation spread from the top of your head to the tips of your toes. Deepen the sensation by visualizing a staircase of ten steps. As you walk down the staircase, the floating sensation doubles with every step. When you get to the bottom, use your visualization exercise.

• Imagine yourself in control. The whole essence of hypnosis is gaining control, and self-hypnosis puts you in perfect control. You're not distracted as at other times, but are totally tuned in to yourself. So use that moment to see yourself in control, able to resist temptation.

Finding a reputable hypnotist...

Hypnosis is a field riddled with quacks. Since anyone can learn to hypnotize another person in five minutes, less-than-competent individuals are attracted.

But to be effective, self-hypnosis must be individually structured. That requires education and training. To find a reputable professional, contact the American Psychological Association or the American Psychiatric Association. They will refer you to a psychologist or psychiatrist who is qualified and experienced in hypnosis. Although a variety of professionals (chiropractors, podiatrists, etc.) and nonprofessionals hold themselves out to the public as hypnotists, you are generally best off going to a qualified mental health professional.

Source: Ronald Jay Cohen, PhD, a clinical psychologist in private practice in New York.

17

Strategies for Success

Obstacles to Success

There are certain obstacles that we all have to deal with before we find success. The problem is in recognizing the obstacles. All too often, ambitious people delude themselves into thinking that the path to success is clear. Then, they wind up stumbling without really knowing why.

Ironically, the lack of a clear goal is the most common obstacle to success, even for people with large amounts of drive and ambition. Typically, they focus on the rewards of success, not on the route they must take to achieve it.

Remedy: Whenever possible, write down your goals, forcing yourself to be specific. Periodically make a self-assessment. Take into account your education, age, appearance, background, skills, talents, weaknesses, preferences, willingness to take risks and languages spoken. Ask for feedback from others. Don't try to succeed at something for which you have no talent. Try out your goal part time. If you dream of owning a restaurant, work in one for a while.

Failure and fear...

Sooner or later, everyone who's ambitious will experience a failure. Many don't recognize, however, that failure is necessary. There are many secret payoffs for failure: The humble poor are never accused of exploiting others. They can feel morally superior to money-grubbing, power-hungry moguls. They're comfortable as part of the culture that supports being a cog in a machine. They get righteous satisfaction from complaining about the system.

To understand failure, evaluate honestly what stands between you and success, both in the outside world and within yourself. Find a mentor who will be open with you about his or her own struggles with such blind spots. Read biographies of people who overcame their own fears to become successful.

Without realizing it, many people fear the *Peter Principle*, which says they'll rise to their level of incompetence and will be exposed as inadequate. Others are so afraid of failure that they become paralyzed. They forget that if they never try anything worthwhile they've already failed.

What everyone must realize is that if you take risks, there's no way to avoid failure. You can't succeed without struggle. But if you're able to learn from what went wrong, you can do it right the next time.

Other obstacles to success:

•Inability to let go. People often stick with a dead-end job out of pride, stubbornness or unwillingness to admit that they made a mistake. Sometimes, the comfort of the familiar is just too seductive. *To start letting go:* Take small, safe steps at first. Start talking to friends and associates about possible new jobs. See what's available during your vacation. Shake things up at the office by suggesting some changes in your current job. Take some courses and learn new skills.

•Lack of self-esteem. This is an enormous stumbling block. But, in fact, you may be judging yourself by excessively high standards. *Example:* An architect who started his own firm realized he was a total loss in math and engineering, and that his only talent was design. If he'd felt inadequate about his deficiencies, he might not have gone into business at all. But as a realist, he simply concentrated on his own area of expertise and hired experts to fill in on the technical end.

•Procrastination. If you delude yourself by thinking something will be easier to do tomorrow, you can avoid looking at why you aren't doing it today. Like alcoholism, procrastination is a subtle, insidious disease that numbs the consciousness and destroys self-esteem. *Remedy:* Catch it early, but not in a harsh, punitive, self-blaming way. Look at what you're afraid of and examine your motives. *Example:* You may not really want to leave your low-level job, but feel you ought to because your spouse is anxious for more money and status. Once you can acknowledge the real cause, you can escape the depressing downward spiral.

•Shyness. If you're shy, the obvious remedy is to choose an occupation that doesn't require a lot of public contact. But even shy salespeople have been known to succeed. As long as they're talking about product lines and business, a familiar spiel can see them through.

Casual socializing seems hardest for the shy person. *Remedies:* Don't put enormous pressure on yourself to socialize if it makes you uncomfortable. Concentrate on getting ahead by doing a terrific job rather than by being Mr. or Ms. Charming. Or, take a Dale Carnegie course. They *are* helpful.

•Unwillingness to look at yourself. If you're not willing to assess yourself honestly, success will probably forever elude you. People tend to avoid self-assessment because they feel they must be really hard on themselves. *How to look at yourself:* Realize you've probably taken the enemy into your own head—you've internalized that harsh, critical parent or teacher from your childhood. Instead, evaluate yourself as you would someone you love, like a good friend whom you'd be inclined to forgive almost anything. *Example:* Anwar Sadat was raised with the teachings of a harsh, judgmental religion. While in prison he read about another religion, which had a loving, forgiving, supportive God. This made all the difference in his life.

Source: Tom Greening, PhD, clinical supervisor of psychology at the University of California at Los Angeles and a partner in Psychological Service Associates

Avoid Sabotaging Your Own Success...or Else

Why do some seemingly sensible people act in ways that harm their own interests?

They set out to succeed but somewhere along the way they either misjudge how to achieve their goals...do not want to face criticism and failure...or defeat themselves with the intention of hurting someone else. *The most common types of self-defeating behavior and how to avoid them...*

Deliberate miscalculation...

Most of us go through life trying to overcome the hurdles set in our way. We avoid doing things that slow us down or increase the odds of failure. Those who exhibit self-defeating behavior choose strategies that will backfire.

Poor decisions are made either because of overconfidence or because the desire for a short-term gain is stronger than the appeal of a long-term goal.

Example I: Jane wanted to study clinical psychology in graduate school. After her initial application was rejected, she decided to show the school she was really a desirable prospect by taking a few courses as a nondegree student at her own expense...a good strategy if carried out correctly. But instead of demonstrating her prowess by taking subjects in which she could easily get A's, she took the hardest courses she could find and scored only C's...dooming her graduate school hopes.

Jane miscalculated because she was overconfident. Had she estimated her strengths and weaknesses more realistically, her chance of success would have been much greater.

Example II: Gary was happily married and prosperous. For many years, he indulged his hearty appetite for eating, drinking and smoking but avoided exercise. Not surprisingly, he suffered a heart attack while only in his early 50s. When the doctor told him he had to change his lifestyle, he did so...for a time.

But after just three months, Gary decided he couldn't do without his vices. Two years later, he had another heart attack...this one fatal.

While it doesn't always lead to such unfortunate results, the same kind of poor trade-off between present benefits and future costs is found in many kinds of self-destructive behaviors—drug addiction...excessive sun exposure...overdependence on credit cards...even procrastination.

To avoid miscalculation mistakes: Evaluate your strengths and weaknesses and the long-term costs and benefits of your actions as realistically as you possibly can...and try to consider all the alternatives.

Trying to avoid the truth...

Many forms of self-defeating behavior occur because people don't want to admit their limitations. They sabotage their own success in ways like these:

• Self-handicapping. This occurs when successful people deliberately construct obstacles for themselves so they will have an excuse for failure.

Example: Whenever French chess champion Deschapelles played, he insisted on giving his opponent the advantage of removing one of Deschapelles' pawns and taking the first move.

Result: Deschapelles increased his chance of losing...but always had a good excuse if he lost.

• Substance abuse. Alcohol and/or drug abuse serves two purposes for self-destructive people. It helps them blot out their own faults and inadequacies...and gives them an external excuse for failure.

Example: Violinist Eugene Fodor was a national hero at age 24 after he won the Tchaikovsky Violin Competition in Moscow. But within a few years, his reputation sank as he turned to drugs and was eventually arrested after breaking into a hotel room.

Reason: Great fame at an early age creates great expectations in audiences...and great stress in performers. Drugs eased the stress Fodor felt and provided an excuse for his failure to perform adequately—but allowed him to believe in his musical ability.

To face the truth: Develop a sense of perspective on yourself, recognize your imperfections and learn to accept criticism.

The quest for revenge...

Sometimes self-defeating behavior is a misguided attempt to redress emotional wounds inflicted in childhood.

Example: Despite obvious talent, Stuart, aged 36, would break rules...steal...drink on the job...in an obvious manner that was sure to be detected. Then his supervisor would reprimand him and threaten his job.

This replicated a pattern from Stuart's childhood, when his father would beat him. After the beating, while Stuart was sobbing, his alarmed mother would scream at his father until his father withdrew into a state of depression. Thus, Stuart would enjoy the sweet taste of victory over his father...even though he was in physical agony himself.

I call this self-defeating strategy Pyrrhic revenge, after the famous "victory" of the Greek king Pyrrhus, who won a battle against the Romans but almost wiped out his whole army in the process.

Pyrrhic revenge is typically found in marriages in which one spouse suffered abuse as a child…often from an alcoholic parent. He seeks out a partner who has the same problem his parent had. He tries to correct the problem and, in doing so, cure his own childhood wounds. This usually doesn't work, so instead he ends up venting the long-repressed anger against the parent…and doesn't mind destroying himself as long as his spouse goes down, too.

To avoid self-destruction via revenge: Realize your own interests…judge whether you are acting to help yourself or to hurt someone else.

Choking under pressure…

Choking is a self-defeating behavior that occurs when people under pressure, striving to do their best, fail because they try too hard to succeed and do not perform as well as they can.

Example: Beth, an outstanding student, had to recite a speech from Shakespeare in front of her high school class. After memorizing it perfectly, she stood up to speak…and nothing came out.

Reason: Smoothly speaking memorized lines is an automatic process. Beth wanted so intensely to succeed that her self-consciousness prevented her memory from working naturally.

The same phenomenon causes sports champions to falter in important matches and winning teams to lose championship games.

To avoid choking under pressure: Develop perspective. Remind yourself that success in life doesn't depend on just one event.

Example: If it's the last minutes of an important event or presentation, and victory or defeat depends on your next move, remember that just being there shows that you already are a success.

Source: Steven Berglas, PhD, clinical psychologist and management consultant, Harvard Medical School, Boston. He is coauthor with Roy F. Baumeister, PhD, of *Your Own Worst Enemy: Understanding the Paradox of Self-Defeating Behavior*, Basic Books, 10 E. 53 St., New York 10022.

Cure for Shyness

Shy people are too preoccupied with themselves, research reports. *How to improve:* Stop focusing on your perceived inadequacies and feelings of anxiety and pay more attention to other people. That way you're concentrating on other people's cues—what they say and do—rather than worrying about how you appear to others.

Developing Your Winning Potential

I used to work in a mental institution where I discovered that motivating some of my patients to speak normally was like getting your coffee table to talk. They have a formula for losing. This started me thinking about whether successful people have a formula for winning.

They do. And there's nothing mysterious about the formula. It's something all of us can learn by bringing out our own winning potential.

Imagine that in every possible area crucial to success there's a scale ranging from 1 to 10. Schizophrenics are at 0 or 1 on the scale, average people are at 5-6, and winners are at 9-10.

How it works: In the area of positive thinking, for example, schizophrenics I treated thought that everyone was out to destroy them, and they spent their time planning the demise of their supposed enemies. Average people often believe that others have insulted them or taken advantage of them. They spend their time blaming and hating those people. Winners, on the other hand, act positively and do something.

The winners' scale…

In a business setting, if something said to them sounds insulting, winners either assume it's their own fault—that they were communicating poorly—or possibly that they didn't hear what was said correctly, or that the others had incorrect information.

The key is that they take responsibility for the problem. *Example:* A politician I interviewed said that whenever he's in a confrontation, he makes an appointment and goes right to the "enemy" to discuss the problem. While the enemy may not become his friend, he's never as cutting or hostile again.

Sensitivity is another crucial measurement on the winners' scale. Schizophrenic patients weren't cruel and insensitive only to others but also hurt and humiliated themselves. Average people are kinder, but winners are considerate, thoughtful, caring and giving.

Attitudes to develop…

The keys to developing your own winning potential:

•Take small steps. I once worked with a catatonic who hadn't moved in 30 years. In 31 days I got him to talk. But he did it in small stages. The first time he twitched his nose, I cheered. I was genuinely positive about it. Winners reinforce their own small successes. *Example:* The loser takes a course in computer programming, doesn't grasp it after the first week and gives up, assuming he's too stupid to learn the subject. The winner who doesn't grasp it after a week assumes he's doing well because he's figured out how to use the keyboard.

•Be willing to fail. Losers assume that winners never make mistakes, that they're just lucky. Often the opposite is true. Winners fail a great deal. One winner, the CEO of a famous company, says his failure rate is 70%. It's the old Babe Ruth story. The year he hit the most home runs, he also had the most strike-outs. Sometimes winners wind up succeeding simply because they stumble on the right answer by trial and error.

•Be kind to yourself. In a sense, you must become your own parent. Losers are brutal to themselves. Average people will lose $10,000 in business and spend years berating themselves for being fools and failures. Winners tell themselves, "Well, I learned what I could from that venture. It's time to move on." When you're feeling down on yourself, lift up your two index fingers, kiss them and plant a kiss on each cheek. Psychologically it works. You'll feel better.

•Listen to the beat of your own drummer. Ignore people who tell you to quit. *Example:* The inventor of tofutti, the popular ice cream substitute, spent all his spare time for years searching for the right formula. His wife got fed up and finally divorced him. Tofutti became a huge success (and its inventor is now happily remarried).

Developing self-esteem…

For those moments when you're not feeling good about yourself, try to realize that everybody else is probably frightened and feeling like two-year-olds. I've treated superstars, royalty, politicians and people on welfare. All of these people, no matter what their accomplishments were, felt insecure and scared as if they were swimming upstream.

Antidote for insecurity: Hard work. There's always room at the top. So get started. No matter how you feel about yourself, hard work will reinforce both your self-esteem and your chance of becoming a winner.

Source: Psychologist and family therapist Irene C. Kassorla, PhD, author of *Go For It: How to Win at Love, Work and Play,* Delacorte Press, New York.

Checking to See If You're On The Right Course

Use your life goals as signposts to indicate you're on the right course. It's the overall direction of your life that counts, not the achievement of specific goals. Getting there isn't just half the fun—getting there is actually what we call living.

Self-Confidence Strategy

How to build self-confidence: Picture yourself a success and dress the part. Appraise yourself realistically—then add 10% to the estimate. In contrast, don't overestimate others. Don't conjure up obstacles for yourself, but learn to tolerate an occasional setback.

Source: *Fail-Safe Business Negotiating* by Philip Sperber, Prentice-Hall, Englewood Cliffs, NJ.

You Don't Have To Be Lucky To Be Lucky

The luck you make for yourself has nothing to do with blind chance. Luck is what the Chinese call it: Opportunity. It knocks every day at your door. But it isn't enough to hear it knock. You have to greet it fearlessly and work with it.

Common obstacle to being lucky: Fear of failure. This fear causes people to put off new projects. Procrastination postpones the possibility of failure. *Secret ingredient of luck:* Willingness to confront the possibility of failure.

To make your own luck:

•Find an idea that offers a new and better way to satisfy people's needs. Start by analyzing your own needs and ways of filling them. You are your own best research laboratory.

•Move forward with your idea before your enthusiasm cools.

•Gather information from people who know most about the subject.

•Build a network of contacts who will help you get the idea off the ground. One contact invariably leads to another.

Characteristics of people who make their own luck:

•They are in touch with their gut feelings. As a result, they realize when a real opportunity is speaking to them. They go out of their way to be friendly. They know how to make contacts and use them.

•They do their homework. They lay the groundwork for their projects, gather facts and prepare in general.

•They take risks and aren't so enslaved by habit that they fear the unorthodox.

•They are skeptical. They never forget that a venture could fail. *Insight:* Being 100% sure of success is not confidence—it is foolhardiness.

•They take failure as a learning experience. They admit their mistakes and are undaunted by previous failures.

•They recognize that the capacity for change and growth exists within them. They know there is no such thing as bad luck that permanently imprisons you within an unsuccessful lifestyle. The only villain who can do that is you.

Source: Bernard Gittelson, author of *How to Make Your Own Luck*, Warner Books, New York.

Self-Defeating Behavior And How to Avoid It

Occasionally we all forget something crucial, come late to an appointment or manage to make a muddle of an important task. But when that type of self-defeating behavior becomes habitual, it signals to people that you're not dependable, that you're not willing to live up to your part of the bargain. Those messages, conscious or not, can have drastic consequences… loss of job, failure of marriage, etc. To understand why we are self-defeating involves a journey into the past. And to change a self-destructive pattern, we must be willing to do some serious self-evaluation.

A child's eye view…

Children are naturally self-centered and aggressive creatures (as is obvious to anyone who has watched small children fighting over toys). But in order to live in the world, the child has to curb his aggressive instincts. He may be furious at mother for toilet training him, but restrains himself from hitting her because he also loves her. As we grow older we must learn to use aggression as well as love to get on with our lives. Competition and the drive to succeed, both come from the aggressive impulse. Living happily in the world requires a very delicate balance between love and aggression, a balance many people never get quite right.

Unresolved aggression turns people into self-defeaters. They haven't learned to modify their aggression in work and love. Or, they've buried their aggression to the point that consciously they don't experience it as a problem, but it bubbles up unconsciously in all kinds of self-destructive ways.

The family drama…

We first learn competition in the family, by competing with siblings, who are symbolic stand-ins for the same-sex parent. We're really competing with the parent for what we perceive him or her as having—power, money, love, respect and so forth. *Conflict:* Feeling guilty about the competition and unconsciously not allowing ourselves to outdo the rival for fear of losing parental love or of inviting parental anger and aggression.

Defying parents' or society's expectations can also invite seriously self defeating behavior. *Example:* A woman became a ballet dancer against her father's wishes. He thought dancing was tantamount to prostitution. She was a marvelous dancer but when she appeared in a ballet that demanded pirouettes, she could only perform well upstage, away from the audience. While pirouetting downstage toward the audience, she'd start to falter and finally fall when she reached the footlights. In this case the audience represented a judgmental father saying, "You're a whore."

Women have a more severe problem since they're trained to be nonaggressive and nurturing. To succeed in business, a woman must become competitive and exhibit behavior commonly thought of as masculine. Many career women become so frightened about losing their feminine identity that they trip themselves up before reaching their full potential.

What to do about it…

• Examine your motives. If you find yourself exhibiting self-defeating behavior, maybe what you're really saying is, "I want out." Ask yourself: Am I successful on my own terms? Am I happy with my life? Wanting a different way of life from what is expected of you is a perfectly valid desire.

Example: Baba Ram Dass, Eastern oriented spiritual leader, started out as Richard Alpert, son of the president of the New Haven Railroad. He gave up an executive position with the railroad because he was frightened by the power of his position. Alpert then became a psychologist and professor at Harvard until, along with Timothy Leary, he was dismissed for distributing LSD to students. A subsequent period of self searching and drug taking was followed by his reemergence as Baba Ram Dass, after a spiritual pilgrimage to India; he became a guru sought after by millions. From his father's perspective, he could be considered a failure and a loony. In his terms, though, he's a smashing success.

• Don't sweat the small stuff. Realistically assess whether a particular behavior is truly self-defeating or merely annoying, and to what degree. If it's just a nuisance, like constantly losing your glasses, it may be better to realize you're making a big fuss over a minor problem and buy some extra pairs. Worry will make it worse. People who worry all the time about any behavior will do it more, not less.

• Become aware of what you're doing. This is difficult in our culture, which doesn't encourage self-reflection. *Helpful:* Keep a journal noting the various activities of your day and how you felt when doing them. Correlate the feelings in the journal with what was going on when you did something self defeating Once you start seeing a pattern, you can adjust for it.

• Pay attention. If things never go well for you in a certain area and you don't know why, ask for feedback from a friend you trust to be objective. Your friend may have noticed a self-defeating behavior that you were totally unaware of. Also, listen to unsolicited feedback from others, without being defensive. If people in your life constantly complain about your lateness, for example, don't keep on giving what seem to you to be perfectly reasonable excuses. Look at the possibly psychic benefits you might be deriving from behavior that is ultimately self defeating.

• Make a virtue out of your weakness. Almost any behavior can be turned to advantage if you acknowledge it and use it. The trick is to be conscious of what you're doing. *Example:* A sloppy dresser can present himself as an intellectual who is too concerned with really important matters to worry about looks. Albert Einstein wasn't known for his sartorial splendor.

• Seek professional help if the self-defeating behavior is a pattern that's out of your control and is adversely affecting your life. You may need therapy to root out the deeper causes and resolve the inner conflict.

Source: Simone F. Sternberg, EdD, a psychoanalyst and psychotherapist who is dean of students and clinical supervisor at the New York Center for Psychoanalytic Training.

When to Make Excuses

Excuses often serve a positive function. They allow us to preserve self-esteem and reduce the stress of failure…maintain harmony with co-workers and friends when we foul up…acknowledge the validity of standards that we've violated…take risks that would otherwise paralyze us.

Source: C.R. Snyder, co-author of *Excuses: Masquerades in Search of Grace.* John Wiley and Sons.

Lateness Can Be Controlled

Rarely is there such a thing as unavoidable lateness. The causes of lateness are many—hostility, fear, contempt, self-destructiveness or the desire for attention. (The attention given to latecomers can be very gratifying and is thus a strong motivation for lateness. All eyes turn to the latecomer when he arrives, and he knows he has been the subject of discussion while the others have been waiting for him.)

Main misconception of latecomers: Their belief that they are late due to circumstances beyond their control. This is usually untrue. *Simple fact:* Some people are in the habit of being on time, and other people are in the habit of being late. Both types are easy to identify. The on-time people are not "lucky." They just know how to get somewhere on time.

Dealing with your own lateness…

•Cutting it close. You leave just enough time to get there, and you're delayed because you miss a bus, or you have to stop for gas, or some other minor "unforeseeable" delay occurs. *Solution:* Assume that the worst conditions will prevail and plan your time with those in mind. Assume bad traffic, trouble finding a parking space, etc.

•Too many appointments. You can make them on time if each goes like clockwork, but they rarely do. *Solution:* Set your appointments with the expectation of the longest possible time for each appointment.

Dealing with lateness in others…

Study people's habits in regard to their lateness as you would study their habits in a poker game. How late is Jones, usually? Most latecomers have a predictable pattern. There are ten-minute-late people, half-an-hour-late people and very late people.

Best ways to cope with the chronic latecomer:

•Never arrange to meet him on the street, and try not to have him come to you. Instead, go to his place.

•Try not to meet for lunch where a reservation is involved. Go to his place and phone the restaurant from there.

•If you must meet a latecomer on neutral turf, be sure it's in a place where you can do paperwork or make phone calls while you're waiting.

•Don't deal with a latecomer by arriving late yourself. It isn't worth the discomfort. Eventually he will beat you at this game, and you will end up with a loss of self-respect.

Latecomers for social engagements: If you want to serve dinner at 8 with cocktails at 7:30, but some of your invitees are latecomers by habit, invite them for different hours. Invite the Joneses, who are ontime people, for 7:30. Invite the Smiths, who are usually late, for 7. Invite the Perrys, the worst offenders, for 6:30. They'll all probably arrive around 7:30.

In case the worst offenders surprise you by appearing considerably earlier than anyone else (on time!), tell them you purposely asked them to come early so you could have some time alone with them. If all else fails and you're still kept waiting at dinner, don't let the latecomers make an issue of their lateness. Cut off their apologies and excuses, and pleasantly but firmly divert the conversation to some other topic. This is the best revenge.

Source: The late Peter Shaw, PhD, associate professor of English at the State University of New York at Stony Brook.

Simple Secrets of Self-Improvement

Most advice about how we can change ourselves concentrates on self-image: Feel confident. Don't sell yourself short. Be relaxed. But some people change—or remain the same—because of repeated acts in a given pattern.

Shyness, for example, is strengthened every time the shy person falls silent after being interrupted. Self-confidence is eroded every time we fail to finish a project, even if we remind ourselves to feel confident.

There's a better way to improve yourself... change by doing.

Encourage friends to criticize you, and learn how to take criticism. Your critics may not always be right. But if you don't get the truth from others, you may never find it out.

Handling criticism:

•Let your critic finish what he has to say before you answer.

•Don't go into the reasons for your actions or behavior. This is really just a way of excusing them.

•Don't jest. It is insulting to the critic.

•Show that you have understood (whether or not you agree) by briefly repeating the criticism in your own words.

•Let your critic know that you understand how your behavior has caused inconvenience or made him feel.

•Don't open yourself to criticism for what you are—only for what you do.

Source: George Weinberg, PhD, author of *Self Creation*, Avon Books, New York.

Overcoming Indecision

Chronic indecision creates enormous stress on the individual. You are, in fact, divided against yourself. This conflict leads to tension, which in turn inhibits positive decision making. It's the most vicious of cycles. *Examples:*

In business, the indecisive manager is a disaster. He gains neither from success nor from setback. Afraid to err, he never learns from mistakes. His paralysis can sink a company.

In relationships we have the aging bachelor. Alienated from his own feelings, he's unwilling to commit himself to one woman. He's afraid to lose his precious freedom. But he never exercises that freedom, so he has lost it anyway. He forgets that freedom means making choices.

Some of us resort to pseudo-decisions—rushed and arbitrary stances that lack commitment or follow-through. But they aren't real decisions unless they are free, unconditional, total and personal...and lead to action relatively quickly...and engender no regrets, rage or emptiness afterward.

Although most people who suffer from indecision don't even realize it, the evidence is clear to those around them. Why do people waffle? Most often they're weighted down by self-hatred. They're terrified of taking responsibility for a decision because there is always the chance they will be wrong, unleashing still more self-hatred.

Another syndrome is rooted in the American Dream—the notion you can have it all without paying a price. But every true decision exacts a price: Giving up the options not chosen. So the dreamer remains inert, refusing to choose, like a child in a toy store.

To overcome indecisiveness, you must first combat self-hatred by ridding yourself of self-glorification. Realize that you have human limitations—and that one of those is making an occasional poor choice. At the same time, it's important to take stock of real assets such as talents, familial love, good health, etc.

To become a decision maker, you must accept what I call "The Big Fact": In very few instances is one decision actually better than another. Unless you're a surgeon deciding whether or not to operate, it probably doesn't matter what you choose. This is particularly true in relationships. After a romance fails, most people choose the same type of partner again and again. Their first choice wasn't bad. *The real fault:* Their lack of commitment—their failure to struggle and grow through communication.

If you're paralyzed by fear of failure, the best course is to meet the fear head-on. After you've failed a few times, you will be desensitized to it—and finally free to choose.

For a complex decision, it helps to assess your priorities. Consider what is most important to you...money, power, prestige, creative activity, pleasure, and so on. You can even assign point values to each category and then see how options stack up.

Make your important decisions when you feel your best. If you're rested and in a positive frame of mind, your decision will be freer. You will know you are making the best choice you can.

Source: Theodore Isaac Rubin, PhD, author of *Overcoming Indecisiveness*, HarperCollins, New York.

How to Get Out of a Rut

There's a hand-written sign next to an old dirt road in Georgia that reads: *Pick your ruts carefully. You're going to be in them for the next 40 miles.*

Unfortunately there's no warning sign for most of us when we land in a rut. Often we don't know how we got into what we're doing or why we stick with it. The one thing we do know is that we don't want to be stuck forever. And no matter how old you are or what kind of rut you're in, there is a way out. At least at first, you don't have to actually do anything. You just have to start thinking differently about who you are and what you want out of life.

First steps...

Before escape is possible, a basic change in attitude is necessary. Most of the people who are stuck in ruts spend their lives complaining about their lot but never doing anything about it. The complaining makes them feel better (usually at the expense of everyone around them), but the end result is the same—nothing changes.

You must accept that no one is going to do anything for you. It is your responsibility, and yours alone, to change your own life. Start thinking constructively about what you want rather than moaning about what you don't have. If you're upset about your career, stop complaining and ask yourself: What do I really want to do? Where do I want to do it? With whom? Under what circumstances? What are my skills? (Include not only business experience but also hobbies, interpersonal skills and non-job related skills.) What are my short-term goals? Long-term goals? Think long and hard and in great detail about what would make you happy. Don't be afraid to fantasize or hatch grandiose schemes. You may be able to make at least parts of your fantasy come true.

Exercise: Give yourself an imaginary $10 million and think about what you would do with it. Be specific. Then use your brain to see how much of your fantasy you can turn into reality. *Sample fantasy:* To live on a South Sea island and spend all my time sunbathing, fishing and picking coconuts. It may not be possible to move to the South Seas and loll about all day, but if you're living in a cold climate and really love the tropics, you might be able to get a job in Florida and spend all the spare time that you choose sunbathing and fishing.

Rut-removal tactics...

People automatically assume that their current job is a given that can't be changed. What escapes their notice is that sometimes you can get out of a rut right in the company where you're now employed. *Examples:*

•A bright young man of 35 was working in New York for a national firm. He'd been dreaming for years about living in California, and, as it turned out, his company had a branch there. Making the change was a little complicated because he was a high producer in New York and his boss didn't want to lose him. But he went to California and got to know the manager of that branch. Then he spoke to his boss, according to a carefully conceived plan, and explained how he would still be doing the company a lot of good in California. He also had a very promising replacement in mind whom he planned to train. His New York boss wound up supporting his move to California, and he's now very happy in the company's San Francisco branch.

•A senior vice president at a big East Coast bank was unhappy because he didn't spend enough time with his family. The family's hobby was sailing, but they often had to go without him since his weekends were spent working He wasn't about to quit his job because, besides enjoying his work, he was in line for the bank presidency. The situation seemed impossible. *Solution:* He redesigned his job. He hired someone to take on his least favorite tasks and concentrated on his areas of expertise, thereby reducing his hours from 80 per week to 50. He started sailing with his kids on the weekends. Recently he got his biggest bonus—and he was truly worth it.

Avoiding extremes...

If you've been in a rut for much too long without doing anything about it, midlife crisis can spark desperate measures. Too many people blindly flee either their job or their marriage, thereby destroying families, hurting children and wiping out the financial gains of a lifetime.

What people don't realize when they're establishing a marriage and career in their twenties is that 25-30 years later, they'll be different people with different ideas, hopes and dreams. If you recognize the inevitability of this process, which is really one of growth, you can factor change into your life. Don't develop tunnel vision about your work, no matter how much you love it. Keep learning and growing in other areas—socially, recreationally and professionally. You'll be less likely to wind up in a rut, and you'll have some means to get out of it if you're in one.

If you need a drastic change...

•Start your own business. This does not have to be a total gamble. *Overlooked clue to success:* Research not only your venture but yourself. Too many people go into businesses they are personally unsuited for. *Example:* The couple who dreams of running a little hotel in the mountains won't make a go of it if they're shy, retiring types.

•Start communicating openly with your family. This hardly sounds like a prescription for drastic change. However, lack of communication is the primary reason for a marital rut. It can be an exciting, startling and totally new experience to find out what your spouse and children really think.

•Alternative to running off with your secretary: Consider going to a weekend marriage workshop, sometimes called a marriage encounter. This is a group of couples with an ex-

perienced leader. Spouses are taught how to be open with each other. It can be more effective than marriage counseling, which is often the last stop before the divorce.

Source: John C. Crystal of the John C. Crystal Center, New York. The Center offers intensive courses in creative life/work planning.

5 Easy Changes Anyone Can Make

To get out of a rut: Go to work by a different route or use another mode of transportation... unplug the TV for a month...take a child to a symphony concert or puppet show...take a bath instead of showering...skip the Valium (or martini) and try a walk in the woods.

Source: *The Psychology of Winning* by Dr. Denis Waitley, Berkley Books, New York.

How to Beat Boredom

Boredom is often a form of emotional anesthesia self-imposed by those who do not want to experience their own feelings. It is also a method by which people keep themselves from changing and growing.

Boredom breeds more boredom. *Hard truth:* People are accountable for their own boredom. Blaming others or one's lot in life is no solution.

Ways out: Growth in areas such as the creative arts, work and study, and involvement with family and friends. This entails struggle, as bored people must use more of themselves than they have previously. And bored people must risk involvement even before a consuming interest materializes. *Point:* Involvement often sparks interest. Waiting for a bolt of lightning to ignite an interest results only in a continuation of apathetic boredom.

Source: *Dr. Rubin, Please Make Me Happy* by Theodore L. Rubin, MD, Arbor House, New York.

Biggest Time Wasters

Guilt: People spend hours moaning and worrying about mistakes they made like missing a bus or taking a wrong turn. This moping about something that has already happened and can't be changed not only uses up unproductive hours—it also incapacitates your mind for coping with the next project. *Better approach:* Accept accidents for what they are, pick up the pieces and go on about your business.

Disorganization: Not taking the time to work out a system for getting regular chores done or filing away important pieces of information can make simple tasks take twice as long. Keep an up-to-date, running shopping list. Put addresses and phone numbers into a book or a card file as you collect them. Schedule routine tasks to keep from wasting a weekend day just deciding what you should do first. (Too many choices will slow you down. Think of how much faster you get dressed on a trip when you only have one or two things to wear.)

Source: Barbara Platcher, PhD, executive director, National Association for Professional Saleswomen, Sacramento, CA.

Importance of Liking Your Job

Chinese proverb: If you would be happy for one hour, take a nap. If you would be happy for a day, go fishing. If you would be happy for a month, get married. If you would be happy for a year, inherit a fortune. If you would be happy for life, love your work.

•Liking your work shouldn't be considered an option or luxury. A compatible job lowers your risk of contracting serious diseases, including cancer. Chronic job stress weakens the body's immune system. If you feel trapped or really unhappy in a job, you should consider moving on—even if it means a cut in pay.

Source: Dr. Roy Walford, professor of pathology, UCLA School of Medicine, Los Angeles.

Why You Should Take Sick Days

Sick days can be therapeutic, even when you're not physically ill. By taking an occasional day off to reduce stress or deal with a pressing problem, you may avoid severe burnout later on. *How to use it:* Read a book, watch a movie, take a long bath. The idea is to indulge yourself.

Source: New York psychologist Don Lewittes, quoted in *Glamour*.

How to Leave the Office At the Office

As more homes begin to look more like offices, complete with telephone answering machines, beepers, computer terminals, tape recorders and coffee-making systems, it becomes difficult to make the break at the end of the workday.

Sometimes it isn't necessary to make the break. Work has its busy seasons and its peak periods. Then, and during ambitious times such as a start-up, it may not be appropriate to think of leaving the office behind every day. But that shouldn't always be the case. Balance is the goal to work toward.

What to turn off…

Make a conscious effort to change your mind-set when you are not at work. Clues that your head is still at the office: You chafe because the host is slow in moving you and other guests to the dining table…You make an agenda before going out to spend the afternoon with your child and stick to the agenda even when something more interesting intrudes. These are business mind-sets, not appropriate to non-office activities.

Give yourself a steady stream of physical cues to help you separate your office from your private world. Don't wear a watch on weekends. If you feel time pressures even when you're at home, don't use digital clocks in the car or home. They pace off the seconds and minutes too relentlessly for many people. Change your clothes as soon as you get home. And if you feel naked without your dictating machine or your briefcase with you at home, experiment with feeling naked!

Use your physical setting to help you keep work in its place. Tell yourself that you can work only at a particular place at home if you must work. Don't bring papers to bed with you. Don't spread them out over the couch, the dining table and the floor.

Making the shift…

The key to making the shift from home to office or office to home is in the transition that happens each morning and evening. Working women especially have trouble giving themselves a 10-minute break when they get home because they're inclined to feel anxious about talking with the children or starting dinner. Take the break. It can make all the difference between experiencing the rest of the evening as a pleasure or as a demand for attention.

Rituals are a useful device for making the switch. Secretaries do this by tidying up the desk or covering the typewriter. Lyndon Johnson symbolically turned off the lights in the Oval Office when he left. For managers, some useful rituals are loosening ties or other constricting clothing, turning a calendar page or making a list of things to do for the next day. They all help make the break. The to do list also helps curb the desire to catch up on tomorrow's tasks while you're at home.

Unwinding kinks…

Resist the growing tendency to abuse the whole winding-down process by taking up activities that create problems of their own… compulsive sex…addictive exercise…overeating or overdrinking…recreational drugs. *Better:* Use the transition time as a period of discovery. Walk or drive home along a different route. Pick up something new at the newsstand instead of the usual evening paper.

The other side of leaving the office at the office is to leave home at home. It may be productive to use lunch times to buy paint, but that's not helpful in keeping the two worlds separate.

The goal of keeping the worlds more separate is to increase understanding of the difference between business friends and other friends. The stimulus of work can be addictive and can leave people feeling helpless when illness, a disability or retirement takes away the only stimulus they know. In the now famous quote of a hard-driving executive: Nobody ever said on his deathbed, "I wish I had spent more time at the office."

Source: Marilyn Machlowitz, PhD, Machlowitz Associates, a management development firm in New York.

Vacation Myth

Not taking vacations isn't necessarily bad, contrary to popular belief. Many chief executives dislike vacations and rarely take them yet are stable, healthy and physically fit. They typically find the preparations needed to get away aren't worth the effort, and they view work involvements as activities that are more creative and pleasing than vacation activities.

Source: Study of 60 chief executives of major companies by William Theobald, professor of recreation studies, Purdue University, Lafayette, IN.

Better Time Managing Can Keep You Healthy

Beating the clock can cause ulcers, high blood pressure, heart attacks and even cancer. Managers who fret or fidget when they're forced to sit for only a few minutes are probably suffering from hurry sickness. They're more prone to disease and early death. *Remedies:* (1) Factor a time cushion into daily schedules. (2) Do things that must be done first and let less important matters wait. (3) Learn to say no to unwanted calls or visitors. (4) Broaden horizons with outside interests.

Source: *Creative Management*, New York.

Shift-Change Warning

Frequent shift changes, from night to day and vice versa, lower productivity. Your body does not have time to adjust its internal clock to the new schedule. It becomes confused on when to sleep and when to wake, resulting in drowsiness on the job. *Solution:* Adhere to a normal 24-hour day and change shifts as infrequently as possible.

Source: Martine C. Moore-Ede, writing in *Natural History.*

Facing Your Own Incompetence

The Peter Principle: *In a hierarchy, individuals tend to rise to their level of incompetence.*

Many people who've read my book *The Peter Principle* have recognized only professional or technical incompetence. But it's more complicated than that. Incompetence has many faces and lurks in some heretofore unsuspected areas:

•Physical incompetence. A person who is professionally or technically competent may develop such anxiety over his work that he gets ulcers or high blood pressure. And that results in a poor attendance record. His boss and co-workers assume he's really very competent but just has health problems. In reality, he is physically incompetent to handle the strain of the job.

•Mental incompetence. This occurs when a person is moved to a level where he can no longer deal with the intellectual requirements of the job.

Example: Stu Pidd was the foreman of the lead sinker casting department. He was a pleasant, kindly person who did a conscientious job. When his company took on more products, he was promoted to supervisor. This job required decisions about the allocation of workers and equipment. Instead of simple orders, Stu received guidelines and policy statements from management. Lacking the ability to deal with these abstractions, he habitually misunderstood

company policy and made illogical decisions, reducing his department's efficiency.

•Social incompetence. A person who is technically competent may be unable to get along with others. Or, problems may arise if he is promoted in an organization where a different class of social behavior is required when moving up the ladder. The Beverly Hillbillies syndrome then tends to set in.

Example: Mal Larkey was a salesman selling lead sinkers to the trade. When his company took on a line of tuning forks, he had to represent a whole different class of product to a tonier group of people. The dirty jokes and breezy manner that worked with the sinker customers didn't go over with the highbrow tuning fork crowd.

•Emotional incompetence. A technically competent person may be too unstable emotionally to deal with a particular job. Creative types, who tend to be insecure, are particularly prone to this type of incompetence when promoted to administrative positions.

•Ethical incompetence. Richard Nixon is a good example. Despite his nickname, Tricky Dick, and even though he had been caught at deceptive practices in earlier campaigns, Nixon was still able to win the presidency in 1968. Only when the White House tapes revealed his dishonesty beyond a doubt was it clear that he had reached his level of ethical incompetence. His brand of manipulative persuasiveness, an asset in local politics, became a liability in the highest office in the land. Nixon Principle: If two wrongs don't make a right, try three.

Why we behave as we do...

The Peter Principle seems to be part of human nature. According to Abraham Maslow, the eminent psychologist, it's human nature to struggle onward and upward through varying levels of needs. First we take care of our survival needs... then our safety needs...then social needs...then esteem or ego needs...and finally self actualization needs. That's why an executive who has reached the top of the ladder in his own company soon gets the itch to start acquiring other companies.

The behavior our parents reinforce in us when we are children always encourages us to strive for bigger and better things. We gain approval for achievement and disapproval for failure. As adults, we keep striving because our developmental makeup says "You've got to have more."

The more recent neurological explanation of left brain versus right brain dominance is also relevant. Left brain-dominant people tend to be the most linear in their thinking and therefore organize life step by step. Left brain types often get into management, where they are good at control but dismal at stimulating creativity. They climb the hierarchical ladder because their natures are linear and methodical.

Escaping the Peter Principle...

Take your life and your job seriously. But don't take yourself seriously. Don't spend your life climbing and acquiring. Instead, combine accomplishment and satisfaction. A climber whose gaze is always focused on the next rung fails to appreciate the view from the rung he's on. *Happiest:* Those who climb to a level that they find fulfilling, stay there for a long period, and then move forward.

To avoid your level of incompetence...

Many organizations exert great pressure on employees to move upward, and an outright refusal of a promotion can be seen as disloyalty, incompetence or cowardice. It might even get you fired. You must approach promotion avoidance indirectly.

Worth trying: The dart strategy. When I was a happy university professor, I had to head off attempts to promote me to department chairman. Whenever the dean dropped into my office to ask me a question, I would reach into the desk drawer, take out a dart, and throw it at a target hanging on the office wall. I wrote down the number of hits, made a rapid calculation...and then proceeded to say no. I knew the dart strategy was a success when I overheard the dean say, "Peter is a genius, but he's a ding-a-ling." The attempts to promote me ceased. When they started up again, I took to strolling over to the window at department meetings and lighting my cigarette by focusing sunlight on it through a magnifying glass. That got me off the hook again.

Source: Dr. Laurence J. Peter, whose latest book is *Why Things Go Wrong, or The Peter Principle Revisited*, William Morrow & Co., New York.

Five Reasons To Quit Your Job

If you're clearly in the wrong job: (1) Why waste time failing? Admit you're licked and find a place to succeed. (2) Why ruin your self-image? The longer you stay, the more you'll feel like a failure. (3) Why wait for the axe to fall? If you know it's coming, don't torture yourself. (4) Why put failure on your record? Quitting is easier to explain than being fired. (5) Why bring others down with you? When managers fail, their subordinates suffer, too.
Source: *The Levinson Letter.*

Why People Change Careers

Mid-life career changes are on the rise for women as well as for men. The average age for the change is in the late thirties. According to Nella Barkley, president of New York's John C. Crystal Center, people are thinking about the trade-offs in their lives much earlier and don't fit old stereotypes and patterns. Although many people are happy and successful in their professions, they're ready for new challenges and actively seek them. *Reason:* People in today's better-educated work force expect more from their jobs than a paycheck. They want to earn a living and fulfill themselves.

10 Rules For Dealing with People

• Remember their names.
• Be comfortable to be with. Don't cause strain in others.
• Try not to let things bother you. Be easygoing.
• Don't be egotistical or know-it-all.
• Learn to be interesting so that people will get something stimulating from being with you.

•Eliminate the "scratchy" elements in your personality, traits that can irritate others.

•Never miss a chance to offer support or say "Congratulations."

•Work at liking people. Eventually you'll like them naturally.

•Honestly try to heal any misunderstandings and drain off grievances.

•Develop spiritual depth in yourself and share this strength with others.

Source: *Time Talk.*

All About Nerds

Unlike wimps, nerds get attention by being obnoxious. They don't pay attention to the signals other people send them. They don't learn about themselves because they seldom stop to listen to others.

How not to be a nerd:

•Let people finish what they are saying.

•Don't always insist that you know more than other people about the subject under discussion.

•Slow down on advice-giving.

•Open up to new ideas.

•Let yourself change your mind once in a while.

When a nerd starts to realize that much of his behavior stems from anxiety about being accepted and loved, he is well on his way to being a nerd no longer.

Source: *The Secret of Charisma* by Doe Lang, New York.

Dale Carnegie's Persuasion Secrets

•Successful criticism. Most people begin their criticism with sincere praise followed by the word "but" and end with a critical statement. That's a trap. The other person feels encouraged until he hears "but" and then questions the sincerity of the original praise. *Better:* Use the word "and" rather than "but." By linking praise to a statement about higher expectations of performance, you're more likely to win the other person's willingness to accept, as well as respond to, your criticism.

•Friends. People spend most of their lives trying to get other people interested in them. The result is that they impress people but don't make many sincere, reliable friends. *Secret:* You can make many more friends faster by becoming genuinely interested in other people. The attention, time and cooperation of even the most sought-after people can be won by showing a genuine interest in their background and work.

•Win support for your ideas by making others think the idea is theirs. *Example:* Instead of urging customers to buy what you have, ask them to give you ideas on improving the product or service. This makes them feel part of the superior quality of the product. Then you don't have to persuade them—they'll feel the idea of buying was their own.

Source: *How to Enjoy Your Life and Your Job*, revised edition by Dale Carnegie, copyright by Dorothy Carnegie and Donna Dale Carnegie, Simon & Schuster, New York.

Incongruous Behavior— How to Read the Signs

People engaged in conversation are often nagged by thoughts contrary to their words. Nor can they always restrain these conflicts. They leak out through incongruous behavior, the sure sign that the speakers are not as comfortable, strong, truthful and sure of themselves as they sound.

There are many forms of incongruous behavior. They often center in the five major areas of nonverbal communication as delineated by Ray L. Birdwhistell more than a decade ago. *The five areas:* Facial expression, hands, feet, posture and eyes. *Another telling area:* The manner in which the words are said.

Incongruity in communication occurs when these areas are not all in agreement with one another. It indicates that some kind of deception, including self-deception, is going on.

You can sharpen your perception of what is troubling a person who consistently practices incongruous behavior. (We are speaking here of people who are basically truthful but who have lapses that are deceptive.)

Here's how:

•Study their lower limbs as they speak. That is where the tension and anxiety show. The person may claim to be relaxed, yet the legs are crossed tightly, and one foot thrusts so rigidly in the air that it appears to be on the verge of breaking off. *Insight:* People concentrate on hiding their tension from the waist up. Their real state is revealed in their legs and feet.

•Be aware of body segmentation, the assumption of closed positions, such as firmly crossed arms or legs, or both. *Contrast:* Someone who takes more open stances, such as moving the arms outwardly during conversation. *Trouble sign:* The person who cannot open body posture even when discussing such intimate subjects as friendship and trust.

•Listen to the voice. People often reveal their inner conflicts by fragmenting their sentences, failing to complete thoughts or skipping key portions.

•Hear the metaphors. A person who is talking of peace and harmony may be depending on metaphors related to war and turbulence.

•Be aware of the volume and rhythm of the voice and the dips in energy in the sentence structure. People tend to speak loudly to convince you of the truth of what they are saying. And they let their voices fall off when they feel they are saying things they do not necessarily want you to hear.

Any of these clues indicates that you are receiving edited versions of a speaker's thoughts, not the full report.

Opportunity…

When you spot the telltale signs of incongruous behavior, ask, "Is there something else you need to tell me?" This gives the person a chance to open up, a chance that would otherwise have remained masked behind the idiosyncratic behavior.

Some incongruous behavior is tied to cultural expectations. *Example:* People may say aggressive things with a smile. In many regions, this is a culturally accepted way for speakers to imply that they are only kidding (even if they aren't). It's more important to understand this type of coding than to confront it. If mixed messages like this are part of the local culture, don't be put off by them.

People who smile all the time, no matter what their message, are permanently incongruous. This suggests character-structure problems that need fuller investigation.

Source: Dr. Martin G. Groder, psychiatrist and business consultant in Durham, NC.

The Power of a Smile

A smile will make people like you better whether they want to or not, a recent study suggests. Subjects' facial muscles were wired with electrodes while videotapes of Ronald Reagan were shown. When Reagan smiled, viewers consistently responded with tiny smiles of their own, even those who disliked his political views. *Hypothesis:* People are disarmed by heavy exposure to a smiling leader.

Source: Roger D. Masters, PhD, professor of government, Dartmouth College, quoted in *Success!*.

How Making Eye Contact Helps

Eye contact helps people in almost any walk of life. *Examples:* Salvation Army Santas claim they almost always get a donation if they make eye contact with pedestrians. Salespeople who use eye contact with customers generate more and larger sales. Hitchhikers stand a better chance of getting rides if they engage in eye contact with passing motorists. Managers and executives who use their eyes when talking with their staffs open communications. And parents often find eyes the most effective means of scolding children.

Source: Study conducted by the University of Utah, Salt Lake City.

Looking Someone In the Eye

Shifty-eyed people aren't necessarily deceitful. Often they're isolated loners who are uncomfortable with closer contact. *If you have this problem:* Try looking at people either just above their eyes or just below. This gives the impression of warmth and openness, even when none exists.

Source: *Medical Aspects of Human Sexuality*, New York.

What Slips of the Tongue Really Mean

Most "Freudian slips" have no hidden motives or meaning, according to recent research. *Why the tongue slips:* A more familiar or simpler word replaces the intended one because of a failure in mental editing.

Source: James Reason, PhD, a psychologist at the University of Manchester, England.

How to Spot a Liar

When we lie, we feel varying degrees of discomfort. Some people feel actual fear—others, the mildest tension. But at least to some degree, our feelings are expressed in our behavior. We may control our words, our voice, our face or our posture. But we cannot control everything. To the astute observer we give ourselves away.

Sometimes the giveaway is only a "micromovement" a brief, minimal change in facial expression. *Example:* I once offered a used-car owner $500. I watched his face and saw a fleeting smile. Although it lasted only a fraction of a second before he resumed his bland expression and proposed a higher price, I knew he was happy with the original offer. I didn't budge. He took the $500.

The voice is a rich source of information. People who are lying tend to talk slowly. (By definition, they're not spontaneous.) They speak in shorter sentences than usual. They realize that the more they talk, the more likely they are to slip up. In fact, they do slip up. *Reason:* Tense people are more error prone in all areas. Liars tend to truncate words and sentences and to express incomplete thoughts. Their voices will be pitched higher than normal, another by-product of tension.

Because liars want to increase their distance from others, they cut back on gestures and eye contact. The less exposure, the better. They tend to sit sideways, rather than face to face. They rarely lean forward toward their listeners.

At the same time, liars are more self-conscious. They shift in their seats, adjust their clothing and scratch themselves. Often they bring a hand to the face—another way to reduce exposure.

A very reliable sign is body stiffness. Look for a rigid posture (whether the person is standing or seated), with strict symmetry of limbs.

Other non-verbal cues are less useful. Certain people—calmer types and men in general—smile more when they lie, since this is a channel they can control. But more anxious people tend to freeze and to smile less than normal when they lie.

A perspiring brow or flushed cheeks are primarily symptoms of high arousal. They may reflect anger, excitement, discomfort or fear. But if a flushed person also speaks in halting sentences and avoids eye contact, you would be wise to doubt his words.

It should be noted that these signals can appear in someone who is not lying. The person may simply be uncomfortable—either about saying something, or about saying it to a particular individual.

Once you suspect someone is lying, there are various ways to smoke him or her out. The key is to frame open ended questions. *Example:* "What were you up to last night?" (not "Did you have a good time?"). Or ask him to repeat an obvious falsehood, saying, "I didn't hear that." He may get flustered enough to change his story. *Another good ploy:* Respond to an answer with silence. Just sit there and wait. The liar won't know whether you expect him to go on or not—a very stressful situation. The more stress you put on a liar, the more information you get.

But what if the tables are turned and you feel the need to lie? My advice is simple…use a letter rather than the phone, and the phone rather than speaking face to face.

But if you must lie to someone in person, avoid major changes in your behavior to mask non-verbal clues. Very few of us are good actors. The more alien your role, the more uncomfortable you'll feel—and the more obvious your lie.

Source: Albert Mehrabian, PhD, a professor of psychology at the University of California at Los Angeles.

4 Clues That Tell You Someone Is Lying

Look for the following signs of distress, fear or anger (typical reactions of people who are attempting to conceal something)…(l) Raised inner eyebrows. (2) Raised, knitted brows. (3) A narrowing and tightening of the red margin of the lips. (4) An asymmetrical smile. (The average persons tells a lie at least twice a day.)

Source: Paul Ekman, a psychologist at the University of California at San Francisco.

Overcoming Embarrassment

Face up to the gaffe. Stop worrying about how silly you appear responding to your mistake. Look for the humor. Don't brood on the past or embarrassments will become inhibitions. *Remember:* Everyone has endured similar humiliations—even the people you fear are laughing at you now.

Source: *Cosmopolitan*, New York.

Face-Reading

Large round eyes indicate bravery, and joined eyebrows reveal a mean and unforgiving nature, according to the ancient Chinese art of siang mien. *Thin lips:* Brutal, selfish (unless tempered by a rounded nose tip). *Smooth, wide forehead:* Clever, decisive. *Cleft chin:* A yen for the limelight. *Large, long ears:* Compassionate, understanding. *Thin eyelashes:* Sharp temper. *Wide space between eyes:* Inner reserves of energy.

Source: *Secrets of the Face* by Lailan Young, Little, Brown & Co., New York.

Walk Talk

A heavy step means you're down to earth but rarely spontaneous, says astrologer Maxine Fiel. *A light step:* Dreamy, optimistic. *A long stride:* Dynamic, forceful. *A quick walk:* Impulsive, alert. *A slow walk:* Contemplative, careful. *Bent forward:* Goal-oriented, serious.

Source: *Mademoiselle*, New York.

Tips for Making Friendships Last

Don't bother criticizing an insecure friend or relative, even in a constructive way. It won't do any good. For a person who lacks self-esteem, any value judgment, no matter how helpful or positive, is seen as an attack.

Source: *Medical Aspects of Human Sexuality*, New York.

•Never try to guess what's troubling a silent friend. Your assumption will probably be wrong and negative. *Instead:* Ask.

Source: *The Love Test* by Harold Bessell, William Morrow & Co., New York.

•To calm a friend who is furious at you, stay calm yourself. Moods are contagious, and it's hard to stay angry at someone who doesn't respond angrily. Keep your voice low and soothing. *Good body language:* An unwrinkled forehead. Relaxed eyebrows and mouth. Uncrossed arms, open hands.

Source: Arnold P. Goldstein, director of the Syracuse University Center for Research on Aggression, in *Vogue*, New York.

Better One-to-One Conversations

We know it's been said before, but the surest way to improve your one-to-one conversations is to become a better listener. Listening skills may seem simple enough, but many people (particularly men) need to work on them.

Live in the present moment. Resist all distractions. Don't let your mind wander to your bank balance or to after-dinner plans. Stay alert and concentrate on what your "partner" is saying—not only the words, but the emotions behind them. Then rephrase what you've heard in your own words (mentally or verbally).

Example: Your friend tells you he's gunning for a promotion but that his boss seems to be favoring a co-worker. *Your response:* "That sounds rough. Is it upsetting you?" This kind of reflection will not only help you understand… it will also make your friend feel you are trying to understand, and encourage him to share more with you.

(Such questions are especially effective for resuming a conversation several days later. You might lead off by asking your friend if the situation at work has changed. This lends continuity to a friendship…and shows you care enough to remember.)

If you follow this technique, you'll naturally become a more empathetic listener. You'll stop interrupting so much, a habit that discourages real communication. And you won't argue so frequently, since you'll be more concerned with grasping the other person's meaning than with scoring some rhetorical point.

Good listening is enhanced by appropriate body language. Consistent eye contact…leaning toward the person if seated…an occasional nod or smile…all can help show that you're an interested listener—if they're natural and timed

correctly. But you can't fake it. If the gestures are forced or perfunctory, it will show.

Even the best listeners occasionally find themselves bored by some long-winded anecdote or complaint. *How to handle it:* Steer the conversation to a mutually interesting subject. Or…approach the old subject from a new angle.

Example: Your friend's complaints about his job have grown tedious. *Your response:* "Have you considered moving to a new company?"

When it's your turn to talk, think about the point you want to make before you start speaking. Then get to it in as few steps as possible. *Important:* Consider your audience. Make what you're saying relevant to the particular person you're addressing.

Beyond that, there are no simple tricks to enrich your conversations. Your talk reflects your life. If you are totally absorbed in your job, your conversations will inevitably stagnate as soon as they get beyond shoptalk. But if you approach life with curiosity and enthusiasm, your speech will range as wide as your mind. *Especially useful:* Reading outside your field… any subject that might spark discussion.

People tend to be more comfortable with others more like themselves. But it's the people outside your clique or specialty who may ask the freshest questions, even if less well informed. (Conversely, don't be afraid to ask a "dumb" question about a subject that's new to you.)

If your conversations seem bland, maybe you're suppressing honest disagreements. A dispute shouldn't hurt an exchange (or a friendship), as long as a certain etiquette is respected.

Useful: Give the other person credit for something before you disagree. Never say, "How can you think something like that?" *Better:* "That's a good point, but I see it differently…." Or first point out areas of similarity: "We agree that world peace is vital—therefore…."

Sometimes intense disagreements should be sidestepped. The old saw "Never discuss politics or religion" can be wisely applied—especially if you don't know the other person very well. An emotional argument can cut short a potential friendship.

Source: Mark Sherman, associate professor of psychology, and Adelaide Haas, associate professor of communications, State University of New York, New Paltz.

Conversation Strategy

"Stop me if you've heard this…" When a friend begins an anecdote already told several times, break in with a summarizing comment. ("Oh, yes, I remember your vivid description of…") Then follow up with a related question. You don't get bored or imposed upon, your friend isn't hurt and you can discuss the subject from a new angle.

Saying No Isn't Easy But It's Important

People who think they can't say no don't realize that they actually do say no all the time —but in indirect and tortuous ways that aren't effective. Instead of refusing directly when confronted with a request they don't want to honor, they say things like "I'll try" and then they fail to follow through. Or they begin to feel that the other person "owes" them, and somewhere along the line, they will try to collect. The other person will experience this as persecution. Then the stage is set for a further round of psychological games.

The programming to say no starts very early. Some people decide, at a very young age, that compliance is the best way to respond to authority. They grow up unable to feel comfortable with saying no. (Others decide early on to respond to authority in a rebellious fashion. Often, they can't feel good about saying yes.)

Those who won't say no openly tend to be vulnerable to frequently recurring fears (such as the fear of rejection) and guilt. They may have a damaged sense of self-esteem, as shown by their need to please others—they feel the need to earn acceptance by being nice all the time. *Result:* They end up carrying around an accumulation of unacknowledged resentment at being "put upon."

People who don't know how to say no also don't know how to accept having others say no to them. Their own wildly disproportionate notions are projected onto other people. *Result:*

When people say no to them, they experience it as an enormous personal rejection.

Learning to say no when you really want to is both healthy and necessary, even though society teaches us that "selfishness" is wrong and that it is virtuous to accommodate others. *The truth:* If you don't take care of your own needs and wishes, neither can you take care of anyone else's needs effectively.

How to say no:

•Be clear about your preferences and feelings before answering a request. If you're not sure about what you want, set aside some time to consider your response. Say, "I'll think it over and let you know tomorrow."

•When you must say no, remember that you have importance for others, as they have for you. They need you, just as you need them. That importance can't be diminished by an instance of your saying no.

•Be aware that it's possible to say no without destroying the other person. There's always a feeling among "pleasers" (people who need to be nice to everyone) that if they refuse a request, the other person will fall apart. This is an illusion.

•Be consistent. Once you decide what you want to do in a given situation, be prepared to repeat saying no and to give additional information. *Examples:* "I won't do it because I don't have time." "If I say yes, I'll feel resentful or manipulated."

•Consider compromise. Compromise is not a dirty word, nor is it a weakness. It's a useful way for two people to get the best outcome without either one suffering. Take time to explore the options. That doesn't mean changing your *no* to *yes*. It means looking for an alternative that might be acceptable to you.

•Practice saying *no* in your head. Whenever anybody asks you for something, try saying no silently, to see how it feels. This is particularly helpful in developing the sense of discrimination that is so necessary for "pleasers."

•Time bomb: When someone tries to persuade you to do something for them that you're really unwilling to do, be aware that if it's bad for you, it's bad for them. You end up with resentment and a muddied relationship.

•Learning to accept no from others objectively is a way to strengthen your own capacity to say no directly and without conflict. Learn to clarify what the other person's *no* means. That way you'll see it in better perspective. *Example:* If someone doesn't return your calls, phone the secretary. Find out if the person you want is just temporarily unwilling to speak with you or is uninterested in what you have to offer. The tendency to distort its meaning, or exaggerate it, is what causes most of the emotional pain of having someone say no to you. If the no is a real rejection of you and objectively painful, it is better to acknowledge it than to keep putting yourself in the position of inevitable rejection.

Source: Gisele Richardson, president of Richardson Management Associates, Montreal, Canada. The firm specializes in assertiveness workshops and consulting.

How to Say No Without Feeling Guilty

Many of us say yes more often than we'd like. Sometimes we feel we have to repay some actual or imagined favor. At other times we acquiesce out of fear of disapproval or out of some misguided idea of politeness. Whatever the reason, if you find yourself saying yes because you feel guilty about saying no, here are some practical measures to help you protect yourself.

The right to stall…

Many people fail to understand that they have a basic human right to say no. Frequently people with assertiveness problems are unsure of their feelings about a particular issue. A request is made of them: On the one hand, they want to help because the asker has done favors for them in the past; on the other, they don't have much enthusiasm for carrying out the request. But they will impulsively say yes because they lack the nerve to give a flat out no.

Stalling is an enormously valuable tactic that gives you precious time to work up an honest rationale for a total refusal. Suggested stalling statements:

•I don't know. I need time to think about it —give me an hour.

•A lot of what you're saying makes perfect sense, but there's something about your request that makes me uncomfortable. I need some time to think it over.

Other helpful tactics…

There are other strategies by which the terminally guilt-ridden can stave off unwanted obligations. Humor is helpful. So is repeating the words, *I can't do that,* over and over. Flattery is another good tactic. White lies are sometimes necessary.

Strategy illustration:

While Loretta was at a co-op board meeting, the president asked her to serve as head of the decoration committee. Despite her initial impulse to say yes, she stalled: "It sounds like a good idea, and I'm sure I could do the job. But I have a few other obligations, and I need a day to think about it." A day later, Loretta called the president back and told him she was flattered that he wanted her for the job but that she just didn't have the time. He then attempted to pressure her by saying, "There's no one else who could do it as well as you." She came back with, "As a matter of fact, you're so artistic, you could do an even better job than I could. If you're too busy, why don't you try Jan or Nancy? They did a bang-up job on the landscaping last year." He then switched to guilt, pointing out that he'd done favors for her when she chaired a committee he was on. She teased him by pointing out that she thought she'd paid back that debt already, and she reminded him that she hadn't signed anything in blood. Finally he gave up good-naturedly.

Saying no to family…

This is the hardest kind of refusal to deal with. You not only need the interpersonal skills to say no gracefully but you also have to rethink your real obligations to your family, so you can say no without guilt. *Suggestions:*

•Resist the hidden-bargain syndrome. Parents often operate under the assumption that since they've done all these wonderful things for their children to bring them up, the offspring owe them everything. Both young and grown children can be manipulated by this assumption. *Remedy:* Recognize that parents do nice things at least as much for their own benefit as for their children's sake. I do a lot of loving and giving to my own child, but primarily because it makes me feel good and gives me satisfaction. I am thus getting my payoff on the spot, through the act of giving itself.

•Recognize that a family member who acts hurt at a turndown is torturing himself. You're not responsible for other people's reactions.

Example: An elderly mother went to visit her son, who lived in an apartment too small for two people to stay in comfortably. When he told her he thought it would be better if he put her up at a hotel, she acted hurt. *Remedy:* The son must recognize that his mother is making herself unhappy by interpreting his hotel offer as a rejection. In truth, he has done nothing thoughtless or inconsiderate. He must point out to his mother that, despite her bad feelings, they would both be more comfortable if they stayed in separate accommodations.

•Don't sit on guilt. As soon as you feel it, share it. Guilt pushers are also guilt buyers, and they know better than anyone how awful it is to feel guilty. In the story above, the son could also tell his mother that she makes him feel terrible when she pushes guilt on him and ask her if that was her intention. Frequently, just pointing out a guilt manipulation makes the other back off. Once that's done, you're free to sit down and honestly discuss how making another person feel guilty hurts a relationship.

•Learn to say no to your children. Parents frequently feel guilty about poor parenting They try to compensate by capitulating easily to their children's requests. More than anything, they want their children to like them. Often the parents themselves grew up in a restrictive environment, and they've vowed not to be as strict with their own children as their parents were with them. But children need structure and limits in order to learn self-discipline and independence. *Helpful:* Remind yourself that saying no to your child is an act of love, not of repression. You're doing your child a favor by teaching him how to grow up rather than remain a perennial emotional infant.

Source: Barry Lubetkin, PhD, a psychologist who is founder and clinical director of the Institute for Behavior Therapy in New York.

Handling Criticism

Properly used, criticism enhances personal growth and relationships. *Hitch:* Even constructive criticism is not always presented in a good way. And learning to accept criticism is hard for most people.

Problem: Criticism is often prefaced with a dogmatic phrase such as "you should." This reveals the rigidity of the critic and makes those being criticized resist change. It also implies the erroneous concept that there is a right way and a wrong way to do things—with no acceptable middle ground.

Result: Critical statements are answered with equally critical rejoinders. Soon, each person is trying to top the other as the tone becomes increasingly personal.

There are ways, however, to avoid this familiar cycle. *A checklist for giving constructive criticism:*

•Target the behavior you want to criticize. Make your criticism as specific as possible.

•Save your critical comments for the appropriate time and place. Never blurt them out in public.

•Verify that the behavior you are criticizing is capable of being changed. If it cannot be, then say nothing.

•Avoid threats and accusations. Keep your comments brief and understandable.

•Do not allow a bad mood to color your words. Listen to your voice for signs of hostility or sarcasm.

•Offer to help in resolving the behavior you are criticizing.

Receiving criticism graciously is equally delicate. *Prime lesson:* Consider the consistency with which a specific criticism is offered. Regularly repeated criticism is probably valid. *Other considerations:*

•Avoid the inclination to defend yourself blindly against criticism. Instead, ask for more information and develop the skill of attentive listening.

•Request solutions to the criticism. Ask the critic, "What would you do in my place?"

•Summarize the criticism and your responses so that communication about the problem is clear. At the same time, plan a definable strategy for correcting the behavior.

Source: *Nobody's Perfect (How to Give Criticism and Get Results)* by Hendrick Weisinger, PhD, Warner Books, New York.

Best Way to Apologize

The one-minute apology: (1) Give it immediately—or as soon as possible—after making a mistake. The longer you wait, the harder it is. (2) Be specific as to what you are apologizing for. A simple "I'm sorry" isn't helpful. (3) Tell the person whom you wronged how you feel (embarrassed, sad, etc). (4) Affirm yourself. Make it clear how unlike you this behavior was (so you can stop feeling guilty).

Source: Kenneth Blanchard, co-author of *The One-Minute Manager*, in *Success!*

Dealing Constructively With Anger

Recent evidence suggests that always getting your anger out and expressing what you're feeling perhaps isn't as cathartic as was once thought, though expressing anger is doubtedly preferable to sitting on your feelings. *Even better:* Learning how to manage your anger so you control it rather than letting it control you. Once you learn to deal effectively with anger, you'll have options. You can express anger when appropriate, stop it from bothering you when inappropriate, or channel it constructively. You won't constantly be at the mercy of this powerful emotion.

Changing your behavior...

Some of us have hot tempers that explode inappropriately, alienating friends, co-workers, bosses, spouses and our children. Others can be boiling inside but act timid when it comes to a confrontation. *The trick:* Expressing anger effectively.

If you have an explosive temper:

•Take time as soon as you begin feeling anger to identify its source. Sit down, close your eyes and visualize as clearly as possible the person you're angry at. See yourself dealing with that person in a reasoned, appropriate manner. As soon as you imagine yourself blowing up, stop and go back to the image of yourself being open, honest and direct—not shouting or being sarcastic or humiliating. This rehearsal will be useful in itself in controlling your anger response. By the time you confront the person, you'll feel less angry and be more effective.

•Do a daily anger assessment. Fill in a chart with three columns: What am I feeling? What am I thinking? What provoked it? The mere act of objectifying your anger will distance you from it and decrease the anger response. Now it's not emerging mysteriously from your system and taking you over. It's something you can rate. It has a beginning, middle and end.

If you're afraid to express anger:

•Visualization will help. See yourself confronting the person you're angry at and expressing your feelings directly and honestly, without retreat or apology. Once the time comes for performance, you'll know your lines well and be feeling comfortable with them.

•Pay attention to body language, so you don't undercut your message. People often smile, giggle, look at the floor or squirm around when they're expressing anger. Look at yourself in front of the mirror to practice what you think anger looks like and check out your body language. You might even ask a good friend to give you feedback.

Changing your outlook...

Tune in to the two types of personality: The requiring and the aspiring. The requiring type demands never to be put down and that the world always be fair. The aspiring type says it would certainly be nice if people never put him down, but he realizes that life is often unfair. You'll find yourself feeling much less angry if you recognize that good luck and bad luck are meted out randomly. Today may be your turn to get a bad break, but maybe tomorrow things will look up. Don't personalize unfairness. Angry people are apt to feel that they're being punished for something they did wrong.

How to be an aspirer:

•Eliminate the word *should* from your thinking ("He should have treated me better, after all I've done for him"). When you're angry or upset, ask yourself: Does life always have to be the way I want it to be? Can I survive as a reasonably happy person even if I don't get what I want in this situation?

•Learn to accept what you can't change. Don't fool yourself that if you somehow magically do something different, the world will play fair with you. *Example:*

You have a boss who always puts you down. You've tried everything to get him to stop, to no avail. You can't quit your job. Accept that he's got the problem, not you, and treat him as you would treat anyone you have to humor to get along with. *Visualization exercise:* He is putting you down. Instead of feeling helpless anger, you are merely disappointed, inconvenienced or sad. You realize that he is a disturbed person, so his behavior doesn't reflect on you.

•Don't invest all of yourself in one aspect of life. If your entire sense of self-worth derives from one area, you may experience enormous anger when it doesn't go well. *Recommended:* Make a list of how you spend your time. You may notice how many other things you do— and do well. Get involved in relationships and activities outside of that area to receive other ego boosts.

•Have a dialogue with yourself: Go back and forth between the part of you that puts up with bullying and the part that always responds with aggression and anger. *Purpose:* When people become angry, they're not aware of anything except the feeling of having to defend themselves. The dialogue will help you get in touch with why you need to defend yourself and why you need to stave off criticism. Your anger will be tempered by understanding.

•Find out where the anger comes from. Look at your anger assessment to see if your anger has a theme. *Example:* You always get angry when criticized by someone in authority. Think back over your childhood. In the past, someone caused you to feel helpless or hopeless because you were not allowed to express anger. You've carried into adulthood a storehouse of bad feelings that gets tapped every time you're con-

fronted by authority. This realization won't necessarily stop you from getting angry, but your anger will be less corrosive once you understand it.

Make anger work for you...

•There's nothing wrong with seeking revenge, particularly if there's no other way of dealing with the situation. But make it classy. Don't get vitriolic or indulge in overkill. Be subtle, yet effective. Often, just thinking about bizarre methods of revenge will dispel your anger, and instead you'll find yourself laughing at your own ingenuity.

•Turn anger into positive energy. The physical feeling of anger produces almost the same bodily response as excitement or enthusiasm. The only difference is the label. Learn to use the energy that anger produces to do something for yourself. *Recommended:* Create an anger-option list with alternative ways to channel your anger. Whenever you feel irrationally angry and know that expressing it is a bad idea, substitute one of the items on your list. *Examples:* Make a phone call to a person who's been intimidating you, jog for a mile, put up shelves, shop for a new suit.

Source: Barry S. Lubetkin, PhD, clinical director, Institute for Behavior Therapy, New York.

How to Manage Your Anger

Avoiding anger, or letting it off in some harmless fashion, are both impossible...contrary to belief. Managing your anger is possible. *Technique:* Don't speak while angry—you're likely to be impulsive or lack judgment. Putting your feelings into a letter helps, but don't send it until you cool down. Ask a trusted friend to help decide whether your anger is appropriate. Sometimes, just talking eases the intensity. If you've really been mistreated, it's crucial to tell the other person clearly.

Source: *The Levinson Letter,* New York.

•Expressing anger is not always a release. Often it simply heightens the feelings. And repressing anger keeps it pent up, which is literally unhealthy. *Best:* Control your anger. *How:* Recognize it and identify it. Usually the object of your current anger is not the source of the problem. Determine how serious the problem is. *Key:* Let trivial upsets pass, and argue only over important matters. When arguing out your anger, never attack the personality or integrity of the other person. State your opinions clearly while keeping to the point. *Worse:* Sulking silently. This is merely another form of anger.

Handling Someone Else's Anger

Don't try to talk to people who are angry. Just listen. Let them blow off steam, and try to understand their feelings. Find a way to reopen talks later, when they have cooled down.

Source: *Supervisory Management.*

• Acknowledge others' anger quickly (ignoring it or laughing it off only adds fuel to the anger). Make it plain that you're concerned. Listen until they run down. Keep calm (don't take them too seriously). Find out what's really wrong. Strive for agreement on a solution with a timetable; then stick to it.

Source: *The Official Guide to Success* by Tom Hopkins, Warner Books, New York.

The Big Little Things In Life

They seem harmless little quirks. The toothpaste tube is squeezed from the middle rather than the end. Or the milk is never returned to the refrigerator after breakfast. Yet at a certain point these bad habits of a spouse, lover, roommate or intimate friend become excruciatingly painful.

Why the exaggerated reaction? *Main reason:* There is already an alienation in the relationship that the bad habit confirms. *Example:* The person who takes extreme offense because the toothpaste tube is squeezed "incorrectly" feels

that the offender does not care enough to be reliable or to be responsive to that person's needs and sensibilities. The careless act is interpreted as a deliberate effort to create pain or a willingness to inflict annoyance.

Often a probing discussion between the parties will uncover the major issues that led to the alienation. Remember, the problem is seldom the bad habit. That is only a manifestation of more serious difficulties. For many, professional counseling may be the only cure.

The ideal expectations of perfectionists cause them to fall prey to this condition. They regard those to whom they are close as minor gods or goddesses. The bad habit, however, is a visible sign of defectiveness which makes the other person unworthy of the perfectionist's feelings.

Perfectionism is sometimes healed by maturity as the sufferers realize there are no perfect people or situations. But severely afflicted perfectionists lose the company of other human beings, since their standards are impossibly high. They usually require psychotherapy. *Problem:* Often they find therapy unsatisfactory because the therapist is imperfect.

The one cause just discussed usually developed over time and grew from an ongoing relationship. There is another category, however, that earns the offender instant dislike. This occurs when the bad habit reminds a person of an important childhood figure who was a tormentor—a parent, sibling, relative or teacher. The habit summons up a traumatic recollection. It is hate at first sight.

The simple solution is to avoid the hated object. If that is impractical, psychotherapy enables the person to discover the memories that were repressed. This leads the way toward healing the fixation.

Simple prejudice spawns extreme reactions in some to the way certain people look and act. Those prejudiced against a race, creed, class or type seize on any identifying characteristic of that group as annoying. *Example:* People may be prejudiced against those with a different accent. The prejudiced claim the others are obnoxious because of the way they talk. *Truth:* It is not the accent that is the problem, but deep seated prejudice.

Cure: If possible, cultural change and human growth. Sometimes discussion groups between conflicting groups can help breed tolerance.

Source: Martin G. Groder, MD, a psychiatrist and business consultant who practices in Chapel Hill, NC.

All About Forgiveness

To forgive another is the greatest favor you can do—for yourself. It's the only way to release yourself from the clutch of an unfair past. Beyond that, it opens the possibility of reconciliation, often a gift in itself.

In its simple essence, forgiving is a new way of remembering a person who has hurt you. When you are first wounded, you remember him only as a person who unfairly injured you. As you begin to forgive, you gradually see him as a weak, needy, silly and somewhat stupid person who tried to cope by being cruel to you. As your memory changes, your hatred gradually recedes and your healing begins.

When you've been unfairly hurt, you paint a mental caricature. If the person who wronged you is a bloated bag of undiluted evil, you feel all the more virtuous by comparison. Hatred can also make you feel strong. It's like a drug—at first.

Still, you need to forgive. If you try merely to forget, to erase a hurt like some cassette, the hatred comes back to haunt you. If you persist in passive hatred, it kills your joy. And if you seek revenge, you'll fail. You cannot even the score because two people in conflict never feel pain to the same degree. Revenge leads to further retaliation and (in retrospect) to guilt.

Forgiving doesn't make doormats out of people. You're not tolerating what was done or excusing the person who did it to you. You are holding that person accountable—and then seeking to go on with your life.

How to forgive…

Every act of forgiveness grows out of unique circumstances. *Guidelines:*

•Take the initiative in forgiving. Don't wait for the other person to apologize. (That cedes control to the one who hurt you in the first place.)

•If the forgiven person wants to re-enter your life, it is fair to demand truthfulness. He or she should be made to understand, to feel the hurt you've felt. Then you should expect a sincere promise that you won't be hurt that way again.

•Be patient. If the hurt is deep, you can't forgive in a single instant.

•Forgive "retail," not "wholesale." It's almost impossible to forgive someone for being a bad person. Instead, focus on the particular act that hurt you. (It might help to write it down.)

•Don't expect too much. To forgive doesn't mean you must renew a once close relationship. (I knew one estranged wife who was afraid that if she forgave her husband, she'd have to go back and be beaten by him again.) Time and circumstances change. Healing yourself won't always end in a warm embrace. You have to begin where you are.

•Discard your self-righteousness. A victim is not a saint. You too will need forgiveness some day.

•Separate anger from hate. Anger is a great gift, a passionate desire to stop a wrong. You can forgive and stay angry. But hate and malice—wishing someone ill—are self-destructive. You can't forgive and still hate.

To dissolve your malice: Face your emotion and accept it as natural. Then discuss it, either with the object of your hatred (if you can do so without escalating the hatred) or with a trusted third party.

Self-forgiveness…

The hardest act of all may be to forgive yourself. When we are genuinely guilty, we feel we deserve our own judgment. It seems outrageous to believe that the terrible wrong we did is irrelevant to who we are. But it's the only way we can deal with the irreversible past.

Self-forgiveness allows us to be freer and to love better. When we're castigating ourselves, it's hard to help, care about and be glad for others.

Again, candor is critical. Admit your fault. Relax your struggle to be perfect. We all need an occasional guilt trip.

Then be concrete and specific about what is bothering you. Your deed was evil. You are not.

Ignore the grudge carriers. If you've fully acknowledged your wrong, you don't need to grovel.

To make self-forgiveness easier: Prime the pump of self-love. Do something unexpected (possibly unappreciated) for a person you care about. By acting freely, you'll find it easier to think freely.

Source: Lewis B. Smedes, author of *Forgive & Forget*, HarperCollins, New York.

Avoiding One Kind Of Family Squabble

When a parent dies, defer for a month the dividing of personal possessions. You'll be far more likely to avoid emotional squabbles.

Source: Avery Weisman, MD, psychiatry professor, Harvard University, Cambridge, MA.

Helping Hypochondriacs

Try to be sympathetic without taking on responsibility. If you're bored, change the subject —but don't be rejecting. It's cruel to say, "It's all in your head." Pain is no less painful when imaginary. *When a new complaint surfaces:* Consider that it might be legitimate. Hypochondriacs are often ignored when they really need medical attention.

Source: *The New York Times Guide to Personal Health* by Jane Brody, Avon Books, New York.

How to Diagnose Yourself

Few experiences are as frustrating as having a chronic health problem that your doctor can't identify.

If the doctor cannot diagnose the problem, you must either learn to live with the symptoms...or go on to another doctor.

Trap: The more doctors a patient consults with, the less seriously each new doctor is likely to take the patient's complaints.

Eventually, even the patient begins to doubt the reality of the symptoms...while remaining debilitated by them. The fear that he/she may be neurotic adds to the problem.

I know about this phenomenon first-hand. I came down with a mysterious and incapacitating illness that turned out—after six years and nearly 30 doctors—to be Lyme disease.

In consulting with a seemingly endless procession of specialists, I learned how important it is to take an active role in the search for a diagnosis. I also found out what to do to get respect and cooperation from doctors—many of whom were skeptical of my symptoms.

The lessons I learned during my search for a diagnosis should be helpful to anyone who is sick but doesn't know why—people in what I call the pre-diagnosis period of a long illness.

Trust your instincts...

Our society has a strong need to categorize. We tend to doubt the reality of anything we can't label.

This is certainly true of most doctors. It's also true of friends and relatives, who may have difficulty being supportive of someone whose condition has no name. It helps to know that you're not alone. Many, many illnesses can take months or years to diagnose.

Recently, I surveyed 180 patients in support groups for five different chronic illnesses. *What I found:* The average time between the onset of symptoms and diagnosis was five years.

Lyme disease isn't the only disease that's often misdiagnosed. Others include lupus, colon cancer, ovarian cancer and Parkinson's disease.

Several things changed once I learned to believe in myself—to accept that I had a real illness even though no one knew what it was. I began to feel less desperate. I learned to cope with my mysterious symptoms. And because I no longer had anything to prove, I stopped acting defensive with doctors.

Example: When a doctor suggested that my illness might be psychogenic (originating in the mind), I no longer jumped to deny it. Instead, I calmly said, *I've had psychological problems at certain times in my life, but I can't believe that is what's causing all of these symptoms.* The doctor considered my symptoms and my attitude, then replied, *You're right. This is not a psychological problem.*

Find the right doctor…

Even if he/she can't diagnose your illness, the right doctor can help you sort out what's wrong.

Your doctor can refer you to specialists, analyze medical opinions and test results and help you manage your symptoms as you await a correct diagnosis and appropriate treatment.

To find the right doctor, get referrals from friends and acquaintances—especially people who work in the medical profession.

Tell them you're looking for a doctor who is compassionate, understanding and willing to take time with patients. Say you want someone who will encourage you to ask questions and be involved in decision-making about your own care.

You're also looking for someone who enjoys being a medical detective. Not every doctor does. You may have to interview several before you find one who takes you seriously and with whom you have a good rapport.

During your first meeting with a prospective doctor, make it clear that you don't expect him/her to have all the answers. Doctors get frustrated, too. If the doctor knows you're looking for someone to help manage your symptoms and guide your search, he/she will be less likely to feel put on the spot—or to brush you off as neurotic.

Examine your records…

Don't assume that you know what's in your medical file. Reviewing your test results and doctors' notes may reveal startling discrepancies…or new avenues to explore.

Problem: Specialists reviewing your file may not always see the big picture—how their findings fit in with those of other specialists. Doctors may record information that's different from what they told you…or from what you meant to relay. Test results may be ambiguous or incomplete.

Example: Three years before my diagnosis, my blood was tested for several illnesses, including Lyme disease. I was told at the time that all the tests came back normal. So, for the next three years I told doctors that I'd tested negative for Lyme. Later, I learned that the Lyme test had never been performed—the state lab had sent a note saying that no such test was available in Minnesota. If I had examined the file, I would have given doctors the correct information and I might have been diagnosed years earlier.

Medical records are usually easy to obtain. Simply request them from the doctor's office or the medical records department of your hospital or clinic. A simple medical dictionary will help you interpret jargon. Some places may ask you to sign a release form and/or pay a small copying fee.

Learn about medications…

Be sure you understand the possible side effects of all drugs prescribed for you. Understand, too, their potential interactions with other medications.

The pamphlets that drug companies put out about their medications are extremely thorough. Ask your pharmacist for copies.

Use the library…

You may discover valuable clues about your illness by doing your own research.

Many hospital and university medical libraries are open to the public. Some general libraries have medical collections. Ask the librarian to steer you toward relevant reference books, journals and databases. Phone the library ahead to find out what times are least busy. Look up your symptoms and their possible causes in diagnostic textbooks.

If your doctor has mentioned possible diagnoses, read about those conditions. Journals frequently include case histories of people with specific diseases or symptoms—the articles are often listed by subject in databases.

Provide your doctor with any scientific article that you think might help him/her with the diagnosis.

Learn to live with uncertainty…

Learn to accept your illness without giving up your search for answers. Acknowledge that your symptoms are real. Don't worry about the future—focus on one day at a time. Try to experience joy even in the midst of uncertainty.

This attitude fosters the relaxed open-mindedness that makes a good detective. It also helps you cope more effectively with your symptoms.

Important: If you stay reasonably relaxed rather than tensing up when symptoms flare up, the discomfort is likely to be of shorter duration and less intense.

Acceptance also helps you notice your body's signals and enables you to respond to them appropriately—whether by eating more nutritiously or taking a nap in the afternoon. You'll be a more effective partner with your body as it works toward healing.

Source: Linda Hanner, coauthor of *When You're Sick and Don't Know Why*, Chronimed Publishing, Minneapolis 55343.

A Mature Ego

When we are faced with life's problems, it is helpful to have other people to help us face them. But even if we don't, we each have an internal pilot that guides our responses. This is the part of the mind that psychologists call the ego.

Because the ego operates subconsciously, we are not aware of the way it works. But by observing others, we can learn about the ways the ego protects us from the pressures we face. The ego reacts to pressures from four sources...

•*Internal:* Our selfish personal desires... and our consciences, which give us conflicting advice on how to behave.

•*External:* The people we deal with...and the events that affect us.

There is no single way to resolve these conflicts, so every individual must find his/her own way. Those with the most mature egos find the ways that are best for both themselves and others.

The pilot mechanism...

Think of the ego as a pilot because it directs us through the turmoil and turbulence of life's journey. A successful airplane pilot must be aware of the dangers he faces in order to take precautions, but he also must remain relaxed in

order to perform his task effectively. Those exceptional pilots who keep calm in the most hazardous circumstances are said to have the right stuff. In turn, those people who handle life with mature egos have the right psychological stuff.

Psychological defenses...

Psychologists have identified a number of different ways—or defenses—that the ego uses to reconcile conflicts and protect against psychological stress. To understand these defenses, consider the ways a teen-ager might deal with a stressful situation.

Peggy, 16, and an 18-year-old boy she recently met are attracted to each other, but her strong religious upbringing tells her that it is wrong to have intimate relations with him. Her possible responses to his urgent pleas can be divided into four groups...

•Psychotic defenses, in which Peggy loses contact with reality.

Example: She might totally ignore her boyfriend...walk by him in the street...insist he was a stranger. Denying reality is one way to avoid unbearable conflict.

•Immature defenses, which are typically employed by teenagers and generally irritate other people.

Example: Peggy might project her own feelings on her boyfriend (Men are all animals)... or fantasize about him...or become a hypochondriac, suffering headaches that keep him safely away from her but still interested.

•Neurotic defenses, which are private and have less effect on other people than immature defenses and are closer to reality.

Example: Peggy might transfer her interest in her boyfriend to a pet or a younger, less emotionally disturbing friend...or repress her feelings by dressing provocatively and talking romantically but still becoming outraged if her boyfriend reacts physically.

•Mature defenses, which recognize and balance harmoniously all the conflicting forces of desire, conscience, people and reality. There are five modes of mature defense—altruism, sublimation, suppression, anticipation and humor. *Examples:*

Peggy might demonstrate altruism by doing volunteer work, so she could use her talents and love to help others...

Or she might sublimate her feelings for her boyfriend by acting opposite him as a romantic lead in a play…

Or Peggy could suppress her impulses while acknowledging her feelings, by postponing the gratification of her yearnings until the appropriate time…

Or she might anticipate by carefully thinking through the course of the relationship…

Or she could use humor to reduce the stress of the predicament.

All the mature defenses give the impression of being consciously planned, even though they are produced by the subconscious workings of the ego.

How a mature ego develops…

The development of a mature ego is a natural, but not inevitable, process. It occurs as we pass through stages of life and successfully navigate a series of challenges.

First, you must learn how to form relationships, which enable you to accept help from others. Then you must master career skills that teach how to be assertive and creative. Finally, in maturity, you are able to pass on wisdom to the next generation and accept your passage into old age.

The maturation process is similar for both men and women. It does not depend on ethnic background…economic status…intelligence… or education.

Example: Since childhood, Stan was observed in a study of youths likely to become delinquent. His father abandoned him at birth, his mother died when he was three years old, and he was raised by elderly aunts in a Boston tenement. He dropped out of school in the eighth grade. At 17, he was in reform school for car theft…at 25, divorced from a wife with whom he used to fight with knives, he was in prison for rape…at 32, already an alcoholic for 15 years, he was in county jail for vagrancy.

But as he matured, he was able to connect with other people and turn himself around. By the time he was 47, he had been out of jail for 15 years, was a nondrinker and a 10-year member of Alcoholics Anonymous, owned his home and was an experienced furniture mover who had bought his own truck. He was happily married and had a close relationship with his adopted son.

There is no magic formula for developing a mature ego…but if you can learn to act as if you have a mature ego, you will.

How to nurture your ego…

• Observe other people. You cannot observe your own ego. By observation, you can appreciate how different egos help other people deal with their problems more or less effectively. Try to behave and think in ways like those who have mature egos.

Suggestions: Try to understand how other people feel and see how you can help them— that's training your ego's altruism. Try to see the humor in life's twists and turns—it helps you cope better with difficulties and provides a little pleasure to alleviate the pain.

• Prepare yourself in the safety of the present to be better able to deal with foreseeable problems in the future—a way to learn anticipation.

• Try to accept the inevitable difficulties of life as they occur and recognize that you don't control the world. This is the mature defense called suppression.

Learning how to act and react in such ways can help your personal pilot acquire the right stuff of ego maturity.

Source: George E. Vaillant, MD, professor of psychiatry at Harvard University Medical School and author of *The Wisdom of the Ego.* Harvard University Press, 79 Garden St., Cambridge, Massachusetts 02138.

How to Reduce Stress

The very best way to reduce the amount of stress in your life is to keep it from building up in the first place. *Suggested:*

• Get up 15 minutes earlier in the morning. The inevitable morning mishaps will be less stressful.

• Make duplicates of all keys. Bury a house key in a secret spot in the garden. Carry a duplicate car key in your wallet, apart from your key ring.

• Plan ahead. Don't let the gas tank go below one-quarter full…don't wait until you're down to your last bus token or postage stamp to buy more.

•Don't put up with something that doesn't work right. If your alarm clock, wallet, shoe laces, windshield wipers—whatever—are a constant source of aggravation, get them fixed or replace them.

Source: Seymour Diamond, MD, executive director of the National Headache Foundation, and director, Diamond Headache Clinic, 5252 N. Western Ave., Chicago 60625.

How to Increase Your Resistance to Stress

In today's fast-moving, success-oriented world, it seems as though one must be able to withstand a very high stress level in order to get ahead and stay ahead. Many ambitious people put themselves under a crushing stress burden for years, eventually paying the price in heart disease, ulcers and so on.

But there are busy, high-achieving people who are seemingly immune to stress. They deal with demanding workloads and high pressure year after year and show every evidence of thriving on their lifestyle. Such people have certain personality traits that insulate them against the ill effects of stress. They have something to teach us on how to increase our own stress-resistance.

Who is stress-resistant?

Studies have determined that people who display three main qualities are the most stress-resistant:

•Seek out and enjoy change. They see it as a challenge. This is extremely important. How we view a stressful event determines how our bodies and minds react. If an event is seen as a threat and we feel victimized, the actual physiology of the body changes to meet the threat. If we see change as a challenge, with potential for growth and excitement, the body's response is entirely different.

Crucial: How we view our past performance. Although some people do as well as others at a particular task, they always feel they haven't done well enough. These are the perfectionists—a very stress-vulnerable group. Perfectionists are always condemning themselves for not having coped well enough in the past. When a new challenge comes along, they view it as just another threat to their self-esteem.

•Feel at one with what they're doing. It's almost as though they've selected or adjusted to what they do so it's an extension of their personalities, rather than something foreign. This quality is important because we don't see stress as dangerous or threatening if we feel that it's something we've chosen—not something that's been laid on us. Identifying with our work enables us to deal with stress.

•Have a sense of control over what goes on in their lives. If you participate in the planning and problem-setting, are then involved with handling your part, and also get a sense of completion at the end of a particular task, there's a clear sense of control. This is why top managers are under less stress than middle managers.

The vicious cycle of stress...

When a situation is viewed as a threat, the body's fight-or-flight syndrome is activated. More energy goes to the muscles and brain, to the exclusion of other organs. Blood pressure, heart rate and blood sugar all go up. The gut tightens and the hormones alter. The body literally tears away at its inner structure to deal with the threat.

This alarm system was programmed into our genes to deal with the actual physical dangers faced by early man. For animals, the fight-or-flight syndrome disappears in a few hours. They rest and regain internal balance. With humans, however, the alarm system is called into play when there's a psychological threat...and then persists. Rebalancing does not occur because we continue to ruminate about the problem.

Even when we rest or sleep, we're still thinking or dreaming about it. We wake up still tight and tense, and therefore less able to deal with the problems of the next day. A perpetual cycle of chronic distress builds up, eventually resulting in body-system breakdowns. Many overstressed people are so accustomed to living with this syndrome that they don't even realize they're under stress until they get physically sick. About 80% of the people who visit physicians are actually suffering from chronic stress.

Building your stress-resistance...

•Change your expectations. The difference between expectations and perception of reality is the measure of how much stress you will experience.

Example: If you begin the day with an attitude of "The world is changing, finances are fluctuating, nothing stays the same," and you perceive that to be so, you'll experience very little stress if you're expectations aren't met. Either the environment or your own performance will displease you.

Remedy: Diminish your expectations and pay attention to your perceptions of reality.

•Ask for feedback. You won't be able to deal with stress if you feel that your past performances have been inadequate. You'll assume that you'll just fail again.

Remedy: Find out the average or expected performance for any given job and gear yourself to that. You may find out you've been failing for very different reasons than you thought. People under stress tend to feel extremely anxious and afraid. These feelings often come across to others as anger rather than fear. If people see you as hostile (even though it is not really so), it may adversely affect any evaluation of your performance.

•Seek a socially cohesive work situation. In England during World War II, there was less illness and higher performance among Londoners who weathered the bombings than before, or after, the war. Great social cohesiveness was provided by an external enemy. That same kind of cohesiveness occurs in any organization geared towards a strong goal.

Learn to relax...

•Do relaxation exercises. The purpose of these is to get the focus on a nonlogical part of the body. It's the constant logical planning and rumination that keeps stress going. *Best:* Approaches that focus on breathing. Proper breathing triggers other parts of the body to relax. The body is born with the innate ability to produce the opposite of the stress response.

These exercises allow you to get in touch with that feeling, and eventually, you'll be able to call upon it at will.

•Make time to do something relaxing. Take some time away from your desk to window-shop or something "silly." Eat lunch out of the office. Plan something pleasurable each week, and then follow through. *Caution:* If you eat while under stress, you'll have a 50% higher cholesterol level after the meal than if you were relaxed.

•Physical exercise helps only if you do it right. For instance, if jogging is just another chore that you don't enjoy, but you squeeze it into a heavy schedule because you feel you should, it only puts an extra load on your heart. Exercise while under stress can be dangerous. But if you see the trees and smell the air and feel high and good after running, you're doing it right. Exercise that makes you feel good is as helpful as any relaxation technique.

Source: Interview with Kenneth Greenspan, MD, psychiatrist and director of the Center for Stress and Pain-Related Disorders, Columbia Presbyterian Medical Center, New York City.

Boredom Can Be Dangerous

Boredom can cause as much personal stress as pressure does, and the effects may be even worse. Drug addiction, for example, can often be traced back to boredom. The best way to avoid general boredom is always to be learning something new...and planning something to look forward to. *Helpful:* Swear off mental opiates such as soap operas and pulp fiction.

Source: David Ruben, PhD, quoted in *Thrive on Stress* by Richard Sharpe, Warner Books, New York.

Handling Pressure

To avoid "choking" under pressure—distract yourself. *One way:* When golfing, count backward from 100 by twos when you need to make a critical putt. *Reason:* "Choking" results from focusing too much attention on yourself. Any means of distraction at times of high pressure can improve performance.

Source: Study of more than 100 Arizona State University students, led by Darwyn Linder, PhD, professor of psychology, reported in *Men's Health,* 33 E. Minor St., Emmaus, Pennsylvania 18098.

Work and Self-Esteem

The who/where/what we do connection has created difficult problems for a growing number of people today who feel trapped in unsatisfying jobs. These people are afraid they won't be able to find another one...or they can't afford to lose seniority and pension rights ...or they can't face the difficulty of relocating their families.

Problem: If you feel unappreciated or taken for granted or inadequately rewarded at work, it has an adverse effect on your work, your relationships with your boss and colleagues... and your own psychological and emotional well-being.

The unresolved anger that you feel in your job may spill over into your private life, with family and friends its innocent victims as you scream at the kids, kick the dog, knock down two fast martinis, etc.

Getting back on track...

Doing nothing only adds to feelings of anger, frustration and exploitation, and victimization will probably continue.

Helpful: Realize that because you have control over yourself, you have control over the situation. Then figure out what you can do to improve the situation. *Questions to ask...*

• *Am I appreciated?* The very fact that you have a job is an important sign that you are valued by your employer. If you're being paid more than people doing similar work elsewhere, that's another good sign.

• *Should I be appreciated?* If your work is marginal or if your achievement level is lower than colleagues in your unit, then it's not realistic to expect compliments and reassurances about the quality of your work.

Try to appraise your real contributions to your employer...and look for ways to bring those to management's attention.

In addition to self-appraisal, it's imperative to get frequent feedback from your boss. If your company doesn't have formal evaluations, request a meeting to discuss your job effectiveness. Work review sessions—in one form or another—should happen much more than once or twice a year, for they give you a good sense of whether you're on the right track.

Try to communicate with your boss about signs of appreciation. If he/she seems to be piling work on you or always giving you the tough tasks, you might interpret it as punishment, while your boss meant to show confidence in your ability. *It helps to talk these things out.*

Also ask colleagues what they think of your work. Assure them that you're not fishing for a compliment, but that you really need an objective appraisal. You may find that you are far more respected than you realize—perhaps for talents or skills you didn't know you had. Team support is a two-way street. Remember to thank and congratulate co-workers when they have done something well, too.

Customers can also be a valuable source of recognition and job satisfaction. When they thank you for your promptness or effectiveness or thoughtfulness, accept the compliments graciously and tell them how much you appreciate the kind words.

But if someone *withholds* praise that you believe you deserve, do not let it cause you to lose confidence in yourself. There's nothing wrong with giving yourself a pat on the back —or a special reward.

Boredom: The bane of self-esteem...

We read frequently about the financial costs of smoking or substance abuse in the workplace, but we rarely hear about the costs of boredom.

Some of boredom's many manifestations: Indifference, anger, disillusionment, procrastination, gossiping, tardiness, absenteeism and physical aches and pains like headaches.

Bored individuals are not stimulated to go to work, to get there on time, to do the job promptly or well, or to remain loyal to the company. People who are bored because they feel their skills or talents aren't being adequately used often become resentful toward their employers.

Boredom is also a classic cause of stress. It is stressful to spend an eight-hour day in an unstimulating environment. It is stressful not to have the opportunity to work on challenging problems. And, it is stressful to realize that you are not growing or developing or reaching the goals you set for yourself. We become spiritless, listless zombies whose minds are on hold.

Solutions to job boredom...

First admit that job boredom does exist and then take personal responsibility for overcoming your boredom. *Some suggestions:*

•Create a log. Chart the activities that you find stimulating and those that are deadly dull. Include contextual information that might help identify whether you're truly bored or simply tired or depressed.

•Analyze your activities and look for patterns. After several weeks of keeping a log, analyze the data to see what patterns emerge. If meetings bore you but you feel stimulated while preparing for and delivering a sales presentation, it may be that you need to perform, to persuade, to be creative. Ask yourself how you can do more of this in your job.

•Reenergize your job. Balance routine, repetitive tasks with work that you find more stimulating. Wherever possible, shuffle the order, break boring patterns and change locations. If you have a morning full of mind-deadening tasks, reward yourself by going out to lunch instead of brown-bagging it. Question whether all routine tasks are really necessary. Take occasional work breaks. Try to rotate jobs or swap responsibilities with a colleague to vary the monotony.

•Stretch—reach beyond your grasp. If you have mastered your job so that it no longer uses your full talents and abilities, ask for a new assignment or see if your job description could be broadened.

Alternative: Transfer to a different job in another department.

•Welcome positive problems at work. Confronting and solving problems adds spice to a job. Finding solutions keeps us emotionally and intellectually alive.

•Shake it up—avoid complacency. If you've become too comfortable in your job, take a new look at it. Look for ways to improve cooperation. Set additional goals. *Bonus:* The fresh excitement new accomplishments generate.

•Do something new. Read new relevant books. Attend a seminar, a workshop, a professional meeting or an educational course. Create or design a new product, a new production process, a new marketing strategy or a new information system and then try to "sell" it to management. Study Continuous Quality Improvement (CQI) to stimulate yourself by planning to do all that you do better—each time you do it.

•Develop a life outside of your job. Thoughts of how you will spend your free time away from the job can provide a mental escape from work that is boring. Pleasurable activities in private life can also provide the excitement and fulfillment that may be missing in your career—and maybe even add to it.

Coaching, reading, working on a political campaign, listening to music, volunteer work, sports and hobbies give balance and verve to your life and put you in control of your emotional well-being. Spend time with people who are energetic and enthusiastic, vital and vibrant ...and thoughtful about their life and work. *Learn from them.*

If it's impossible to eliminate boredom and reenergize your enthusiasm for the job, face the fact that it's time to move on. You've grown and changed and are now ready for new challenges...new beginnings...new dreams.

Source: John Sena, PhD, professor of English and Stephen Strasser, PhD, associate professor, division of hospital and health services administration, both at Ohio State University. They are authors of *Work Is Not a Four Letter Word*, Business One Irwin, 1818 Ridge Rd., Homewood, Illinois 60430.

Modesty Traps

Being overly modest is as bad as unabashed bragging. In either case, the people who should be aware of your accomplishments either won't learn about them (if you're too modest) or won't believe you (if you brag). *Best:* Share your accomplishments matter-of-factly, in casual conversation. For example, tell how a customer was satisfied, a crisis averted or a problem solved. And when someone compliments you, express your appreciation.

Source: Ted Pollack, management consultant, Old Tappan, New Jersey, writing in *Production*, 6600 Clough Pike, Cincinnati 45224.

Healthy Stress

Some stress actually keeps you healthy. *Positive stress* is produced by experiences that are challenging, exciting, arousing or fun...or that give life purpose and meaning. Healthful stress is the body's way of adapting to the constant changes of life.

Source: Harriet Braiker, PhD, author of *Lethal Lovers and Poisonous People*, Pocket Books, 1230 Avenue of the Americas, New York 10020.

The Power of Positive Relationships

People who build constructive relationships with their personal friends and family members gain important benefits...

- •They are healthier.
- •They live longer.
- •They succeed in most of their activities.

A Duke University study of 1,300 patients who had suffered coronary attacks showed that those patients who were socially isolated...unmarried, with no confidants...had a death rate three times as high as those with stronger social ties. *How positive relationships help...*

- •Sociable people take better care of themselves. People who value their friendships with others are more likely to stop smoking...continue to take required medications...go to the doctor more often when they're ill. That's

because even when they are tempted to let things slide, their friends get after them.

Example: In a support group for women with breast cancer observed by Dr. David Spiegel of Stanford University, when one woman mentioned new pains, the other women in the group convinced her to report it immediately to the doctor even though she was inclined to wait until her next appointment.

- •Sociable people are physically healthier. Researchers have found that social ties have physiological effects that make people healthier. Sociable people feel less depressed...notice fewer aches and pains...have lower levels of stress-related hormones.

Psychologist James Pennebaker found that when people discussed stressful events with others, even with strangers, their blood pressure declined.

Building better relationships...

Obviously, it's in everyone's self-interest to build good relationships with others...and, fortunately, it's a skill that can be learned even if it doesn't come naturally.

If you want to form more positive relationships but have always found it difficult because of your personality, your best strategy is to begin by changing your behavior, not your attitudes. Strategies that can help you improve your relationships...

- •Practice listening. At least once a day, when someone is talking to you, force yourself to let that person finish what he/she is saying. Even if you find it hard to pay attention, don't interrupt or disconnect...at least, look attentive.

It may be difficult at first, but gradually you will learn that other people may have something worthwhile to say, you can learn something from them...and when you show them that you recognize that, you'll get through to them better, as well.

You will gradually come to appreciate where other people are coming from, become more tolerant, and find relationships with others easier to make and more enjoyable.

- •Get involved with community affairs or volunteer work. If you don't already have satisfying personal relationships, one good way to make connections is to participate in community-service activities. Research studies have found that men who volunteered had greater longevity and reported better health than their non-volunteer counterparts.

Volunteering to help other individuals or groups is not only an excellent way to learn specific caring behaviors, it also enlarges your capacity for empathy with others, and helps reduce your social isolation.

Helpful: Seek out opportunities for about two hours a week of one-on-one helping...try to help strangers...look for problem areas where you can feel empathy with those you are helping...look for a supportive formal organization so you can feel part of a team...find a service that uses a skill you possess...and when you are volunteering, forget about the benefits you are giving or receiving—concentrate on enjoying the feeling of closeness with the person you're helping.

•Have a confidant. The best source of personal support is an intimate relationship with at least one person. A spouse or best friend with whom you share your inner life can help you carry out your duties...act as a sounding board to help you make important decisions...and comfort you when you are feeling down.

If you already have a confidant, cultivate the relationship to forge even closer ties. If you don't, try to find someone suitable.

•Get a pet. If you're initially uncomfortable with people...or live in socially isolated circumstances...positive relationships with animals can produce dramatic health benefits. A University of Maryland study of coronary patients showed that only 6% of the pet owners died within a year...compared with 28% of those without pets.

Source: Redford Williams, MD, director of behavioral research at Duke University. He is coauthor of *Anger Kills: Seventeen Strategies for Controlling the Hostility that Can Harm Your Health*, Times Books, 201 E. 50 St., New York 10022.

All About Civility

The great lack of civility in America is the major factor behind the breakdown in family life, unethical practices in business, selfishness and dishonesty in politics.

Civility means much more than politeness. Civility is all-embracing—a general awareness by people that personal well-being cannot be separated from the well-being of the groups to which we belong...our families, our businesses and our nation.

Lack of civility is tied to unreasonable expectations in recent decades of constant happiness and constant comfort. When real life presents us with painful experiences...when something hurts us...when we feel unfulfilled—we feel cheated. And too many of us—too often—reach for instant happiness by illegitimate means that disregard the interests of other people.

Consciousness and civility...

The route to improved civility begins with greater awareness of our shortcomings and our tendencies to manipulate others.

Greater awareness leads to a willingness to accept pain in the short term, recognizing that it is an unavoidable part of any growth process, leading to significant personal growth. Learning how to handle pain realistically is a prerequisite for warmer, more meaningful relationships over the long term. Civility does not happen automatically. You have to train yourself to be aware of your true motives, to be honest with yourself and others, and to judge yourself first.

Civility in the family...

The first training ground for civility is the family. Children learn how they are expected to behave by observing their parents' behavior, not just by listening to their words. So if you want your children to demonstrate civility now and later in life, you have to practice it yourself.

Example: Your two kids are having a disagreement and your six-year-old son slugs his little sister. Then you tell him, *Don't ever hit your sister!* and hit him.

That will deliver quite a different message than you want to give: *It's OK to hit someone else ...but don't hit your sister when your mother or father is around.*

With that kind of discrepancy prevalent between parental educational words and actions, it's not surprising that so many people grow up with an internal moral code that tells them,

You can do whatever you want as long as you don't get caught doing it.

Civility in business...

Successful businesses are built on cooperation. Businesses have a right to both demand and expect cooperation from their employees, because the main purpose of any business is to make a profit. But companies also have a responsibility to treat their workers fairly and honestly in the process.

Example: Some companies that vest workers with pension benefits only after a long period of employment save money by laying the workers off only a short time before they become vested.

This is uncivil. It is obviously unfair to the workers and may also hurt the company by encouraging the best employees to leave.

Better way: Set up a system that recognizes both the company's interest in dedicated, hard-working employees and the employees' interest in security and fair compensation. This will only work when both sides honestly keep their parts of the bargain.

Honest communication...

Companies, families and all types of organizations become more civil when they encourage honest, two-way communication—straight talk and listening. That is not easy, but it can be done if you follow these principles:

•Don't expect perfection...just do your best and learn from your mistakes.

•Set aside time for communication.

•Clear your mind and listen to the other person.

•Be honest...with yourself and others.

•Judge yourself first. Look into your real motives.

•Take time to respond and think. Don't be afraid of silence.

•Be willing to be hurt—and to risk hurting others by speaking honestly. If someone is too fragile to respect your point of view, he/she cannot be a part of your community.

•Try to be as gentle as possible. Don't make any unnecessarily painful statements...yet don't be so subtle that the point is completely missed.

•Speak personally and specifically. Don't talk about "the system" or some impersonal authority. Don't generalize. Document what you say.

•Don't analyze other people's motives. Don't play psychologist.

•Speak when you are moved to speak. Don't cop out.

Bottom line: It takes hard work to get an organization to operate in a mode of civility. But those who have made the transition do not want to go back.

Source: M. Scott Peck, MD, a founder of the Foundation for Community Encouragement. He is author of *The Road Less Traveled* and, most recently, *A World Waiting to be Born*, Bantam Books, 1540 Broadway, New York 10036.

All About Selficide

Many people do not find satisfaction in today's world. They find life to be a flat, unreal experience. They cannot enjoy intimate relationships with others. They are not in touch with their own selves. I use the word *selficide* to describe this state of being unable to learn and grow from life's experiences.

As we age, we increasingly need to understand who we are and how to behave as responsible, caring adults. Important questions to ask yourself to see if you are on the right track...or on the road to *selficide*...

Do you control your own behavior...or are your actions governed by a need to rebel or comply with other's rules? My patient Denise was anorexic. She ate sensibly—but whenever she reached a healthy weight, she stopped eating and lost weight again.

Her eating problem was the symptom of an internal struggle between her perception of the voice of her parents, which told her she must eat to be loved, and her desire to be herself.

She was able to solve her problem when, with encouragement, she disciplined herself not to control her eating habits. Instead she focused on doing something that she really *wanted* to do...*not* what she felt she *should* do.

Are your thoughts, feelings and actions consistent with each other? We all know the old joke about the Boy Scout who took an hour to help an old lady across the street…because she didn't want to go. His behavior was inconsistent with his goal—to do good.

Do you truly play a meaningful part in your own activities and dealings with others…or are you often just there physically? Some people are so involved in regret over the past that they can't think about what they should be doing *now*. Others are so busy *daydreaming* about the *future* that they aren't acting now to make their dreams possible.

Do you willingly surrender yourself to reality …or do you begrudge it? Can you ever leave a discussion without having the last word?

Are you able to give and take…or do you insist on only one direction? Do you feel like a martyr…and let everyone know it?

Do you accept others as they are…or do you always feel the need to judge them?

Do you act naturally, without pretension… or are you dishonest or phony?

Do you take joy in your experiences…not just look at life as a series of tasks to accomplish?

Example: Ned, a patient of mine, wondered why his business was always outperformed by a small rival company, so he went to check on it. He noticed that the owner of the company was an exceedingly enthusiastic individual. When Ned asked him, "You really enjoy what you do, don't you?" he replied, "Yeah, it sure beats the hell out of working!"

Do you have an inner aesthetic sense of morality that makes it seem repellent to you to do something wrong?

Are you willing to take risks—to try something new to satisfy your real inner desires…or are you afraid of doing anything that people don't expect of you?

• Do you exercise your creativity—the willingness to dismiss old ways or experience to be free to grow in new directions…or are you afraid to lose the security provided by always repeating the same pattern—even when you find it to be unsatisfactory?

How to avoid *selficide*…

People who cannot give positive answers to any of the questions are well on their way to selficide. But selficide is not the same as suicide …life always contains the possibility of growth.

If you are willing to look into yourself as you confront the issues of everyday living and examine your inner feelings, you can find new responses that better satisfy your needs and those of the people close to you.

Those new responses will develop as you embrace new experiences and adopt less fearful ways of dealing with the world. That joyful approach is not really alien to anyone's nature, because it represents a return to the way everybody starts out life.

Babies explore the world fearlessly and joyfully…they accept bumps and falls as the price of growth. They learn to walk and talk at their own pace…nobody else can make it happen faster or slower. Before babies learn to walk, they crawl…but when they learn to walk they stop crawling.

As long as they are able to act naturally, children continue to learn and grow because they are *open to new experiences*…willing to *acknowledge their true feelings*…able to *react in new ways*.

Many adults have forgotten those natural instincts.

As analyst Erich Fromm said: "We listen to every voice and to everybody but not ourselves. We are constantly exposed to the noise of opinions and ideas hammering at us from everywhere…motion pictures, newspapers, radio, idle chatter. If we had planned intentionally to prevent ourselves from ever listening to ourselves, we could have done no better."

But if we pause as we go about our daily activities and look carefully at the world around us…at the people we are with…and most of all deep into ourselves…we can find what we want from life and we can achieve it.

Source: Patrick Thomas Malone, MD, medical director of Mental Health Services at Northside Hospital in Atlanta, and a psychotherapist at the Atlanta Psychiatric Clinic. With his father, Thomas Patrick Malone, MD, PhD, he wrote *The Windows of Experience: Moving Beyond Recovery to Wholeness*, published by Simon & Schuster, 1230 Avenue of the Americas, New York 10020.

What Ever Happened To Loyalty?

Loyalty is out of fashion these days. People would sooner switch than fight…not only in the marketplace, where customers rapidly switch to suppliers who offer better deals…but also in their personal, social and political lives.

As soon as they think they might do better elsewhere, baseball players change teams…professors leave their colleges…voters desert their parties…husbands abandon their wives and vice versa.

Rather than trying to build better relationships where they are, people abandon their old associations and enter into new ones…which are likely to be temporary, too.

What happened to loyalty?

The breakdown of loyalty is not only a result of selfishness—it also has ideological roots.

For the past 200 years, giants of philosophy, particularly Immanuel Kant and Jeremy Bentham, have argued that people should not make decisions based on what is best for themselves but instead based on an impersonal calculation of what would be best for the entire society.

These ideas have had a powerful effect on the way many educated people think, but they certainly have not produced a society in which people act better…or even feel better. That is because the world is too complicated for people—even philosophers—to figure out what is best for humanity at large.

Result: Many people reject the old-fashioned belief that we owe loyalty to those who are close to us and helped to make us what we are. They also do not believe we owe loyalty to the nation whose benefits we enjoy. In the short run, this disregard of loyalty hurts some people. In the long run, this attitude hurts everyone.

Advantages of loyalty…

Loyalty in marriage, family life, social interactions and politics strengthens bonds between people. It assumes that the relationships we are born into—or choose voluntarily—should continue. It encourages us to accept the other party's good faith and so includes a willingness to accept mistakes.

Under these conditions, with time to correct mistakes and a healthy degree of flexibility, relationships can become stronger. Each partner is willing to allow the other to change previous patterns of behavior without fear of immediate abandonment, so each can help the other to grow.

A one-sided, individualistic approach to life may work as long as things are going well, but it is likely to fail when problems arise. Loyalty builds strong, long-lasting mutual relationships that can help overcome temporary setbacks…it leaves both sides better off in the long term.

Loyalty in families…

Successful families are built on a web of loyalty between father, mother and children. Today's emphasis on personal happiness over loyalty to others is a major cause of family breakdown.

The same emphasis on self that leads to divorce also corrodes the relationship between parents and children.

Example: A huge number of divorced fathers who have remarried simply abandon the children from their first marriage…therefore, a new generation fails to learn how to practice loyalty and enjoy the satisfaction it provides.

How to build loyalty…

Loyalty stands us in good stead when times are tough…but it should be established when things are still going well. *Five steps to loyalty:*

• Affirmation. Think about the good things others are doing for you. Show them how much you appreciate them…in both word and deed.

• Confrontation. Show that the relationship is important to you by pointing out how it can be improved. When you disapprove of your partner's behavior, don't be afraid to say so…but always constructively.

• Complicity. I use this term, which is translated from the French, to mean the sense that you and your partner(s) are separate from the rest of the world. You possess something nobody else has. Feel very happy about it.

• Ritual. Find ways to do things for the special people in your circle.

Example: When loved ones are coming to visit, meet them at the airport.

• Privacy. Keep the details of your shared relationship away from outsiders. How you make decisions is nobody else's business. Never complain to outsiders about your partner.

The tendency today is to think of intimate relationships in political terms. Both men and women are excessively concerned about whether their private conduct meets the standards of behavior set by their friends. Traditional men are concerned about whether they look like they are "wearing the pants in the family." Liberated women worry about whether their sisters would approve of their cooking and washing dishes. This manner of looking over one's shoulder reflects a conflict of loyalties. Loyalty to one's spouse comes into tension with loyalties to those outside the relationship. This conflict undermines trust and destroys intimacy.

Conclusion: Be loyal to your spouse and forget how your private way of doing things may look to outsiders.

The toughest challenge of personal loyalty is to stand by another when the going gets tough. Loyalty becomes important only when we are tempted to "jump ship." Fair-weather loyalty is but convenience. The next time you are tempted to leave, think, *This is the time to show my loyalty.*

Source: George P. Fletcher, Beekman Professor of Law at Columbia University and author of *Loyalty: An Essay on the Morality of Relationships,* Oxford University Press, 200 Madison Ave., New York 10016.

Get More Out of Your Dreams

Dreams can be a rich resource for creativity, decision making, problem solving and self-understanding.

We actually do much of our information processing at night. Dreaming helps us integrate emotional and intellectual material from the day —without the defensiveness that characterizes our waking thoughts. Because we're more honest with ourselves when we are asleep, we're often more insightful as well.

Recalling dreams…

You may not remember your dreams, but that doesn't mean you didn't have any. Everyone dreams at least four times a night. You can learn to recall your dreams by trying to "catch" them first thing in the morning.

Opportunity: Keep a pencil and pad by your bed. Jot down the date each night before you go to sleep. Immediately after waking up in the morning, write down a few lines about whatever is on your mind—even if all you write is, *There is nothing on my mind.* Within a week or two, you'll find that you're remembering plenty of your dreams.

Using dreams to solve problems…

Everyone has had the experience of "sleeping on a problem"—and waking up with the solution. We can make this process more deliberate by practicing what I call *dream incubation.* Here's how you can do it…

Before you go to bed, write down a one-line phrase that clearly states an issue you want to understand better, a problem you'd like to resolve or the kind of idea you need.

Don't worry about or try to solve the problem at this time. Turn out the light and repeat the phrase over and over—as calmly as though you were counting sheep—until you fall asleep. *Bonus:* This will also help you fall asleep more quickly.

As usual, when you wake up, write down what's on your mind. Sometimes the answer will be straightforward—in the form of a simple idea rather than a dream.

People have used dream incubation to find ways of resolving conflicts with a friend or colleague…streamlining office paperwork…turning around a marketing campaign…coming up with ideas for a presentation.

Other answers may require more interpretation. You might have a dream that helps you understand the situation better, even if you don't have the information to solve it completely. Or your dream may reframe the question. In rare cases, the dream incubation may not work—if another pressing problem comes up at the same time.

With my clients, I have found that dream incubation leads to helpful insights as much as 95% of the time. It sounds hard to believe, but it's true.

Interpreting your dreams…

Many people think of dream interpretation as a system of rigid Freudian symbols. Sigmund Freud and Carl Jung were on the right track in taking dreams seriously, but they drew on their cultural prejudices and attached specific meanings to various dream images.

Actually, each individual's dream metaphors are very private and personal. I encourage people to dismiss their preconceptions about dream symbols and discover for themselves what they think about the images in their dreams. It's not necessary to analyze every detail of a dream in order to understand it. Record the main ideas and themes.

Then set up a *dream interview* with a friend, a therapist—*or even yourself* as interviewer—to clarify the dream's meaning. *The dream interview has three major steps…*

•Description. Describe each of the major elements—people, animals, objects, setting, action and feelings—in the dream as if you were describing them to someone who comes from another planet and has never heard of them. If you are doing a self-interview, you might find it helpful to write down the descriptions the first few times.

•Bridge. For each element, ask yourself, *Is there anything in my life—or anything about myself—that's like this figure or action in my dream, which I describe as…?*

•Summary. Tie together what you've learned by reviewing each description and its bridge. Think about how the dream as a whole could be a parable about your life.

To use the insights you've gained, consider taking a fourth step:

•Action. Reread your dream several times, and keep it in mind during the day. Your dream may give you the insight and courage to make important changes.

Caution: Never act based on a dream without first evaluating the option in your conscious mind. Dreams aren't commands from the supernatural—at best, they're new ways of viewing issues. Any action you take based on a dream insight should also make perfect sense in waking life…and should seem so obvious that you can't believe you didn't think of it before.

Common dream themes…

Though each person's dream symbolism is highly individual, certain themes often have connotations that are common to many people. *Examples:*

The examination. In the dream, you're about to take an important test and you haven't studied all semester…or you can't find the examination room. In waking life, you may be facing a challenge for which you don't feel prepared.

If you *are* prepared, the dream may reflect simple anxiety. But it could also be a warning that you need to take steps to meet the challenge. Another possibility is that you're living under such pressure that you never feel quite ready for anything. You may need to reevaluate whether you want to keep functioning that way.

Falling. Dreams in which you are falling often have to do with loss of control. Are there areas in which you're out of control? Does this present a danger to your career or a personal relationship?

Having sex with a surprising partner. This *doesn't* usually mean that you harbor a secret attraction for the person you dreamed of making love with. More often, when you describe your dream partner, you'll find you're describing some aspect of yourself…or of your real-life partner.

Source: Gayle Delaney, PhD, codirector of the Delaney & Flowers Center for the Study of Dreams, 337 Spruce St., San Francisco 94118. She is author of *Breakthrough Dreaming* (Bantam Books, 1540 Broadway, New York 10036) and the forthcoming *Sexual Dreams*, Fawcett Columbine, 201 E. 50 St., New York 10022.

How to Increase Your Creativity

You don't have to be an artist or writer to be creative. Creativity involves your ability to use your brain to change, renew and recombine aspects of your life. Creativity means sensing the world with vigor and making new use of what you have perceived.

Frederic Flach, MD, a New York psychiatrist who has made a specialty of studying the creative process, believes that the source of a creative idea is the preconscious. According to Dr. Flach and other psychoanalysts…

•The preconscious includes all ideas, thoughts, past experiences and other memory impressions that, with effort, can be consciously recalled.

•To be conscious means to be aware and to have a perception of oneself, one's acts and one's surroundings.

•The subconscious is a state in which mental processes take place without conscious perception.

When we are conscious, we are aware of our surroundings, Dr Flach explains—but we are limited by the our sense of reality and the restrictions of conscious language. In our subconscious, our feelings are so buried they are inaccessible. Our painful past experiences and emotions are locked up.

In our preconscious, however, things are close to the surface. It's our computer data center, where we put things together—memories, fantasies and the vibrations we pick up from other people. It's where we are in touch with ourselves.

How to tap into your preconscious and increase your creativity...

•Talk about yourself and your past. It is a process that's similar to psychotherapy. You can uncover new facts or new relationships among new and old data and rid yourself of inhibitions caused by people and circumstances you faced in the past—the teacher who told you that you were inadequate or your teasing sibling.

•Don't be a character actor. If you select a defined role, such as button-down executive or superwoman, you may be unable to do things another way.

•Think like a child. Youngsters are filled with wonder, curiosity, playfulness and imagination. Pursue activities that you have always wondered about. Play a new game. Daydream. As famous psychologist L.S. Vygotsky observed, "Imagination is the internalization of children's play."

•Verbalize or write down all your ideas for a particular project or problem. Don't judge as the ideas are flowing, no matter how far out or silly your conscious side may be telling you they are.

•Write or tape your frustrations. If you are having trouble coming up with ideas, record what is bothering you. It can help free up the creative flow.

•Change your environment. If you are still having difficulty starting the flow of ideas—change the room in which you are working—or change your clothes. Take a "mental excursion" by thinking about a place you'd like to go.

•Review and analyze. Once you have unclogged your creative-idea flow, you can evaluate whether any of them are workable.

•Don't be afraid to make mistakes. If you fail, learn what doesn't work. Try a new approach. If you are not failing, you are not being very creative, because new trails are unmarked and full of pitfalls. Many mistakes, though, can be eliminated by a higher round of creativity. Write out your ideas—in precise detail. Look for the flaws. Then, through more creative thinking, you can develop new solutions.

•Don't make excuses. Age, infirmity and lack of time are frequent reasons given for not being able to create. They are rarely valid. Picasso, at 91, kept art supplies by his bed in case he awoke during the night and had an idea. George Bernard Shaw wrote *The Millionairess* in his eighties. William Carlos Williams, the physician-poet, suffered his first stroke at age 68. In spite of paralysis and a transient inability to speak, he published three books of verse before his death at age 79.

•Associate with encouragers, not discouragers. Many a wet blanket has smothered another person's creativity. Choose associates who will support your efforts.

Source: Arthur Winter, MD, director, New Jersey Neurological Institute's Memory Enhancement Clinic. Dr. Winter is co-author with his wife, Ruth Winter, of *Build Your Brain Power*, St. Martin's Press, 175 Fifth Ave., New York 10010.

The Alertness/ Effectiveness Connection

In today's 24-hour world, workers are given extensive training, equipped with very reliable automated machinery and provided with comfortable surroundings. But that doesn't guarantee effective performance around the clock.

Bizarre example: In the cockpit of a Boeing 707 en route to Los Angeles, the entire crew fell asleep while the autopilot continued to fly the plane westward...far over the Pacific Ocean. When air traffic controllers on the ground noticed the wayward plane, their verbal inquiries went unanswered. The desperate controllers averted disaster when they managed to wake up the crew by triggering loud chimes in the cockpit.

Alertness is key to effective performance...

That near-disaster was caused by the failure of one critical human factor—alertness. Like so many systems today, the airplane was designed to perform so well automatically that it was hard for the pilots to remain alert.

But alertness is vital for people to perform effectively. Only in that state are people fully aware of their surroundings...able to think clearly...consider all options...make sensible decisions.

Physiological basis...

To physiologists, alertness represents a desirable state of balance between two human nervous systems.

One of these nervous systems—*the sympathetic nervous system*—automatically triggers the fight-or-flight response...heart pounding... blood pressure rising...pupils dilating...hair standing on end.

It represents a peak of alertness vital for dealing with emergency situations...but it usually can't be sustained for too long.

Minimum alertness occurs when the body is highly relaxed...under control of the *parasympathetic nervous system*. Consider someone dozing by the fire after a heavy meal...heart beating slowly...blood pressure dropping... pupils constricting. It is essential for the body and mind to rest sometimes...but a state of total relaxation is bad news if you're supposed to be working...studying...even observing.

In a state of alertness, the brain is engaged and ready to react appropriately to evolving situations. But we're often not alert when we need to be because our external environment or our internal state—or a combination of both—work to disengage our brain.

Nine switches of alertness...

Research into the physiology of alertness has shown there are nine switches that control alertness. We can improve our alertness by learning what they are and how to switch them on or off. *They are:*

1. *Sense of danger, interest or opportunity:* Nothing switches us faster from drowsiness to alertness than awareness of imminent danger. The brain can also be woken up in a less extreme way by other forms of stimulation.

Helpful: If you're in a meeting about a subject that's not too exciting and feel yourself dozing off, try to stimulate yourself. Ask questions...make comments...take notes...bring others into the discussion.

2. *Muscular activity:* Vigorous exercise can improve alertness for an hour or more. Many people performing tasks where alertness is vital cannot move around—pilots, drivers, nuclear plant operators. But they can find other types of muscular activity to help keep them alert.

Helpful: Stretch in place...chew gum...take periodic breaks to walk around.

3. *Time of day on the biological clock:* Humans have their own biological clock that tells when it's time to wake and to sleep. If you're on shift work or traveling between different time zones, it's not easy to adjust your built-in clock to match the environment.

Helpful: If you're running a meeting with people from all over the country, or the world, be aware of their biological clocks. Try to schedule a compromise time that helps as many as possible stay awake. Remember that people feel drowsy after lunch and are most alert when their body tells them it's mid-morning or late afternoon.

4. *Sleep bank balance:* Alertness depends on how long it is since we last slept. It is possible to restore the balance in our sleep bank by a good single night's sleep or by a number of brief naps at strategic intervals.

Interesting: A short nap of 10–15 minutes provides more benefit than one of 30–40 minutes, which leaves you drowsy. Research has shown that people can work 22 hours a day for extended periods if they get a 20-minute nap every four hours.

5. *Ingested nutrients and chemicals:* Stimulation by food, drink or chemicals can improve our alertness. In moderation, it may be sensible, but it's often a poor way to cope. Two or three cups of coffee are fine to help you stay awake, but any more than that stays in the sys-

tem and makes it hard to sleep after work, and it makes you more tired the next day. Similarly, people who pop too many stay-awake pills develop insomnia and then become dependent on sleeping pills.

Helpful: A 10-minute coffee break. But if you have the choice, a 10-minute nap is better.

6. *Environmental light:* Bright light keeps people alert, but to be truly effective, it must be about the level of natural light at dawn—about the level of a hospital operating room, which is twice as bright as a well-lit office. This level of light doesn't just help you see well, it stimulates the brain. Today, exploiting light for alertness is on the technological frontier.

7. *Environmental temperature and humidity:* We all know that a cold shower wakes us up… a warm bath puts us to sleep…and that when driving on a boring highway, one of the best ways to wake up is to open the window and get a blast of cold air.

8. *Environmental sound:* The rolling surf at the beach or the smooth rushing of a mountain stream can lull us to sleep. These are examples of "white noise" that is also generated by machines that people use to help them go to sleep …and resembles the background noise produced by much equipment found in industrial control rooms where operators are expected to stay awake at night.

Helpful: In control rooms, try to use irregular sources of sound that vary in pitch and intensity…allow workers to listen to stimulating radio programs when possible.

9. *Environmental aroma:* Although this switch has not been scientifically investigated as much as the other eight switches, there are intriguing reports that aromas like peppermint may help alertness.

With an awareness of how these nine switches work, you can improve your own alertness. By learning to put them in the "off" position, you can learn how to relax better, as well.

Source: Martin Moore-Ede, MD, PhD, associate professor of physiology at Harvard Medical School, Director of the Institute for Circadian Physiology. He is the founder and CEO of Circadian Technologies, consultants to industry worldwide on enhancing alertness in the workplace and author of *The Twenty-Four-Hour Society: Understanding Human Limits in a World that Never Stops*, Addison-Wesley, Jacob Way, Reading, Massachusetts 01867.

How to Complain… Successfully

Complaining is a normal part of human life, especially among people who live together. Without complaining, our resentments fester into permanent barriers to communication. But even though they are essential, complaints have two strikes against them…

• They convey that there is something wrong with the other person's behavior, which no one likes to hear.

• They contain a command or a request—which is an indirect command—that the other person's behavior be changed.

Most adults have knee-jerk negative reactions to commands from other adults. *Result:* Rather than considering the content of the complaint, they respond with denials, defensiveness and counter-accusations.

To complain more effectively, it's important to define the goal of your complaint. If you're simply venting your anger, it doesn't matter what you say. But if you want the other person to change his/her behavior, you should use a different technique.

The three-part message…

I use a verbal tool for complaining that works so well it seems almost magical. I call it the "three-part message": When you [X]…I feel [Y] …because [Z].

The point of the three-part message is to avoid triggering the listener's resentment. It succeeds by targeting a specific, verifiable behavior and then linking that behavior to the speaker's feelings and a real-world consequence.

Example I: "When you forget to water the tomato plants, I feel angry, because the plants die."

Example II: "When you overdraw our checking account, I feel embarrassed, because our checks bounce."

Example III: "When you bring the car home with no gas, I feel anxious, because I might run out on the way to work the next morning."

The three-part message works only when you absolutely stick to the pattern.

Ground rules…

•*Part One/When you X:* Cite one—and only one—specific behavior, which must be verifiable and beyond dispute. *Useful:* "When you yell at the children…" *Not useful:* "When you act like some tyrant…."

•*Part Two/I feel Y:* The emotion should be stated simply and without any exaggeration. *Useful:* "I feel distressed…" *Not useful:* "I feel like a second-class citizen…."

Pitfall: Drawing conclusions about your partner's feelings. *Not useful:* "I feel as if you don't respect me…."

•*Part Three/because Z:* Complainers must prove their right to complain…by describing a nondebatable consequence that reasonable people would want to avoid.

Useful: "When you leave all the lights on, I feel frustrated, because our utility bills get so high." *Not useful:* "…because it means you don't care about how hard I work for my money."

The three-part message is not suited for intimate or complex issues. But if you use this to-the-point tool for your everyday problems, your partner may become more receptive to longer discussions as the need arises.

Source: Suzette Haden Elgin, PhD, founder of the Ozark Center for Language Studies in Forum, Arkansas. She is the author of 23 books. Her latest book is *Genderspeak: Men, Women and the Gentle Art of Verbal Self-Defense,* John Wiley & Sons, 605 Third Ave., New York 10158.

Since Almost Everything in Life Is a Negotiation

Too often we walk into a negotiation unprepared—and consequently uncertain. Whether we are going to be talking about a raise, a job, a house, the rent, summer plans or where the kids go to school, it's unrealistic to expect to get everything we want.

That's because each person involved in a negotiation has different interests. Being well-prepared will help you understand the different interests. There is always the prospect that each side would do better by working out an agreement. The basic question is how to pursue that possibility—as a form of warfare or as joint problem solving.

Traditional haggling, in which each side argues a position and either makes concessions to reach a compromise or refuses to budge, is not the most efficient and amicable way to reach a wise agreement.

Better: Principled negotiation, or negotiation based on the merits of what's at stake, which is a straightforward negotiation method that can be used under almost any circumstances.

Checklist for principled negotiations…

Separate the people from the substantive problem. Think of preserving the relationship. Attack the problem, not the person. If the other side attacks you, as often happens, call him/her on it and ask him to return to the problem.

Focus on interests, not positions. Negotiating positions often obscure what people really want. Try to determine the true interests on both sides—usually you can find some common ground.

Generate a range of options before deciding upon one. Having a lot at stake inhibits creativity. Do not try to determine a single, correct solution. Instead, think of a wide range of possibilities that could please both sides. Look for a solution that benefits everybody.

Insist on using some legitimate standard of fairness. By choosing some objective standard—market value, the going rate, expert opinion, precedent, what a court would decide—neither party loses face by conceding. He is merely deferring to relevant standards. Never yield to pressure, only to principle.

Develop your best alternative to a negotiated agreement. If you haven't thought through what you will do if you fail to reach an agreement, you are negotiating with your eyes closed. You may be too optimistic about your other options—other houses for sale, buyers for your used car, plumbers, jobs, etc.

The reality is that if you fail to reach an agreement, you will probably have to choose just one option.

An even greater danger lies in being too anxious to reach an agreement because you haven't considered your other options. It may be better to walk away.

Consider what kind of commitment you want. It's a mistake to think that every meeting has to result in a final decision. It's much smarter to view a meeting as an exploratory session. You can draw out what interests motivate the other side and draft promises without nailing anything down. This gives you a chance to sleep on the alternatives or consult others. If the other side comes back with new demands, you have the right to renegotiate as well.

Communicate. Without communication, there is no negotiation. But whatever you say, expect the other side to hear something different.

Solutions: Listen actively, paying close attention and occasionally interrupting to make sure you understand what is meant. Ask that ideas be repeated if there is any ambiguity or uncertainty. It's very important to understand perceptions, needs and negotiating constraints.

Understanding is not agreeing. You can understand the other side's position—and still disagree with it. But the better you understand the other side's position, the more persuasively you can refute it.

Negotiating strategies…

•Marital roles. Learn to disagree without being disagreeable. You can disapprove of someone's behavior but still love that person. Discuss problems in a caring way. Make a joint list of issues that need to be addressed. Be firm but reasonable. Don't try to decide right away… mull things over for a few days.

•Requesting a raise. As with all negotiations, prepare beforehand. Find out what others at your level are earning, both inside and outside your company. Be ready to explain why you deserve more—you've been coming in every Saturday to help with the workload…you're dealing with the company's toughest customers…or you've been offered more elsewhere. Your boss needs a rationale that he can use with his boss or other employees who also want raises.

•Buying a house. Often, by exploring various options and payment schedules, an agreement can be reached that provides maximum tax advantage and financial satisfaction for both the buyer and the seller.

•Divorce negotiation. Suppose you are a wife who doesn't trust your husband to make his agreed child-support payments. Fearing that you will have to keep going back to court to get payment, you ask your lawyer to negotiate for equity in the house instead. Your husband's lawyer says that's ridiculous. He's certain that your husband will meet his obligations. OK, says your lawyer, then the husband won't object to signing a contingent agreement—if he misses two payments for any reason, his ex-wife will automatically get the equity in the house and he will be off the hook for future child-support payments.

Source: Roger Fisher, director of The Harvard Negotiation Project and Williston Professor of Law Emeritus, Harvard Law School, 1563 Massachusetts Ave., Cambridge 02138. He is co-author of *Getting to Yes.* Viking Penguin.

How to Make More Good Decisions

Behind nearly every bad decision is wishful thinking. To improve your decisions at work and at home, you have to replace guesswork with a new method of evaluation.

I have found a reliable system that teaches us to make better decisions than the trial-and-error method that most people use nowadays.

Many leading business organizations have found that managers and workers trained in this system consistently make smarter corporate decisions…and when they get home and try it with their spouses and children, they make better personal decisions as well.

Half-decisions don't work…

Most people today don't think through their decisions with their heads and their hearts…so they only make half-decisions—and they're not happy with the results. But I have found that by asking ourselves a few questions that can be answered with a simple yes or no, we can arrive at decisions that satisfy both our intellects and our emotions.

Think ahead: When faced with a decision of any kind, we must first analyze what we really need…not merely what we want. There's an easy way to do this—don't look at what you want to do now, but what you would like to have done when you look back at the decision.

Once we decide what we need, we have to think through our options—and list them. We can usually find options that we had not considered by gathering information…not only facts, but information about how people feel about the facts.

Armed with the knowledge of our needs and options, we can think each option through. For each option, imagine what situation may occur.

Ask yourself: What would probably happen then?…and then what?

Thinking options through will take some time. But if you make the wrong decision because you didn't want to spend that time at the beginning, you will spend a lot longer straightening it out.

The heart helps…

So far, I have explained the first half of better decision making—using our heads to determine whether our decisions rate a yes or a no answer to the practical question—*am I meeting the real need, informing myself of the options and thinking it through?*

A *yes* to that question alone is not enough. To make a better decision, we must also use our hearts to see if our decisions fit our personal beliefs.

For most of us, that's not easy. We have become uncomfortable about looking deeply into ourselves. But we can be sure our decisions are better if they reflect our true character. A good decision depends on three character traits…

• *Integrity:* We don't fool ourselves.

• *Intuition:* We feel that we can trust ourselves.

• *Insight:* We know that we really want to do better.

We need all three characteristics to make the right decision.

Integrity…

Though our ego often encourages us to fool ourselves, we can replace illusions with reality if we put our egos aside and ask for advice from others—people who aren't attached to our illusions…people whom we admire.

Or we can ask ourselves what decisions we would advise a friend to make.

Parking our ego can help us arrive at the truth and make better decisions much sooner because we are honest with ourselves.

Intuition…

Our experience with past decisions that worked—or didn't work—gives us an intuition that makes us feel better not only about the decision when we have made it but also about the way we decided.

Intuition signals our body to give an answer in terms of feeling. If our intellect tells us that the answer to the practical question we first asked is only maybe, then we must rely on our intuition for a better answer.

Our intuition tells us when we're making a sound decision by making us feel clear rather than confused about the problem…calm rather than stressed about the process…and enthusiastic rather than afraid about the outcome.

Insight…

In addition to integrity and intuition, we need to develop insight. Otherwise, we may go ahead with a decision we know is not the best one…or we may not bother to get all of the information we need.

We may sabotage ourselves because, in our hearts, we don't really want to make the best decision. We don't really believe we deserve it. To consistently make good decisions, we must really believe we deserve to succeed.

Putting it all together…

A good decision is one that lets us give yes answers to both the practical and personal questions we must ask ourselves. *Does my head tell me that it meets my needs…not merely my wants? Have I explored all my options? Have I thought it through? Does my heart tell me I am being honest with myself? Do I trust my intuition? Do I believe I deserve better?*

Once you're able to ask the questions automatically and answer them rapidly, you'll be able to size up situations and make the right choices.

Source: Spencer Johnson, MD, who has written more than two dozen books dealing with the behavioral sciences and has more than 11 million copies of his books in print.

18

Your Emotional Health

How Everyday Low-Level Tension Can Kill Us... And How to Avoid It

Psychological stress means much more than just sweaty palms, headaches and a queasy stomach. Stress can contribute to all sorts of serious health problems, including insomnia, chronic diarrhea or constipation, high blood pressure, stroke, heart disease and depression.

A decade ago, scientists believed that the most harmful form of stress was that resulting from major life crises—the death of a spouse, the loss of a job, divorce, etc. Now it's clear that while stress associated with these events is often severe, it is usually short-lived. Consequently, it has little time to cause damage to our bodies.

Far worse, scientists now theorize, is the everyday stress to which all of us are routinely subjected—being late for work, arguing with a loved one, etc. Each little frustration that oc-

curs throughout the day speeds the heart rate, dilates the pupils and floods the bloodstream with powerful hormones, setting the stage for stress-related problems.

The best way to fight stress is by adopting a more relaxed attitude about everything...a state of mind that can be achieved by taking advantage of the many relaxation techniques now available.

Benefits: Increased happiness, reduced vulnerability to illness and increased creativity and productivity at work.

The causes of stress...

Don't blame stress on your environment. No matter how hectic your job or family life, stress has less to do with your immediate surroundings than with your psychological makeup. It is not eliminated through a better job, a more supportive spouse or fewer money problems.

Example: Some people experience a great deal of stress even in the calmest environment, while others remain stress-free—even when things are collapsing around them.

Clearly, stress is not something external but a product of the mind—and therefore something that each of us can control. Here's how:

Self-defense...

• Avoid stress-promoting forms of thought and speech. If someone cuts you off in traffic, or speaks to you with disrespect, you can become enraged...or you can accept the fact that you have no direct control over the actions of others.

Most of us explode rather than catch ourselves before being consumed by stress. This occurs not out of any character flaw, but because we're victims of stress-promoting ways of thought and speech...

• Catastrophic thinking. This occurs when you describe unpleasant situations with words like "awful," "terrible" or "horrendous." Such extreme labels usually overstate the reality of the situation and needlessly create stress. *Remedy:* Avoid these words. In their place, use less dire descriptions.

• Absolutist thinking. This is marked by the use of "must," "should," "ought" and other words that set up standards of behavior. Typically, these codes are difficult, if not impossible, to live up to. Absolutist thinking encourages us to expect too much of ourselves and those around us...and leads to undue frustration and stress. *Remedy:* Cut these words from your vocabulary. Accord yourself and those around you greater compassion.

Relaxation techniques...

• Make daily use of relaxation techniques. These range from biofeedback and sensory deprivation to meditation. Some, such as biofeedback, require equipment. Others require little more than a quiet room.

Recommendation: Experiment with several techniques before settling on one or more. Be sure to use them every day, not just when you're feeling particularly frazzled. Of all the relaxation techniques, three are especially powerful...

• Progressive relaxation. The most common form of relaxation, this method involves alternate tensing and relaxing of each of the body's 16 major muscle groups. It can be done with or without the supervision of a therapist.

Procedure: Sit or lie with your eyes closed in a dimly lit room. Adopt a relaxed, passive attitude.

Clench the muscles of your right hand and forearm as tightly as possible. Hold this tension for seven seconds, then relax your hand and arm for about 45 seconds. Do this several times until your muscles feel warm and relaxed. Then move on to your right biceps, your left hand and forearm, left biceps, forehead, middle portion of your face, lower portion of your face, your neck, upper back, chest and abdomen, right thigh, right calf, right ankle and shin, left thigh, left calf, left ankle and shin.

Once you've completed all the muscle groups, your entire body should feel relaxed and warm. If any areas of tension remain, repeat the appropriate tensing/relaxing exercise until it disappears.

• Meditation. This family of techniques includes yoga and transcendental meditation. It offers a systematic method for eliciting a profound state of relaxation.

Procedure: Sit or lie in a quiet, soothing environment. As you breathe slowly and rhythmically, softly recite "peace," "calm," "om" or some other word or sound of your choosing. Adopt a passive attitude. As you focus on this word and your respiration, troubling thoughts will gradually subside. For maximum relief from stress, meditate twice daily for 10 to 20 minutes at a time.

• Autogenic training. This technique, used with or without a therapist's supervision, involves adopting a passive, relaxed attitude and focusing on a set of six relaxation themes—heaviness, warmth, regular heartbeat, regular breathing, abdominal warmth and cooling of the forehead.

Procedure: Sit or lie in a quiet, dimly lit room. Close your eyes and envision yourself in a comfortable, relaxing environment—stretching out on a sandy beach, for instance, or sitting in a warm, sunny meadow. Repeat to yourself, "I am at peace." Chant this phrase softly again and again, until you really do begin to feel at peace. Next, repeat the following line: "My arms and legs are heavy and warm." Do the same for the following phrases: "My breathing is calm"..."My abdomen is warm"..."My forehead is cool." Repeat these phrases for 20 to 30 minutes. Try not to let your mind wander, but don't be bothered if it does. Again, a passive attitude is essential.

Also helpful…

•Hold your breath. Meditation and other stress-reduction techniques are powerful—but they can be time-consuming and their effects short-lived.

For an effective and convenient "touch-up" during the course of the day, try controlled breath-holding. It not only distracts you from the source of your annoyance, but also temporarily boosts bloodstream levels of carbon dioxide, which has a calming effect on the brain.

The technique can be practiced anywhere, anytime, whether you're alone or in a crowd—whenever you feel yourself angry or frazzled.

What to do: Inhale deeply, hold it for a few seconds, then exhale slowly. If you prefer, say "relax," "calm" or another soothing word or syllable as you exhale. This may be said aloud or silently. Inhale and exhale slowly four more times. Your tension will ebb.

•Take regular vacations. A long, uninterrupted run of routine activities eventually saps your ability to cope with stress. One way to boost your "coping" behavior is to take regular breaks from the daily routine. *Good news:* These vacations need not be long or costly. A weekend in the country is often enough.

•Take good care of your body. Some people quickly fall prey to the deleterious effects of stress—developing headaches, ulcers or other stress-related ailments. Others seem immune to such problems no matter how stressful the environment. Similarly, individuals capable of coping well with stress at one time of the day may succumb at another time.

While heredity plays a key role in determining your ability to avoid and to withstand stress, it's by no means the only factor. *Also important:* Good nutrition, regular exercise and proper sleep patterns. You're far more vulnerable to stress when you're tired, hungry and lethargic than when you're in tip-top shape. Don't allow yourself to become run down.

Source: Kenneth L. Lichstein, PhD, professor of psychology and former director of clinical training, department of psychology, Memphis State University, Tennessee. He is the author of *Clinical Relaxation Strategies*, John Wiley & Sons, 605 Third Ave., New York 10158.

Stress Buster

Diminish stress by learning to slow your pulse and breathing rate. Design triggers that work for you. *Examples:* Count to 10 and imagine yourself on a beach with your hand in warm sand—then count back down to zero. Or close your eyes and imagine a dial set on high to indicate tension—then imagine turning the dial down. *Key:* Develop imagery that you find restful. It will help you gain control of stress—and reduce pulse rate and blood pressure.

Source: *The Joy of Stress* by family practitioner Peter Hanson, MD, Andrews and McMeel, 4900 Main St., Kansas City, Missouri 64112.

The Simple Secrets of Controlling Your Temper

When you feel yourself losing control, take a deep breath. Inhale slowly and exhale slowly. And remember this when you get angry with others…

•An angry response is not very likely to persuade, but is likely to make the other person angry. This is why a heated exchange changes few minds for the better.

•If the other person remains calm while you get angry, that person's presence of mind is likely to defeat you.

•Believe it or not, the person who is attracting your anger feels justified, just as you feel when you make others angry. Try to understand the reason for the person's behavior. Become analytical and you won't get angry.

•Talk about your anger. Directing yourself to your feelings will help you to calm down, and it will allow the conversation to move gradually to a more rational tone.

•Call a break for a cooling-off period whenever emotions flare. The moment you feel you're about to lose control, your rational brain is talking. Listen to it. It's telling you that you're on the verge of doing or saying something you'll later regret. Remember, three things cannot be recalled: Time passed, the spent arrow and the spoken word.

• Finally, get out of the reach of incorrigible people and those who delight in getting to you. Work through intermediaries or buffers, if possible. When all else fails, separate from them. Give them the rejection they've earned.

Source: *What to Say to Get What You Want,* ©1991, by Sam Deep and Lyle Sussman. Reprinted with permission of Addison-Wesley Publishing Co., Jacob Way, Reading, Massachusetts 01867.

How to Boost Your Mental Energy

We'd all like more mental energy—the drive and focus that help us go after what we really want. But many of us try to boost that energy in the wrong ways.

Examples: Smoking cigarettes, eating sugary foods, drinking coffee. These give a short-term burst of energy, but can drain resources over the long run.

Boosting basics…

• Get out of your rut. Do something different from what you did yesterday. It doesn't have to be drastic—very simple changes will stimulate your mind. If you usually read biographies, try a mystery. Take a new route into the city.

• Take more risks. Exercise your mind with greater challenges.

Examples: Take a course in Latin. Learn all about the new business systems.

• Give yourself a "mental health" day. You don't have to be physically sick to take a day off from responsibility—once in a while. Spend it on whatever renews you mentally, whether it's browsing for antiques or just lying on the beach.

• Believe in yourself. Worry and self-criticism are mentally fatiguing. Never put yourself down. Give yourself frequent pep talks instead. Rather than twisting yourself into a pretzel to please other people, make sure you are satisfied with your life and actions.

• Visualize your goals. Picture them vividly. Fill your environment with reminders of prizes for achievement—such as a picture of your dream house on your bulletin board. Visualizing what you want will help sustain the energy you need to go after it.

• Improve your ability to focus. We exhaust ourselves by scattering our attention among many different projects and ideas at once…instead of concentrating on the task at hand. Dr. Mihaly Csikszentmihalyi of the University of Chicago has written about the highly satisfying flow state experienced by artists, athletes, musicians and others who concentrate on performing an action to the best of their ability.

You can achieve flow in everyday activities, too. Absorb yourself in each task—no matter how mundane it seems. Say to yourself: *This is the most important project on Earth. Ask yourself: How can I do this better…more efficiently …more pleasingly?*

• Meditate. Sit quietly, relax your entire body and concentrate for 10 minutes on your breathing, a favorite proverb or a syllable such as the word "one." When other thoughts intrude, let them drift away. If you do this at least once a day, you will find yourself feeling calmer and more mentally energetic.

• Take care of your body. Physical energy affects mental energy, and vice versa. Keep a regular sleep schedule…eat a variety of healthful foods…gradually cut back on fat and caffeine…exercise regularly. A five-minute walk will give you greater and longer-lasting mental energy than a cup of coffee.

• Reflect on your mission in life. Who and what are most important to you? When you have a strong sense of inner direction, you will bring more energy to everything you do.

Source: Russell Wild, senior editor of Prevention Magazine Health Books and coauthor of *Boost Your Brain Power,* Rodale Press, 33 E. Minor St., Emmaus, Pennsylvania 18098.

How to Get Rid Of Phobias

A phobia is an irrational or exaggerated fear of something that isn't frightening to most other people.

Between five million and 10 million people in the US experience phobias. And, contrary to popular misconception, most are treatable. Available techniques are moderately to very effective 80% of the time. (A very small number of patients do not respond because they appear interested in holding onto the phobia, or because the phobia is a part of depression, which must be addressed.)

•Simple phobias. Involve fear of the object or situation—snakes, elevators, flying, etc.

•Complex phobias. Involve fear of fear—the person is afraid of the way he/she will react to the anxiety-producing situation.

Example: Someone who's afraid of tunnels might not fear the tunnel itself, but that he'll lose control if his car breaks down inside one.

Where phobias come from…

•Traumatic events. These usually happen in childhood.

Simple example: A 12-year-old who was stuck in an elevator for hours goes to great lengths to avoid elevators.

•Parallel life experience. An anxiety-producing event occurs close to a previously neutral situation.

Example: Just before a business trip, a woman who has always been comfortable flying learns that her husband is about to leave her. As the plane takes off, she begins to panic. Her anxiety is even worse on the return trip, and the woman becomes afraid of flying.

•Parental modeling. We learn many things from our parents…and not all of them are good.

Example: A child's mother or father panics in the presence of dogs, and he becomes afraid of dogs, too.

Common thread: Avoidance. When a person avoids a feared situation, the anxiety is reduced—further reinforcing the tendency to avoid the situation in the future.

Treating phobias…

•Systematic desensitization. The person is gradually exposed to the feared situation—first through imagery, then in real life.

He and his therapist construct a hierarchy of fear-producing images, from the least to the most anxiety-provoking.

Example: For someone afraid of public speaking, the hierarchy may include 15 to 20 items—from being invited to give a lecture…to reviewing notes for the lecture…all the way up to standing at the podium and being heckled by someone in the audience.

The person is taught a relaxation technique, such as deep breathing, self-hypnosis or meditation.

After becoming completely relaxed, he creates a mental image of the least-threatening item in the hierarchy, and pictures the scene for three minutes, while remaining relaxed. He repeats this process several times.

When that situation no longer elicits much anxiety, he imagines the next item on the list.

When each scene in the hierarchy can be vividly imagined without anxiety, we move on to real-life exposure, again beginning with the least-frightening situation, and with plenty of support from the therapist.

Example: The person afraid of public speaking might give a presentation to several therapists at the clinic.

•Education. People gather information from books and other sources regarding the feared situation. The additional information helps them to challenge their misconceptions.

Examples: Someone who is afraid of flying may attend a lecture by an airline pilot…a person who's afraid of bugs could go to a natural history museum and speak to the curator.

•Self-statements. Each time the person notices an irrational thought that concerns the phobia, it's replaced with a rational, positive one.

Examples: "The audience wants to hear what I have to say"…"The elevator isn't likely to get stuck."

•Looking for a secondary gain. Sometimes the phobia has an underlying cause.

Example: The person afraid of public speaking may actually be terrified of the promotions that could result from a higher professional profile. It may be necessary to explore the ways that long-ago competition with siblings or others affected present-day attitudes toward achievement.

•Medication. Phobic reactions resistant to other forms of treatment sometimes respond to anti-depressant or anti-anxiety medication.

Source: Barry Lubetkin, PhD, director of the Institute for Behavior Therapy, 137 E. 36 St., New York 10016. He is the author of *Bailing Out: The Healthy Way to Get Out of a Bad Relationship and Survive,* Prentice-Hall Press, 15 Columbus Circle, New York, New York 10023.

The Importance Of Solitude

Many Americans admire the rugged individualists in novels and films who take on the system or overcome adversity single-handedly.

Yet, we don't feel comfortable with those who keep to themselves. We tend to distrust contemplation and view solitary people and pursuits with suspicion.

Opportunity: We would be better off if we engaged in positive solitude—time alone that is used thoughtfully to benefit mind and soul. Positive solitude is an important element of self-discovery and growth.

Solitude provides the opportunity to identify your most cherished goals and develop ways of achieving them. Regular reflection contributes to a sense of inner peace…and makes you feel more in control of your life.

The problems of being alone…

Positive solitude takes conscious effort, whether you live with others or alone.

•People who live with others are often so caught up in the demands of family life that they don't take time for self-reflection. Time alone feels like an expendable luxury to them. Thus, they're in danger of defining themselves through others.

These people need to make private time a priority and be creative about ways of finding it.

Examples: Evaluate work and community responsibilities, and determine which are essential—and which can be cut back. Join a baby-sitting co-op so someone else can look after your children one or two days a week. Plan a solitary retreat to a quiet place for a few days to reflect on what's really important to you.

•People who live alone may feel left out in a world of couples and families. They may fight solitude by compulsively seeking company, filling their days with "busy-ness" that isn't very satisfying…and missing a wonderful opportunity for self-discovery and growth.

They need to challenge the belief that having a family is the only way to be happy…look for ways to nurture themselves instead of waiting for a partner to make life satisfying…and take advantage of the chance to learn more about their own values and perceptions.

I believe that living alone doesn't have to be lonely—nor should it be viewed as a way station on the path to "coupledom." Living alone can be a deeply rewarding lifestyle in its own right.

Positive solitude actually enhances relationships when people do come together. People who are not afraid of solitude can meet as strong wholes instead of incomplete halves that are desperate for fulfillment.

Turn off the TV…

One of the biggest threats to positive solitude is television. It's the easiest, but possibly least-satisfying, way to fill up your time.

Watching television does not put you in contact with other people or yourself. Instead, it bombards you with the agenda and values of the TV programmers and advertisers.

Spending a lot of time in front of the TV feeds loneliness. It encourages us to let someone else decide what's interesting, discourages us from looking inward and takes up time that could be spent developing original ideas or actively challenging or supporting the ideas of others.

Ways to use private time…

In solitude, we can explore what's most meaningful to us—free from other people's expectations. We can begin to develop a personal philosophy or life plan.

This isn't an easy task, but it's an exciting one. *Key:* Ask yourself the kinds of questions that don't have simple answers…and be prepared to return to them again and again. *Examples…*

"What contribution do I want to make to the world?" Focus on what's significant to you—not to your parents, spouse or boss. *Possibilities:* Create a new variety of rose…raise healthy, loving children…comfort people in distress…make music…gather and analyze information about nature or politics.

"What are the gaps in my life?" Are there things you'd like to understand better or have more control over? Goals you've abandoned out of fear—but still wonder about? What are some ways to address these gaps?

Tools that can help in your exploration include a journal…walking…meditation…quiet time in a natural environment. *Exercises:*

•Write for 15 minutes about a topic of your choice, without stopping or censoring yourself. You'll be surprised at the ideas that come up.

•Write about a dream you had recently, the emotions it stirred and the messages it might have. Dreams often introduce important themes we haven't yet faced consciously.

Moving outward…

Quietly thinking and writing aren't the only ways to discover meaning. In fact, planning and taking part in challenging activities can be an outgrowth of positive solitude. We can try activities that reveal new aspects of ourselves—physical, intellectual and spiritual. The key is to identify and follow those pursuits that engage you—not to please friends or family or because you've always done them. *Exercises:*

•Write down 10 or 20 activities that you used to love but haven't done for a long time. What did you most enjoy as a child or adolescent? Try some of these activities again.

•Make a list of activities you always wanted to try but never got around to. Pick one—and do it.

Planning is essential for this stage. If we don't plan, then the easiest things will happen, not the most fulfilling. We'll come home and switch on the TV instead of going to a concert or arranging a kayaking trip.

Make activity dates for yourself…pencil them into your calendar…and make sure you keep them.

Be patient…

Don't be surprised if this self-analysis feels uncomfortable at first—or if you don't make dramatic discoveries right away.

Getting to know yourself takes some time. Challenging and reexamining your assumptions do not happen in a day. But the effort will bring satisfying rewards…including a deeper understanding of your values and needs…increased confidence in your capabilities…a richer enjoyment of life…and a greater receptivity to others.

Source: Rae André, PhD, associate professor of management psychology at Northeastern University. A consultant, lecturer and workshop leader, she is the author of *Positive Solitude: A Practical Program for Mastering Loneliness and Achieving Self-Fulfillment.* HarperCollins, 10 E. 53 St., New York 10022.

About Depression

Many Americans share a tragic misconception about depression—that people who are depressed could "snap out of it," if they wanted to. As a result, more than 30 million Americans troubled by emotional illness never get the help they need.

The result is devastating. Sufferers feel hopeless, inadequate and unable to cope with daily life. Their self-esteem is shattered—and so are their ties with family and friends. What's more, depression is often lethal. Up to 30% of people with serious mood disorders kill themselves.

Feeling "blue" from time to time is a normal part of life—we all experience the sadness of failed relationships, the loss of loved ones, etc. Periods of sadness that are mild and short-lived do not require medical help.

Understanding…

But if enjoyable activities, the passing of time and confiding in friends, family or even psychotherapists fail to alleviate emotional pain, you may be suffering from a biological form of depression. Such disorders, triggered by chemical changes in the brain, call for medical treatment. They cannot be cured by talking to a therapist or reading a self-help book.

While the causes of depression are not fully understood, new technology has provided insight. Scientists believe that depressed people have decreased amounts of certain mood-regulating chemicals called neurotransmitters.

In most cases, depressive illness caused by such chemical imbalances is inherited. *Evidence:* Children of depressed parents have a 20% to 25% risk of having a mood disorder.

Children of nondepressed parents have a 5% risk.

Warning signs of depression...

If you have felt sad or down in the dumps in recent weeks, or if you've lost interest in many or all of your normal activities, you may be suffering from depression. *Warning signs:*

- Poor appetite or overeating
- Insomnia
- Sleeping more than usual
- Chronic low energy or fatigue
- Restlessness, feeling less active or talkative than usual, feeling "slowed down"
- Avoidance of other people
- Reduced interest in sex and other pleasurable activities
- Inability to derive pleasure from presents, praise, job promotions, etc.
- Feelings of inadequacy, low self-esteem or an increased level of self-criticism
- Reduced levels of accomplishment at work, school or home
- Feeling less able to cope with routine responsibilities
- Poor concentration, having trouble making decisions

If you're experiencing four or more of these, consult a doctor immediately.

Kinds of emotional illness...

The most common type of depression is unipolar illness, in which the person's mood is either normal or depressed. *Other common types:*

- Dysthymia. This condition is marked by a chronic mild state of depression. Sufferers of dysthymia experience little pleasure and are chronically fatigued and unresponsive. Sadly, many people suffering from dysthymia mistake their illness for a low-key personality...and never get the help they need.
- Manic depression. Patients whose periods of depression alternate with periods of euphoria are suffering from manic depression (bipolar disorder). During the "high" periods, manic-depressives may also have an inflated sense of self-esteem...a decreased need to sleep...a tendency to monopolize conversations...the feeling that their thoughts are racing...increased

activity...impulsive behavior (including buying sprees, promiscuity, rash business decisions).

Though manic episodes sometimes occur when a person has never been depressed, they are frequently followed by severe depression. *Danger:* Manic-depressives often do not realize that they're ill, even though the problem may be obvious to family and friends. As with all forms of biological depression, manic depression calls for immediate treatment.

- Cyclothymia. A variant of manic depression, this disorder is characterized by less pronounced ups and downs. Like manic-depressives, cyclothymics are often unaware of their problem and must be encouraged to seek help.

Diagnosis and treatment...

First, have a complete physical exam to rule out any medical disorders. Certain ailments including thyroid disease and anemia can produce various symptoms that mimic depression.

If the exam suggests no underlying medical problem, ask for a referral to a psychopharmacologist—a psychiatrist who is trained in biological psychiatry. *Caution:* Nonphysician therapists, such as psychologists and social workers, lack medical training and cannot prescribe medication...and may be less adept at distinguishing between biological and psychological forms of depression.

When a biological form of depression is diagnosed, antidepressants should almost always be used as the first line of treatment. They completely relieve or lessen symptoms in more than 80% of people with severe emotional illness... and they are not addictive, nor do they make people "high." Once medications have brought the depression under control, however, psychotherapy often proves helpful—especially to patients embarrassed or demoralized by their illness.

Antidepressants...

Among the oldest and most effective antidepressants are the so-called tricyclics and monoamine oxidase inhibitors (MAOIs). These drugs are often very effective, but they must be used with caution.

Tricyclics have a wide range of side effects, including dry mouth, constipation, blurred vision and sexual difficulties. MAOIs must never be taken in combination with foods containing high levels of tyramine—such as aged cheese. Doing so causes a potentially dangerous rise in blood pressure. Other side effects include low blood pressure, sleep disturbances, weight gain and sexual difficulties.

Although these medications are still valuable in the treatment of depression, newer classes of drugs, including fluoxetine (Prozac), sertraline (Zoloft) and paroxetine (Paxil), are often superior. These new medications have few side effects, although some people who take the drugs complain of drowsiness or anxiety. *Note:* Despite one recent report claiming that Prozac caused some patients to attempt suicide, follow-up studies have not confirmed this finding.

For manic depression, the clear treatment of choice is lithium. Common minor side effects include diarrhea, a metallic taste in the mouth, increased frequency of urination, hand tremor and weight gain.

For seriously depressed or suicidal patients who do not respond to antidepressants, electroconvulsive therapy (ECT) is often a lifesaver. In this procedure, electrical current is applied to the brain via electrodes.

Sad: Many patients who stand to benefit from ECT refuse it altogether—because they consider it a brutal form of treatment. Today, however, patients receive a general anesthetic and a muscle relaxant prior to the application of current, so there's no emotional or physical trauma. Side effects—including slight confusion for several hours after treatment and occasionally memory loss—generally fade with time.

How to find the right help…

If your family doctor cannot recommend a good psychiatrist, contact the nearest medical school or teaching hospital. Many have a special treatment clinic for depression. Local branches of the American Psychiatric Association will provide names of psychiatrists in your area, but they cannot evaluate the psychiatrist's training in biological psychiatry.

The National Foundation for Depressive Illness (800-248-4344) gives referrals to psychiatrists interested in pharmacological treatment of mood disorders. Finally, additional information can be obtained from the National Depressive and Manic-Depressive Association (312-642-0049).

Source: Donald F. Klein, MD, professor of psychiatry at the Columbia University College of Physicians and Surgeons and director of research at the New York State Psychiatric Institute, both in New York City. Dr. Klein is coauthor of *Understanding Depression: A Complete Guide to Its Diagnosis and Treatment,* Oxford University Press, 200 Madison Ave., New York 10016.

The Amazing Power Of Writing to Yourself

Keeping a diary or a journal has been recommended for years by therapists because most of us aren't aware of our feelings except when they are extreme.

Journal-writing is an antidote to our culture's excessive emphasis on the denial of feelings that is required to be successful. No matter what you do for a living, writing provides a soothing, relaxing way to get in touch with the feelings of the day.

Why be in touch?…

Many achievement-oriented people work very hard to get where they are. However, most kinds of work that lead to achievement require effort that isn't in time with our natural rhythms. In order to tolerate the pain of working when we don't feel like it, we suppress our negative feelings and keep working. The price, however, is steep. Unexpressed feelings are the cause of most psychosomatic illnesses, including some life-threatening ones.

Feelings are the greatest source of a person's motivation. So people who are not in touch with their feelings don't know why they're doing what they're doing and often don't know why they're going through conflicts or pain.

Why keep a journal?…

Expressing your feelings in the haven of your own journal not only reduces stress and promotes good health, but enables you to understand yourself and make better decisions in business, personal life and relationships. Each time you write you have the opportunity to get to know yourself better.

Journal-writing gives you an opportunity to reflect on positive as well as negative things that you may be ignoring. You may start to become more sensitive and notice people who would like to become your friends...and people you've been at odds with who want to reconcile.

If you have a place to reflect and feel your feelings, it's more likely you'll be aware of dangerous situations in which people are trying to undermine or manipulate you. Sometimes both positive and negative signals are so low in the static of everyday noise that they're only discoverable in the quiet of journal-writing.

Since so much of our time with people involves doing things together rather than sharing feelings, we often have feelings, positive and negative, that we're afraid to express with friends, lovers, spouses, relatives. There's a comfort in acknowledging and affirming that you really have these feelings. This is especially true for men, who often have trouble expressing feelings. They can benefit most from journal-writing.

The most popular relaxation tool is the television. But TV distracts us from our feelings. Journal-writing may be the only way for chronic television addicts to find out who they really are.

Another issue has to do with trust. These are paranoid times. Urban living crowds us and the general level of trust among people is low. Telling your problems to your journal is even more safely anonymous than telling them to a bartender.

In a hectic lifestyle, journal-writing is like meditation or taking long walks, one of the few sources of solitude. It's safe, available and you can do it on a rainy day. Journal-writing may be the only solitude a high-achieving person or working parent gets.

The final advantage is a personal record. Very often people's problems escape them because they don't have an adequate perspective. I've often found that when people do journal-writing over time they can look back and discover very important things about themselves.

Common: Discovering that you've been having the same problems and feelings over and over and getting nowhere. Or alternatively, that you're making progress. It's a different perspective from memory, which is quite unreliable.

With more and more of us becoming cosmopolitan and living far from the culture and geography we grew up in, many of us are like refugees to other countries. We develop divided personalities to adjust to new circumstances.

The city-dweller behaves differently with different people throughout the day, in ways that are different from how he/she grew up. Also, we have fewer lifelong friends that can help us maintain a sense of continuity.

Journal-writing enables the divided self to note how many people he/she has to be today and what all their thoughts and feelings and opinions are about whatever is going on.

Example: An internal conflict between your vulgar, risk-taking, obnoxious self and your careful, conservative, bean-counting self.

Suggested: Use multiple colors for journal-writing. The risk-taker might write in red, the conservative self in black and the romantic in purple. *Result:* You'll get a sense of how many people are on "your committee," who they are, and what they agree and disagree about. As the chairperson of your personality, you can make better choices taking into account all the aspects of yourself.

Example: Changing jobs. The conservative self might write about how scary it is and how he doesn't like change. The risk-taker might write that he'd rather go into business for himself and get rich. The romantic might write about wanting to chuck work altogether to become a beach bum. Becoming aware of these aspects of your personality makes it more likely that you'll make a decision you can live with.

How to keep a journal...

Don't just list events in your life. Share your feelings, concerns, opinions and reflections on the meaning of actions.

To avoid list-making: Just write down events that elicited strong feelings. You don't have to make an entry of anything that didn't have an impact in terms of feelings, negative or positive.

To get to your feelings: Write down fantasies. Write a review of how a performance related to your life. Write about other people's lives and how they're similar or dissimilar to yours. Read a compelling novel and write about it. Do volunteer work with children or sick people—and write about it.

Pick a comfortable place to write. It should be a place where you feel safe to express yourself.

You don't have to write every day, though that probably is the most effective way to tune into the fine details of feelings. Some people do more journal-writing during a single weekend at the beach than they did in the entire three weeks before.

Find the kind of journal you want to write in. I like a highly tactile book with a corduroy cover. I always look forward to touching it. Other people like silk, velvet or the kind of black-and-white speckled notebook they used in the first grade. Some people prefer a computer. *Also:* Pick up something you like to write with, whether it's a felt tip or a fountain pen...or a pencil.

Important: Take appropriate security measures to make sure that what you write will be private.

Source: Martin G. Groder, MD, a psychiatrist and business consultant in Chapel Hill, North Carolina. His book, *Business Games: How to Recognize the Players and Deal With Them*, is available from Boardroom Books, PO 2614, Greenwich, CT 06836.

Secrets of Appreciating Life

Despite the ever-growing amount of information we have about human nature, the soul is still impossible to define in pragmatic terms and still remains an enigma.

Unlike the brain, the soul has no physical or material reality. Yet it governs our values, relatedness and personal substance. Lose touch with your soul and the effects can be debilitating... even devastating.

For example, many people who are in perfect physical health and have attained wealth and fame feel a deep sense of unease when they neglect their souls.

Not knowing how to care for your soul leaves you at a serious disadvantage, since painful experiences are unavoidable. Confronting them and learning from them are the ways to nurture the soul.

Most of us recognize that some of the more simple aspects of life are particularly satisfying. That is why we refer to them as "food for the soul" and "music that is good for the soul."

But every aspect of life—family, love, work... even dark aspects like jealousy, depression and illness—can provide spiritual food for the soul if we approach them in a receptive way.

Family and the soul...

Many people today who regard themselves as self-sufficient have lost the important truth, which was taught by traditional societies, that we must honor our families.

Honoring the family helps the soul because the family is a source of religious awareness. A family forces you to realize that you did not create yourself...that you have a unique place in the world. Within your family, you can be who you really are and learn to appreciate the individuality of others.

To help family appreciation: Don't expect too much from your family. Try to appreciate each member's unique qualities. If you are miserable and feel it's because of the way you were treated by your family when you were young, try a different perspective. Ask yourself, *Where did my good qualities come from?* It's highly likely that your family had a great deal to do with them.

Love and the soul...

Many people have unrealistic expectations of love—within the family, with spouses, with friends. Love isn't perfect and eternal. It passes through different stages...and often ends.

To satisfy your soul, a loving relationship must honor the other person's soul as well. That means recognizing who the other person really is...and allowing that person to change. You must pay attention and allow the relationship to develop.

For soul-satisfying relationships: Spend time together...write letters to each other...visit friends together. When you talk to each other, don't just talk about work—talk about what's in your heart.

Work and the soul...

Work is a major part of life. Few things satisfy the soul more than a fulfilling vocation. But if the work you do conflicts with your soul— because of your sense of ethics or aesthetics— it may make you very unhappy, no matter how much you earn.

If you are in that position, look into a career change. If a change isn't immediately feasible, don't despair. Look around...for years, if necessary. And meanwhile, even though you are unhappy in your current work situation, practice other ways to care for your soul.

To help your soul if you are unhappy at work: First, acknowledge your situation. Then, make the best of it by putting more effort into areas that do satisfy your soul...family, friendships, hobbies, sports, travel, etc.

Soul and the darker side of life...

Anyone who thinks that life's only goal is happiness will be troubled. The less-pleasant parts of life cannot be avoided.

If you reflect on your unhappy experiences, you will find that they offer their own gifts... and contribute to the development of your soul. These experiences include...

• Jealousy, which comes with intense relationships. It teaches that relationships are demanding...and deepens your understanding of both the self and the relationship.

• Depression, which deepens the personality, leaving you better able to cope with future problems. People who have only seen the sunny side of life may be overwhelmed when something bad happens...those who have gone through depression look at the world in a more realistic, accepting way.

• Illness, which forces you to reflect on your own mortality and teaches that you are not as strong or as independent as you thought.

To benefit from troubles: When you suffer physical, social or economic setbacks, see what you can learn from the experiences. Acknowledge your human frailties...don't be afraid to ask others for help. You will gain a richer perspective on friendship and the meaning of life.

The art of life...

Modern society pursues functionality and efficiency at all costs, but the human soul craves beauty. Much of the unhappiness in today's world comes from a neglect of the beauty of life in favor of acquiring things and getting results quickly.

Since schools don't often teach the arts, your soul is starved of the imaginative diet it needs. You can make up this deficiency by striving to bring beauty into your life.

To feed your soul in everyday life: Even if you don't consider yourself artistic, you can use your imagination to enrich the way you live.

When you decorate your home, for example, don't settle for someone else's taste...even if it's advice from a high-priced interior decorator. Your home should express your feelings and imagination. Think about the location, the furnishings and the decorations, so they satisfy you emotionally and express your soul's individuality.

By living in a way that cares for your soul faithfully every day, you can let your individual genius emerge and discover in full measure who you really are.

Source: Thomas Moore, PhD. A former monk with academic degrees in theology, music and philosophy, Dr. Moore is author of the best-seller *Care of the Soul: A Guide for Cultivating Depth and Sacredness in Everyday Life.* HarperCollins, 10 E. 53 St., New York 10022. 800-242-7737.

The Simple Secret of Sabotaging Self-Sabotage

If we routinely fall short of our goals... and/or make decisions that interfere with our personal, professional or financial growth... and/or feel inadequate to meet the challenges in our daily lives—we may be victims of our own self-defeating behaviors.

Self-defeating behaviors are responses that originally protected us and helped us to cope with life...but which now work against us.

Example: A child who is subjected to excessive criticism learns to keep a low profile—to avoid notice or possible derision. Such a child is apt to mature into a painfully shy adult, incapable of making friends or achieving career goals.

By coming to understand these negative patterns and the purposes they once served, we can learn to replace our destructive behaviors with constructive ones.

Variety of self-defeating behaviors...

The average person in our culture regularly indulges in a dozen or so self-defeating behaviors.

These range from serious threats to health, such as smoking or drug abuse...to more subtle forms of self-sabotage like perfectionism, procrastination, hostility, compulsive worry or shyness.

Displaying a self-defeating behavior does not mean you're "sick." It simply means that you're still being controlled by negative external forces that have been internalized—family members, church, school, etc. These institutions are too often sources of criticism, prejudice, unrealistically high expectations and even abuse.

We may have been victims of these environmental influences earlier in our lives. But as adults, we victimize ourselves—by continuing to behave in ways that are no longer helpful.

Dangerous patterns…

Because these destructive patterns are learned and reinforced unconsciously, it's sometimes hard to spot the danger they pose. Two powerful forces keep these destructive patterns alive…

•A promise of protection. For example, you might think to yourself, *If I worry all the time, I'll be prepared when disaster strikes.*

•Fear. This is often expressed as an almost superstitious thought—*If I stop worrying, disaster will surely strike.*

Unfortunately, the behavior doesn't deliver on the promise…and people wind up being ruled by the fear.

Example: Chronic worry undermines both your health and your enjoyment of life. When bad things do happen, you're too tied up in knots to deal with them effectively.

Five steps for changing self-defeating behaviors…

Step 1: Identify the behavior. We'll continue to use the example of compulsive worry.

Step 2: Identify the situations that trigger the behavior. You may feel as if you fret constantly. But give the matter some thought and you may notice that you worry only under certain circumstances—for example, when you're trying to fall asleep…when your child comes home late from school…when a major project is due at work.

Step 3: Observe how you build the behavior. Self-defeating behaviors aren't floating around in space waiting to attack us. We create them by following a specific pattern of thoughts and behaviors. Breaking down the parts of this sequence can help us to regain control.

There's always a split-second between the triggering situation and the moment we begin to construct the behavior.

In this instant we choose to think a self-defeating thought…focus on that thought…and begin behaving so as to reinforce the thought.

Example: You come home early from work and are enjoying the afternoon paper. *Trigger:* You glance up at the clock and notice that your 13-year-old daughter is 15 minutes late. A split second later you think that something terrible may have happened to her.

You may also hear an inner voice saying, *If I continue to enjoy myself, and something awful does happen to her, it will be my fault.*

Panic sets in, and you imagine all of the horrible possibilities—What if she's been mugged… kidnapped…hit by a car?

Finally, you cement the behavior by disowning it—you find a way to shift the responsibility for your reaction to a source outside yourself. *If only she would call when she's going to be late, I wouldn't feel this way.*

It's nearly impossible to change this pattern once it's been set in motion—one step follows automatically on the heels of another. But—by repeatedly observing the sequence of mental events, you can learn to break this pattern of behavior in the future.

What once happened automatically will gradually become a conscious process—and will therefore lose much of its power.

Key: In the split second before you build the self-defeating behavior, you'll begin to ask yourself, *What can I do instead?*

Step 4: Find a healthy replacement behavior. Simply trying to stop the self-defeating behavior is a recipe for certain failure—you cannot replace something with nothing. Instead, you must substitute another, more constructive action.

Examples:

•Engage in gardening, weight-lifting or another physical activity that leaves you no mental energy for worrying.

•Force yourself to repeat to yourself reassuring, rather than catastrophic, statements.

•Calm yourself with deep breathing exercises.

•Call an upbeat friend.

•Organize a messy drawer.

•Read.

•Take a nap.

•Plan your weekend.

Where to find replacement behaviors:

• Your past. What did you do before negative experiences led you to create the self-defeating behavior?

• Role models. What would one of your "heroes" do in a similar situation?

• Your body. What would feel good physically in this situation?

• Your wiser self. Often, we already have the answers we need—if we can only trust ourselves.

• Feedback from others. Ask friends and other people you trust for suggestions.

Step 5: Practice replacing the old behavior with the new, healthier one. At first you'll need to be vigilant. It will feel unnatural not to slip into the old pattern.

But if you persist, you'll reprogram your unconscious mind…and the new, self-enhancing behavior will become as automatic as the self-defeating behavior once was.

Source: Robert E. Hardy, EdD, a licensed psychologist affiliated with Personnel Decisions, Inc., a Minneapolis-based international consulting firm that applies the principles of behavioral science to building successful organizations. He is coauthor, with Milton R. Cudney, of *Self-Defeating Behaviors*, Harper/San Francisco, 10 E. 53 St., New York 10022. Or call 800-633-4410 for more information.

Emotional Factors That May Make Some People More Vulnerable to Cancer

A rapidly growing body of research suggests that psychological factors play a role in physical disease. My own research, including studies of patients with malignant melanoma (a virulent and often deadly form of skin cancer), provides strong evidence that cancer is one of these diseases. Its development and progression—or the body's resistance to it—can be affected by emotions and behavior. I call this behavior pattern Type C.

The Type-C pattern…

The core of the Type-C pattern is a striking lack of emotional expressiveness—especially where anger is concerned. It seems that Type Cs do not express anger—or other emotions such as anxiety, fear, sadness and even joy—and they are often unaware of even feeling these emotions.

Type Cs tend to be remarkably nice people. They're patient, cooperative and highly focused on meeting other people's needs, while showing little or no concern for their own. There's nothing wrong with being nice, cooperative or considerate of others. These are admirable traits. But Type Cs carry this behavior to extremes.

Example I: Ask a Type C, Will you help me move today? and he/she will agree without thinking twice—even though he's exhausted and suffering from a sore back.

Example II: Most people would expect to be angry, sad and/or fearful upon receiving a diagnosis of cancer. But when a Type C who's newly diagnosed with melanoma is asked what is most upsetting about the situation, a typical response is: "I'm not upset personally, but I'm very concerned about how my husband/wife/children will deal with this. I don't know what they will do without me."

For some people, a serene, unflappable approach is a healthy way of coping with the world. But for Type Cs, this unruffled exterior does not arise out of a sense of inner peace. It hides unacknowledged anger and anxiety… even despair.

The roots of Type-C behavior…

These findings don't mean Type Cs make themselves sick. People with cancer did not want to get the disease…nor did they give it to themselves…nor do they allow it to happen by not thinking "positively enough." There is no data to support such misconceptions.

Like other human beings, Type Cs have developed their behavior patterns unconsciously, in order to deal with the environment as best they can.

Example: The passiveness of Type Cs is often an adaptive response to growing up in an abusive family. A child may hope to avoid harsh punishment by focusing on whatever the other person wants. Even in nonabusive homes, many parents unwittingly encourage Type C patterns with messages such as, Big boys don't cry. Good little girls don't get angry. Children learn from this that their natural responses are bad and should be disregarded or suppressed.

Type C and the body...

Behavior patterns don't cause cancer. They are among the elements that may contribute—along with other factors over a period of time—to predisposing someone to an illness or pushing someone already at risk over the edge. Type-C behavior appears to influence physical illness in two major ways...

•Stress. Type Cs tend to stay in stressful situations—such as a bad marriage or frustrating job—longer than other people. Because they don't recognize their emotions, they may not even know they're under stress. But the body knows—it produces stress hormones, including cortisol, which have been shown to suppress the immune system when chronically present in the body.

•Natural opiates. Part of the process of emotional suppression seems to involve production by the body of natural opiates (brain chemicals that have a pain-killing effect similar to artificial drugs like morphine). These opiates hook up with receptors on certain immune cells in the body, giving them the message to "turn off."

Plenty of healthful activities, including exercise, cause these natural opiates to be produced on a temporary basis. But in the case of emotional suppression, the opiates are chronically present...and continue to have a dampening effect on the immune system.

Self-defense...

Recognizing Type-C behavior can be empowering. Studies have shown that people who work to reverse destructive behavior patterns can improve their resistance to disease. If you notice aspects of the Type-C pattern in yourself, here are some new options to explore...

•Become more aware of your emotions. They are giving you important information. Respect them. You wouldn't run on a painful ankle —you know that would make it worse. Yet we often ignore similar emotional messages...and continue to act in ways or spend time with people who cause us emotional pain.

I strongly recommend therapy as a way for Type Cs to learn about their emotional lives and cope more effectively. Group therapy can be especially useful—hearing other people talk about their experiences and feelings can help you recognize your own.

If your emotions are a complete blank to you, be alert for slight twinges of discomfort—a clenched jaw, a vague feeling that something isn't right, etc. *Ask yourself:* What happened just before I noticed this sensation? What other sensations am I experiencing? What do I need right now? What are my options for dealing with this situation?

•Say "no" more often—and ask for support when you need it. Challenge the belief that asserting yourself will lead to rejection—or that the consequences of rejection would be unbearable.

•Learn to express anger and other emotions in a constructive way. It's true that it isn't always in your best interest to express yourself—there are times when getting angry may cost you your job or cause you to be physically attacked.

But there are also situations in which anger can help you get what you want. Various kinds of assertiveness training can help you learn to stand up for your rights without blowing your top all the time. Have a range of responses available so your automatic reaction is no longer, *What can I do for you?*

•Learn to relax. Regular practice of relaxation and body awareness techniques can strengthen immune response and enhance sensory awareness, which is helpful in learning to identify what you feel.

Source: Psychologist Lydia Temoshok, PhD, director of the US Military's Behavioral Medicine Research Program on HIV/AIDS. A former faculty member at the University of California School of Medicine, she is the coauthor of *The Type C Connection: The Behavioral Links to Cancer and Your Health.* Random House, Inc., 201 E. 50 St., New York 10022.

How We Can Keep a Lid On Emotional Upset

Events and other people don't truly upset us. We upset ourselves by what we tell ourselves about these events. *How to think and feel better:*

•Acknowledge...that the event or person you are upset with did not upset you—you, for the most part, upset yourself.

•Look for the "should" and/or the "must"… with which you made yourself upset.

Example: "I should have made a better impression on the interviewer. I must get a job this week. The world should give me what I want when I want it."

•Dispute, challenge and question those "must" thoughts and statements. Change them to preferences.

Example: "I would prefer to have aced the interview, but it didn't work out that way. I'll learn what I can and try to do better next time."

You may have to voice these new statements very strongly, in order to fight the strength of your habitual, gloom-and-doom response.

With practice, however, the rational way of thinking will become your automatic reaction. You'll find that you'll be telling yourself immediately…"That was unpleasant, but it's not the end of the world. I can probably succeed next time."

Source: Albert Ellis, PhD, originator of Rational-Emotive Therapy and founder of the Institute for Rational-Emotive Therapy, which has branches throughout the US and around the world. He has written more than 50 books, including *How to Stubbornly Refuse to Make Yourself Miserable About Anything—Yes, Anything!*, Lyle Stuart/Carol Publishing Group, 600 Madison Ave., New York 10022.

What Color To Paint What Room

Warm colors (yellow, rose, earth tones) create a cozy sense of well-being in the home. But soft green, off-white and cool blue can make you feel melancholy if they're overused. *Where cool colors work best:* In rooms that are intended for study or meditation.

Source: Jacquelyn Yde, a Miami designer and color consultant, in *USA Today.*

Interior Lighting: Key to a Peaceful Home

Innovations in fixtures and even in the types of bulbs available make the lighting of rooms as important as the furniture or color scheme in achieving the effect you want.

Proper lighting can make the rooms of a house work efficiently and feel comfortable. Bad lighting in a room imposes psychological stresses on the people who spend time there, leaving them with a vague feeling of tension and strain.

Living room…

Because it is used for so many purposes, this focal area of the house needs several lighting systems. *Best:* To keep lighting flexible, use dimmer switches on the main lamps and fixtures.

For entertaining, general brightness is important. That can be achieved with indirect lighting fixtures such as torchiere lamps. Dark-colored walls and furniture require more wattage.

Track lighting is good for spotlighting paintings and plants. Halogen or quartz bulbs give the clearest, most natural light for art works. (However, they are more expensive and burn hotter than incandescent bulbs.)

Plants can be made dramatic at night with underlights. Use small floor or table fixtures that hold reflector bulbs. Experiment with using these lights to throw interesting patterns on the walls and ceiling.

New low-voltage spotlights or floodlights throw soft light on prized objects such as sculpture or an antique table, or they can illuminate an heirloom rug. Low-voltage lights use a transformer to produce 5½-volt or 12-volt beams made up of cool rays that will not harm fabrics or wood.

For reading, writing or playing board games in the living room, individual lamps need to be strategically placed to give good, strong light on the work areas. When the television is on, the indirect lights can be turned low to prevent eye strain. Sharp contrasts between dark and light areas are the most fatiguing.

Kitchen…

Bright, even lighting is most beneficial to the cook. Fluorescent bulbs—the longer the better—are a practical, economical choice. If the room is L-shaped, use two fixtures. For natural color, use cool white bulbs in blue or green kitchens and warm white bulbs in red or yellow ones. Warm white deluxe bulbs have extra yellow for a sunnier effect. Although under-cabinet lights shouldn't be necessary in a properly lighted kitchen, they give a cozy glow for midnight raids of the refrigerator when the overhead lights seem too much.

Bedroom...

Convenience dictates. Bedside lamps should be controlled by easy-to-reach switches and directed so that one person can sleep while another is still awake and reading. "Task lighting" (a separate fixture for each need) is best.

Dining room...

This is the one room where a chandelier makes sense (unless the entryway is considered a room and has the necessary height). A shimmering glass fixture will catch light and play with reflections from your table silver and crystal. For a softer mood, use low-voltage indirect lights on dimmers.

Bathroom...

For women who apply makeup at the bathroom mirror, fluorescent lights are a poor choice because they distort colors. To get even, wide-spectrum light, use strips of 25-watt incandescent bulbs. Most bathrooms can be well lighted with a total of 200 watts spread the length of the room. Strips made up to specified lengths have recently become available.

Source: Miri Small-Kesten, vice president of Lighting Associates, a designer-lighting showroom in New York.

Lessons from the Late Dr. Norman Vincent Peale

Editor: As I passed your church the other day, I saw the notice of your upcoming sermon: "Have a wonderful time living." And I thought, what does "wonderful time" mean? And what does "living" mean?

Dr. Peale: "Wonderful" means something happy, pleasant, exciting, satisfying. And living, of course, is the act of survival, from cradle to grave. But there are gradations. Some people merely exist their way through life. Some have

pain all the way and never find themselves. So it's what level you're living on that counts.

To me, "living" would be vigor, enthusiasm, vitality, joy—everything that is positive in nature. I've seen people who are crippled in wheelchairs and who at the same time rise above that because their spirit is victorious. With an indefatigable spirit, you can have a wonderul time living.

Ed.: But perhaps you're raising our expectations too much. Isn't it unreasonable to expect every day to be wonderful? There's an awful lot of the day that has to be mundane and ordinary, at best.

Dr. Peale: It all depends on the attitude with which you wake up. A man I once knew—he used to write for the old *New York Herald Tribune*—was a philosophical sort of character. When he got out of bed, he projected his day as far as he knew it, and he resolved to do everything that day as best he could. He would be contented and happy, no matter what came along. Then, when he went to bed, he'd go through his day—his "little world," as he put it —and drop out all the unpleasant things. He'd say, "I commit them to oblivion."

Ed.: I'm not sure I'd find that so simple.

Dr. Peale: You can't always do it. But if you make the effort, you can take the sting out of anything.

The main thing is to keep your attitude up, no matter what. I'm not a Pollyanna, but I go on the theory that everybody is greater than anything that happens to them. If you've got a sound concept of what life is all about—that is, a mixture of laughter and tears, pain and pleasure—you'll be all right.

Ed.: Given the mixture, what can we reasonably expect from life?

Dr. Peale: You expect the best, and usually you get the best, but anybody's a fool who thinks he won't have a lot of trouble mixed in. Maybe the best day of all is when you have some trouble or pain and overcome it.

You see, life is a mixture of opposites—negatives and positives, good and bad, dark and light. But you can draw out the positives and make them work for you. Every day you'll meet a scoundrel or a fool, but every day you'll also meet a delightful person. Once, in

Rome, I was at the foot of the Spanish Steps. The crowds were surging around, and there was a little boy eight or nine years old with a daisy in his hand. He was studying this flower, totally oblivious to all the confusion around him. And he didn't just tear it apart, either. He'd just lift up a petal and look underneath. So, I'd say he had a wonderful day, and he certainly contributed to mine.

Ed: Speaking of opposites, it seems that people's strengths often turn out to be their weaknesses. If a person is forceful, he forgets he has a softness as well.

Dr. Peale: That's true. But the way I see it, even your negatives can be turned around. Years ago, someone said: We become strongest at our weakest place. When a piece of metal breaks, that's its weakest place—the spot where it broke. If you want to put it back together again, you apply heat and weld it. Now, even if that metal broke again, it would probably do so at a different point, because the weakest place is now the strongest one.

If a person has a weakness in his makeup, and he really works on that weakness, in the end he can make it his strongest element. Which is part, I'd say, of living a wonderful life.

Source: The late Reverend Dr. Norman Vincent Peale, author of more than 45 books, including *The Power of Positive Thinking* (Fawcett Books, 201 E. 50 St., New York 10022), *The Power of Positive Living* (Doubleday, 1540 Broadway, New York 10036) and most recently, *Positive Thinking Every Day* (Simon & Schuster, 1230 Avenue of the Americas, New York 10020).

Looking at Joy, Pleasure and Life

To take full pleasure from life, you must be spontaneous. Most of us are raised to dredge up the past and prepare for the future, rather than simply to enjoy today. And that's a mistake.

When we go to a party, some of us look over our "partner's" shoulder to check who else is coming in, to see where we could be having more fun. We miss so much. When my students ask me, "What are we going to do?" I tell them, "We're already doing it." The only reality is the present. Yesterday is gone, and we can't predict tomorrow. If we lose *now*, we've lost the essence of living.

To enjoy relationships…

As you embrace the moment, so you must accept people as they are. Nothing kills a relationship faster than the expectation that you can change someone. It's impossible. Trying to change someone else is a lost cause. The best you can do is to become more tolerant and flexible yourself, to encourage an atmosphere for change, and then hope for the best.

When you meet someone you want to share your life with, stop a moment. Ask yourself: *Is this person enough just the way he or she is?* If not, watch out. Don't expect strong, silent types suddenly to become demonstrative just because you love them.

Remember that you can never own people, even (and especially) a lover. You have to merit those you care about and work at the relationship. It's a forever process.

When you give, give freely. If you expect people to give the same back, measured by the cup, you'll always be disappointed. If they respond, that's great. And if they don't, that's all right, too.

The importance of honesty…

At the same time, you need to be honest with the people you care about. I knew a case where one spouse's insistence on squeezing the toothpaste tube in the middle, a classic little problem, became an "irreconcilable difference" that led to divorce. Get rid of petty irritants. Don't suffer in silence until you finally explode. Say what you mean and feel. If the other person turns out to be hopeless in the tube-squeezing department, work out a compromise. (You might buy two tubes, one for each.)

Honesty needn't be cruel. *Good rule:* Be as tactful with your spouse and children as you are with friends and distant relatives. We're wonderful in courtship. But later we get careless. Love is not a license for rudeness.

We also tend to use our families as alibis when we fall short of our own goals. Stop underestimating these people. They're much more flexible than we assume. We can make our dreams real if we want them enough—and share them with the people we love. But if you never say, "Let's go to Nepal!" you'll never get there.

Of course, you're taking a chance. If your family picks up the challenge, you'll still have to work to achieve that goal. No fairy godmother will simply wave her wand and give you your heart's desire.

Many years ago, I dreamed of building a big institute to study the dynamics of human relationships. A very wealthy woman finally said she'd endow the school if I'd be president. Suddenly I was faced with my dream...and I didn't take the reality. I decided I wasn't ready to sit behind a desk. It was a good decision—but if I hadn't been confronted with it, I still might be moaning about the institute that I never really wanted.

Living with risk...

Above all, you must accept that life is, by definition, always in flux. Everything is perpetually in a state of change. There is no real peace out there, no wall high enough to protect you. You must be your own anchor and have the courage to risk. Every moment is a risk. When you accept that, you'll be filled with the invigoration of your own power.

The biggest risk of all is to love. We're scared to death of expressing ourselves. When you meet people on the street, don't be afraid to greet them—your tongue won't fall off. Hug people—your arms won't fall off. I'm not ashamed to show that without love, I would die of loneliness. It's a gamble to be vulnerable. But you never really lose because the risk itself reminds you how richly you are living.

Source: Leo Buscaglia, author of *Loving Each Other*, Holt, Rinehart and Winston, New York.

What Makes A Person Happy?

Twenty-five years ago, men defined happiness as a steady job with a future, while the typical woman looked to a secure marriage with children. But a recent survey found that difference has blurred. Women depend more

on work for their satisfaction than they used to, and men depend more on family life. *Bottom line:* A sense of well-being is conditioned more by society than by any basic difference between the sexes.

Source: Study by psychologist Joseph Veroff, PhD, reported in *Vogue*, New York.

All About Happiness

Sometimes happiness seems like a terribly elusive goal. We tend to forget that it doesn't come as a result of getting something we don't have, but rather of recognizing and appreciating what we do have. Some steps on the pathway to happiness:

•When you think about time, keep to the present. My research suggests that thinking too much about events far in the future or in the distant past leads to unhappiness. Very often those who are future-oriented tend to score very high in despair, anxiety, helplessness and unhappiness. As much as is practical, focus on the here and now.

•Don't dwell on past injustices. You'll be unpopular company. No one wants to hear about how your boss doesn't appreciate you. Bill Bradley once said that one of the biggest problems a basketball player could have was to keep on replaying the game in his head after it was over. This is also true of life. If you keep doing instant replays, you'll lose your chance to enjoy the present.

•Check your goals. Many of us get so wrapped up in the means that we forget about the ends. Ask yourself from time to time: "Why am I doing this? Am I working hard because I love my work, or because I think money will buy happiness?" Maybe you'd really like peace of mind or recognition or job satisfaction. These can be more immediate, attainable goals. If you're working yourself to the bone because you think money will eventually buy contentment, maybe you can discover that you don't really need a million dollars. Making enough money to buy a small country retreat might do the trick.

•Drop your bucket where you are. Legend says that an explorer's sailing ship was becalmed in the mouth of the Amazon River. Thinking they were in the salty ocean, he and the crew were dying of thirst. Out of the sky a voice commanded, "Drop your bucket where you are." They did so, pulled up fresh water, and were thus saved. *Lesson:* Take advantage of what you already have. There are interesting, stimulating adventures waiting in your own backyard. Get to know your own children, for example.

•Develop the habit of noticing things. An active mind is never bored. While I walk to work every morning, I always try to pick out a house to look at carefully—one I haven't really paid attention to before. Make a resolution to notice new things each day—about nature, people, or anything else that interests you. Ask questions. Don't assume you know all the answers or that showing curiosity will be considered prying. Most people love to talk about themselves or their interests. *Example:* Talk with old people about their childhoods. You may have the fascinating experience of finding out about another world.

•Make some time for yourself. Everyone needs at least 20 minutes a day for quiet reflection—just-thinking time. If you think while walking or running, leave the radio home. Let your thoughts drift to who you are, how you feel, what you're doing, how your life is going.

•Exercise. It's good for the mind. I don't mean jogging 10 miles a day. But a brisk walk, maybe during your self-reflection time, will put you in a better frame of mind. And it's important to do it regularly, as part of your daily routine, just as you shower and eat at certain times.

•Establish a regimen for yourself. This will give you a feeling of control. If you can stop smoking, lose weight, exercise, stick to a schedule, etc., you'll gain a sense of mastery. Anything that proves you can affect your own life will give you a positive sense of self.

•Listen to the old saw about accepting what you cannot change. As we get older, we have to accept our limitations. At some point in life, we all must recognize that we'll never be president of General Motors, a Nobel Prize winner, a

Time cover subject, a perfect "10" or whatever else we thought was crucial to happiness. At this point, you have to be able to say sincerely, "So what!"

•Learn to like yourself. The best way to think positively about yourself is to think positively about others. They will then reflect back to you how wonderful you are, which will make it a lot easier. Our sense of self is a reflection of other people's responses to us. *Exercise:* Pay three sincere compliments a day to others. You'll soon see yourself. The key word is *sincere*. Finding things you really like will change how you think about people, which will, in turn, make you a lot more likable.

•Don't wear too many hats. Focus on one thing at a time. Make policy decisions ahead of time about situations such as taking work home. Set time aside for your family, yourself, your golf game, etc.—for having fun. If you set your priorities in advance, you avoid the anxiety of making moment-to-moment decisions. These priorities don't have to be carved in stone, but they'll help you cope. *Also:* If you stick to your plans, you don't have to feel guilty because you're having fun and not working.

•Keep your sense of humor. A good laugh goes a long way in making almost any situation bearable. It also lightens the impact of life's inevitable tragedies.

Source: Frederick Koenig, PhD, professor of social psychology, Tulane University, New Orleans, LA.

Happy People Are Unselfish

To prove it, make a list of 10 people you know well. Write *H* for happy or *N* for not happy after the name of each. Then go down the list again and write *S* for selfish or *U* for unselfish beside each name. *Odds:* You will find that most people you rate as happy will also be considered unselfish.

Source: Surveys by psychologist Bernard Rimland at the Institute for Child Behavior Research in San Diego, as reported in *Psychology Today*, New York.

Smiling Troubles Away

You may be able to alter your mood with a grin or a frown. *Reason:* Facial expressions lead to changes in the involuntary nervous system, reinforcing the appropriate emotion. *For better empathy:* Mimic the expression of the person you're dealing with.

Why Laughing Is Good For Your Health

A good guffaw is more than a great tension reliever. *It also can:* Aid digestion, lower blood pressure, stimulate the heart and endocrine system, activate the right brain hemisphere (your creative center), strengthen muscles, raise pulse rate, soothe arthritic pain, work out internal organs and keep you alert. No joke!

Source: William F. Fry, Jr., MD, professor of psychiatry, Stanford University, quoted in *American Health.*

To Stop Unwanted Thoughts

The average person has more than 200 negative thoughts a day—worries, jealousies, insecurities, cravings for forbidden things, etc. (Depressed people have as many as 600.) You can't eliminate all the troublesome things that go through your mind, but you can certainly reduce the number of negative thoughts. *Here's how:*

1. When a negative thought begins to surface in your mind, pause. Just stop what you are doing for a few seconds. Don't say anything—talk will reinforce the bad feeling.

2. Take five deep, slow breaths. By taking in more oxygen, you flush out your system and lower your level of anxiety. If you do this correctly, you will approach a meditative state.

3. Concentrate on a pleasant, relaxing scene —a walk on a breezy beach, for example. Take two to three minutes for a minor trouble, up to 10 minutes for a serious upset.

Best: Use this technique continuously until the upsetting thoughts begin to decrease. Then practice is intermittently.

Source: Elinor Kinarthy, PhD, professor of psychology, Rio Hondo College, Whittier, CA.

Dealing with Loneliness

Virtually everyone is lonely from time to time, but chronic loneliness is a matter of more serious psychological dimension. Most people have no trouble describing what loneliness feels like. Emptiness, tightness in the throat, anxiety or feelings of "deadness inside" are among the phrases that recur when people talk about their lonely feelings. The trouble people do have is in locating the sources of their loneliness. *The most common error:* People who feel lonely blame themselves for their condition. In fact, it is usually some situation or external problem that causes the loneliness, rather than some inner psychological mechanism. No one is "genetically lonely" or "naturally lonely."

Social forces have a good deal to do with being alone, the most common cause of loneliness. Being alone is in good part the product of the high divorce rate and the fact that wives outlive husbands. It is also a product of our culture's emphasis on "self-sufficiency" and independence.

Popular fallacy: That old people are the most lonely members of our society. Just the opposite is true. They are the least lonely. (Research shows that young people are the most lonely and also the most unhappy, the most often bored and the lowest in self-esteem of the entire population.) Old people are the least lonely because we become wiser and psychologically sturdier as we age. It's also possible that the unhappy, lonely people die off sooner, leaving the more optimistic, cheerful ones to survive and be counted. *Another fallacy:* Women need men more than men need women. *Fact:* Indications are clear that men tend to be more dependent on women. *One reason:* Women are far

411

more skilled than men at establishing intimacy and at creating nurturing relationships.

What to do about loneliness…

•Recognize that there are ways in which you may have become accustomed to dealing with loneliness that can in fact exacerbate it and be harmful in other ways. *Examples:* Solitary drinking, taking tranquilizers or other drugs, or watching television. The last is a particularly insidious (because ostensibly harmless) diversion that, like many other escapist solutions, can reduce your capacity to be alone and introspective. (It's no accident that in a study of high-school students, the ones who had the lowest social status and self-esteem were the ones who watched television most often.) Television tends to serve as a substitute for social life, not a route into it. It's potentially more harmful than smoking a little marijuana on occasion.

•Learn the benefits of solitude by undertaking some of its more active forms, such as journal writing, letter writing or reading. Such activities contribute to your sense of personal strength and your level of awareness, and they enhance your sense of creativity. These are all vital contributions, since low self-esteem is a central factor in loneliness. It's important to learn the positive benefits of being alone. It's a mistake to spend time with people to cope with feelings of emptiness. Surrounding yourself with people you don't like is just bad as stuffing yourself with food you don't need in order to cope with loneliness. They are narcotics, not solutions to the problem of the void you feel.

•Remember that the way in which you perceive being alone is the decisive factor in whether you feel lonely. People who equate loneliness with being alone are the ones who end up actually feeling lonely in solitary circumstances. There are, after all, many people who have been living alone all their lives, yet are among the least lonely people.

•Consider how to establish more intimate ties with other people. This is, above all, the prime factor in avoiding feelings of loneliness. Such feelings reflect the fact that you have insufficient or inadequate personal ties in your life.

Source: Carin Rubenstein, PhD, senior editor of *Psychology Today* and coauthor (with Phillip Shaver) of *In Search of Intimacy*, Delacorte Press, New York.

How to Self-Indulge

It's been a grueling week. Meetings, deadlines, pressure, crises—and now, finally, Friday is almost over. M. feels the tension begin to melt. His eyes focus on some distant point outside his office window. *This week should be Mozart or Mendelssohn?* he wonders. *A concerto for flute or for violin? Jean-Pierre Rampal or Itzhak Perlman or maybe Rosalyn Tureck playing Bach?* He smiles at the decision that lies ahead.

M. is getting ready to self-indulge. Every Friday he pops into a record store and buys a classical music tape as a gift to himself for making it through the week.

It happens that M. can afford to order the entire Columbia Masterworks Library in a single stroke. Obviously, he can also buy his tapes on Monday or Wednesday or by mail order. But that is not the point: M. is not methodically pursuing a hobby or building a music collection. He is practicing artful self-indulgence. That is why he chooses to savor his purchases, one by one.

Artful self-indulgence is a ritual. It is theater (because the anticipation is as satisfying as the performance itself). It is a reward for good behavior bestowed by the person who knows you best—you.

The difference between artful self-indulgence and spoiled-brat hedonism lies in moderation and self-knowledge. For example, the person who pigs out on a quart of Haagen-Dazs mocha chip is usually following a false messiah. It is rare to find salvation in an act so gross, guilt-producing and common as eating too much ice cream. On the other hand, the person who rewards herself with a Shiatsu massage once a month may enjoy a sense of physical peace that nourishes her for weeks.

I've found that practitioners of this art, or survival skill, fall into two broad categories: Those who self-indulge by buying and those who self-indulge by doing.

The buyers…

B. buys accessories: A streamlined coffee maker that plugs into the car cigarette lighter, state-of-the-art earphones for his stereo, a fancy carrying case for his floppy disks, you name it. B. is convinced that each accessory is absolutely necessary to the usefulness of his existing machines or appliances. That belief gives him psychological permission to self-indulge.

R. buys stationery. She likes choosing paper to match her subject and her moods. She buys everything from lined pads at the dime store to monogrammed notepaper from Tiffany's. When she's depressed, she buys antique postcards. She doesn't call her habit self-indulgence. She calls it "buying myself a clean slate."

W. buys courses. At the moment, it's a writing seminar. Before that, it was an all-day conference on "Selling Yourself." Next, he's considering either conversational Chinese, "The Wines of California" or flying lessons. He says he sets aside a strict percentage of his paycheck for these courses—not to earn college credit or Brownie points with the boss, but to "keep on growing."

A. is a hardware-store freak. She buys tools and gadgets; the more obscure their function, the better. She buys electrical supplies—and hooks, screws, nails and every manner of fastener. Nothing delights A. more than having precisely the right item for any fix-it job. Her idea of lip smacking self-indulgence is spending Sunday afternoon hanging a 40-pound picture on a hollow wall.

The doers...

Most of us reward ourselves after an exhausting day by flaking out in front of the TV set or going to sleep right after dinner. But there's another breed of humans who treat themselves well by going into action. I don't mean your ordinary 12-miles-a-week jogger or daily health-club fanatic. I'm talking about people who give themselves an occasional well-planned, very special treat. Here are a few virtuoso self-indulgers:

The New York Times recently featured an investment banker who goes hot-air ballooning, a computer consultant who plays "Ultimate Frisbee," a croquet player, and several race walkers, boccie players, rock climbers and parachute jumpers. But they didn't name my personal self-indulgence: Motor scootering. Despite the known hazards of New York City traffic, I find a ride around Central Park or a run up and down Riverside Drive to be among the most refreshing activities available to an urban dweller.

E. gets his jollies by making weekend brunches. He spends many daydreaming moments during the work week planning his invitation list and a unique menu. Although he sees the creativity as self-indulgence (and a costly one if he chooses something like a caviar omelet party), he says, "I have fun twice: Once while I'm cooking and then while I'm with my friends."

B. considers her volunteer work as self-indulgent as anyone else's luxuries because it gives her so much pleasure. B. is a black woman who owns her own business. On weekends, she is a Big Sister to a 13-year-old black girl. Together they go to the movies, to the beach, to museums, shopping, bike riding, whatever. And they talk. When a school holiday coincides with a work day, B. takes her Little Sister to the office with her. "I want her to form an image of her own future possibilities," she says.

H. writes in his journal. He doesn't expect ever to get published, but that's not his goal. His goal is to slow down his life, to observe and to record his feelings and experiences before everything blurs in his memory. Since he started writing in his journal, he says, he has become much more sensitive about noticing the things around him and understanding himself and the people he loves.

To each, his or her own. Happily, artful self-indulgence is a private transaction between you and your passions. So, if you can afford it and it makes you feel good and it doesn't hurt anyone—go to it!

Source: Letty Cottin Pogrebin is the author of *Family Politics*, McGraw-Hill, New York.

Learning the Virtues Of Endless Patience

Endless patience is a discipline that takes time, practice and, yes, patience to learn. It means having enough patience for a crucial project even when it is unclear how much will be required.

Goal: To undertake long, complex, open-ended personal and business ventures and bring them to a conclusion without being consumed with unnecessary anxieties and worries.

Problem: Most people are easily overcome by petty concerns and spend many wasted hours fretting. *Result:* They pay a huge emotional price in turmoil about things over which they have little control.

The route to mastering endless patience starts with understanding the concept of risk taking. Most ventures have, at best, a 50% chance of success. People tend to forget this. They pray to Lady Luck that every project will turn out well. Then they are disappointed—and shocked—at the failures. They must learn to wait patiently to see which projects will survive and which will go under.

Trap: Blind faith, whose followers fervently believe that they will succeed. They hang on to any undertaking, no matter how clear the signs that it will fail. *Contrast:* People with endless patience are willing to pay the price to achieve the goal only as long as it is feasible. When feasibility dies, the practitioner of endless patience knows it is time to quit.

Secret weapon of achieving endless patience: A calm, analytical state of mind. The mystical writer Carlos Castaneda give this explanation of what makes a good warrior-hunter-stalker: "The warrior never frets."*

To avoid fretting: Identify the real problems. Make sure that everything humanly possible is being done to solve them. Then, sit back and stop worrying. *Insight:* Your patience does not expire until the project succeeds, dies or is killed.

Most innovation has a long portion of the exponential curve, in which there is hardly any incremental value during long months or years. Then it might suddenly swerve upward and keep climbing. Impatient people do not hang in long enough to witness this upturn.

Helpful analogy: Practicing endless patience is similar to setting out in unknown territory to find diamonds. You know from research that the diamonds are out there. You are even familiar with the type of ground in which they may be located, though you lack a map marking

The Eagle's Gift by Carlos Castaneda, Simon & Schuster, New York.

their site. You plan for the expedition, anticipate your problems and set out in the hope of succeeding.

Endless patience prevents you from fretting over a missed turn, sprained ankle or minor setback. You press on toward your goal without agonizing over small annoyances or uncontrollable events. You may find the diamond field—or you may at some point decide the search is no longer feasible. Either way, you will have exercised the correct approach.

Patience must also be exercised in short-term dealings with people and situations. Understanding the basic concepts of endless patience ends much unproductive behavior.

Another way out: Develop the practice of focused attention. Concentrate on the problems that cause you real concern. Puzzle out ways to solve these problems, and then relax.

Source: Martin G. Groder, MD, a psychiatrist and business consultant who practices in Durham, NC.

Importance of Sadness

Showing sadness on a hospital visit is perfectly acceptable, even positive. *Reason:* It helps validate the patient's own feelings and reflects sincere sympathy. It doesn't pay to strain to cheer someone up. A person who's sick and away from home is entitled to feel unhappy. *Recommended:* Let the patient set the emotional tone for the visit.

Source: Ellen Martin, director of patient relations, St. Luke's-Roosevelt Hospital, New York, quoted in *McCall's*, New York.

Jogging vs. Depression

Jogging can be an effective treatment for depression. Doctors discovered that jogging often leads to a natural high which can be effective as a treatment for depression. Forty-five minutes of moderate to heavy exercise or an hour of brisk walking four to six times a week is adequate to produce this high. In addition, many drug-addicted individuals have used the exercise program with great success.

Source: Dennis Coffee, MD, Del Amo Hospital, Torrance, CA.

Do-It-Yourself Depression Test

If you're depressed for no good reason, it might be a hormone deficiency. *How to check:* Place an oral thermometer on your bedside table. As soon as you awaken, tuck the thermometer into your armpit for 10 minutes. A temperature below 97.8 may point to low thyroid or adrenal activity. *Possible treatment:* Prescribed medication.

Source: Dr. Stephen Langer, Berkeley, CA, quoted in *Family Circle.*

Why Sunlight is Necessary for Your Mental Health

Natural-light deprivation causes depression. The less you are exposed to natural unfiltered light, the more depressed you are likely to feel. Sunlight appears to stimulate the production of melatonin, a hormone that influences mood, sleep and fertility. Normal artificial light does not provide the spectrum of light needed. *Solution:* Try to spend at least 15 minutes a day outside, or install a full-spectrum light bulb that provides light similar to the sun's.

Source: Duro-Lite Lamps, Inc., North Bergen, NJ.

Why Unemployment May Be Bad For Your Health

Unemployment greatly increases the risk of hospitalization. Workers who are unemployed more than 50% of the time are seven times more likely to enter a psychiatric clinic than those who are regularly employed. And the chance of admission to medical and surgical wards is almost twice as high among the chronically unemployed.

Source: A survey of bricklayers in Risskov, Denmark, as reported in the *Journal of the American Medical Association*, Chicago, IL.

Survival Technique

Denying the seriousness of an illness often helps a patient survive. This denial is a coping mechanism that enables some people to put aside their fears. *Result:* Less stress, which encourages healing. Those with the ability to deny are usually born so.

Source: Thomas P. Hackett, MD, professor of psychiatry at Harvard Medical School and chief of psychiatry at Massachusetts General Hospital, Boston.

Kiss of Death

Strong, supportive families have always been assumed to sustain the chronically ill. *Surprise:* In a recent study of dialysis patients, those who enjoy close family ties suffered more complications and died sooner. *Probable reason:* When family members interact well, a chronic illness is a more profound stress on the entire unit. In such a case, death may represent a collaboration—the patient dies so that the family can survive.

Source: Research by David Reiss, MD, of the Family Research Center, George Washington University, in *Medical World News,* New York.

Grief Kills

Husbands whose wives died still had suppressed immune systems two months after the deaths. Their systems were still acting somewhat subnormally a year later, making the men vulnerable to illness and earlier death. *Suspected cause:* Dysfunction of the hypothalmus, which is also linked with depression and anxiety.

Source: Study at Mount Sinai Hospital in New York.

Why It Pays to Panic

Executives who are least prone to panic may be most susceptible to stress. The most competent decision makers are those who approach problems from a variety of perspectives, combining all plausible ideas into one effective action plan. Studies show these multidimensional managers have fewer psychiatric problems than others but a higher incidence of intestinal upsets and cardiac irregularities.

Source: Siegfried Streufert, professor of behavioral science, Pennsylvania State University's College of Medicine, cited in *Management Focus,* New York.

Killer Jobs

People whose work takes the worst physical toll are laborers, secretaries, inspectors, clinical laboratory technicians, office managers, foreman, managers and administrators. Their jobs are the high-stress occupations. *Criteria:* Rates of death, heart and artery disease, hypertension, ulcers, nervous disorders and mental health admissions.

Source: Study by the National Institute for Occupational Safety and Health in *Workrights* by Robert Ellis Smith, E. P. Dutton, Inc., New York.

•The job stress that puts workers most at risk for heart disease is a combination of high psychological demand and low control over how the job is done, according to recent studies in both the US and Sweden. *Example:* Machine-paced assembly line workers were found to be 70%–200% more likely to develop heart disease than low-level managerial personnel. *Other occupations with dangerously low decision control and high psychological demand:* Fireman, waiter/waitress, salesclerk, telephone operator, cashier, cook, freight handler, garment stitcher and mail worker. Jobs traditionally thought to be most stressful—manufacturing or sales manager, real estate agent, physician, policeman, high school teacher—were found to be less damaging to physical health. Individuals in these jobs are in a position to make their own decision about what needs to be done and how to go about doing it.

Source: Robert A. Karasek, PhD, director of the studies and assistant professor of industrial engineering, Columbia University, quoted in *The New York Times.*

Best Days of the Week

Blue Mondays are a myth. In tests to learn about stress in married men, a tangential discovery was made—that Mondays are no more difficult (for those interviewed) than any other day of the week. *Upbeat days:* Saturday and Sunday. Maybe Mondays only seem blue by comparison.

Source: Findings of psychologists Arthur A. Stone and John Neale at the Long Island Research Institute and the State University of New York at Stony Brook.

Guidelines for The Overworked

Busy people incur more than their share of dangerous stress. *If you have more work than you can handle:* Get better organized. Establish priorities, and then concentrate on doing one job at a time. Recognize your limitations. Don't dwell on failure. Remember past successes. Ask for and use help when you need it. *Bottom line:* The American Medical Association reports that 80% of our diseases are either caused by or aggravated by stress.

•Job involvement can be overdone. Obsessive people create elaborate (but impractical) systems, work by formula, can't take criticism and often immerse themselves in details to avoid big decisions. They lie awake worrying about their jobs, too. But the only result is lost sleep and decreased mental alertness.

Source: *Insight,* Waterford, CT.

To Reduce Stress At Your Desk

- Make certain that your chair is comfortable.
- Quiet your telephone's ring.
- Alter the lighting to reduce glare…or increase brightness.
- Personalize your work space with photos, posters, etc.
- Adopt at least a partial closed-door policy for your office. (If you have no way to be alone in your office, find a place elsewhere in the building where you can take breathers.)
- Avoid tight shirt collars…they can cut blood flow to the brain and result in lightheadedness and panic attacks. Tightly cinched belts are troublesome, too.
- Establish a regular time for meals, especially lunch.

Source: *The Termination Trap* by Stephen Cohen. Williamson Publishing.

Want to Relax? Get a Fish Tank

The aquarium in your dentist's office is not just decoration. Watching fish swim lazily about can have a positively tranquilizing effect. In fact, recent tests showed that fish-watching is as calming as hypnosis or meditation before a tooth extraction.

Source: Study by Aaron Katcher, MD, associate professor of psychiatry, University of Pennsylvania.

- Although tropical fish won't fetch your slippers, they can relieve stress. Watching fish lowers blood pressure for most people.

Source: *Medical Self-Care,* Inverness, CA.

Colors Affect Emotions

Darker colors make most people feel peaceful and less stressed. Brighter colors spark energy and creativity, as well as aggressive and

nervous behavior. *Interesting:* Gray is, for everyone, neutral—it leads to no response.

Source: *Office Biology: Or Why Tuesday Is Your Most Productive Day and Other Relevant Facts for Survival in the Workplace* by Edith Weiner, futurist, strategic thinker and cofounder of the New York consulting firm Weiner, Edrich, Brown, Inc. MasterMedia Limited.

How to Protect Yourself Against Toxic Ideas

Most people—including perfectly intelligent people—subscribe to at least a few misleading opinions, beliefs or philosophies that I call toxic. These toxic ideas lead to frustration, anxiety and even depression instead of the success they promise.

Toxic ideas are often unquestioningly passed on by well-meaning parents, teachers, bosses and friends. I'm not talking about obvious lies like *It's a good idea to intimidate one's subordinates* or *All fat people are jolly.* Toxic ideas are more insidious. They seem true, or they contain a kernel of truth. But when followed automatically or to extremes, they steer us off the path of happiness—and toward misery.

To determine whether a particular idea or belief is toxic, take a good, hard look at the evidence of its validity. A toxic idea collapses under close scrutiny.

Once you've held a toxic belief up to the light, replace it with a healthy counterbelief—and continue to remind yourself of that healthier belief until it becomes second nature.

Most common toxic ideas…

- *Toxic idea:* People can achieve anything they set their minds to. This belief is basic to the American dream—the Horatio Alger rags-to-riches promise that hard work inevitably pays off in success.

This belief is especially destructive because it leads people to feel guilty when they fail to achieve something beyond their capacities. People in this position must cope not only with failure, but also with the feeling that they're lazy and unmotivated.

Accepting your weaknesses is just as important as building on your strengths. Believe in yourself, but be realistic.

Example: As an adolescent, I was interested in architecture and engineering. But my visual/spatial perception was, and still is, very poor. If I had set out to become an architect or engineer, buildings and bridges would now be collapsing.

Instead, I cultivated my skills in problem-solving and working with people—and launched a satisfying and successful career in psychology. I've never regretted it.

I'm not condemning all positive thinking. The power and benefits of optimism are well-documented. But silly, empty positive thinking leads inevitably to grief. Accepting a challenge is quite different from continually bashing your head against a granite wall. *Healthy:* Identifying your assets and making the most of them. *Unhealthy:* Making a commitment to a goal that simply lies beyond your grasp.

Healthy counterbelief: I can achieve a great deal if I set realistic goals and work toward them.

• *Toxic idea:* Kindness always overcomes unkindness. You cannot compel a nasty, vicious person to change his/her ways through your own kindness. Thinking that you can leads only to physical or psychological abuse.

That doesn't mean you should go looking for a fight. In most cases, it makes more sense to walk away. But behavior is often reinforced by its immediate results. If you repay nastiness with niceness, you're simply encouraging the person to continue being nasty.

Instead: If you repay niceness with niceness and stand up to people when they're unkind, they may be prompted to shape up. In the long run, standing up for yourself may require you to avoid the abusive person altogether—even if it means leaving a job, marriage or other relationship.

Healthy counterbelief: I am entitled to courteous and fair treatment.

• *Toxic idea:* Never break a promise. Someone who routinely breaks promises will quickly lose friends. But believing that you must never back out of an agreement can cause you to do things that hurt you…and others.

Example: A young man who was having serious second thoughts about his impending marriage went through with the ceremony anyway …and was soon divorced. Why did he get married even though he had come to realize that he and his fiancée were wrong for each other? Because he had given her his word. Breaking off the engagement would have been painful—but not as painful as getting divorced.

Avoid making promises you can't keep—especially unconditional promises…the kind that begin, *No matter what happens…*

Healthy counterbelief: I'll keep my promises …unless serious, unanticipated circumstances prevent me from doing so.

• *Toxic idea:* An ultimatum is the best way to settle a dispute. Ultimatums can be effective on the battlefield—or in legal matters. Telling an adversary, If you don't call off your troops by noon, our air force will commence bombing…or I'll call the police if you don't stop is sometimes the only way to get results.

In ongoing relationships, however, ultimatums do more harm than good. They are coercive and adversarial—qualities that have no place in intimacy.

Your goal in any disagreement with a loved one—or even a colleague—should not be to vanquish your opponent. It should be to talk about the issue and seek an equitable solution.

Ultimatums must be considered a last resort —to be used only in extreme circumstances.

Healthy counterbelief: I am more likely to resolve everyday disagreements through negotiation and compromise.

• *Toxic idea:* Trust your gut feelings. Intuition is an important source of information and guidance—but it's only one source, and a fallible one. *Examples:*

•Someone who first strikes you as cold and aloof may indeed be remote…or may simply be shy. You can't tell for sure without seeing the person in a variety of circumstances.

•If a business investment feels like a money-maker, you may be sensing an important trend …or may be letting your dreams of fortune blind you to a potential disaster. Take time to evaluate the opportunity rationally before risking your savings.

Healthy counterbelief: I take my hunches seriously—but I always check them against other evidence.

• *Toxic idea:* When in doubt, always say "no." In recent years, a host of popular books have urged us to assert ourselves by saying "no" to other people's requests.

Certainly, giving in to someone's every whim is unhealthy—no one wants to be a doormat. But between intimates, saying "no" too often can kill a relationship.

I've found that where loved ones are concerned, it makes sense to say "yes" whenever you can. Of course, one person shouldn't do all of the yessing. If you have a valid reason not to grant a particular request, by all means explain it. But in general, the word "yes" contributes far more to an atmosphere of trust, closeness and cooperation than the word "no."

Healthy counterbelief: With people I care about, I say 'yes' as often as I can.

Source: Arnold A. Lazarus, PhD, distinguished professor of psychology, Graduate School of Applied & Professional Psychology, Rutgers University, New Brunswick, New Jersey. Dr. Lazarus's latest book is *Don't Believe It for a Minute! Forty Toxic Ideas that Are Driving You Crazy.* Impact Publishers.

How Not to Let Oprah, Sally Jessy and Geraldo Drive You Crazy

If you watch daytime talk shows, you probably get the impression that we're all victims of emotional trauma. Not true. This is an imaginary world, one designed more to entertain than to enlighten.

Danger: By immersing unsuspecting viewers in this imaginary world, daytime talk shows…

• Give viewers the impression that emotional illness is ubiquitous. Implication: Without the help of a therapist, we may not even be aware of our problems.

• Promote bad psychotherapy. Therapists who appear regularly on TV are often "trauma hunters" who espouse simplistic views of human emotion.

The easiest way to defend yourself against the daytime talks is not to watch. If you insist on watching, remember…

• The human spirit is resilient. Holocaust survivors who managed to put their lives back together again did so not by bemoaning their cruel fate—but through determination and hard work. The rest of us would do well to adopt the same strategy.

• Help is close to home. Professional help may be needed for severe emotional problems. But often all it takes to feel better is to surround ourselves with caring friends.

• Problems and solutions lie in the present. People who experience trauma almost never have difficulty remembering it. The talk shows would have you believe otherwise.

For most of us, the real "villain" in our lives isn't an abusive parent or spouse, but simply change. If you are feeling sad or anxious, ask yourself, "What's going on in my life now that is substantially different from five years ago? What resources have helped me through previous difficulties, and how can I use them to help me now?"

If you believe you could benefit from psychotherapy, be sure to get the right kind.

Research has shown that a therapist's degree is less important than his/her approach to the therapeutic process. It's best to interview several therapists before making a choice.

Find someone who answers "yes" to these questions…

• During your training, were you observed by a supervisor? Therapists who have not had such training may be less effective than those who have.

• Will you encourage me to seek help from friends, family and other important people in my life? Some therapists are so eager to assume an important role in their clients' lives that they keep their clients from asking others for help.

• Will you outline specific courses of action that I can undertake to alleviate my distress? Watch out for therapists who are so eager to explore the "whys" of your problems that they are unable to help you take steps to get better.

Source: Terence W. Campbell, PhD, a clinical and forensic psychologist in private practice in Sterling Heights, Michigan. He is the author of *Beware the Talking Cure: Psychotherapy May Be Hazardous to Your Mental Health.* Upton Books.

Proven Ways to Stay Well

There is a heavy price to be paid when feelings are denied or repressed. Lethargy, boredom and a lack of enthusiasm toward life may be the consequences. Those who are unaccustomed to dealing with feelings in healthy ways often seek out other means to cover up those feelings or distract themselves, such as alcohol, food, drugs, TV, unhealthy relationships or compulsive work.

Befriend your emotional self. Accept emotions as valuable signals that tell you something is in need of attention. *How to acknowledge emotions...*

- Write an angry letter and then tear it up.
- Compose a poem about your grief.
- Draw, paint or even dance to express your feelings.
- Exercise vigorously.
- Talk about your feelings.
- Let fear be there.
- Let discouragement be there.

Don't try to chase these emotions away. Look at them. Express them when it is appropriate to do so. Then move on.

Simplify your life...

Becoming well in body, mind and spirit is not nearly as difficult as it may seem. Wellness is not a matter of accumulating something, like more research or experience.

Rather, wellness is realized by unburdening yourself of all those things that prevent the natural state of healthiness from being present. To become well is to appreciate simplicity. *Examples:*

- Simplify your life.
- Simplify your diet.
- Take time to rest your mind.
- One breath is precious...one smile...one day of seeing the sun.

Honor your body's wisdom...

Inhabit your body. Learn to start listening to what it is saying to you and to trust what you hear.

Listening to others instead of yourself...or saying *yes* when you mean *no* are just two examples of the many ways you shortchange yourself. Wellness is about "coming home"—taking up residence inside your own body once again.

Reprogram yourself...

Current research in the field of psychoneuro-immunology verifies what folk healers have known for centuries—that thinking and emotions have a direct impact on the strength of the immune system.

The immune system is the first line of defense against disease. Strengthening your immune system consciously, through the use of imagery or nurturing self-talk, gives you a much better chance of maintaining whole-body health.

Connect to the earth for healing...

When was the last time you sat on the ground or touched the earth in some way? This may seem silly, but physical contact with soil, natural waters, sunlight and fresh air is healing.

When stress has built up, a walk around the block is often all that is needed to restore perspective.

Beyond that, you connect with forces stronger than the individual self in nature, and this puts everything in perspective.

A partnership in healing...

There will be times in your life when you need the care and attention of a helping professional—a doctor, psychologist, social worker, etc.*

When you're looking for such professionals, it's important to find people willing to take the time to answer questions and listen to your concerns. If you find someone who is unwilling to do this, switch to someone who will.

Bottom line...

Getting started on these small changes will help you make a difference in your life. We hope that you will experience increased self-awareness and self-appreciation...have a sense of greater inner strength...and, above all, live a healthier life.

*Helping professionals interested in learning more about developing partnership relationships with their patients or clients can contact Wellness Associates, 707-937-2331. A book, *Wellness for Helping Professionals: Creating Compassionate Cultures*, is available from Wellness Associates.

Source: John Travis, MD, and Regina Sara Ryan, co-authors of *Wellness: Small Changes You Can Use to Make a Big Difference*. Ten Speed Press.

19

Simple Stress-Busters

New Ways to Have Fun In the 1990s

In the next few years, we'll see dramatic shifts in the way we have fun, whether it's pursuing recreation or being entertained.

Driving the changes: Aging of the baby boom generation, plus a wider rift between those who have money and those who don't... and between those with plenty of spare time and those who don't have enough time to take care of job and family.

What to expect...

•A closer link between health and pleasure. Jogging, for instance, will be on the decline, while aerobic therapy is on the way in. In a sense, pastimes will become more pleasurable.

Reason: Until recently, things we enjoyed often had to with overindulgence and were bad for our health. Today, more pastimes are becoming good for our health, or at least not harmful.

On the way out: Big dinners, evenings of drinking, spending the day at the beach (since we've learned about the harmful effects of radiation). Shopping for the fun of shopping will also lose much of its appeal since many of us will be under greater economic pressure.

Fun-time activities for the future...

Bird watching (already a fast-growing hobby), food gardening, structured relaxation for stress management, and hanging out at "brain bars" (establishments where nonalcoholic drinks are laced with nutrients that supposedly help our cerebral abilities) and networking with people on computer systems.

In the coming years, we'll see a continuation of the trend where some people have a great deal of time and money while others have too little. That means fun will become more closely linked to the ability to find time for it.

Many Americans will have to relearn the art of having fun with their children, an activity that was largely shoved aside in the last two decades. And most of us will have to take greater care in scheduling a scarcer amount of fun time with family and friends.

The goal: To enjoy taking time off without losing ground professionally.

Many of us are already relying on new technologies to help with this aspect of time management. Cellular phones, for instance, often show up at football games and restaurants.

Prediction: Most people will soon tire of trying to have fun while they're electronically tethered to the office.

Source: Edith Weiner is president of Weiner, Edrich, Brown, Inc., futurists and strategic planning consultants, 200 E. 33 St., New York 10016.

25 Ways to Be Good to Yourself

Little things can make a significant difference in improving your health and your outlook on life. The following are simple suggestions for revitalizing your energy and personal productivity…

1. Establish uninterrupted quiet time—each day—to accomplish specific tasks. You will find that your production level will increase and your stress level will decrease—because you are actually getting something done.

2. Take a walk instead of a coffee break. Physical activity vents excess pressure. Walking is one of the most effective aerobic exercises and one that almost everyone can do. It is also a wonderful way to stimulate creative thinking. And when there's time to get past that first mile, you'll find your mind just flows with ideas.

3. Make a checklist for tomorrow. At the end of each day—before you leave your work area—make a list of the six most important things to do the following day. Arrange these tasks in the order of their importance. Each morning, begin with the first item on your list and scratch it off when you are finished. Work your way right down the list. If you don't finish an item, put it on the list for the following day.

4. Take a mini-vacation every four hours during the day. Get up. Walk around. Look out the window. Daydream for a few minutes. Get a drink of water. The purpose is to move yourself around both mentally and physically for just a few minutes.

5. Get the sleep that you need. Lack of sleep can make you more susceptible to stress—and more irritable. The amount of sleep you require may be very different from that of others. Don't try to judge how much sleep or rest you should have based on someone else's needs. Get the amount that you need. You know your body better than anyone else. *Pay attention to it.*

6. See failures as learning experiences instead of roadblocks. Look at the situation as another experience that can help you grow.

7. Unclutter your life. Get rid of the stuff you never use—those clothes you never wear, books that only sit on your shelf. Drop memberships in organizations in which participating has become an unpleasant chore. Cancel subscriptions to magazines you don't read.

8. Spend time with special friends. Do something enjoyable with the special people in your world at least twice a month. Remember to smile, laugh, have fun and enjoy life with each other. Enjoy dinner with "thinking" friends. *Important:* Set aside specific time for each other. If you don't, other things will fill your schedule.

9. Be kind to others. What goes around comes around. When you are kind to other people, they will be kind to you.

10. Don't be afraid of change. Don't let anyone tell you that you can't do something because it has never been done. That's the time to *begin.*

11. Explore your talents. Are you great at building friendships? Making peace? Do you make people feel good? Make a list of what you are good at and post it where you can see it first thing every morning. Start the day knowing how special you are.

12. Create a wish bank. Find a special box or jar and create a wish bank for yourself. Make a list of things you would like to do but just never seem to get around to. Put some five-minute items in there. Add some 10-minute items or maybe some 15- or 30-minute items. Then periodically draw out a wish card and make it come true.

13. Give the gift of time. The greatest gift you can give to anyone, including yourself, is the gift of time. We all receive 86,400 seconds a day. We either use them—*or lose them.* Because time is so precious and cannot be expanded, when

we share it with someone else, we give them a rare and beautiful gift.

14. Be a kid again. Sometimes, as adults, we are so afraid that someone is going to see us that we forget how to enjoy and just be. Find a pile of dried leaves and listen to them crunch as you walk through them. Walk barefoot on grass that is still covered with early-morning dew. For one day, leave your inhibitions behind and be a child again.

15. Touch the earth. Plant some flowers in your flower bed or window box. Improve the beauty in your world. Dig in the dirt. Let the soft, moist soil run through your fingers. There is something very peaceful about working with the earth.

16. Daydream. Take a moment now and then to dream about something that you very much want to have happen. Visualize it in the greatest of detail—the colors, the sounds, the smells, the sights—exactly as you wish it to happen.

17. Buy a gift for yourself—*for no reason at all*. Have it gift-wrapped and then take your time unwrapping it.

18. Take a joy break. Sometimes we just need to laugh. Keep a drawer or box with articles, jokes and stories that will tickle your funny bone. Your mind will work better and you will be much more productive when you laugh while you work.

19. Think in terms of *right now*. During the day, stop and ask yourself, *Is there a better way, right now, for me to take care of me?* The answer to this question may be to relax your shoulders, take a walk, switch projects, tackle something you have been putting off, have someone help you lift something or maybe take a lunch break.

20. Act enthusiastic. Don't save enthusiasm for special occasions. Use it now. Share it with everyone you meet.

21. Send yourself flowers. And don't forget the card. Write a very special message on it and sign it "An admirer."

22. Unplan an evening. Set aside one evening a week that is totally unplanned—time when you can do anything you want to.

23. Limit your *pity parties*. If you must have one at all, limit it to one a week and make sure it lasts no longer than 15 minutes. Put on some sad music and really get in tune with your emo-

tions. Cry. Feel sorry for yourself. Review all the depressing situations you can come up with. But be sure to set a timer, because when 15 minutes have passed, you are through for the week.

24. Live in the moment. Too often we try to live yesterday, today and tomorrow at the same time. We can't do that. Tomorrow is only a promissory note. All we have is today...right now. We need to learn to live one day and even one moment at a time because this is all we have. Nothing else is certain.

25. Believe in you. You are unique. You can do things no one else can do. You can be things no one else can be. You touch the lives of other people in a way that only you can. You are here for a very important reason. Your purpose in this world can be fulfilled by no one else.

Source: Donna Watson, PhD, president of the Donna Watson Group in Oklahoma City. Dr. Watson conducts 150 workshops annually on stress management. She is the author of *101 Ways to Be Good to Yourself*, Energy Press, 5275 McCormick Mt. Rd., Austin, Texas 78734.

How to Make the Most Of Your Time...Without Driving Yourself Crazy

People have less free time than they did a generation ago—37% less than in 1973, according to a recent Harris survey. There is, though, more time available than you think.

Three general rules...

•Eliminate slave-of-habit routines. *Example:* Spending 45 minutes each morning with the daily paper...when you can get the news you need with a quick scan of the front page or 10 minutes with an all-news radio station.

•Change your schedule so that you're at your best for your most important and challenging tasks. Many executives waste the start of their work day—when they may be freshest —by going through their mail. They'd do better by plunging into a tough report and saving the mail for later in the day, when they're slowing down.

•Learn to do two or three things at the same time. When you go to the bank, always bring something you need to read on the inevitable line. When you make a call and are placed on hold, switch to your speaker phone and take care of some paperwork. When your party comes on the line switch back.

Most time-saving ideas are small in scale—but those minutes add up. In most cases, a newly efficient person can save an hour a day—and that is a significant amount of time.

The morning routine:

•Pop out of bed as soon as you wake up, rather than lingering under the covers. *Incentive:* Think of the most pleasant activity on your schedule that day.

•Plan a pre-breakfast work segment—30 to 60 minutes of uninterrupted concentration in some quiet part of your home.

•Write a "to-do" list in your daily organizer book—a schedule of the high-priority tasks you need to address. Do it the night before. Less urgent tasks should be listed under "Things to Be Done This Week" and "Things for Following Weeks."

•Schedule tasks that require others' actions for early in the day. By reaching people early, you're more likely to get them to do what you need that day.

Organizing your office:

•Angle your desk away from open doorways, busy corridors or windows—all sources of distraction.

•Keep your desk neat. Clear away everything unrelated to the project at hand. *To dispose of clutter:* Eliminate dispensable items, including photos, gadgets and magazines. Put in a few inexpensive bookshelves you can get to without rising.

•Install the largest wastebasket your office can gracefully contain.

Communications:

•Use a dictation device, rather than a secretary's shorthand. *Advantages:* More speed and flexibility...simpler changes...enhanced concentration.

•Computerized electronic mail eliminates much time-wasting telephone tag. *For maximum efficiency:* Note when you'll be available for a return phone call.

•Rely on your answering machine to screen incoming calls. Your highest priority should always be the most important item on your schedule...which is rarely attending to the telephone.

The media:

Read selectively. Concentrate on one general newspaper. *Before you start reading:* Examine the general and business news indexes for stories of interest.

•If you find an item of interest in a newspaper or magazine, rip it out and read it when appropriate—and throw the rest of the publication away.

•Read for 15 to 30 minutes before bedtime. This is a good time for books that inspire or entertain.

Source: Ray Josephs, public-relations pioneer and author of the newly revised *How to Gain An Extra Hour Every Day.* Penguin USA, 375 Hudson St., New York 10014.

Planning Your Leisure Time

If you're like most people, there are lots of activities you'd like to do in your leisure time, but you never seem to get around to them. The solution is to plan—not so much that you feel like you're "on the job," but not so little that you fail to accomplish whatever is important to you, whether that means learning French or going dancing. *Recommended:*

•Create a "to do" list for your spare time just as you might for your workday. You probably don't want every hour accounted for, but you should at least list what you most want to do with each leisure evening or weekend.

•Allot some specific times on a regular basis when you will pursue the leisure activities that are most important to you. A scheduled time will help ensure the successful fulfillment of your plan.

•If it's culture you're after, consider getting at least one subscription series to eliminate some of the paperwork and phone calling that often accompany even leisure-time plans. (You will also avoid wasting time in line!)

• Set up regular social contacts, like monthly Saturday dinner with specific friends, so you spend less time coordinating your meetings and more time enjoying them.

• If you use too much of your recreation time for household chores, try delegating those tasks to professional help or family members. Or do it more efficiently and less frequently.

• If you often work in your leisure hours, consider that you may be more efficient if you plan, and carry out, pleasurable activities that energize you (and prevent work burnout).

• To keep your leisure-time plans active (not reactive to other people's demands on you), make appointments with yourself. You will be less inclined to give up your plans if someone else asks you to do something, since you have a previous commitment to yourself.

• Just as a "quiet hour" of uninterrupted time at the office increases your work efficiency, a "quiet" leisure hour enhances your nonwork time. On a fixed schedule, if possible, take some time each evening and weekend to meditate, listen to music, reflect, or just plain old "unwind."

• How can you find more hours for recreation? By setting your alarm clock only half an hour earlier on weekends you'll gain four hours a month. Become more efficient at work, so you can leave earlier (and not have to take work home as often). To find the time to read that mystery novel, try switching from showers to baths, and read in the tub.

Source: J. L. Barkas, Ph.D., author of *Creative Time Management*, Prentice-Hall, Englewood Cliffs, NJ.

47 Inexpensive Ways To Have a Good Time

Having fun can't be calculated in dollars and cents. Sometimes the less money you spend, the more you enjoy yourself.

Here are some inexpensive ways to have fun:
• Explore the beach and collect seashells.
• Visit the zoo and feed the monkeys.
• Go to a free concert in the park.
• Pack a picnic and drive to an attractive spot for lunch.

• Go skiing at your local park or a nearby mountain.
• Window-shop at your favorite stores.
• Eat early-bird-special dinners at local restaurants. Then go home and see a movie on TV.
• Hug each other more.
• Dress up with your favorite person and enjoy a formal dinner at home with fine food and wine.
• Go camping or backpacking.
• Go gallery-hopping. See the latest art exhibits.
• Enjoy your public library. Go to the reading room and catch up on the new magazines.
• Go for a drive on the back roads to just enjoy the scenery.
• Visit friends in a nearby city. (Arrive around lunchtime.)
• Eat dinner at home. Then go out for dessert and coffee.
• Instead of eating dinner out, eat lunch out over the weekends. It's less expensive.
• Seek out discount tickets and two-fers for local entertainment.
• Take in the local museum's cultural events, including low-priced lectures and concerts.
• Invite friends in for drinks when a good movie is on TV.
• Take an afternoon walk in the park.
• Row a boat on the lake.
• Have a beer-and-pizza party for friends.
• Go back to the old family board games.
• Raise exotic plants or unusual herbs in a window box.
• Learn to paint or sculpt.
• Learn calligraphy.
• Take a long-distance bus ride.
• Go out to the airport and watch the planes.
• Visit the local amusement park and try the rides.
• Have friends over for a bring-your-own-specialty dinner.
• Become a do-it-yourselfer.
• Take an aerobic exercise course.
• Join a local political club.
• Go shopping for something really extravagant. Keep the sales slip and return the item the next day.
• Play cards for pennies, not dollars.

- Go to the races and place $2 bets.
- Explore your own city as a tourist would.
- Learn to be a gourmet cook.
- Treat yourself to breakfast in bed.
- Hold a family reunion.
- Attend religious services.
- Learn a foreign language.
- Join a local chorale or dramatic club.
- Watch local sports teams practice.
- Play golf or tennis at local parks or courses.
- Read everything in your area of interest at the library.
- Buy books. Get many hours of pleasure (and useful information) for still relatively few dollars.

Keeping Street Noise Out of Your Home

Noise intrusion is a constant and nagging problem in many buildings because of thin walls and badly insulated floors and ceilings.

How to noise-proof walls:

- Hang sound-absorbing materials, such as quilts, decorative rugs, carpets or blankets. *Note:* Cork board and heavy window draperies absorb sound within a room but do not help much with noise from outside.
- If you don't want to hang heavy materials directly on your walls, consider a frame that attaches to the wall. Insulation goes on the wall within the frame, and then a fabric is affixed to the frame.

How to noise-proof ceilings:

- Apply acoustical tile directly to the ceiling with adhesive for a quick and inexpensive fix.
- If you can undertake more extensive work, put in a dropped ceiling of acoustical tile with about six inches of insulation between the new and existing ceiling.

How to noise-proof floors:

- Install a thick plush carpet over a dense sponge rubber padding.
- *Key:* The padding must be dense, at least three-eighths of an inch thick. Your foot should not press down to the floor when you step on the padding.

How to Ease Long-Distance Driving

For a safe, healthy trip when you're driving a long distance...

- Do most of your driving during daytime hours. Visual acuity is lessened at night.
- Be particularly careful to check out your car's exhaust system before leaving—a leak can send odorless but deadly gases into the car.
- To insure sufficient fresh air inside the car, leave both a front and a back window open. Tailgate windows should be kept closed. Use your air conditioner. It provides fresh air and quiet inside the car. Although it reduces gas mileage, the loss is not much more than the loss from open windows' drag.
- Use seat belts and shoulder harnesses to relieve fatigue, as well as to boost safety.
- Take 20- to 30-minute rest breaks after every one-and-a-half or two hours of driving.
- Exercise during your breaks.
- Eat frequent high-protein snacks for improved driving performance.
- Don't stare straight ahead, even if you're the only car on the road. Keep your eyes moving.

Car Games

To make the ride less tedious, here are some games to play:

Educational games...

- Spelling Bee. Take along a dictionary.
- Discover America. As someone keeps score, riders name the states of the union and their capitals.
- Add a Letter. Start with a single letter and go around building a word.
- I'm a Famous Person (also known as Botticelli). Pretend to be a celebrity—living or dead. Give clues to your personality as others try to guess who you are.
- Quiz Kids. Before the trip, collect an assortment of difficult questions and answers. (You can use Trivial Pursuit cards.)

•Words. Select a long word, such as separation, and then see how many words can be made from its letters. Have pencil and paper handy.

Silly games…

•Famous Pairs. Within a given period of time, perhaps half an hour, reel off the first names of famous couples. *Examples:* George and Martha, Ron and Nancy, Bill and Hillary.

•Don't Say That Word. Prohibit certain words from the conversation, such as *it, no, yes.* Try to maintain a dialog without using them.

•What Time Do We Arrive? Each person guesses the time of arrival at various places along the route—the next big city on the map, when you stop for lunch or gasoline.

•Animals. See who can spot the most cows, horses, etc. in the fields by the side of the road.

•Name That License Plate. Look for funny personal license plates that have names, initials or unusual numerical combinations.

•Plates and States. Keep lists of cars from different states. The person who gets the most states within a set period wins.

•Sign Games. Think up lines to rhyme with interesting billboards or signs.

•Let's Find It. Agree to look for one special thing—a covered bridge, a bright red automobile. The first one to spot it wins and then selects the next thing to look for.

•If I Were a Millionaire. Ask what people would want if they were millionaires. Then ask them for second wishes.

•Favorite Books and Movies. Review the books and movies you have liked best. Tell what makes them enjoyable.

•Sports Favorites. Prepare a series of questions about sports events and stars before you depart. Then quiz sports fans while on the trip.

•Where Am I Going? Mentally select a place where you are headed. Give hints about your imaginary destination, and let the other passengers guess where you are going.

Song games…

•Sing-Along. See how many songs you can sing by different composers—Cole Porter, Irving Berlin, Billy Joel, The Beatles.

•Sing Along With Me. Bring a book of popular songs and lead the car in an old-fashioned sing-along.

•Tap-a-Song. Tap out the rhythm of a famous song. Give each person three guesses.

Semi-serious games…

•Personal History. Spin tales of family remembrances—a time spent with grandparents, a favorite birthday, a lovely trip taken in the past. Give each person a chance to share an experience.

•Play Psychiatrist. Ask everyone what bothers them most about their lives. Try to help them resolve their problems.

How to Fight the Blahs

•Count your blessings.
•See a funny movie or TV show.
•Read a joke book.
•Go for a long, brisk walk.
•Spend a weekend in a deluxe hotel with breakfast in bed.
•Listen to beautiful music.
•Read a very good and engrossing novel.
•Exercise a lot.
•Rent a convertible and ride with the wind around you.
•Go to the airport and watch the planes land and take off.
•Buy a new and exciting game for your video machine.
•Look at old family albums.
•Sing songs around the piano with friends.
•Get a haircut.
•Go for a swim.
•Buy a dog or cat to keep you company.
•Get some new tapes or records.
•Buy something you have always wanted.
•Fix up your house.
•Go to an art museum.
•Meditate.
•Clean out your closets or bureau drawers.
•List your assets and accomplishments.
•Call a special friend who always makes you feel happy.
•Take a deep, warm, bubbly bath.
•Eat a large piece of chocolate cake.
•Blast the stereo and sing along at the top of your lungs.
•Spend some time at a religious retreat.

Fighting Holiday Blues

Visits to psychiatrists and physicians jump 25% or more during the holiday season that lasts from Thanksgiving to New Year's. *The most common underlying causes of distress:* Holiday depression, boredom, and burnout. *Specifically:*

• A longing for happier holidays (real or imagined) in days past.

• Loneliness. This is especially true for those in a new location or those who have recently lost a loved one or gone through a divorce.

• The feeling that holidays should be a happy time, that family life should be perfect, and that presents will bring your heart's desires.

• For those whose health is frail, a primitive fear of not getting through the cold, dark winter.

The best ways to combat the blues…

• Don't expect too much. Unrealistic anticipation only breeds disappointment. As expectations are reduced, every pleasant surprise becomes a bonus.

• Be selective about the festivities you attend. Enjoy the fellowship more than the alcohol.

• Try not to be alone. But spend your time with people who are comfortable and easy to be around.

• When the holidays seem too grim, take a trip or try some totally new experience. Perhaps volunteer work in a hospital, where the emphasis will be on bringing cheer to others.

• Skip those Christmas-shopping crowds by ordering your gifts by mail and visiting small, local shops or those in out-of-the-way places.

• Keep holiday entertaining simple. If traditions become too much of a burden, try something offbeat (for example, decorating with cut flowers instead of ornate evergreens). Or, go out. Above all, don't try to give huge, exhausting affairs.

• Unless you love to receive cards from others, save the bother and expense of sending them yourself.

How to Really Appreciate Movies

If you really want to appreciate movies, stray a little from the heavily beaten track. There are a number of good critics in small or specialized magazines who can alert you to fine—and unusual—new films, as well as notable revivals.

Movie buffs typically go through three stages in their appreciation of films:

• First, they find movies awe-inspiring magic.

• Second, they begin to realize those are actors up there and that all kinds of technology are involved. In this stage, which some people never leave, they become "fans." Many fans don't care about movies—they're just interested in following their favorite actors.

• Third, they realize movies aren't magic, that it may be a miracle they ever get made, but that they're a human achievement that also happens to be marvelous. At this stage they can start to look at movies critically.

To get the maximum enjoyment from movies…

• Watch a lot of them. Make a special effort to see foreign films. You'll begin to see what's original and fresh and what's stereotyped.

• Learn about movie forms and genres and the unique visual language of cinema.

• Read, follow other art forms. Read about psychology, politics, history and other branches of knowledge.

• Avoid the rush. Don't dash off to see the latest blockbuster. It'll be around a while. See a film more likely to close soon, even though it was well-reviewed.

• Watch movies on cable TV and on cassettes. Both these forms have done a lot to make film scholarship possible and good movies accessible.

• Go to foreign films. More than a few are worth seeing, but most people aren't interested in them anymore. In the past, the "ooh-la-la" factor drew viewers. But now that American films are no longer censored, foreign films have lost their cachet.

Source: Andrew Sarris, film critic for *The New York Observer*, a professor of cinema at Columbia University, and author of *The American Cinema: Directors and Directions*, Octagon Press, New York, and *Politics and Cinema*, Columbia University Press, Irvington, NY.

Don't Let Your Vacation Home Cut Into Your Leisure Time

The most desirable thing to look for in a weekend house is ease of maintenance.

- Get rid of rugs in the summer.
- Ask the landlord to remove his accumulations of dust-catching peacock feathers and other decorator touches.

Keep your own importations to a minimum.

- Cut down on weekend cleaning chores and outdoor work with hired help.
- Consider expanding leisure time by commuting with the laundry. That's cumbersome, but better than hours in a laundromat on a sunny afternoon.
- Cultivate the fine art of list-making. Shopping and menu planning can be almost painless if the list is done right.
- If you're planning a Saturday dinner party, don't rely on the local supermarket for the perfect roast unless you've ordered (and confirmed) in advance. The accompanying wines might be better purchased at home, too, unless you're sure of your local supplier.
- Don't forget to take the same precautions as you would for a trip—extra reading glasses and copies of prescriptions might save you an unwanted journey home.

Unusual and Adventuresome Vacations

- Backpack in the West.
- Visit Australia's haunting Great Barrier Reef Islands.
- Take an air safari to East Africa.
- Heli-ski in the Canadian Rockies.
- Visit native villages in New Guinea.
- Canoe down the Amazon River.
- Balloon in California.
- Cruise the Mississippi.
- Ride the Colorado River on a raft.
- Barge through the rivers of Europe.
- See the unspoiled wildlife on the Galapagos Islands.
- Study-tour in Mexico.
- Go on a religious retreat.
- Work on a kibbutz in Israel.
- Explore Australia's outback regions.
- Visit the ancient city of Machu Picchu in Peru.
- Join an archaeological dig in China or Tunisia.
- Climb the Himalayas and visit Nepal.
- Go deep-sea fishing off the coast of Baja, California.
- Visit Bali and learn about its ancient music.
- Learn a foreign language by living with natives.
- Explore the coral reefs of the West Indies.
- Visit Alaska's national parks.

The Wonderful New Art Of Dining at Home

Gone with the extravagant 1980s is the nonchalant going out for $100 dinners-for-two several nights a week.

Today's two-wage-earner families are tired at the end of the day. Their idea of fun is to entertain at home—but in small numbers and serving simple food.

In contrast, at-home chefs from the previous generation took great pride in being able to turn out culinary triumphs like Beef Wellington with Sauce Perigueux that were the rage in the 1960s and 1970s when everyone aspired to be like Dione Lucas or Julia Child. Today's twenty- and thirtysomethings often can't cook at all and may never really need to. Despite the seemingly endless number of cookbooks published each year, very few are best sellers and many have a very short life.

Fresh and healthy…

What is undeniably true today, however, is a tremendous emphasis on health. We are all watching our weight and cholesterol, and many of us don't want to eat beef, much less the rich duxelles and foie gras stuffing that

429

goes between the filet and the pastry wrapping in a classic Beef Wellington.

Among the favored entrees today: Fish and chicken...and even totally vegetarian creations.

Also popular: Chili, pasta dishes and such homey American favorites as chicken pot pie—and good ones can often be purchased ready-made.

Instead of serving three or four courses, most of today's hosts and hostesses settle for a light starter—perhaps a cold or hot soup—or maybe just a few simple hors d'oeuvres, an entree accompanied by a vegetable or salad and a small but elegant dessert, followed by decaf espresso.

A little help...helps a lot...

What's made entertaining at home a lot more doable for working people these days is the wide variety of foods and specialties that can be purchased from outside sources.

From freshly made pastas (with sauces and trimmings) to crispy cooked chicken...to an endless array of tempting precut salad ingredients...a whole meal can be put together with very little chopping or time-consuming preparation by the hosts.

If you're throwing something on the grill, for example, it's very easy to foil wrap a few sliced vegetables like eggplant, onions and zucchini with colorful peppers and roast them, too. Pick up one of the interesting premade pasta or potato salads to serve on the side.

While almost everyone loves a rich little dessert treat, almost no one has to make one anymore. Virtually every town or suburban hamlet has a patisserie or a special bakery that turns out tiny little fruit tarts or sinfully rich chocolate truffles. Or serve mixed fruit with some elegant cookies. Even some supermarket frozen desserts are becoming quite acceptable. *Examples:* Chocolate-covered ice cream bonbons, frozen cheesecake that can be dressed up with fresh berries and a raspberry sauce.

Concentrate on the ambiance...

Although there are many fine small caterers around these days who are more than willing to prepare at-home dinners, my sense is that few people are using them. Even those who could afford to use a caterer perceive that they cannot ...or feel that this would seem pretentious in the hard-pressed 1990s.

As we go forward in this decade, there will be less and less need for people to learn to cook, unless they just love cooking as a creative outlet.

Where most of us will use our creativity, however, is in concocting an interesting menu, putting various food items together and setting a pretty table. *Important:* Offering a warm and inviting environment in which guests can relax and unwind from the cares of the day.

Helpful: Choose a nice wine and serve it in appropriate stem glasses...have a few flowering plants or fresh flowers around.

Put some thought into the presentation of foods that have been purchased elsewhere. If you're serving deli potato salad, for example, be sure to garnish the platter with leafy green lettuce or radicchio. Snip a little fresh parsley, dill, basil or tarragon over salads.

For those who feel somewhat more adventurous this summer, try putting together a hearty salad meal such as tuna nicoise—with fresh broiled tuna, green beans, tomatoes, anchovies and black Kalamata olives with sliced new potatoes vinaigrette. Take a cue from the many fine restaurants that are now serving salad meals using various combinations of fresh vegetables and baby lettuces with warm sliced broiled chicken or fish.

Bottom line...

When entertaining at home today, almost anything goes—so long as it's fresh, looks pretty, has color and texture and, of course, tastes good. After all, the point is to get together with friends, not to prove you can outdo Julia Child.

Source: Irena Chalmers, a food writer and author of many cooking/food books. Her latest is *The Great American Food Almanac*, HarperCollins, 10 E. 53 St., New York 10022. She is currently at work on a massive new project, the *Whole Earth Book of Food*.

Enjoy an Amusement Park Visit

Go on Monday or Tuesday when it's least crowded...check the opening hours (some actually open a half hour before the posted time)

...aim first for the ride or activity that's most important to you and then work your way around in a circular pattern...check ahead for special admission packages and discounts (entering after 4 p.m, groups of 10 or more, affinity group discounts)...call before you go to be sure that the park is open (they can be booked for company parties).

Source: *AAA World*, 12600 Fair Lakes Circle, Fairfax, Virginia 22033.

Super Bathtubs for Fun... For Health

Whirlpools—tubs with jets—are more popular now than ever—and come in more varieties than ever.

Inexpensive whirlpools resemble standard tubs (as small as 5' by 32") equipped with four jets. *More expensive:* Tubs with up to eight jets ...usually larger ovals or rectangles—and those that come in designer colors. They may take deep, free-form shapes and are as large as 8' by 8'. Some seat four. *Details:*

Cost: For basic whirlpools—$1,000–$3,000. For high-end whirlpools—up to $8,000.

Material: Lighter weight acrylic tubs are easier to install than those of enamelled cast iron, but acrylics scratch more easily if cleaned with abrasives.

Brands: Jacuzzi, Kohler and American Standard are three widely respected brands. Kallista offers only high-end tubs, has unique shapes and will produce any color the buyer desires.

Possible problems...

•*Need for more hot water:* Most homes have 40-gallon hot water heaters. A big tub demands that much, leaving none for other uses. *Solution:* Put in a larger (60- to 75-gallon) hot water heater. *Cost:* $600 + labor (*labor rates differ:* $40/hr.–$100/hr.).

•*Vibration:* Without proper installation, the tub can cause noise in the room below it. Discuss this with your contractor very thoroughly.

•Access to the motor is essential if repairs are needed. Usually—but not always—this can be managed without great trouble. Often, the motor is installed near a closet or in a cabinet.

•Structural problems caused by the weight. A structural engineer should check an old house (pre-1930s) before a tub is installed.

•*Electrical:* In most states, a whirlpool must be run on a special circuit that blocks any surge of current into the tub—to protect against electrocutions.

Source: Sheldon Malc, general manager of Davis & Warshow, the largest distributor of whirlpools in the New York area, 150 E. 58 St., New York 10155.

How to Take Better Vacation Photographs

Point-and-shoot and automatic/auto focus cameras have made it easier for travelers to take pictures. Yet, many people are not happy with the results. Blurry images, dull color and badly exposed subjects are just a few of the problems.

Ways to help you take better photographs...

•Be sure your camera works properly and that you know how to use it. You would be surprised by the number of people who take old cameras to their travel destinations, only to find that they no longer work. Others take new cameras and forget the instruction manuals. Then, they can't figure out how to use the cameras.

Self-defense: Test your camera before you leave by shooting and developing a roll of film.

•Think about what you want to say with your photographs before you take them. If you love the glamorous, glittery side of New York, for instance, photograph glitzy subjects, like fancy store windows, neon lights or skyline views.

•Compose your photographs through the camera lens. Don't view a subject with your eyes and then quickly put the camera up to shoot. Instead, look through the viewfinder while moving around to see how the three-dimensional view you see with your eyes translates into the two-dimensional view of the lens.

•Be aware of the background before you snap the shot. Many people don't notice unattractive signposts or utility lines in the backgrounds until their photographs are developed.

•Be patient. Wait, with your camera ready, for a child to laugh, a sailboat to go under a bridge or ducks to settle on a lake.

•On sunny days, photograph early or late in the day. Overhead sun at noon causes shadows underneath people's eyes. In early and late afternoon sunshine, you get lovely textures and softer colors. Low sun behind your back onto the front of the subject almost always produces good pictures.

•Choose the correct film speed. For your basic outdoor shots in nice weather, a safe choice is 100 ASA film. For low-light shots, switch to 400 ASA film. For indoor shots without a flash, use 400 ASA film...and with a flash use 100 ASA film.

•Shoot subjects from a distance of no more than four feet to reduce the red-eye effect. Red eye is caused by a flash bouncing off the retina of the eye. The closer you are to your subject, the less reflection there will be. To completely eliminate the red-eye effect, either have subjects turn their eyes away from the camera or use an off-camera flash.

•Put a clear plastic bag over your camera—leaving a hole for the lens—when shooting in inclement weather. Gray skies, mist, fog, rain and falling snow can result in beautiful pictures.

•To avoid silhouettes at sunset, use your flash and stay within about four feet of your subjects. You can get some nice effects this way.

Buying a camera...

A good-quality point-and-shoot camera can go a long way. But, purchase one that isn't too complicated—and that has a fairly fast lens (F/4 and F/3.5 are good).

Point-and-shoot cameras worth considering: The Canon Sure Shot Max, the Pentax IQ90WR Zoom, the Konica Off Road and the Konica Hexar are great values and can produce great results.

Source: Susan McCartney, New York-based professional travel photographer who conducts how-to workshops on photography. She is author of *Travel Photography: A Complete Guide to How to Shoot and See*, Allworth Press, 10 E. 23 St., New York 10010.

Fascinating Dates For You and Your Mate

•Blue highways date. Take a one-day drive into the country together, resolving not to use any major roads. (We call this a blue highways date after the color of the small roads on most American maps.) No fast-food places are allowed. The fun of this date lies in exploring the unknown, including unlikely places to eat and shop. What looks like a rough country bar can turn out to have top-notch homemade food, and what looks like a junk sale may turn out to have an unnoticed treasure. As you search, there's plenty of time for conversation and reminiscence.

•Dancing lesson. Have a dance lesson date at a local dance studio. Call around to see which studio may be offering a special. After your dancing lesson, you may want to ask your spouse to a dancing-out date.

•Honeymoon memory. Ask your spouse to join you for an overnight date at the place where you went on your honeymoon—even if this means staying at a cheap motel. Take the time to recall your honeymoon and the history of your marriage. You may decide to improve on what you did the first time. Make a date to go someplace entirely different to have honeymoon memories.

•We're just too tired to talk date. Make a date to do almost nothing—not even talk. If you're both particularly tired, and don't feel like doing anything or seeing anyone, arrange a lazy evening at home. Set yourselves up to be comfortable, watch television and not have to talk.

The only preparation necessary for this date is having some videotapes on hand, and the telephone numbers for local pizza or Chinese restaurant delivery. Let the answering machine take your calls, and wordlessly relax.

Source: Dave and Claudia Arp, directors of the Marriage Alive Workshops, a national marriage enrichment network, Box 90303, Knoxville, Tennessee 37990. They are the authors of *52 Dates for You and Your Mate*. Thomas Nelson, Nelson Pl. at Elm Hill Pike, Nashville 37214.

Andrew Sarris Finds Lost Movie Treasures

Movie revenues from videocassettes are now—for the first time—exceeding box-office receipts from theaters. For the most part, the best-renting and best-selling movie videos have tended to be favorites in theaters as well. Hence, many worthy films slip through the cracks because of insufficient publicity or inadequate and misleading reviews. To correct this oversight, here are some suggestions for your home-video entertainment.

•*Billy Bathgate:* The reviewers were hypnotized by the star power of Dustin Hoffman and Bruce Willis as Cagney-Bogart-type gangsters to the point that they overlooked the adolescent infatuation of Loren Dean's Billy Bathgate with Nicole Kidman's high-society moll, which culminates in his chivalric rescue of his beloved from a gang rub-out. This rescue is the heart and soul of the movie, adapted from E.L. Doctorow's novel. *Director:* Robert Benton.

•*The Miracle:* This low-budget romantic whimsy from Ireland touches delicately on the incestuous feelings of a young man for a touring American actress who turns out to be his long-lost mother. Beverly D'Angelo as the mother and Niall Byrne as the painfully confused son achieve a magical rapport, aided in no small measure by Donal McCann, as the eternally resentful father and husband, and Lorraine Pickington as the boy's sweetly jealous girlfriend. Miraculously, the mood remains light and charming. *Director/Writer:* Neil Jordan.

•*The Hand That Rocks the Cradle:* Both a thriller and a dark comedy, this tale of a demonic baby-sitter, from a screenplay by Amanda Silver, was a big hit, though it was widely misunderstood as being carved from the *Fatal Attraction* mold. Rebecca De Mornay as the devilish poltergeist in a yuppie household gives a star-making performance, and Annabella Sciorra provides a solid representation of supermom burn-out. *Director:* Curtis Hanson.

•*Let Him Have It:* This film was based on the real-life story of the last man to go to the gallows in Britain—in what amounted to a clear and outrageous miscarriage of justice. A mostly obscure British cast discouraged attendance during its American theatrical release. Chris Eccleston, Paul Reynolds, Tom Courtenay, Tom Bell, Eileen Atkins and Clare Holman are all superb in this heart-wrenching drama from a screenplay by Neal Purvis and Robert Wade. *Director:* Peter Medak.

•*Rush:* Jennifer Jason Leigh and Jason Patric are two highly talented performers who have not yet reached bankable stardom. They are so convincing as two narcs becoming cocaine addicts after trying to infiltrate a drug operation that they depressed audiences in the theatres. Home video may be kinder to the movie's gripping realism. From a screenplay by Pete Dexter, based on the book by Kim Wozencraft. *Director:* Lili Fini Zanuck.

•*The Inner Circle:* Tom Hulce plays Stalin's film projectionist, with sterling support from Lotita Davidovich, Bob Hoskins as Beria and Aleksandre Zbruyev, who is nothing less than uncanny as Stalin. *Director:* Andrei Konchalovsky.

•*The Man in the Moon:* Reese Witherspoon is enchanting as a tremulous tomboy in love with the quiet farm boy next door. When he takes up with her older sister (Emily Warfield), she is torn between jealousy and loyalty to her sibling with whom she has spent so many nights on the porch looking at the man in the moon. A cruel, senseless accident resolves the conflict sadly but lyrically. *Director:* Robert Mulligan.

•*Truly, Madly, Deeply:* This gem of a realistic fantasy presents the absurdist problem of a dead lover (Alan Rickman) returning to the apartment of his grieving girlfriend (Juliet Stevenson), along with a bunch of his ghostly movie-buff pals who spend all their time looking at videos and commenting on them. Rickman and Stevenson are both funny and moving. *Director:* Anthony Minghella.

•*White Dog:* This anti-racist cult movie about a dog who has been conditioned to attack blacks was pulled from theaters ironically because of protests from civil rights groups over the blunt treatment of racial prejudice. Not for the squeamish, this is a first-rate melodrama with adroit performances by Kristy McNichol, Paul Winfield, Burl Ives and Jameson Parker. *Director:* Samuel Fuller.

• *Trust:* Hal Hartley has been described as the cinematic poet-laureate of Long Island, and as the American version of Eric Rohmer. With unfamiliar performers such as Adrienne Shelly and Martin Donovan, he has fashioned a goofy but powerful love story in a seeming casual style. *Director/Writer:* Hal Hartley.

• *Point Break:* The New Age surfing and sky-diving rhetoric spouted by Patrick Swayze as a grandiose beach philosopher and bank robber gave the reviewers ammunition to dismiss one of the most brilliantly choreographed and photographed action movies in recent years. Keanu Reeves, Gary Busey and Lori Petty offer a strong moral counterweight to Swayze's windswept delusions. *Director:* Kathryn Bigelow.

• *What About Bob?:* This is the funniest movie ever about the grotesque symbiosis of psychoanalysts and their more demanding analysands. Bill Murray's mental basket case of a patient fastens like fungus to Richard Dreyfuss's hapless analyst to the point of invading his August vacation sanctuary and winning over his family and professional colleagues. *Director:* Frank Oz.

• *Impromptu:* Great fun in period costumes from Judy Davis as George Sand, Hugh Grant as Frederic Chopin, Mandy Patinkin as Alfred de Musset and Emma Thompson, the dazzling revelation of *Howard's End,* as the silly Duchess d'Antan. *Director:* James Lapine.

• *Mortal Thoughts:* Demi Moore and Glenne Headly make a more realistic Thelma and Louise pair as they dispose of the male chauvinist pig husband, Bruce Willis, while detective Harvey Keitel tries to figure out who has done what to whom. *Director:* Alan Rudolph.

Source: Andrew Sarris, the noted film critic for *The New York Observer*, is professor of film at Columbia University and the author of 10 books on film, including *The American Cinema, Confessions of a Cultist* and the forthcoming *The American Sound Film*.

Wonderful Lesser-Known Holiday Videos

Most of us are familiar with the traditional Christmas classics. Of the three screen versions of Dickens' *A Christmas Carol,* the 1951 British version with Alastair Sim as Scrooge enjoys a slight edge over the 1984 version with George C. Scott as Scrooge and the 1938 Hollywood version with Reginald Owen as Scrooge.

The spirit of Santa Claus has still not found a more endearing embodiment than Edmund Gwenn's in the 1947 *Miracle on 34th Street,* and Frank Capra's 1946 *It's a Wonderful Life* with Jimmy Stewart has lost none of its power to move us over the past few decades.

But if you're a little weary of these old standbys, along with Bing Crosby singing "White Christmas" in the 1942 *Holiday Inn,* "Turaluralura" in the 1944 *Going My Way,* and the title song in the 1945 *The Bells of St. Mary's,* here are a few offbeat suggestions to tap the deeper feelings of the season…

• *A Christmas Story* (1983). A little gem of a memory movie from humorist Jean Shepherd. Peter Billingsley plays a little boy with a yen for a Red Ryder rifle, but the real story is that of a family facing a variety of ridiculous situations, evoking warm feelings that are never too sweet and gooey. Directed by Bob Clark, with Melinda Dillon, Darren McGavin and Peter Billingsley.

• *The Holly and the Ivy* (1953). A beautifully acted drama of an English parson and his three troubled children, and the emotional epiphany that reaches its climax on Christmas Day. Directed by George More O'Ferrall. With Ralph Richardson, Celia Johnson, Margaret Leighton, Denholm Elliott.

• *Christmas in July* (1940). The winner of a bogus contest brings joy to his whole neighborhood before his good luck is exposed as a coworker's prank. In his darkest moment, his girlfriend makes an eloquent speech for her man, a speech that saves the day. Directed by Preston Sturges. With Dick Powell and Ellen Drew.

• *A Holiday Affair* (1949). In the background is the Christmas shopping season in New York. In the foreground is a war widow forced to choose between a good provider and a free spirit as her husband and as father to her fatherless son. In the end the child virtually makes the decision for his mother. Directed by Don Hartman. With Robert Mitchum, Janet Leigh, Wendell Corey.

• *The Apartment* (1960). A brilliant love story for mature viewers, this pairing of Jack Lemmon and Shirley MacLaine takes place over the Christmas and New Year's Holidays, and projects true love, self-sacrifice and emotional nobility in a situation that begins with the sordid and ignoble attitudes that flourish in the midst of our moral posturings. Directed by Billy Wilder.

• *Love Affair* (1939). The Christmas spirit pervades this almost miraculous love story involving two pleasure-seekers who achieve self-purification. Directed by Leo McCarey. With Irene Dunne and Charles Boyer.

• *Penny Serenade* (1941). Cary Grant and Irene Dunne experience the joys and heartbreaks of adopting children in the midst of a Christmas season with its childhood pageants. Directed by George Stevens.

Source: Andrew Sarris, professor of film at Columbia University and author of 10 books on film, including the forthcoming *The American Sound Film.*

The Most Romantic Videos

Although love is what is supposed to make the world and movies go round and round, remarkably few memorable love stories have materialized on the screen. Somehow we never lose our childhood giggles or embarrassment when the kissing scenes come on the screen. Hence, despite the omnipresence of "sex appeal" and "love interest" in the casting, writing and directing of motion pictures, most movies pretend to be about something else.

Significantly, the two most famous love films, *Gone With the Wind* (1939) and *Casablanca* (1942) profess to be concerned with Great Wars rather than the chemistry between Vivien Leigh's Scarlett and Clark Gable's Rhett in the former, and Ingrid Bergman's Ilsa and Humphrey Bogart's Rick in the latter. In neither romance do the lovers live happily ever after. But that is consistent with most of the great love stories of literature and music.

Most of my favorite love stories on film are somewhat more optimistic, though true love doesn't run smoothly in any of them, least of all in my all-time favorite, *That Hamilton Woman*

(1941), in which Vivien Leigh's Emma Hamilton and Laurence Olivier's Horatio Nelson bring more passion and feeling to their ill-fated adulterous love affair than the historical originals ever did.

On a happier note, Wendy Hiller and Roger Livesey brought civilized grace and humor to a wartime romance in the Scottish Isles in the haunting *I Know Where I'm Going* (1945).

The great male lover of the 1930s and 1940s in Hollywood was, fittingly enough, a Frenchman, Charles Boyer. Three of his most charismatic partners in passion were Irene Dunne in *Love Affair* (1939), Margaret Sullavan in *Back Street* (1941) and Jean Arthur in *History Is Made at Night* (1937), one of the most adventurously romantic titles in the history of the cinema.

The lost art of letter-writing to one's beloved is preserved in the epistolary eloquence of *Shop Around the Corner* (1940) in which Margaret Sullavan and James Stewart carry on an anonymous romance by mail after placing ads in the personals columns...and *Love Letters* (1945) in which Jennifer Jones becomes victimized through a Cyrano-like imposture by which the Right Man writes love letters for the Wrong Man. A murder must intervene before a twentieth-century Roxanne finds happiness with Joseph Cotten's handsome Cyrano.

Life imitated art in *Woman of the Year* (1942) in which Katharine Hepburn and Spencer Tracy began their enduring love affair off-screen as they were making love on-screen in a movie ahead of its time in celebrating the emotional electricity generated by two highly competitive career people of opposite sexes. The picture was marred by a studio-tacked-on ending in which Ms. Hepburn gets her comeuppance in a disastrous kitchen sequence. For the most part, however, Hepburn and Tracy's characters bickered in the exhilarating manner of Beatrice and Benedict in Shakespeare's *Much Ado About Nothing.*

Billy Wilder has given us two magical romances in two very different decades with *The Major and the Minor* (1942) in which Ginger Rogers plays a faux Lolita to Ray Milland's chivalrously susceptible Major Kirby—and *Love in the Afternoon* (1957) in which Audrey Hepburn as an impressionable virgin chooses as her first lover Gary Cooper's much older and disreputably promiscuous playboy-businessman. In one of the great endings in film history, the first love of her life almost miraculously becomes the last love of his.

You may have noticed that most of my favorites date back to the 1930s and 1940s, the most tightly censored period in Hollywood's history. There were no nude scenes back then, no rollicking between the bed sheets, but instead an eroticism of the heart, which is what Valentine's Day is all about, or at least should be.

Source: Andrew Sarris, the noted film critic for *The New York Observer*, is professor of film at Columbia University and the author of 10 books on film, including *The American Cinema, Confessions of a Cultist* and the forthcoming *The American Sound Film.*

Seven Quick Stress Busters

1. Stick colored dots on all your clocks. Whenever you check the time, use them as a reminder to take a deep, relaxing breath.

2. Instead of hitting the shower the moment your alarm goes off, lie quietly in bed for a few minutes, listening to sounds from inside the house or outdoors.

3. Let the phone ring two or three times before answering. Use the time to pause and become aware of your breathing.

4. Try driving with your radio turned off. Concentrate on the act of driving—the feel of your hands on the wheel, the sound of the road, the images in your visual field.

5. At least once or twice a week, eat lunch by yourself, in quiet contemplation.

6. Pay attention to the walk to your car after work.

7. To ease the transition from office to home, change clothes when you get home.

Source: Saki F. Santorelli, EdD, associate director, Stress Reduction Clinic, University of Massachusetts Medical Center, Worcester.

Quick Stress Relief

A five-minute mini-meditation session lowers blood pressure, reduces levels of stress hormones and boosts feelings of well-being. *What to do:* Sit comfortably, straight and tall… become aware of your breathing…visualize a mountain scene, noticing all the details…imagine changes taking place, the sun arcing across the sky, violent storms whipping up…focus on the mountain's stillness and calm throughout these events and carry this calm with you all day.

Source: Jon Kabat-Zinn, PhD, director, Stress Reduction Clinic, University of Massachusetts Medical Center, Worcester, Massachusetts.

20

Getting the Most for Your Medical Dollar

How to Be a Savvy Medical Consumer

While it's no surprise that Americans spend too much on medical care, few consumers are aware of just how much money they're wasting on diagnostic tests, drugs, doctor's visits, etc. *Biggest areas of overspending:*

Doctors' fees…

Patients often forget that doctors are businesspeople. While the services they offer are different from those offered by car dealers and real estate brokers, your goal should be to get the best service for the lowest price.

Every day we negotiate prices with suppliers. The same should be true with those who supply our medical care. Ask questions and negotiate with your physician. The more you ask, the more information you'll receive—and the better decisions you'll make.

If you think you're being overcharged by your doctor for office visits or medical procedures, discuss your concerns with the doctor.

Try to get a better price. Don't allow yourself to be steered to an assistant or bookkeeper. The *physician* is supplying the services, and he/she is responsible for what they cost.

Diagnostic tests…

Even the most routine examination often results in the physician suggesting one or more diagnostic tests.

Some tests are useful and necessary—for example, an X-ray or MRI scan to check for a broken bone. But 40% are unnecessary. Close to half of the $20 billion a year Americans spend on diagnostic tests is wasted.

Scandal: Many doctors have a financial stake in diagnostic labs, either through direct ownership of the lab or because they may receive a payment for each referral patient.

To protect yourself: Never leave the doctor's office without asking the rationale for the recommended diagnostic test. Find out what the test is intended to find—or to rule out. If you're told that one test might prove inconclusive and that a second test might need to be done, ask your doctor to consider skipping straight to the second test.

Also, make sure you receive a copy of test results directly. Don't let your doctor call you "only if there's trouble." Reviewing test results with your doctor will help ensure that no problems have been overlooked.

Be especially careful if you are hospitalized. When patients check into their rooms, staff doctors often order a new round of diagnostic tests —without first checking to see if these patients have already undergone these tests.

Trap: Hospital patients wind up having to pay for duplicate tests—which can easily cost thousands of dollars.

To avoid duplicate tests, ask your physician to share with the hospital staff the results of *all* medical tests he/she ordered. And double-check with the hospital physician about what any newly ordered test is supposed to do.

Follow-up office visits…

Doctors often suggest a follow-up visit just to check up on a patient's progress—and they often charge the standard fee even if no additional treatment is necessary.

Example: A pediatrician prescribes a drug to treat your child's ear infection, then tells you to bring the child back for an office visit in 10 days. You pay $40 for the first visit and $20 to $30 for the follow-up—even though it consists of nothing more than a 10-second peek in your child's ear. If that's all there is to the follow-up visit ask your doctor if he/she would be willing to accept a reduced fee. Rather than haggling, many doctors will agree to look in an ear or listen to a set of lungs for $10 or less—perhaps even for free.

Prescription drugs…

There are several ways to save money here…

•Buy generic drugs. They cost as much as 80% less than brand-name drugs.

Caution: A generic drug may be slightly more or less potent than its brand-name counterpart. If you have a chronic heart condition or another ailment that requires a very precise level of medication in the bloodstream, be sure to ask your doctor if switching medications is safe.

Bottom line: If your doctor insists on a brand name, ask why. If you're not convinced, go generic.

•Buy only a two- to three-day supply of drugs. Doctors often prescribe 10 days or more of a particular drug—even though you might have an adverse reaction to the drug after only a day or two. *Result:* You wind up being stuck with a week's worth of a drug you cannot take. *Lesson:* Don't overbuy.

•Inform your doctor of any medical condition that might affect your tolerance to a particular drug—or if you're taking another drug that might interact with the newly prescribed drug. About $2 billion a year is spent on drugs that treat the adverse effects of other drugs.

•Comparison-shop. Call several pharmacies, especially those in discount stores. Some offer prescriptions below cost to entice customers into the store. Your doctor might have some ideas on finding the best deals.

Medical specialists…

Just because you've used a high-cost specialist in the past doesn't mean you must return in the future.

Example: If you consult an ear, nose and throat specialist for a difficult sinus problem, there's no need to go back to that specialist for a simple cold or allergy. A general practitioner (GP) can take care of those problems for far less. Women often go to gynecologists for complaints that a GP could easily handle—doubling or even tripling the cost of the office visit.

Bottom line: Pick your doctor on the basis of your problem—see a general practitioner whenever possible. If the GP recommends a specialist, ask why. Doctors occasionally "hand off" patients to specialist colleagues—just to give their friends a little business.

Billing errors…

Although it's easy to check a simple bill from your personal doctor, hospital bills are often so confusing that they defy comprehension. That's too bad, because 90% of these bills contain errors— *75% of which favor the hospital.*

Common mistakes: Being billed for a private room when you actually had roommates…being billed for a circumcision—when you gave birth to a girl. And hospitals routinely charge thousands of dollars under the category of "pharmacy" with no itemization of the drugs for which they're billing you.

Many patients are so intimidated that they blindly pay bills—squandering hundreds or thousands of dollars.

Better: Delay paying the hospital bill until several days after the day you are discharged. When you check out, tell the billing office you'll pay it after you've had a chance to scrutinize the bill. For any charge you don't understand, call the billing department and request an explanation. Be sure to get an itemized list of all charges —and don't pay up until you're satisfied that all charges are accurate.

Payoff: With some hospital stays costing tens of thousands of dollars, catching just a few errors can produce big savings for you.

Hospital administrators are aware of billing problems, and in many cases they'll adjust your bill when you challenge their fees. If the hospital refuses to adjust your bill, withhold payment for that portion under dispute. If that fails, contact your insurance company and ask for help.

If you're still unhappy, ask your congressional representative to intervene on your behalf. With the health-care industry under fire, insurance companies are particularly sensitive to the threat of negative publicity.

You can also reduce hospital bills by taking a few prudent steps *before* you check in. Hospitals are notorious for overcharging for simple items—anywhere from $1 for an aspirin to $16 for a plastic water pitcher. To avoid these exorbitant charges, bring your own pitcher, aspirin, pillow, etc. If possible, have your prescriptions filled by a less expensive pharmacy outside the hospital.

Source: Charles B. Inlander, president of the People's Medical Society, a consumer advocacy group based in Allentown, Pennsylvania. His most recent book is *Good Operations, Bad Operations*, Viking Books, 375 Hudson St., New York 10014.

What You Need to Know About Health Insurance

Millions of Americans have no problems with their health insurance. They file the necessary forms...their claims are paid...and all parties are satisfied.

But thousands of Americans do have serious complaints regarding health claims. Frequently, policyholders are abandoned by their insurers when they most need the coverage. *Problem:* The higher the ultimate amount of your claim, the more likely you are to encounter a violation of your insurance contract by your insurer.

Due to the complexity of the laws governing insurance, what insurers can—and what they can't—do is often unclear. Here are some of the most common questions policyholders must face...

Can my insurer change or reduce my coverage? Unfortunately, yes. *Key:* The insurer must give policyholders early notice of the changes. *Recommended:* Read all mail from your insurer —carefully. Often, such notices are buried in communications that appear to be junk mail.

Self-defense: If the reduction in coverage is made before you have a health problem, complain to your employer or union or switch policies.

What if the coverage is reduced after I have filed a claim? It is unclear if insurers can legally reduce coverage once a policyholder is "on claim" for a particular accident or disease. However, insurance companies have recently been getting away with it in court.

Reason: Every state has consumer protection rules that limit an insurer's ability to change coverage in midstream. But for individuals insured through their employers, state laws are preempted by a federal law, ERISA (the Employee Retirement Income Security Act). ERISA makes no provisions for arbitrary reductions or changes in coverage.

Some courts are sympathetic to insurers rather than individual policyholders in the belief that premiums will rise if insurers are forced to pay all of the claims they have contracted to pay.

Example: Recently, a man who was insured under his employer's self-insurance plan had the $1 million AIDS coverage his policy promised reduced to a mere $5,000—after he became ill. The court allowed the reduced benefit to stand.

In this controversial area, trial attorneys take the position that this is a vesting issue...that once a person is "on claim," it is illegal to reduce benefits.

Self-defense: Seek legal advice if your benefits are reduced after you are on claim.

Can I be dropped from a group, or can my health insurance be cancelled? Generally, no. If you are insured as a member of a group, the insurer would have to cancel the entire group. It is illegal to single out just one person.

Exception: If you are insured through your employer and become so seriously injured or ill that you cannot work, your insurer may try to claim that your employment relationship has ended. Thus you are no longer part of the group —and can be cancelled in mid-claim.

Again, this is a gray area. Many states prohibit this type of cancellation, but the state laws are negated under ERISA. Trial attorneys say that a person is vested if he/she becomes injured or ill while employed. Case law precedent holds that the insurer must continue to cover claims resulting from that particular illness or injury. However, some courts have held otherwise.

Self-defense: Check your insurance contract for conditions under which you can be dropped. They are usually headed "Termination of Coverage." Don't automatically accept a cancellation if it occurs. This area of law is technical and esoteric. Insurance companies are making up the rules, generally to their advantage and policyholders' disadvantage, and thereby forcing policyholders to challenge them in court. Seek an attorney who is experienced in this area.

There are cases in which an insurer has dropped an entire group of policyholders, claiming it's discontinuing its group health coverage business. State laws that once required insurers to provide alternate coverage for such policyholders have been negated under ERISA, leaving large numbers of people uninsured, and uninsurable, in mid-claim.

When can my insurer decide that my new claim was a preexisting condition? This is an area where policyholders frequently fail to get the coverage they believe they are paying for. Carefully check your policy for conditions that are excluded for either a certain amount of time, or altogether.

General rule: For an insurer to deem a condition "preexisting," you must have seen a doctor for the condition, and had a symptom the doctor could diagnose as indicating that condition, previous to your insurance policy taking effect.

Everyone may have the symptomless beginnings of an undetected health problem. But some insurers stretch their definition of "preexisting."

Example: A man is denied coverage for his heart attack because his doctor told him he had high cholesterol three years earlier and recommended that he watch his diet.

Self-defense: Challenge the denial. Your condition must have been diagnosable to be considered preexisting. If it wasn't diagnosed, you have a strong case for coverage. Even if it was diagnosed, you may be able to prove it wasn't preexisting.

Can insurers apply exclusions in unfair or illegitimate ways? They can, and they do. Coverage exclusions are legal, and common for entire categories of treatment, such as alcoholism, drug dependence and psychiatric care.

Caution: Insurers may try to "weasel out" of coverage related to these exclusions. *Example:* An insurer may deny coverage for a liver ailment, claiming it was a result of alcoholism and is therefore excluded.

Self-defense: Challenge the denial. It's the liver that's being treated, not the alcoholism.

Insurers also tend to deny coverage based on broad interpretation of legitimate exclusions.

Examples: Experimental treatment...medical versus "custodial" care...treatment or hospital days that are "not medically necessary."

Danger area: Policies that pay for accidents but not sickness. *Catch:* You file a claim for injuries resulting from a fall, the insurer says the fall was caused by dizziness resulting from a disease, so the fall was not accidental.

Can the insurance company's doctor's opinion overrule my doctor's judgment? Usually, yes. A number of insurance policies even state that the insurer reserves the right to have its own "medical director" make a final determination when benefits are being disputed.

Problem: As an employee of the insurer, this medical director almost always rules against the policyholder.

Self-defense: The best insurance contracts state that the deciding opinion in a claim will be by the policyholder's treating physician.

Reality: Most insurers will not put this issue in writing, and most insurance policies say nothing about who decides in the event of a dispute.

Exception: A union or large corporation may be able to negotiate an appropriate clause in its contract.

What can I do to protect myself? It's impossible to be totally secure, no matter what your insurance contract says. But there are ways to minimize risk. *Suggestions:*

• If your employer offers a choice of insurers, investigate the claims records of each company.

Best source: Whoever handles claims for your employer. Inquire about each insurer's history of paying claims, delays versus timeliness, invoking exclusions and preexisting conditions, etc.

Reason: There is no way to access an insurer's records on how well it pays claims. Your state department of insurance may keep records of complaints filed, but many don't keep records.

• To ensure more clout when contesting a claim, consider buying additional group insurance that is not provided through an employer and thus does not fall under the jurisdiction of ERISA.

Such policies are regulated by state insurance law and are therefore easier to take recourse on if problems arise.

Examples: Plans offered through professional associations, organizations such as AARP, NOW and many others.

Source: William M. Shernoff, a specialist in consumer claims against insurance companies, and author of *How to Make Insurance Companies Pay Your Claims.* Hastings House. His Claremont, California law firm, Shernoff, Bidart & Darras, has a staff of insurance analysts who specialize in insurance coverage, disputes and ERISA.

The Worst Problems You're Likely to Face With Your Insurer

Insurance companies are in the business of selling security and peace of mind. But when it comes to settling claims, most insurance companies are in the business of saving money.

While millions of policyholders have their claims settled with a minimum of fuss, there are many areas in which abuses by insurers are widespread.

Rule of thumb: The higher the cost of your claim, the more likely you are to have trouble with your insurer.

The most common ways insurers shortchange policyholders—and how to defend yourself...

• Unwarranted rescissions. Attempts by an insurer to rescind—or cancel—a policy *after* a claim has been filed are common in all insurance and widespread in health claims. Wrongful rescissions comprise 25% of the cases I handle.

How it works: Many insurers don't investigate your insurance application until you've filed a claim. This procedure is called *post-claims underwriting.* An adjuster audits your medical records, not for the purpose of paying your claim—that's a separate department—but to see if you forgot to include something on your application.

Example: A woman who had cancer hadn't disclosed that she had consulted a doctor several years before about problems with irregular menstrual periods, a normal symptom of menopause. The insurance company attempted to rescind coverage, and a dispute ensued.

Self-defense: Case law on this subject is clear. If you had no knowledge of a medical problem at the time of your policy application, if you failed to appreciate the significance of an omission or if the omission is immaterial or trivial to the underwriting of your policy, your coverage cannot be rescinded.

Example: An insurer can't rescind your policy when you make a claim for knee surgery on the grounds that you didn't disclose an insignificant problem, such as an allergy.

When applying for insurance: Answer all questions honestly, *yourself.* Insurance agents often paraphrase questions.

Example: The agent says, *Any problems with your blood pressure?* when the question actually reads, *Have you* ever *been treated for high blood pressure?*

• Failing to fully investigate claims. According to consumer protection laws in almost every state, it is the insurer's duty to investigate policyholders' claims *in good faith*. But insurers are sometimes adversarial when it comes to paying claims.

Result: Insurers may deny claims without consulting the appropriate experts—doctors, appraisers, contractors—or do so only to find a reason *not* to pay.

Example: A dying woman who required 24-hour skilled nursing care was denied health coverage on the grounds that the care was *custodial*. The family sued, complaining that the insurer did not discuss her condition with her doctors or the nurses who cared for her and allowed unqualified claims investigators to make medical decisions. The family won the case—unfortunately, after the patient had died.

Self-defense: If your claim is unfairly denied, enlist the help of your insurance agent and submit statements from experts who can support your claim. If your claim is for property damage, visual documentation—photographs, videotape—can help as well. If the insurer refuses to consider your evidence, contact a trial attorney.

• Overturning medical opinions. Insurers must often review medical questions—*Was this treatment really necessary? Is this person really disabled?* For this purpose, most insurers use in-house medical examiners or hire "independent" medical examiners who may not be unbiased since they have ongoing business arrangements with the insurers.

Result: Thousands of claims are unjustly denied every year when insurers' "medical experts" override the opinions of policyholders' doctors.

Example: A man was hospitalized with symptoms of a heart attack. After running a series of tests, his doctor found he had a less serious condition. Thus, the insurer decided the hospitalization was "not medically necessary." His doctor contested the decision and won, claiming that it would have been negligent not to treat the case as potentially life-threatening—not to mention the insurer's bad faith in denying a claim due to hindsight.

Self-defense: Most major medical policies pay for a second opinion—be sure to get one whenever possible. Choose doctors who are willing to go to bat for you if their opinions are contradicted.

• Narrowly defining *disability*. Most state laws and employers define *disability* as the inability to perform steadily in a job to which you are reasonably suited by education, training, experience, opportunity, and physical and mental capacities.

But most disability insurance policies ignore state law and define *disability* as the inability to perform *any* job. By this definition, an executive who suffers a debilitating stroke would not be considered disabled if he/she could still wash dishes and, therefore, could be denied the benefits he expects based on his salary.

Self-defense: Look for a disability policy that covers you for your "own occupation," not just "any occupation." When filing a disability claim, describe the nature of your work to your doctor and precisely how your injuries affect your ability to work. Make sure this information is included in your doctor's report to the insurance company.

• Denying health claims that have been *preapproved*. Thousands of policyholders follow their insurers' instructions. They call the insurer for "preapproval" of a medical procedure—but are turned down when they file the claim, often on the grounds that the procedure was *experimental, not medically necessary* or *excessive treatment.*

Reason: Policyholders may actually have spoken with a clerk who did not approve the procedure but simply verified the policy is active or that a certain procedure is covered. Clerks are not claims adjusters and do not preapprove the amount the insurer is willing to pay or whether the procedure was necessary for *you*.

Self-defense: Be sure that you speak with a *claims adjuster* and get preapproval for the specific procedure and amount covered in writing. If you are denied approval of a formerly *experimental* procedure, such as a bone-marrow transplant for cancer, have your doctor call the insurer and explain why you are a good candidate for such treatment. If necessary, contact an attorney.

• Using false or deceptive advertising practices. Some insurers train their agents to sell policies based on advertising or brochures that seriously misrepresent the actual contents of the policies.

Example: A self-employed client bought what he believed was a major medical policy with a lifetime maximum of $1 million from a subsidiary of a major insurance company. When he filed a claim for treatment for non-Hodgkins' lymphoma, the company paid only $3,420 of $47,000 in medical and hospital bills.

Result: He sued and showed that the company's brochures radically overstated what turned out to be a bare-bones policy. In the policy, doctors' visits were excluded for the first four weeks following surgery, for example, and only a small percentage of surgeons' fees were paid—not 100%, as stated in the brochure. The jury found the company guilty of fraud and awarded the plaintiff $25 million in punitive damages.

Self-defense: It can't be said too often—*take the time to read your insurance policies.* If you find there are discrepancies between a company's ads, brochures or booklets and the actual policy, the courts will generally rule in your favor—but it's always better not to have to go that far.

Source: William M. Shernoff, an attorney specializing in consumer claims against insurance companies. His law firm, Shernoff, Bidart & Darras (600 S. Indian Hill Blvd., Claremont, California 91711, 909-621-4935) provides free answers to questions from consumers nationwide about insurance coverage and disputes. Mr. Shernoff is author of *How to Make Insurance Companies Pay Your Claims*, Hastings House, 141 Halstead Ave., Mamaroneck, New York 10543.

What to Do About Preexisting Medical Conditions

For many people suffering from heart disease, cancer, diabetes and other chronic medical conditions, obtaining health insurance is difficult or even impossible. Insurance firms just don't want to assume the financial risk of covering such people, and no law forces them to do so.

At one time only serious ailments were grounds for refusal of coverage...but no more.

Insurers now refuse coverage even for minor problems, such as mild hypertension or depression—in some cases even for such things as having once sought psychological counseling. Sadly, federal regulations governing the insurance industry are notoriously spotty...and state regulations are not much better.

Scandalous: In many parts of the country, state insurance agencies are staffed by former insurance company executives—hardly an unbiased group.

While such problems defy easy solutions, certain steps do bring you some protection...

• Hold on to your existing health insurance. If you're covered by an employer's health plan but are considering switching jobs, determine in advance whether you're eligible for coverage under the new employer's plan.

Some insurers refuse coverage for any preexisting conditions. Some accept persons with preexisting conditions, but only if they've been managing without treatment for a specified length of time. Others accept such people but will not honor any claims for that condition made within the first year of coverage.

Bottom line: Get the terms of your prospective employer's insurance plan in writing before you quit your job. If you're not guaranteed adequate coverage in advance, you may want to hold on to your current job.

If your employer switches insurers, the new insurer is required by law to accept all employees for coverage. If you quit or get fired, federal law dictates that you can keep your existing health plan for 18 months if there are more than 20 members in your group health plan.

• Be honest about your health. Hiding a preexisting medical condition when applying for coverage is fraudulent and foolish. Even if doing so did enable you to get coverage, it might mean big problems later on.

Reason: Insurers scrutinize applications at the time of the first significant claim. If even a hint of dishonesty is found, the claim is usually denied…and the coverage dropped.

•Don't let yourself be mistreated. Some insurers mistreat their policyholders, confident that few people have the wherewithal to fight shabby treatment. Don't let them get away with it. If you've been unfairly denied coverage, or if your insurer fails to honor a legitimate claim, you have many potential allies—local media, elected officials, the state insurance commissioner, etc.

Some states now publish a list of health insurers—and many states publicize complaints against these carriers. A few now publish rankings of health insurers from "good" to "bad."

•Go to court. If all else fails, find a lawyer experienced in health insurance issues. If your case has merit, the lawyer may suggest a lawsuit.

Good news: In many cases, insurers will pay up at the very hint of a suit.

An insurer that loses such a "bad faith" lawsuit is liable not only for the amount of the claim, but also for potentially astronomical damages.

Few insurers are eager to risk losing a $1 million judgment over a $20,000 claim. Insurers also fear the negative publicity that could be generated by media coverage of such a lawsuit.

Source: William M. Shernoff, a senior partner with the law firm of Shernoff, Bidart & Darras, Claremont, California. Shernoff, whose firm has represented thousands of consumers seeking settlements from insurance companies, is the author of several books on insurance fraud, including *How to Make Insurance Companies Pay Your Claims* and *Payment Refused: How to Combat Unfair Insurance Practices*, both published by Hastings House, 141 Halstead Ave., Mamaroneck, New York 10543.

Get Your Medical Claim Paid

While about 90% of insurance claims are handled smoothly and routinely, millions of unjustly rejected claims, though a small percentage of the total, are costing consumers billions of dollars. *Encouraging:* Most policyholders who dispute claim denials either win their case or improve their settlement.

Trap: The larger your claim, the more likely it is to be delayed, reduced or denied.

The person with the power to pay, settle or refuse your claim is the claims adjuster. *Problem:* Some adjusters may be looking for reasons not to pay legitimate claims.

If your claim is unfairly denied: First question the decision with a call to the adjuster handling the claim. Then contest it in writing—write first to the adjuster who handles the claim. Refer your complaint to the department's supervisor if necessary.

For best results: Assemble as much documentation as possible to support your position.

If you are still unsatisfied, contact your state department of insurance. If you don't get a response, see a qualified trial attorney.

Unfortunately, medical claims is the area in which policyholders encounter the worst and most frequent insurance nightmares.

•Cancer: Most health insurance policies provide for cancer surgery, radiation and chemotherapy.

Biggest problem area: Bone marrow transplants, long considered by doctors to be standard effective treatment for patients who need more aggressive therapy when the first round has failed.

Common tactic: Insurers claim the procedure is still "experimental" and therefore not covered. Most alternative therapies are also refused on the grounds of being "unproven."

•AIDS or other catastrophic illness: The more costly or long-term the anticipated treatment, the more likely your insurer will deny your claim or cancel your policy, shifting the burden of care to the public.

Common tactics: The insurer claims you have a "preexisting condition," or that the medications and treatment prescribed are unproven and experimental. Often, if you have been insured as part of a group policy, the insurance company cancels the group, leaving you uninsurable elsewhere.

•Long-term progressive illness: If the condition is long-term, serious and/or deteriorating, you are likely to have frequent claims refused.

Examples: Coma victims, patients with multiple sclerosis, Alzheimer's disease.

Common tactic: The insurer claims the victim requires "custodial" rather than "medical" care.

•Work-related disability: Any ongoing claim is likely to be flagged for cancellation or reduction.

Common tactics: The insurer offers a flat settlement if the disabled person agrees to give up rights to collect under the terms of his/her policy. The insurer accuses the person of malingering and tries to prove that the person is not really disabled.

Problem: You are disabled if you are unable to perform the type of work you are qualified for. But an insurer may claim you can work if you can function just minimally. *Example:* A roofer who is confined to a wheelchair following an accident is clearly disabled. Yet, an insurer may claim he is mobile and therefore able to work.

•Nursing home or rehabilitative care: Many insurance policies exclude "long-term or custodial care." But, patients receiving medical care in a facility that meets the definition of a hospital may be covered.

Common tactic: The insurance company claims the care is not medical but custodial, or that the facility is not a "hospital."

•Minor claims: Insurance companies make enormous profits by refusing to pay small sums to legitimate claimants.

Caution: Check your insurance policy and follow up on any discrepancies you find if a small part of a larger claim is refused. Don't be lazy, and don't settle for less than you are due.

While a complex or costly claim is far more likely to be reduced than a modest one, filing a small claim is no guarantee it will be paid.

Example: Several years ago, I had a client who sued his insurance company over a $48 unpaid claim. During the trial, a pattern of fraud perpetrated against policyholders was revealed. *Result:* The jury ordered the insurer to pay $4.5 million in punitive damages.

Source: William M. Shernoff, specialist in consumer claims against insurance companies, and author of *How to Make Insurance Companies Pay Your Claims.* Hastings House. His Claremont, California law firm, Shernoff, Bidart & Darras, has a staff of insurance analysts insurance coverage, disputes and ERISA.

Ten Questions to Ask When Evaluating a Health Insurance Policy

Most people wouldn't buy a car without researching their options, test-driving several models and comparing dealers' prices. As personal circumstances change—the birth of children, divorce, relocation, etc.—so do the cars we buy. But when it comes to health insurance, many people fail to spend much time thinking about whether their policy best suits their needs.

There are guidelines to use in evaluating your health coverage—whether you are thinking about changing your insurer, supplementing your current policy, dropping yours in favor of your spouse's…whether you are part of a group or shopping for an individual policy …if you are changing jobs or your company is changing policies…or you are weighing choices in a "cafeteria plan." *Questions to ask:*

1. What is covered? While cost is always a consideration in health insurance, *comprehensiveness* is just as important in determining value.

Recommended: A major-medical or medical-surgical policy that covers expenses related to illness or injury, starting with the first day in the hospital and including doctors' visits, surgical procedures and outpatient care.

Optional: Routine physicals, prescription drugs. *Aim:* At a minimum, to protect yourself and your family from a catastrophic financial loss in the event of a medical emergency.

Not recommended: Accident insurance or disease-specific policies, which are limited in coverage and usually duplicate coverage you already have.

2. What is the maximum benefit provided by the policy? An unlimited benefit is ideal, but avoid buying one that is worth less than $1 to $2 million in maximum lifetime benefits.

Recommended: Some policies restore a portion of the maximum benefits following an illness if you can document that you're well and haven't filed a claim for a certain period of time.

3. Are the premiums deductible—and co-payments affordable? Take the highest deductible you can afford, to keep premiums low. Look for a health-insurance policy with a deductible that is annual rather than per illness. This reduces out-of-pocket expenses. Look for a co-payment schedule in which the insurer pays at least 80% of costs incurred after the deductible has been met—and the insured pays 20%. *Helpful:* Premiums that are reduced if paid annually rather than monthly or quarterly.

4. What is your maximum out-of-pocket expense? Look for a policy with a "stop-loss" provision in which your annual out-of-pocket expenses are capped at a certain amount—usually several thousand dollars for a family—and the insurer pays subsequent costs.

5. Is the policy a service-benefit plan or an indemnity plan? A service-benefit plan pays "usual, customary and reasonable" fees directly to the hospital or doctor who provides your care. This enables you to avoid steep, out-of-pocket expenses. Insurers and member-providers usually have contracts that set acceptable fees in your area.

Example: A typical policy offered by most employers.

Indemnity plans pay a specific amount for hospital rooms and medical procedures. *Caution:* Indemnity plans can be deceptively written and often pay much less than the current rate for a day in the hospital or a given surgical procedure. Before buying an indemnity plan, check on the hospital-room rate in your area and canvass a few surgeons to compare their "usual and customary" fees with what is covered.

6. What is not covered? Carefully read the clauses called "exclusions." If something that is important to you or your family is excluded from coverage, the policy is probably useless.

Examples: Psychiatric care, chiropractic care, services from "alternative providers." Preexisting conditions may be excluded for one or two years, or even permanently.

7. Is the policy guaranteed to be renewable? Many policies are guaranteed to be renewable until a specific cutoff date—usually age 65. Avoid policies that are optionally renewable by the insurer or "conditionally" renewable,

provided you have complied with the conditions in the policy. *Aim:* To avoid unwarranted cancelations.

8. Does your group policy contain a conversion clause? If you are covered through a group plan, such as a plan offered by an employer, a conversion provision allows you to continue some individual coverage for a set period of time if you become unemployed or are no longer part of the group. *Caution:* The cost of your insurance may increase, and coverage may be reduced.

9. Can coverage be extended to your family at a reasonable cost? This factor can be significant, especially in families with two working spouses, both of whom can elect to participate in either employer's group plan. *Helpful:* According to federal law, in the event of death, divorce or retirement of the employed party, the covered spouse and dependent children can continue coverage for up to three years. Unemployed workers and their families can extend coverage for 18 months.

10. Is an HMO an option? Health Maintenance Organizations (HMOs) provide comprehensive health care to member-subscribers for a fixed monthly fee. The comparison between an HMO and standard major-medical insurance can be complex, and HMOs or other managed-care plans are not for everyone. But the choice may be offered in some employers' "cafeteria plans," which allow employees to select from several different types of coverage.

Advantages: HMOs often pay for routine checkups, preventive care and other general services, which can be particularly useful for a family with young children.

Disadvantages: Choice is limited, since services must be provided by member physicians, hospitals and clinics. For someone who travels a lot, an HMO may be a poor choice, since most plans will only pay for care within the provider area, except in cases of serious emergency.

Source: Charles B. Inlander, president of the People's Medical Society in Allentown, Pennsylvania. He is co-author, with Karla Morales, of *Getting the Most For Your Medical Dollar*, Pantheon, 462 Walnut St., Allentown, Pennsylvania 18102.

Shrewder Long-Term Care Insurance Buying

Key features of a good long-term care policy…

•A prior stay in a hospital is not required before you collect your benefits.

•Coverage for Alzheimer's disease or related illnesses or disorders is guaranteed.

•Home care is included as a regular benefit or available with an extra premium. *Best:* A policy that allows you to alternate between home and a nursing home.

•Benefits are adjusted, at least partially, for inflation.

•The policy is guaranteed renewable for life.

•The policy has a "waiver of premium" clause that allows you to make no payments if ill—and after receiving benefits for a specified period of time.

•There's a "window" that allows you to change your mind and cancel the policy at no cost within the first 30 days.

Source: Daniel Kehrer, a Los Angeles-based business and finance writer and author of *Kiplinger's 12 Steps to a Worry-Free Retirement.* Kiplinger Books.

Medicaid Alert

Medicaid rules have been revised to make it harder for older people to shield their assets so that Medicaid will pay their nursing home bills.

Old law: A patient who gives assets to children or relatives or puts them in an irrevocable income-only trust must act 30 months before entering a nursing home, otherwise he/she becomes ineligible for nursing home benefits for a period not to exceed 30 months.

New law: Assets must be transferred 36 months before a patient enters a home. A longer look-back period of 60 months applies to transfers involving certain types of trusts. And, income-only trusts may no longer work. But the language of the statute as it affects trusts is un-

clear and confusing, as is the effective date of the new rules in the various states—stay tuned.

Source: Elder law attorney Peter J. Strauss, partner, Epstein Becker & Green, 250 Park Ave., New York 10177.

Money for the Very Ill

Cash needs of the terminally ill can be met by taking a loan against a life insurance policy with cash value, such as a whole life policy. *Alternatives:* If a policy does not have cash value, it's possible to borrow from family members or friends and pledge to use the policy proceeds to repay the loan. About 150 insurers now offer "living benefits" to terminally ill policyholders. *Important:* The entire family should be involved in this decision, since money taken now will not be there for the beneficiaries after the policyholder's death. *Also:* Some insurers and "viatical settlement" companies that will pay before death charge a great deal of interest on the amount withdrawn…and may even deduct from the principal—as much as 25% of the policy.

Source: Robert Hunter, head, Consumer Federation of America, 1424 16 St., NW, Washington, DC 22207.

Health Club Secrets

More than 10 million Americans work out in 15,000 health clubs and spas across the country. They pay substantial amounts for the privilege—but things don't always turn out as planned.

Health club members face three common pitfalls—insolvency, incompetence and injuries. *To protect yourself:*

•Check with consumer watchdog groups. Call your state or local consumer protection agency and the Better Business Bureau. Ask whether any negative reports have been filed against the club you have in mind. At least 36 states have enacted legislation designed specifically to protect the interests of health club members.

447

For additional information, contact the Association of Physical Fitness Centers, 600 E. Jefferson St., Rockville, MD 20852. This trade group monitors member clubs to ensure that they meet minimum standards.

Caution: Never join a health club before it opens, no matter how sterling its prospects or how luxurious its facilities. Look for a club with at least three years of continuous operation—or a new branch of an established chain.

•Conduct a thorough inspection of the club. Go at peak time—at lunch, for example, or after work. If the place is wall-to-wall with people, there is probably a lack of equipment or instructors. If it's empty, something else is wrong. *What else to look for:* The pool, bathrooms, locker rooms and weight rooms all should be clean and well-maintained. Equipment should be in good repair. Faulty or worn equipment can cause injuries. As you walk around the club, find out what members like most about the club—and what they like least.

•Make sure the club is bonded. Some states require health clubs to post a minimum bond of $500,000. While that's hardly enough for a large club, it suggests at least some financial security on the part of the owner. Request evidence of bonding from the club or from the consumer protection agency.

•Insist upon qualified instructors. Though many fine trainers lack formal credentials, competent ones often will be certified by one of three sanctioning bodies...

•American Council on Exercise, 800-825-3636.

•American College of Sports Medicine, 317-637-9200.

•Aerobics and Fitness Association of America, 800-445-5950.

•Resist hard-sell tactics. An eager salesperson may offer you a special membership contract that expires "at midnight tonight." Don't take the bait—no matter how interested you are in the club. Instead, request a one-day trial membership. *Cost:* No more than a few dollars—perhaps free. If possible, try a sample session with a personal trainer.

•Negotiate your membership fee. Annual fees range from several hundred dollars for a family all the way up to $3,500 for an individual. Some clubs tack on a nonrefundable initiation fee of several hundred dollars. But no matter what the initial quote, membership fees and conditions are almost always negotiable.

•Insist on a short-term contract. Sad but true—90% of health club members stop coming after three months. To avoid paying for workouts you never get, arrange to pay on a monthly basis...or sign up for a 90-day trial membership. *Important:* Don't sign on the spot. Take the contract home and review it with a friend or family member.

•Read the fine print. A typical contract is two pages. Each portion must be scrutinized not only for what it includes, but also for what it *omits.* Make sure you will have full access to all facilities that interest you...swimming pool, squash courts, etc. Avoid contracts that limit the hours you can use the club—unless that fits your schedule.

If the contract does not include an "escape" clause, insert one. It should stipulate that you will get a prorated refund if you move or become disabled before the term is up. *Caution:* Watch out for the *club's* escape clause—a waiver of liability in case you are injured. Such clauses are illegal in many states, but cross it off and initial it before signing just to be sure. If possible, get the club to guarantee that it won't move.

Finally, make sure the contract covers everything that you've discussed with club employees. *Never* rely on verbal agreements.

If you have second thoughts about joining a health club, ask for a full refund. Most states mandate a three-day "cooling-off" period, during which consumers can back out of contracts and major purchases.

Source: Stephen L. Isaacs, JD, professor of public health at Columbia University and a practicing attorney in New York City. He is coauthor of *The Consumer's Legal Guide to Today's Health Care: Your Medical Rights and How to Assert Them,* Houghton Mifflin, 215 Park Ave. South, New York 10003.

Home Health Care Visits

Home health care visits are covered by Medicare provided each of the following four conditions are met: The care includes intermittent skilled nursing care, physical therapy or speech therapy...the patient is confined to home...home care is approved and arranged by a doctor...the agency providing the care to the patient is a Medicare participant.

Source: *Retiring Right: Planning for Your Successful Retirement* by independent retirement and financial management planner Lawrence J. Kaplan, Manhasset, New York. Avery Publishing Group, 120 Old Broadway, Garden City Park, New York 11040.

Faster Filing of Health Insurance Claims

Prepare a master form for each of your policies. Use a blank insurance company claims form and fill in the policy number...your name and address...insured's Social Security number ...additional health coverage carried by the family...the signature of the insured. When you need to file a claim, simply photocopy the master form and add details on the bills you are submitting.

Source: *The Health Insurance Claims Kit* by Carolyn F. Shear, MSW, medical claims agent, health insurance claims processor, Deerfield, Illinois. Dearborn Financial Publishing, 520 N. Dearborn St., Chicago 60610.

Costly Procrastination

Delays can be costly in submitting health insurance claims. Most policies have a 90-day time limit—and claims will be rejected if filed after that point. Also, in most states insurers *must* begin action on claims within a set period of time after submission. The sooner a claim is filed with the insurance company, the sooner it will be reviewed and paid.

Source: *Health Insurance: How to Get It, Keep it, or Improve What You've Got* by Robert Enteen, adviser on health insurance policy issues. Paragon House, 401 Fifth Ave., New York 10016.

Vitamin-Buying Basics

A month's supply of vitamin/mineral supplements should cost no more than $5. Brand-name supplements are no better than less costly store brands...and synthetic vitamins are just as good as "natural" vitamins. *Exception:* Vitamin E. Natural vitamin E is believed to be better utilized by the body than synthetic vitamin E.

Source: Bonnie Liebman, MS, director of nutrition, Center for Science in the Public Interest, Washington, DC.

Hospital Bill Overcharges

Hospital bill overcharges can be minimized if you inform the facility in writing before you're admitted that you will only pay for treatment and equipment that you have preapproved. Errors can also be reduced by asking that an itemized bill be sent to you before it is mailed to your insurance company. *Strategy:* Show the bill to your doctor, who should be able to interpret the codes and assess the costs.

Source: Frederick Ruof is president of the National Emergency Medicine Association, a consumer group, 306 W. Joppa Rd., Baltimore 21204.

Cost-Cutting Secret

Get free drugs simply by asking for them. Doctors are constantly visited by salespeople from drug companies who leave samples. And the samples usually sit forgotten in a desk or filing cabinet. At today's prices, they're worth asking about.

How to Beat The Deduction Limit

Everyone has medical expenses and everyone faces a limit on deducting them—you can only deduct those expenses in excess of 7½ percent of your adjusted gross income. But there are ways to beat the limit…

•Double up. Maximize your medical deductions by bunching payments in alternate years. If you're not going to meet the threshold percent this year, defer paying medical bills until next year, when your combined expenses may put you over the limit.

On the other hand, if you're clearly going to meet the limit this year, stock up on medicine and drugs, pay outstanding medical and dental bills before year-end, and consider having planned dental work and voluntary surgery done (and paid for) this year, rather than next.

•Hold off. If you plan not to itemize your deductions this year, but know that you're going to itemize next year, hold off paying medical bills until January. You'll get no deduction for them this year, while next year you might.

•Charge it. Medical and dental expenses paid by credit card are deductible in the year you sign for the charge, rather than in the year you pay the credit card company. You can boost your deductions this year by putting year-end medical expenses on your credit card.

•Drugs. Only prescription drugs and insulin can be deducted as medical expenses. *Tip:* Many over-the-counter drugs can also be bought on prescription. Ask your doctor for prescriptions for patent drugs you use. *Trap:* The price, as a prescription, may be higher.

•Dependents. You are entitled to include in your deductions medical expenses you pay on behalf of a dependent. *Bonus:* You can deduct medical expenses for a family member who meets all the requirements for being claimed as your dependent except that he or she has too much income (over $2,450). *Suggestion:* Make your support dollars do double duty by paying the medical bills of a person you're helping support. Those payments could get you both a dependency deduction and a medical expense deduction.

•Life care. The medical expense portion of a lump-sum life care fee paid to a retirement home for a parent is fully deductible as a medical expense in the year the fee is paid. You may be better off taking a deduction now for future medical care rather than making annual payments.

•Separate returns. It is sometimes advantageous for a married couple to file separate returns when one spouse, but not the other, has heavy medical expenses. On a joint return, medical expenses must exceed 7½ percent of a couple's combined adjusted gross income. But if separate returns are filed, only the income of the spouse with the big medical bills is considered for the deduction limit. (The only way to tell for sure whether it's better to file jointly or separately is to work out the figures both ways).

Doctor's orders…

Obvious medical expenses include prescription drugs, doctor, dentists and psychiatrist bills, hospital costs and laboratory fees. *Less obvious expenses include:*

•Transportation costs back and forth to the doctor's office or the dentist's, by cab, train or bus. If you drive, you can deduct as a medical expense either your actual car expenses or the IRS mileage allowance (plus tolls and parking, whichever method you use).

•Lodging. A patient and an individual accompanying him can each deduct up to $50 per night of lodging expenses—but not meals—on a trip to an out-of-town hospital facility to get necessary medical care.

•Marriage counseling is deductible if performed by a licensed psychologist or psychiatrist. So is sex therapy.

•Home improvements that are medically required are deductible to the extent they do not increase the value of your property. (If a pool for an arthritis sufferer costs $10,000 to install, and increases the value of the house by $6,000, the deduction is limited to $4,000.)

•Travel simply for a change of scenery is not deductible. But trips recommended by a doctor to treat a specific ailment are deductible. *Example:* A trip to Arizona by an asthma victim or by a person whose postoperative throat condition is aggravated by cold weather.

•Weight-loss programs prescribed by a doctor as treatment for a specific medical condition such as hypertension are deductible. *Not deductible:* Weight loss to improve general health and well-being. Get a letter from your doctor recommending a specific program as treatment for a specific disorder.

Also deductible if prescribed by a doctor as treatment for a specific medical condition are:

- Stop-smoking programs.
- Speech therapy.
- Health-club visits.
- Special filters for air conditioners. Ionizers to purify the air. Filters to purify drinking water.

Other deductible medical expenses include:

- Birth-control pills, abortions that are legal under local laws, vasectomies.
- Acupuncture, hearing aids, eyeglasses, contact lenses, dentures and braces.
- Orthopedic shoes, medically required shoe lifts, support hose and surgical belts.

Source: Edward Mendlowitz, partner, Mendlowitz Weitsen, CPAs, Two Pennsylvania Plaza, New York 10121.

Tax Deductions Confidential

Keep a diary of your medical expenses. Include doctor and dentist bills and prescription drugs. The diary can be used both as proof for the IRS in case you are audited and as a reminder to yourself when filing your return.

Some not-so-obvious medical expenses that have been allowed by the courts and the IRS:

- A health club membership when prescribed as treatment for a specific medical condition. *Strategy:* Ask your doctor to put this in writing as he would any other prescription. This way, if you are audited a few years later, you'll have the prescription and be safe from the risk that you or your doctor may not remember the exact circumstances of the health club membership.
- A trip taken for the relief of a specific medical condition.
- Transportation to and from your doctor's office.
- Clarinet lessons taken on a doctor's advice to correct a dental defect.
- A dust-free room for an allergy sufferer.

- Legal fees for committing a mentally ill spouse.
- A wig bought to alleviate stress caused by hair loss—when prescribed by a doctor.
- Maintenance costs of a home swimming pool. (Has been approved when recommended by a doctor for people suffering from medical problems such as emphysema, heart problems, back problems…)
- Trained cat to alert its hearing-impaired owner to unusual sounds.
- New house siding for a person allergic to mold.
- Reclining chair bought on a doctor's orders to alleviate a heart condition.

For Corporations Only

One of the healthiest tax benefits you can provide for yourself or your key employees is a corporate medical reimbursement plan under Section 105(b).

You get full reimbursement of medical expenses without reduction for the percent of adjusted gross income limitation on medical expenses.

Medical expenses that are reimbursed to you or paid directly for your benefit are fully deductible by the corporation as compensation.

The amounts reimbursed to you or paid for your benefit are not included in your gross income.

Simply put, all medical expenses for you and all your dependents can be paid by your corporation without your having to pay one penny of income tax on the benefits.

Uninsured (self-insured) medical expense reimbursement (pay) plans have to meet the breadth-of-coverage requirements applicable to qualified pension plans. In order for medical expense reimbursements to be excluded from the employee's income, the plan must not discriminate in favor of key employees (highly compensated individuals and certain stockholders).

Source: *The Book of Tax Knowledge.* Irving L. Blackman. Boardroom Books.

Medical Insurance Tip

Medical expenses are deductible to the extent they exceed 7½ percent of your adjusted gross income…and weren't reimbursed by insurance. *Included:* The cost of medical insurance.

Insurance Trap

Insured medical expenses are not deductible, whether or not a claim is filed with your insurance company. In one case, a person didn't file a claim because of the paperwork involved. *IRS ruling:* The taxpayer could have recovered his costs through insurance, so he was entitled to no deduction.

Source: *Letter Ruling* 8102010.

Double Tax Benefit

The IRS denied medical-expense deductions taken by a quadriplegic taxpayer who won a $4 million lump-sum damage award in a malpractice suit. *IRS:* The tax-free award covered future medical expenses. If he also deducted his medical expenses, he would get a double tax benefit—the right to exclude the award from income and tax deductions. *Court of Appeals:* For the taxpayer. Tax law permits the double tax benefit.

Source: *Kelly B. Niles*, CA-9, No. 82-4278.

About Dependents

You can deduct medical bills paid for a dependent, even if you can't take a dependency exemption for that person, as long as you paid more than half that person's support in either the year the bills were run up or the year they were paid. Similarly, you can deduct bills paid now for a former spouse, as long as you were married when the bills were incurred.

Nursing Home Deductibles

Nursing home residents pay a "resident fee" and a "monthly service fee." A portion of both fees is used for medical care. *IRS ruling:* The part that is used for medical care is deductible as a medical expense.

Source: *Letter Ruling* 8502009.

Motheraid

A son paid his mother's medical expenses with money he withdrew from her bank account under a power of attorney. The IRS disallowed the son's deduction for these expenses, saying the money was really the mother's. But the Court of Appeals allowed the deduction. The money was legally his—a gift from his mother to him.

Source: *John M. Ruch*, CA-5, 82-4463.

Lifetime Care

A one-time medical payment for a lifetime of medical care was fully deductible in the year paid. It didn't matter that treatment might take place in later years.

Source: *Acquiescence in Estate of Smith*, 79 TC 313.

Prepaid Institution Fees

• A taxpayer prepaid a fee for the lifetime institutional care of his mentally retarded dependent son. The IRS ruled that the entire fee was deductible in the year it was paid, even though the taxpayer will receive a refund if his son dies within five years. The refund, of course, will have to be declared as income.

Source: *Letter Ruling 8310057.*

•The parents of an autistic child planned to make a lump-sum payment to an institution for lifetime care of the child. The payment would be partially refunded if the child died within 10 years. *IRS ruling:* The full prepayment is deductible as a medical expense despite a possible refund.

Source: *Letter Ruling 8309011.*

A Change of Scene For a Depressed Child

A teenage girl suffered from depression. After conventional therapy failed, her parents decided to take her on trips that would provide her with new experiences. The girl's condition improved, but the Tax Court said that the travel costs were not a deductible medical expense. *Reason:* The trips were not prescribed by a doctor and did not amount to standard medical care.

Source: *Joseph R. Levene*, TC Memo 1982-5.

When a Trip Is Deductible and When It's Not

A doctor suggested that a change in environment could improve a taxpayer's parents' condition. So, the taxpayer sent them on an all-expenses-paid trip to Houston, Texas. Can he deduct the cost?

The IRS will usually allow a medical trip to be deducted if it is made on the advice of a doctor to treat a specific condition, when a change in locale is medically recognized as treatment for

that condition. *Example:* A trip to Florida by a person recovering from throat surgery in a northern city, when cold air could aggravate his condition. *Limit:* Only travel costs (including meals and lodging en route) are deductible. Living costs at the destination are not.

Trips to promote general health are not deductible. So a doctor's recommendation that "change of scenery" might help one's general condition won't get a deduction.

Finally, to get a medical deduction for your parents' expenses, you must have provided more than half of their financial support for the entire year.

Medical Trips

Parents who drove their disabled son to an out-of-state clinic for treatment could deduct travel costs plus expenses for lodging on the trip.

Source: *William L. Pfersching*, TC Memo 1983-341.

•A taxpayer's dependent adult son had an operation in an out-of-state clinic. The parent flew to the clinic each day during the post-operative period. *IRS ruling:* The parent's airplane fare was a deductible medical expense. So was the cost of renting a car to drive to the clinic and hospital. *Key:* The clinic required someone to attend patients during their post-operative period.

Source: *Letter Ruling 8321042.*

Long-Distance Telephoning

Telephone counseling was deductible as a medical expense when a person's psychologist was located 350 miles away. The long-distance telephone bills were a necessary part of a post-drug addiction recovery program.

Source: *Letter Ruling 8034087.*

Three Special Schools That Were Deductible And One that Wasn't

•Taxpayers were advised by psychiatrists to put their emotionally disturbed child in a psychiatrically oriented boarding school with a strong guidance program. *IRS ruling:* Since the school fit the tax law's definition of a "special school," the tuition was deductible as a medical expense.

Source: *Letter Ruling* 8447014.

•The cost of a special school for a child with a specific learning disability was deductible. *Key:* The school has a specialized curriculum, and it required neurological and psychological testing before admission.

Source: *Letter Ruling* 8445032.

•The IRS ruled that parents could deduct the cost of sending their child, who suffered from dyslexia, to a special school for children with learning disabilities. *Key:* The school had a specialized professional staff providing services that weren't available in regular schools. *Also deductible:* The cost of transporting the child to and from school.

Source: *Letter Ruling* 8401024.

•Two children suffering from language learning disabilities were sent to a special school. Costs were $1,800 above regular tuition. The parents deducted that amount as a medical expense. But the IRS disallowed the deduction because the school had no trained psychiatrists or psychologists on staff and because the special schooling had not been recommended by a doctor. *Tax Court:* For the parents. The childrens' disorders were severe enough to make normal education impossible. And, while the school's staff members did not qualify as medical personnel, they had been trained in special-education techniques.

Source: *Lawrence F. Fay,* 76 TC 408.

Home Improvements Are Deductible...But

Medically required home improvements, such as elevators, air conditioners and swimming pools, qualify in part as deductible medical expenses. But, in order to get the deduction, the taxpayer making the improvements must have a property interest in the home. *Recent ruling:* A polio victim who had a specially designed swimming pool installed at his parents' home could not deduct part of the cost. Although he lived in the house, he had no ownership interest in it.

Source: *Letter Ruling* 8249025.

Child Safety

The cost of removing lead-based paint from areas within a child's reach was ruled to be deductible as a medical expense when the purpose was to prevent the lead poisoning of a child who had been exposed to the paint. *Not deductible:* The cost of removing the paint from areas not within the child's reach, and the cost of repainting.

Source: *Revenue Ruling* 79-66.

When Swimming Is Allowed

•A patient with emphysema and bronchitis was advised by his doctor to exercise by swimming. Because local pool hours didn't coincide with his work schedule, he built his own indoor pool. He deducted the cost of fuel, electricity, insurance and other maintenance expenses. *IRS position:* The existence of a diving board and the lack of medical equipment showed that the pool was for nondeductible personal use. *Tax Court:* Expenses were deductible. The patient's need to exercise his lungs didn't require any medical equipment except the pool. Recreational use by his family was incidental.

Source: *Herbert Cherry*, TC Memo 1983-470.

•A special "lap" swimming pool for a sufferer of osteoarthritis was a deductible medical expense to the extent that the cost of the pool exceeded the resulting increase in the value of the property.

Source: *Revenue Ruling* 83-33.

•Swimming pool fees are a deductible medical expense when the pool is used following a doctor's recommendation. A couple could deduct the $100 a year they paid for their son to have access to a local pool, when a doctor had prescribed swimming as therapy for the son's arthritis.

Source: *Letter Ruling* 8326095.

When Your Doctor Puts It in Writing and When He Doesn't

•A taxpayer with high blood pressure was urged by his doctor to take a 13-day diet and exercise program at a health institute. *IRS ruling:* The cost of the program was a deductible medical expense. *Key:* The course was prescribed as treatment for a specific physical illness. The doctor put his recommendation in writing.

Source: *Letter Ruling* 8251045.

•Spa fees didn't reduce taxes. A woman claimed she was told by her doctor to join a health club. But she couldn't prove it because he died. *Tax Court:* Disallowed a medical deduction. *Reason:* Lack of doctor's proof that the payments were directly related to her medical care. Expenditures made for general health benefits aren't deductible.

Source: *May Gayle Strickland*, TC Memo 1984-301.

•Roy Disney, Walt's brother, claimed a medical expense deduction for a mechanical exercise horse. Disney's doctor had suggested more exercise and had recommended various kinds of gym equipment. But the doctor had not specifically prescribed use of a mechanical horse. *Result:* Deduction denied. *Lesson:* Have

your doctor put his recommendations in writing and make sure they are specific.

Source: *Roy O. Disney*, DC-Calif., 413 F. 2d 783.

How to Stop Smoking, Lose Weight and Get a Deduction

No-smoking and weight-reduction programs to improve your general health are not deductible, even when recommended by a doctor. But a weight-reduction program prescribed as treatment of hypertension, obesity, and hearing loss was ruled deductible. *Key:* The program was prescribed to treat specific ailments. The IRS would probably rule the same way on a no-smoking program prescribed by a doctor for a specific ailment, such as emphysema.

Source: *IRS Revenue Ruling* 79-162; *IRS Letter Ruling* 8004111.

When a Special Car Isn't Deductible

A back injury made it difficult for Donald Robb to drive a normal car, so a doctor recommended the purchase of a specially equipped van which made driving easier. *Tax Court:* The cost was not a deductible medical expense because the van had no therapeutic value.

Source: *Donald G. Robb*, TC Memo 1982-687.

If Vitamins Are Prescribed

The cost of vitamins was deductible when they were prescribed as treatment for a specific medical condition...in this case, arteriosclerosis and related heart ailments.

Source: *Garnett Neil*, TC Memo 1982-562.

Unusual Medical Deductions

- Whiskey prescribed for heart disease.
- The cost of electrolysis qualifies as a deductible medical expense.

Source: *Letter Ruling* 8442018.

- A clarinet and clarinet lessons were deductible medical expenses when prescribed as treatment for a child's dental defects.

Source: *Letter Ruling* 62-210.

- A doctor prescribed a wig to relieve the mental distress of a person whose hair fell out. The cost of the wig was a deductible medical expense.

Source: *Revenue Ruling* 62-189.

- Sex therapy treatments are deductible as a medical expense.

Source: *Revenue Ruling* 75-187.

- Legal costs related to the commitment of a taxpayer's mentally ill spouse to a hospital were held to be deductible as a medical expense.

Source: *Carl A. Gestacker,* 414 F2d 448.

For Much Lower Medical Costs

The most sensible way to balance your medical budget begins with an eye on good health…

- Eat a nutritionally balanced diet…and exercise regularly.
- See your doctor regularly. Preventive maintenance helps keep both your body and your wallet fit. Get a thorough physical exam once a year—it can nip a problem before it turns into a costly illness.
- Quit smoking. Not only will you save on the ever-increasing cost of cigarettes, but your chances of suffering from smoking-related diseases will decrease.
- Get an annual flu shot. Even if it doesn't stop the flu, it will at least make the illness less severe.
- Be wary of con artists promoting miracle cures. Check with a physician, pharmacist or other health care professional before buying health care products or programs.
- Don't purchase insurance coverage that duplicates what you already have. This is an area where scammers often travel. Be wary of direct mail pitches and read all the fine print.
- Shop for a doctor who'll accept you as a patient "on assignment," if you are on Medicare. That way the doctor will bill Medicare and not make you pay up front.
- Take advantage of free or discounted services—vision and dental care are often available from universities where students, supervised by instructors, do the work.
- Buy cheaper medicines. If your prescriptions aren't covered by insurance, ask your doctor for generic equivalents.

Source: Diane Warner, author of *How to Have a Great Retirement on a Limited Budget,* Writer's Digest Books.

21

Health Research at Your Fingertips

Toll-Free Numbers for Health Information

The federal government operates many clearing houses and information centers that focus on specific topics. Their services include distributing publications, providing referrals and answering inquiries. Many offer toll-free numbers.

AIDS/HIV...

AIDS Clinical Trials Information Service:

Provides current information on federally and privately sponsored clinical trials for AIDS patients and others with HIV infection. Sponsored by the Centers for Disease Control, the Food and Drug Administration, the National Institute of Allergy and Infectious Diseases, and the National Library of Medicine. 9 a.m–7 p.m.

800-874-2572
800-243-7012 TDD

National AIDS Hotline:

Provides general information to the public

on the prevention and spread of AIDS.

800-342-2437 24 hours
800-344-7432 Spanish, 8 a.m.-2 a.m.
7 days a week, except holidays
800-243-7889 TDD, 10 a.m.-10 p.m.

CDC National AIDS Clearinghouse:

Collects, classifies, distributes up-to-date information and educational materials; provides expert assistance to HIV and AIDS prevention professionals. A service of the Centers for Disease Control. 9 a.m.–7 p.m.

800-458-5231; 800-243-7012 TDD
800-342-AIDS Hotline

National Criminal Justice Reference Services AIDS Clearinghouse:

Distributes a series of AIDS bulletins. Also maintains a literature database. 8:30 a.m.–7 p.m.

800-851-3420; 301-251-5500 in Maryland

National Indian AIDS Hotline:

Provides printed materials and information about AIDS and AIDS prevention in the Indian community. 8:30 a.m.–12 p.m. and 1 p.m.–5 p.m.

800-342-2437

Project Inform Hotline:

Provides treatment information and referral for HIV-infected individuals. Information on clinical trials. No diagnosis. 10 a.m.–4 p.m. (Pacific) Monday–Saturday.

800-822-7422, 800-334-7422 in California

Adoption...

Bethany Christian Services:

Services for women considering adoption. Free testing and counseling. 8 a.m.–1 a.m. every day.

800-238-4269

National Adoption Center:

Promotes adoption opportunities throughout the US, particularly for children with special needs. Links all state adoption agencies through a telecommunications network. Addresses adoption and child welfare issues. 9 a.m.–5 p.m.

800-862-3678; 215-735-9988 in Pennsylvania

Aging...

National Eldercare Institute on Health Promotion:

Supports State Units on Aging and other organizations in the field of aging and health in developing and implementing health promotion programs for older adults. Maintains a health promotion library, disseminates information on health promotion for minority populations and provides resource lists and referrals to health-promotion organizations. Library materials may be viewed by appointment only.

601 E St. NW, Fifth Floor
Washington, DC 20049
202-434-2200; 202-434-6474 (Fax)

National Institute on Aging Information Center:

Provides information and publications on topics of interest to older adults, to the public and to doctors, nurses, social activities directors and health educators.

Box 8057
Gaithersburg, Maryland 20898-8057
800-222-2225

National Council on Aging:

Provides information and publications on topics such as family caregivers, senior employment, long-term care. 9 a.m.–5 p.m.

800-424-9046

Alcoholism/Drug Abuse...

Toxic Substances Control Act Assistance Information Service:

Provides information and referrals to government officials, the public and the press.

401 M St. SW
Washington, DC 20024
202-554-0515; 202-554-5603 (Fax)

Al-Anon Family Group Headquarters:

Provides printed materials specifically aimed at helping families dealing with the problems of alcoholism. 9 a.m.–4:30 p.m. (EST)...24-hour hotline.

800-356-9996

Alcohol and Drug Helpline:

Provides referrals to local facilities where adolescents and adults can seek help 24 hours.

800-821-4357; 801-272-4357 in Utah

Office for Substance Abuse Prevention's National Clearinghouse for Alcohol and Drug Information:

Gathers and disseminates information on alcohol and other drug-related subjects. Distributes publications. Services include subject searches and provision of statistics and other information.

Box 2345, Rockville, Maryland 20847-2345
800-729-6686, 301-468-2600
800-487-4889 (TT); 301-468-6433 (Fax)

National Council on Alcoholism and Drug Dependence Hopeline:

Refers to local affiliates for counseling and provides written information on alcoholism. Operates 24 hours.

800-622-2255
212-979-1010 9 a.m.-9 p.m. in New York

American Council on Alcoholism:

Offers treatment referrals, counseling and advice for recovering alcoholics. 24 hours.

800-527-5344

Alzheimer's Disease...

Alzheimer's Disease and Related Disorders Association:

Refers to local chapters. Offers information on publications available from the association. 8 a.m.–5 p.m. (Central).

800-272-3900

Alzheimer's Disease Education and Referral Center:

Sponsored by the National Institute on Aging. Provides information and publications on Alzheimer's disease to health and service professionals, patients and their families, caregivers and the general public.

Box 8250, Silver Spring, Maryland 20907-8250
800-438-4380; 301-495-3334 (Fax)

Arthritis…

National Arthritis and Musculoskeletal and Skin Diseases Information Clearinghouse:

Identifies educational materials about arthritis and musculoskeletal diseases and serves as an information exchange for individuals and organizations involved in public, professional and patient education. Conducts subject searches and makes resource referrals.

Box AMS, 9000 Rockville Pike
Bethesda, Maryland 20892
301-495-4484; 301-587-4352 (Fax)

Arthritis Foundation Information Hotline:
Provides publications, information and referrals to local organizations. 9 a.m.–7 p.m.

800-283-7800

Cancer…

American Cancer Society Response Line:
Provides publications and information about cancer and coping with cancer. Refers callers to the local chapters of the American Cancer Society for support services. A service of the American Cancer Society. 8:30 a.m.–4:30 p.m.

800-227-2345

Cancer Information Service (CIS):
Answers cancer-related questions from the public, cancer patients and families and health professionals. Spanish-speaking staff members are available. A service of the National Cancer Institute. 9 a.m.–10 p.m.

800-4-CANCER, 800-422-6237

National Marrow Donor Program:
Provides information about marrow donation and transplantation. Answers questions and can refer inquiries about patient issues, medical research and recruitment to potential donors or people interested in becoming donors. Lists local donor centers. Operates 8 a.m. to 6 p.m. (Central). M–F.

800-MARROW-2

Chemical Products/Pesticides…

CHEMTREC Center:
Provides nonemergency referrals to companies that manufacture chemicals and to state and federal agencies for health and safety information and information regarding chemical regulations. 9 a.m.–6 p.m. (EST).

800-262-8200

National Pesticide Telecommunications Network:

Responds to nonemergency questions about the effects of pesticides, toxicology and symptoms, environmental effects, disposal and cleanup, and safe use of pesticides. Also responds to emergency questions from home owners, medical professionals and veterinarians. A service of the Environmental Protection Agency and Oregon State University. 9:30 a.m.–7:30 p.m. (EST). M-F.

800-858-7378

Child Abuse/Missing Children…

Child Find of America, Inc.:
Looks for missing and abducted children. Operates 24 hours.

800-426-5678

Professional Mediation Services:
800-AWAY-OUT (800-292-9688)

Covenant House Nineline:
Crisis line for youth, teens and families. Locally based referrals throughout the United States. Help for youth and parents regarding drugs, abuse, homelessness, runaway children and message relays. Operates 24 hours.

800-999-9999

National Child Abuse Hotline:
Provides crisis intervention and professional counseling on child abuse. Gives referrals to local social service groups offering counseling on child abuse. Has literature on child abuse in English and Spanish. 24 hours.

800-422-4453

National Child Safety Council Childwatch:
Answers questions and distributes literature on safety, including drug abuse, household dangers, and electricity. Provides safety information to local police departments. Sponsor of

459

the missing kids milk carton program. Operates 24 hours.

800-222-1464

National Clearinghouse on Child Abuse and Neglect Information:

Serves as a major resource center for the acquisition and dissemination of child abuse and neglect materials; free publications catalog upon request. Provides information services to professionals who work to prevent child abuse and assist its victims. 8:30 a.m.–5:30 p.m.

800-394-3366; 703-385-7565

National Hotline for Missing Children:

Operates a hotline for reporting missing children and sightings of missing children. Offers assistance to law enforcement agents. A service of the National Center for Missing and Exploited Children. 7:30 a.m.–11 p.m.

800-843-5678
703-235-3900 in Virginia/DC

National Resource Center on Child Abuse and Neglect:

Provides general information and statistics about child abuse. Sponsored by American Humane Association. 8:30 a.m.–1:30 p.m.

800-227-5242

National Runaway Switchboard:

Provides crisis intervention and traveler's assistance to runaways. Gives referrals to shelters nationwide. Also relays messages to, or sets up conference calls with, parents at the request of the child. Operates 24 hours.

800-621-4000

National Youth Crisis Hotline:

Provides counseling and referrals to local drug treatment centers, shelters and counseling services. Responds to youth dealing with pregnancy, molestation, suicide and child abuse. 24 hours.

800-448-4663

Child Development…

National Center for Education in Maternal and Child Health:

Responds to information requests from consumers and professionals, provides technical

assistance, and develops educational and reference materials.

2000 15 St. N, Suite 701
Arlington, Virginia 22201-7802
703-524-7802; 703-524-9335 (Fax)

National Maternal and Child Health Clearinghouse:

Centralized source of materials and information in the areas of human genetics and maternal and child health. Distributes publications and provides referrals.

8201 Greensboro Dr., Suite 600
McLean, Virginia 22102
703-821-8955, ext. 254 or 265
703-821-2098 (Fax)

Human Growth Foundation:

Provides parent education and mutual support, supports research and promotes public awareness of the physical and emotional problems of short-statured people. Offers brochures on a number of child growth abnormalities. 8 a.m.–5 p.m.

800-451-6434, 703-883-1773 in Virginia

Family Life Information Exchange:

Provides information related to family planning issues and distributes publications on these subjects. Makes referrals to other information centers in related subject areas. Produces a directory of family planning grantees, delegates and clinics supported by the Office of Population Affairs.

Box 37299, Washington, DC 20013-7299
301-585-6636

Child Education…

National Association for the Education of Young Children:

Sponsors workshops, conferences, and public awareness activities concerning the education of young children, birth through age 8. Publishes books, posters and brochures for teachers and parents of young children. 9 a.m.–5 p.m.

800-424-2460; 202-232-8777 in DC

Diabetes/Digestive Diseases…

American Diabetes Association:

Provides literature, a free newsletter, information on health education and refers to local affiliates for support-group assistance. 8:30 a.m.–5 p.m.

800-232-3472; 703-549-1500 in Virginia/DC

Juvenile Diabetes Foundation International Hotline:

Answers questions and provides brochures on juvenile diabetes. Refers to local chapters, physicians and clinics. 9 a.m.–5 p.m.

800-223-1138; 212-785-9500 in New York

National Diabetes Information Clearinghouse:

Collects and disseminates information about patient and professional education materials related to diabetes and its complications. Distributes its own publications and other diabetes-related materials. Maintains a registry of meetings pertaining to diabetes and an automated database of patient and professional materials. Library collection is open to the public, although materials do not circulate.

Box NDIC, 9000 Rockville Pike
Bethesda, Maryland 20892
301-468-2162

Drug Abuse...

Adcare Hospital Helpline

Provides information and referral for alcohol and other drug concerns. 24 hours. Nationwide.

800-252-6465

Drug Free for a New Century Hotline

Provides alcohol and other drug statistics, information and referrals. Prerecorded messages targeted to the media, community leaders, and the general public. Operates 24 hours. (8 a.m.–5 p.m. to speak with information specialists.)

800-487-4890

Drug-Free Workplace Helpline

Offers general information, publications, and referrals to corporations, businesses, industry, and national organizations on assessing the drug abuse within an organization and developing, and implementing drug abuse policy and programs. A service of the National Institute on Drug Abuse. 9 a.m.–8 p.m.

800-843-4971

NIDA Hotline

Provides general information on drug abuse and on AIDS as it relates to intravenous drug users. Offers referrals to drug rehabilitation cen-

ters. A service of the National Institute on Drug Abuse. 9 a.m.-3 a.m. Mon.-Fri.; 12 p.m.–3 a.m. Sat. and Sun.

800-662-4357; 800-662-9832 Spanish

Fire Prevention...

National Fire Protection Association:

Develops fire protection codes and standards and provides technical information on fire prevention, firefighting procedures and the fire loss experience. 8:30 a.m.–8 p.m.

800-344-3555; 617-770-3000, ext. 416

Fitness...

Aerobics and Fitness Foundation:

Answers questions from the public regarding safe and effective exercise programs and practices. Offers general information on the association for educators and certification for aerobic teachers and professionals. 10 a.m.–5 p.m. (Pacific).

800-233-4886

YMCA of the USA:

Provides information about YMCA services and locations. 8:30 a.m.–5 p.m. (Central).

800-872-9622

Food Safety...

Meat and Poultry Hotline:

Provides safety hints on proper handling, preparation, storage and cooking of meat, poultry and eggs. Sponsored by the US Department of Agriculture. 10 a.m.–4 p.m. (EST).

800-535-4555

Food and Nutrition Information Center:

Provides information on human nutrition, food service management and food technology. Acquires and lends books and audiovisual materials.

Department of Agriculture
National Agricultural Library, Room 304
10301 Baltimore Boulevard
Beltsville, Maryland 20705-2351
301-504-5719; 301-504-6409 (Fax)

General Health...

Agency for Health Care Policy and Research Clearinghouse:

Distributes publications produced by the agency, including clinical practice guidelines on a variety of topics, reports from the National

Medical Expenditure Survey and health care technology assessment reports.

Box 8547
Silver Spring, Maryland 20907-8547
800-358-9295
301-594-1364 x 169

Office of Minority Health Resource Center:

Responds to information requests from health professionals on minority health issues and locates sources of technical assistance. Has developed a Resource Persons Network, and provides referrals to relevant organizations. Bilingual staff members are available to serve Spanish-speaking requesters.

Box 37337
Washington, DC 20013-7337
800-444-6472; 301-589-0884 (Fax)

ODPHP National Health Information Center:

Helps the public and health professionals locate health information through identification of health information resources, an information and referral system and publications. Uses a database containing descriptions of health-related organizations to refer inquirers to the most appropriate resources. Collection of journals, newsletters, references and educational materials is available for use by the public; advance arrangements are recommended. Prepares and distributes publications and directories on health promotion and disease prevention topics.

1010 Wayne Ave., #300
Silver Spring, Maryland 20910
800-336-4797
301-565-4020; 301-565-5112 (Fax)

National Center for Health Statistics:

Provides professionals with information about the development of health measures. Offers referral services and distributes annotated bibliographies. Access to the library of 4,000 documents and journals is available by appointment.

6525 Belcrest Rd., Room 1064
Hyattsville, Maryland 20782
301-436-8500

National Heart, Lung, and Blood Institute Education Programs Information Center:

Serves as a source of information and materials on risk factors for cardiovascular disease.

Box 30105
Bethesda, Maryland 20824-0105
301-251-1222; 301-925-1223 (Fax)

Federal Information Center Program:

Provides information about the federal government's agencies, programs and services. Current government reference materials and service directories are used to respond to inquiries.

General Services Administration
Seventh and D Streets SW
Washington, DC 20407
202-708-5804

Medic Alert Foundation:

Provides emergency service for people who cannot speak for themselves by means of a unique member number on a Medic Alert bracelet or necklace.

800-432-5378

Handicapping Conditions...
See also Hearing and Speech

Heath Resource Center:

Provides information on postsecondary education for the handicapped and on learning disabilities. 9 a.m.-5 p.m.

800-544-3284; 202-939-9320 in DC

Clearinghouse on Disability Information, Office of Special Education and Rehabilitative Services Department of Education:

Responds to inquiries on a wide range of topics, especially in the areas of federal funding, legislation and programs benefiting people with disabling conditions. Provides referrals.

330 S St. SW, Switzer Building, Room 3132
Washington, DC 20202-2524
202-205-8241; 202-205-9252 (Fax)

Job Accommodation Network:

Offers ideas for accommodating handicapped persons in the workplace and information on the availability of accommodation aids and procedures. 8 a.m.–8 p.m. Monday-Thursday; 8 a.m–5 p.m. Friday.

800-526-7234 Voice/TDD
800-232-9675 Voice/TDD

National Center for Youth with Disabilities:

Identifies appropriate resources to guide youths with disabilities through the transition from adolescence to adulthood. Offers a variety of bibliographies and pamphlets and runs the National Resource Library Database, which provides model programs, consultants, and training materials. 8 a.m.–4:30 p.m. (Central).

University of Minnesota
800-333-6293; 612-626-2825

National Information Center for Children and Youth with Disabilities (NICHCY):
Information and referral service dedicated to disabled and handicapped children. 10 a.m.–5 p.m. or leave recorded message after hours.

800-695-0285; 202-884-8200

National Information Clearinghouse for Infants with Disabilities and Life Threatening Conditions:
Makes referrals to support groups and sources of financial, medical, and educational assistance for families having infants with disabilities (ages 0–3). 9 a.m.–5 p.m.

800-922-9234, ext. 201
800-922-1107 in South Carolina

National Rehabilitation Information Center:
Provides rehabilitation information on assistive devices and disseminates other rehabilitation-related information related to disabilities. 8 a.m.–6 p.m. (EST).

800-346-2742; 301-588-9284 in Maryland

Head Injury/Headache…

National Injury Information Clearinghouse:
Collects, investigates, analyzes and disseminates information on the causes and prevention of death, injury and illness associated with consumer products.

CPOC
Washington, DC 20207
301-504-0424; 301-504-0124 (Fax)

National Headache Foundation:
Sends literature on headaches and treatment and offers membership information. 9 a.m.–5 p.m. (Central).

800-843-2256; 800-523-8858 in Illinois

National Brain Injury Association Family Helpline:
Dedicated to improving the quality of life of people with head injury and their families. 9 a.m.–5 p.m. (EST).

1776 Massachusetts Ave. NW, Ste. 100
Washington, DC 20036
800-444-6443

Hearing and Speech…

American Speech-Language-Hearing Association:
Offers free information on speech, language and hearing disorders. They also certify audiologists and speech language pathologists. 8:30 a.m.–5 p.m.

800-638-8255; 301-897-5700 in Maryland

Deafness Research Foundation:
Funds research into prevention of deafness and its treatment. 9 a.m.–5 p.m.

800-535-3323; 212-768-1181 Voice/TTY

Dial a Hearing Screening Test:
Answers questions on hearing problems and makes referrals to local numbers for a two-minute hearing test, as well as ear, nose and throat specialists. Also makes referrals to organizations that have information on ear-related problems, including questions on broken hearing aids. 9 a.m.–5 p.m. (EST).

800-222-3277

Hear Now:
Provides hearing aids, cochlear implants and related services for the hearing impaired who do not have the financial resources to purchase these devices. Collects and distributes reconditioned hearing aids. Applications for assistance available. For individual assistance, call 8 a.m.–5 p.m. Leave recorded message after hours.

800-648-4327 Voice/TDD

Hearing Aid Helpline:
Provides information and distributes a directory of hearing aid specialists certified by the International Hearing Society. 10 a.m.–4 p.m. (EST).

800-521-5247

Hearing Helpline:
Provides information on better hearing and preventing deafness. Materials are mailed on request. A service of the Better Hearing Institute. 9 a.m.–5 p.m.

800-327-9355; 703-642-0580 in Virginia

John Tracy Clinic:
Provides free diagnostic, habilitative and educational services to preschool deaf children and their families through on-site services, and to preschool deaf and deaf-blind through

worldwide correspondence courses in Spanish and English. 8 a.m.-4 p.m. (Pacific). Leave message after hours.

800-522-4582

Tripod Grapevine:

Offers information on deafness, including raising and educating a deaf child. Refers callers to parents, professionals, and resources in their own communities nationwide. 8 a.m.-5 p.m. (Pacific) or leave recorded messages after hours.

800-352-8888 Voice/TDD
800-287-4763 in California, Voice/TDD

Hospital/Hospice Care…

Children's Hospice International:

Within a community, provides support system and information for health care professionals, families, and the network of organizations that offer hospice care to children with life threatening conditions. Distributes educational materials. 9 a.m.–5 p.m.

2202 Mt. Vernon Ave., Ste. 3C
Alexandria, VA 22301
800-242-4453; 703-684-0330

Hill-Burton Hospital Free Care:

Provides information on hospitals and other health facilities participating in the Hill-Burton Hospital Free Care Program. A service of the Bureau of Resource Development, US Department of Health and Human Services. 9:30 a.m-5:30 p.m. or leave recorded message after hours.

800-638-0742; 800-492-0359 in Maryland

Hospice Education Institute Hospice Link:

Offers general information about hospice care and makes referrals to local programs. Does not offer medical advice or personal counseling. 9 a.m.–4 p.m.

800-331-1620; 203-767-1620 in Connecticut

Shriners Hospital Referral Line:

Gives information on free hospital care available to children under 18 who need orthopedic care or burn treatment. Sends application forms to requesters who meet eligibility requirements for treatment provided by 22 Shriners Hospitals in the United States, Mexico, and Canada. 8 a.m.–5 p.m.

800-237-5055

Impotence…

Impotence and Prostate Information Center:

Provides free information to prospective patients regarding the causes of and treatments for impotence and prostate problems. 8:30 a.m.–5 p.m. (Central) or leave recorded message after hours.

800-843-4315

Recovery of Male Potency:

Self-help group assisting patients. Distributes information packet. A service of Grace Hospital, Detroit, and affiliated with 23 hospitals nationwide. 9 a.m.–5 p.m.

800-835-7667; 313-357-1216 in Michigan

Medicare Telephone Hotline:

Gives information on medigap insurance and policies. A service of the Health Care Financing Administration, U.S. Department of Health and Human Services. 8 a.m.–8 p.m., year round.

800-638-6833

National Insurance Consumer Helpline:

Represents life, health, property and casual insurance companies. Consumer awareness on policies and technical language. 8 a.m.–8 p.m.

800-942-4242

Justice…

National Criminal Justice Reference Service:

Provides research findings and documents from bureaus within the Office of Justice. 8:30 a.m.–7 p.m. (Eastern).

800-851-3420

Learning Disorders…
See also Handicapping Conditions

The Orton Dyslexia Society:

Clearinghouse that provides, through its 44 branches, information on testing, tutoring, and computers used to aid people with dyslexia and related disorders. 9 a.m.–5 p.m. Leave recorded message after hours.

800-222-3123; 410-296-0232 in Maryland

Library Services…

Modern Talking Picture Service, Inc.:

Provides free loan of captioned film for the deaf and hearing impaired. 8:30 a.m.–5 p.m.

800-237-6213 Voice/TDD

National Audiovisual Center:

Provides information on a variety of government-produced materials, including slides, videos, 16mm films, books and cassettes. 8:30 a.m.– 4 p.m.

800-788-6282

National Library Service for the Blind and Physically Handicapped:

A network of 56 regional and over 100 local libraries that work in cooperation with the Library of Congress to provide free library service to anyone who is visually or physically impaired. Provides both audio and Braille formats through a network of state libraries. 8 a.m.–4:30 p.m. (Eastern).

800-424-8567; 202-707-5100 in DC

Recording for the Blind:

Serves people who cannot read standard print because of a visual, learning, or physical disability. Provides text books on tape and on computer diskettes. One-time registration fee of 525 entitles user to lifetime borrowing privileges. 8:30 a.m.–9 p.m. Leave recorded message after hours.

800-221-4792

Liver Diseases…

American Liver Foundation:

Provides information, including fact sheets, and makes physician and support group referrals. Liver disease information brochure available upon request. 9 a.m.–5 p.m. (Eastern).

800-223-0179; 201-256-2550 in New Jersey

Lung Diseases/Asthma/Allergy

Asthma and Allergy Foundation of America:

Provides general information, publications and videos and referrals to physicians. Operates 24 hours.

800-727-8462

Asthma Information Line:

Provides written materials on asthma and allergies. A service of the American Academy of Allergy and Immunology. Operates 24 hours.

800-822-2762

Lung Line National Asthma Center:

Answers questions about asthma, emphysema, chronic bronchitis, allergies, juvenile rheumatoid arthritis, smoking and other respiratory and immune system disorders. Ques-

tions answered by registered nurses. A service of the National Jewish Center for Immunology and Respiratory Medicine. 8 a.m.-5 p.m. (Mountain).

800-222-5864

Lupus…

American Lupus Society:

Provides a 24-hour recording for callers to leave their names and addresses to receive information on services provided.

800-331-1802

Mental Health…

National Clearinghouse on Family Support and Children's Mental Health:

Distributes publications on parent/family support groups, financing and early intervention services.

Portland State University
Box 751, Portland, Oregon 97207-0751
800-628-1696

National Foundation for Depressive Illness:

A 24-hour recorded message describes symptoms of depression and gives an address for more information and physician referral.

800-248-4344

National Mental Health Association:

Makes referrals to mental health groups. Educational brochures available. 9 a.m.–5 p.m.

800-969-6642

Myasthenia Gravis…

Myasthenia Gravis Foundation:

Provides information regarding services for myasthenia patients. Promotes public awareness. 8:45 a.m.–4:45 p.m. (Central).

800-541-5454

Nutrition…

American Dietetic Hotline:

Provides dietetic and nutrition information. Callers wishing to speak to a dietitian call between 9 a.m. and 4 p.m. A recorded message is available 24 hours.

800-366-1655

National Dairy Council:

Develops and provides educational materials on nutrition. 8:30 a.m.–4:30 p.m. (Central).

800-426-8271

Organ Donation...
See also Vision and Urological Disorders

The Living Bank:
Operates a registry and referral service for people wanting to commit their tissues, bones or vital organs to transplantation or research. Informs the public about organ donation and transplantation. Operates 24 hours.
800-528-2971

Organ Donor Hotline:
Offers information and referrals for organ donation and transplantation. Answers requests for organ donor cards. Operates 24 hours.
800-243-6667

Paralysis and Spinal Cord Injury...
See also Handicapping Conditions, Stroke

National Rehabilitation Information Clearinghouse:
Supplies publications on disability-related topics, prepares bibliographies tailored to specific requests and assists in locating answers to questions. Open to the public, the center has a collection of materials on rehabilitation and documents on professional and administrative practices and concerns. The center also publishes a directory of librarians specializing in rehabilitation and a free quarterly newsletter. 8 a.m.–6 p.m. (Eastern).
8455 Colesville Rd., Suite 935
Silver Spring, Maryland 20910
800-346-2742; 301-588-9284
301-587-1967 (Fax)

National Spinal Cord Injury:
Makes referrals to local chapters and other organizations. Produces the National Resource Directory, which deal with topics helpful to handicapped individuals. 9 a.m.-5:30 p.m.
800-962-9629 for members and individuals with spinal cord injuries; no vendors
617-935-2722 for nonmembers, general public, professionals

Parkinson's Disease...

National Parkinson Foundation:
Answers questions about the disease: Staffed by nurses. Also makes physician referrals and provides written materials. 8 a.m.–5 p.m.
800-327-4545; 800-433-7022 in Florida
305-547-6666 in Miami

Practitioner Reporting...

Practitioner Reporting System:
Offers a service for health professionals to report problems with drugs or medical devices. A service of the Food and Drug Administration. 8:30 a.m–4:30 pm.
800-638-6725

Pregnancy...

ASPO/Lamaze (American Society for Psychoprophylaxis in Obstetrics):
Offers a list of local certified childbirth educators for those interested in this type of birth method. The Washington, DC, number gives information on local Lamaze classes and on becoming a certified Lamaze educator. 9 a.m.–5:30 p.m. Leave recorded message.
800-368-4404; 202-857-1128 in DC

International Childbirth Education Association:
Provides referrals to local chapters, support groups, membership information, certification and mail-order service. 7 a.m.–4:30 p.m. (Central).
800-624-4934; 612-854-8660

Rare Disorders...

Cystic Fibrosis Foundation:
Responds to patient and family questions and offers literature. Provides referrals to local clinics. 8:30 a.m.–5:30 p.m.
·800-344-4823; 301-951-4422 in MD

The Epilepsy Foundation of America:
Provides information on epilepsy and makes referrals to local chapters. 8:30 a.m.–5:30 p.m.
800-332-1000; 301-459-3700 in MD

Huntington's Disease Society of America:
Gives information on the disease and provides referrals to physicians and support groups. Answers questions on presymptomatic testing. 9 a.m.–5 p.m.
800-345-4372; 212-242-1968 in NY

National Down Syndrome Society Hotline:
Offers information on Down syndrome and gives referrals to local program. Provides free information packet upon request. 9 a.m.–5 p.m.
800-221-4602

National Organization for Rare Disorders:

Provides information on symptoms, standard and investigative therapies, statistics and voluntary agencies for all rare disorders. Offers information on networking programs and provides referrals to organizations for specific disorders. 9 a.m.–5 p.m. (Eastern). Leave message after hours.

800-999-6673; 203-746-6518 in CT

National Reye's Syndrome Foundation:

Provides awareness materials to the public and medical community and offers guidance and counseling to victims of Reye's syndrome. 8 a.m.–5 p.m. (Eastern). Leave message after hours.

800-233-7393

National Tuberous Sclerosis Association:

Answers questions about the disease and makes parent-to-parent contact referrals. Literature is provided to families and professionals. 8:30 a.m.–5 p.m.

800-225-6872; 301-459-9888 in MD

Sarcoidosis Family Aid and Research Foundation:

Information mailed to callers. Staff available for counseling. 24 hours.

800-223-6429. Leave recorded message

Sickle Cell Disease Association of America:

Offers genetic counseling and an information packet. 8:30 a.m.–5 p.m. (Pacific).

800-421-8453; 213-736-5455

Spina Bifida Information and Referral:

Provides information to consumers and health professionals and referrals to local chapters. A service of the Spina Bifida Association of America. 9 a.m.–5 p.m.

800-621-3141; 202-944-3285

Tourette Syndrome Association:

Provides a 24-hour recording for callers to request information and leave name and address. To speak with a staff member, call the local number 9 a.m.–5 p.m. (Eastern).

800-237-0717; 718-224-2999 in NY

United Cerebral Palsy Association:

Provides literature about cerebral palsy. 9 a.m.–5:30 p.m. (Eastern).

800-872-5827; 202-842-1266

United Scleroderma Foundation:

Provides list of publications, chapters throughout the United States and general information. 8 a.m.–5 p.m. (Pacific).

800-722-4673

Safety...

See also Chemical Products/Pesticides

Clearinghouse for Occupational Safety and Health Information:

Provides technical information support for National Institute of Occupational Health and Safety (NIOSH) research programs and disseminates information to others on request. Services include reference and referral, interlibrary loans and information about NIOSH studies.

4676 Columbia Parkway
Cincinnati, Ohio 45226
800-35-NIOSH
513-533-8326; 513-533-8315 (Fax)

Office of Navigation Safety and Waterway Services:

Provides safety information to recreational boaters; assists the public in finding boating education classes; answers technical questions; distributes literature on boating safety, federal laws and the prevention of recreational boating casualties.

US Coast Guard Auxiliary; Auxiliary Boating and
Consumer Affairs Division (G-NAB)
2100 Second St. SW
Washington, DC 20593-0001
800-368-5647 (Boating Safety Hotline)
202-267-0780 (in metropolitan Washington, DC)

National Highway Traffic Safety Administration Auto Safety Hotline:

Provides information and referral on the effectiveness of occupant protection, such as safety belt use and child safety seats, and auto recalls. Staffed by experts who investigate consumer complaints and provide assistance to resolve problems. Gives referrals to other government agencies for consumer questions on warranties, service, and auto safety regulations. 8 a.m.–4 p.m.

800-424-9393; 202-366-0123 in DC

Consumer Product Safety Commission Hotline:

Maintains the National Injury Information Clearinghouse, conducts investigations of alleged unsafe/defective products, and establishes product safety standards. Assists consumers in evaluating the comparative safety of products and conducts education programs to increase consumer awareness.

4330 Eastwest Highway, Room 519
Bethesda, Maryland 20814
800-638-2772, 800-638-8270 (TT)
800-492-8104 (TT, in Maryland only)
301-504-0580; 301-504-0046 (Fax)

National Safety Council:

Provides posters, brochures, videocassettes and booklets on safety and accident prevention. 8:30 a.m.–4:45 p.m. (Central).

800-621-7619; 312-527-4800 in IL

Sexually Transmitted Diseases...

CDC National STD Hotline:

Information regarding 20 sexually transmitted diseases. Referral to community clinics offering low-cost examination and treatment. 8 a.m.–11 p.m.

800-227-8922

Stroke...

Courage Stroke Network:

Provides information to stroke patients and receives catalog orders for products, exercise tapes and equipment. 8 a.m.–4:30 p.m. (Central).

800-553-6321

Sudden Infant Death Syndrome...

American SIDS Institute:

Answers inquiries from families and physicians, distributes literature and makes referrals to other organizations. 8 a.m.–5 p.m.

800-232-7437

National SIDS Foundation:

Provides literature on medical information and referrals, as well as information on support groups. 8:30 a.m.-5:30 p.m. or leave a recorded message after hours on emergency line.

410-653-8226 in Maryland

Surgery/Plastic Surgery...

American Academy of Facial Plastic and Reconstructive Surgery:

Provides physician referral list and publication list. 24 hours.

800-332-3223

American Society for Dermatologic Surgery, Inc.:

Provides information about certain disorders and procedures as well as referrals to dermatologic surgeons in local areas. 8:30 a.m.–5 p.m. (Central).

800-441-2737

Urological Disorders...

American Association of Kidney Patients:

Helps renal patients and their families to deal with the physical and emotional impact of kidney disease. Supplies information on renal conditions. 9 a.m.-5 p.m. (Eastern).

800-749-2257

American Kidney Fund:

Grants financial assistance to kidney patients who are unable to pay treatment-related costs. Also provides information on organ donations and kidney-related diseases. 8 a.m.–5 p.m. (Eastern).

800-638-8299

National Kidney Foundation:

Provides information and referrals to general public and professionals regarding kidney disorders. 8:30 a.m.–5:30 p.m. (Eastern).

800-622-9010; 800-228-4483

Vision...

National Library Service for the Blind and Physically Handicapped:

A network of 56 regional and over 100 local libraries that work in cooperation with the Library of Congress to provide free library service to anyone who is visually or physically impaired.

Library of Congress
1291 Taylor St. NW, Washington, DC 20542
800-424-8567

American Council of the Blind:

Offers information on blindness. Provides referrals to clinics, rehabilitation organizations, research centers and local chapters. Publishes resource lists. 9 a.m.–5:30 p.m. Leave message after hours.

800-424-8666; 202-467-5081 in DC

Guide Dog Foundation for the Blind:

School for blind individuals requiring guide dogs. 8 a.m.–5 p.m. (Eastern).

800-548-4337; 516-265-2121 in NY

National Federation of the Blind; Job Opportunities for the Blind (JOB):

Answers questions from blind individuals seeking jobs, teachers. 12:30 p.m.–5 p.m. (Eastern).

800-638-7518

A Beginner's Guide To On-Line Medical Information

Just by pushing a few buttons on a personal computer, it's now possible to obtain up-to-the-minute information on new drugs...join a support group...track down the best cancer specialists...and more.

If you're intimidated by computers, don't worry. Finding your way around on the Information Superhighway isn't as hard as you might imagine. You just need to know where to look—and *how* to look.

What you'll need to go on-line:

•*Personal computer.* A bare-bones system runs $800 to $1,000, a used system even less.

•*Modem.* This device allows your computer to communicate with other computers via telephone.

Look for a modem rated at least 9,600 baud (that's the rate at which the modem transfers digital information over the phone lines). If you can afford it, get one rated at 14,400 baud —or higher.

Cost: $100 and up. Although slower modems cost less initially, they may keep you connected to the on-line service for a longer period. Most on-line services charge hourly.

• *Communications software.* Each of the three leading services (America Online, CompuServe and Prodigy) will send you software that allows you to log on to their systems. Other types of communication software must be used for a direct connection to the Internet.

Commercial services:

The Internet can be *very* confusing to navigate. If you're new to computers, you should probably opt for one of the commercial on-line services, which are easier to use.

In addition to software, each of the Big Three services will provide you with a password and a free 30-day trial. After that, basic service costs about $10 a month. That typically includes five hours of "connect time." Each additional hour costs about $3.

All three services offer "bulletin boards" that let you post questions and read responses from other users. But after that, the services differ greatly in their offerings...

America Online (AOL):

America Online (800-827-6364) is the leader in "chats," live discussion groups in which participants send messages back and forth at a set time in a designated area. It's an excellent service for beginners, because its software is so easy to use.

Places to look for health information on AOL include...

•*Better Health and Medical Forum.* Articles and reports on all sorts of ailments, from psychological stress to dental hygiene. Under the "Mental Health" heading, for example, you can choose "Stress Management" to obtain a questionnaire for evaluating your stress level...and find instruction in stress-reduction techniques.

•*Health Message Center.* A collection of on-line message boards covering a variety of health topics. Under "Diet, Exercise and Fitness," for example, you can choose from a number of boards ranging from "Exercise Planning and Maintenance" to "Healthy Eating and Nutrition."

•*Health and Medical Chat.* Attending a live "chat" on the health topic of your choice is a great way to get started. You can join a discussion/support group on everything from attention-deficit disorder to chronic illnesses.

CompuServe:

CompuServe (800-848-8199) provides more reference materials—medical journals, a health library and a cancer resource center—than the other on-line services. It's harder to use, but its databases offer more in-depth information, including...

•*PaperChase.* Citations and abstracts from *Medline*, a government database that contains articles from more than 4,000 medical journals.

•*Physician's Data Query.* A directory of cancer centers and cancer specialists, protocols for cancer treatment and general cancer information—for both physicians and laypeople.

• *Health Database Plus.* Abstracts and articles from a wide range of health-related publications, including popular consumer magazines like *Shape*...the epidemiology journal *Morbidity and Mortality Weekly Report*...and top medical journals such as the *Journal of the American Medical Association* and *The New England Journal of Medicine.*

Also available: Articles from medical texts on diseases, medical tests and drugs and pamphlets from health organizations such as the American Cancer Society and the Arthritis Foundation.

• *HealthNet Reference Library.* An on-line encyclopedia of diseases, with topics referenced by name and by symptom.

Example I: Under "Diseases and Disorders," find "Urinary." This leads to articles on kidney stones, kidney failure, prostate and bladder problems, etc.

Example II: Under "Symptoms," select "Emotional" to get explanations of depression and anxiety, plus treatments.

Prodigy:

Prodigy (800-776-3449) provides several bulletin boards where you can post questions and read responses from other subscribers. You'll also find articles on a variety of health topics under "Health and Fitness" in the "Home/Family/Kids" area.

• *Health bulletin boards. Examples:* Foot care, homeopathy and women's health.

• *Health articles.* Look under "Health Topics" for articles and expert advice on "Wellness," "Children," "Diseases" and "Hot Topics."

• *Health news.* New stories about current health issues.

The Internet:

This vast network contains seemingly limitless amounts of information on all aspects of health. The only problem is navigating your way around without getting lost.

Most Internet services are now accessible through the Big Three on-line services. Or, you can get an account with a private access provider.

Cost: $20 a month, plus the cost of special networking software.

Several different Internet services are available. To find information on the Internet, punch in the "address" of the information site you want.

One of the hottest and easiest-to-use internet Services is called the World Wide Web. To access information on this part of the Internet, you need "web browser" software that lets you punch in the appropriate "universal resource locator" (URL). All three computer services now offer this software.

The web presents information in "pages" shown on your computer screen. By clicking your mouse on words within these pages, you can find related information on other parts of the Internet.

For a directory of health-related resources on the web, go to the web page called "Yahoo." *Address:* http://www.yahoo.com/health.

Other Internet resources:

• *Go Ask Alice.* This database contains health- and psychology-related questions (and answers) posted by students at Columbia University. *Address:* http://www.columbia.edu/cu/healthwise/all.html.

• *Medlars.* This vast database is made up of more than 30 databases from the National Library of Medicine. *Address:* gopher://medlars.nlm.nih.gov.

• *Oncolink.* This is an invaluable cancer resource from the University of Pennsylvania. *Address:* http://cancer. med.upenn.edu/.

• *USENET newsgroups.* The following health-related discussion groups are available…

- Sci.med.aids
- Sci.med.nutrition
- Misc.health.diabetes
- Misc.kids.health
- Alt.support.cancer
- Alt.support.depression
- Alt.support.obesity
- Alt.support.mult-sclerosis
- Alt.support.asthma
- Alt.health.ayurveda

Source: Tom Ferguson, MD, a senior associate at the Center for Clinical Computing, Harvard Medical School, Boston. He is the author of several books, including *Health Online: How to Go Online to Find Health Information, Support Forums and Self-Help Communities in Cyberspace.* Addison-Wesley.

Do Your Own Medical Research...Help Save Your Own Life

A doctor's advice is usually accepted at face value. Yet when it comes to treating a serious illness, that advice should be given close scrutiny.

Reason: Even the most caring, compassionate physician is ultimately performing a job. He/she has less at stake than the person who's sick—and whose life may be on the line. In a world where medical breakthroughs occur on an almost daily basis, no doctor can be expected to be up-to-date on every new treatment for every illness.

If you assume that your doctor has all the pertinent information, and accept his suggestions about the "best" course of action without providing any input of your own, you're behaving dangerously.

When your well-being is at stake, you must be your own best advocate. To do that, you must educate yourself about your condition—the various treatment options...and what the latest research reveals about new and possibly experimental treatments. You must then work with your care-givers to assure optimal care.

How I saved my life...

Four years ago my doctor told me I had a rare and incurable form of leukemia. What he did not know—and what my own research revealed—was that a new anti-leukemia drug had become available three months before my grim diagnosis.

This new drug was especially effective against the rare form of leukemia I was suffering from—80% of those treated achieved a complete and lasting remission. Because of that new treatment I am alive and cancer-free today. *Here is how you or a loved one can learn what you need to know about a serious illness:*

Second opinions...

If you heed no other advice in this article, be sure to get a second opinion. It can literally spell the difference between life and death.

Example: Six years ago, a friend of mine was diagnosed with advanced liver cancer. My friend's doctor offered him no treatment and gave him only months to live. But on the advice of his brother-in-law, a hospital administrator, Frank sought a second opinion from a major cancer research center. The doctors there recommended a new type of surgery. Frank got the surgery—and he is now healthy and cancer-free.

Moral of this story: Medicine is an inexact and rapidly evolving science. Doctors vary widely in their knowledge. Some are diligent about keeping up with advances in their field. Others aren't. By seeking out a second or perhaps even a third or fourth opinion, you boost your odds of finding a practitioner knowledgeable about every form of therapy that might prove beneficial to you.

Caution: The choices garnered from multiple opinions aren't always clearly black or white, right or wrong. One doctor might recommend a treatment that has an 80% cure rate—but a 20% risk of serious long-term adverse effects. Another might recommend a treatment with a 50% cure rate—but with only a 5% chance of serious side effects. Which is the better option? It's up to the patient to decide.

Using a medical library...

Medical information—including information on the latest developments in treatment for virtually every illness, is readily available. The key is knowing how—and where—to find it.

Libraries affiliated with medical schools or major hospitals tend to have the most complete information.

If you're already hospitalized, federal law requires that you be given access to the hospital library—and that the hospital librarian respond to your requests for help in doing research.

If you're not hospitalized, call the library and find out if it's open to the public. If not, ask which local medical libraries are. If none are, ask about exceptions to the restricted access policies. In most states, at least one health library is open to the public.

In addition, at least two medical libraries in the US are geared specifically to lay people...

•Center for Medical Consumers, 237 Thompson St., New York 10012. 212-674-7105.

•Planetree Health Resource Center, 2040 Webster St., San Francisco 94115. 415-923-3680.

Pinpointing information...

Pinpointing information in a medical library can be a daunting task to the uninitiated.

To start, ask the librarian to help look up relevant studies in the *Index Medicus*, the master index of medical information. Copy down the names of relevant articles in respected medical journals—such as *The New England Journal of Medicine*, the *Journal of the American Medical Association* and *The Lancet*, a British periodical.

What are you looking for? A general overview of your illness, plus details of the latest research. In particular, you'll want to know different methods of treatment—including their success rates and their possible complications—and whether there's been any recent development that your primary physician may not yet know about.

You also want to know about clinical trials —experiments that test new treatments at the cutting edge of medicine. Participating in these experiments carries some risk, but it also offers hope where previously none existed. Despite the risks, far more people have been helped than hurt by clinical trials in this country.

If you find an article that details a promising new treatment, call the author of the article—or ask your doctor to call for you. Some researchers prefer talking to other medical professionals rather than to patients.

On-line medical data bases...

Thanks to powerful computers and high-speed modems, medical information is now readily available from large medical databases held on government and private computers.

Benefit: Research that might take days of labor in a library can now be compiled in a matter of minutes using on-line databases.

Many medical libraries now provide access to these computer databases. To do on-line searching on your own, you'll need a modem, communications software and an account with a database provider. *Useful resource: Grateful Med,** a program designed to provide easy, user-friendly access to Medline, a vast compilation of medical articles, as well as many other important medical databases.

Via the popular on-line service Compu-Serve,† you can gain limited access not only to Medline but also to Physician's Data Query (PDQ), a database that provides detailed information about new drugs and other treatments for all types of cancer.

Through CompuServe or by mail you can also check out the database maintained by the National Organization for Rare Disorders (NORD), Box 8923, New Fairfield, Connecticut 06812. 203-746-6518. By mail, the first report is free. Additional reports cost $3.25 apiece.

Caution: As efficient as they are, on-line databases are neither user-friendly nor cheap. If you're not familiar with the arcane search techniques required to access these databases, consider hiring a medical research firm to do the research for you. Three excellent services:

•The Health Resource, 564 Locust St., Conway, Arkansas 72032. 501-329-5272. $275 for research on cancer, $175 for other topics.

•Planetree (see above for address). 415-923-3581. $100 per report.

•Schine On-Line, 39 Brenton Ave., Providence, Rhode Island 02906. 800-346-3287 or 401-751-0120. $189 for cancer research, $100 for other illnesses.

*Grateful Med is available from the US Commerce Department, National Technical Information Service, Springfield, VA 22161. 703-487-4650. *Cost:* $29.95. All prices are subject to change without prior notice.

†To sign up for CompuServe, call 800-848-8199. *Cost:* $8.95 a month for unlimited access. Extended services can cost up to $9.50/hr. $39.95 for optional software. There may be additional fees for accessing Medline, PDQ or NORD.

Source: Gary Schine, president of the medical research agency Schine On-Line, Providence, RI. He is the author of *If the President Had Cancer....* Sandra Publications.

22

New Horizons in Good Health

Alternative Therapies— Does Your Doctor Know?

In 1990, alternative therapies were being used by one in three Americans, according to a Harvard study. And 72% of those using alternative therapies failed to tell their doctors they were doing so.

I guess these patients were afraid their doctors would ridicule them or try to get them to stop using unconventional forms of treatment.

If you're using alternative therapies, be sure to let your doctor know. Tell him/her what other health-care practitioners you see and what supplements, herbs, etc. you take. Don't be surprised if your doctor is supportive. He may even admit he sees an acupuncturist or chiropractor himself!

For optimal care, your conventional and alternative health-care providers must communicate and cooperate with one another. Good communication helps you to…

…*find out which therapy is working.* Say your

doctor gives you a painkiller for arthritis. You decide to have acupuncture—but don't tell your doctor. You improve, and your doctor keeps you on the painkiller because he thinks that's what's working. You may be running all the risks of long-term painkiller use even though it's the acupuncture that's really helping.

…*avoid interactions between therapies.* Herbs sometimes interfere with drugs. If you take Coumadin or another anticoagulant, for instance, it can be very dangerous to take an anticoagulant herb like red clover.

…*facilitate sharing of information.* Conventional and alternative practitioners can learn from one another. For example, your chiropractor may want to look at the X rays your doctor took for your low back pain—or vice versa.

How can you encourage this interaction? *Tell your doctor about your alternative practitioner.* If his response seems hostile, don't react with hostility. Just say you find the therapy helpful and would be happy to discuss it when he is ready. Don't bring it up again. Wait until he does.

If your doctor seems curious, suggest that he call the alternative practitioner and introduce himself. Then call your alternative practitioner and tell her to expect the call. Explain your doctor's perspective and concerns.

If your doctor flat-out disapproves of alternative therapy, don't try to force him to talk to the alternative practitioner. It won't do anyone any good if the two practitioners just scream at each other.

If your doctor remains hostile, it might be time to find a new doctor. You might even ask your alternative practitioner to recommend someone. A list of doctors who practice alternative medicine—or who work with alternative practitioners—is available for $5 from the American Holistic Medical Association, 4101 Lake Boone Trail, Ste. 201, Raleigh, North Carolina 27607, 919-787-5181.

Write a note to your doctor telling him why you're leaving. If enough patients do that, doctors may be forced to reexamine their perspective.

Of course, it might be the alternative practitioner who is hostile to doctors. In such cases, the same advice applies. Try to get them to talk, but if the practitioner remains hostile, consider trying someone else.

Remember, no single therapy works for everything. Most people derive the greatest benefit from a combination of therapies.

Don't trust anyone who seems to have a "religious commitment" to one treatment modality, whether it's traditional Chinese medicine, homeopathy, chiropractic—or mainstream Western medicine.

Source: Adriane Fugh-Berman, MD, a Washington, DC-based medical researcher who specializes in women's health and alternative medicine. She is the author of the forthcoming book *Alternative Medicine: What Works.* Odonion Press.

What You Can Do to Avoid Being Caught in America's Health-Care Morass

Are Americans really facing a health-care crisis? Yes—but it's not the sort of crisis most of us believe it to be. Most Americans believe the crisis stems from a lack of ready access to health care.

Assumption: Simply by cutting the cost of medical insurance and thereby making quality medical care accessible to more people, our health will improve.

In fact, access to good doctors and hospitals has surprisingly little to do with our health.

How can that be? Even if all Americans were instantly granted free top-notch health care, the same maladies that beset us now would continue to beset us. That is as true, for example, for heart disease, cancer and diabetes, as it is for drug abuse, violent crime and teenage pregnancy.

We might save some lives and alleviate some symptoms, but we still would not have dealt with the causes of these health problems.

If not medical care, what is effective at keeping us healthy? It comes down to how we choose to live our lives—how much and what sorts of foods we eat...how often we exercise ...whether we wear our seat belts or drink when we drive.

Of greatest importance: The number and quality of our relationships with others. The sense of love and of belonging that defines these relationships serve as both the bedrock of American democracy and as a power buffer against the inevitable threats to our health.

Numerous studies have shown that persons who are enmeshed in mutually supportive relationships are much less vulnerable to illness than persons who feel isolated, unloved and unloving. Caring relationships also help speed recovery from illness and injury...and in the case of chronic illness or disability, such relationships help us come to terms with our situation.

Bottom line: Good health is not a product or service to be bought. It's the payoff for living wisely and deliberately and in close emotional contact with friends, family members and members of the larger community.

How do such relationships help keep us healthy? The short answer is that they protect us from loneliness—an emotional state that apparently underlies all sorts of serious health problems, including heart disease, cancer, accidental injuries, stroke, suicide and homicide. To get a sense of just how fatal loneliness can be, consider the death rate of middle-class European-American men living in Nevada:*

Although these men are sufficiently well-off to afford quality medical care, they have a remarkably high rate of premature death from heart disease.

Probable explanation: These men are often divorced, widowed or uprooted—and therefore lonely. They lack the stability, companionship and sense of belonging necessary for good health.

Similarly, Dr. Bernie Siegel, the Yale surgeon and strong proponent of mind-body medicine, has said that all disease is the absence of love. In the individual, a lack of love can translate into anything from heart disease to psychological depression.

On a societal level, alienation between neighbors and other members of the community plays itself out in ways such as an increased rate of violent crime, drug abuse and infant mortality.

Lesson: Those who act out of selfish interests, as though they need not be concerned about the welfare of others, are spiritually impoverished. It is this experience that puts these individuals at grave risk for poor physical health and early death.

If medical care is no guarantee of good health, why do so many Americans seem to want more of it? Three factors are involved. First, and most significant, is what has been called the deification of doctors. This phenomenon stems from the misguided belief—common among Americans—that physicians have the power to eliminate all suffering and to rescue us from illness and death.

Of course, under certain circumstances doctors can and do rescue us. However, they are by no means omnipotent. Believing that they are leads us to take unnecessary chances with our health.

Example: Americans know (cognitively) that smoking is hazardous to their health, yet they

*A phenomenon that was discussed by psychologist James Lynch in his fascinating book *The Broken Heart: The Medical Consequences of Loneliness.*

persist in smoking both because they believe they won't be harmed, and, if they are, doctors can cure them.

All humans are mortal, and some degree of pain is inevitable no matter how good a physician is. The body is not simply a machine that can always be repaired.

What are the other factors that lead us to desire more medical care? The second factor is our penchant for defining problems that are clearly societal in nature as being medical.

Examples: Drug abuse, excessive drinking, teenage pregnancy, etc.

We seem to think that increased access to health care could solve these problems. But these problems actually stem from the tears in our social fabric—such as racism, sexism and economic oppression.

Example: A teenage girl who is poor, black, uneducated and pregnant. If we focus all our efforts on providing her with good prenatal care, we lose sight of the social problems that threaten her pregnancy to begin with.

Lesson: Though it might sound trite, the only way to mend these tears in our social fabric is via greater love and compassion for one another. We must replace the uniquely American credo of "rugged individualism" with one that stresses both autonomy and interdependence. After all, humans are by their nature social beings.

And the third factor? That is our tendency to exaggerate the severity of minor ailments. Americans tend to call the doctor at the first sign of pain or fever, when there's rarely any benefit in doing so. Of course, doctors and other members of the health-care industry have a financial stake in perpetuating these bad habits. Once I heard a radio advertisement that urged persons with a simple sore throat to visit an urgent care center. That is totally irresponsible.

Better way: Health care providers could teach their clients how to distinguish between ailments that need treatment and those that do not. Patients should be willing to learn.

Payoff: Reduced medical expenses for patients. *Bonus:* Reduced demand for doctors' services might ultimately help drive down the costs of medical care.

Bottom line...

By taking active steps to live a healthier life—eating nutritious foods, exercising regularly, giving up alcohol and tobacco and forming strong, healthy relationships with others—you are doing much more to promote your own good health than any government policy or mandate ever could.

Ultimately, the solution to Americans' health-care problem lies with the care and attention we give to our own bodies, minds and relationships.

Source: Ronald David, MD, lecturer in public policy, John F. Kennedy School of Government, Harvard University, Cambridge, Massachusetts. A former deputy secretary of health for the State of Pennsylvania, Dr. David is board-certified in both pediatrics and neonatal medicine.

Alternative Medicine ...And You

Alternatives to conventional medical treatments are attracting widespread attention.

Fact: More than one-third of Americans used an unconventional therapy for serious medical conditions in 1990, according to a survey published in *The New England Journal of Medicine.*

Major medical schools are introducing programs in alternative medicine into the curriculum. And the National Institutes of Health opened an Office of Alternative Medicine last year.

While each area of alternative medicine is different from the other, all share a common approach...

•The healer—or practitioner—looks at all aspects of the patient's life—not only the physical but also the social, psychological and spiritual.

•The healer-patient relationship is a collaborative partnership.

In many cases, the preferred healing methods are those that patients can learn to do themselves.

Manipulative therapies...

Practitioners in this field are trained to use their hands to move or otherwise affect muscles, joints and soft tissue. The therapies are often used to help reduce back pain and other musculoskeletal problems. *The most common forms...*

•Spinal manipulation. Practitioners include osteopaths and chiropractors, who believe that the cause of musculoskeletal pain and problems with internal organs may be malpositioned vertebrae impinging on nerves.

Osteopaths, or DOs, receive a four-year course of education similar to that of MDs. Coursework covers anatomy, physiology, chemistry and hospital work. There is also a year-long internship—in addition to training in manipulation. They take the same licensing examinations as MDs, and they can prescribe drugs.

Chiropractors, or DCs, specialize in manipulation and anatomy, but don't receive the extensive training in basic sciences that osteopaths do. Most chiropractors are also knowledgeable about nutrition, exercise and other healthful practices.

•Massage therapy. This can reduce muscle tension and overall stress, increasing circulation, improving the mobility of joints, and promoting healing of some injuries. *Most common:* Swedish massage, which combines long strokes, kneading, gentle slapping and other techniques.

While massage should not be considered a stand-alone treatment for serious illness, it can be helpful as an adjunctive treatment. Physical therapists and registered massage therapists are among those who perform massage.

•Reflexology. This is based on the yet-unproven theory that all parts of the body are represented by particular points on the feet and hands...and that stimulating those points can promote healing elsewhere in the body.

Acupuncture...

Acupuncture is part of the Chinese system of medicine—a philosophy of healing—developed over thousands of years. During acupuncture, fine needles are inserted at points along the body that are believed to connect—via lines or meridians—to specific organs and bodily functions. The needles are not usually painful but can create a heavy or pulling sensation.

Studies have found that acupuncture points have different electrical potential than the surrounding points, suggesting that acupuncture works by stimulating the body's electrical energy —which affects physiological and biochemical processes. Acupuncture has been shown to release endorphins, the body's natural painkillers …improve the vital capacity of the lungs…increase immune-system function…induce relaxation…and help in the treatment of addiction, alcoholism and asthma.

Practitioners: Licensing requirements vary by state. The American Academy of Medical Acupuncture (5820 Wilshire Blvd., Suite 500, Los Angeles, California 90036, 213-937-5514) has strict membership criteria and can supply a list of members in most localities.

Important: To guard against transmission of disease, be sure the practitioner uses disposable needles or sterilizes them carefully.

Relaxation therapies…

Many types of relaxation training induce what Harvard researcher Herbert Benson, MD, has termed the *relaxation response*—a state of mental and physical calm elicited through focused concentration. Methods vary but usually involve having the patient sit quietly and silently repeating a word or sound to oneself. The resulting physiological state is characterized by a slowing of heart and respiratory rates and decrease in blood pressure.

Relaxation therapies can be useful complements to the treatment of physical disorders, such as hypertension, migraine headaches, chronic pain, spastic bowel, insomnia and possibly even infertility. Practiced regularly, focused relaxation can also increase mental awareness and produce a healthy detachment from daily anxieties. *The most common therapies…*

•Meditation. A spiritual as well as physical practice involving commitment to a philosophical path. Forms range from the vigorous physical activity of Sufi whirling to quiet contemplation.

•Biofeedback uses special devices to measure and convey to the patient signs of stress, such as muscle tension and blood circulation. Sensors are attached painlessly to the skin.

Example: A particular tonal sound may indicate tension in the forehead…and change pitch as the forehead muscles relax.

The feedback helps the patient learn to change those internal processes, ultimately without the aid of the device.

Practitioners: Instructors in relaxation techniques need not be licensed. The methods are commonly taught at stress-management clinics, holistic-education centers and some hospitals and medical centers.

Nutritional and herbal therapies…

Beyond the minimum requirements for basic nutrients, such as vitamins, minerals and amino acids, there is very little agreement in the medical community about what nutrients and in which amounts are essential for optimum health.

However, research has suggested that diets high in certain nutrients may be conducive to long life and better health. *Warning:* Patients should be cautious about taking large doses of vitamins. Some can produce unpleasant side effects, or even be toxic in large amounts. Before going on a vitamin regime, discuss with your physician so he/she can be alert to any reactions.

An emerging area of nutritional therapy is *food sensitivities.* Though controlled studies have yet to prove this, many patients report feeling better after eliminating foods to which they may be sensitive (common culprits are wheat, milk and sugar).

Practitioners: Licensed nutritionists, chiropractors and some physicians are among those who provide nutritional counseling. Clinical ecologists specialize in identifying and eliminating irritating substances, including food and inhalants, from a patient's environment.

Herbal medicine…

This is based on thousands of years of empirical findings that certain herbs can be helpful in treating certain conditions.

Many of the medications we use in Western medicine are derived from herbs. Herbalists believe that using the herb itself, rather than the derivative, may be more effective and less potentially toxic.

Combinations of small amounts of herbs are thought to be safer than single herbs—which in large doses can give rise to problems with toxicity just as drugs can.

Practitioners: There is substantial scientific literature on herbs but no certification or licensing procedure for herbalists. Your best bet is probably someone who has been working with herbs for many years, is modest about what he can do and is willing to show you the research to back up recommended treatment.

As with any medication, exercise caution, be alert for side effects and don't stay on the regimen for more than a month or two without consulting an herbal specialist.

Homeopathy…

Homeopathy was developed about 200 years ago by a German physician, Samuel Hahnemann. He came to the conclusion that certain substances, which when given in large doses create symptoms such as redness or inflammation, could be used in microdoses to relieve those same symptoms. Contrary to conventional medical theory, practitioners of homeopathy believe that the smallest possible doses are most potent.

Although homeopathy seems to violate all canons of our accepted medical perspective, several scientific studies suggest that it can be helpful in treating fever and arthritis, among other conditions.

Practitioners: Only licensed medical professionals can practice in the US, but the requirements vary by state. Ask the practitioner where he studied, whether he has passed the certification exam and how long he has been practicing.

Finding a practitioner…

First see a physician for a medical diagnosis. Some medical doctors are willing to recommend nontraditional therapies for certain conditions.* Friends who have had successful alternative treatment are another source of recommendations.

Important: Make sure the practitioner you're considering has received significant, recognized training. Find out how long he/she has been in practice. Ask others who have been to this person if the treatment has been helpful. If you feel uneasy about the practitioner or treatment, look for assistance elsewhere.

*For a list of doctors in your area familiar with alternative therapies, send $5 to the American Holistic Medical Association, 4101 Lake Boone Trail, Suite 201, Raleigh, North Carolina 27607. 919-787-5181. Specify the desired state. *Maximum request:* Three states.

Source: James S. Gordon, MD, clinical professor in the departments of psychiatry and community and family medicine at Georgetown Medical School. A physician and acupuncturist, Dr. Gordon is founder and director of the Center for Mind-Body Studies, 5225 Connecticut Ave. NW, Suite 414, Washington, DC 20015.

All About Homeopathic Medicine

Unlike other non-western medical systems such as Chinese or Ayurveda, homeopathy isn't an ancient practice rooted in thousands of years of tradition. It was invented in the late l9th century by one man, Samuel Hahnemann, as a direct reaction to the barbaric medical practices of his time—particularly bleeding and purging. Until the l920s, one-third of all American medical schools taught homeopathic medicine. However, with the advent of modern technology-based medicine, including drugs such as antibiotics, homeopathy fell into disrepute. While considered quackery now by mainstream physicians, homeopathy is also undergoing a revival with the growing movement toward holistic, alternative medicine.

The fact that homeopathy is very popular in England and is the medicine of the British royal family has added to its legitimacy. Its appeal resides in that homeopathic medicines are gentle, noninvasive, and aid the body's own healing process rather than substituting for it.

What is homeopathy?…

Homeopathy believes there is a vital force—an energy field—that given the proper stimulation, can restore the physical, emotional and mental equilibrium that has been disturbed by illness.

In an ideal state of health, the vital force would always be able to cure its own imbalances, but distorted by chronic illness, the channels through which the self-healing energies flow have been blocked. The blockage has a characteristic pattern which the homeopath figures out by analyzing the patient's symptoms.

The doctor then selects an extremely diluted version of a remedy that is capable—in standard strength—of producing in healthy individuals the same symptoms that the patient is suffering from.

This remedy temporarily aggravates—instead of relieves—the patient's symptoms, showing the body's vital force the pathways along which it must act to restore equilibrium.

Homeopathy bears some resemblance to Chinese medicine, which also believes that the body's energy field has to be restored in order for healing to take place. Both acupuncture and homeopathic remedies are meant to stimulate the body's energy and get it flowing in the correct pathways.

Homeopathy versus allopathy…

Hahnemann called the orthodox medicine of his day allopathy, from the Greek words *allos* for different, and pathein for disease. *Homeo* is the Greek word for similar.

Today, as in Hahnemann's time, orthodox or allopathic medicine proceeds on the principle that a disease, or a symptom of a disease, is cured by using a medicine that opposes the symptoms.

Example: Aspirin for pain.

But homeopathy goes on the principle that "like cures like." In a process called provings, homeopaths test their medications on healthy people. A collection of the symptoms experienced by a large number of provers produces a full picture of the disease-producing effects of the drug. Then the drug can be matched to similar symptoms reported by sick people.

Example: A substance that induces vomiting in a healthy person might be used to treat a sick person who exhibits vomiting as a symptom.

Hahnemann called this the "Law of Similars." The idea wasn't original with him—it had been advanced by philosophers and physicians from time to time for thousands of years. It was in the writings of Hippocrates, too—2,400 years ago. Hahnemann, however, was the first to build a consistent system of therapeutics based on it.

Traditional medicine also uses this principle. Synthetic hormones are used for hormone replacement therapy. And…vaccines contain a tiny amount of the killed virus.

However, the overwhelming majority of drugs that modern medicine uses today are allopathic.

Examples: Antibiotics, tranquilizers, sleeping medications, laxatives and antihistamines. Even the descriptive terms for such drugs, which use the prefix "anti," indicate the principle on which they're based.

The problem with many allopathic medicines is that they only treat the symptoms of disease, without confronting the underlying condition.

Example: Pain treatment. Conventional drugs dull pain, while common sense would tell us that pain has a value—it's a sign that something is wrong.

Homeopathic practices…

•One disease—one medicine. Since the aim of homeopathy is to treat a patient's complex symptom-picture with a remedy whose known effects most closely resemble the symptoms of the disease, no more than one remedy is given at a time. Homeopaths believe that only one drug fits the symptoms presented by any particular patient. Unlike allopathic medicine, where the patient may go home with prescriptions for half a dozen different drugs, homeopaths insist on a single remedy.

•Dilution. This is one of the most controversial aspects of homeopathy. *Principle:* The more a medicinal substance is diluted, the better it works, while at the same time reducing the undesirable aggravation of a patient's symptoms. Many homeopathic remedies have only a trace of the therapeutic substance. Some are so diluted that the trace cannot be found by current scientific equipment. Although such extreme dilution makes no sense in terms of western medicine, it works.

Questions and answers…

What's actually in homeopathic remedies?

The active ingredients range from mild herbs such as chamomile, to poisonous substances such as belladonna and arsenic, to minerals such as sulfur and calcium carbonate, to mundane ingredients like table salt.

The homeopathic *Materia Medica* comprises some 21,000 different substances. In practice, however, only about 50 "broadly recognizable" remedies are utilized.

Can homeopathic remedies replace antibiotics?

Yes. Homeopaths believe that bacteria is only part of the problem. The underlying problem is the weakened immune system that makes the patient more susceptible to infection. The homeopathic remedy is chosen to remove that inner susceptibility and create an environment no longer hospitable to the infecting organism.

Ideally, the homeopath shouldn't have to resort to antibiotics. In practice, however, if the patient is gravely ill, many homeopaths will give antibiotics if there isn't enough time to find the proper homeopathic remedy.

What conditions can homeopathy cure?

Homeopathy can cure most illnesses. *Exceptions:* Gross trauma requiring surgical intervention, psychosis and cases where the disease process is so very advanced.

Note: This doesn't mean that homeopaths have the cure for cancer, or any other disease. Because a homeopathic physician has successfully cured one case of cancer with a certain remedy, it doesn't mean that homeopathy can cure all cases of cancer. It simply means that the homeopath has come up with the right remedy to eradicate the underlying problem that led one particular patient to get a malignant tumor.

What distinguishes homeopathy from the placebo effect?

Three of the world's leading research journals have recently published results supporting the effectiveness of homeopathy over a placebo. One study found that hay fever patients receiving a homeopathic mixture of grass pollen suffered 50% fewer symptoms than those receiving a placebo. Another found that 82% of rheumatoid arthritis sufferers improved after receiving a homeopathic remedy compared with 21% receiving a placebo. A third study showed that homeopathic doses of silica stimulated the immune system.

Also, homeopathy has successfully treated infants and animals, where the placebo effect is highly unlikely.

Source: Michael Weiner, PhD, editor of *Dr. Weiner's Alternative Medical Newsletter*, 6 Knoll La., Mill Valley, CA 94941. He has written 15 books, including *The Complete Book Of Homeopathy*. Avery Publishing Group.

All About Chiropractic Medicine

While more recently, chiropractic medicine was lumped with such offbeat practices as crystal healing and shamanism—it has emerged as an effective medical therapy and has gained acceptance by mainstream physicians and the public. What it is…

Many perceptions of chiropractic medicine are tainted by images of mysterious bone manipulations and outrageous claims for cures of serious illnesses.

Its responsible practitioners, however, explain chiropractic medicine in less sensational terms. The chiropractic approach treats the whole person, rather than just a particular injury or illness. It relies on neither drugs nor surgery and seeks to take advantage of your body's self-healing processes and capacities for self-regulation.

Chiropractors also promote good body mechanics, nutrition and healthy emotional relationships with others. These factors combined, they have found, play a major role in healing and keeping us well.

A typical visit…

Most people initially seek a chiropractor because of a musculoskeletal problem—back pain, chronic muscle ache, the proverbial "crick" in the neck. What to expect:

Chiropractors rely heavily on extensive patient histories. Your chiropractor will want to know about your work and exercise habits and how long you've had your particular problem. Then, he/she will examine you thoroughly, just as a typical physician would do.

You may also be X-rayed and have blood taken. A chiropractor emphasizes the importance of diagnosis. His first task is to determine the nature of your complaint and, if it's beyond the scope of his practice, to refer you immediately to an appropriate specialist.

Should the chiropractor decide to treat you, he may employ massage techniques designed to work on soft tissue and muscle.

He may use ice packs if there's swelling.

He may use ultrasound, a device that stimulates muscles and nerves through painless electronic vibration.

If your condition has impeded some movement, a chiropractor may manipulate nearby joints to restore the normal range of motion.

He will almost certainly advise you about exercise. If you incurred the problem working or during some other physical activity, he'll have suggestions for less stressful ways of moving your body to prevent a recurrence.

It is, of course, spinal manipulation and adjustment for which chiropractic medicine is best known.

The "backbone" of chiropractic therapy stems from the theory that our spines are vitally integral to our health. Through manipulation, the spinal column can energize the nervous system and normalize body functions.

Spinal manipulation, however, is not always a necessity in chiropractic treatment. And before such treatment, a responsible chiropractor will explain some potential problems possible with spinal adjustment.

Finding a chiropractor…

The first step is to get a referral from someone you know. If you don't know anyone who has visited a chiropractor, call your local chiropractic society for suggestions. Most chiropractors are members of the American Chiropractic Association in Washington, DC.

Chiropractors are certified as chiropractic physicians in about half the states in the US. Being recognized as competent professionals in the medical community has been a longtime goal.

A good chiropractor should…

• Do a health history and physical as part of your initial consultation.

• Be trained to do spinal adjusting. You should ask before any treatment is given.

• Be able to diagnose and, if necessary, refer you to the correct specialist.

• Release you when you are well without pressuring you for follow-up treatment.

Like any area of health care, chiropractic medicine has its share of ambulance chasers and unscrupulous types. As a potential chiropractic patient, you should be wary of chiropractors who:

• Insist upon X rays, even if they don't seem to be indicated by your problem.

• Make "instant" diagnoses.

• Schedule weekly or monthly visits without a clear explanation about their necessity.

• Are reluctant or unwilling to refer you to other medical authorities or profess to be able to cure a suspiciously wide range of illnesses and injuries.

Source: James Winterstein, DC, chiropractic radiologist and president of The National College of Chiropractic, 200 E. Roosevelt Rd., Lombard, Illinois 60148. He is also president of the Council on Chiropractic Education in Des Moines.

What Your Doctor Won't Tell You About Very Modern Medicine

People are inundated with exhortations to be screened for high cholesterol…and cancer …to control high blood pressure…and have regular checkups.

People who strive to follow these recommendations feel guilty when they don't. That's unfortunate. *Surprising:* Medical advice of this type is not only hard to follow, it's often dangerous.

Hazards include faulty diagnoses… inaccurate medical tests…botched surgical procedures… hazardous medications…and more.

Doctors aren't always to be avoided. Anyone with chest pains or other acute health problems, for instance, should call an ambulance immediately. But regular contact with doctors is not only unnecessary, it's hazardous to your health.

The common notion that modern medicine is all-powerful is but one of many fallacies that victimize all of us.

Major medical fallacies…

• *Fallacy:* If cancer and other diseases are cured, people will live much longer. Even if cures for heart disease and cancer were found, human longevity would not significantly increase. Most people would still die in their seventies or eighties.

Humans are mortal. Sooner or later, we all die. But instead of fearing illness and death, we should accept them as inevitable consequences of being alive—in the same way we accept hurricanes, earthquakes and other acts of God.

Living a good life is about passion and joy and love and work, not about slogging it out week after week on the treadmill or in the aerobics class.

• *Fallacy:* Modern medicine makes us healthier. Doctors tend to stress objective measures of health—the number of white blood cells, blood-pressure readings, etc. *More important:* How healthy we feel. *Surprising:* Medical breakthroughs have not improved such subjective evaluations of well-being.

Example: Fifteen years ago, about 40% of Americans polled reported not feeling well.

Today, despite myriad advances in diagnosis and treatment, that figure has climbed to 60%. More people feel sick more of the time than in the previous generation.

• *Fallacy:* The patient's health is a doctor's sole concern. Doctors often have a financial interest in ordering lots of X-rays and other tests, in performing surgery and in prescribing medications.

Pharmaceutical companies shower physicians with gifts, free travel and free medical equipment. Can doctors really prescribe drugs only when necessary?

Obstetricians make much more money from cesarean sections than from vaginal deliveries. Is it any wonder that C-section rates are far higher in countries with for-profit medical care?

Many physicians own X-ray machines and other sophisticated diagnostic equipment and profit from its use.

And there's always the specter of malpractice if a doctor fails to order a test that might conceivably have proven helpful. Is it surprising that doctors are especially zealous in their ordering of expensive diagnostic tests?

These are only a few examples of the ways in which a doctor's judgment can be influenced by outside factors.

• *Fallacy:* Medical tests are invaluable. In recent years, people have been led to believe that it's imperative to undergo routine testing for high cholesterol, high blood pressure and more. Respected experts all but coerce us to submit to these tests.

Reality: Being tested generally is not a good idea. Early diagnosis helps only if effective treatments exist. But cancer, heart disease and many other ailments are notoriously hard to treat even when caught early.

In such cases, early diagnosis does little more than extend the time span during which the patient knows of—and worries about—the disease. Additionally, screening programs often miss the ailments they're supposed to spot.

Worst of all, many perfectly healthy people are told they are ill. Such false positives lead to needless biopsies, operations and more, taking great financial and emotional tolls.

Unless you've already begun to experience symptoms, be wary of medical tests. If your doctor recommends a test, request more information. Find out not only the potential benefits of the test, but also the risks.

• *Fallacy:* Doctors have all the answers. In reality, doctors often have little idea what's wrong with their patients—although they're often reluctant to say so.

Instead of admitting their uncertainty, doctors maintain a facade of knowledge. *Rationale:* Patients expect quick diagnoses and aggressive treatment of their ailments. They view with considerable suspicion any physician who does otherwise—and physicians know it.

In truth, many ailments are hard to diagnose. Even with an accurate diagnosis, existing treatment often fails.

• *Fallacy:* Only medical experts have the key to health. The single most important rule for maintaining good health is—all things in moderation. Don't eat too much, don't drink too much, get regular, moderate exercise and so on. It's basically the same advice my grandmother gave me.

Much has been made of research linking smoking to lung cancer. But the connection isn't new. As early as 1882, cigarettes were referred to as coffin nails.

• *Fallacy:* Modern medicine has vanquished most diseases. Some medical problems—including smallpox, tuberculosis and death in childbirth—have been almost completely eradicated in America by modern medicine. But these are the exceptions. The vast majority of ailments—perhaps up to 90% of them—remain mysterious.

• *Fallacy:* Doctors treat disease and only disease. In fact, many diseases aren't diseases at all.

Example: Hypertension. Although doctors warn their patients about high blood pressure, they fail to explain that the cutoff between normal and high blood pressure is arbitrary. True, the higher the pressure, the greater one's risk of heart attack and stroke. But to call one person's blood pressure normal and another's high is inappropriate, given how hard it is to get an accurate reading—blood pressure varies greatly at different times and under different circumstances.

Each day, thousands of people walk into doctor's offices feeling normal and walk out labeled sick—all because of arbitrary rules. That's a big problem.

Being called hypertensive causes anxiety... and many anti-hypertensive medications have unpleasant side effects—including impotence. Hypertension and many other fabricated illnesses get lots of attention in part because many drugs are available to treat them.

• *Fallacy:* It takes good medical care to overcome most ailments. Wrong. Most recoveries occur naturally, with or without the help of high-tech medical intervention. Natural body defenses are usually sufficient to conquer illness...if we allow them to work through rest and relaxation.

People who recover from a sore throat after taking an antibiotic may conclude the antibiotic was responsible. Chances are they would have recovered just as quickly without medication.

Source: Petr Skrabanek, MD, PhD, senior lecturer in community health, Trinity College, Dublin, Ireland. He is coauthor of *Follies & Fallacies in Medicine*. Prometheus Books.

Can Acupuncture Work for You?

Can acupuncture work for you? The answer is probably yes. Numerous studies have shown this ancient healing art to be effective for pain, addiction, nausea and rehabilitation after a stroke.

According to Chinese medical theory, acupuncture works by correcting the balance of energy in the body. This energy—called qi (pronounced chee)—flows through 59 invisible channels called meridians. Here in the West, we've shown that acupuncture boosts production of endorphins, the brain's own "feel-good" chemicals. This finding helps explain temporary pain relief—but not acupuncture's effects on other conditions.

Before undergoing acupuncture, patients often ask, "Will it hurt?" The answer is, "Not much." Acupuncture needles are nothing like hypodermic needles. In fact, they're as thin as hairs. Some points on the body—along the hands and feet, for instance—are tender. But even at these points, needle insertion hurts no more than a mosquito bite.

For kids or people with a morbid fear of needles, acupressure should be used instead of acupuncture. As its name suggests, acupressure uses pressure instead of needles. Acupressure isn't quite as effective as acupuncture—but it does work.

Fact: Acupuncture is very safe. Side effects are rare, and the most common ones—relaxation and a heightened sense of well-being—aren't too bad. Internal injuries are almost unheard of, although bruising is not uncommon. Hepatitis and other blood-borne diseases can be spread by dirty needles. Make sure your acupuncturist cleans your skin before needle insertion...and uses disposable needles (most already do).

Acupuncture runs about $40 to $90 a session. For chronic conditions, 10 or more sessions may be necessary. An average session lasts 30 minutes. Some insurance companies cover acupuncture, others don't. For a list of qualified acupuncturists in your state, send $3 to the National Commission for the Certification of Acupuncturists, Box 97075, Washington, DC 20090-7075. 202-232-1409.

Source: Adriane Fugh-Berman, MD, senior researcher at one of the world's major research institutions and author of a forthcoming book on alternative medicine.

Index

H

491